STUDIES ON VOLTAIRE
AND THE
EIGHTEENTH CENTURY

188

General editor

HAYDN MASON
School of European Studies
University of East Anglia
Norwich, England

GRAHAM GARGETT

VOLTAIRE
AND
PROTESTANTISM

THE VOLTAIRE FOUNDATION

AT THE

TAYLOR INSTITUTION, OXFORD

1980

ISSN 0435-2866
ISBN 0 7294 0243 6

Printed in England by Cheney & Sons Ltd,
Banbury, Oxfordshire

For my parents

Contents

Contents

Acknowledgements

This study grew out of a doctoral thesis presented at the University of East Anglia in May 1974 and from research carried out in 1975 while I was on study leave from the New University of Ulster. My thanks must go to m. Olivier Dessemontet, director of the Archives cantonales vaudoises at Lausanne, where the material I required was made available to me speedily and efficiently, and where I was treated with great courtesy. The inter-library loans services of the University of East Anglia and the New University of Ulster were of great assistance to me, and I wish to thank particularly mrs. K. Hutchings and miss V. Fletcher for their help in obtaining books at Coleraine. M. Michel Baridon, of the University of Dijon, contributed useful information on several occasions and the conversations I had with him provided me with a valuable stimulus. Nor can I miss this chance of expressing my thanks to miss G. Edwards, dr M. Bond and dr D. Hanley, my former colleagues in the Department of West European Studies at the New University of Ulster: without their friendly co-operation and comradely assistance, it is unlikely that I would ever have finished this study. I am also indebted to the English department of the University of Créteil (Paris XII), particularly mlle Christiane d'Haussy and mlle Claire Guichard, for the opportunity they gave me to spend an extended period of time in Paris (1978-1980) while I was preparing my work for publication. It is difficult to say how impressed I have been by the help given to me by the staff of the Voltaire Foundation. I wish to thank both Andrew Brown, for his initial advice and continuing guidance, and Martin Smith, for his remarkably accurate and painstaking checking of my manuscript. Any mistakes which remain are entirely my own responsibility. Finally, my unbounded gratitude must go to professor H. T. Mason of the University of East Anglia: it was he who first suggested the subject to me, and over the years his painstaking supervision, his friendly advice and encouragement, have been quite invaluable.

G.G.

Prefatory note

'Deism versus theism'

SOME critics, when writing about the *philosophes* of the eighteenth century, make a distinction between deism and theism. The most notable example is professor René Pomeau, in whose opinion a theist held a more elaborate set of beliefs than a deist (see below, p.453, n.1). Despite such examples, I have not attempted in this study to distinguish between the two, since it seems to me that it was basically Voltaire's *attitude* to Christianity which arguably changed somewhat as he grew older rather than the *content* of his own beliefs. The terms 'deist' and 'theist', 'deism' and 'theism' will not therefore be sharply differentiated in meaning in this book.

Table of abbreviations

I

Introduction

'Dans l'histoire de l'esprit humain, le protestantisme était un grand objet', proclaims Voltaire at the beginning of his pamphlet *Du Protestantisme et de la guerre des Cévennes* (M.xxiv.570), written, as René Pomeau tells us, in 1763, during the Calas affair (*Oh*, p.1737). But is this statement characteristic of Voltaire's usual attitude? Is Protestantism a major theme in his historical works? Moreover, was Voltaire's own life personally affected to any great extent by Protestantism or by his contacts with individual Protestants, and is there clear evidence of this in the *philosophe*'s printed works and in his private correspondence? Or had the Calas campaign momentarily exaggerated the importance of a topic which did not usually claim Voltaire's interest to more than a limited extent?

To answer these questions it would seem natural to consult one of the many works in which distinguished critics have studied Voltaire's religious position and analysed his anti-Christian campaign. But here a surprise is in store, for comparatively little has been said about his relations with Protestantism. Particular episodes have, of course, received attention, notably the Calas and Sirven cases.[1] Critical editions of the *Lettres philosophiques* seek to assess the significance and accuracy of those passages in which Voltaire describes the various English Protestant denominations. His continuing interest in Quakerism has been ably studied by miss Edith Philips[2] and professor W. H. Barber.[3] René Pomeau includes a section on Voltaire's dealings with Genevese

---

[1] one of the most interesting recent studies on the Calas case is David D. Bien, *The Calas affair: persecution, toleration and heresy in eighteenth-century Toulouse* (Princeton 1960), which contains a full bibliography of earlier scholarship on the subject. The most comprehensive study on the Sirven affair remains Elie Galland, *L'Affaire Sirven* (Mazamet 1911).

[2] see 'Le Quaker vu par Voltaire', *Rhl* (1932), xxxix.161-77, which reappears virtually unchanged as chapter 2 of *The Good Quaker in French legend* (Philadelphia 1932), by the same author.

[3] 'Voltaire and Quakerism: Enlightenment and the inner light', *Studies on Voltaire* (1963), xxiv.81-109.

and Swiss pastors in his masterly book *La Religion de Voltaire* (Paris 1956, pp.292-300, 339-40), and in Paul Chaponnière's *Voltaire chez les calvinistes* (Geneva 1932) we have a valuable biographical account of the same period in the *philosophe*'s life. A little-known thesis published in 1919 explores Voltaire's connections with his French Protestant contemporaries, but the treatment of this study is rather superficial and its scope limited.[4] Besides, although it is now almost a commonplace to point this out, recent advances in scholarship, in particular the publication of Theodore Besterman's monumental edition of Voltaire's correspondence, have provided a wealth of fresh information and made it necessary to reassess even the partial studies which have been attempted. In any case, it remains true to say that there has been no comprehensive investigation into Voltaire's changing attitude towards Protestants throughout his life, still less into his attitude toward the various forms of Protestantism and their intellectual content and significance.[5]

But perhaps we are begging the question. If Protestantism was indeed a topic of little interest to Voltaire, why should critics have bothered to study his opinion of it, or its effects on him? Yet evidence is not lacking to show that many of his contemporaries did not take such a negative view. One of the most prominent cries during Voltaire's 'apotheosis' in Paris in 1778 was 'Gloire au défenseur des Calas'.[6] In the eyes of the populace at least, Voltaire's reputation probably depended as much on his efforts to help the oppressed and persecuted, of whom a substantial number had been Protestants, as on his literary achievements. Nor were the French Protestants themselves slow to express their gratitude.[7]

[4] Edouard Champendal, *Voltaire et les protestants de France* (Geneva 1919).

[5] an exception to this is R. E. Florida, *Voltaire and the Socinians*, Studies on Voltaire (1974), cxxii, which represents an important contribution to the subject. I shall have occasion to refer to this study more than once.

[6] Alfred Noyes, *Voltaire* (London 1938), p.599. Cf. mme Du Deffand's comment to Walpole: 'Il est suivi dans les rues par le peuple, qui l'appelle *l'homme aux Calas*' (letter of 12 April 1778, quoted in Best.D21151, commentary).

[7] cf. Best.D14577, Gal-Pomaret to Voltaire, 7 November 1767: 'Ce n'est pas pour le bien de quelque peuple particulier que vous avés travaillé, mais pour celui de l'humanité en général [. . .] Eh! qui d'entre les anciens & les modernes s'éleva jamais aussi fortement contre l'avilissante superstition, & contre le cruel fanatisme que vous l'avés fait, & que vous le faites. Puissiés vous donc vivre, Monsieur, pour concourir de plus en plus à amener ces tems fortunés, où les hommes convaincus que le meilleur culte qu'on puisse rendre à dieu, c'est de lui offrir une âme pleine de sentimens de bienfaisance, ne s'égorgeront plus les uns les autres, et vivre assés pour voir vos généreux travaux couronnés du plus heureux succès.'

And a moment's thought will show that a man who visited Protestant countries so extensively and spent a considerable amount of time there is likely to have formed strong opinions about their religious institutions, one of the fundamental differences which distinguished them from the land of his birth. Moreover, a *philosophe* who has also been called 'the most typical and the most universal of the historians of the Enlightenment'[8] surely made clear his attitude to the Reformation, claimed by many to be the ancestor of the *siècle des lumières* (cf. below, p.21, n.1).

The aim of this book is thus to investigate not only Voltaire's opinion of Protestantism as a historical phenomenon, but also the possible interaction of ideas between him and the Protestants he came to know during his own lifetime. Yet how is one to set about this task? With an author so prolific as Voltaire the basic requirement is clearly a full acquaintance with the relevant sections of his printed works and correspondence, but even then there are pitfalls for the critic too eager to demonstrate a particular interpretation of Voltaire's ideas. Dr Theodore Besterman has given us a useful reminder of 'methodological requirements' in such a study,[9] and examples to show the wisdom of his advice could be multiplied.[10] Again, should one attempt to form a synthesis of Voltaire's ideas regarding Protestantism as a whole, or trace chronologically the ups and downs of his relationships with the

---

[8] cf. J. H. Brumfitt, *Voltaire historian* (London 1958), p.1.

[9] 'Voltaire's god', *Studies on Voltaire* (1967), v.31: 'It is, indeed, by no means easy to pin down Voltaire's views on such sensitive subjects as this [i.e. his religious opinions]. It is necessary, for instance, to distinguish between his avowed works and his clandestine writings at various levels, and between these and many kinds of letters. Beyond these again are the private *Notebooks*. There is also the often insoluble problem presented by his tales, his poems, his plays: what parts of them can be regarded as expressing his views, and to what extent?'

[10] the following extract could be quoted from the *Traité sur la tolérance* (1763) to show that Voltaire was basically in sympathy with the Protestants: 'Ne dissimulons point que, malgré leurs erreurs, nous leur devons le développement de l'esprit humain, longtemps enseveli dans la plus épaisse barbarie' (*Mélanges*, pp.573-74). But a very different picture is painted at one point of the *Avis au public sur les parricides imputés aux Calas et aux Sirven* (1766): 'Les catholiques répondent à tous ces reproches que les protestants en méritent d'aussi violents. Les meurtres de Servet et de Barneveldt, disent-ils, valent bien ceux du conseiller Dubourg. On peut opposer la mort de Charles 1er à celle de Henri III. Les sombres fureurs des presbytériens d'Angleterre, la rage des cannibales des Cévennes, ont égalé les horreurs de la Saint-Barthélemy' (*Mélanges*, pp.843-44). Voltaire is expressing a Catholic point of view here, but the tone of the passage suggests that it is an opinion with which he has some sympathy. Passages like these, taken in isolation and out of context, could be used to give a completely false impression of Voltaire's overall attitude.

Protestant individuals and groups he came to know during his life?

Neither of these methods would be entirely satisfactory if applied in a systematic way. The chronological approach would probably tend to concentrate on biography, relegating ideas to a relatively unimportant level. But a synthetic approach also has its drawbacks: it is impossible to give a genuine insight into Voltaire's complex and frequently changing attitude toward Protestantism without seeking an explanation of these changes in the events of his own life. Yet so many and varied were his contacts with Protestants of all kinds that a synthesis which tried to take account of them to any meaningful extent would tend to become hopelessly bogged down with digressions.

The method I have adopted represents something of a compromise. Voltaire's most comprehensive appraisal of the Reformation and of many other parts of Protestant history is contained in the *Essai sur les mœurs,* whose first complete publication in 1756 (Brumfitt, pp.61-62) coincided with Voltaire's 'honeymoon' period in Geneva, when he may have hoped to achieve some measure of co-operation with liberal Protestants (cf. below, pp.118ff). In a preliminary section I shall thus attempt to outline his attitude to the Reformation, the Reformers and the Protestant religion: its doctrine, morality and general ethos, taking the views expressed in the *Essai* as my starting point. Then later chapters will consider Voltaire's reactions to the reality of Protestantism as he personally experienced it in four centres: Holland, Switzerland, France and England. It must however be made clear that this is merely a division of convenience, and that no strict separation of material will be made. Thus in the preliminary section Voltaire's later attitudes to a particular phenomenon will be explained if this seems relevant, and points will sometimes be illustrated by reference to his correspondence and other works, of whatever date. Similarly, the later section on specific Protestant centres will include an examination of Voltaire's attitudes to the history of the countries concerned, even if the relevant material is often to be found in the *Essai sur les mœurs.* Such a method may seem artificial and somewhat self-contradictory, but it is essential to adopt some division enabling the enormous amount of material to be organised in a comprehensible way, and this should at least enable us to reach a certain number of general conclusions at the end of our study.

The *Essai sur les mœurs* was not the first work in which the sixty-two year old Voltaire had expressed opinions about Protestantism: *La*

Henriade and the *Lettres philosophiques* are so well known in this respect that they spring to mind immediately, and a brief review of these and other writings in which there are relevant comments may serve to illustrate the emergence of many themes later to become characteristic of Voltaire's attitude to the Protestants and their religion. In the case of *La Henriade*,[11] the theme of Protestantism is, of course, inevitably present, since the subject of the epic poem is the conversion of good king Henri IV to Catholicism, played out against a backcloth of the religious wars of the sixteenth century and including, in the second canto, a description of the St Bartholomew's Day massacre, Voltaire's favourite example of religious fanaticism. Though the poet's attitude in the epic is nominally that of a Catholic and the Protestants are said to be in the wrong,[12] Voltaire came in for a deal of criticism[13] for condemning the political pretensions of the papacy, for making some of the Protestant characters virtuous,[14] and above all for the celebrated line put in the mouth of Henri IV (before the latter's conversion): 'Je ne décide point entre Genève et Rome.'[15]

The *Essay upon the civil wars of France* (1727) is also generally favourable to the Huguenots (cf. below p.237), but Voltaire's next important work, the *Histoire de Charles XII*, conceived and begun during his exile in England in about 1727 and first published in 1731 (*Oh*, p.1659), indicates that the sympathy apparently shown to Protestantism in *La Henriade* was not to be a permanent feature of the *philosophe*'s writings. Though the *Histoire* as a whole contains few references to Protestantism, and these present religion mainly as a pretext for political action,

[11] the poem was originally printed in 1723 under the title of *La Ligue* (Brumfitt, p.6), but the first nine cantos were ready by October 1721 (*La Henriade*, ed. O. R. Taylor, Voltaire 2 (Geneva 1970), p.37).

[12] cf. the hermit's speech in the first canto: 'J'ai vu naître autrefois le calvinisme en France [. . .], Enfin mes yeux ont vu, du sein de la poussière, Ce fantôme effrayant lever sa tête altière, Se placer sur le trône, insulter aux mortels, Et d'un pied dédaigneux renverser nos autels' (lines 233, 237-40, Taylor, p.378).

[13] cf. a long anonymous letter to the *Journal de Trévoux*, written about May 1731 (Best.D410), which takes Voltaire to task for his shortcomings in *La Henriade*: the poet should not have ventured into the field of theology, which he did not properly understand; moreover, he should have distinguished between the rebellious *Ligue* and the loyal Catholics who took up arms only at the legitimate bidding of their king.

[14] Duplessis-Mornay is perhaps the best example: cf. first canto, lines 151-84: 'Mornay, son confident, mais jamais son flatteur, Trop vertueux soutien du parti de l'erreur, Qui, signalant toujours son zèle et sa prudence, Servit également son église et la France' (Taylor, pp.373-74).

[15] second canto, line 5 (Taylor, p.391).

there are one or two significant passages. For example, in connection with queen Christina of Sweden, whom Voltaire praises as 'aussi illustre en quittant le trône, que ses ancêtres l'étaient pour l'avoir conquis ou affermi', he remarks caustically (p.61): 'Les protestants l'ont déchirée, comme si on ne pouvait pas avoir de grandes vertus sans croire à Luther.' And in his *Notes sur les 'Remarques' de La Mottraye*, replying to a criticism that he had 'plus étudié l'ancienne mythologie que les systèmes des théologiens', Voltaire gives a correct account of the attitude of Luther and his disciples toward free will and says that this is not the only point which divides them from the Calvinists. He concludes ironically: 'Au reste, M. de Voltaire connaît les mythologies anciennes et nouvelles et en fait le cas qu'il doit.'[16]

Indifference and scepticism, then, seem to be his attitude towards Protestants as well as Catholics. Confirmation is provided by the *Lettres philosophiques* (1734), which, despite their relatively favourable tone in describing the Quakers, dismiss the various Protestant sects while praising the principle of toleration which allows them to exist. An attitude of amused curiosity is evident, but it is tempered by the more serious purpose which Voltaire had in writing the work, the implied criticism of the French Church and France's religious intolerance. The Quakers provide valuable ammunition for this since they are simple, peace-loving and virtuous – a perfect foil for the contemporary Catholic Church, in Voltaire's opinion. Given their commendable qualities, he might almost be tempted to admire them seriously, were it not for their ostentatiously bizarre manners and their 'enthousiasme', in fact if only 'les hommes pouvoient respecter la vertu sous des apparences ridicules'.[17] Voltaire's attitude later changed somewhat, but in the *Lettres philosophiques* mockery is one of the most important elements in his description of the Quakers. The other Christian denominations mentioned are given short shrift: the Anglicans are grasping and intolerant, whereas the Presbyterians are sanctimonious and pleasure-hating, though it is conceded that they both have better morals than Catholic priests and abbés. Only the Socinians and Unitarians are spoken of with more indulgence, presumably because their opinions are nearer to, or synonymous with, those of the deists, and Voltaire is anxious to show that 'les plus grands Philosophes & les meilleures plumes de leurs tems',

[16] *Oh*, p.288. Mxvi.361, is much shorter, but to the same effect.
[17] *Lettres philosophiques*, ed. Gustave Lanson (Paris 1909), i.45.

Newton, Clarke, Locke and Leclerc, were members of this select band (ed. Lanson, i.80).

One of Voltaire's most private writings, the *Traité de métaphysique*,[18] shows that two English Protestant thinkers, Clarke and Locke, had exercised a very profound influence on Voltaire's metaphysical speculations, although this is very different from saying that he was brought any nearer to the Protestant faith as far as his religious views were concerned. A similar comment would be in order as regards the *Eléments de la philosophie de Newton* (1740): Voltaire's reverence for Newton's scientific achievements in no way tempted him to share his idol's confessional beliefs (cf. below, pp.425-26): he was interested in Protestant sects and influenced by Protestant thinkers, but the connection went no further than that.

Yet although Voltaire doubtless rejected Protestantism as a belief, this by no means reduced his interest in it as a phenomenon. The *Histoire de l'empire de Russie* (probably begun in 1737) dismisses the idea that the repeal of the Edict of Nantes did no harm to France (*Oh*, p.408), and compares the authority of Peter the Great in church affairs to that of the kings of England in their rôle as heads of the Anglican Church (*Oh*, p.428), an early example of Voltaire's enthusiasm for Erastianism. These references, though interesting, are few in number. But during the 1730s and 1740s Voltaire was working on his major contributions to historical writing. The *Siècle de Louis XIV*, first published in 1751 (Brumfitt, p.48), contains an important chapter entitled 'Du calvinisme au temps de Louis XIV', where Voltaire recounts in detail the events leading to the repeal of the Edict of Nantes and comments on the tragedy which this turned out to be both for the Protestants and for France.[19] The *Essai sur les mœurs*, as already pointed out, provides a wealth of material relevant to our study, and was certainly the work in which Voltaire discussed Protestantism most fully and in a manner most likely to make a lasting impression on his readers. Besides sketching its pre-history and causes, Voltaire devotes eleven chapters – fifty pages in the Moland edition (M.xii.283-334) – to describing the Reformation as it took place in various parts of Europe, and then traces the

[18] 'Composée vraisemblablement au milieu de 1734, remaniée plusieurs fois entre 1734 et 1738' (*Mélanges*, p.1366); cf. also *Traité de métaphysique*, ed. H. Temple Patterson (Manchester 1937), pp.v-vi.

[19] Gustave Lanson has traced the various additions which Voltaire made to this chapter in his 'Notes pour servir à l'étude des chapitres 35-39 du *Siècle de Louis XIV* de Voltaire', *Mélanges offerts à m. Charles Andler* (Strasbourg, Paris 1924), pp.171-95.

development of Protestantism, where this seems to him relevant in a world history, until the end of the reign of Louis XIII, giving special consideration to the religious wars in France and in England. Completed by the *Siècle de Louis XIV* and the *Précis du siècle de Louis XV*, this immense historical survey gives us a panorama including almost every important topic in the history of Protestantism.

Perhaps some provisional conclusions may be drawn from this brief summary of the more significant references to Protestantism in the works Voltaire wrote before settling at Geneva. The first and most obvious point is that there can be no doubt that Protestantism in its various manifestations is an important subject in his writings. Once this has been said, however, it is difficult to advance to any more positive conclusions. No clear patterns yet emerge, rather a picture of fluctuating attitudes and opinions. Our first task will be, therefore, to attempt to form an overall view of Voltaire's position and to see whether, by and large, the Protestants are favoured with his approval, or whether on the contrary they incur the same withering scorn as the Catholics.

Finally, I do not propose to make a detailed study of the sources which inspired Voltaire's comments on Protestantism and helped him to form his mature opinions about it, although these will be mentioned when relevant and known. Such a study would no doubt be very desirable, but it certainly falls outside the scope of this book. The extent of the task involved in covering all Voltaire's works would be immense: one has only to consult Lanson's article on five chapters of the *Siècle de Louis XIV* to realise this. My main objectives are to explore Voltaire's views about Protestantism, to trace the development of his opinions, to evaluate the influence which Protestantism may have had on him, and vice-versa. Among other things, we may hope to see whether, from the evidence provided by his works and his correspondence, Voltaire lives up to the claim he makes in his pamphlet *Du protestantisme et de la guerre des Cévennes* (*Oh*, p.1277), already mentioned at the beginning of this introductory section:

Quelques protestants ont reproché à l'auteur de l'*Essai sur les mœurs* de les avoir souvent condamnés; et quelques catholiques ont chargé l'auteur d'avoir montré trop de compassion pour les protestants. Ces plaintes prouvent qu'il a gardé ce juste milieu qui ne satisfait que les esprits modérés.

2

Voltaire and the Reformation

~~~⚜~~~

IT might seem a reasonable assumption that Voltaire would describe the Reformation with some indulgence, if not enthusiasm. Was not the spirit of free enquiry, which he so outstandingly embodied, a direct consequence, or at least an offshoot of the revolution in thinking and religious behaviour which shook sixteenth-century Christendom to its foundations? In short, does Voltaire acknowledge himself to be in any way a spiritual child of the Reformation?[1] Is his attitude to it one of enthusiasm, hostility, or merely indifference?

There are in fact several accounts of the Reformation in Voltaire's works, and not only do they enable us to analyse the *philosophe*'s opinion of Protestantism and its origins, they also provide us with an excellent opportunity to assess his qualities as a historian. Pierre Bayle, who influenced Voltaire in so many ways[2] and who was himself at least nominally a Protestant, had laid down very high standards for those who would attempt to interpret the past:

Un historien ne saurait être trop sur ses gardes, et il ne peut presque pas s'échapper des pièges de la prévention. Il y a des formes de gouvernement, il y a des maximes de morale ou de politique qui lui plaisent ou qui lui déplaisent. Ce préjugé le porte à favoriser un parti plutôt qu'un autre, lors même qu'il fait l'histoire d'un ancien peuple ou d'un pays éloigné.[3]

Did Voltaire accept these standards and attempt to observe them in his description of the Reformation, or was he tempted, as in other places,

---

[1] cf. W. H. Barber's positive statement: 'Whatever its manifold other affinities, the Enlightenment is essentially a child, or if one prefers a younger sister, of Protestantism, and Voltairean theism, one of the more spiritual formulations of Enlightenment thought, naturally lies close to the most radical of all Protestant forms of religious belief' ('Voltaire and Quakerism', p.108). For a discussion of the second part of this claim, see below pp.456-61.

[2] cf. H. T. Mason, *Pierre Bayle and Voltaire* (London 1963).

[3] *Dictionnaire historique et critique*, article 'Rémond (Florimond de)', rem. D.

to sacrifice strict impartiality for propaganda reasons, the need to be prudent, or other tactical considerations?[4]

In his article 'History and propaganda in Voltaire', J. H. Brumfitt divides the *philosophe*'s works into two classes:

those which he regarded as his serious contributions to historiography and which he published under his own name (the *Siècle*, the *Essai*, and the *Histoire de Russie*, for example) and works like the *Histoire du parlement* and *La Philosophie de l'histoire*, which were published anonymously and which were more obviously works of political and religious controversy. The works in the former category are no doubt those by which Voltaire would wish to be judged.[5]

If this distinction is valid, it will be necessary to consider briefly the circumstances in which particular works mentioning the Reformation were written, although whether such works fall into the first or second of professor Brumfitt's categories, one might in any case expect Voltaire's interpretation to be less tendentious than, say, his description of the Inquisition or religious orders, where his hostility to the phenomenon under consideration is all too obvious, sometimes making his attitude completely unacceptable to a modern historian.

As we have seen, the longest and most important account of the Reformation in Voltaire's works appears in the *Essai sur les mœurs*, classified by professor Brumfitt as one of Voltaire's 'serious contributions to historiography'. Moreover, since the critic adds (p.282) that Voltaire was usually able to make clear his real opinions on all major issues despite the need to tone down his views for reasons of prudence, it is obvious that this section of the *Essai* is extremely significant for an understanding of Voltaire's views on the Reformation, and that it ought not to be clouded by excessive propaganda. Another account occurs in the *Annales de l'empire*, written in 1753 at the request of the duchess of Saxe-Gotha.[6] This fact is, however, unlikely to have made Voltaire change or distort his attitude to the Protestants in any way, for Louise-Dorothea, although an ardent worshipper of divine pro-

---

[4] his writings on Jewish history (cf. *La Philosophie de l'histoire*, chapters 38-49), the early Church (cf. *Essai sur les mœurs*, chapters 8-10), and on monastic orders (cf. *Essai sur les mœurs*, chapter 139), would seem to be prime examples of history with a philosophical bias.

[5] *Studies on Voltaire* (1963), xxiv.276-77.

[6] cf. Best.D5298 (Voltaire to mme von Buchwald, 28 May 1753): 'C'est un ouvrage qu'il faut finir, puisque la Minerve de l'Allemagne me l'a ordonné.'

vidence[7] and for many years a believer in Leibnizian optimism,[8] was also a great admirer of Voltaire, on occasion paying him compliments which showed quite clearly that she no longer had any Protestant susceptibilities to be humoured.[9] The *Histoire du parlement de Paris* (1768) has often been regarded as a propaganda work, 'closely linked with the ministerial campaign against the *Parlement* in the late sixties', and perhaps 'written at the government's request' (Brumfitt, *Voltaire historian* p.70) but Voltaire himself, in a letter to mme Denis of 3 July 1769 (Best.D15727), hotly denied the charge, and his distinguished editor, Theodore Besterman, states (Best.D15727, n.1) that 'it derives ultimately from the *Mémoires secrets* (17 juillet 1769), and is as insubstantial as it is improbable'. Though the *Histoire du parlement* contains only the briefest of accounts of Luther's Reformation, this is nonetheless interesting, and there is also a description of the reasons for François I's rejection of the Reformation in France, a detail which is absent from the other accounts. These then are the three main sources on which our study of Voltaire's view of the Reformation will be based, though passages from other works may also be quoted if this seems relevant.

i. *The background to the Reformation*

Voltaire does not see the Reformation as an isolated event; for him it is the culmination of a long series of heresies, all of which sought, to a greater or lesser extent, to restore Christianity to its simple and unpretentious origins.[10] The first heresy he normally mentions in this connection is that of the Vaudois (or Waldensians), who followed 'les dogmes de Bérenger,[11] de Claude, évêque de Turin, et de plusieurs

[7] cf. Best.D10655 (to Voltaire, 16 August 1762): 'J'aime et j'adore la Divinité de toutes mes facultés.'

[8] cf. Best.D8048, D8098, D8343, D10032.

[9] cf. Best.D5713, 9 March 1754: 'Vous [. . .] lui [the Church] faite plus de tort que Luther et tous ses partisans: Luther n'a qu'un peu ébranlé l'édifice et Vous le sapéz.'

[10] cf. *Essai sur les mœurs*, ed. René Pomeau (Paris 1963) (henceforth referred to as *Essai*), i.487: 'L'opinion de Scot, de Ratram, de Bérenger [unfavourable to transubstantiation], ne fut pas ensevelie; elle se perpétua chez quelques ecclésiastiques; elle passa aux Vaudois, aux Albigeois, aux Hussites, aux protestants.' Ratramnus (d.868) was a monk who took part in most of the theological controversies of his day. His most celebrated writing is a treatise on the Eucharist, *De corpore et sanguine Domini*, condemned by the Synod of Vercelli on 1 September 1050 (*Oxford dictionary of the Christian Church*, ed. F. L. Cross (London 1958), s.v. 'Ratramnus').

[11] Berengar, or Bérenger, was born at Tours about 1000 A.D. He became archdeacon of Angers about 1040 and some ten years later was imprisoned by Henri I of France for his views on the Eucharist. The Synod of Vercelli (1050) censured his opinions, and other

autres' (*Essai*, ii.217). Claudius is cited several times by Voltaire as a forerunner of the Protestants, and in the *Essai sur les mœurs* he describes the Bishop's position as follows:

On vit, au VIIe siècle, Claude, archevêque de Turin, adopter la plupart des sentiments qui font aujourd'hui le fondement de la religion protestante, et prétendre que ces sentiments étaient ceux de la primitive Eglise. Il y a presque toujours un petit troupeau séparé du grand; et, depuis le commencement du XIe siècle, ce petit troupeau fut dispersé ou égorgé, quand il voulut trop paraître.[12]

The parallel account of the *Histoire du parlement* is very similar, and clearly links Claudius's ideas with those professed by the Waldensians and Albigensians:

Il y avait sur les confins de la Provence et du comtat d'Avignon des restes de ces anciens Vaudois et Albigeois qui avaient conservé une partie des rites de l'Eglise des Gaules, soutenus par Claude, évêque de Turin, au VIIIe siècle, et perpétués jusqu'à nos jours dans les sociétés protestantes.[13]

The *Siècle de Louis XIV* makes the same point, then goes on to list explicitly the forerunners of the Reformation (*Oh*, p.1043):

Les anciens dogmes embrassés par les Vaudois, les Albigeois, les Hussites, renouvelés et différemment expliqués par Luther et Zuingle, furent reçus avec avidité dans l'Allemagne.

A further passage of the *Essai*, again dealing with the Waldensians, includes Wyclif as one of the spiritual predecessors of the Reformation.[14]

The proto-reformers and their doctrines are described in chapter 73 of the *Essai sur les mœurs* (i.697-702) and in the *Annales de l'Empire* (M.xiii.431-37). Wyclif is portrayed as the most violent of these doctors: Voltaire says that the main point of his preaching, which was contem-

---

condemnations followed. Berengar made various retractions but his real views are difficult to ascertain (*Encyclopaedia of religion and ethics*, ed. James Hastings (Edinburgh, Newcastle 1909), *s.v.* 'Berengar').

[12] i.484. Cf. Best.D7488 (Voltaire to Augustin Fangé, 1 December 1757): 'Croyez vous que Claude de Turin ait regardé la confession des laïcs, comme un sacrement nécessaire? Il me semble que cet évêque pensait à peu près comme ceux qu'on appelle réformés, et que son opiniâtreté à rejetter les nouveaux usages fut l'origine de la plupart des schismes qui ont divisé les chrétiens occidentaux.' Cf. also Best.D10616 and D12450. Claudius, bishop of Turin (d. *c*.830-40), made an attack on image-worship, relics, adoration of the cross, pilgrimages and intercession of saints. He also showed scant respect for the see of Rome (*Oxford dictionary of the Christian Church, s.v.* 'Claudius').

[13] M.xv.499. Cf. also *Annales*, M.xiii.236, and *Essai*, i.361.

[14] ii.275. Cf. also i.698: 'Ce que les Vaudois enseignaient alors en secret, il [Wyclif] l'enseignait en public.'

poraneous with the schism of popes Urban v and Clement,[14a] was that the Church should follow the example France had given for a time and not recognise a pope at all. In this he was supported by many lords who were tired of seeing England treated like a province of Rome, but he was opposed by 'tous ceux qui partageaient le fruit de cette soumission' (*Essai*, i.698), presumably the clergy. His theology, which denied transubstantiation, and his attempt to abolish confession and indulgences and to reform the hierarchy 'éloignée de sa simplicité primitive', received less support than his political proposals, but his doctrines were merely repressed, not stamped out altogether. Indeed, they spread to Bohemia and were adopted by John Hus, a doctor of theology and the queen's confessor. He rejected the doctrinal part of Wyclif's ideas, but was at one with him in attacking the abuse of ecclesiastical power by the pope and the bishops: 'La doctrine de Jean Hus consistait principale-ment à donner à l'Eglise les droits que le saint-siège prétendait pour lui seul' (*Annales*, M.xiii.431). Summoned to give an account of his doctrine at the Council of Constance in 1414, he went, relying on a safe-conduct given him by the emperor, Sigismund. This, however, was not honoured, and after refusing to retract, Hus was burned at the stake on 6 July 1415:

Voici les propositions principales pour lesquelles on le condamna à ce sup-plice horrible:[15] 'Qu'il n'y a qu'une Eglise catholique, qui renferme dans son sein tous les prédestinés; que les seigneurs temporels doivent obliger les prêtres à observer la loi; qu'un mauvais pape n'est pas vicaire de Jésus-Christ.'[16]

In fact, Voltaire goes on to say that the Council Fathers were obviously determined to kill Hus, for the latter 'n'adoptait aucune des propositions de Wiclef, qui séparent aujourd'hui les protestants de l'Eglise romaine'. The only reason Voltaire can give for Hus's execution is 'cet esprit d'opiniâtreté qu'on puise dans les écoles' (*Essai*, i.700). Yet Voltaire is obviously presenting Hus as a forerunner of the Reformers, even if his theological doctrine is not the same as theirs; the fact that Hus adopts and continues Wyclif's attacks against the abuses of the papacy is

---

[14a] the popes in question would seem actually to have been Urban vi and Clement vi (Robert of Geneva).

[15] elsewhere (Best.D7584, to Théodore Tronchin, 15 January 1758), Voltaire refers to Hus's death in a list of 'assassinats', which also includes those of Dubourg, Servetus, Antoine, and Barneveldt, all regarded by the *philosophe* as victims of *l'infâme*.

[16] M.xiii.436; cf. *Essai*, i.699-700.

sufficient to establish his credentials, as far as Voltaire is concerned. Moreover, the manner in which Hus dies recalls vividly that of many later Protestant martyrs: 'il loua Dieu jusqu'à ce que la flamme étouffât sa voix' (*Annales*, M.xiii.436). His disciple, Jeremy of Prague, 'un homme bien supérieur à Jean Hus en esprit et en éloquence', condemned for sharing Hus's ideas, dies with the same heroism and his death is compared to that of Socrates. In fact, by denying that these two critics of the Church, unlike Wyclif, had anything of the Reformer in them, and by emphasising the manner of their death, Voltaire scores doubly at the expense of the Catholic Church, portrayed not only as intolerant but also as needlessly cruel and severe.

The general tone of Voltaire's description of these three 'docteurs' is favourable. Not only do they highlight abuses in the Church hierarchy, Wyclif also demonstrates that its theology is no longer that of primitive Christianity, and, perhaps dearest of all to Voltaire's heart, claims that the Church should be subject to the state rather than vice versa. This has been the *philosophe*'s contention as he has described at length the Guelf-Ghibelline dispute between the papacy and the emperors. Indeed, Erastian principles and ideals are one of Voltaire's favourite weapons in his attacks against the Catholic Church, and we shall see many examples of its use relevant to the topic we are studying (cf. especially pp.91-94 below).

Since Voltaire seems to be saying that the teaching of Wyclif, Hus and Jeremy of Prague was justified, and that they themselves possessed a high degree of moral integrity and dignity, one might expect his favourable attitude to be maintained or even strengthened when he comes to describe the Reformation. But this would be to reckon without Voltaire's underlying suspicion that most forms of organised Christianity were characterised both by priestly hypocrisy and popular superstition. For the earlier heretics, as well as the Reformers, were believing Christians, and although their grievances were justified and therefore useful for propaganda purposes, their motives were suspect to Voltaire, and he appears to think that they were probably fanatics of one sort or another. This point is made in connection with the Manicheans, of he Voltaire says (*Essai*, i.483):

On ne les appela manichéens que pour leur donner un nom plus odieux [. . .] C'était probablement des enthousiastes qui tendaient à une perfection outrée pour dominer sur les esprits: c'est le caractère de tous les chefs de sectes.

Such a *chef de secte* was Savonarola, a fine example of a domineering fanatic who caused a lot of trouble and who came to a deservedly bad end:

Il y avait à Florence un dominicain nommé Jérôme Savonarole. C'était un de ces prédicateurs à qui le talent de parler en chaire fait croire qu'ils peuvent gouverner les peuples, un de ces théologiens qui, ayant expliqué l'*Apocalypse*, pensent être prophètes. Il dirigeait, il prêchait, il confessait, il écrivait; et dans une ville libre, pleine nécessairement de factions, il voulait être à la tête d'un parti.[17]

So we are given a glimpse of a very different type of pre-Reformer, self-interested, power-seeking, and worse still a theologian who has dabbled in interpreting the Apocalypse, which even the great Newton was unable to do with impunity![18] It remains to be seen whether, in Voltaire's opinion, the great Reformers will resemble Savonarola rather than Hus or Jeremy of Prague.

ii. *Luther's reform*

Chapter 127 of the *Essai sur les mœurs* is entitled 'De Léon x, et de l'Eglise' and examines at some length the causes of the Reformation. Voltaire comments briefly on the struggles everywhere between Church and state, 'excepté dans les Etats où l'Eglise a été et est encore souveraine' (*Essai*, ii.208), and says that after the reigns of Alexander vi and Julius ii the temporal power of the popes in Italy was firmly established. He stresses the general moral dissolution of the times (*Essai*, ii.211):

Tous les écrivains protestants et catholiques se récrient contre la dissolution des mœurs de ces temps: ils disent que les prélats, les curés et les moines, passaient une vie commode; que rien n'était plus commun que des prêtres qui élevaient publiquement leurs enfants, à l'exemple d'Alexandre vi.

But the most scandalous abuse, 'ce qui révoltait le plus les esprits', was the shameful traffic of indulgences:

Toutes les impudicités les plus monstrueuses avaient leur prix fait. La bestialité était estimée deux cent cinquante livres. On obtenait même des dispenses,

[17] *Essai*, ii.84. According to H. T. Mason (*Pierre Bayle and Voltaire*, p.42), several details of Bayle's *Dictionnaire* article 'Savonarola' are 'reproduced by Voltaire with many similarities in the *Essai sur les mœurs*'.

[18] cf. especially a 1739 addition to the *Lettres philosophiques* (ed. Lanson, ii.61). Cf. also M.xix.2, xx.230; *Dictionnaire philosophique*, ed. Julien Benda and Raymond Naves (Paris 1954), pp.33, 451; and below, p.426.

non seulement pour des péchés passés mais pour ceux qu'on avait envie de faire [. . .] Les prédicateurs disaient hautement en chaire que 'quand on aurait violé la sainte Vierge, on serait absous en achetant des indulgences'.[19]

It was a painful experience for the 'grand nombre de pères de famille qui travaillent sans cesse' and for those 'qui gagnent leur pain à la sueur de leur front' to see the immense riches possessed by the monks and difficult to convince the 'peuples indignés' that the Church needed to be reformed, rather than abolished altogether (*Essai*, ii.213).

The reasons given so far seem to show that Voltaire approved of the Reformation's motives, and this is as we might expect in such a dedicated enemy of the Catholic Church, yet he goes on to qualify these statements very radically. In the first place, he says that even if the abuses had been more excessive, they were 'moins dangereux sans doute que les horreurs des guerres et le saccagement les villes'. This is ostensibly one of the excuses given by Catholic apologists, but it is clear from the context that Voltaire shares the same view.[20] Moreover, Leo x's court, though sumptuous and immoral, performed a beneficial function: 'Le faste de la cour voluptueuse de Léon x pouvait blesser les yeux; mais aussi on devait voir que cette cour même policait l'Europe, et rendait les hommes plus sociables'.[21] In fact, there is a fundamental ambiguity in Voltaire's attitude to the Church and more especially to the papacy at this time. In so much as it represents Catholic Christianity, he is stoutly behind the reforms introduced by the Protestants and applauds them loudly. On the other hand, he cannot see all these reforms in a vacuum. To him they are part of a logical process which the Protestants have never taken far enough, the progression to pure deism which ensures the absence of all superstitions. As it is, they remain Christians, and as such incur his wrath almost as much as the Catholics. In fact, in some ways, as we shall see later, he reserves a particular dislike for certain Protestant characteristics: the stern moral teaching of the Reformers and the importance

---

[19] *Essai*, ii.212, 215. It appears that this was not a purely Voltairean exaggeration: cf. E.-G. Léonard, *Histoire générale du protestantisme* (Paris 1961), i.48.

[20] moreover, he also claims that crimes committed at the papal court did not affect the Italians as a whole, and that the clerical ambition which existed before the Reformation was very different from 'cet acharnement de la haine théologique qui produisit tant de meurtres' (*Essai*, ii.213).

[21] *Essai*, ii.214. Cf. Best.D17796, Voltaire to Shuvalov, 27 June 1772: 'Je trouve Monsieur le Prince Galitzin bien bon de quitter Rome pour Genêve. Il quitte le sein des beaux arts pour des écoles un peu sèches.'

of the Old Testament in Protestantism, to give only two examples (cf. below, pp.66ff., 84ff.).

The next significant fact is that at the time he is describing, the Church was the main patron of the arts. Voltaire's loyalties are obviously divided. In the first place he clearly feels much more sympathy for the cultured Leo x than for the infamous Alexander vi or the warlike Julius ii. We are told that 'le pape surtout joignait le goût le plus fin à la magnificence la plus recherchée' (*Essai*, ii.209), and that he encouraged geniuses in all branches of the arts. Indeed, one has the impression that although Voltaire is ostensibly expressing disapproval, and pointing to the extravagance of Leo's court as one of the causes of the Reformation, he really admires the pontiff who caused the plays of Plautus, Ariosto and Machiavelli to be performed before him.[22] A contradictory picture of the times seems to be emerging, diametrically opposed to the one we have just traced:

La religion n'avait rien d'austère, elle s'attirait le respect par des cérémonies pompeuses; le style barbare de la daterie était aboli, et faisait place à l'éloquence des cardinaux Bembo et Sadolet, alors secrétaires des brefs, hommes qui savaient imiter la latinité de Cicéron, et qui semblaient adopter sa philosophie sceptique.

Despite the abuses mentioned earlier:

Il y avait cependant partout des hommes de mœurs tres pures, des pasteurs dignes de l'être, des religieux soumis de cœur à des vœux qui effraient la mollesse humaine: mais ces vertus sont ensevelies dans l'obscurité, tandis que le luxe et le vice dominent dans la splendeur.[23]

For it was not only the Roman Church and its curia that were favoured with good times (*Essai*, ii.214):

[22] there is in fact substantial evidence in Voltaire's correspondence to support this view. On 23 December 1760 he mentioned Leo x as one of the men who had restored the fortunes of the theatre in Italy (Best.D9492, to Capacelli), and about August 1765 he returned to the same theme: 'L'Italie au commencement de notre seizième siécle vit renaître la tragédie et la comédie, grâce au goût du pape Léon x, et au génie des prélats Bibiena, la Casa, Trissino' (Best.D12832, to mlle Clairon). As early as 27 June 1743 Voltaire had remarked that the 'Sage Lambertini' (Benedict xiv) 'De Leon dix est successeur' (Best.D2776, to Cideville), and when Benedict was dying in 1756, the *philosophe* referred to him in the most generous of terms, which perhaps redound a little also to the pope to whom Voltaire had earlier compared him: 'Si tous ses prédécesseurs luy eussent ressemblé, il n'y eût point eu de guerres de relligion dans le monde' (Best.D7062, to Jean Robert Tronchin, 24 November 1756).

[23] *Essai*, ii.213-14.

La plupart des chrétiens vivaient dans une ignorance heureuse. Il n'y avait peut-être pas en Europe dix gentilshommes qui eussent la *Bible*. Elle n'était point traduite en langue vulgaire, ou du moins les traductions qu'on en avait faites dans peu de pays étaient ignorées.

In fact, what, according to Voltaire, was one of the principal causes of the Reformation he extols as 'une des plus belles entreprises qui puissent illustrer des souverains', and it claims his unqualified admiration. He is referring to the completion of the great church of St Peter's at Rome, begun by Julius II, 'cette merveille de la métropole de l'Europe', to which every Christian ought to have contributed. Yet this, together with a projected war against the Turks, was what induced the by now impoverished pope to declare a new sale of indulgences and to spark off 'la révolution la plus sérieuse' (*Essai*, ii.215).

According to Voltaire, Leo x was warned by cardinal Polus that his encouragement of learning, though commendable, was a dangerous policy.[24] The development of printing, too, marked the beginning of the collapse of the Church's spiritual ascendancy. Then Erasmus covered the monks with a ridicule from which they did not recover, and Germany laughed at the Italians with the authors of the *Lettres des hommes obscurs*.[25] The ambiguity in Voltaire's attitude has now become plain. While praising Leo x's patronage of the arts, he says that the pontiff was warned about the danger of increasing knowledge, yet still seems loath to admit that, by his own arguments, the spread of learning

---

[24] *Essai*, ii.214. Cf. Best.D7171, to Lévesque de Burigny, 24 February 1757: 'Le cardinal Polus pourait bien avoir écrit la lettre à Léon dix longtemps avant d'être Cardinal. C'est de mylord Bollingbroke que je tiens l'anecdote de cette lettre, il en a parlé souvent à feu mr de Pouilly votre frère et à moy.'

[25] *Essai*, ii.214-15. These were 'the *Epistolae obscurorum virorum*, a satire on monastic ignorance [. . .] first published in 1515, they were, at least in part, by Ulrich von Hutten' (Best.D8720, n.2). There is a brief reference to their author in Voltaire's Piccini notebooks (Voltaire 82, p.563; most of this material dates from 1750-1755), but Voltaire had apparently not read the work before the beginning of 1760, when he expressed his enthusiasm to Elie Bertrand (Best.D8720, 22 January 1760). Voltaire's reference to the *Epistolae* is part of a passage he added to the *Essai* in 1761 (ii.214 – in his edition Pomeau indicates the changes which occurred in the *Essai*'s text in 1761, 1769, 1775 and the Kehl edition). His slighting comment regarding sixteenth-century literature, together with the fact that he had consulted von Hutten's work so late in life, provide an apposite illustration of the point made by Brumfitt, *Voltaire historian* p.62) that 'his reliance on second-hand sources, only partial in the *Siècle*, became almost total in the *Essai*'.

Voltaire later (1767) devoted the second of the *Lettres à s.a. mgr le prince de* **** to 'les prédecesseurs de Rabelais en Allemagne et en Italie, et d'abord au livre intitulé *Epistolae obscurorum virorum*'.

fostered by the Renaissance and by causes independent of the pope, made the Reformation virtually unavoidable. In fact, Voltaire goes as far as to say, in one extreme statement, that Italy was saved for arts only because the Reformation failed there:

Les beaux-arts continuèrent à fleurir en Italie, parce que la contagion des controverses ne pénétra guère dans ce pays; et il arriva que lorsqu'on s'égorgeait en Allemagne, en France, en Angleterre, pour des choses qu'on n'entendait point, l'Italie, tranquille depuis le saccagement étonnant de Rome par l'armée de Charles-Quint, cultiva les arts plus que jamais.[26]

When Voltaire is in this frame of mind, he sees the Reformation as merely the latest of a series of abstruse arguments about incomprehensible dogmas, encouraged by the fanaticism of the mob and by the political opportunism of those in high places. Perhaps this explains the spare and cynical account he now proceeds to give of Luther's Reformation.

In a thesis entitled *Voltaire et les protestants de France* (cf. above, p.14), Champendal claims that Voltaire attributes the Reformation to trifling causes such as an amorous whim of Henry VIII and maintains (p.17) that:

Il ignore ou veut ignorer que tout le mouvement de la Réforme n'est pas autre chose qu'un immense effort de restauration de l'Eglise chrétienne dans sa pureté primitive [. . .] et il n'en parle que pour le dénigrer et le traîner dans la boue.

And indeed the beginning of the chapter dealing with Luther's reform tempts one to agree unreservedly with Champendal's opinion. Everything seems reduced to a monks' quarrel. Can Voltaire really be taken seriously as a historian?

Vous n'ignorez pas que cette grande révolution dans l'esprit humain et dans le système politique de l'Europe commença par Martin Luther, moine augustin que ses supérieurs chargèrent de prêcher contre la marchandise qu'ils

---

[26] *Essai*, ii.173. Cf. ii.222: 'Peu de personnes prirent le parti de Luther en Italie. Ce peuple ingénieux, occupé d'intrigues et de plaisirs, n'eut aucune part à ces troubles.' Voltaire's analysis of the situation is woefully inadequate here. The Reformation in Italy was in fact suppressed mainly owing to the systematic persecution which was applied there: cf. Owen Chadwick, *The Reformation* (*The Penguin history of the Church*, vol.iii) (Harmondsworth 1964), pp.267-68. It is indeed strange to find Voltaire accepting with approval a state of affairs brought about by the Italian Inquisition, although he was apparently unaware that this was the case or had not thought out the full implications of his position as expressed in the *Essai*.

n'avaient pu vendre. La querelle fut d'abord entre les augustins et les dominicains.[27]

It is true, however, that this statement is qualified by 'd'abord', implying that other reasons will be given to explain later developments, but that Voltaire's main purpose is to belittle the causes of the Reformation at the very beginning of his account is made quite clear by a paragraph added in 1761, which Voltaire inserted into his text immediately after the controversial remarks I have just quoted. Not only does he imply that the origins of the Reformation were trivial and devalue any spiritual significance its descendants might claim for it, he also has an excellent opportunity to make a jibe against priests in the most typical Voltairean manner: 'Vous avez dû voir que toutes les querelles de religion étaient venues jusque-là des prêtres théologiens' (*Essai*, ii.217). The Reformation, it appears, was just one more of these pointless disputes, and its philosophical credentials were conspicuous by their absence.[28]

Yet Voltaire is not always so cynical, and the shorter account of the Reformation given in the *Histoire du parlement de Paris* is much fairer than the one we have just been considering. Briefly and tellingly, he outlines the abuses in the Church and makes them entirely responsible for subsequent events (M.xv.498):

Enfin les débauches, les assassinats et les empoisonnements du pape Alexandre VI, l'ambition guerrière de Jules II, la vie voluptueuse de Léon X, ses rapines pour fournir à ses plaisirs, et la vente publique des indulgences, soulevèrent une partie de l'Europe. Le mal était extrême, il fallait au moins une réforme: elle fut commencée, mais par une défection entière, en Allemagne, en Suisse, et à Genève.

Likewise, in the *Annales de l'empire*, though mentioning the quarrel between the Dominicans and Augustinians, Voltaire gives it less prominence than in the *Essai* and makes clear that it was only 'la première étincelle qui embrasa l'Europe' (M.xiii.479).

The *Essai* too gives other reasons, though at first they are not very convincing. Luther did not expect to destroy Catholicism in half of

---

[27] *Essai*, ii.217. Voltaire explains earlier, in chapter 127, that the Augustinians, deprived of their traditional right to sell Indulgences, were jealous of the Dominicans to whom it had been transferred.

[28] cf. an earlier comment in the *Essai*: 'Les disputes de religion qui agitèrent les esprits en Allemagne, dans le Nord, en France, et en Angleterre, retardèrent les progrès de la raison au lieu de les hâter: des aveugles qui combattaient avec fureur ne pouvaient trouver le chemin de la vérité' (ii.173).

Europe, but after condemning indulgences he went on to investigate the authority of the pope. Though no one had doubted it in the past, 'les temps étaient changés; la mesure était comblée' (ii.217). This must be one of the weakest reasons a historian could give for any event. True, Voltaire apparently subscribed to a theory that events must happen at exactly the right time if their potential importance was to be realised. In the *Lettres philosophiques*, for example, he says that Socinianism 'prend très-mal son tems de reparoître dans un âge où le monde est rassasié de disputes & de Sectes', and goes on to remark (ed. Lanson, i.80):

n'est-ce pas une chose plaisante, que Luther, Calvin, Zuingle, tous Ecrivains qu'on ne peut lire, aient fondé des Sectes qui partagent l'Europe, que l'igno-rant Mahomet ait donné une Religion à l'Asie & à l'Afrique, & que Messieurs Newton, Clarck, Locke, le Clerc, &c, les plus grands Philosophes & les meilleures plumes de leurs tems, aient pu à peine venir à bout d'établir un petit troupeau qui même diminue tous les jours.

Here, at least, a reason is given, but in the *Essai* Voltaire is merely avoiding the difficulty. To say that the times had changed gives not the slightest indication as to *why* they had changed. So far Voltaire's explanation of the Reformation is unconvincing, to say the least.

Fortunately he soon advances some more plausible reasons. He says that economic motives were more important than theological ones: 'On sentait assez que les hommes puissants ne se réforment pas. C'était à leur autorité et à leurs richesses qu'on en voulait: c'était le joug des taxes romaines qu'on voulait briser', and then puts forward his most telling explanation, the fundamental importance of political inter-vention: 'Pour parvenir à cette scission, il ne fallait qu'un prince qui animât les peuples. Le vieux Frédéric, électeur de Saxe, surnommé le Sage [. . .] protégea Luther ouvertement' (*Essai*, ii.218). Unlike the purely religious disagreements, this succeeded in provoking a complete separation. The *Annales de l'empire* presents Frederick's motives as follows:

Frédéric, duc et électeur de Saxe, était, comme on l'a dit, le protecteur de Luther et de sa doctrine. Ce prince avait, dit-on, assez de religion pour être chrétien, assez de raison pour voir les abus, beaucoup d'envie de les réformer et beaucoup plus peut-être encore d'entrer en partage des biens immenses que le clergé possédait dans la Saxe.[29]

[29] M.xiii.479-80. Voltaire is always cynical about the religious sincerity of princes and others in high places: even Henri IV's abjuration is constantly claimed to be a result of political expediency (cf. M.xxiv.509; M.xxv.484, 486; M.xxvii.289; Best.D7875). This is

33

Allied with Frederick's greed and political opportunism was the cause of German nationalism, for when Luther burned a papal bull in Wittemberg: 'une partie de l'Allemagne, fatiguée de la grandeur pontificale, était dans les intérêts du réformateur, sans trop examiner les questions de l'école' (*Essai*, ii.220). The spiritual grievances, in fact, were 'des choses très peu intelligibles,' and apparently not enough to cause a schism (ii.218).

Leo x, though secretly despising these disputes, was obliged to condemn the Reform movement, and the events seem to follow one another inexorably in Voltaire's limpid prose. Luther's power grew, he criticised more and more points of Roman doctrine, and soon the only common ground left between them was the trinity, baptism, the incarnation and the resurrection (ii.220). Memories of the pope-emperor disputes were renewed and some of Voltaire's own indignation is apparent as he recounts the indictments levelled against the papacy: 'De quel front un Alexandre vi, l'horreur de toute la terre, avait-il osé se dire le vicaire de Dieu?'[30] For the moment the Reformation was limited mainly to Germany and Switzerland: the polished Roman court had not expected a revolution from this part of the world (ii.222). Voltaire wonders if the emperor Charles v was really opposed to the Reformation and concludes that, though he may have basically agreed on some points, political considerations decided him against embracing it.[31]

normally in order to refute Catholic historians who claimed that Henri had undergone a true conversion, but Voltaire makes the same point in the *Essai* (ii.537-40), expounding in some detail the political advantages which made the step necessary. Moreover, in connection with Henri's first abjuration at the time of the St Bartholomew's Day massacre, Voltaire remarks caustically: 'Les princes, en qui la religion n'est presque jamais que leur intérêt, se résolvent rarement au martyre' (ii.516). And earlier, speaking about William of Orange and the Reformation in the Low Countries, he says quite explicitly: 'la nécessité le fit calviniste: car les princes qui ont ou établi, ou protégé, ou changé les religions en ont rarement eu' (ii.441-42). Similarly, Voltaire was always very sceptical about the motives which had prompted Turenne to become a Catholic (cf. Best.D882, D4761, D4784, D4817, D14495, *Oh*, p.735).

[30] *Essai*, ii.221. The whole paragraph, of which this quotation is the penultimate sentence, was added to the text in 1761.

[31] the second and most interesting part of the paragraph first appeared in the Kehl edition of Voltaire's works. The *philosophe* implies that Charles was wrong in his calculations: 'il lui eût été facile, en excluant le pape et ses sujets du concile, d'en obtenir des décisions conformes à l'intérêt général de l'Europe; qu'il en eût été le maître, surtout du temps de Paul iv, pontife également sanguinaire et insensé.' It is perhaps not fanciful to see here an echo of the increasing militancy with which Voltaire viewed the papacy's position from the late 1760s when concerted action by the Catholic powers, especially by

The events of the Diet of Worms and Luther's appearance there are described (ii.223-24). Since the Diet was composed of princes rather than priests, Luther was able to trust their honour and rely on the emperor's safe-conduct. The chapter ends with a re-emergence of the more ironical, polemically-minded Voltaire, anxious to score a few extra points against the Catholic Church. For Luther, having decided to abolish the mass, pretended that the Devil had appeared to him to reproach him for his idolatrous practices, an expedient which, Voltaire comments, 'dans un temps plus éclairé, n'eût pas trouvé beaucoup d'applaudissements' (ii.224). But not only is Voltaire able to illustrate the unenlightened nature of the methods used by Luther in his Reformation, some of Luther's critics, the *philosophe* adds (ii.225), remarked that

celui qui avait consulté le diable pour détruire la messe témoignait au diable sa reconnaissance en abolissant les exorcismes, et qu'il voulait renverser tous les remparts élevés pour repousser l'ennemi des hommes.

This provides the opportunity for an onslaught against the superstition of Catholic countries where exorcism continued to be a regular practice. In this matter the Reformers were two hundred years ahead of the Catholics, claims Voltaire. Yet so far, this is about the first thing he has said to the Protestants' advantage.[32] The picture he has painted of Luther's Reformation has not been a very edifying one, relying as it has mainly on the working of greed and power-politics, sparked off by a quarrel between some monks.

iii. *The Reformation spreads*

Luther and Germany, however, are not the whole story. The next chapter contains a more approving account of Zwingli's Reformation at Zurich. In this case, after Zwingli's ideas on the eucharist had been criticised by the local clergy, the affair was referred to the Senate of Zurich: 'On alla aux voix: la pluralité fut pour la réformation [...]

---

the Bourbon *pacte de famille*, seemed likely to limit severely the pope's traditional powers, (cf. *The New Cambridge modern history*, vol.viii, (Cambridge 1968) p.391).

[32] even this is modified by a 1769 addition at the end of the chapter: 'car si dans nos derniers temps les protestants du Nord ont été encore assez imbéciles pour faire brûler deux ou trois misérables accusés de sorcellerie, il est constant qu'enfin cette sotte abomination est entièrement abolie' (ii.225). The Reformation did not cure the Protestants of irrationality, it appears.

tout le peuple fut dans le moment de la religion du sénat' (*Essai*, ii.226). Such an example of Erastianism in action could hardly fail to arouse Voltaire's admiration and he recounts with equal satisfaction a similar event in Berne.[33] However, when a stolid nation like the Swiss changes religion so suddenly, 'il y a infailliblement une cause qui doit avoir fait une impression violente sur tous les esprits' (ii.227). This Voltaire suggests, was the result of another quarrel between monks! The Dominicans, refusing to accept the doctrine of the immaculate conception of Mary which was preached ardently by the Franciscans, deceived a young lay brother, called Yetser, into believing that the Virgin had appeared to him to assure him that she had, in fact, been born 'dans le péché originel'. However, poor Yetser's suspicions were eventually aroused after he had been given five supposed stigmata, and he denounced the Order to the magistrates. Exemplary justice was meted out by Rome itself, but this fact was soon forgotten: 'On ne se souvenait que du sacrilège' (ii.229). Voltaire probably found this story in Burnet's *Voyage de Suisse, d'Italie et de quelques endroits d'Allemagne et de France, fait ès années 1685 et 1686* (Rotterdam 1687), pp.61-84 (ii.227, n.3), and it enables him both to provide himself with a satisfactory reason for the Swiss Reformation and at the same time to fire another broadside at the evils of monasticism (cf. *Oh*, pp.840-41).

At length, then, we see examples of the Reformation as a wholly beneficial occurrence, a step forward in reason and common sense jointly approved of by both magistrates and people.[34] Similar triumphs for 'la religion évangélique' took place in Sweden and Denmark where Catholicism is utterly discredited because it is the religion of the tyrant king Christiern and the infamous archbishop Troll of Upsala (*Essai*, ii.231-32). After Gustav Vasa's victory in Sweden, Catholicism is quickly abolished in both countries. In all this, however, one still has the impression that Voltaire's satisfaction is caused by the more negative side of the Reformation, the abolition of Catholicism and its abuses, rather than by the positive religious alternatives offered by the various Reformers. It is the assumption of effective control over Church affairs

[33] the passages summarised from this point until the end of the paragraph were added in 1761.

[34] Voltaire's enthusiasm for the manner in which the Swiss Reformation was brought about seems to have lasted until the end of his life: cf. Best.D20745, to Catherine the Great, 1 August 1777: 'Ce furent autrefois ces braves Suisses qui commencèrent à démolir le vaste édifice de la tyrannie de Rome.'

by various governments (consisting of laymen and *not* priests) which is his main cause for rejoicing. This is made clear when Voltaire comments significantly that Zwingli, 'en établissant sa secte, avait paru plus zélé pour la liberté que pour le christianisme' (ii.230). The English Reformation is not depicted so favourably, brought about as it was by a whim of 'le barbare et capricieux Henri VIII',[35] a representative of secular power hardly comparable in dignity with the august Swiss magistrates. Basically, however, it has Voltaire's sympathy, for he lists the abuses the English Church had been subjected to, and describes Catholicism in England as 'ce grand monument dès longtemps ébranlé par la haine publique' (ii.251).

The Protestants, then, were becoming 'recommendables aux yeux des peuples par la manière dont leur réforme s'établit en plusieurs lieux' (*Essai*, ii.241). Singled out for the highest praise is Geneva:

Les magistrats de Genève firent soutenir des thèses pendant tout le mois de juin 1535. On invita les catholiques et les protestants de tous les pays à venir y disputer: quatre secrétaires rédigèrent par écrit tout ce qui se dit d'essentiel pour et contre. Ensuite le grand conseil de la ville examina pendant deux mois le résultat des disputes: c'était ainsi à peu près qu'on en avait usé à Zurich et à Berne, mais moins juridiquement et avec moins de maturité et d'appareil. Enfin le conseil proscrivit la religion romaine.[36]

The moral severity which characterised the Reformation is not, on this occasion, spoken of disapprovingly. Voltaire justifies it by describing the scandals which had been rampant under the Catholic régime: public brothels administered by the prince bishop, secret passages from

---

[35] *Essai*, ii.261; cf. ii.251: 'On sait que l'Angleterre se sépara du pape parce que le roi Henri VIII fut amoureux.'

[36] one of Voltaire's early letters had expressed similar sentiments. Writing to Isaac Cambiague about the possible places of publication of the *Henriade*, he mentions London, Amsterdam and Geneva, and goes on: 'Mon admiration pour la sagesse du gouvernement de cette dernière ville, et surtout pour la manière dont la réforme y fut établie, me font pencher de ce côté' (Best.D259, *c*.December 1725). There is no real reason to suppose that Voltaire subsequently changed his favourable opinion of Geneva's Reformation. What he admired was the dignified and reasonable way Catholicism had been abolished in the city, and later disputes with the pastors of Geneva appear not to have altered this. At any rate, he did not revise the text of the *Essai* as he could so easily have done, and in fact did in many other places. The *philosophe*'s hostility is reserved for Calvin and the way in which he influenced Geneva's Reformation, and this hostility is already complete in the first edition of the *Essai*, before Voltaire's disagreements with men like Vernet. Indeed, as we shall see, it was some of his comments about Calvin which started the trouble: cf. below, pp.128ff.

monasteries to nunneries, and at Lausanne a little door behind the altar in the bishop's chapel leading to a nearby convent. The political motive is again strongly stressed – 'les Genevois recouvrèrent en effet leur vraie liberté' – but this liberty is not retained for long, however, and the idyllic Genevese Reformation is soon spoiled by the sanctimonious and tyrannical Calvin, who, although he took no part in the original Genevese Reformation, 'y retourna ensuite, et s'y érigea en pape des protestants' (ii.242).

Moreover, although the Reformation was spreading in a praiseworthy and respectable way in some places, Voltaire is not slow to draw attention to a very different phenomenon, the growth of another type of Protestantism whose adepts 'méritaient qu'on sonnât le tocsin sur eux de tous les coins de l'Europe' (*Essai*, ii.241). These were the Anabaptists, 'les premiers enthousiastes dont on ait ouï parler dans ces temps-là' (ii.236). Voltaire's antipathy for them as they were in their origins is predictable, since they were not only fanatical but of the lowest social class. Yet he does show a certain sympathy for their demands while utterly condemning their methods: 'A la vérité, le manifeste de ces sauvages, au nom des hommes qui cultivent la terre, aurait été signé par Lycurge [. . .] ils réclamaient les droits du genre humain; mais ils les soutinrent en bêtes féroces.'[37] Once again, however, his qualified sympathy is only for political and social grievances. As so often happens, Voltaire is unwilling to accept as genuine the religious aspirations of any type of 'enthousiastes'; he is not even prepared to admit that they have any. He has been able to explain the motives of Luther and the other Reformers as an alliance between the political opportunism of princes and the theologian's desire to dominate. Now, confronted with the sort of religious manifestation which the Enlightenment in general and he in particular were at a complete loss to understand, Voltaire resorts to arguments which seem more than a little unconvincing in the present context. Applied to the leaders of the Anabaptists, the explanation of hypocrisy could conceivably be adequate, since they might hope to gain power and influence from the revolt: 'Deux fanatiques, nommés Stork et Muncer, nés en Saxe, se servirent de quelques passages de l'Ecriture qui insinuent qu'on n'est

---

[37] *Essai*, ii.236. This passage was added in 1761, but the original text also clearly stressed the political content of the Anabaptists' demands: 'Ils développèrent cette vérité dangereuse qui est dans tous les cœurs, c'est que les hommes sont nés égaux, et que si les papes avaient traité les princes en sujets, les seigneurs traitaient les paysans en bêtes.'

point disciple du Christ sans être inspiré: ils prétendirent l'être.' Yet the fact that there must have existed a widespread religious vacuum before two men like Stork and Muncer could have received such an enormous response is completely ignored. After all, if they had merely preached equality and revolution, why should the religious part of their message have been so important? Earlier revolts in the Middle Ages had not relied on this catalyst.[38] Yet Voltaire is quite categorical in insisting that religion was only a hypocritical pretext: 'ils se dirent inspirés, et envoyés pour réformer la communion romaine et luthérienne' (*Essai*, ii.236), whereas by saying something like 'ils se croyaient inspirés, et dirent', he could have legitimately criticised their actions without implying that their motives were equally indefensible.

It really seems as if the only religious experience Voltaire was capable of fully understanding and approving was that of the deist, who worshipped the Supreme Being in a 'reasonable' way, devoid of any distasteful manifestations of subliminal religious or spiritual fervour. Indeed, one could go as far as to say that the concept of a spiritual life, equally important to both Catholic and Protestant traditions, is completely alien to the *philosophe*: he not only condemns, but appears to doubt the very existence of the forms of religious experience covered by this term. For him they are indistinguishable from fanaticism or superstition, merely the pretext to gain power by preying on the ignorance of the lower classes. Voltaire's religious beliefs have been the subject of much heated debate, and even now it cannot be claimed that a final position has been reached.[39] At this stage of our study, it is

---

[38] Voltaire himself seems to have realised this inconsistency: originally he said in the *Essai* that the Anabaptists were preaching 'l'égalité *et* la réforme' (ii.963-64, my italics), but in 1761 he replaced this phrase with a much longer passage (of which the quotation on p.38 is an extract) outlining the peasants' political grievances. The *Annales de l'empire* seems to fluctuate between two attitudes: on the one hand, Voltaire paints what is really a very sympathetic picture of the Anabaptist leader Hutter, concluding: 'il prêchait la réforme et l'égalité, et c'est pourquoi il fut brûlé' (M.xiii.500), but a little earlier (p.489) he has been extremely cynical about the motives of Muncer. In the 1761 additions to the *Essai* Voltaire seems to have followed passages of the *Annales* closely (cf. the quotation given below, p.43, which is identical with a passage in M.xiii.489), and probably under the influence of his campaign against *l'infâme* abandoned those parts of his narrative which appeared to be sympathetic to the Anabaptists or which mentioned their religious motivation.

[39] for two widely differing opinions, see Theodore Besterman, 'Voltaire's god', *Studies on Voltaire* (1967), iv.23-41, and W. H. Barber, 'Voltaire and Quakerism'. These articles will be discussed at a later stage (below, pp.453ff).

worth quoting at some length the end of the section dealing with the Anabaptists, for Voltaire's interpretation of the facts allows him to make propaganda both against religious 'enthusiasm' and in favour of deism. Nor is it necessary to assume that he is being hypocritical in this passage, using the deist position merely for reasons of prudence or in order conveniently to ridicule Christianity. The additions of 1761 and 1775 clearly illustrate Voltaire's determination to stress the 'redeeming' rôle of deism, thinly disguised here as Unitarianism. Moreover, the beliefs ascribed (in the 1761 addition) to the Unitarians, 'qui ne reconnaissent qu'un seul Dieu, et qui, en révérant le Christ, vivent sans beaucoup de dogmes et sans aucune dispute,' are remarkably similar to the opinions with which d'Alembert, perhaps under Voltaire's influence, credited the Genevese pastors in his notorious *Encyclopédie* article 'Genève' (1758).[40] Here, surely, is evidence of a constructive side to Voltaire's generally critical analysis of the Reformation, an attempt, even after many disappointments, to stress that the difference between philosophical deism and the relatively advanced theological position reached by some Protestant theologians was not unbridgeable.[41] At any rate, though there is indeed satire of orthodox Christianity in this passage, the emphasis is progressively placed on the concrete advantages to be gained from a simple, unsuperstitious belief in God, even when the starting point has been with a sect originally as cruel and fanatical as the Anabaptists (*Essai*, ii.240):

Cependant la secte subsiste assez nombreuse, cimentée du sang des prosélytes, qu'ils appellent *martyrs*, mais entièrement différente de ce qu'elle était dans son origine: les successeurs de ces fanatiques sanguinaires sont les plus paisibles de tous les hommes, occupés de leurs manufactures et de leur négoce, laborieux, charitables. Il n'y a point d'exemple d'un si grand changement; mais comme ils ne font aucune figure dans le monde, on ne daigne pas s'apercevoir s'ils sont changés ou non, s'ils sont méchants ou vertueux.

[1761 addition:]
Ce qui a changé leurs mœurs, c'est qu'ils se sont rangés au parti des unitaires, c'est-à-dire de ceux qui ne reconnaissent qu'un seul Dieu, et qui, en révérant le Christ, vivent sans beaucoup de dogmes et sans aucune dispute; hommes condamnés dans toutes les autres communautés, et vivant en paix au milieu d'elles.

[40] cf. below, pp.135 ff., for a discussion of this article and of reactions to it.
[41] cf. below, pp.182, 194. The 1775 addition would seem to represent a renewed hardening of attitude on Voltaire's part.

[1775 addition:]

Ainsi ils ont été le contraire des chrétiens; ceux-ci furent d'abord des frères paisibles, souffrants et cachés, et enfin des scélérats absurdes et barbares. Les anabaptistes commencèrent par la barbarie, et ont fini par la douceur et la sagesse.

It is impossible not to be struck by the total difference in position of Bayle and Voltaire on the important matter of religion and conduct. Voltaire is saying clearly in this passage that what transformed the bestial Anabaptists into exemplary citizens was their change in beliefs, whereas Bayle's contention that religious beliefs have no effect whatsoever on human conduct is almost too well known to need reiterating.[42]

Chapter 136, 'Suite de la religion d'Angleterre', contains a similar development in connection with the English Anabaptists (*Essai*, ii.262). Voltaire stresses that

ils ressemblaient très peu par les dogmes, et encore moins par leur conduite, à ces anabaptistes d'Allemagne, ramas d'hommes rustiques et féroces que nous avons vus pousser les fureurs d'un fanatisme sauvage aussi loin que peut aller la nature humaine abandonnée à elle-même.

but one has the impression that, although their beliefs and conduct may have been very different from those of the original German Anabaptists, their religion is remarkably similar to that developed by the latter's peaceable descendants. The connection between these English Anabaptists and the Quakers is expressly stated and Voltaire goes on to explain their beliefs, which were deistic, whether they realised this or not (ii.262):

Ceux qu'on appelait alors anabaptistes en Angleterre sont les pères de ces quakers pacifiques, dont la religion a été tant tournée en ridicule, et dont on a été forcé de respecter les mœurs [...] mais ce qui est très extraordinaire, c'est que, se croyant chrétiens, et ne se piquant nullement de philosophie, ils n'étaient réellement que des déistes: car ils ne reconnaissaient Jésus-Christ que comme un homme à qui Dieu avait daigné donner des lumières plus pures qu'à ses contemporains.

Thus, in a few generations, deism, closely connected with the Anabaptists and Quakers, has achieved little short of a miracle, and Voltaire is clearly implying that similar transformations could occur elsewhere if such reasonable tenets were adopted by other Christian denominations.

[42] however, H. T. Mason, *Pierre Bayle and Voltaire*, p.89, shows that Bayle is sometimes inconsistent in this respect.

The element of propaganda is indeed strong in many parts of Voltaire's narrative. My contention has been that this was not a purely negative attack on Christian or Protestant belief, written from a completely sceptical viewpoint. In his provocative and stimulating article 'Voltaire's god', Theodore Besterman concludes that: 'Voltaire was at most an agnostic; and were any tough-minded philosopher to maintain that this type of agnosticism is indistinguishable from atheism, I would not be prepared to argue with him' (p.41). But this attitude is surely hard to square with the comments about the Anabaptists which are found in the *Essai sur les mœurs*. After describing the English Anabaptists, for example, Voltaire goes on immediately to sing the praises of deism, and he emphasises its superiority not only over other religions, but also over 'un athéisme funeste, qui est le contraire du théisme' (*Essai*, ii.263). Voltaire's attitude toward certain aspects of the Reformation can only be fully understood as the reaction of a man who genuinely believed in the merits of deism, but, as I have already remarked, was unable to comprehend what is usually referred to as the 'spiritual life' of a Christian and its accompanying manifestations. In his opinion, the two extremes meet: it is the spread of deism that has defeated atheism, but the latter had been a real danger in the sixteenth century when the Reformation was engendering widespread scepticism. As he says quite specifically in the *Essai* (ii.264): 'cette opinion pernicieuse' (atheism) has been almost completely wiped out by 'la vraie philosophie, la morale, l'intérêt de la société': 'mais alors elle s'établissait par les guerres de religion; et des chefs de parti devenus athées conduisaient une multitude d'enthousiastes'. The last part of this quotation is really an extraordinary statement for a historian of the Reformation to make: so unable or unwilling is Voltaire to distinguish genuine religious feeling from 'enthusiasm', superstition and fanaticism that he actually claims that the Reformers themselves were atheists. Had he restricted such accusations to the Anabaptists, his position would at least have been defensible, for as A. G. Dickens remarks: 'The Anabaptists had no great spiritual leader, no generally-accepted epitome of doctrine, no central directive organs.'[43] A hostile commentator might conceivably be justified in regarding the Anabaptist leaders as 'des chefs de parti devenus athées' whose followers were nothing but 'une multitude d'enthousiastes'. But it is little short of perverse to extend this

[43] *Reformation and society in sixteenth-century Europe* (London 1966), p.135.

description to the Lutheran, Zwinglian and Calvinist Reformations, all of which claimed at least some followers of the more respectable and moderate kind, and fostered ordered types of religious life worlds away from the Anabaptists' bizarre experiments. Nonetheless, we shall have to look a long way in Voltaire's works before finding the Reformation attributed to any genuinely religious motive, as opposed to idle theological disputes or cynical manipulation of the masses.

Be this as it may, the appeal of a rational, peaceful religion like deism is enhanced by the account Voltaire gives of the Anabaptist excesses during the Peasants' Revolt. The hypocrisy of Muncer is brought out: 'Muncer s'empare de Mulhausen en Thuringe en prêchant l'égalité, et fait porter à ses pieds l'argent des habitants en prêchant le désintéressement.'[44] All the gentlemen the Anabaptists met were massacred. Despite Muncer's death, they continued to ravage Germany 'au nom de Dieu' and took over the town of Munster after chasing out its bishop: 'le fanatisme n'avait point encore produit dans le monde une fureur pareille'. In many ways, as we shall see later, 'tous ces paysans, qui se croyaient prophètes, et qui ne savaient rien de l'Ecriture sinon qu'il faut massacrer sans pitié les ennemis du Seigneur' (*Essai*, ii.238), resemble the Camisard rebels for whom Voltaire generally expressed so little sympathy.[45] Moreover, they had a predilection for the Old

[44] *Essai*, ii.237. The passage quoted was added in 1761: cf. above, p.39 n.38.

[45] cf. Best.D12425, D13274, D13325. The similarity is mentioned explicitly by Voltaire in a letter to Frederick the Great of 20 December 1740 (Best.D2386): 'Ceux qui diront que Les tems de ces crimes sont passés, qu'on ne verra plus de Barcochebas, de Mahomets, de Jeans de Leide [. . .] font ce me semble trop d'honneur à la nature humaine. Le même poison subsiste encore quoyque moins dévelopé [. . .] N'a t'on pas vû de nos jours les prophètes des Cevenes tuer au nom de dieu ceux de leur secte qui n'étoient pas assés soumis?' As we shall see shortly, John of Leyden (Jan Beukels) was one of the Anabaptists' leaders, who became 'king' of Munster (cf. A. G. Dickens, *Reformation and society in sixteenth-century Europe*, pp.133-34).

It is interesting to note that throughout his life Voltaire continued to maintain a dual attitude toward the Anabaptists. On the one hand, they could represent the personification of religious fanaticism, as in Best.D14039, textual notes (to Linguet, 14 or 15 March 1767), where, speaking of the development of reason in a much more optimistic frame of mind than he showed in Best.D2386, Voltaire says: 'Je défierais aujourd'hui [. . .] Jean de Leide de se faire roi de Munster.' Cf. also Best.D20447. On the other hand, Voltaire often refers to the 'bons anabaptistes', those peaceful descendants of the original fanatics, whom he describes in the *Essai sur les mœurs* as exemplary theists. The 'bon anabaptiste Jacques' of *Candide* is the best-known example of this tendency, but cf. also Best.D2341, D15985 and D16069 (Voltaire to Moultou, 1 January 1770): 'Je pense bien fermement qu'il n'y a de chrétiens primitifs que les bons Quakers et les anabatistes.'

Chapter 2

Testament, a fact not likely to increase his esteem for them (ii.238-39):

Ils voulaient d'abord établir la théocratie des Juifs, et être gouvernés par Dieu seul; mais [. . .] un garçon tailleur, nommé Jean de Leyde [. . .] assura que Dieu lui était apparu, et l'avait nommé roi: il le dit et le fit croire.

Like the kings of Israel, he wished to have several wives, and was himself both monarch and prophet. One of his spouses having spoken against his authority had her head cut off in front of the others, who then, 'soit par crainte, soit par fanatisme', danced round her corpse with their master (ii.239). Despite these moral aberrations, John was valiant and defended the town for a year against its bishop. His eventual capture and death did not prevent other Anabaptists from being on the point of taking Amsterdam. Finally, however, they were massacred everywhere, 'comme [. . .] des monstres dont il fallait purger la terre' (ii.239, 1761 addition).

By this time, the progress of the Reformation could no longer be stopped. Fourteen towns and several princes protesting against the moderate proposals of the Diet of Spire (1529) gave the name of Protestants to all enemies of Rome, regardless of their denomination. As yet, 'le sang ne coulait point encore dans l'empire pour la cause de Luther', apart from that shed by the Anabaptists (*Essai*, ii.238). Yet it was really Luther who was responsible for their outbursts, 'puisque le premier il avait franchi la barrière de la soumission', but he lost none of his influence, 'et n'en fut pas moins le prophète de sa patrie' (ii.237).

iv. *Voltaire's attitude to the Reformation*

This attribution of the real responsibility for the Peasants' Revolt to Luther is yet another reminder of Voltaire's generally unenthusiastic attitude towards the Reformation, and at the same time indicates his main grievance against it. For when the attention of Voltaire's social and humanitarian conscience is drawn to the scandal of war, other factors and considerations fade in comparison. The shortcomings of the Reformation are, in fact, usually forgiven in view of the amelioration of the human condition for which it was responsible: the shattering of monolithic Roman ecclesiastical power, the subjection of Church to state and the abolition of many religious abuses were no small achievement, and Voltaire is ready to mark his approval. At the same time he cannot forget the price which was paid for these changes in terms of suffering humanity. 'Il n'y a point de pays, en effet,' he observes sadly, 'où la religion de Calvin et de Luther ait paru sans exciter des persécutions et des guerres' (M.xv.39). *Dieu et les hommes* (1769) puts the deaths caused by the Reformation and its aftermath high on the list of 'barbaries chrétiennes': Voltaire estimates that about two million people lost their lives 'pour la transsubstantiation, la prédestination, le surplis et l'eau bénite' (M.xxviii.235). Again and again he returns indefatigably to the same theme, which reappears like a refrain in every chapter dealing with the Reformation. It is in this frame of mind that he describes Luther's Reformation as 'ce petit intérêt de moines, dans un coin de la Saxe', but such an apparently trivial dispute 'produisit plus de cent ans de discordes, de fureurs et d'infortunes chez trente nations' (*Essai*, ii.216). Elsewhere he admits that: 'le clergé a été corrigé par les protestants, comme un rival devient plus circonspect par la jalousie surveillante de son rival', but a 1761 addition comments tellingly: 'mais on n'en a versé que plus de sang, et les querelles des théologiens sont devenues des guerres de cannibales' (*Essai*, ii.218). Likewise, a rather flippant discussion of Philip of Hesse's bigamy and the approval which Luther was forced to give this (cf. below, pp.52-54), ends with the comment: 'Si les nouveautés n'avaient apporté que ces scandales paisibles, le monde eût été trop heureux; mais l'Allemagne fut un théâtre de scènes plus tragiques' (*Essai*, ii.235). In fact, Voltaire's seeming reluctance to admit to the necessity of a major reform, though owing much to the reasons discussed earlier (cf. above, pp.29-31), springs mainly from this hatred of bloodshed. The more he thinks about the disasters which occurred, the more prepared he becomes to condone the various abuses which existed in the Church before admitting that the Reformation was inevitable. Granted that the loose morals of the clergy were a scandal:

il faut aussi convenir que ce n'était pas une raison pour autoriser tant de guerres civiles, et qu'il ne fallait pas tuer les autres hommes parce que quelques prélats faisaient des enfants, et que des curés achetaient avec un écu le droit d'en faire.[46]

Yet there is no doubt that the legacy of the Reformation, or more strictly that part of it which Voltaire sees as beneficial to humanity at large, is accepted, albeit with the severe restrictions just mentioned – the tone of the chapters dealing with the Reformation in Switzerland,

---

[46] *Essai*, ii.211-12. The last clause of this quotation was added by Voltaire in 1761.

Scandinavia and England makes this sufficiently clear. The motives of the Reformers, however, receive no such acceptance.

The historical shortcomings of Voltaire's account are obvious and need not be stressed. He is not impartial and indeed would probably not have wished to be. His desire was to point a lesson for his times,[47] and the humanitarian concern he felt in considering the wars caused by the Reformation is surely understandable, as are also his attempts to establish religious toleration in a France which had, within living memory, seen the repeal of the Edict of Nantes, and where according to the letter of the law any Protestant minister was liable to be executed if he were unfortunate enough to be discovered.[48] One wonders, indeed, whether the division of Voltaire's historical works into two categories, suggested by professor Brumfitt (above, p.22), is not a little too clear-cut. In dealing with great events like the Reformation, the *philosophe* certainly follows in the main what he believes to be the judgement dictated by reason and humanity, but the resulting synthesis is far from what a modern historian would consider to be acceptable.

Perhaps the most serious defect, from a historical point of view, in Voltaire's appraisal of the Reformation, is the one which has already been discussed in connection with the Anabaptists: his complete lack of appreciation of the more positive religious motives of the Reformers, and his seeming unawareness of any fundamentally religious cause for the Reformation. This point must obviously not be laboured, but it is

[47] cf. H. T. Mason, *Pierre Bayle and Voltaire*, p.32: 'History is for him another weapon in the fight against "l'infâme", in the course of which enlightened reason may triumph over the forces of obscurantism. It can help to educate the "philosophes" and those who share their views.' Bayle, on the other hand, 'despite the didactic value he attaches to historical writing [. . .] promises [. . .] not to be partial'. Professor Mason's point is perfectly illustrated by the reflection Voltaire added in 1761 to the end of his chapter on Savonarola: 'Vous regardez en pitié toutes ces scènes d'absurdité et d'horreur; vous ne trouvez rien de pareil ni chez les Romains et les Grecs, ni chez les barbares. C'est le fruit de la plus infâme superstition qui ait jamais abruti les hommes, et du plus mauvais des gouvernements. Mais vous savez qu'il n'y a pas longtemps que nous sommes sortis de ces ténèbres, et que tout n'est pas encore éclairé' (*Essai*, ii.86).

I personally find it difficult, for the reasons I have explained, to agree with Dieter Gembicki when he speaks of 'l'extrême hardiesse de la vision voltairienne de la Réforme' ('La Réforme allemande vue par Voltaire', *Historiographie de la Réforme*, ed. Philippe Joutard (Paris, Neuchâtel, Montreal 1977), p.153). This article makes a useful survey of Voltaire's historical sources, as also does Louis Trenard, 'Voltaire, historien de la Réforme en France' (*Historiographie de la Réforme*, pp.156-70).

[48] cf. Shelby T. McCloy, *The Humanitarian movement in eighteenth-century France* (Lexington, Kentucky 1957), pp.11-17.

nonetheless basic to our discussion. Though various schools of historical thought have stressed differing aspects of the economic, social and political causes of the Reformation, few have denied that religious feeling held an important place among them. The distinguished Protestant historian, E.-G. Léonard, claims moreover that non-religious explanations should not be overemphasised, and underlines the central importance, in his opinion, of the rediscovery of personal piety at a time when, for various temporal reasons, the Roman Church was unable to respond to this deeply and widely-felt need:

L'appel aux intérêts matériels des princes et des seigneurs qui se décidèrent pour ou contre la Réforme refuse de tenir compte du fait qu'ils avaient, eux aussi, une âme et une intelligence ouvertes aux problèmes spirituels, et qu'ils restèrent le plus souvent fidèles à la position prise, lorsque ces intérêts leur conseillaient de profitables conversions [. . .]

Au total, l'élimination, dans la recherche des motifs de la Réforme, de ceux qui ne porteraient que sur telle classe et telle région et la constatation qu'elle intéressa tous les pays et tous les milieux obligent à lui reconnaître des causes valables pour tous les hommes. De ces causes générales aucune n'est plus universelle que le sentiment religieux [. . .] Aussi bien est-il naturel de chercher à une révolution religieuse des motifs spécifiquement religieux [. . .]

Je tiens à marquer dès maintenant [. . .] que *la Réforme, bien plus qu'une révolte contre la piété catholique, en fut l'aboutissement, la floraison.*[49]

Yet Voltaire mentions no genuine religious motive in his account, apart from destructive 'enthusiasm', and the major reformers lack even that. Perhaps Voltaire not only suspected the latter's motives but also disagreed with their tactics. If he ever attempted to imagine himself in the reformers' shoes, would he not have considered their task better fulfilled by a rational, sustained, perhaps ironic attack on Church abuses from within, rather than by a complete rupture followed by a violent confrontation from outside, very much as he himself harried *l'infâme* and spread deist propaganda while yet remaining a nominal Catholic? For Voltaire no doubt saw his own situation as in many ways similar to that of the sixteenth-century Reformers: the part of their work which he supported, namely the abolition of the Catholic Church's temporal power, remained incomplete in many countries. Had Luther and Calvin resembled Erasmus, they might never have

[49] *Histoire générale du protestantisme* (Paris 1961-1964), i.9-10. It will be noticed that Léonard's position is directly opposed to that of Voltaire on the subject of princely conversion: cf. above, p.33, n.29.

become such great figures in the history of religious thought, but they would at least have been more likely to gain Voltaire's approval.

Be this as it may, it is indubitable that the chief defect of the Reformation in Voltaire's eyes is that it was a disruptive social force and a source of bloody wars. When he remembers that these were a direct fruit of theological speculation, 'cet acharnement de la haine théologique qui produisit tant de meurtres',[50] his anger knows no bounds. The Scots, for example, 'auraient bien mieux fait de s'appliquer à fertiliser par leur travail leur terre ingrate et stérile, et à se procurer au moins par la pêche une subsistance qui leur manquait, que d'ensanglanter leur malheureux pays pour des opinions étrangères et pour l'intérêt de quelques ambitieux' (*Essai*, ii.268). The fact that the Reformers were theologians damns them in Voltaire's estimations – usually they incur his wrath equally with the Catholic clergy, and in his mind they conform to the same archetypal figure of the power-crazed, hypocritical priest. A passage from chapter 171 of the *Essai*, 'De la France sous Charles ix' (ii.491), will make this clear:

Chacun cherchait à dévorer une partie du gouvernement. Le clergé d'un côté, les pasteurs calvinistes de l'autre, criaient à la religion. Dieu était leur prétexte; la fureur de dominer était leur dieu: et les peuples, enivrés de fanatisme, étaient les instruments et les victimes de l'ambition de tant de partis opposés.

Yet extreme though this statement is, one should not necessarily conclude that the sentiments expressed are entirely characteristic of Voltaire. Sometimes, as we shall see, Protestant ministers are treated with slightly more indulgence in his writings than the Roman priesthood, and Voltaire was certainly readier to compromise with the former than with the latter. The next section of this study will consider Voltaire's views on the main Reformers and their doctrines, for although he affected to despise theology, he discussed it on many occasions. We shall then be in a better position to decide what facets, if any, of the new religion Voltaire accepted, and whether his attitude to Protestantism as a whole was more enthusiastic than the very limited approval he was willing to grant to the Reformation.

[50] *Essai*, ii.213. An exception to Voltaire's usual attitude on this point is to be found in notebook fragment no.25, where he states categorically: 'Il n'y eut des guerres de relligion que parce que les princes voulurent être despotiques. Ni les lutheriens ni les calvinistes ne commencèrent la guerre. Ce n'était pas une nécessité qu'il y eût une guerre civile parce qu'il y avait une nouvelle relligion' (Voltaire 82, pp.632-33).

3

Voltaire, the Reformers, their doctrines, and the ethos of Protestantism

DESCRIBING Calvin in chapter 133 of the *Essai sur les mœurs*, Voltaire comments (*Essai*, ii.242):

il écrivait mieux que Luther, et parlait plus mal: tous deux laborieux et austères, mais durs et emportés; tous deux brûlant de l'ardeur de se signaler et d'obtenir cette domination sur les esprits qui flatte tant l'amour-propre, et qui d'un théologien fait une espèce de conquérant.

The two major reformers, then, are summarily characterised; if this is typical of Voltaire's attitude to them, it is obvious that they are made in the image of Savonarola rather than of John Hus or Jeremy of Prague. And, indeed, it must be confessed that Voltaire's opinion of Luther and Calvin is singularly low. They are typical *chefs de secte*, devoid of any sort of wider spiritual insight or message, thirsting only after power and the domination of men.[1] That this is their *primum mobile* is shown by the fact that, like princes, they change their opinions to suit the circumstances in which they find themselves. Calvin, for example, had at first held a different doctrine from the Genevese on the eucharist: 'Calvin se brouilla d'abord avec ceux de Genève qui communiaient avec du pain levé; il voulait du pain azyme.' Later, however, he returned to the city, 'et communiant avec du pain levé comme les autres, il y acquit autant de crédit que Luther en avait en Saxe' (ii.243). Luther's doctrine also evolves, and Voltaire's remark in this case illustrates the extent of his scepticism in theological matters: 'Ce moine n'avait pas encore de doctrine ferme et arrêtée. Mais qui jamais en a eu?' (*Annales*, M.xiii.479).

---

[1] 'La vanité d'être chef de secte est la seconde de toutes les vanités de ce monde: car celle des conquérants est, dit-on, la première' (1770 addition to the article 'Arius', *Dictionnaire philosophique*, ed. Benda and Naves, p.453).

49

Chapter 3

i. *Luther*

The account of the beginnings of the Reformation in the *Annales de l'empire* is very similar to that in the *Essai sur les mœurs*, but there is a very slight difference in connection with Luther. The *Annales* adds a sentence giving the briefest of biographical sketches, then continues in the same vein as the *Essai*: 'Le fils d'un forgeron, né à Islèbe, fut celui par qui commença la révolution. C'était Martin Luther, moine augustin, que ses supérieurs chargèrent de prêcher contre la marchandise qu'ils n'avaient pu vendre' (M.xiii.479). The purpose of this extra information is probably to discredit Luther in the eyes of the reader by emphasising his humble origins, and, indeed, the description of him as a 'moine augustin' would certainly have stigmatised him in Voltaire's own opinion without any further compromising details. Actually, whether Voltaire was aware of it or not, Luther was already doctor of theology and vicar-general of his order in the Wittemberg district,[2] so the *philosophe*'s account of the circumstances is a little inaccurate, to say the least. Luther's scholarship is belittled (*Essai*, ii.219-20; 1761 addition):

Les luthériens voulurent d'abord de nouvelles versions de la *Bible* en toutes les langues modernes, et des versions purgées de toutes les négligeances et infidélités qu'ils imputaient à la *Vulgate* [. . .] Luther traduisit, d'après l'hébreu, la *Bible* germanique; mais on prétend qu'il savait peu l'hébreu, et que sa traduction est plus remplie de fautes que la *Vulgate*.

We have already seen that Voltaire despises the pretext Luther used for abolishing the Mass (cf. above, p.35). He also detests the vulgar and ungentlemanly way Luther addressed his adversaries, above all the pope (*Essai*, ii.221):

'petit pape, petit papelin, vous êtes un âne, un ânon; allez doucement, il fait glacé, vous vous rompriez les jambes, et on dirait: Que diable est ceci? Le petit ânon de papelin est estropié' [. . .]

Ces basses grossièretés, aujourd'hui si dégoûtantes, ne révoltaient point des esprits assez grossiers. Luther, avec ces bassesses d'un style barbare, triomphait dans son pays de toute la politesse romaine.

Yet, despite such criticisms and the fact that Luther is held responsible for the Peasants' Revolt and much bloodshed, Voltaire cannot help expressing a certain amount of reluctant admiration for this man who

[2] Léonard, *Histoire générale*, i.35.

wrought such a change in the world. Referring to Luther's action of burning a papal bull at Wittemberg, he exclaims: 'On voit par ce trait si c'était un homme hardi', though the statement is immediately qualified: 'mais aussi on voit qu'il était déjà bien puissant' (ii.220). Voltaire also admits that by appearing at the Diet of Worms, Luther was 's'exposant hardiment au sort de Jean Hus', but he implies that there was no real comparison, as the members of the Diet were very different from the fathers of the Council of Constance: they were princes not priests. Nevertheless, 'il parla devant l'empereur et devant la diète, et soutint sa doctrine avec courage' (ii.223). Even after his condemnation, Luther 'ne s'étonna pas: caché dans une forteresse de Saxe, il brava l'empereur, irrita la moitié de l'Allemagne contre le pape, répondit au roi d'Angleterre comme à son égal, fortifia et étendit son Eglise naissante' (ii.224). These are not the terms of complete condemnation or scorn. Voltaire also approves Luther's demands that monastic vows be abolished and that priests be allowed to marry, although the point has to be made obliquely in order to preserve the fiction that Voltaire is writing as an orthodox Catholic (ii.224-25):

La même impartialité doit reconnaître que Luther et les autres moines, en contractant des mariages utiles à l'Etat, ne violaient guère plus leurs vœux que ceux qui, ayant fait serment d'être pauvres et humbles, possédaient des richesses fastueuses.

The disguise does not prevent the meaning from remaining crystal-clear. Voltaire cannot really make up his mind what to think of Luther. He admires the great man in him, though he is reluctant to express this too readily, for he cannot forget that Luther was at one time a monk, and remained a theologian all his life.[3] The ambiguity in his attitude shows clearly at the end of chapter 130 of the *Essai sur les mœurs*, 'Progrès du Luthéranisme', where he adopts a rather detached, flippant tone in harmony with the nature of the subject he is treating (ii.231-35). For

[3] the most critical references to Luther are in Voltaire's notebooks, where the following anecdote is recorded twice, presumably because it emphasises both Luther's pride and his basic insincerity: 'Luther, dans un de ses sermons, dit: "On ne me considère pas comme on le doit: si on m'inquiète encore, sachez que je me dédirai. C'est moi qui ai mené le branle, c'est moi qui le romprai." Est-ce un si grand mal de dire la messe? Bossuet le lui reproche' (Voltaire 82, 525; repeated almost identically on p.596). However, Voltaire does not appear to have used this damning material in his published works, and was thus perhaps not completely convinced of its accuracy himself: it would certainly be surprising if he regarded Bossuet as a reliable authority.

this is the story of Philip of Hesse's bigamy, approved by Luther and the Reformers. Two standpoints would seem to be open to Voltaire: either he could take the part of the Reformers and claim that marriage was merely a civil contract (at the same time tacitly condemning the position of the Catholic Church), or he could argue that the law that a man should take only one wife was recognised by everyone and that the Reformers were being hypocritical in allowing a powerful prince to transgress a rule which was binding on other Christians. In point of fact, Voltaire takes neither position: he tries both to discredit Luther and to deny the inviolable sanctity of monogamy.

At the beginning of the episode, Voltaire seems to take the anti-Reformer view (ii.232-33):

ils dispensèrent d'une loi reconnue, laquelle semblait ne devoir plus recevoir d'atteinte; c'est la loi de n'avoir qu'une femme, loi positive sur laquelle paraît fondé le repos des Etats et des familles dans toute la chrétienté

yet Voltaire immediately qualifies this in a manner which would seem to absolve the reformers:

mais loi quelquefois funeste, et qui peut avoir besoin d'exceptions, comme tant d'autres lois. Il est des cas où l'intérêt même des familles, et surtout l'intérêt de l'Etat, demandent qu'on épouse une seconde femme du vivant de la première, quand cette première ne peut donner un héritier nécessaire. La loi naturelle alors se joint au bien public; et le but du mariage étant d'avoir des enfants, il paraît contradictoire de refuser l'unique moyen qui mène à ce but.

The changing and non-universal nature of Catholic doctrines is implied by the assertion that pope Gregory II in 726 allowed a second marriage if the first wife was incapable of bearing children.[4] Yet this piece of information is not used to absolve the Reformers, for Catherine de Saal, Philip's first wife, 'n'était point infirme' (ii.233), and he had had children by her. One of the reasons given by the synod Luther assembled in Wittemberg ought to have commanded, and probably did command, Voltaire's approval: 'Le synode de Vittemberg ne regardait pas le mariage comme un sacrement; mais comme un contrat civil.' Yet there

---

[4] ii.233. This passage, like the previous quotation, was added in 1761, and seems to indicate that Voltaire's attitude toward monogamy was becoming less enthusiastic, a conclusion also supported by his letter of 13 March 1764 to Arthur Hill-Trevor: 'Such a double wedding is contrary to our western laws, not to eastern, nor to the law of nature, and much less to good nature' (Best.D11767).

is such capital to be made out of the inconsistencies of the 'réformateurs d'Allemagne, qui voulaient suivre l'Evangile mot à mot' (ii.232), that Voltaire concentrates on bringing out their hypocrisy judged by their own standards rather than their correctness judged by the light of reason (ii.234):

il [the synod] disait que la discipline de l'Eglise admet le divorce, quoique l'Evangile le défende; il disait que l'Evangile n'ordonne pas expressément la monogamie; mais enfin il voyait si clairement le scandale, qu'il le déroba autant qu'il put aux yeux du public.

The Reformers are therefore shown to have broken their own rule of accepting the literal truth of the Bible, and their motives in doing this are equally damning. For although Voltaire cannot understand the naïvety of Philip of Hesse who, 'd'ailleurs sage et politique, semblait croire sincèrement qu'avec la permission de Luther et de ses compagnons il pouvait transgresser une loi qu'il reconnaissait', he points out that 'il fait sentir adroitement à ses docteurs que, s'ils ne veulent pas lui donner la dispense dont il a besoin, il pourrait bien la demander au pape' (ii.233).

Luther, then, is convicted beyond doubt of sacrificing his beliefs to expediency, and his sincerity as a religious teacher is called completely into question. Yet this is done in a way which leaves Voltaire open to the accusation of scandalmongering; the episode after all takes up two-thirds of the chapter in question, and the flippant tone in which parts of it are written could be claimed not to belong to a serious history, still less to an important matter such as the one in question. For example, Voltaire cannot restrain himself from suggesting one more fact in favour of Philip, a singularly racy piece of information which would hardly be out of place in a Sunday newspaper: 'La loi naturelle parlait seule en faveur du landgrave; la nature lui avait donné au nombre de trois ce qu'elle ne donne aux autres qu'au nombre de deux; mais il n'apporta point cette raison physique dans sa requête' (ii.233; 1761 addition). The story obviously tickled Voltaire's fancy, as he repeats it in the *Fragment sur l'histoire générale* (1773), promoting its importance in the affair very considerably (M.xxix.231-32):

Nous sommes loin d'insinuer qu'on doive établir la polygamie dans notre Europe chrétienne [. . .] Luther et Melanchthon permirent au landgrave de Hesse, deux femmes, parce qu'il avait au nombre de trois ce qui chez les autres se borne à deux [. . .] mais ces exemples sont rares.

It is easy to see how the myth of the 'sourire hideux' arose!

More important, perhaps, is that Voltaire gives no clear statement of his own views on the subject of polygamy. Had he done this, the attacks on Luther and the other Reformers need have lost none of their force, for as Voltaire points out, they were breaking 'une loi reçue dans leur parti même' (*Essai*, ii.233), and he would have appeared more in the guise of an impartial judge of the Reformers' case than as a counsel for the prosecution. Yet even here, where Voltaire falls more than usual from his claimed impartiality as a historian, there remains a slight note of admiration for Luther's audacity: 'ce que, depuis Grégoire, jamais n'avaient osé les papes, dont Luther attaquait le pouvoir excessif, il le fit n'ayant aucun pouvoir'.[5] Despite all his faults, he remains a great man, for although Luther was a theologian, Voltaire finds no major crime of intolerance with which he can reproach him, and all indignation on this score is reserved for Calvin. He attempts to describe Luther patronisingly, and sometimes affects to despise him, but an element of admiration for one of the world's great revolutionaries is never entirely absent from Voltaire's attitude.

ii. *Zwingli and the minor Reformers*

Zwingli is the only great Reformer whom Voltaire describes at all enthusiastically. Though he was killed in the 'première guerre de religion entre les catholiques et les réformés [. . .] à la tête de l'armée protestante', thus laying himself open to Voltaire's disapproval as just one more bloodthirsty theologian, Zwingli's responsibility is not over-emphasised and the Catholics are blamed for starting the war.[6] He is also made the

---

[5] ii.234. There would appear to be an inconsistency here with what Voltaire says a little earlier in the *Essai* – cf. above, p.51: 'on voit qu'il [Luther] était bien puissant' – but there is surely a difference in the types of power to which the *philosophe* is referring. In the earlier passage he means that Luther had a lot of political support in Germany and was therefore fairly secure in his attacks on the papacy. But in the second passage he is talking about theological or spiritual power, and the paradox is certainly clear in a situation where the popes, despite their wide powers to interpret dogma and discipline, had never gone as far as to permit bigamy, whereas Luther, who claimed none of the papal powers in this field, and who was anyway supposed to be bound by scriptural teaching, nonetheless took it upon himself to sanction an act universally condemned by the rest of Christendom.

[6] *Essai*, ii.229. Cf. the *Sermon prêché à Bale* (1768): 'Je sais bien que nous ne voyons plus renaître ces jours déplorables où cinq cantons, enivrés du fanatisme qui empoisonnait alors l'Europe entière, s'armèrent contre le canton de Zurich, parce qu'ils étaient de la religion romaine, et Zurich de la religion réformée. S'ils versèrent le sang de leurs compatriotes après avoir récité cinq *Pater* et cinq *Ave Maria* dans un latin qu'ils n'entendaient pas: s'ils firent, après la bataille de Cappel, écarteler par le bourreau de Lucerne le corps

father of Calvinism, and Voltaire implies that Calvin merely reaped the benefits of the work really done by Zwingli: 'Calvin lui donna son nom [i.e. to Zwingli's religion], comme Améric Vespuce donna le sien au nouveau monde, découvert par Colomb.'[7] But Zwingli is not singled out for praise merely in order to emphasise the defects of Calvin; he has positive merits of his own. Firstly, he was a convinced Erastian and did not seem over-preoccupied with Christian dogma. Most important of all: 'il croyait qu'il suffisait d'être vertueux pour être heureux dans l'autre vie, et que Caton et saint Paul, Numa et Abraham, jouissaient de la même béatitude' (*Essai*, ii.230). Voltaire's digust at the opinion of some theologians that even virtuous pagans would be damned is a constant theme in his work,[8] and the assertion of saint Augustine that the pagans' good actions were merely 'péchés splendides' is often ridiculed.[9] A typical statement of Voltaire's position is to be found in the poem *Les Trois empereurs en Sorbonne* (1768), prompted by the Sorbonne's censure of Marmontel's *Bélisaire* (M.x.154):

> Princes, sages, héros, exemples des vieux temps,
> Vos sublimes vertus n'ont été que des vices;
> Vos belles actions, des péchés éclatants.
> Dieu, juste selon nous, frappe de l'anathème
> Epictète, Caton, Scipion l'Africain,
> Ce coquin de Titus, l'amour du genre humain,
> Marc-Aurèle, Trajan, le grand Henri lui-même,
> Tous créés pour l'enfer, et morts sans sacrement.
> Mais, parmi ses élus, nous plaçons les Cléments.

mort du célèbre pasteur Zwingle: s'ils firent, en priant Dieu, jeter ses membres dans les flammes, ces abominations ne se renouvellent plus' (*Mélanges*, pp.1272-73).

[7] *Essai*, ii.230. Cf. Best.D7534 (Voltaire to Vernes, 24 December 1757): 'Ce n'est point Calvin qui fit votre relligion. Il eut l'honneur d'y être reçu.' Cf. also a 1770 addition to the article 'Arius': 'ni Arius ni Calvin n'ont certainement pas la triste gloire de l'invention' (*Dictionnaire philosophique*, ed. Benda and Naves, p.453).

[8] cf. M.viii.171-72; M.ix.454; M.xxvi.170, 457, 535; M.xvii.25. The lists of virtuous philosophers sometimes given by Bayle, La Mothe Le Vayer and others (see Mason, *Pierre Bayle and Voltaire*, p.87, especially n.1) fall into a rather different category, since they are intended to demonstrate that unbelievers can be virtuous. Voltaire himself sometimes lists such philosophers, including for example moderns like Spinoza and Vanini. But his intention in the references I have mentioned at the beginning of this note is rather to emphasise the absurdity of a theology which teaches that such men are irremediably damned, however excellent their actions might have been.

[9] cf. a comment in one of Voltaire's Leningrad notebooks: 'Le splendida peccata des payens, (dans st Augustin) est l'origine de cette impertinente opinion que les vertus des payens, étoient des crimes', Voltaire 81, p.349; cf. also M.xviii.74; M.xxvii.25, 26; M.xxix.243.

Zwingli had, at least, avoided the preposterous injustice and narrow-mindedness of the Catholic theologians, and he is duly praised. Moreover, two comments from Voltaire's correspondence of the 1760s show that, as time went on, his favourable opinion of Zwingli in no way diminished. On 23 January 1765 he commented to Moultou: 'Zuric me parait plus raisonnable que le tripot de Calvin. Zwingle était un bon et brave Déïste qui a laissé son esprit à ses compatriotes, Dieu soit béni' (Best.D12343). And three years later Voltaire ended a letter to the same correspondent in a similar vein: 'Je vous embrasse en Zwingle qui pensait que toutes les religions étaient bonnes excepté la tirannie romaine.'[10] Zurich's Reformer has thus become for Voltaire the symbol of that rarest of species, an enlightened and tolerant religious leader.

Another reformer whom Voltaire did not condemn out of hand was Melanchthon, 'l'un des fondateurs du luthéranisme' (*Essai*, ii.194). He points out in the *Lettres à s.a. mgr le prince de* **** (1767) that Melanchthon was one of the few non-fanatical theologians of his time, and was consequently misunderstood completely by his contemporaries: 'Mélanchthon [...] etait modéré et tolérant [...] Il passe pour indifférent. Etant devenu protestant, il conseilla à sa mère de rester catholique.[11] De là on jugea qu'il n'était ni l'un ni l'autre' (*Mélanges*, p.1187). The article 'Pierre' of the *Dictionnaire philosophique* is written in the same vein, and 'un fameux luthérien d'Allemagne', who 'avait beaucoup de peine à digérer que Jésus eût dit à Simon Barjone, Cepha ou Cephus: "Tu es Pierre, et sur cette Pierre je bâtirai mon assemblée, mon Eglise," ' was probably Melanchthon, in Voltaire's opinion.[12] Thus, another

---

[10] Best.D14878, 23 March 1768. Exceptionally, however, Voltaire was prepared to reprove the intolerance of Zwingli's Protestant successors by placing the Reformer's name not among those who thought virtuous pagans would be saved, but side by side with the pope, representing the theological obscurantism in the name of which such men as Cato and Marcus Aurelius were condemned. Writing to Formey in connection with a 'théologien de Bâle', Voltaire observed: 'On prétend que de bonnes lois & de bonnes troupes ne valent rien si l'on n'a pas une foi vive pour les dogmes de Zwingle & de Calvin. Or, comme Titus, Marc Aurèle, Trajan, Nerva, Julien, &c.&c.&c. avaient le malheur de ne croire pas plus à Zwingle qu'au pape, & que cependant tout allait assez bien de leur temps, on a cru à Potsdam ne devoir pas être tout à fait de l'avis du révérend docteur suisse' (Best.D5061, 4 November 1752).

[11] there is a marked resemblance between him and Sully, who advised Henri IV to change his faith: 'Il est nécessaire, lui disait Rosny, que vous soyez papiste, et que je demeure réformé' (*Essai*, ii.538; cf. also M.xxiv.510).

[12] '(C'était, je pense, Mélanchton)' (ed. Benda and Naves, p.348). The Moland edition is more emphatic, and says quite simply: '(c'était Mélanchthon)' (M.xx.214).

Reformer apart from Zwingli gained some measure of approval from the *philosophe*.[13]

Voltaire was in fact as well informed regarding the leaders of the Reformation as he was about the widely differing kinds of Protestant denominations.[14] Beza,[15] Farel,[16] Œcolampadius,[17] Bucer (cf. *Annales*, M.xiii.500), and many other minor figures are cited when the need arises. But in general Voltaire's sympathy is with none of them. It is perhaps worth quoting at this point the account given, in the *Lettres à s.a. mgr le prince*, of Erasmus, disliked equally by Protestants and Catholics because of his independent stand, and to whom Melanchthon is compared. A clear reflexion of the difficulties Voltaire himself experienced is surely apparent from this description of the famous Rennaissance scholar (*Mélanges*, p.1187):

Le célèbre Erasme fut également soupçonné d'irréligion par les catholiques et par les protestants, parce qu'il se moquait des excès où les uns et les autres tombèrent. Quand deux partis ont tort, celui qui se tient neutre, et qui par conséquent a raison, est vexé par l'un et par l'autre. La statue qu'on lui a dressé dans la place de Rotterdam, sa patrie, l'a vengé de Luther et de l'Inquisition.

Perhaps Voltaire could already see his own statue in the *Panthéon*.

iii. *Calvin*

In his thesis *Voltaire et les protestants de France* Edouard Champendal attempts to sum up and explain Voltaire's attitude to Calvin: 'Un

[13] despite this, he is sometimes condemned like all the others; cf. M.xiii.500: 'Mais Luther et Mélanchthon furent inflexibles, et montrèrent en cela bien plus d'opiniâtreté que de politique.'

[14] Voltaire frequently indulges in enumerating long lists of Protestant sects, usually, no doubt, with the purpose of showing that the truth could not be divided among so many different denominations. But there is more to Voltaire's interest than mere polemics: one could almost say that he was a 'collector' of sects. Perhaps such manifestations of religious diversity were rather exotic to a man brought up in strictly Catholic France and for Voltaire always retained something of this flavour: cf. M.ix.457; M.xxvii.29, 80, 111; M.xxviii.200, 240.

[15] as might be expected, Voltaire's attitude to the lieutenant of Calvin was hostile: cf. Best.D10133. Beza is mentioned twice in the *Dictionnaire philosophique* (ed. Benda and Naves, pp.19, 37).

[16] cf. *Traité sur la tolérance* (*Mélanges*, p.591); Notebook fragment no.6 (Voltaire 82, p.614).

[17] cf. *Questions su·· les miracles* M.xvv.445); *Histoire de Jenni* (ed. Brumfitt and Davis (Oxford 1960), p.65); *Catéchisme de l'honnête homme* (*Mélanges*, p.667); Best.D13232.

dominateur, un conquérant imbu d'amour-propre, un rêveur fanatique [. . .] Voilà Calvin pour Voltaire' (p.26). But why such a harsh
judgement? Because: 'Voltaire aime volontiers rapetisser les grands
hommes [. . .] Calvin, qu'il déteste, est tout entier dans la mort de
Servet' (p.19). The first part of the explanation is scarcely plausible in a
man who had written the *Siècle de Louis XIV* in order to praise the
supreme artistic achievement of an epoch personified and typified by the
roi soleil. Why should Voltaire have objected to Calvin simply because
he was a great man, when 'il note à propos d'Alfred le Grand que "le
genre humain [. . .] sans ces hommes extraordinaires, eût toujours
été semblable aux bêtes farouches" [. . .] Incontestablement, Voltaire
voit dans l'action de tels personnages l'une des forces motrices de
l'histoire'?[18] The second part of Champendal's diagnosis, however, is
very much nearer the truth. Servetus's execution is not the only episode
of Calvin's career with which Voltaire concerns himself, but it is certainly the one which characterises the Reformer in his mind as the very
incarnation of intolerance.

References to the Spaniard's death are widespread in Voltaire's works
and in his correspondence,[19] and an entire chapter is devoted to it in the
Essai sur les mœurs (ii.244-50). Moreover, Voltaire made substantial
additions to this chapter in 1761, and these passages clearly indicate
that worsening relations with the pastors of Geneva had strengthened
his hostility to Calvin, although in an early letter to Jacob Vernet,
Voltaire had already crystallised his attitude regarding Geneva's great
Reformer: 'j'aimerais Calvin, s'il n'avait pas fait brûler Servet' (Best.
D653, 14 September 1733).

It is in general no part of this study's scope to approve or condemn
the opinions expressed by Voltaire about particular incidents of Protestant history. However, since I have pointed out that his account of
the Reformation may be unacceptable to many because of the lack of
attention given to spiritual factors, it would also seem fair to indicate
that, on the contrary, Voltaire's hostility toward Calvin in connection
with the fate of Servetus has been echoed by numerous other critics[20]

[18] *Essai*, Introduction, pp.xliv-xlv; cf. also Brumfitt, *Voltaire historian*, p.68; H. T.
Mason, *Voltaire* (London 1975), pp.38-39, 43-44.
[19] cf. for example, M.i.54, 98 ff.; M.vii.183; M.xxiv.479, 518; M.xxv.373, 381, 420,
429, 440, 448; M.xxviii.247; Best.D7579, D7584, D7913, D8158, D9247, D9523,
D9787, D12819, D13651, D13659, D14779, D14832, D16153.
[20] cf., among recent critics, G. R. Elton, *Reformation Europe 1517-1559* (New York
1963), p.230: 'It is perfectly true that all denominations of the day united in abhorrence of

and would probably be shared by the modern reader. One of Calvin's most distinguished biographers, François Wendel, admits that 'The death of Servetus, for which Calvin bears a large share of the responsibility, has given rise to an abundant literature ever since the day after his execution', but he nonetheless insists that Calvin was merely following the conviction shared by most of his contemporaries 'that it was the duty of a Christian magistrate to put to death blasphemers who kill the soul, just as they punished murderers who kill the body'.[21] This indeed was the argument put forward by Haller in the course of his correspondence with Voltaire at the beginning of 1759: 'Pour le triste sort de Servet il a souffert par des loix, qui étoient en vigueur alors dans toute la Chrétienneté', stated the Bernese spokesman of orthodoxy: 'qu'est-ce qu'un Servet vis-à-vis des milliers de Protestans, qui ont été brûlés par l'Eglise Romaine?' (Best.D8259, 11 April 1759). But this attempt to disculpate Calvin is categorically rejected by Voltaire, even though he is willing to admit on this occasion that the Catholics had committed worse atrocities than their Protestant brethren (Best. D8266, 17 April 1759):

Je ne vous passerai jamais qu'on ait été excusable de brûler avec des fagots verds un pauvre diable de médecin, pour avoir pensé à peu-près comme on pensait dans les trois premiers siècles, cela me paroitra toujours très cannibale. Les monstres Papistes, qui firent pis, étoient des démons déchaînées.

In Calvin's condemnation of Servetus, Voltaire sees the betrayal of all the values which a sincere reformer ought to have defended. The Roman Church was at least consistent in its policy of persecuting heretics, since it considered itself to be infallible, but the Protestant innovation of free examination surely implied that no one man could lay claim to a primacy of truth, and that all sincere religious opinions should be tolerated (cf. below, pp.185-86). The affair revealed Calvin as an intolerant coward, lacking even the courage to do his own dirty

Servetus' views, that Servetus was tactless and violent and, in coming to Geneva, very foolish; but none of this reduces the guilt of Calvin in denouncing him and pursuing him to the death'; Henry Kamen, *The Rise of toleration* (World University Library 1967), p.76: 'Calvin acted in accordance with the dictates of the time and of his own conscience [. . .] At the same time, however, little can be said in extenuation of Calvin. The martyrdom of Servetus set the seal on his reputation as an intolerant leader.' Cf. also Owen Chadwick, *The Reformation*, p.90. Voltaire's heart would no doubt have rejoiced had he known that in later times a group of Calvinists would set up an expiatory column near the place where Servetus was executed (Kamen, p.76).

[21] *Calvin*, tr. Philip Mairet (London 1965), p.97.

work. First of all he denounced Servetus, but circumvented the Genevese law that the accuser should commit himself to prison with the accused by having one of his 'disciples' act on his behalf.[22] Then,

Quand son ennemi fut aux fers, il lui prodigua les injures et les mauvais traitements que font les lâches quand ils sont maîtres. Enfin, à force de presser les juges, d'employer le crédit de ceux qu'il dirigeait, de crier que Dieu demandait l'exécution de Michel Servet, il le fit brûler vif, et jouit de son supplice, lui qui, s'il eût mis le pied en France, eût été brûlé lui-même; lui qui avait élevé si fortement sa voix contre les persécutions.[23]

It seems fairly certain that by stressing Calvin's intolerance and describing in detail the death of Servetus, Voltaire hoped to encourage Protestant pastors of the eighteenth century, and more especially the Genevese clergy, to renounce their great Reformer and to take a step forward on the road of deism. Evidence for this exists in the chapter itself, where at one point Voltaire suggests that Calvin's spirit no longer dominates Geneva, that the beliefs of its pastors and the *philosophes* are not really so far apart, and that future cooperation under the banner of those Unitarian saints Servetus and Sozzini would really be feasible:

Il semble aujourd'hui qu'on fasse amende honorable aux cendres de Servet: de savants pasteurs des Eglises protestantes, et même les plus grands philosophes, ont embrassé ses sentiments et ceux de Socin. Ils ont encore été plus loin qu'eux: leur religion est l'adoration d'un Dieu par la médiation du Christ.[24]

But, as we shall see later (below, pp.118-55), the pastors were not to be tempted, and a series of disagreements with them drove Voltaire, by the end of the 1750s, into an irreconcilable hostility toward Geneva's religious establishment. One of the *philosophe*'s reactions was to multiply his attacks against Calvin and broaden their scope even further. Thus the additions made in 1761 to the *Essai* chapter 'De Calvin et Servet' tend to shift the emphasis a little from the Reformer's intolerance to

[22] this detail is perfectly correct; cf. François Wendel, *Calvin*, p.95: 'Calvin [. . .] had no hesitation: he charged one of his disciples to lodge the complaint of heresy and blasphemy and to allow himself to be imprisoned as the law required.'

[23] *Essai*, ii.246. Here, and elsewhere, Voltaire appears to be unaware of, or ignores, the fact that Calvin wished Servetus to be executed in a more humane way: cf. Wendel, p.97; Chadwick, p.90.

[24] *Essai*, ii.247. For the other efforts made by Voltaire to wean Geneva's pastors from Calvin, cf. below, pp.128 ff. Cf. also pp.135 ff. for a discussion of d'Alembert's *Encyclopédie* article 'Genève' which expressed ideas very similar to the passage just quoted.

his shameless hyprocrisy,[25] which now symbolises for Voltaire the trait inherited by nearly all Calvin's successors in the Genevese pastorate. Voltaire finds the case against Calvin unanswerable, for the Reformer's declarations on this score had been quite explicit (*Essai*, ii.245):

on voit ces propres mots dans une de ses lettres imprimées: 'En cas que quelqu'un soit hétérodoxe, et qu'il fasse scrupule de se servir des mots *trinité* et *personne*, etc., nous ne croyons pas que ce soit une raison pour rejeter cet homme; nous devons le supporter, sans le chasser de l'Eglise, et sans l'exposer à aucune censure comme un hérétique.'

The same passage is to be found written in one of Voltaire's notebook fragments as an extract from Calvin's *Epîtres*,[26] so the fact that Calvin had expressly recommended toleration had made a great impression on Voltaire.[27] This convincing evidence of the Reformer's hypocrisy could tend only to confirm his prejudice against religious leaders in general.

Voltaire's work in favour of Calas and Sirven and increasing contacts with French Protestantism during the 1760s did nothing to soften his attitude toward Calvin.[28] Two letters written to the président Hénault in connection with the latter's *Abrégé historique* show that Voltaire had taken up an even more extreme position over Calvin's treatment of Servetus. He no longer retains any semblance of self-control: Servetus's death was a murder, pure and simple, 'un véritable assassinat commis en cérémonie'. Moreover, it represented a criminal violation of international law, 'qui devait attirer sur les assassins le

[25] Voltaire also mentions the breach of international law committed by the Genevese authorities and emphasises even more clearly Servetus's belief in the divinity of Christ: 'il déclara dans le cours de son procès qu'il était fortement persuadé que Jésus-Christ était le fils de Dieu, engendré de toute éternité du Père, et conçu par le Saint-Esprit dans le sein de la Vierge Marie' (*Essai*, ii.246).

[26] Voltaire 82, p.620; cf. also M.xx.542; M.xxiv.479.

[27] cf. Best.D9247, to the chevalier de R...x, 20 September 1760, where Voltaire comments to his correspondent: 'si vous songez que le républicain Jean Calvin, ce digne théologien, après avoir écrit qu'il ne fallait persécuter personne, pas même ceux qui niaient la trinité, fit brûler tout vif & avec des fagots verts un Espagnol qui s'exprimait sur la trinité autrement que lui', then he will conclude that there is no more virtue in republics than in monarchies. The discussion is clearly in connection with the theories expressed in *De l'esprit des lois*, and Voltaire gives other examples to back up his assertion; cf. below, p.108.

[28] Voltaire was active in campaigning for the release of the remaining Protestant galley-slaves; he also attempted to intervene with the authorities when particular cases of injustice or persecution came to his notice, and he corresponded with pastors like Paul Rabaut and Jean Gal-Pomaret see below, especially pp.283 ff.

châtiment le plus terrible'. Indeed, Voltaire claims, had the emperor Charles v not been put off by the word 'Arian' applied to Servetus, or rather, had he not been on the point of abdicating, 'il aurait puni sévèrement cet outrage fait dans Genêve, ville impériale, à la nation espagnole'. Not only did Calvin commit this 'brigandage', but he forced 'le misérable conseil de Genêve à faire brûler Servet à petit feu avec des fagots verts, et il jouit de ce spectacle. Il n'y eut point dans votre st Barthélemi d'assassinat plus cruellement exécuté', Voltaire exclaims in disgust (Best.D14779, 26 February 1768).

The unfortunate Hénault having been imprudent enough to defend his article 'Servet', Voltaire sent him another letter in which his detestation of Calvin reached its peak (Best.D14832, 14 March 1768):

J'ai donc lu *Servet*, et j'ai été bien affligé. Je le suis d'autant plus que je sais certainement que Servet était un fou très honnête, et Calvin le plus malhonnête fanatique qui fut en Europe. C'était un maraud fait pour être grand inquisiteur, une âme atroce et sanguinaire, un monstre d'orgueil et de cruauté [...] D'ailleurs il ne s'agissait pas de tolérance entre Servet et lui. Servet n'était ni de son église, ni de sa ville; il passait son chemin sur la foi du droit des gens. C'était un voyageur tombé dans une caverne de voleurs.

So violent is Voltaire's revulsion at the fate suffered by Servetus that he makes an astonishing statement:

Je vous répète que le meurtre de Calas est une action très pardonnable en comparaison de l'assassinat juridique commis sur la personne de Servet. Les juges de Calas ont été trompés par de faux indices; mais les juges de Genêve violèrent ouvertement tous les droits des nations. Servet ne demandait point la tolérance pour sa doctrine; il ne demandait qu'à passer vite. Des cannibales en manteau noir se saisissent de lui, de son argent, et le brûlent à petit feu pour plaire à Calvin qui gouvernait la multitude.

Geneva's reformer has thus become for Voltaire the symbol of fanatical intolerance and injustice, worse even than the detested parlement de Toulouse and the perpetrator of a deed which equals in horror the St Bartholomew's Day atrocities.

Champendal's assertion (p.19) that Voltaire championed Servetus because the latter was a 'libre penseur' whereas the other martyrs were 'chrétiens imbéciles' is quite absurd, not only as far as the *Essai sur les mœurs* is concerned, but also in respect of Voltaire's other works. In the *Essai*, Servetus is praised by Voltaire for having been a 'très-savant médecin', and for having discovered the circulation of the blood, but then we are told that 'il négligea un art utile pour des sciences dangereuses', in other words, theology. Voltaire quotes a passage from Servetus's work on the trinity to show how incomprehensible it was (*Essai*, ii.244). Yet the Spanish theologian 'était de si bonne foi dans sa métaphysique obscure' that he entered into a correspondence with Calvin on the subject of the trinity (ii.245). Although Voltaire is sympathetic to Servetus as a victim of Calvin's cruelty, there is no indication that he despised the Spaniard's theories any less than those of the other theologians he so gleefully ridiculed. In fact, there are at least two occasions in Voltaire's correspondence where he refers to Servetus as 'mad'.[29] Moreover, in the *Poème sur le loi naturelle*, Voltaire claims that Servetus would probably have acted just like Calvin had he been in the Reformer's position (M.ix.453):

> Servet fut en personne immolé par Calvin.
> Si Servet dans Genève eût été souverain,
> Il eût, pour argument contre ses adversaires,
> Fait serrer d'un lacet le cou des trinitaires.

What then are the motives which Voltaire attributes to Calvin's action? They are the usual anti-clerical reasons we might expect, for Calvin did not differ from, but epitomised, other examples of priestly intolerance. Theology, as usual, is the basic offender: 'De la dispute Calvin passa aux injures, et des injures à cette haine théologique, la plus implacable de toutes les haines' (*Essai*, ii.245). From this moment Servetus's fate was sealed, Voltaire concludes in one of his 1761 additions to the *Essai sur les mœurs*, for Calvin changed his mind about tolerance 'dès qu'il se livra à la fureur de sa haine théologique' (ii.245). He even went as far as to publish a book proving that heretics should be punished, a complete reversal of his earlier attitude.[30] Theological disputation, then, encouraged in Calvin pride and hatred for those who disagreed with his opinions. His persecution of Servetus was the prime, but not the only example of this; he also caused the exile of Castellio, 'homme plus savant que lui', of whom he was jealous,[31] and Voltaire

---

[29] cf. Best.D14832 and D7913 (to the président de Brosses, 21 October 1758), where Voltaire speaks of 'le pays où ce brigand de Calvin fit brûler ce fou de Servet au sujet de l'*omousios*'.

[30] ii.245-46. This was the *Declaratio orthodoxae fidei*, published in January 1554. Later in the same year Calvin's disciple Theodore Beza brought out his *De haereticis a civili magistratu puniendis*, a work also attacking toleration (Kamen, pp.79-80).

[31] *Essai*, ii.243. This passage was in the 1756 edition of the *Essai*, and the same is true of other passages quoted from it until the end of this section of Calvin, unless otherwise stated.

makes him responsible too for the death of Gentilis, who escaped Servetus's fate in Geneva by a timely retraction but was later arrested and condemned as an Arian in Berne.[32]

The other fundamental trait of Calvin's character was a desire to dominate others, for although 'sa religion est conforme à l'esprit républicain,[33] Calvin avait l'esprit tyrannique' (*Essai*, ii.243). His influence in Geneva reached such a point that he not only forced the wife of the future first syndic, who had committed the heinous crime of dancing in her own home, to 'paraître en personne devant le consistoire, pour y reconnaître sa faute', but also caused 'Pierre Ameaux, conseiller d'Etat, accusé d'avoir mal parlé de Calvin, d'avoir dit qu'il était un très méchant homme, qu'il n'était qu'un Picard, et qu'il prêchait une fausse doctrine', to be condemned 'à faire amende honorable, en chemise, la tête nue, la torche au poing, par toute la ville', even though he had asked for mercy.[34]

Voltaire's dislike for Calvin drives him to emphasise snobbishly Calvin's origins as he does Luther's. Yet he has less scope than with Luther who was only 'fils d'un forgeron' (*Annales*, M.xiii.479). For Calvin's father, 'légiste et financier', was 'chargé des intérêts de l'évêque'.[35] 'Son nom propre était Chauvin; il était né à Noyon, en 1509; il savait du latin, du grec, et de la mauvaise philosophie de son temps' (*Essai*, ii.242). Yet somehow Voltaire contrives to make him sound contemptible: 'Nous ne sommes plus au temps de Jean Chauvin, Picard qui avait l'impertinence de précéder dans les cérémonies le

---

Sebastian Castellio (1515-1563) disagreed with Calvin over the canonicity of the *Song of songs* and over whether Christ's descent into Hell had actually occurred or was merely a symbolic description of his sufferings. After much dispute between the two men Calvin lodged a complaint against Castellio with the Petit conseil, which at first admonished, then later expelled Castellio from Geneva (Wendel, pp.82-83; Elton, pp.228-29).

[32] M.xvii.364; cf. also Best.D17580. Gentilis was an Italian antitrinitarian who arrived in Geneva in 1556. Two years later he was arrested and forced to make an act of submission, after which he fled the city. Then followed years of wandering, ending in imprisonment at Gex and Lyons. Calvin was dead by the time that Gentilis was condemned and executed in Berne in 1566 (Wendel, pp.100-101; Kamen, pp.81-82).

[33] this is a characteristic of Calvinism constantly remarked on by Voltaire. Cf. for example M.xxviii.244: 'Les papistes sont des esclaves qui ont combattu sous les enseignes du pape, leur tyran. Les luthériens ont combattu pour leurs princes; les calvinistes, pour la liberté populaire.' Cf. also Best.D1359, D10897; M.xviii.294.

[34] *Essai*, ii.247-48. Voltaire also recorded this incident in one of his notebooks (Voltaire 82, p.525), and the account he gives of it is quite correct (cf. Wendel, p.86). As we shall see shortly, Voltaire himself often echoed the tone of Ameaux's assertions.

[35] Léonard, *Histoire générale*, i.259.

magnifique conseil [...] Les temps sont un peu changés', the 'vieux capitaine Durost' is made to exclaim in the *Questions sur les miracles* (1765) (M.xxv.393), and Voltaire usually insists on correcting the Reformer's name to 'Chauvin', presumably because he finds it more ridiculous,[36] as well as on stressing his Picard origins.[37]

The portrait of Calvin which Voltaire gives in the *Essai* is almost entirely one-sided, but not quite. He does recognise Calvin's genius for organisation (ii.243):

Il régla les dogmes et la discipline que suivent tous ceux que nous appelons *calvinistes*, en Hollande, en Suisse, en Angleterre, et qui ont si longtemps partagé la France. Ce fut lui qui établit les synodes, les consistoires, les diacres; qui régla la forme des prières et des prêches: il institua même une juridiction consistoriale avec droit d'excommunication.

A grudging admission is also made that Calvin's character was not merely an amalgam of every conceivable vice (ii.248):

Les vices des hommes tiennent souvent à des vertus. Cette dureté de Calvin était jointe au plus grand désintéressement: il ne laissa pour tout bien, en mourant, que la valeur de cent écus d'or. Son travail infatigable abrégea ses jours, mais lui donna un nom célèbre et un grand crédit.

One paragraph, however, is hardly enough to efface the idea which Voltaire has been instilling in his readers for the better part of two chapters: in the *Essai sur les mœurs* Calvin personifies all that is worst in a religious leader, more especially as he is a so-called Reformer. In fact, it is not going too far to say that he is cast as the arch-villain of the Reformation,[38] and Voltaire makes his feelings on this score

[36] the modern sense of the word had not yet developed, however. Cf. Paul Robert, *Dictionnaire alphabétique de la langue française* (Paris 1965), p.733.

[37] in Best.D7945 Voltaire uses the form 'Jean Chauvin', and Theodore Besterman (Best.D7945, n.1) explains that 'in contemporary documents the name is said to be written indifferently Caulvin, Cauvin, Chauvin, Chauve, Calvus, Calvinus'. This was no doubt the case, but it is also clear that Voltaire uses some of these forms, or stresses Calvin's Picard origins with the express intention of making the reformer appear ridiculous, or a mere usurper of power in Geneva: cf. especially the reference in Best.D8120 to 'Jehan Chauvin, picard réfugié à Geneve sous le nom de Calvinus'. Cf. also Best.D8992, D9497, D13158, D13500, D17580.

[38] cf. Best.D14832, to the président Hénault, 14 March 1768: 'Il n'y avait pas dans le parti opposé un homme plus haïssable que lui, et c'est beaucoup dire. J'ai été à portée dans mon voisinage d'apprendre des particularités de sa conduite qui font frémir.' Entries in Voltaire's notebooks evoking Calvin's egotistical cruelty (p.614) and fanaticism (pp.525, 676) confirm this judgement.

65

transparently clear in the *Dictionnaire philosophique* article 'Dogmes'.[39] This contains a very amusing account of a Voltairean vision of the Last Judgement where the judges turn out, perhaps not so surprisingly, to be Confucius, Solon, Socrates, Titus, the Antonines, Epictetus, 'tous ceux qui ont fait du bien aux hommes' (ed. Benda and Naves, p.172). The tone of amused irony in the first part of the article does not prevent Voltaire from forcibly expressing his feelings on the subject of Calvin, and they could hardly be more damning (p.173):

Vis-à-vis du cardinal de Lorraine était Calvin, qui se vantait, dans son patois grossier, d'avoir donné des coups de pied à l'idole papale, après que d'autres l'avaient abattue. 'J'ai écrit contre la peinture et la sculpture, disait-il; j'ai fait voir évidemment que les bonnes œuvres ne servent à rien du tout, et j'ai prouvé qu'il est diabolique de danser le menuet: chassez vite d'ici le cardinal de Lorraine, et placez-moi à côté de saint Paul.'

Comme il parlait, on vit auprès de lui un bûcher enflammé; un spectre épouvantable, portant au cou une fraise espagnole à moitié brûlée, sortait du milieu des flammes avec des cris affreux.

'Monstre, s'écriait-il, monstre exécrable, tremble! reconnais ce Servet que tu as fait périr par le plus cruel des supplices, parce qu'il avait disputé contre toi sur la manière dont trois personnes peuvent faire une seule substance.' Alors tous les juges ordonnèrent que le cardinal de Lorraine serait précipité dans l'abîme, mais que Calvin serait puni plus rigoureusement.

So, despite a Reformation attempting to correct the abuses of the Roman Church and its corrupt prelates, one of the leading Reformers is judged by Voltaire to merit harsher punishment than a prime mover of the detested *Ligue*. A comment in one of his notebooks sums up Voltaire's hostility to Calvin, briefly listing those who fell victims to the reformer's zeal: 'Calvin persécuta Servet, Castalion, Bolsec, Bertelier, Blandrole, Alecat, Gentilis' (Voltaire 82, p.675). There is no saving grace: Calvin is the archetype of priestly intolerance and hypocrisy, and he and all his works are anathema to Voltaire.

iv. *Protestant morality*

As we have seen (above, p.49), Voltaire characterises Luther and Calvin as 'laborieux et austères, mais durs et emportés', a mixture of good and bad, but with the bad clearly predominating. The same could be said of

---

[39] first published in the Varberg edition, printed in Amsterdam in 1765: cf. ed. Benda and Naves, p.172.

Voltaire's view of the Reformers' followers and of the moral teaching of Protestantism in general. On the one hand, the 'laborieux' element would refer to the industry exhibited by the Protestants after the Reformation, a quality probably necessary for their very survival, and one which has often been linked with the growth of capitalism.[40] Voltaire was obviously in favour of this characteristic: it is one of his reasons for praising the Quakers[41] and for the idealisation of English trade and commercial enterprise which first found expression in the *Lettres philosophiques*.[42] Moral austerity is remarked on in the *Essai sur les mœurs* as a quality shared by religious reformers throughout the centuries. Voltaire quotes a Provençal poem about the Waldensian heretics:

> Que non voglia maudir ne jura ne mentir
> N'occir, ne avoutrar, ne prenre de altrui,
> Ne s'avengear deli suo ennemi,
> Loz dison qu'es Vaudes, et los feson morir,

and comments: 'Cette citation a encore son utilité, en ce qu'elle est une preuve que tous les réformateurs ont toujours affecté des mœurs sévères.'[43] This quality is sometimes a useful propaganda weapon against the shortcomings of the Roman Church and its ministers: an obvious example is again that of the Quakers, but in the *Lettres philosophiques* the ministers of the Church of England are also praised because 'à l'égard des mœurs le Clergé Anglican est plus réglé que celui de France', despite the fact that they exhibit other, less laudable, qualities (ed. Lanson, i.63). Yet when Voltaire considers moral austerity as it was actually put into practice, in men who were at the same time inflexible and passionately dedicated supporters of a strict, evangelical religion, it is something very little to his taste, indeed one of the features of the Reformation which he most dislikes. Voltaire soon makes his position clear in the *Essai sur les mœurs*, for he is at pains to explain that although Luther, Calvin and Zwingli married, and despite the scandalous affair of the Landgrave of Hesse, the opinion of uneducated

[40] for a recent consideration of this question see Philippe Besnard, *Protestantisme et capitalisme: la controverse post-Weberienne* (Paris 1971).

[41] *Lettres philosophiques*, ed. Lanson, i.1, 11, 51.

[42] Lanson i.74, 120-22; cf. the *Dictionnaire philosophique* article 'Tolérance' (ed. Benda and Naves, p.401).

[43] *Essai*, i.763. According to Pomeau (i.763, n.1), Voltaire must have found this quotation from the *Nobla leyczon* in Samuel Morland, *History of the evangelical churches of the valleys of Piemont* (1658).

Catholics, '[qui] pensent que ces fondateurs s'insinuèrent par des séductions flatteuses, et qu'ils ôtèrent un joug pesant pour leur en donner un très léger', is quite mistaken. The moral zeal of the Reformers was real enough and did not merely consist in idle preaching: 'ils avaient des mœurs farouches; leurs discours respiraient le fiel' (*Essai*, ii.242). Their austerity, however, even when presented as genuine, is rejected absolutely. For it is not merely a standard of conduct which makes demands on the individual attempting to practise it, but one which is also imposed on others in an authoritarian and repressive manner (ii.242-3):

S'ils condamnaient le célibat des prêtres, s'ils ouvrirent les portes des couvents, c'étaient pour changer en couvents la société humaine[44] [. . .] Ils proscrivirent la confession auriculaire, mais ils la voulurent publique: dans la Suisse, dans l'Ecosse, à Genève, elle l'a été, ainsi que la pénitence.

Voltaire could hardly have described strict Protestant ideals more disparagingly, for to a *philosophe* who considered pleasure to be a good thing in itself, the convent and the monastery were one of the Christian religion's greatest crimes against humanity.

In point of fact, however, Voltaire rarely speaks as if he considers an attitude favourable to repressively strict moral severity to be the logical consequence of an honestly held set of beliefs. Usually it appears to him as just one more example of how priests or religious fanatics have attempted to influence and dominate a creduluous populace: 'On ne réussit guère chez les hommes, du moins jusqu'aujourd'hui, en ne leur proposant que le facile et le simple; le maître le plus dur est le plus suivi.'[45] And of all the reformers, Calvin, 'pape des protestants', with his thirst for power, understood this best: 'Les jeux, les spectacles, furent défendus chez les réformés: Genève, pendant plus de cent ans, n'a pas

[44] Voltaire often refers disparagingly to Geneva as a *couvent*: cf. below, p.171.

[45] *Essai*, ii.243. This quotation inevitably prompts the question as to why, in Voltaire's opinion, men react in such an unreasonable way. The *philosophe* appears to give no precise answer to this enigma, but one may speculate that he was thinking somewhat on the lines of Montesquieu who, in *De l'esprit des lois*, commented: 'Par la nature de l'entendement humain, nous aimons en fait de religion tout ce qui suppose un effort, comme, en matière de morale, nous aimons spéculativement tout ce qui porte le caractère de la sévérité. Le célibat a été plus agréable aux peuples à qui il sembloit convenir le moins, et pour lesquels il pouvoit avoir de plus fâcheuses suites. Dans les pays du midi de l'Europe, où, par la nature du climat, la loi du célibat est plus difficile à observer, elle a été retenue; dans ceux du nord, où les passions sont moins vives, elle a été proscrite' (*Œuvres complètes*, ed. Roger Caillois (Paris 1951), ii.740).

souffert chez elle un instrument de musique.'⁴⁶ Here, artistic reasons and personal rancour reinforce Voltaire's annoyance at what he sees as, in effect, a bigoted prejudice and unwonted tampering with the freedom of the individual. His subsequent *démêlés* with the Genevan authorities over the private theatrical performances he insisted on mounting at *Les Délices* and Ferney (or Tournay) further intensified his dislike of this aspect of Protestantism in general and of Calvinism in particular.⁴⁷ It is not surprising that Voltaire frequently uses the weapon of irony to discredit the Calvinist position: to show how innocent the prohibited activities are, and to emphasise how little they have to do with real virtue. A typical example is to be found in the *Dictionnaire philosophique* article 'Dogmes' quoted a little earlier: ' "J'ai écrit contre la peinture et la sculpture", disait-il [i.e. Calvin] [. . .] "et j'ai prouvé qu'il est diabolique de danser le menuet" ' (ed. Benda and Naves, p.173). At the end of his life, in the *Dialogues d'Evhémère* (1777), Voltaire is still poking this kind of fun at Calvin's repressive conception of morality. Not only is it ridiculous, but a direct result of uncivilised ways of thinking and of unenlightenment (M.xxx.501):

EVHEMERE: [. . .] il est arrivé à la philosophie même chose qu'à la danse.
CALLICRATE: Comment cela?
EVHEMERE: Les druides, dans un des petits pays les plus sauvages de l'Europe, avaient proscrit la danse, et avaient sévèrement puni un magistrat et sa femme pour avoir dansé un menuet. Depuis ce temps, tout le monde a appris à danser.

Strict Protestant morality is thus completely rejected by Voltaire to whom it is an entirely alien concept. In the *Conversation de m. l'intendant des menus avec m. l'abbé Grizel* (1761), he dismisses it with utter contempt (M.xxiv.250, n.1):

Je ne veux point faire un tableau de toutes les contradictions de ce monde [. . .] La pire espèce de toutes, je l'avoue, est celle des prétendus réformateurs. Ce sont des malades qui sont fâchés que les autres se portent bien; ils défendent les ragoûts dont ils ne mangent pas.

⁴⁶ *Essai*, ii.243. Cf. Henri Vuilleumier, *Histoire de l'église réformée du pays de Vaud sous le régime bernois* (Lausanne 1927-1933), iv.116-17. Even organs were looked on with suspicion, and were only gradually reintroduced into the pays de Vaud's churches during the course of the eighteenth century.

⁴⁷ cf. below, pp.119, 167-71. The different policies of Lausanne and Geneva on the matter of theatrical performances strengthened Voltaire's belief that the Genevese clergy's position was hypocritical, especially since some members of the pastorate had on occasions attended the performances: cf. below, p.124-25.

Voltaire gives what amounts to two explanations of the moral austerity of Protestantism, yet both are products of the same common cause, the attempts of ambitious ecclesiastics to influence and dominate others. For he can never quite believe that those who mortify themselves are disinterested in their motives: even heretics like the Waldensians and the Manicheans who protested against the scandals of the Roman Church, and whom we would expect to have Voltaire's sympathy, are often described as 'affecting'[48] severe morals, as if they had some ulterior motive.[49]

The first explanation that Voltaire gives suggests that the preoccupation with a stern morality is a type of compensatory factor for those Protestant clerics who, for one reason or another, have lost political influence and economic power. It enables them to retain a strict spiritual ascendancy over their flock. For the Protestant clergy had hamstrung themselves by their denunciations of the riches of the Roman clergy, and

ils s'imposèrent à eux-mêmes la bienséance de ne pas recueillir ce qu'ils condamnaient [. . .] Partout où leur religion s'est établie, leur pouvoir a été restreint à la longue dans des bornes étroites par les princes, ou par les magistrats des républiques.

Only the Anglican clergy are more or less well-off, whereas "les pasteurs calvinistes et luthériens ont eu partout des appointements qui ne leur ont pas permis de luxe' (*Essai*, ii.248-49). Their natural reaction has therefore been to condemn riches and luxury and to affect a stern attitude of moral severity which is really no more than a kind of sour grapes. This theme is found in Voltaire's works as early as the *Lettres philosophiques*, in the letter 'Sur les Presbitériens', where it is expressed quite explicitly and at some length (ed. Lanson, i.72):

Comme les Prêtres de cette Secte ne reçoivent de leurs Eglises que des gages très-médiocres, & que par conséquent ils ne peuvent vivre dans le même luxe que les Evêques, ils ont pris le parti naturel de crier contre les honneurs où ils ne peuvent atteindre.

[48] *Essai*, i.763. A comment made in connection with the English Civil War shows the same attitude: 'La fureur de la guerre civile était nourrie par cette austérité sombre et atroce que les puritains affectaient' (*Essai*, ii.666).

[49] the Manicheans were 'probablement des enthousiastes qui tendaient à une perfection outrée pour dominer sur les esprits' (*Essai*, i.483). Even when Voltaire accepts that the morality of strict religious leaders is genuine, he still tends to reject some of its manifestations: cf. Best.D13651, Voltaire to Vernes, 4 November 1766, where he refers to the 'faquirs de l'Inde et des brachmanes qui ont assurément la morale la plus pure et la plus sainte, mais qui la déshonorent par leurs folies'.

The Presbyterian minister (i.73):

affecte une démarche grave, un air fâché, porte un vaste chapeau, un long manteau par dessus un habit court, prêche du nez & donne le nom de la prostituée de Babilone à toutes les Eglises, où quelques Ecclesiastiques sont assez heureux pour avoir cinquante mille livres de rente.

Any resemblance between the Presbyterians and the Quakers (because of similarity in dress or beliefs) is ruled out, because the latter, most of whom are successful businessmen, practise their idea of virtue through choice, and not through spiteful hypocrisy caused by economic necessity. They are, moreover, tolerant of the opinions of others.

The connection between the Scots Presbyterians and the Calvinists is made clear by Voltaire: 'Ce Presbiterianisme n'est autre chose que le Calvinisme pur, tel qu'il avoit été établi en France & qu'il subsiste à Genève' (ed. Lanson, i.72), and it is above all those sects which trace their origin to Calvin that Voltaire specifically dislikes because of the sanctimonious attitude shown by their ministers, and the humourless conviction of their own moral superiority that he found among the laity. But the qualities which, though irritating, are merely ridiculous in a pedantic kill-joy and busybody, present a very sinister phenomenon when they are found in a powerful religious leader like Calvin. For the ecclesiastical tyrant is much more absolute than the political tyrant, and his influence extends to private actions and thoughts. Not only may he show his intolerance by persecuting those who do not agree with his theological opinions, but, as we have seen, he can conduct a sort of inquisition into the most harmless activities of the private citizen (cf. above, p.64). Voltaire can surely be seen here as a true representative of the liberal tradition, for the target of his attack, ecclesiastical interference in the individual's life, was in many ways a predecessor of those systems of political thought which seek to control the minds, as well as the bodies, of those they rule. Be this as it may, Voltaire often expressed the fear that a spirit akin to that engendered by Calvinism might overtake the French nation, with disastrous consequences. In a letter to Damilaville of 30 January 1764 (Best.D11670) he wrote:

Tout ce que je crains c'est qu'un esprit de presbytérianisme ne s'empare de la tête des Français, et alors, la nation est perdue. Douze parlements jansénistes sont capables de faire des Français un peuple d'atrabilaires.[50]

[50] cf. below, p.168, especially n.140.

Voltaire is perhaps further suggesting that, in some circumstances, the affectation of poverty and severity by men such as Calvin may represent a type of power more unbearable in its naked reality than that which is somewhat disguised or made more natural and easier to bear by the pomp, circumstance and outward display surrounding a king, or even a tyrant. The brilliance of Louis xiv's court and the extraordinary flowering of the arts which accompanied his reign may have made the monarch's authority more acceptable, or at least more respectable, in the eyes of his subjects. The spurning of these normal accessories of rule perhaps indicates a pride even more absolute, delighting only in the exercise of power for its own sake and which, moreover, is not ashamed that this be apparent. One may surely draw a parallel between Calvin and Voltaire's judgement of the Spanish cardinal Ximenes (*Essai*, ii.211):

esprit né austère et dur, qui n'avait de goût que celui de la domination absolue, et qui, revêtu de l'habit d'un cordelier quand il était régent d'Espagne, disait qu'avec son cordon il saurait ranger tous les grands à leur devoir, et qu'il écraserait leur fierté sous ses sandales.

Dogmatic inflexibility and sanctimonious moralism are both, therefore, potential and equally detestable elements of the priest-dictator, personified for Voltaire in Calvin (cf. Voltaire 82, p.614).

There is, however, another reason why Voltaire could never have accepted wholeheartedly a severe type of Protestant morality: the obvious incompatibility of his idea of virtue with that of the Reformers. The conflict is in fact irreconcilable, for in Voltaire's opinion, morality, although a divine gift, is to be seen primarily in a social context, and what is good is what is useful to the community as a whole.[51] This is why an entertainment like the theatre can be beneficial, in that it may be able to influence favourably the subsequent actions and opinions of those who attend it (cf. below, p.168). The Protestant ideal of a direct relationship between the individual and God, and of a morality consequently based on a standard transcending human expediency, which makes demands in opposition to what he sees as harmless social practices and conventions, is complete anathema to the *philosophe*. Voltaire's god is usually cast in the rôle of a majestic but remote first cause:[52] he has presumably had some connection with humanity, for

[51] cf. the *Dictionnaire philosophique* article 'Vertu'.
[52] cf. René Pomeau, *La Religion de Voltaire*, pp.211-18, 312-13.

the light of reason is latent in every individual, and natural morality, thinks Voltaire, is common to all cultures. But the deity does not intervene in particular cases: there is no providence, and there are no miracles. Nor are certain men 'chosen' by God. In fact Voltaire has nothing but total scorn for the strict Calvinist teaching that the 'elect' have been predestined for salvation from all eternity, and its corollary that the rest of mankind are irremediably damned.[53] In the fifth of the *Discours en vers sur l'homme* (1734), Voltaire directs his muse to showing that this doctrine is not merely repellent, but actively turns people against virtue:

> Jusqu'à quand verrons-nous ce rêveur fanatique
> Fermer le ciel au monde, et d'un ton despotique
> Damnant le genre humain, qu'il prétend convertir,
> Nous prêcher la vertu pour la faire haïr?
> Sur les pas de Calvin, ce fou sombre et sévère
> Croit que Dieu, comme lui, n'agit qu'avec colère.
> Je crois voir d'un tyran le ministre abhorré,
> D'esclaves qu'il a faits tristement entouré,
> Dictant d'un air hideux ses volontés sinistres.
> Je cherche un roi plus doux, et de plus doux ministres.[54]

Similarly, in *Candide*, it is the unassuming, undogmatic Anabaptist who helps out the young protagonist, rather than the Calvinist pastor 'qui venait de parler toute une heure de suite sur la charité dans une grande assemblée'.[55] This representative of orthodoxy deems it a necessary preliminary to action to put a whole series of theological questions to the unfortunate Candide, and when he receives what he considers an unsatisfactory reply, promptly forgets his charitable precepts and reviles the suspected heretic, ably assisted by his spouse (*Candide*, ed. Morize, p.19). Moreover, in a very significant passage of the *Essai sur les mœurs*, Voltaire claims that Calvin's own conduct fell very short of the standard required in a civilised and genteel society. Not only were the trappings of Calvinism disagreeable and unnecessary in fostering virtue, they were clearly less effective than the school of polite society. For Calvin had

---

[53] cf. below, pp.453ff, for a fuller discussion of these questions.

[54] M.ix.409; cf. also M.xxv.367. These comments can also be taken to refer to Jansenist teachings, as an anecdote in one of Voltaire's Leningrad notebooks makes clear: 'Cavois disoit, le dieu des calvinistes est un roy qui entrant dans sa capitale dit, que la moitié de mes sujets soupe avec moy, et qu'on pende l'autre. Le dieu des jansénistes ordonne que tout le monde le suive, et fait pendre ceux qui ont la goute. Le dieu des jésuites pardonne aux gouteux, et donne à souper à ceux qui l'ont bien servi' (Voltaire 81, p.378).

[55] *Candide, ou l'optimisme*, ed. André Morize (Paris 1957), p.17.

helped in Servetus's condemnation at Lyons by sending to the French ecclesiastical authorities incriminating letters written to him by the Spaniard, 'action qui suffirait pour le déshonorer à jamais dans la société, car ce qu'on appelle l'esprit de la société est plus honnête et plus sévère que tous les synodes'.[56]

The real fruits of Calvinist morality are thus not so much an increase in virtue as in bigotry and dogmatism. Voltaire can only explain the success of such unpalatable teaching by invoking the unreasonableness of the masses: 'c'est ainsi que les princes, en fait de religion, obéissent plus aux peuples que les peuples ne leur obéissent', he observes in the *Essai sur les mœurs*.[57] 'Partout le peuple est peuple', he sighs in the *Siècle de Louis XIV*; 'le fanatisme rend la science même sa complice et étouffe la raison' (*Oh*, p.1062). Once again, fanaticism, that hydra of ignorance and superstition, is Voltaire's explanation for every religious manifestation which he finds rationally inexplicable.[58] It is perhaps one of the most overworked words in Voltairean prose.

v. *Protestant theology*

'Ils ôtaient aux hommes le libre arbitre, et l'on courait à eux' (*Essai*, ii.243): a harsh theology no more turned people away from Calvinism than its strict morality. By the time he came to write the *Essai sur les mœurs*, Voltaire himself had rejected his earlier belief in free will, and it comes therefore as no surprise that he does not indulge in a major attack on predestination. He does however express his disapproval of Calvinist teaching regarding the uselessness of good works unaccompanied by faith,[59] which is perhaps somewhat inconsistent in one who on occasion expressed a belief that men were little more than automata.[60] Yet in general one may say that Voltaire and the Calvinists were in broad

[56] *Essai*, ii.245. Calvin did in fact behave as Voltaire claims: cf. Wendel, p.95, Kamen, p.76.

[57] in connection with Charles I (*Essai*, ii.665).

[58] a cryptic though interesting comment in one of Voltaire's notebook fragments describes 'enthousiasme' as a 'maladie approchante des vapeurs, épidémique' (Voltaire 82, p.627).

[59] cf. Best.D13932, Voltaire to cardinal de Bernis, 9 February 1767: 'je hais ces maudits enfans de Calvin qui prétendent avec les jansénistes, que les bonnes œuvres ne valent pas un clou à souflet. Je ne suis point du tout de cet avis.' Cf. also *Dictionnaire philosophique*, ed. Benda and Naves, p.173, quoted above, p.66.

[60] cf. Best.D18333, to mme Necker, 23 April 1773, where Voltaire refers to us as 'les marionettes de la providence infinie'.

agreement on this point: both believed that the universe was governed by an immutable destiny, whose decrees were often quite incomprehensible to mere humans.[61] It would thus seem useful, at this point, to consider Voltaire's opinion of other aspects of Protestant theology, to see just how far this temporary agreement continued.

The first point to be borne in mind is that Voltaire did not consider religious reasons for the Reformation to be the most important. In his opinion, it was primarily a phenomenon of political, economic and social interest (*Essai*, ii.218):

Il n'y avait point encore de séparation marquée en se moquant des indulgences, en demandant à communier avec du pain et du vin, en disant des choses très peu intelligibles sur la justification et sur le libre arbitre, en voulant abolir les moines, en offrant de prouver que l'Ecriture sainte n'a pas expressément parlé du purgatoire.

Does this mean that Voltaire merely dismissed Protestant theology without trying to understand it, or that he simply avoided discussing it? The answer should already be apparent from the list just quoted of Luther's religious grievances. Voltaire was quite aware of the issues at stake, although he despised them as 'des choses très peu intelligibles'. Theological speculation was both a frivolous and a harmful activity, in Voltaire's opinion, but he was usually correct when describing the doctrines of the various Reformers or their position on a particular question. Luther, for example, 'nia le libre arbitre, que cependant ses sectateurs ont admis dans la suite' (ii.220), and as early as 1732 Voltaire had shown himself aware of this internal contradiction of Lutheranism (*Oh*, p.288):

C'est une chose rare de voir le sieur de la Motraye assurer que la prédestination n'est pas le dogme de Luther [...] C'est une chose certaine et connue que Luther dans ses livres nie le libre-arbitre et le mérite des bonnes œuvres, et admet la prédestination absolue. Les luthériens se sont depuis écartés de ce dogme, et ils ont fait comme tous les sectateurs qui ont changé la religion de leur fondateur.

Discussing Henry VIII's attack on Lutheran doctrine, he says the king defended seven sacraments against the reformer, 'qui alors en admettait trois, lesquels bientôt se réduisirent à deux' (*Essai*, ii.222). That these

---

[61] it is perhaps not fanciful to detect a personal note, as well as an attack on theology, in Voltaire's rueful description of free will as 'cet [...] écueil de la raison humaine' which was a 'source intarissable de querelles absurdes' (*Essai*, ii.220).

assertions are correct may not seem very remarkable, but the fact that Voltaire is equally well-informed on the other questions of Protestant theology is worthy of note in one who so despised theologians and expressed such profound hostility toward the object of their study.[62] Luther is praised for attacking Aristotle, who was 'alors le maître des écoles', but the main purpose of this accolade seems to be the fine opportunity it provides for attacking the obscurantism of the Sorbonne, since 'Luther ayant affirmé que la doctrine d'Aristote était fort inutile pour l'intelligence de l'Ecriture, la sacrée faculté de Paris traita cette assertion d'erronée de d'insensée' (*Essai*, ii.221). The venerable body was in fact so enraged by Luther's position on free will that it suspended 'l'examen de la dispute s'il y a eu trois Magdeleines, ou une seule Magdeleine, pour proscrire les dogmes de Luther' (ii.220).

Perhaps the most important basis of Protestant theology as developed at the time of the Reformation was the primacy accorded to the biblical text over Church tradition and later accretions, and Voltaire is no more ignorant of this than of the other important theological questions. In fact, he takes it for granted to the extent of hardly bothering to enunciate it formally. Apart from one passing reference in chapter 128 of the *Essai sur les mœurs* ('De Luther. Des indulgences'),[63] we have to wait until Voltaire is about to discuss the marital problems of Philip of Hesse before coming across the brief reference to 'les réformateurs d'Allemagne, qui voulaient suivre l'Evangile mot à mot' (*Essai*, ii.232). One or two other equally brief passages recall the reader's attention to this fundamental teaching of Protestantism. Unfortunately, Voltaire sees in the principle of literal interpretation only a source of confusion and disaster. Indeed, for him this is perhaps the weakest point in the whole Protestant position, an infallible cause of divisions and wars, for 'ce n'est qu'après Luther que les séculiers ont dogmatisé en foule, quand la *Bible*, traduite en tant de langues, et différemment traduite, a fait naître presque autant d'opinions qu'elle a de passages difficiles à expliquer' (ii.217). In this difficulty Voltaire sees the crux of the Christian

---

[62] Voltaire's hostility to theological disputes is characteristically expressed in a letter to Théodore Tronchin: 'Ce sont [. . .] des disputes puériles qui ont fait couler ces torrents de sang, et qui troublent encor la terre. C'est cet amas de dogmes absurdes toujours expliquez et toujours contredits, qui est encore le fléau du genre humain' (Best.D7584, 15 January 1758).

[63] Luther 'demanda [. . .] que l'on communiât avec du vin, parce que Jésus avait dit: "Buvez-en tous"; qu'on ne vénérât point les images, parce que Jésus n'avait point eu d'image' (*Essai*, ii.220).

religion's insoluble problem (*Essai*, ii.232): the Roman Church certainly needed reforming, but 'il n'est pas moins certain que s'il n'y avait pas eu dans le monde chrétien une autorité qui fixât le sens de l'Ecriture et les dogmes de la religion, il y aurait autant de sectes que d'hommes qui sauraient lire [...] presque chaque mot peut susciter une querelle'. Unfortunately, this would leave the way clear for papal pretensions, for 'une puissance qui aurait le droit de commander aux hommes au nom de Dieu abuserait bientôt d'un tel pouvoir'. And Voltaire sums up cynically: 'le genre humain s'est trouvé souvent, dans la religion comme dans le gouvernement, entre la tyrannie et l'anarchie, prêt à tomber dans l'un de ces deux gouffres' (ii.232). The Reformers, in Voltaire's opinion, were inconsistent in their reasoning, for they condemned the abuses of the Roman Church, but according to the wrong criterion. Instead of relying on the Bible as their supreme guide, they should have continued the process they had initiated and interpreted the text of the Bible itself according to the dictates of reason. For this was how they judged the Catholic Church, its teachings and its institutions. Why then should the book which formed the basis of their religion be examined and criticised any less carefully than the vehicle through which its teachings had been proclaimed to the world for so many centuries? In any case, the huge number of mistakes 'qu'ils imputaient à la Vulgate' should have taught them to accept any version of the biblical text with extreme caution.[64] Voltaire seems to have overlooked the possibility that the early Protestants might have used their reason, not, as he would have wished, to condemn their faith in the Bible, but to construct their own systems of theology. He sees this as just one more example of their inconsistency: they had begun a worthwhile reform, but ruined it because of their blind faith in a book which they should have seen was no more sacred than those who for so long had been its only depositories.

Of course, Voltaire agrees with some of the conclusions reached by Protestants who had judged the Roman Church from a biblical standpoint: attacks on papal pretensions, the abolition of monasteries and convents, the marriage of priests, the ending of the veneration of images, all these he warmly welcomed (*Essai*, ii.220), but not because the Bible contained no mention of them. He was in favour of them

[64] *Essai*, ii.219. Voltaire's own publication of apocryphal gospels (the *Collection d'anciens évangiles*, M.xxvii.439-556) and his biblical criticism, especially *La Bible enfin expliquée*, were further to emphasise the difficulties encountered by anyone who would accept the truth of the Bible word for word.

because they were reasonable reforms in themselves, the economic and social advantages of which were obvious to him. This did not prevent Protestant theology from being just as senseless as that of any of the Catholic doctors: 'Les thèses les plus vaines étaient mêlées avec les plus profondes, et des deux côtés les fausses imputations, les injures atroces, les anathèmes, nourissaient l'animosité des partis' (ii.221). In fact, in the *Annales de l'empire*, Voltaire delights to show that the Reformers could not make up their minds just what to believe (M.xiii. 489):

Les différents sectaires savaient bien ce qu'ils ne voulaient pas croire; mais ils ne savaient pas ce qu'ils voulaient croire. Tous s'accordaient à s'élever contre les abus de la cour et de l'Eglise romaine; tous introduisaient d'autres abus.

The differences between the various Protestant factions were most obvious in their positions regarding the eucharist, and this question is examined in detail by Voltaire, providing as it does an ideal opportunity for ridiculing Catholic beliefs at the same time. In fact, the first discussion of the matter in the *Essai sur les mœurs* begins by stating that transubstantiation was rejected by the reformers 'comme un mot qui ne se trouve ni dans l'Ecriture ni dans les pères'. It was, Voltaire adds, a late development and not universally adopted by the Church until the time of Gregory vii. Luther, a typically inconsistent Reformer, retained one part of the mystery and rejected the other: 'Il avoue que le corps de Jésus-Christ est dans les espèces consacrées; mais il y est, dit-il, comme le feu est dans le fer enflammé; le fer et le feu subsistent ensemble' (*Essai*, ii.219). In the earlier versions of the *Essai sur les mœurs*, Voltaire recounts this theologian's analogy with a straight face. But in 1769 he added to the end of the paragraph what are surely two of the most *brûlable* sentences he ever wrote, amounting to the most complete and blatant blasphemy in a Catholic. This addition, which could have had very serious consequences for Voltaire just a few years earlier, expresses his growing confidence toward the end of the 1760s that the battle against *l'infâme* was being won. He sets forth with calculated irony and insolence the Catholic, Lutheran and Calvinist theories of the eucharist. It is necessary to quote the preceding sentence also, in order to give an idea of the extraordinary change in tone (*Essai*, ii.219):

Luther se contente de dire que le corps et le sang étaient dedans, dessus, et dessous, *in, cum, sub*.[65] Ainsi, tandis que ceux qu'on appelait papistes mange-

---

[65] Voltaire sometimes uses this formula elsewhere as a shorthand way of referring to Lutheranism: cf. Best.D8414.

aient Dieu sans pain, les luthériens mangeaient du pain, et Dieu. Les calvinistes vinrent bientôt après, qui mangèrent le pain, et qui ne mangèrent point Dieu.

During the 1760s, Voltaire's feelings against the Catholic doctrine of transubstantiation seem to have reached their height, and an equivalent passage from the *Dictionnaire philosophique* may also be quoted to show how Voltaire sometimes expressed himself in terms of the most violent indignation, though it is doubtful whether this is any more devastating than the detached irony of the *Essai*:

Les protestants, et surtout les philosophes protestants, regardent la transubstantiation comme le dernier terme de l'impudence des moines, et de l'imbécilité des laïques [...] Leur horreur augmente, quand on leur dit qu'on voit tous les jours, dans les pays catholiques, des prêtres, des moines qui, sortant d'un lit incestueux, et n'ayant pas encore lavé leurs mains souillées d'impuretés, vont faire des dieux par centaines, mangent et boivent leur dieu, chient et pissent leur dieu.[66]

Voltaire seems to view the Calvinist position on the eucharist with least disfavour, but this is because it is more reasonable than the Catholic or Lutheran doctrines, not because it is more biblical (cf. below, p.81, n.70). It is true, however, that in the *Cinquième homélie*, 'Sur la Communion' (1769), Voltaire seems to be arguing that the eucharist should be retained because it has clear biblical support (M.xxvii.559):

nous nous en tenons à la partie de la loi qui est la plus clairement énoncée. Or qu'y a-t-il, je vous prie, de plus raisonnable et de plus lumineux que ces mots: *Faites ceci en mémoire de moi*? C'est donc en vertu de ces paroles que nous sommes assemblés. Nous nous acquittons d'une cérémonie que nous croyons nécessaire, parce qu'elle est ordonnée, parce qu'elle nous inspire la concorde, parce qu'elle nous rend plus chers les uns aux autres.

But it must not be forgotten that Voltaire was at this time becoming increasingly disturbed by the atheist productions of the *coterie holbachique*.[67] Although as hostile as ever to the Catholic Church, he showed some signs of a possible compromise with the more reasonable forms of Christianity, provided they rid themselves of their remaining superstitions. The passage I have quoted from the *Cinquième homélie* may represent a Voltairean concession to some of the philosophical

[66] *Dictionnaire philosophique* article 'Transubstantiation', ed. Benda and Naves, p.411.
[67] cf. Best.D16540, D16549, D16666, D16786, D17066.

pastors he discussed such matters with in Switzerland (cf. below, pp.192-97). In any case, the passage stresses the benefits which result from the practice of communion just as much as, if not more than its biblical origins, and the word *raisonnable* occupies a notably prominent place in the argument. Voltaire further makes clear that no doctrinal or denominational interpretations are to be imposed on the ceremony; it must serve as a means of reconciliation for all Christians rather than a ground of division between them: 'Nous ne comprenons rien aux idées ou plutôt aux paroles des uns et des autres; mais nous les regardons comme des frères dont nous n'entendons pas le langage' (M.xxvii.560). It is obviously reason that is Voltaire's guide in this matter, for are we to imagine that he would have suggested retaining the eucharist merely because its institution was clearly to be found in the Bible if he had not thought it might be turned to beneficial uses? He was, in fact, approaching the question from a point of view diametrically opposed to that normally held by Protestants.

Yet it would perhaps be useful to point out that although, on these questions, Voltaire's thinking is completely divorced from that of Protestant orthodoxy, the works of a notorious, but sincere,[68] Anglican clergyman, Jonathan Swift, express remarkably similar views. The *philosophe* would surely not have disavowed the explanation of one cause of European wars given by Gulliver to his Houyhnhnm master. Here is the same scorn for trifling details of dogma, dress and ritual, the same emphasis on the devastation brought about by unimportant scholastic quibbling:

Difference in opinions hath cost many millions of lives: for instance, whether *flesh* be *bread*, or *bread* be *flesh*; whether the iuice of a certain *berry* be *blood* or *wine*; whether *whistling* be a vice or virtue; whether it be better to *kiss a post*, or throw it into the fire; what is the best colour for a *coat*, whether *black, white, red* or *grey*; and whether it should be *long*, or *short, narrow* or *wide, dirty* or *clean*, with many more. Neither are any wars so furious and bloody, or of so long continuance, as those occasioned by difference in opinion, especially if it be in things indifferent.[69]

One explanation as to how such an obvious similarity in ideas could exist between Swift and Voltaire is that Protestants were less subjected

---

[68] for the sincerity of Swift's religious convictions see Ricardo Quintana, *Swift: an introduction* (London 1953), p.33.

[69] *Gulliver's travels*, Penguin English Library (Harmondsworth 1967), p.292.

to a monolithic system of dogma than Catholics. But if this is true, was Voltaire himself not aware of the many Protestant thinkers who had protested against theological disputes and religious intolerance? Do his works pay tribute to such men, or are his comments restricted to criticism of Protestant orthodoxy?

Voltaire was certainly well aware of the diverging views of Protestants on many questions, and this probably explains why his normal purpose in mentioning their various ideas on the eucharist was to stress the divisions between the reformers: 'Ni Luther, ni Calvin, ni les autres, ne s'entendirent sur l'eucharistie: l'un, ainsi que je l'ai déjà dit, voyait Dieu dans le pain et dans le vin comme du feu dans un fer ardent; l'autre, comme le pigeon dans lequel était le Saint-Esprit.'[70] It also provides a convenient way of differentiating the sects he is talking about:[71] the chapter on Zwingli and the Swiss Reformation begins with a description of his conception of the Eucharist – 'il n'admit point que Dieu entrât dans le pain et dans le vin' (*Essai*, ii.226) – even though Voltaire later suggests that the 'curé de Zurich' was more interested in liberty than Christianity (ii.230). Theological disputes are seen to be just as much the bane of the Protestants as of Christianity in general. Disagreement between theologians prevents the attempted reunification of all the Protestant sects, instigated by Philip, Landgrave of Hesse; this would have spared Europe a lot of bloodshed, but 'Luther et Mélanchthon furent inflexibles, et montrèrent en cela bien plus d'opiniâtreté que de politique'.[72] And, of course, in Voltaire's opinion this is

[70] *Essai*, ii.243. Here we see that Voltaire was just as ready to make fun of Calvin's theological ideas as of those of the other Reformers, although another passage from the *Essai sur les mœurs* (quoted above, pp.78-79) tends to look more favourably on Calvin's interpretation of the eucharist than on the views of Lutherans or Catholics. The explanation of this apparent inconsistency is probably that in the latter passage Voltaire is concerned to make maximum propaganda at the expense of transubstantiation, and in the context of Catholic beliefs, Calvin's position on the eucharist does indeed appear more reasonable to a *philosophe*. But in the former passage only Lutherans and Calvinists are mentioned, and Voltaire makes clear that, despite the apparent reasonableness of Calvin's teaching, it is conceived of according to a theological frame of reference which appears nonsensical to a rational man.

[71] cf. *Annales*; M.xiii.494-95: 'Le conseil de Berne fait plaider devant lui la cause du catholicisme et celle des sacramentaires, disciples de Zuingle. Ces sectaires différaient des luthériens, principalement au sujet de l'eucharistie, les zuingliens disant que Dieu n'est dans le pain que par la foi, et les luthériens affirmant que Dieu était avec le pain, dans le pain et sur le pain; mais tous s'accordant à croire que le pain existe.'

[72] *Annales*; M.xiii.500. Cf. a letter of about 5 November 1742 to Frederick the Great, in which Voltaire points out that Sanchez's speculations on the Virgin Mary and the Holy

just the opposite of what Protestants should do. Before they can expect tolerance, they must be tolerant themselves. In the *Remontrances du corps des pasteurs du Gévaudan* (1768), Voltaire, speaking in the guise of a Protestant, expresses himself as follows:

Vous attaquez vos sauveurs, ceux qui ont prêché la tolérance; ne voyez-vous pas qu'ils n'ont pu obtenir cette tolérance pour les calvinistes paisibles sans inspirer l'indifférence pour les dogmes, et qu'on nous pendrait encore si cette indifférence n'était pas établie? Remercions nos bienfaiteurs, ne les outrageons pas.[73]

This pamphlet is one of Voltaire's propaganda productions, seeking to show that Protestants should have only feelings of gratitude towards the *philosophes* after the Calas affair, but it also has a wider significance in that it stresses the direct relationship between the progress of tolerance and the growing indifference to dogma.[74] It also makes clear that, in Voltaire's opinion, Protestants were no more tolerant than Catholics.[75]

But what is particularly noteworthy is that, although he refers briefly to Sebastian Castellio, expelled from Geneva at Calvin's instigation (cf. above, p.63), and to other victims of Protestant persecution, Voltaire makes no attempt to summarise or even mention the tolerant ideas disseminated by the author of *De hæreticis, an sint persequendi*[76] and by not a few other Protestant writers and personalities. This is surely a surprising and a very significant omission from the writings of a man recognised by common accord as the Enlightenment's greatest champion of religious toleration, for it is clear that omission there is. Luther himself supported the policy of toleration, although he

Ghost, despite their rather bizarre conclusions, caused no disputes and no men were burned because of them: 'Si les partisans de Luther, de Zuingle, de Calvin et du pape avaient usé de même,' he concludes, 'il n'y aurait eu que du plaisir à vivre avec ces gens-là' (Best.D2681). Cf. also Best.D4984.

[73] M.xxvii.108. Cf. *Essai*, ii.248.

[74] Voltaire explicitly outlined this theory to his correspondent Moultou in connection with the attitude he had adopted in the *Traité sur la tolérance* (cf. Best.D10885 and D10897).

[75] cf. Voltaire's warning to the Protestant Végobre, who was a member of the committee formed to help the Calas family: 'Il faudra bien en venir à la fin au dogme abominable de la Tolérance. Mais souvenez vous un jour, vous autres ennemis des usurpations papales d'être tolérants à vôtre tour' (Best.D13994, 25 February 1767).

[76] this was an attack on Calvin over the burning of Servetus, which Castellio published in March 1554, under the pseudonym Martin Bellius (Kamen, *The Rise of toleration*, p.77).

later took up a position radically opposed to his former views.[77] But Philip of Hesse, whose bigamy Voltaire recounts in such detail (cf. above, pp.52-54), was also notably liberal in religious matters, never at any time confirming a death sentence for heresy.[78] Was this fact not at least as important as his matrimonial adventures? Sebastian Franck, quoted by Castellio, in *De haeriticis*, expressed himself in terms which would not have appeared foreign in Voltaire's own mouth:

My heart is alien to none. I have my brothers among the Turks, Papists, Jews and all people. Not that they are Turks, Jews, Papists and Sectaries or will remain so; in the evening they will be called into the vineyard and given the same wage as we.[79]

It is difficult to avoid the conclusion that Voltaire must have been aware of at least some of these tolerant Protestants, and that he deliberately avoided mentioning them. What can explain this apparent perversity?

At the end of a correspondence which had included its share of home truths for both participants, the Swiss poet Haller dismissed Voltaire's complaints over the execution of Servetus, and declared (Best.D8282, April/May 1759):

C'est chez l'Eglise protestante que la tolérance est née: inconue aux Chrétien avant eux, elle a peu à peu éclairé jusqu'à Vos yeux Monsieur où sans elle, et sa liberté de penser, d'écrire, ces idées brillantes d'amour Universel n'eussent peut être jamais penché.

This claim was a commonplace of Protestant apologetics and had no doubt been encountered by Voltaire even before Haller drew it so forcibly to his attention. Perhaps the *philosophe*, concerned above all with outbreaks of intolerance symbolised by the fate of Servetus, was angered by such statements and consequently determined, in the *Essai sur les mœurs* and many other works, to emphasise the non-liberal

[77] the distinguished Protestant historian E.-G. Léonard paints a glowing picture of the Reformer's sentiments (*Histoire générale*, i.80). Unfortunately, Luther's liberal position changed fundamentally against the background of the Peasants' Revolt and the alarming proliferation of sects, and when 'in 1530 [...] Melanchthon [...] gave his written opinion that the death penalty should be retained for all offences against civil and ecclesiastical order', Luther expressed his approval (Kamen, p.39).

[78] it must be added, however, that 'on the political side, Philip was as ruthless as Luther. He helped to suppress the Knights' rising under Sickingen in 1523, and in 1525 he suppressed the main body of the peasants at Frankenhausen with a ferocity that echoes through history' (Kamen, p.41).

[79] quoted by Kamen, p.78.

aspects of Protestant history and teaching, with the double aim of shaming liberal Protestants into renouncing Calvin while at the same time
making further propaganda against the Christian religion as a whole.
Whatever the explanation, one can say quite confidently that approbatory references to liberal Protestants in Voltaire's works are few and
far between. A handful of latitudinarian Anglican divines, particularly
Clarke and Tillotson, provide something of an exception, and so also
do two unorthodox Protestant thinkers of the eighteenth century,
Marie Huber and Jean Barbeyrac, who are discussed by Voltaire in the
Lettres à s.a. mgr le prince de****. In their case, however, the aim is purely
one of propaganda against *l'infâme*, for the title makes clear that these
are authors 'accusés d'avoir mal parlé de la religion chrétienne', and
none of what Voltaire says about them is made to redound to the credit
of Protestantism.[80] Thus one can say that his dislike of Calvinism and
the more extreme manifestations of Protestantism leads Voltaire to
ignore many of those thinkers and writers who were in a very real
sense his own predecessors and who laid the foundations of religious
toleration.

We have seen that Voltaire regarded literal acceptance of the Bible's
contents as a source of disaster, and there is yet another way in which
the important place of scripture in Protestant thought incurred his
wrath. Worse still even than the calculating theologians were the
'enthusiasts' who, convinced that they were inspired, twisted various
biblical passages to support their claims or justify their actions. This was
a constant policy of various kinds of Protestant *illuminés*. Indeed, it
was even practised by the peace-loving and respectable Quakers,[81]
though in their case it did little harm and was merely ridiculous. Usually,
however, the grotesque element was accompanied by the most frightful
and sanguinary fanaticism, as we have seen in the case of the Anabaptists, and an unreasonable veneration of the Bible had been the cause of
some of the most bloodthirsty events in human history. Voltaire's
description of the Presbyterians at the time of the English Civil War
well illustrates his conception of this phenomenon, and the clear link
established in his mind between fanaticism, biblical justification and
violence (*Essai*, ii.667; 1761 addition):

[80] cf. below, pp.148-49; the same comment is true of Voltaire's remarks on Swift and
Warburton.
[81] *Lettres philosophiques*, ed. Lanson, i.3-4.

Ce ridicule, que les réformateurs avaient tant reproché à la communion romaine, devint le partage des presbytériens. Les évêques se conduisirent en lâches; ils devaient mourir pour défendre une cause qu'ils croyaient juste; mais les presbytériens se conduisirent en insensés: leurs habillements, leurs discours, leurs basses allusions aux passages de l'Evangile, leurs contorsions, leurs sermons, leurs prédictions, tout en eux aurait mérité, dans des temps plus tranquilles, d'être joué à la foire de Londres, si cette farce n'avait pas été trop dégoûtante. Mais malheureusement l'absurdité de ces fanatiques se joignait à la fureur: les mêmes hommes dont les enfants se seraient moqués imprimaient la terreur en se baignant dans le sang; et ils étaient à la fois les plus fous de tous les hommes et les plus redoubtables.

What better proof could one ask for that the Bible should be interpreted only in the light of reason?

Worse still was that, being so much better versed in the Bible than the Catholics, the Protestants were more likely to remember the cruelty and treachery shown so often in the Old Testament by the chosen people of God, the detested Jews, and to imitate actions which had received divine approval. There is no doubt, in Voltaire's opinion, that this did actually happen and a clear link exists in his mind between the fanatical and heartless Jewish prophets, and, for example, the Anabaptists, Cromwell's supporters, and the Camisard rebels,[82] or even the exiled Calvinist theologian, Jurieu.[83] Although in the *Essai sur les mœurs* Voltaire says that, during the English Civil War, all denominations were in good faith (*Essai*, ii.667), the *Examen important de milord Bolingbroke* probably gives us a more characteristic expression of his opinions. There Voltaire says that the various types of 'prophets' who have appeared in religious history were quite probably hypocrites as well as fanatics:

Nous avons vu arriver à Londres, par troupe, du fond du Languedoc et du Vivarais, des prophètes, tout semblables à ceux des Juifs, joindre le plus horrible enthousiasme aux plus dégoûtants mensonges. Nous avons vu Jurieu prophétiser en Hollande. Il y eut de tout temps de tels imposteurs, et

---

[82] cf. Best.D13274, to the d'Argentals, 30 April 1766: 'Je fais une histoire des proscriptions [Voltaire is referring to *Octave*] à commencer depuis celle des vingt trois mille Juifs que les Lévites égorgèrent pieusement du temps de Moÿse, et à finir par celle des prophètes des Cévennes, qui faisaient une liste des impies que Dieu avait condamnés à mourir par leurs mains.' Cf. also Best.D13325.

[83] cf. the *Siècle de Louis XIV* (*Oh*, p.1057).

non seulement des misérables qui faisaient des prédictions, mais d'autres misérables qui supposaient des prophéties faites par d'anciens personnages.[84]

Almost at the end of his life, recalling the excesses of the Cévenol prophets, Voltaire is prompted to make one of his most extreme anti-Protestant statements and in his anger to resolve the problem of biblical interpretation in an unexpected and uncharacteristic way:

les temps sont changés. Il est vrai que, dans la guerre des fanatiques des Cévennes, ces malheureux avaient une prophétesse nommée *la grande Marie*, qui, dès que l'esprit lui avait parlé, condamnait à la mort les captifs faits à la guerre; mais c'était un abus horrible des livres sacrés. C'est le propre des fanatiques qui lisent l'Ecriture sainte de se dire à eux-mêmes: Dieu a tué, donc il faut que je tue: Abraham a menti, Jacob a trompé, Rachel a volé: donc je dois voler, tromper, mentir. Mais, malheureux, tu n'es ni Rachel, ni Jacob, ni Abraham, ni Dieu; tu n'es qu'un fou furieux, et les papes qui défendirent la lecture de la *Bible* furent très-sages.[85]

Increased knowledge of the Bible, and more particularly of the Old Testament, had therefore caused very pernicious effects among the Protestants. Even familiarity with the Book of psalms, for which the Huguenots were noted, was likely to lead to a hardening of their hearts in view of the cruel sentiments expressed in some of the poems. These are listed in *Dieu et les hommes* (1769). It will be sufficient to quote the most damning:

Vous sentez combien il est indécent de ne chanter à Dieu que des chansons juives, et combien il est honteux de n'avoir pas eu assez d'esprit pour faire vous-mêmes des hymnes plus convenables [. . .] Ne rougissez-vous pas de dire à Dieu [. . .] Bienheureux celui qui prendra tes petits enfants, et qui les écrasera contre la pierre.[86]

The same psalm is recalled in the *Discours de me Belleguier* (1773), and the relation between biblical inspiration and bloodshed is vividly

---

[84] *Mélanges*, p.1038. A similar anecdote to that recounted at the beginning of this quotation can be found in one of Voltaire's Leningrad notebooks (Voltaire 81, pp.67-68).

[85] M.xxx.136, n.1.

[86] M.xxviii.241-42. Voltaire's disgust for the content of such psalms is presumably responsible for a somewhat unexpected remark in one of his notebooks: 'Ne valoit il pas mieux réciter les psaumes en latin que de faire chanter aux femmes dans l'église les psaumes impertinents de Marot et de Bèze?' (Voltaire 81, p.412). As in the case of the passage quoted above, exasperation at the extent of Protestant 'fanaticism' drives Voltaire into making an illiberal, apparently pro-Catholic statement, but these outbursts should certainly not be interpreted as in any real way favourable to the Catholic position.

illustrated by the fact that the offending verse is spoken by Cromwell, in Voltaire's opinion one of those cynics who manipulate the fanaticism of others:

Cromwell, à la tête de son régiment des frères rouges, portait la Bible à l'arçon de sa selle, et leur montrait les passages où il est dit: 'Heureux ceux qui éventreront les femmes grosses, et qui écraseront les enfants sur la pierre.'[87]

In *Dieu et les hommes* Voltaire goes on to attack the immorality of the respected author of the Psalms, David, 'l'homme selon le cœur de Dieu' (M.xxviii.242). Elsewhere he recalls the persecution conducted by Jurieu and the theologians of the Refuge against Bayle, who had treated David harshly in one of his dictionary articles. Voltaire describes the Protestant position and emphasises its untenability: 'Quoi donc! les ennemis de Bayle auraient-ils voulu que Bayle eût fait l'éloge de toutes ces cruautés et de tous ces crimes?' (M.xx.198).

Yet how much more harmful was the justification provided by Old Testament precedents for political assassinations! In the *Essai sur les mœurs* Voltaire states explicitly that the murder of the duc de Guise by Poltrot de Méré was the first event of its kind in France and that the Huguenots were therefore responsible for this new horror (ii.490):

Le meurtre de ce grand homme fut le premier que le fanatisme fit commettre en France. Ces mêmes huguenots qui, sous François 1er et sous Henri II, n'avaient su que souffrir ce qu'ils appelaient le *martyre*, étaient devenus des enthousiastes furieux: ils ne lisaient plus l'Ecriture que pour y chercher des exemples d'assassinats. Poltrot de Méré se crut un Aod envoyé de Dieu pour tuer un chef philistin. Cela est si vrai que le parti fit des vers en son honneur, et que j'ai vu encore une de ses estampes avec une inscription qui élève son crime jusqu'au ciel.

Voltaire stresses that the motive was religious and not political by clearing Coligny and Beza from any responsibility for the assassination, and later in the *Essai* the resemblance between Jacques Clément and Poltrot de Méré is made clear.[88] In the *Histoire du parlement de Paris*

---

[87] M.xxix.16. In an article written in 1748, Voltaire further explained his attitude toward Cromwell. The latter was not a hypocritical rogue all his life – he became one after realising the folly of his former beliefs: 'Je pense qu'il fut d'abord enthousiaste, et qu'ensuite il fit servir son fanatisme même à sa grandeur' (M.xviii.294); cf. below, pp.404-409.

[88] *Essai*, ii.527. Poltrot and Clément (the assassin of Henri III) or Ravaillac (the assassin of Henri IV) are included together in several lists of religious assassins which occur from time to time in Voltaire's correspondence: cf. Best.D2106, D2386, D13651.

(1768) Voltaire has changed his position slightly and states that 'ce n'était pas le premier assassinat que la rage de religion avait fait commettre', but he emphasises its special character: 'Celui-ci fut le plus signalé, par le grand nom de l'assassiné et par le fanatisme du meurtrier, qui crut servir Dieu en tuant l'ennemi de sa secte' (M.xv.516). Moreover Voltaire reflects bitterly on the event and the conclusions he reaches illustrate perfectly his opinion that the practice of accepting the Bible as literal truth is an 'abus de la religion chrétienne', as dangerous as it is absurd and unreasonable:

Tout ce qu'on put enfin conjecturer de plus vraisemblable c'est qu'il [Poltrot] n'avait d'autre complice que la fureur du fanatisme. Tels ont été presque tous ceux à qui l'abus de la religion chrétienne a mis dans tous les temps le poignard à la main, tous aveuglés par les exemples de Jael, d'Aod, de Judith, et de Mathathias qui tua dans le temple l'officier du roi Antiochus, dans le temps que ce capitaine voulait exécuter les ordres de son maître, et sacrifier un cochon sur l'autel. Tous ces assassinats étant malheureusement consacrés, il n'est pas étonnant que des fanatiques absurdes, ne distinguant pas les temps et les lieux, aient imité des attentats qui doivent inspirer l'horreur, quoique rapportés dans un livre qui inspire du respect.[89]

The exploits of the Scottish Presbyterians after another assassination inspired by the Bible, that of the archbishop of St Andrews, give Voltaire a fine opportunity to exercise his irony upon their fanaticism and the Old Testament idea that the Jews were the people of God (*Essai*, ii.694; 1761 addition):

Cette armée s'appelait *l'armée du Seigneur*. Il y avait un vieux ministre qui monta sur un petit tertre, et qui se fit soutenir les mains comme Moïse, pour obtenir une victoire sure. L'armée du Seigneur fut mise en déroute dès les premiers coups de canon.

Although Voltaire frequently recalls massacres and executions of Protestants, his purpose is usually to discredit the actions of their Catholic persecutors, and to emphasise the fundamental violence of Christianity itself. Normally, while sympathising with their cruel deaths, he seems to have rather a low opinion of the 'martyrs', as this

[89] M.xv.517; cf. also M.xxviii.239. On Frederick the Great's accession, Voltaire expressed in verse the fear that some Catholic inspired by Old Testament examples might assassinate his hero! (Best.D2462). And an anecdote in one of the Leningrad notebooks sums up with characteristic wit and brevity his argument against imitation of scriptural examples: 'Un évêque reprochoit à la reine Elisabeth, une action peu conforme à l'écriture. Je voi bien, dit elle, que vous n'avez pas lu le livre des rois' (Voltaire 81, p.384).

extract from the *Conseils raisonnables à m. Bergier* well illustrates: 'Le détail de ces horreurs vous fait dresser les cheveux; mais la multiplicité en est si grande qu'elle ennuie. On faisait périr ainsi des milliers d'*imbéciles*, en leur disant qu'il fallait entendre la messe en latin.'[90] Even one Protestant, whom Voltaire considered to be far from an imbecile, and whose execution is frequently referred to in his works as a prime example of the intolerance of the Catholic Church (cf. M.xxv.373, 381; M.xxvii. 49), is shown to be mistaken in believing that his death was a religious duty. The *Discours du conseiller Anne Dubourg à ses juges* (1771) recounts how a Protestant gentlewoman, mme de Lacaille, persuaded Dubourg not to abjure his faith in order to save his life. Voltaire comments wryly:

Il n'était pas bien démontré que Dieu, qui a soin de tant de globes roulants autour de leurs soleils dans les plaines de l'éther, voulut expressément qu'un conseiller-clerc fût pendu pour lui dans la place de Grève; mais Mme de Lacaille en était convaincue.
Le conseiller en crut enfin quelque chose.[91]

We have already seen that, in the *Essai sur les mœurs* and his other historical works, Voltaire neglects almost entirely the specifically religious aspects of the Reformation. His dismissal of the actions of men like Dubourg also demonstrates that he had little appreciation of the 'âmes en mal de salut',[92] who longed for the spiritual nourishment provided by Luther and the other Reformers. Voltaire is incapable of understanding the Protestant's need of witness, the Christian duty to testify to one's faith which has brought about the willing acceptance of martyrdom by so many Protestants and other believers during the Church's history. This inability can only be attributed to the different attitudes to God held by Voltaire and the Protestant. For the latter, an intimate relationship with the divinity is not only possible but an overriding necessity. If once achieved, it will obviously be the most important fact of an individual's life and will condition all other aspects

[90] M.xxvii.51, my italics. Voltaire's attitude on this point is summed up in a brief comment made twice in his notebooks: 'persécution, abominable; martyr, fou' (Voltaire 82, p.534; cf. also Voltaire 82, p.613).

[91] M.xxviii.469-70. In one of his Leningrad notebooks Voltaire records a similar example of Huguenot attachment to martyrdom: 'Un bon huguenot parlant des persécutions de ses frères, dit de l'un d'eux qui s'étoit sauvé, enfin dieu l'abandonna, il ne fut pas pendu' (Voltaire 81, p.369).

[92] E.-G. Léonard, *Histoire générale*, i.16.

of his existence. For Voltaire, however, no such contact is feasible, indeed the very suggestion emanating from a creature so insignificant as man is presumptous and constitutes an affront to God's dignity and majesty.[93] This unwillingness to concede any direct relationship between God and the individual, at any rate in a sense meaningful to Christians, lies at the heart of Voltaire's opposition to many features of traditional Protestantism. Examples illustrating this attitude could be multiplied, and it can perhaps help us to understand more easily why Voltaire reacted so violently against the morality and theology of Protestantism, for not only did he hold the Reformation responsible for an enormous amount of bloodshed and misery, he also rejected the fundamental religious premises on which it was based.

What of the Reformers, whom Voltaire has by and large made out to be sanctimonious hypocrites and intolerant power-seekers? In the *Essai sur les mœurs* he himself states clearly that 'les catholiques ne peuvent comprendre que les protestants reconnaissent de tels apôtres' (*Essai*, ii.248), implying, it would at first appear, that he agrees with such critics. However, he is preparing one of those passages which not only give a plausible reason for the objection he has just put forward, but also tend to include Christianity as a whole in the opprobrium originally intended for one of its denominations (ii.248):

Les protestants répondent qu'ils n'invoquent point ceux qui ont servi à établir leur réforme, qu'ils ne sont ni luthériens, ni zwingliens, ni calvinistes; qu'ils croient suivre les dogmes de la primitive Eglise; qu'ils ne canonisent point les passions de Luther et de Calvin; et que la dureté de leur caractère ne doit pas plus décrier leurs opinions dans l'esprit des réformés que les mœurs d'Alexandre VI et de Léon X, et les barbaries des persécutions, ne font tort à la religion romaine dans l'esprit des catholiques.

Cette réponse est sage, et la modération semble aujourd'hui prendre dans les deux partis opposés la place des anciennes fureurs.

In other words, both sides have skeletons in their cupboard, but despite the quarrels and bloodshed of the past, peace has at last come about

---

[93] as Voltaire told Fyot de La Marche on 19 May 1762 (Best.D10457): 'la chaîne des évènements est immense, éternelle. Les acceptions de personnes, les faveurs et les disgrâces particulières ne sont pas faites pour une cause infinie; et dans la quantité prodigieuse de globes qui roulent les uns autour des autres par des loix générales, il serait trop ridicule que l'Eternel architecte changeât, et rechangeât continuellement les petits évènements de nôtre petit globule, il ne s'occupe ni de nos souris, ni de nos chats, ni de nos Jesuites, ni de vos flottes, ni même des tracasseries de vôtre Parlement.' Cf. below, pp.453 ff.

thanks to the growth of philosophy. Yet although it has been just as guilty as Catholicism in causing these disasters, the Protestant faith has in some ways helped the cause of reason, a fact Voltaire himself is willing, on occasion, to recognise.

vi. *The benefits of Erastianism*

A belief that the Church and all aspects of its life and worship should be entirely subject to state control is commonly called Erastianism in English-speaking countries,[94] and although, in his works, Voltaire appears to make no reference to Erastus, the principle associated with this Protestant divine was one of those dearest to his heart. For Voltaire, indeed, the one great strength of the Reformation was that in many Protestant countries it encouraged the state to take up a dominant position in the religious establishment, and a brief review of the advantages which flowed from this principle will now be made.

The Reformation, despite its defects, had enabled a certain amount of intellectual progress to be achieved, and Protestant countries figure prominently and consistently in the lists Voltaire gives of enlightened nations. On 13 August 1760 he told Helvétius: 'la lumière se répandra en France comme en Angleterre, en Prusse, en Hollande, en Suisse, en Italie même' (Best.D9141). Twelve years later he asked Jacques Du Pan: 'Par quelle fatalité faut il que les plus beaux climats de la terre, le Languedoc, la Provence, l'Italie, l'Espagne, soient livrés aux superstitions les plus infâmes, lorsque la raison règne dans le nord?'[95]

In a letter to prince Golitsuin in 1773 Voltaire was even more complimentary to Protestant countries: 'On goûte depuis longtemps ce bonheur [religious concord] en Angleterre, en Hollande, en Brandebourg, en Prusse, & dans plusieurs villes de l'Allemagne, pourquoi donc pas dans toute la terre?'[96] Reason herself, speaking in *L'Homme aux*

---

[94] cf. Owen Chadwick, *The Reformation*, p.150. Erastus was the humanist name of Thomas Luber, who was a pupil of Bullinger and opposed the introduction of Calvinist discipline into the Palatinate.

[95] Best.D17710, 24 April 1772. Cf. Best.D10285, D13046 and D1320, to Frederick the Great, *c.* 25 April 1737: 'Les pays du nord ont cet avantage sur le midy de l'Europe, que ces tirans des âmes y ont moins de puissance qu'ailleurs. Aussi les princes du nord sont ils pour la plus part moins superstitieux et moins méchants qu'ailleurs.' Whether or not Voltaire actually believed this, he actively canvassed the idea of making the Holy Roman emperors alternately Catholic and Protestant, clearly hoping that such a possibility would appeal to Frederick: cf. Best.D1574 and D1999.

[96] Best.D18431, 19 June 1773; cf. Best.D12660.

quarante écus (1768), explains the situation as follows: 'Je suis très-bien reçue à Berlin, à Moscou, à Copenhague, à Stockholm. Il y a longtemps que, par le crédit de Locke, de Gordon, de Trenchard, de milord Shaftesbury, et de tant d'autres, j'ai reçu mes lettres de naturalité en Angleterre' (M.xxi.362). Here England, a Protestant country, is seen as the home of philosophers who have, in their turn, encouraged the progress of reason, and a similar development appears to have occurred in other Protestant nations. Was this a mere coincidence? No, explains Voltaire: the reform of the Roman Catholic religion is a necessary preliminary to the development not only of philosophy, but also of the economic and social well-being of a country.[97] Again England illustrates the point (M.xxi.342):

L'exemple de l'Angleterre et de tant d'autres Etats est une preuve évidente de la nécessité de cette réforme. Que ferait aujourd'hui l'Angleterre si, au lieu de quarante mille hommes de mer, elle avait quarante mille moines? Plus les arts se sont multipliés, plus le nombre des sujets laborieux est devenu nécessaire. Il y a certainement dans les cloîtres beaucoup de talents ensevelis qui sont perdus pour l'Etat.

Sometimes Voltaire's enthusiasm for Protestant countries leads him to rather doubtful conclusions: 'Les théologiens ne donnent des décrets ni en Angleterre ni en Prusse,' he exclaimed to Marmontel on 1 January 1763, 'aussi les Anglais et les Prussiens nous ont bien battus' (Best. D14636; cf. Best.D9931). Voltaire's reasoning might in this instance appear a little specious to some, especially when one remembers that it was a monk[98] who is often credited with the discovery of gunpowder! Nevertheless, this letter gives characteristic expression to his belief that Protestant nations are better off materially and more efficient generally because they have fewer priests than their Catholic counterparts: 'Il faut de bons laboureurs et de bons soldats', he concludes, 'et le moins de théologiens qu'il soit possible' (Best.D14636).

Indeed the economic and social benefits of the Reformation cannot be denied. The abolition of monasteries has led to a beneficial increase in population:

---

[97] cf. Best.D14668, 13 January 1768, Voltaire to Servan: 'Il me semble que l'Angleterre n'a de véritablement bonnes loix que depuis que Jacques 3 [sic] alla toucher les écrouelles au couvent des Anglaises à Paris.'

[98] the Franciscan Francis Bacon (*c.*1220-*c.*1292), often known as the *doctor admirabilis* (cf. *Encyclopaedia britannica*, 1967, *s.v.* 'Gunpowder').

Il y a des quartiers entiers à Londres qui ne formaient autrefois qu'un seul couvent, et qui sont peuplés aujourd'hui d'un très grand nombre de familles. En général, toute nation qui a converti les couvents à l'usage public y a beaucoup gagné, sans que personne y ait perdu.[99]

The marriage of clerics has had the same beneficial effect. Discussing polygamy with James Marriott, Voltaire commented: 'Je voudrais seulement que chacun de nos prêtres en eût une [a wife], et surtout de nos moines' (Best.D13224, 28 March 1766). Moreover, the education normally received by the sons of the Protestant clergy is also commendable, to judge from the *Doutes sur l'histoire de l'empire* (1743): 'on ne voit guère de meilleure éducation que celle des enfants des pasteurs en Angleterre, en Allemagne, en Suède, en Danemark, en Hollande' (M.xxiv.36).

These then are some of the advantages enjoyed by Protestant countries as a direct consequence of their more reasonable religion. But even now Voltaire's strictures on Catholic nations are not at an end, for his experience as a landowner at Ferney led him to protest time and again against the large number of uneconomic feast-days which hampered the development of agriculture and provoked disbelieving amusement among his Swiss neighbours. In a letter to the d'Argentals (Best.D9837, 21 June 1961) he thundered: 'le roy devrait, je ne dis pas permettre les travaux champêtres ces jours là, mais les ordonner. C'est un reste de nôtre ancienne barbarie, de laisser cette grande partie de L'œconomie de l'Etat, entre les mains des prêtres.' Moreover, other religious restrictions are also harmful in this respect (Best.D16079, 5 January 1770):

Si jamais il y eut une chose qui dut dépendre de la grande police, c'est assurément la nourriture des cultivateurs. Mais à la honte de la raison et de la magistrature c'est un Evêque qui permet ou qui deffend de manger des œufs pendant quarante jours à des gens qui ont à peine des œufs.

State control of the clergy would bring immeasurable benefits: 'il n'y a pas un seul exemple d'un pasteur protestant qui ait eu un procez avec ses paroissiens', Voltaire lectured Deschamps de Chaumont in 1758,[100]

---

[99] *Essai*, ii.249. The same point is made in a letter to Shuvalov, again to the advantage of England: 'Les prêtres désolent l'Italie. Les pays d'Allemagne gouvernés par les prélats sont pauvres et dépeuplés, tandis que l'Angleterre a doublé sa population depuis deux cents ans, et décuplé ses richesses' (Best.D14450, 30 September 1767).

[100] Best.D7981, 16 December 1758. Chaumont was the titular bishop of Geneva, residing at Annecy, in whose diocese Ferney was situated.

notably changing his tune from the one he often played to Calvinist pastors.[101] Nonetheless, the reason for which he thinks discord is less widespread in Protestant countries, although mistaken,[102] is still significant: 'C'est que ces curés [i.e. the Protestant clergy] sont payés par l'état qui leur donne des gages: ils ne disputent point la dixième ou la huitième à des malheureux' (Best.D7981).

The abolition of feast-days, lenten fasting and tithes would represent a considerable step forward, but the fatal mistake of Catholic princes is much more fundamental. Although they have begun to attack fanaticism, 'ils reconnaissent encor deux puissances, ou dumoins ils feignent de les reconnaître. Ils ne sont pas assez hardis p^r déclarer que l'église doit dépendre uniquem^t des loix du souverain' (Best.D15349, 3 December 1768). The nefarious principle of two powers exists neither in Catherine the Great's Russia, nor in Protestant countries, a fact which prompts Voltaire to record his enthusiastic approval: 'Je ne connais que les princes protestants qui se conduisent raisonablement', he told the Duchess of Saxe-Gotha, wife of just such a ruler. 'Ils tiennent les prêtres à la place où ils doivent être, et ils vivent tranquiles (quand la rage de la guerre ne s'en mêle pas)' (Best.D11313, 19 July 1763).

The good side of Protestantism makes Voltaire all the more impatient with what he sees as its defects and illogicalities. For example, he considers the remaining anti-Catholic laws at Geneva and in various other Protestant countries to be a result of continued clerical influence, and since these affected him personally, his attack on them is especially bitter (cf. below, p.121). In the *Avis au public sur les parricides imputés aux Calas et aux Sirven* (1766), he goes as far as to imply that Protestant countries are more intolerant than Catholic ones in some ways (*Mélanges*, p.836):

Qu'on ne dise donc point qu'il ne reste plus de traces du fanatisme affreux de l'intolérantisme: elles sont encore partout, elles sont dans les pays mêmes qui passent pour les plus humains. Les prédicants luthériens et calvinistes, s'ils étaient les maîtres, seraient peut-être aussi impitoyables, aussi durs, aussi

---

[101] cf. especially some of his comments in the *Questions sur les miracles* (1765).

[102] as Voltaire himself had pointed out in the *Lettres philosophiques* (ed. Lanson, i.44), the Anglican Clergy collected tithes from their parishioners, and this income could in no way be regarded as state 'gages' of the type described by Voltaire in Best.D7981. Similarly in Germany, another largely Protestant land, the clergy were supported by tithes (see W. H. Bruford, *Germany in the eighteenth century: the social background to the literary revival* (Cambridge 1935), p.253).

intolérants, qu'ils reprochent à leurs antagonistes de l'être. La loi barbare qu'aucun catholique ne peut demeurer plus de trois jours dans certains pays protestants n'est point encore révoquée. Un Italien, un Français, un Autrichien, ne peut posséder une maison, un arpent de terre, dans leur territoire, tandis qu'au moins on permet en France qu'un citoyen inconnu de Genève ou de Schaffouse achète des terres seigneuriales.

In this obviously extreme statement, Voltaire goes further than his normal position, but it is nonetheless a useful reminder of how uneasy the alliance between the *philosophe* and Protestantism was, and how quickly he was liable to turn on his temporary allies. It only needed a reminder of past or present intolerance, or evidence of unwillingness to progress to a more reasonable form of religion, for Voltaire to forget the practical benefits of the Reformation and to subject Protestantism to the same withering scorn as its rival, Catholicism. Perhaps, after all, this is not so surprising: a priest was always a priest to Voltaire, and the Reformers had been theologians, not *philosophes*. Their Protestant successors were likely, at best, to be uneasy and unreliable converts to the Enlightenment.

In summing up, then, we may say that Voltaire's attitude to the morality, theology, and general ethos of Protestantism reflected the view he took of the main Reformers. There were some good points in Zwingli and Luther, and likewise he praised Protestantism for its healthy Erastianism, its abolition of superstitious practices, and its contribution towards the progress of reason and the human spirit. Yet this contribution was more an accidental side-effect of the Reformation than an aim of the Reformers. They were determined to subject their reason blindly to the Bible, thus laying themselves open to the harmful influence of the Old Testament Jews. Intolerance and fanaticism, epitomised by Calvin, characterised Protestants just as much as Catholics, whose defects the Reformers had so severely criticised. The harsh, unpalatable, and socially irrelevant morality imposed on Protestants was a consequence of the hypocrisy and insatiable desire for power exhibited by their leaders, but even more so it was the price they paid for following reason only half-way, and showing themselves unwilling to accept complete enlightenment.

In the first part of this study I have tried primarily to present a synthesis of Voltaire's attitudes to Protestantism in general, based largely on his descriptions, in historical works like the *Essai sur les mœurs*, of the Reformation, the Reformers and their teachings. It would not be unfair to say that Voltaire's views on many of these topics were somewhat theoretical before he settled in Geneva in 1754. Admittedly he had come into contact with Protestantism in England and Holland, but these experiences, though important, had been of comparatively short duration, and there were still substantial gaps in his knowledge. His views on the French Huguenots were sketchy and ill-informed, though there is some evidence that he was beginning to be aware of the problem.[103] Similarly, although his attitude to Calvin had already emerged clearly, it was his years in Protestant Geneva which strengthened Voltaire's hostility to the authoritarian Reformer and all he represented, while showing the exiled author at the same time that contemporary Protestants had many laudable features and were capable of a remarkable degree of enlightenment on certain matters. We have glimpsed some of the factors which, on occasion, caused Voltaire to modify his original opinions about Protestant characteristics, beliefs or personalities. In describing the benefits Voltaire considered to have been brought about in certain countries by their adoption of the Protestant faith we have further widened our horizons and indeed anticipated to some extent the second part of our study. Now it remains for us to investigate in detail Voltaire's reactions to his personal experiences in Protestant environments and the contacts he had with Protestants in four main centres: Holland, Switzerland, France, and England. The sections on Switzerland and France particularly will enable us to appreciate how extensive was the interchange of ideas between the *philosophe* and some of his Protestant contacts and acquaintances. Voltaire was to learn much, but we shall also see that he clung on occasion to beliefs and prejudices he had formed as a young man, attributing a large measure of blame for Geneva's political troubles to clerical interference, although it seems clear that this was at best a minor factor. All the sections will indeed show that Voltaire's view of the Protestant religion was significant, if not decisive, in determining his general view of the countries concerned. Whenever he could, moreover, Voltaire did his best to encourage and promote those Protestant values of which he approved, though more often than not his attitude was hostile; as must already have become clear, the Enlightenment's most typical and universal historian was to be a harsh and in many ways uncompromising judge of the Reformation and its heirs.

[103] cf. Best.D4561 and D6037, and below, pp.256-59.

4

Protestantism in Holland

⚜

VOLTAIRE's opinion of the religious situation in Holland can be reduced to quite a simple theme: the well-deserved reputation of the Dutch for tolerance was ruined, in the sixteenth century, by a recurrence of fanaticism and theological persecution culminating in the death of a great political leader, an event which the Dutch ought eternally to regret. The naïve enthusiasm of Voltaire's early letter to the marquise de Bernières[1] is later coloured by a growing disillusion with the Dutch character. Sometimes he maintained that the people of Holland, as opposed to their ministers, were basically in favour of tolerance. Yet on other occasions the Dutch nation in its entirety incurred his anathema. This more general condemnation became apparent, however, only after the late 1750s and Voltaire's earlier attitude, in which hostility was mainly restricted to the ministers and general optimism was expressed regarding the consolidation of Dutch toleration, is well represented in a passage from the *Histoire des voyages de Scarmentado* (1756) (M.xxi. 126-27):

J'allai en Hollande, où j'espérais trouver plus de tranquillité chez des peuples plus flegmatiques. On coupait la tête à un vieillard vénérable lorsque j'arrivai à la Haye. C'était la tête chauve du premier ministre Barneveldt, l'homme qui avait le mieux mérité de la république. Touché de pitié, je demandai quel était son crime, et s'il avait trahi l'Etat. 'Il a fait bien pis, me répondit un prédicant à manteau noir; c'est un homme qui croit que l'on peut se sauver par les bonnes œuvres aussi bien que par la foi. Vous sentez bien que, si de telles opinions s'établissaient, une république ne pourrait subsister, et qu'il faut des lois sévères pour réprimer de si scandaleuses horreurs.' Un profond politique du pays me dit en soupirant: 'Hélas! monsieur, le bon temps ne

---

[1] 'On ne voit ici que des prairies, des canaux, et des arbres vers; c'est un paradis terrestre depuis la Haie à Amsterdam; j'ai vu avec respect cette ville qui est le magasin de l'univer [. . .] On ne voit la personne qui ait de cour à faire, on ne se met point en haie pour voir passer un prince, on ne conoit que le travail et la modestie' (Best.D128, 7 October 1722).

97

durera pas toujours; ce n'est que par hasard que ce peuple est si zélé; le fond de son caractère est porté au dogme abominable de la tolérance, un jour il viendra: cela fait frémir.'

Thus, despite such a classic example of religious intolerance, Voltaire's conclusions are nonetheless favourable as far as the future development of Holland is concerned. We shall see shortly how he was to revise somewhat his opinion of the Dutch people's sterling qualities and 'le fond de son caractère'.

The whole subject of Voltaire's connections with Holland and its people has been ably studied in an important work by J. Vercruysse,[2] whose conclusions obviously have great relevance to our present investigation. On Voltaire's admiration for Dutch political institutions, the absence of rigid class distinctions in Holland and the freedom of thought and speech enjoyed there, little remains to be said. M. Vercruysse's account of the effect Holland had on the young Voltaire's philosophical development is particularly clear and well argued, and these qualities are characteristic of the work as a whole. Yet there are some errors,[3] and the glowing picture painted of the place of Holland in Voltaire's affections, though attractive and at first sight convincing, fails notably to attribute sufficient importance both to the religious dimension and to the evolution of his opinions, which became consistently less favourable to Holland and the Dutch as the years went by. Altogether we shall see that Voltaire's attitude is far less enthusiastic than represented by m. Vercruysse at the end of his study:

Le jugement que Voltaire porte donc sur la Hollande est nettement favorable, et souvent élogieux [. . .] même s'il n'est pas l'esclave, comme d'autres, d'un mythe, la Hollande reste pour lui cet état libéral qui représente ce qui devrait être fait et qu'on ne fait pas en France.[4]

[2] *Voltaire et la Hollande*, Studies on Voltaire (1966), xlvi.

[3] for example, m. Vercruysse (p.72) mistakenly interprets Best.D7729 as implying that Amsterdam's theatre was superior to that of Geneva; in fact, no theatre was permitted in the latter city. M. Vercruysse also comments (p.161): 'Voltaire suit de près les remous suscités à Genève par l'affaire de l'article "Trinité" de l'*Encyclopédie*.' The article which caused so much controversy was in fact 'Genève', by d'Alembert: cf. below, pp.153 ff.

[4] p.188. The last part of m. Vercruysse's comment is almost certainly correct, and this in itself is a good reason why one should hesitate to take at their face value all Voltaire's statements regarding Holland. M. Vercruysse himself goes on to point out that 'Tout éloge devient ainsi une critique indirecte.' As in the case of England, Voltaire's most enthusiastic remarks about the country he was describing may indeed have been sometimes rather uncritical or exaggerated with the express intention of criticising by implication the very different situation which existed in France.

The ambit of this study being Voltaire's contacts with Protestantism, it will obviously not be possible to indulge in an extended discussion of m. Vercruysse's conclusions, especially since it is precisely Voltaire's unfavourable opinion of Dutch Calvinism which he most neglects. Yet to the extent that other topics, particularly Voltaire's judgement of the Dutch character and its financial preoccupations, impinge on the religious question, these will also be discussed, and we shall see that m. Vercruysse's views may have to be substantially qualified on several points.

i. *The enigma of Dutch toleration*

Towards the end of his section on 'Tolérance et liberté' (p.169) m. Vercruysse comments judiciously: 'L'opinion de Voltaire sur la tolérance hollandaise n'est donc pas aussi simple qu'on pourrait le croire.' It is indeed here that the basic ambiguity in Voltaire's attitude to the Dutch and their religion becomes most apparent, yet although m. Vercruysse draws attention to some of the *philosophe*'s unfavourable remarks, especially in connection with the execution of Barneveldt and the de Witt brothers, he does not make clear the fundamental dilemma. Calvinism was accepted by the Dutch, Voltaire thinks, because it suited their frugal character and the economically backward state of their country at a particular stage of its development. In turn, many features of Protestantism produced economic and social benefits enjoyed by the Dutch and admired by Voltaire. But it is evident that, in the latter's opinion, the toleration he found so commendable in Holland and the fact that numerous sects flourished there in apparent harmony owed nothing whatsoever to the official religion of Calvinism. On the contrary, Calvinist pastors and theologians resembled the priests of other Christian denominations in their determination to persecute those who disagreed with their teachings. How then did Dutch toleration come about, bearing in mind the fact that Protestant writers have often claimed that this development was a consequence of Holland's status as a Protestant country? Such a claim would doubtless have been categorically rejected by Voltaire, yet at the same time he gives no real explanation for the growth of toleration in Holland, as a brief survey of his historical works will show us.

In chapter 164 of the *Essai sur les mœurs*, Voltaire describes the circumstances of the Reformation in the Low Countries. As we might by now expect in view of his accounts of what happened in other countries, religious causes for the event are conspicuous by their absence. He concentrates on political motivation: after all, the Flemings were a stolid people and would never have changed their practices so quickly had it not been as a reaction against the tyranny of Philip II (*Essai*, ii.441):

les Flamands sont naturellement de bons sujets et de mauvais esclaves. La seule crainte de l'Inquisition fit plus de protestants que tous les livres de Calvin chez ce peuple, qui n'est assurément porté par son caractère ni à la nouveauté ni aux remuements.

The abolition of Catholicism was further caused by hatred of Spain: 'on abolit la religion romaine, afin de n'avoir plus rien de commun avec le gouvernement espagnol' (ii.442-43). In stressing these political causes, however, Voltaire gives no explanation as to why, already, 'le calvinisme dominait dans les provinces maritimes des Pays-Bas' (ii.441). Indeed, he mentions this fact only in order to stress the religious opportunism of the prince of Orange's conversion to Calvinism. The prince 'ne pouvait armer que les Protestants en sa faveur; et pour les animer, il fallait l'être'. In describing one of the prince's armies, Voltaire explicitly links 'l'enthousiasme de la religion et l'espoir du pillage' (ii.442), a characteristic example of his attempts to play down or discredit religious emotion whenever he comes across it. Once again he has succumbed to the temptation of omitting all legitimate religious reasons, explaining everything in terms which, as a historian, he found so much more satisfactory – the terms of political or social motivation.

The limitations of Voltairean historiography are here apparent, for the next time he deals with Holland in the *Essai sur les mœurs*, we find that religious toleration is firmly established as a principle of the nation, yet Voltaire has given no reason why this should be so. He has not even traced its development. All he has done is to describe the growing strength of Calvinism. Indeed, the only reference in the previous chapter on Holland[5] of any relevance to the subject of religious toleration represented a step in the opposite direction, namely the abolition of Catholicism. Voltaire is fascinated by the resemblance between the United Provinces and the republics of antiquity, especially Sparta (*Essai*, ii.449), and religion fades into the background until it is

---

[5] the two chapters in question are 164: 'Fondation de la république des Provinces-Unies' and 187: 'De la Hollande au XVIIe siècle'.

invoked as the cause of something harmful. Chapter 2 of the *Siècle de Louis XIV* gives a brief survey of the country's history since its independence, which may be quoted usefully to show how entirely religious developments are neglected (*Oh*, p.625):

Ce petit Etat des sept Provinces-Unies, pays fertile en pâturages, mais stérile en grains, malsain, et presque submergé par la mer, était, depuis environ un demi-siècle, un exemple presque unique sur la terre de ce que peuvent l'amour de la liberté et le travail infatigable. Ces peuples pauvres, peu nombreux, bien moins aguerris que les moindres milices espagnols, et qui n'étaient comptés pour rien dans l'Europe, résistèrent à toutes les forces de leur maître et de leur tyran, Philippe II, éludèrent les desseins de plusieurs princes, qui voulaient les secourir pour les asservir, et fondèrent une puissance que nous avons vue balancer le pouvoir de l'Espagne même. Le désespoir qu'inspire la tyrannie les avait d'abord armés: la liberté avait élevé leur courage, et les princes de la maison d'Orange en avaient fait d'excellents soldats. A peine vainqueurs de leurs maîtres, ils établirent une forme de gouvernement qui conserve, autant qu'il est possible, l'égalité, le droit le plus naturel des hommes.

Not a word about religion in all this. Chapter 187 of the *Essai sur les mœurs* also describes briefly the liberty owed by the Dutch to their work and sobriety, and the growing importance of their commerce, before mentioning religious toleration, a phenomenon which now seems to be taken for granted by Voltaire (*Essai*, ii.728):

La douceur de ce gouvernement, et la tolérance de toutes les manières d'adorer Dieu, dangereuse peut-être ailleurs,[6] mais là nécessaire, peuplèrent la Hollande d'une foule d'étrangers, et surtout de Wallons que l'Inquisition persécutait dans leur patrie, et qui d'esclaves devinrent citoyens.

But although other denominations are tolerated, Calvinism remains the dominant one, and it is duly praised by Voltaire as being beneficial to Holland. The arguments he puts forward to justify his approval are, however, purely economic in nature: Protestantism provided a needy country with extra manpower by abolishing the monasteries, a sure method of increasing the population, and spared it the expensive luxury of maintaining an ecclesiastical hierarchy. While these comments may be significant in their embryonic grasp of the sociology of religion, reminding us more than a little of Montesquieu's speculations in the

---

[6] Pomeau notes that this 'formule de prudente concession, évidemment peu sincère', appears because Voltaire was following a similar passage from the *Siècle de Louis XIV*, and forgot to correct it. Cf. also Beuchot's note, M.xiii.117.

Lettres Persanes and *De l'esprit des lois*, they surely betray a somewhat inconsistent attitude on Voltaire's part, for nowhere is it suggested that Calvinism had anything to do with the establishment of toleration (*Essai*, ii.728):

La religion réformée, dominante dans la Hollande, servit encore à sa puissance. Ce pays, alors si pauvre, n'aurait pu ni suffire à la magnificence des prélats, ni nourrir des ordres religieux; et cette terre, où il fallait des hommes, ne pouvait admettre ceux qui s'engagent par serment à laisser périr, autant qu'il est en eux, l'espèce humaine. On avait l'exemple de l'Angleterre, qui était d'un tiers plus peuplée depuis que les ministres des autels jouissaient de la douceur du mariage, et que les espérances des familles n'étaient point ensevelies dans le célibat du cloître.

In fact it is religion, and more specifically Calvinism, which destroys the idyll of peace and tolerance in Holland (ii.729):

cette république fut près de détruire elle-même la liberté pour laquelle elle avait combattu, et [. . .] l'intolérance fit couler le sang chez un peuple dont le bonheur et les lois étaient fondés sur la tolérance.

Theology was again the cause of division and bloodshed, and as usual the quarrel was over predestination, liberty, grace, 'sur des questions obscures et frivoles, dans lesquelles on ne sait pas même définir les choses dont on dispute'. This unhappy affair caused a national crisis (*Essai*, ii.729):

Deux docteurs calvinistes firent ce que tant de docteurs avaient fait ailleurs. (1609 et suiv.) Gomar et Armin disputèrent dans Leyde avec fureur sur ce qu'ils n'entendaient pas, et ils divisèrent les Provinces-Unies.

Voltaire is, however, fairer towards religion here than he is sometimes elsewhere, for although he makes it responsible for the outbreak of civil unrest, he does not attribute to it the entire blame for subsequent events. It was the adoption of the cause of the Gomarians by the prince of Orange and that of the Arminians by the chief magistrate Barneveldt which made the situation really serious. Voltaire makes this clear in the *Siècle de Louis XIV* when he draws a parallel between the Dutch dispute and a similar disagreement on grace between the Jansenists and the Jesuits in France (*Oh*, p.1069):

C'était précisément le fond de la querelle des gomaristes et des arminiens. Elle divisa la Hollande comme le jansénisme divisa la France; mais elle devint en Hollande une faction politique plus qu'une dispute de gens oisifs [. . .]

Cette dispute ne produisit en France que des mandements, des bulles, des lettres de cachet et des brochures, parce qu'il y avait alors des querelles plus importantes.

Voltaire again shows us two statesmen using religion as a pretext to further their ambitions; in Barneveldt's case this was more pardonable, since he wished only to safeguard the country's republican institutions, but prince Maurice hoped to acquire 'un pouvoir souverain' and thus became Barneveldt's implacable enemy: 'il y eut des séditions sanglantes dans quelques villes (1618), et [. . .] le prince Maurice poursuivait sans relâche le parti contraire à sa puissance' (*Essai*, ii.730). To further his ends, the stadtholder convoked a Calvinist synod at Doordrecht; but although this was, therefore, a politically inspired assembly, Voltaire makes it clear that the assembled theologians needed no prompting from prince Maurice to exercise their rigour on their Arminian opponents. This was clearly a betrayal of the principles of Protestantism and Voltaire does not hesitate to point out the hypocrisy of the Calvinist ministers (ii.730):

Les pères de ce synode, qui avaient tant crié contre la dureté des pères de plusieurs conciles, et contre leur autorité, condamnèrent les arminiens, comme ils avaient été eux-mêmes condamnés par le concile de Trente. Plus de cent ministres arminiens furent bannis des sept Provinces.

The prince of Orange had Barneveldt tried by a joint commission of the nobility and the magistrature, and he was condemned to death and executed. One of his sons later shared a similar fate merely for having been aware of the existence of a plot against prince Maurice. 'Si ces temps d'atrocité eussent continué, les Hollandais libres eussent été plus malheureux que leurs ancêtres esclaves du duc d'Albe', Voltaire comments bitterly (*Essai*, ii.731). Although a little earlier he has placed the main responsibility for the crisis on political exploitation of a religious disagreement, Voltaire is already wavering in his attitude, so fundamental is his dislike of theological disputes and so basic his belief that they can do nothing but harm. Indeed, by 1769 the tragedy had again become primarily a religious affair in Voltaire's mind, for in that year he rounded off the paragraph, of which the last quotation was originally the end, with the following comment:

Ces persécutions gomariennes ressemblaient à ces premières persécutions que les protestants avaient si souvent reprochées aux catholiques, et que toutes les sectes avaient exercées les unes envers les autres.

Religion is once again the cause as well as the pretext.

Fortunately, this disaster did not for long impair the solid virtues of the Dutch nation. Amsterdam still championed toleration and prince Maurice's action was eventually punished by his son's exclusion from the stadtholderate, a direct result of his own cruelty. Voltaire draws a wise lesson from all this in the *Siècle de Louis XIV* (*Oh*, p.1069): the death of Barneveldt was a

violence atroce que les Hollandais détestent aujourd'hui après avoir ouvert les yeux sur l'absurdité de ces disputes, sur l'horreur de la persécution, et sur l'heureuse nécessité de la tolérance, ressource des sages qui gouvernent, contre l'enthousiasme passager de ceux qui argumentent.

As elsewhere (cf. above, p.82, n.74), Voltaire claims that it is the lack of interest in dogma which has strengthened toleration, and that the happy state of affairs in Holland is a political, rather than a religious achievement. This toleration was certainly due in no way to the Dutch clergy, represented by the bigoted Calvinist ministers[7] portrayed in the *Histoire des voyages de Scarmentado* and *Candide*. In the latter *conte* the protagonist has heard that 'tout le monde était riche dans ce pays-là, et qu'on y était chrétien' (ed. Pomeau, p.92), but the only charitable treatment he receives is not meted out by the representative of the dominant church, who displays a predictably fanatical and intolerant attitude, refusing to help him because Candide does not agree without question that the pope is the Antichrist.

Voltaire's explanation of the rise and persistence of religious toleration in Holland is thus sketchy and uninformative and his attitude toward the important Dutch Calvinist church is overtly hostile in most of the references he makes to it. Neither of these points is brought out in m. Vercruysse's study,[8] and we shall see that his remarks on Voltaire's view of the Dutch character are similarly distorted by a failure to realise that this growing destestation of Calvinism was probably one of the most important reasons for Voltaire's increasing disenchantment with aspects of the Dutch personality.

[7] or 'fétiches hollandais' as they are called in *Candide*, ed. René Pomeau (Paris 1959), p.160.

[8] it is only fair, however, to point out that m. Vercruysse is well aware that Voltaire had some reservations about Dutch Protestantism: 'Aux yeux de Voltaire, si la Réforme est, à tout prendre, préférable à Rome, elle n'en est pas moins un élément suspect de fanatisme. Son insistance sur les déboires d'Oldenbarnevelt prouve suffisamment qu'il n'a pas été dupe du mythe de la tolérance absolue' (*Voltaire et la Hollande*, p.186).

ii. *The Dutch character*

Despite Voltaire's enthusiasm after his first acquaintance with Dutch freedom, his attitude towards the 'Bataves' soon included a note of hostility, and the Dutch in general, not merely their theologians and pastors, seem to incur Voltaire's growing distaste as he grows older: their formerly praised mercantile spirit has now become mercenary in his eyes. As often as not it is turned to the disadvantage of poor authors, a fact which now rankles with him and diminishes his enthusiasm for the 'Bataves' as a nation.[9] As early as 1740 Voltaire expressed his criticism of the Dutch character in the following often-quoted ditty composed for Frederick the Great, which is obviously not to be taken as a measured judgement of his opinions, but which nonetheless clearly illustrates that the Dutch have lost their initial fascination for Voltaire:

> Un peuple libre et mercenaire,
> Végétant dans ce coin de terre
> Et vivant toujours en Batau,
> Vend aux voyageurs l'air et l'eau,
> Quoyque tout deux n'y valent guère;
> Là plus d'un fripon de libraire
> Débite ce qu'il n'entend pas
> Comme fait un prêcheur en chaire;
> Vend de l'esprit de tous états
> Et fait passer en Germanie
> Une cargaison de romans
> Et d'insipides sentiments,
> Que toujours la France a fournie.[10]

It is true that in *La Princesse de Babylone* (1768) Voltaire gives a more favourable picture of Holland, but his protagonist, Amazan, finds that Dutch women are frigid. This may appear a frivolous reason for cri-

---

[9] m. Vercruysse is surely mistaken when, after discussing in detail Voltaire's *démêlés* with Dutch publishers, he nonetheless concludes (p.145) that these relations were no worse than those he had with other publishers and that they did not affect his judgement of the country as a whole. On the contrary, his quarrels, especially with van Duren, appear definitely to have soured his view of the Dutch: cf. Best.D2270 and D13600.

[10] Best.D2270, July 1740. This attitude is confirmed by a brief, though significant, comment in the *Lettre à l'occasion de l'impôt du vingtième* (16 May 1749): 'Je ne parlerai point des autres capitales. Amsterdan, la plus peuplée de toutes après Londres, est le pays de la parcimonie' (M.xxiii.306). Cf. also Best.D16159, to Choiseul, where Voltaire refers to 'la Hollande que je vomis de ma bouche parce qu'elle est tiède'.

ticising a nation, but it seems to serve here as a sort of focus for a wider, undefined feeling of disenchantment on Voltaire's part. The virtues of the Dutch are praised, but in such a pedestrian way as to make them seem insipid (M.xxi.406):

Amazan arriva chez les Bataves; son cœur éprouva dans son chagrin une douce satisfaction d'y retrouver quelque faible image du pays des heureux Gangarides; la liberté, l'égalité, la propreté, l'abondance, la tolérance; mais les dames du pays étaient si froides qu'aucune ne lui fit d'avances comme on lui en avait fait partout ailleurs; il n'eut pas la peine de résister.

The Dutch are insensible to beauty, and judge everything by its monetary value: 'à l'égard du phénix, elles [the Dutch women] n'en firent pas grand cas, parce qu'elles jugèrent que ses plumes ne pourraient pas se vendre aussi bien que celles des canards et des oisons de leurs marais'. They have no imagination of their own: 'mais, comme ils étaient les facteurs de l'univers, ils vendaient l'esprit des autres nations, ainsi que leurs denrées' (M.xxi.407). What can possibly have caused the formulation and expression of such damning views?

The explanation put forward by m. Vercruysse seems once more inadequate. After faithfully cataloguing the hostile references which are reasonably abundant in Voltaire's works,[11] he comments (p.75):

On peut s'interroger sur les motifs de cette hostilité de Voltaire au caractère hollandais. C'est parce qu'il y a rupture avec son propre caractère. Les défauts qu'il reproche aux Hollandais, sont radicalement opposés aux traits de sa nature, toujours en éveil, souple, bavarde.

Unfortunately, this conclusion takes no account of the fact that one of the traits criticised by Voltaire was one which he himself shared and indulged in with great enthusiasm – the ability to make money. It is indeed rather surprising to find someone like Voltaire, who in the *Lettres philosophiques* and in so many other works praised the importance and utility of commerce, using words like 'facteurs' and 'marchands' in a derogatory sense.[12] Yet the conclusion is inescapable. He really seems to have come to despise the self-satisfied materialism of the Dutch, and, while still appreciating the value of their tolerant

---

[11] the main defects mentioned by m. Vercruysse (pp.75-76) are avarice, taciturnity and coldness.

[12] Voltaire displayed a similar attitude in the face of Genevese commercial enterprise: cf. below, p.168, n.139.

attitude to religion, is inclined to blame them, as well as their Calvinist clergy, for past atrocities.

This claim may at first sight appear somewhat far-fetched, yet it is possible to back it up with a fair amount of telling evidence. Voltaire had already learned at the time of the 'Genève' controversy that the Dutch Calvinist clergy were antipathetic to 'liberal' reforms in Protestant theology: at any rate he told d'Alembert on 8 January 1758 that they had considered condemning Vernet's *Catéchisme*.[13] It is true that about the same time he was also claiming that 'la moitié de la Hollande' shared the Genevese pastor's liberal opinions,[14] but the clergy presumably belonged to the other half. Some doubt might remain in Voltaire's letter to Théodore Tronchin of 12 January 1758 (Best.D7579) as to whether Voltaire was criticising the Dutch clergy alone, but a few days later he made his attitude crystal clear to the same correspondent (Best.D7584, 15 January 1758):

Quelques beufs de Hollande, quelques prédicants d'un peuple qui foule aux pieds le crucifix quand il va vendre du gérofle au Japon, ne flétriront pas la réputation d'une ville de gens d'esprit et d'honnêtes gens.

Here, significantly, the opprobrium at first reserved for the clergy is extended to the Dutch people as a whole. Voltaire's attitude thus appears to fluctuate somewhat: sometimes his hostility is confined to the clergy, but on other occasions, as in the *Poème sur la loi naturelle* (1752), it is the entire nation which is held responsible for the tragic death of the De Witts (M.ix.448):

> Là, le froid Hollandais devient impétueux,
> Il déchire en morceaux deux frères vertueux.

In a work which dates from the year after *La Princesse de Babylone*, the pamphlet *De la paix perpétuelle par le docteur Goodheart*, the duality of Voltaire's attitude is apparent; the Dutch as a whole were responsible for the Synod of Doordrecht and the death of Barneveldt. Religion has been their downfall as well as their triumph:

Les Hollandais de nos jours pourraient leur [i.e. to the Tyrians] être comparés, s'ils n'avaient pas à se reprocher leur concile de Dordrecht contre les bonnes

[13] 'est ce en secret que les autres impertinents prêtres de Hollande ont voulu le condamner?' (Best.D7564). Vernet was perhaps the most influential Genevese theologian at the time Voltaire was writing: cf. below, pp.120-22, 129 ff., 173-77.

[14] Best.D7570, to Diderot, probably written on about 8 January 1758. Cf. also Best. D7579, to Théodore Tronchin, 12 January 1758.

œuvres, et le sang du respectable Barneveldt, condamné à l'âge de soixante et onze ans pour avoir *contristé au possible l'Eglise de Dieu*. Ô hommes! ô monstres! des marchands calvinistes, établis dans des marais, insultent au reste de l'univers! Il est vrai qu'ils expièrent ce crime en reniant la religion chrétienne au Japon.[15]

Nor must it be imagined that these are isolated statements, made by Voltaire in a moment of uncharacteristic *pique* against the Dutch. Unfavourable references to Holland in the correspondence begin as early as April 1737, when Voltaire, discussing the persecution of Bayle with Frederick of Prussia, comments angrily: 'Qu'importoit à la Hollande que Baile eût raison?' (Best.D1320, *c.* 25 April). As usual in this connection it is Jurieu who bears the brunt of Voltaire's attack, but the tolerant Dutch as a whole are also clearly implicated. Although, as we have seen, Voltaire sometimes remarked that there were many enlightened people in Holland and specifically told d'Alembert on 25 February 1758 that Socinians were numerous in Amsterdam (Best.D7651), by the 1760s his tone has become almost consistently hostile. On 20 September 1760 he used the fact that 'les Hollandais ont mangé sur le gril le cœur des deux frères de Witt' as one of several examples intended to convince the chevalier de R. . .x 'qu'il n'y a pas plus de vertu dans les républiques que dans les monarchies' (Best. D9247). 'Barnevelt a péri comme Jean Hus,' he told Bertrand at the end of 1763: 'Le synode de Dordrecht vaut il mieux que celui de Trente' (Best.D11580, 26 December). And in a letter to Philibert de Fénille of 17 December 1765 Voltaire summed up his feelings once more, referring to 'le Barnevelt hollandais, immolé à la liberté de sa patrie sous l'abominable prétexte de je ne sais quelle hérésie calviniste' (Best.D13047).

It seems reasonably clear that Voltaire's growing distaste for Holland cannot be explained merely by the fact that the characteristic traits of his personality were diametrically opposed to those of the Dutch. His change in attitude was no doubt a reflection of his dislike for the Calvinist religion, whose privileged position he describes in the *Lettre civile et honnête à l'auteur malhonnête de la Critique de l'Histoire universelle de m. de Voltaire* (1760): 'On appelle la *religion dominante* celle qui domine [. . .] Le calvinisme domine en Hollande, quoiqu'il y ait plus de catholiques que de protestants' (M.xxiv.148). Thus, although his

---

[15] M.xxviii.107. Voltaire reveres Barneveldt to such a point that in the same work he calls Socrates 'ce Barneveldt d'Athènes'.

original enthusiasm for Holland was already diminishing by the late 1730s, probably as a result of disputes with publishers like van Duren, the factor which may have confirmed this tendency was Voltaire's increasing detestation of the Calvinist clergy of Geneva. It would seem more than likely that the disappointments experienced by Voltaire in Switzerland affected his opinion of Holland, another country he knew to be Calvinist dominated and whose clergy had in past times paralleled the fanaticism and intolerance of Servetus's murderers. This might have enabled him to make a division in his mind between the unchartable, fanatical, unimaginative and grasping features of the Dutch temperament attributable to Calvinism, and its better aspects: love of liberty, equality, hard work and tolerance, which would constitute the leaven supplied by members of the less dogmatic sects, witness the good Anabaptist in *Candide*. Voltaire's fundamental opposition to Calvinism and its morality might also explain why, in stark contrast to England, Holland plays such a small part in Voltaire's theistic propaganda of the 1760s and 1770s. It is unnecessary to labour the point: English names and spokesmen abound in works of this period,[16] but one would be hard pressed to find a single example of the Dutch being used in a similar way. Surely this disparity is to be explained simply through Voltaire's identification of Holland with Calvinism, incorrigibly narrow-minded and intolerant, whereas England was fortunate to possess the Anglican Church, which, although endowed with faults common to all Christian denominations, was strictly subordinated to state control and increasingly seemed to Voltaire a model for other countries.

In conclusion one can thus see that in determining Voltaire's attitude toward the Dutch, religion was an extremely important factor. His distaste for Calvinism encouraged a waning of his original enthusiasm for Dutch institutions and liberty. He never completely forgot the good features of Dutch life, but these were mentioned less frequently in his works, and even when, as in *La Princesse de Babylone*, 'la liberté, l'égalité, la propreté, l'abondance, la tolérance', of the Dutch are mentioned, Voltaire still contrives to damn Holland as a 'nation insipide' (M.xxi.406). One is tempted to glimpse in Voltaire's changed attitude to the Dutch a reflection of the increasing importance which religious

[16] cf. for example *Homélies prononcées à Londres* (1767), *Lettre de l'archevêque de Cantorbéry* (1768), *De la paix perpétuelle par le docteur Goodheart* (1769), *Histoire de Jenni* (1775), *Les Oreilles du comte de Chesterfield* (1775).

factors exercised on his opinions as the years progressed. Be this as it may, it is certain that for Voltaire Holland was at the same time a triumph and a warning – a triumph of politically inspired toleration, but a warning that this was always potentially threatened by quarrelling theologians, who were equally dangerous whether they be Catholic or Protestant.

5
Voltaire and Switzerland[1]

IF there is any doubt that Voltaire considered Calvinism to be the source of Holland's woes, it is absolutely certain that he held it responsible for the discords which bedevilled Geneva. For this was Calvin's town, and it was necessarily associated in Voltaire's mind with the man who had made it a world centre of Protestantism, but who had also engineered Servetus's death there: 'Je vois de mes fenêtres la ville où régnait Jean Chauvin, le Picard, dit Calvin, et la place où il fit brûler Servet pour le bien de son âme', he comments in the *Mémoires pour servir à la vie de m. de Voltaire* (1759) (M.i.54). Another passage in the *Mémoires* gives the key to Voltaire's attitude toward Calvin's successors, the pastors of Geneva: they are Socinians,[2] yet they hypocritically persist in denying a fact which should be to their credit (M.i.54):

Presque tous les prêtres de ce pays-ci pensent aujourd'hui comme Servet, et vont même plus loin que lui. Ils ne croient point du tout Jésus-Christ Dieu; et ces messieurs, qui ont fait autrefois main basse sur le purgatoire, se sont humanisés jusqu'à faire grâce aux âmes qui sont en enfer[. . .] C'est une assez jolie révolution dans l'histoire de l'esprit humain.

But this is to anticipate. As all students of the Enlightenment know, Voltaire was at first overcome with enthusiasm for the city of Geneva. On 10 March 1756 he wrote to Sébastien Dupont (Best.D6774): 'Il

---

[1] strictly speaking, one should not use the word 'Switzerland' to refer to eighteenth-century Geneva, as the city was at that time an independent republic. Nonetheless, I have not thought it unduly anachronistic to adopt modern usage on this point, except where a clear distinction must be made, since undue repetition of the phrase 'Geneva and Switzerland' appears stylistically inelegant as well as unnecessary.

[2] I use this term perhaps loosely, but in the way I think it was employed, in the eighteenth century, by Voltaire, d'Alembert and others: that is I mean by it people who, while they in some way associated Jesus Christ with their worship of God, had abandoned one or more of the fundamental doctrines subscribed to by both the Catholic and Protestant traditions (e.g. the trinity or eternal punishment), and who submitted both their beliefs and their interpretation of the Bible to the criterion of reason. See below, p.458, n.12, for a fuller discussion of this question.

n'y a point de ville où il y ait plus de gens d'esprit et de philosophes qu'à
Genève. Ma maison ne désemplit pas, et j'y suis libre.' Yet less than
two years later he poured out his scorn for Geneva's clergy in the most
violent terms: 'Fanatiques papistes, fanatiques calvinistes, tous sont
pétris de la même m... détrempée de sang corrompu' (Best.D7512,
12 December 1757). Commenting on this abrupt change, in his stimulating article 'Voltaire and the ministers of Geneva', André Delattre
attributes it to 'the publication of the famous article "Geneva", written
by d'Alembert for the *Encyclopédie*, and the storm it aroused by its
account of the ministers' faith'.[3] These events were certainly the immediate cause of Voltaire's outburst to d'Alembert, but his basic
change of attitude cannot be put down to any one factor. Though many
critics have covered the same ground,[4] we must examine once more the
sequence of events which brought about Voltaire's disillusionment with
the clergy of both Geneva and Lausanne.

Broadly speaking, one can distinguish two distinct phases in Voltaire's
contacts with Geneva and Switzerland. The first, from the time of Voltaire's arrival in Switzerland at the end of 1754 until 1760-1761, covers
the period when he was primarily involved with the clergy: his initial
attempts to co-operate with them, the skirmishes over his theatricals,
then following each other closely, the *âme atroce* affair, the controversy
over d'Alembert's article 'Genève', and finally the Saurin affair in
Lausanne. During these years Voltaire's chief grudge was thus against
the Calvinist ministers, and despite official action against his theatre,
an event also described in the *Mémoires* helped him to retain his respect
for the government of the city, so that his contempt did not fall on
Geneva as a whole but only on its clergy:

Ils [the pastors] ont voulu me prouver que Calvin était un bonhomme; ils
ont prié le conseil de Genève de leur communiquer les pièces du procès de
Servet: le conseil, plus sage qu'eux, les a refusés; il ne leur a pas été permis
d'écrire contre moi dans Genève. Je regarde ce petit triomphe comme le
plus bel exemple des progrès de la raison dans ce siècle.[5]

A precedent was thus established whereby Voltaire could regard the
Genevese government as the supporter of reason and progress and the
clergy as the instruments of prejudice and intolerance, who sought

[3] *Church history* (1944), xiii.244.
[4] one of the best accounts is R. E. Florida, *Voltaire and the Socinians*, pp.141 ff.
[5] M.i.55; cf. below, pp.130 ff.

moreover to influence and control the civil authorities. This linked up with his usual theme of the necessity for Erastianism, and enabled him to recall in miniature the quarrels between the popes and emperors. But the convenient distinction between Geneva's priests and politicians was shattered in the 1760s when Voltaire began to take an active interest in the city's politics. Suspicions that he was behind the persecution of Rousseau, exasperation at his support first of the *bourgeois représentants* and then of the lower-class *natifs*, and finally the setting up of a colony of exiled Genevese watchmakers at Ferney, estranged Voltaire from many sections of the Genevese population, making it seemingly impossible for him to regard the clergy as his only enemies. Yet to the end, even after he had experienced violent hostility from some members of the Genevese government, Voltaire continued to attribute religious causes to events which would appear to us primarily political in significance. He seemed determined to regard the clergy with especial distaste and, characteristically enough, in works like the *Questions sur les miracles* and *La Guerre civile de Genève*, it is they who are cast as the chief villains.

Recent years have seen great advances in Voltairean scholarship. Many myths have been exploded. We now know, for example, from information available concerning Voltaire's library and reading habits,[6] that he was far better informed than had previously been supposed, and that the learned references in his works are not usually mere attempts to overawe the reader by appeals to authorities which Voltaire himself had never consulted.[7] It is surely no longer sufficient, therefore, to gloss over so complicated a relationship as that which existed between Voltaire and the Swiss pastors, merely attributing events which occurred to 'well known' traits of his character, such as his superficiality or his uncontrollable irony. An understanding of Voltaire's character is naturally vital in any study of his life or works, but we must also seek

[6] for information on Voltaire's library see G. R. Havens and N. L. Torrey, *Voltaire's catalogue of his library at Ferney*, Studies on Voltaire (1959), ix; Vladimir S. Lyublinsky, 'La Bibliothèque de Voltaire', *Rhl* (1958), lviii.467-88; M. P. Alekseyev and T. M. Kopreeva, *Bibliothèque de Voltaire: catalogue des livres* (Moscow 1961). Various studies of Voltaire's marginalia have, moreover, demonstrated the thoroughness of his reading habits.

[7] cf. the conclusion of René Pomeau, who checked the reliability of Voltaire's references in about 150 pages of the *Essai sur les mœurs*: 'Parfois Voltaire se trompe; mais il est faux que son texte soit truffé d'erreurs flagrantes. Il est pareillement faux qu'il se soit contenté dans sa hâte de compiler quelques ouvrages facilement accessibles' (*Essai*, i.xxiv).

to show how his attitude toward the Swiss clergy was connected with his earlier intellectual development, and how the various events which shaped his opinion of the pastors were interrelated and cannot be considered in isolation. Some critics have unfortunately persisted in regarding Voltaire as a sort of incorrigible mischief-maker whose actions and motives are always suspect. It will be sufficient to cite one example. Louis Roulet's otherwise excellent study[8] is marred by his pervasive scorn for Voltaire the man, a standpoint which leads him to adopt a consistently patronising attitude toward the *philosophe,* and a readiness to accept the least creditable explanations of his motives (cf. below, pp.125-28). Other critics, though trying harder to understand Voltaire's position, have usually given unsatisfactory explanations of his contacts with the Swiss clergy. Even René Pomeau oversimplifies the issue: in his opinion Voltaire was wrong in thinking the Genevese clergy were thinly disguised deists. His mistake came from the fact that:

Inconsciemment, il raisonne toujours en catholique, concevant le christianisme comme un bloc dogmatique. Parce que ceux-ci ont renoncé à des articles qu'il juge essentiels, Voltaire se flatte qu'ils ne sont plus chrétiens, et il sera scandalisé quand certains refuseront de le suivre.[9]

At first sight this may seem a very tempting argument, but a moment's thought will remind us that, throughout the centuries, doctrinal disputes have been at least as characteristic of Protestantism as of Catholicism. The historian of the Reformation, who scornfully pointed out the failure of Calvinists and Lutherans to agree on the eucharist and other dogmas (see above, pp.78-79), the chronicler of the Synod of Doordrecht (see above, pp.102-103) and of religious disputes between Protestants all over Europe, was hardly unaware of this. It is clearly unsatisfactory to present Voltaire as a *naïf* theoriser who had no idea of Protestantism on his arrival in Geneva, and who through his upbringing and prejudices failed to grasp the spirit of this liberal form of Christianity.

The more extremist Protestant explanation of Voltaire's stormy contacts with the Swiss clergy and his often expressed opinion of their beliefs is, as one might expect, that the impious *philosophe* was not only completely mistaken in his interpretation of the religious situation he was confronted with, but that he also spitefully falsified the position of

---

[8] *Voltaire et les Bernois* (Paris, Neuchâtel 1950).
[9] *La Religion de Voltaire,* p.288.

Geneva's Calvinist clergy. Such dishonesty on Voltaire's part would explain uncomfortable rumours about the unorthodoxy of certain pastors. Thus Gaberel paints mid-eighteenth-century Geneva as an evangelical bulwark against the spread of philosophic ideas: 'Les magistrats, les savants et les pasteurs genevois s'unirent étroitement pour préserver leur ville d'un matérialisme grossier, et leurs efforts furent couronnés de succès positifs.'[10] He claims that Voltaire tried for twenty years to transform Geneva, but without success (pp.2-3). If Voltaire had contacts with some ministers, this was only after concessions on his part. In the case of Jacob Vernes, Voltaire wanted to know him because the pastor was an important literary figure (p.157). Moreover, Vernes defended revelation triumphantly before Voltaire's friends at Ferney (pp.158-61). As for Paul Moultou, Gaberel maintains that there is no reason to suspect his orthodoxy (pp.82-84): Voltaire understood his friend's religious principles and did not attempt to shock them! Similarly, Charles Coquerel, although admitting that 'les rapports [. . .] de Voltaire [. . .] avec le pasteur Moultou, de Genève, sont fort singuliers, et d'après nos lettres laissent quelque chose de louche', concludes: 'Il est bien probable [. . .] que le ministre Moultou ne méritait pas, sous tous les rapports, les compliments philosophiques dont Voltaire se plut à l'accabler.'[11] Coquerel's judgement is less categorical than Gaberel's, and other nineteenth-century Protestant historians, aware of unorthodox developments in Swiss and French Protestantism before the evangelical revival (*Réveil*) which took place at the beginning of the nineteenth century, were disinclined to investigate closely Voltaire's relations with the pastors, beyond generally attributing the growing atmosphere of secularisation to his baleful influence.[12] The *Réveil* itself complicated matters even farther, for its supporters vied in decrying those whom they considered as the lukewarm or unfaithful Christians of the eighteenth century, whereas its opponents saw in the same 'liberal' pastors the forerunners of a modern theology which would liberate Protestantism from the straightjacket of orthodoxy.[13] The wheel has now turned full circle, and in his *Histoire*

[10] *Voltaire et les Genevois*, 2nd ed. (Paris, Geneva 1857), p.2.

[11] *Histoire des églises du désert*, ii.340.

[12] cf. Edouard Champendal, *Voltaire et les protestants de France*, pp.78-81; Léon Maury, *Le Réveil religieux dans l'église réformée à Genève et en France (1810-1850)* (Paris 1892), i.7.

[13] for a hostile reaction to eighteenth-century Protestantism in France and Geneva, see Maury, *Le Réveil religieux*; Daniel Benoît, *L'Etat religieux du protestantisme français dans la seconde moitié du XVIIIe siècle* (Montauban 1909); H. von der Goltz, *Genève religieuse*

générale du protestantisme, far from denying Voltaire's assertions about the beliefs of Geneva's clergy, E.-G. Léonard speaks of 'un parti voltairien' which 'tendait [. . .] à donner le ton, en la personne notamment des pasteurs Moultou et Jacob Vernes' (iii.56).

Yet despite tacit or overt admissions by many Protestant writers that the doctrinal views of at least some pastors were not very different from those described by Voltaire, literary critics have seemed largely unaware of this and have continued to present a mitigated form of what might be called the Gaberel thesis: that Voltaire fundamentally misunderstood the situation and went further than the facts justified. Paul Chaponnière, for example, explains that 'le protestantisme genevois ne représentait plus guère qu'un moralisme chrétien rationalisant' (*Voltaire chez les calvinistes*, p.43). He shows how dogmas like predestination and original sin were often left in the background, even affirming that the Genevese pastors and the encyclopedists 'tendaient au même but et ne différaient d'opinion que sur le meilleur moyen d'y parvenir' (p.46). Yet despite these admissions Chaponnière does not agree that Voltaire was correct in his opinion of the Genevese clergy: even though he proves that the *philosophe*'s assertions were substantially justified, he still contrives to make it appear that Voltaire was somehow mistaken, and he concludes complacently (p.47):

Le clergé se glorifait de passer pour libéral et éclairé, assuré de rester ainsi dans la ligne de sa tradition et satisfait d'avoir trouvé, pour défendre le christianisme éternel, une position fortifiée par la philosophie du siècle.

In one of the most closely argued accounts of Voltaire's contacts with the Genevese clergy, André Delattre does not go as far as Chaponnière in admitting the similarity between the aims of the Swiss pastors and the *philosophes*, though he shows that important developments in Genevese theology had taken place at the beginning of the eighteenth

---

au XIXe siècle (Genève 1862). J.-E. Cellérier, *L'Académie de Genève* (Geneva 1872), pp.51 ff., is more charitable, and in *L'Eglise de Genève à la fin du XVIIIe siècle* (Geneva 1892), L. Vallette attempts a positive, though not entirely convincing rehabilitation of Geneva's church during the revolutionary years.

A good example of the split between 'evangelicals' and 'moderns' in nineteenth-century Protestant circles can be seen in reactions to the antitrinitarian Esaïe Gasc, whose teaching caused controversy in the Académie de Montauban in 1811-1812. Charles Dardier, *Esaïe Gasc, citoyen de Genève, sa politique et sa théologie* (Paris 1876), describes Gasc's views with obvious approval, whereas Ch.-L. Frossard, *L'Orthodoxie et l'Eglise réformée de France* (Paris 1864), condemns him out of hand.

century. Like René Pomeau he asserts that 'even though Voltaire rejected Christian faith, his conception of Christianity remained invincibly dogmatic' (Voltaire and the ministers', p.250). According to Delattre (pp.244-45):

Protestant theologians have often been hard pressed in their efforts to reconcile both the principle of a free individual interpretation of the Scriptures and the normal development, within their denomination, of tradition and authority.

In the Protestant churches there are 'cycles': one generation will formulate a doctrinal corpus, a later one will reject it and go through an antidogmatic phase. This was the situation in Geneva at the time of Voltaire's stay. Jean-Alphonse Turretini (1671-1737), Geneva's greatest theologian of the eighteenth century, had considered dogma to be a Catholic rather than a Protestant characteristic. He reduced the truths necessary for salvation to a very small number.[14] These might even vary, depending on each individual's character. Turretini further drew a complete distinction between faith and the science of religion, that is theology, and insisted on the necessity of tolerance, encouraging reunion between various Protestant denominations. According to Delattre, Voltaire fundamentally misunderstood the movement which had occurred in Geneva: 'Voltaire refusa de concevoir qu'un mouvement qui s'éloignait du dogmatisme n'allât pas nécessairement vers le rationalisme, alors que ni l'un ni l'autre n'avait de véritable critère religieux pour Turretini' (*Correspondance avec les Tronchin*, p.xxvii).

Delattre's assertions provide an excellent basis for our investigation of Voltaire's contacts with the Swiss clergy. Is it correct to maintain that the pastors of Geneva had not in many cases passed the borderline between Christianity and deism, and that their beliefs merely represented one stage of a recurrent cycle normal within Protestantism? In any case, did pastors like Vernet, Moultou and Vernes, as Delattre seems to think, hold views similar to those of Turretini, or had their opinions become even more 'liberal'? To put it bluntly in Delattre's own words: 'did the ministers of Geneva lack the courage to admit their real beliefs, or lack of beliefs, or was Voltaire carried away by his own brand of fanaticism?' ('Voltaire and the ministers', p.244).

[14] *Correspondance avec les Tronchin*, ed. André Delattre (Paris 1950), p.xxvii; cf. below, pp.147-48.

Chapter 5

i. *The first months: uneasy peace*

Voltaire's perfectly genuine enthusiasm on his arrival in Geneva is normally assumed to have been caused by the atmosphere of security and freedom he found there compared with the court of Frederick or Jesuit-ridden Colmar. This was certainly the case, but another factor which helps us to understand his reaction is the discrepancy between what he actually experienced in Geneva and his earlier, distinctly unfavourable impression of Calvinism as a historical phenomenon. As we have seen, Voltaire had already described the Reformation and its consequences in two major works.[15] Not only did he detest Calvin as a domineering and persecuting theologian, but the picture he painted of Calvinist morality was also grim by any standards. Austere and repressive, it condemned the most harmless pastimes (cf. above, pp.68-70). Public confession and penance had been established in Switzerland, Scotland and Geneva (*Essai*, ii.243). Voltaire knew that times had changed and had expressed his admiration for the city before arriving there,[16] but nonetheless the relief he experienced at finding Genevese life so liberal and enlightened can only have been heightened by its contrast with the picture he had drawn of Calvin's Geneva. Restrictions still existed, but many of them were ignored (cf. Best.D15324) and it must indeed have seemed to Voltaire that the city and its clergy had undergone a considerable revolution to depart so far from the precepts and practice of their great Reformer.[17]

At the beginning of his stay in Geneva Voltaire was extremely prudent. The reason for his caution is obvious: fear that any unfortunate incidents might cause the government to expel him from their territory. Yet would it be completely naïve to detect at the same time a kind of

---

[15] the *Essai sur les mœurs* and the *Annales de l'empire*. Although the *Essai* was first published in a complete form in 1756 (cf. above, p.16) when Voltaire had been in Geneva for some time, it seems extremely likely that most of it had already been written before Voltaire's arrival in Switzerland, and in any case we have seen (above, p.58) that his attitude to Calvin had crystallised many years earlier.

[16] it seems as if he may have genuinely admired the democratic and orderly way the Reformation was effected in Geneva (cf. *Essai*, ii.243; cf. also Best.D259, quoted above, p.37, n.36), but the fulsome praise contained in Best.D6107 (to François Tronchin, 25 January 1755) would appear to be a *compliment de circonstance*: 'Il me serait doux de vivre et de mourir auprès de vous dans le sein de la liberté, du repos et du bon esprit qui fait le caractère de vos concitoyens.'

'Je révère votre gouvernement, j'adore la liberté.'

[17] 'Geneve n'est plus le Geneve de Calvin, il s'en faut beaucoup', (Best.D6821, Voltaire to Cideville, 12 April 1756).

good faith, a willingness to try to live with the annoying features of Genevese life because it possessed so many which were manifestly excellent and had greatly impressed the *philosophe?* Be this as it may, Voltaire's attitude toward the authorities, both secular and ecclesiastic, was at first very conciliatory. No word of protest is to be found anywhere in his correspondence regarding the condemnation of the *Délices* epistle. Official action against his theatricals was also accepted without a murmur, despite the fact that Voltaire had apparently been led to believe that they would be allowed[18] and had boasted to d'Argental on 18 July 1755: 'Geneve aura la comédie malgré Calvin' (Best.D6340). The worrying affair of *La Pucelle* was also smoothed over – Voltaire sent an explanation to the *Compagnie des pasteurs* who accepted that he was not the author of lines uncomplimentary to Calvin which he denied having written and which he claimed had been inserted in the poem by his enemies.[19] In fact Voltaire's co-operative attitude met with a favourable response on the part of the authorities. Not only was the *Compagnie des pasteurs* prepared to give him the benefit of the doubt, the Council acted on his behalf in imprisoning Grasset, the unauthorised publisher and hawker of *La Pucelle*.[20] Voltaire had also made a good impression generally, according to Elie Bertrand.[21] At any rate the influential councillor Du Pan did not seem too worried by the irreligion of *La Pucelle*, though he confided to the Bernese magistrate Freudenreich that it must be condemned officially (Best.D6384, 4 August 1755). And later in the year he admitted to the same correspondent that 'La Pucelle nous a bien diverti, elle fait faire de beaux éclats de rire à nos femmes' (Best.D6617, 7 December 1755). Voltaire's policy of conciliation would seem to have been an outstanding success, gaining for him both security and acceptance in his city of refuge.

18 cf. mme Denis's letter to Jean-Robert Tronchin of 23 July 1755: 'J'ai crains dans le premier moment que quel que personne dans Geneve ne désaprouve le peti plaisir que nous voulons nous donner. Tout le monde m'a assuré que cela seroit trouvé très bon et que même nous aurions à notre petite assemblée des ministres qui y viendroient' (Best.D6352).

19 cf. Best.D6384, Du Pan to Freudenreich, ?4 August 1755, and Best.D6391, Jean Jallabert to Charles de Brosses, 6 August 1755.

20 cf. Best.D6397 and D.app.149.

21 Best.D6390, to Formey, 6 August 1755. Yet it is only fair to point out that this opinion was not shared in all quarters. On the same day Végobre wrote to Antoine Court: 'Je ne sais si l'on nous envie en Suisse l'avantage que nous avons d'avoir ici le fameux Poëte. Ce qu'il y a de vrai c'est que son crédit diminue un peu ici, et que bien des gens le verroient partir sans regret' (Best.D6393).

But there were clouds on the horizon. Jacob Vernet, perhaps the most influential pastor and theologian in Geneva, had corresponded intermittently with Voltaire for many years.[22] But on Voltaire's arrival in his native city, Vernet saw fit to write him a long letter pointing out the merits of Geneva's enlightened, evangelical Christianity (Best. D6146, 8 February 1755). Emphasising that society needed a religion, Vernet guardedly warned Voltaire against attacking it, and expressed the hope that he would actively support the pastors in their efforts. Voltaire replied evasively in general terms (Best.D6149, 9 February 1755):

Mon cher monsieur, ce que vous écrivez sur la religion est fort raisonnable. . . .
Je déteste l'intolérance et le fanatisme, je respecte vos lois religieuses. . . .
J'aime et je respecte votre république.

And there the matter seemed to drop. We might explain Voltaire's vagueness and lack of enthusiasm by his being somewhat taken aback that a Genevese pastor, rather than he himself, should open the debate on religion between them, for the *philosophe* intended that in any projected *rapprochement* between deism and Protestantism, his would be the terms discussed. Moreover, the letter, though moderate in tone, went straight to the heart of the matter and contained none of the polite formulae and expressions of respect Voltaire had received from other Swiss pastors. In point of fact, Vernet's letter worried Voltaire considerably, and he had to be reassured by François Tronchin that it need not be taken too seriously. It is not difficult to see why. Such a message from a man of Vernet's status might seem tantamount to an official warning. The fact that it was written at all appeared to constitute a threat to someone in Voltaire's precarious position, a threat of which he was only too painfully aware.[23]

Voltaire's hatred for Vernet was no doubt conceived at this time, and although it was suppressed for the present, two letters written soon

[22] cf. Pomeau, *La Religion*, p.294; Florida, pp.145-46. The first letter from Voltaire to Vernet is Best.D653, dated 14 September 1733.

[23] though the correspondence for 1755 betrays none of this, Voltaire reminded Tronchin on 4 September 1757 of 'la plaisante lettre qu'un certain tartuffe [Vernet] m'écrivit lorsque j'étais prest de signer à Prangin avec mr de la Bat. Souvenez vous combien cette lettre me donna d'ombrage, et combien vous me rassurâtes' (Best.D7367). This letter would appear to refute convincingly those critics who have interpreted Vernet's warning as a friendly or conciliatory gesture.

after Voltaire's reply to the influential pastor sound a note of defiance which can probably be attributed directly to the anger provoked by Vernet's warning. Before settling in Switzerland Voltaire had been disturbed by the anti-Catholic laws of both Lausanne and Geneva, especially those preventing Catholics from owning land in the two towns.[24] As a distinguished guest Voltaire was enabled to bypass these confessional restrictions, but such a blatant instance of Protestant intolerance was not lost on him. Several references to it occur in his writings.[25] At the height of his quarrels with the Swiss clergy, on 5 January 1759, Voltaire was to emphasise this and other similar cases in an important letter to Bertrand, claiming that 'Il n'est pas moins nécessaire [. . .] de prêcher la tolérance chez vous que parmi nous' (Best. D8029; cf. below, p.185). A premonition of his disputes with the pastors and a latent opposition to the Calvinist establishment of Geneva uncharacteristic of Voltaire's honeymoon period with the city are already evident in a letter of 13 February 1755 to Richelieu: 'Il est plaisant que je n'aye de terres que dans le seul pays où il ne m'est pas permis d'en acquérir. La belle loy fondamentale de Geneve est qu'aucun catholique ne puisse respirer l'air de son territoire.'[26] As far as Voltaire was concerned, the Protestant clergy in the shape of Vernet had struck the first blow in the battle which was soon to oppose them, and this he did not forget.

At the beginning of his stay in Switzerland, Voltaire's position in relation to the clergy was indeed ambiguous. Vernet's warning came a little too late, for had the *philosophe* not been urged to seek exile in Switzerland by members of the pastoral *corps* as well as by laymen? On 24 February 1759 Voltaire reminded the seigneur d'Hermenches in a slightly piqued tone of the circumstances regarding his establishment at Lausanne: 'Il est vray comme vous le dites monsieur, que ce n'est pas vous ny mr de Gentil qui m'avez proposé de m'établir à Lausane, mais dès l'an 1751 Mr Polier m'en avait prié par ses lettres, lors que j'étais

---

[24] cf. Best.D5942: 'Je me figure qu'un papiste peut posséder et hériter dans le territoire de Lausanne. Me serais-je malheureusement trompé?' (to de Brenles, 6 October 1754). Voltaire repeated his request for information on 18 October (Best.D5960), and on 20 December he told de Brenles: 'Je crois qu'il ne peut plus être question d'Alaman ny d'aucune autre terre seigneuriale, puisque les loix de votre pays ne permettent pas ces acquisitions à ceux qui sont aussi attachez aux papes que je le suis' (Best.D6038).

[25] cf. Best.D7875 and D17906; also above, pp.94-95.

[26] Best.D6159; cf. also Best.D6150, to de Brenles.

auprès d'un roy'.[27] Even Vernet himself, if we are to believe Voltaire, invited him to Geneva: 'Il n'y a personne dans votre ville sur l'indulgence de qui j'aurais dû compter autant que sur la sienne. C'est lui qui le premier m'engagea à venir dans votre république' (Best.D7396, 23 September 1757, to Théodore Tronchin).

Whatever the exact facts of the matter, pastors like Polier and Vernet could not have been unaware of Voltaire's European reputation as a deist and freethinker. And he, in his turn, must have considered quite justifiably that the invitation extended to him indicated some measure of agreement with or at least toleration of his views. He may have thought that the pastors would be willing to meet him halfway on some points. Even if he was mistaken, Voltaire can surely be pardoned for believing this. His impression that the Genevese pastors were not severe Calvinists can only have been strengthened by the letters he received from some of their colleagues in other parts of Switzerland at the beginning of his stay in Geneva. Allamand wrote to him on 19 August 1755 commiserating over the condemnation of his *Délices* epistle (Best.D6421). In an earlier letter (20 June 1755) Allamand had referred to his ministry in a slightly flippant tone, and Voltaire had replied sympathetically: 'Quel chien de métier vous faittes!' (Best.D6331). He had also assured Polier de Bottens: 'J'attends avec impatience le moment où je pourai être votre diocésain' (Best.D6189, 28 February 1755), and was rewarded with a scholarly letter which, according to Theodore Besterman, helped him to write his article 'Fornication' for the *Encyclopédie* (Best.D7106, 1756/1757, textual notes). Cordial relations were also established with Elie Bertrand, pastor of the French Church at Berne.[28] With evidence like this of Calvinist 'liberalism', it was inevitable that Voltaire should begin to wonder why anachronistic regulations against the theatre and other amusements persisted in Geneva. If the children of Calvin, especially the clergy, had really changed for the better, why should they not accept the socially useful

[27] Best.D8138. Voltaire was no longer on the best of terms with his friends in Lausanne because of the Saurin affair. D'Hermenches had required Voltaire not to make their correspondence public.

[28] cf. Best.D6046, 28 December 1754 (Voltaire to Bertrand), which refers to Bertrand's 'lettre obligeante, et aussi remplie de bonté que d'esprit'. It would seem that this earlier letter from Bertrand had opened the correspondence between the two men. We shall see later how useful a contact Bertrand was to be. Voltaire realised this immediately, and on 12 September 1755 sent him a presentation copy of the *Orphelin de la Chine* for 'm. Tshifely', secretary of the Bernese Consistory (Best.D6484).

role of dramatic entertainment, unless they had adopted the mask of hypocrisy, no longer sharing Calvin's opinions but afraid to depart from them lest the clergy itself be rendered obsolete and its ministers lose the power and influence they still possessed in Geneva?

ii. *Lausanne*

It is often forgotten that Voltaire's contacts with Switzerland were not confined to Geneva and that he rented a fine house in the suburbs of Lausanne where he hoped to take advantage of the milder winter climate. Thus he arrived in the pays de Vaud at the end of December 1755 for his first stay there. His impassioned reaction to the Lisbon earthquake which had occurred on 1 November provided a good opportunity to test how real was the *modus vivendi* achieved between him and the Swiss clergy. 'Il a fait une pièce en vers sur la catastrophe du Portugal, elle est, dit-on, Philosophique et non Théologique', reported Du Pan to the Freudenreichs on 7 December (Best.D6617). Thus far Voltairean propaganda seemed to be working well. But there was also opposition in Lausanne to his views. Leresche and some other ministers preached against the *Epître à Uranie* and the *Lisbonne* poem.[29] Moreover, Voltaire received an anonymous letter which he at first wrongly attributed to Haller.[30] Yet despite these setbacks Voltaire contrived as in Geneva to produce a mainly favourable impression on the clergy and people of Lausanne, and for his part was well satisfied with his hosts. On 29 January 1756 he told Jacob Vernes that the ministers of Lausanne were 'fort aimables et très instruits' (Best.D6709). And on 27 March Seigneux de Correvon informed Haller that Voltaire had won over those people who at first would not visit him. Correvon himself found the *Lisbonne* poem 'belle et grande' and added that he would not attempt to express 'toutes les belles choses qu'il [Voltaire] nous dit à la gloire du Christianisme' (Best.D6806). One would dearly like to know what these compliments were, but before taxing Voltaire with hypocrisy we should remember that he was following Vernet's advice to the letter.[31] However questionable this conduct may appear to us, it was a solution

[29] Best.D6802, May to Haller, 23 March 1756.

[30] see Best.D6791, commentary, D8193, D8210, and Heinrich Dübi, 'Altmann, Voltaire und Haller', *Blätter für bernische Geschichte, Kunst und Altertumskunde* (December 1909), v.255-64.

[31] 'Vernet se rendait-il compte qu'il recommandait à son correspondant une double doctrine non dénuée d'hypocrisie' (Pomeau, *La Religion de Voltaire*, p.296).

both Voltaire and most Swiss or Genevese pastors were prepared to accept. Elie Bertrand, for example, took Voltaire to task for the views he had expressed in the *Lisbonne* poem and on his religious position in general, but this did not prevent the pastor from using his good offices to arrange the trip to Berne which greatly strengthened Voltaire's position at Lausanne. Voltaire continued to praise Geneva as the most philosophic of towns, and he reached a new peak of enthusiasm when the heads of the Council and Church gave their unqualified approval to two of his poems which had been read to them.[32] On 27 May he told Thieriot: 'je suis si heureux que j'en ai honte', and the rest of 1756 was relatively uneventful as far as his relations with Swiss Protestantism were concerned.[33] There seemed no reason why the sometimes uneasy truce between Voltaire and the pastors should not continue.

Yet this was merely the calm before the storm. Voltaire's second winter at Montriond was decisive in the development of his relations with the pastors of Geneva. A letter to Jean-Robert Tronchin of 4 or 5 February 1757 gives the key to this change of attitude: 'On joue tous les jours la comédie à Lausanne. Ce n'est pas comme dans votre ville de Calvin' (Best.D7142). Later in the month, probably on 27 February, Voltaire urged the Genevese pastor Jacob Vernes that he and Claparède should quit their ministers' dress and attend a performance of *L'Enfant prodigue*: 'On ne se scandalize point à Lausan[ne; on] y respire les plaisirs honnêtes, et [les douceurs] de la société' (Best.D7174). And in fact Voltaire's theatricals were proving an immense success. On 16 March Seigneux de Correvon wrote an entirely approbatory letter to Haller in connection with them. Voltaire reacted to this welcome development by redoubling his enthusiasm for Lausanne, and by making sure the lesson was not lost on Geneva's pastors: 'La piété n'est point ennemie des plaisirs honnêtes', he declared to Vernes on 20 March, pointing out that ministers had attended his theatricals and even taken

[32] Best.D6821, to Cideville, 12 April 1756. The works in question were the 'religion naturelle' and perhaps *L'Orphelin de la Chine*.

[33] René Pomeau gives a mistaken idea of this period when, after quoting from Voltaire's enthusiastic letter to Cideville (Best.D6821, mentioned above), he comments (p.301): 'L'interdiction de jouer la comédie aux Délices, signifiée par le Consistoire, le 31 juillet, ne réussit pas à rompre le charme.' It could evidently have had no such effect since this ban had been pronounced the previous year, on 31 July 1755, as Pomeau's own note 122 indicates. Voltaire did receive Rousseau's celebrated letter on providence during this period, but it seems unlikely that this had any direct effect on his relations with the clergy of Lausanne and Geneva.

part as musicians (Best.D7209). There is as yet no tone of rancour in Voltaire's letter on the subject (cf. Best.D7186). He was obviously enjoying himself thoroughly, but it is also evident that he could hardly avoid making unfavourable comparisons with Geneva, where Calvinist severity persisted in this matter. As he observed to Pierre Pictet on 27 March: 'Il faut avoüer que Lausanne donne d'assez beaux exemples à Geneve' (Best.D7217).

Nor were these examples confined to the field of drama. Polier de Bottens, *premier pasteur* of Lausanne, was becoming an encyclopedist. On 4 February Voltaire told d'Alembert that 'un prêtre hérétique de mes amis, savant et philosophe, vous destine *Liturgie*' (Best.D7139). After receiving the article Voltaire was even more enthusiastic: what progress reason had made, he exclaimed, when it was necessary for him to tone down the work of a theologian![34] Modern scholarship has shown that Voltaire was not exaggerating in his estimation of Polier's unorthodoxy.[35] In fact, the beliefs of the Lausanne pastoral *corps* as a whole were somewhat suspect in 1757. A commission consisting of Albert Haller and Victor de Bonstetten was appointed by the Bernese government to enquire into the Academy's teaching. The two men duly arrived in Lausanne on 9 February and set to work. Their conclusions were far from reassuring: Christian dogma was being neglected, and many pastors were guilty of preaching a moralism indistinguishable from that of Plato, Epictetus, Seneca or Cicero (Vuilleumier, iv.232). An unnamed minister 'n'avait pas craint d'exposer ouvertement des principes sociniens' (Roulet, p.99).

In his study *Voltaire et les Bernois* Louis Roulet is at pains to prove that Voltaire bore at least some responsibility for the appearance of unorthodoxy among the Lausanne pastors. After commenting quite correctly that 'les jeunes ministres qui n'avaient pas craint, du haut de la chaire, d'émettre des jugements rappelant étonnamment les principes condamnés [i.e. Socinian principles], s'apparentaient consciemment ou non à Voltaire', he agrees (p.101, n.1) that neither Haag[36] nor Vuilleumier make any 'rapprochement direct entre l'enquête et la

[34] Best.D7165: 'J'ai eu toutes les peines du monde à rendre cet article chrétien.'

[35] cf. Raymond Naves, *Voltaire et l'Encyclopédie* (Paris 1938), pp.28-33, 185-94. Naves shows that Polier was indeed the author of many 'philosophical' articles, and that, although these may have been comprehensively edited by Voltaire (as in the case of 'Messie'), their fundamental content and orientation were not changed.

[36] 'La mission d'Albert de Haller à Lausanne en 1757', *Neues Berner Taschenbuch* (1900), translated into French by Ed. Payot, *Revue historique vaudoise* (1900), viii.65-72.

présence de Voltaire à Lausanne'. Yet, despite this, he finds enormously significant the fact that, in his *Mémoires*, Bonstetten mentions that Voltaire was in Lausanne at the time the enquiry took place.[37] Pointing out that Voltaire was on excellent terms with de Brenles and Polier de Bottens, and that he was visited by 'plusieurs pasteurs éclairés', Roulet feels able to conclude: 'Dès lors, il est permis de soupçonner Voltaire, de le rendre, en partie, responsable de la mésentente qui régna parmi les ministres de l'Evangile' (p.101). Pressing his argument further in a memorable footnote, Roulet indicates that Voltaire told Bertrand he was aware of the doctrinal disagreements between members of the clergy and denied responsibility for them. After a passing appeal to the proverb 'Qui s'excuse s'accuse', Roulet asks (p.101, n.1) if it would be going too far to 'présumer que la présence de Voltaire n'est point étrangère à cette subite aggravation du malaise?'[38] Was it not curious that the crisis occurred just when Voltaire appeared in Lausanne?

The evidence adduced by Roulet to back up his assertions is flimsy, to say the least. Voltaire's mere presence in Lausanne at the time the enquiry took place can hardly be taken to prove he was responsible for the situation which had rendered such an investigation necessary. Moreover, as Roulet himself admits, the crisis 'n'est point récent', and Voltaire had been at Lausanne for only a very short time when he referred to the clergy's disagreements in the letter to Bertrand mentioned by Roulet. Could he, in three or four months, have worsened the situation among the pastors to such an extent that the Bernese government intervened, but without its representatives taking the slightest action against Voltaire or even mentioning his responsibility in their report?[39] In any case, there is no reason to doubt what Voltaire

[37] Roulet's logic deserves to be quoted: 'Certes, le patricien bernois [...] ne fait pas d'allusion directe; mais les deux événements étant rapportés l'un à la suite de l'autre, un rapprochement s'établit par là même' (pp.100-101).

[38] 'il ressort des lettres envoyées par Voltaire à Bertrand que le patriarche était au courant de la mésentente qui régnait parmi les ministres de l'Evangile', is Roulet's comment (p.101, n.1). The letter in question is Best.D6818 (6 April 1756), in which Voltaire tells Bertrand: 'Je sais qu'il y a bien des tracasseries à Lausanne, mais je ne m'en mêle point. Je n'ai été qu'une seule fois dans cette ville. On m'a dit que de jeunes ministres n'ont pas pour leurs anciens toute la considération qu'ils leurs doivent; que quelquefois même ils prêchent les uns contre les autres; mais ce n'est pas à moi à prendre connaissance de ces petits scandales.' Surely this is no more than the amused comment of an interested bystander.

[39] Roulet in fact admits that no reference was made to Voltaire by the commissioners, and he even recounts how Haller 'ne fit pas grise mine au philosophe et accepta son invitation. "J'ai été à Lausanne, écrivait-il à Charles Bonnet [letter of 23 March 1759], j'ai

says in the letter to Bertrand. Just before his visit to Berne he is concerned to show that the policy of conciliation he had adopted in Geneva was also being practised in Lausanne. Voltaire was aware that opposition to him existed, and there is no reason to believe that he would immediately have set about intensifying the hostility of men like Leresche by stirring up a revolt among younger members of the clergy.

Fortunately, one of the works cited by Roulet himself contains evidence suggesting that Voltaire did not play any significant part in this affair. Henri Vuilleumier tells us that the enquiry of Haller and Bonstetten in 1757 had been occasioned primarily by the teaching of J.-P. Secrétan, appointed *professeur de théologie élenchtique* in 1751. Secrétan wished to combat the growing tide of atheism and deism rather than concentrating on inter-sectarian disputes. Vuilleumier comments (iv.233):

La question était seulement de savoir si la théologie à la mode, celle d'un christianisme 'raisonnable' qui mettait au premier rang les articles de la religion et de la morale naturelles et reléguait à l'arrière-plan ce qu'on appelait les mystères de la religion révelée, si une théologie comme celle-là était de taille à combattre victorieusement la philosophie sensualiste et déiste.

Although as yet taking no active part in these matters, Voltaire must have been encouraged by the obvious hold of unorthodoxy among the Lausanne clergy, and confirmed in his belief that the Swiss clergy were, in the main, enlightened Calvinists more than ready to take a few steps into the deist fold.

To imagine that Voltaire's appearance in Lausanne could immediately effect such a dramatic change in the clergy is, in any case, to betray a surprising ignorance of the *pays romand*'s religious development in preceding decades. What is now the canton of Vaud was administered until the end of the eighteenth century by Berne. Even if it is probably going too far to claim with Delattre ('Voltaire and the ministers', p.248) that 'to oppose official orthodoxy became a way of taking a stand against the oppression of the German-speaking rulers, a form of political resistance', it is true that frequent controversies and 'rebellions'

fait l'aimable connaissan ce de M. Tronchin, j'ai vu représenter M. de Voltaire: c'était allier agréablement le plaisir aux peines d'une commission assez difficile"' (Roulet, p.101). What could be more posi tive? Haller's letter contains not the slightest note of censure, and he makes no *rapprochment* whatsoever between Voltaire's presence and the situation he was investigating.

were caused by the intransigent policy of the central government. Pastors were required to accept the *Formula consensus*, an extreme Calvinist formulation of doctrine directed against Arminian and Pietist beliefs, and the clergy of the *pays romand* were expected to follow the directives of their German-speaking counterparts. Many pastors signed the *Formula*, adding the words *quatenus scripturae consentaneae*, and this practice, censured by the Bernese government, caused further controversy (cf. Vuilleumier, iii.572-84). The development of views considered heretical by the strictly Calvinist Bernese authorities is therefore no surprise. It was a periodic occurrence until the *Formula* was finally abandoned, and there is thus no difficulty in understanding the 1757 commission of enquiry without any particular reference to Voltaire or his views.

iii. *The first shots against Calvinism: 'l'âme atroce'*

The presence in Lausanne of a commission to enquire into the clergy's orthodoxy and a successful season of theatricals probably combined to encourage Voltaire to take a more positive stand over Geneva's Calvinist restrictions. He was now convinced, and not without reason, that many clergymen in both towns subscribed to an enlightened form of Christianity. If the Lausanne pastors could show themselves so liberal, their Genevese colleagues must be prodded into realising that their own beliefs were identical, and that anachronistic regulations in their city should be abolished. Voltaire did not choose to fight the battle on the issue of the theatre; he went straight to the heart of the matter. Calvin, whom he had already painted in the blackest of colours as the intolerant murderer of Servetus and the fanatical preacher of austerity, was for Voltaire the evil genius of Geneva. The pastors, who no longer shared Calvin's beliefs but maintained his moral and social restrictions, must be induced to renounce any remaining allegiance to the reformer, if not in so many words at least tacitly and by implication. Thus at the beginning of 1757 we see Voltaire complimenting Jacob Vernes because in Geneva it was possible to print that 'Servet était un sot, et Calvin un barbare. Vous n'êtes point calvinistes', he went on significantly, 'vous êtes hommes' (Best.D7119, 13 January). On 24 February Voltaire repeated his praise of Geneva, this time to Pierre Rousseau, at the same time intensifying his criticism of Calvin. He claimed to have been able to print 'avec l'approbation universelle que Calvin était un très méchant homme, altier, dur, vindicatif et sanguinaire' (Best.D7172). Finally, to Thieriot (Best.D7213, 26 March), Voltaire was even less cautious in his expressions, asserting that it was no small example of the progress of philosophy and tolerance 'qu'on ait imprimé à Genève [...] avec l'approbation publique, que Calvin avait une âme atroce aussi bien qu'un esprit éclairé. Le meurtre de Servet paraît aujourd'hui abominable.' How can we see this as anything other than an intentional campaign with the references to Calvin becoming progressively more violent? At first Voltaire wrote to a Genevese pastor who, he had reason to believe, would not take his letter amiss. In the absence of unfavourable reaction the *philosophe*, emboldened, obviously intended to publicise his views in the hope that the Genevese clergy as a whole would react like Vernes. The choice of correspondents makes this abundantly clear: Pierre Rousseau was editor of the *Journal encyclopédique*, and Thieriot was hardly likely to keep any correspondence received from Voltaire to himself, as the subsequent publication of Best.D7213 in the *Mercure* demonstrates. The phrase 'avec l'approbation publique' in the letter to Thieriot ensured that, unless the Genevese pastors specifically denied Voltaire's assertions, they could be considered to have tacitly endorsed his views on Calvin and Servetus.

That Voltaire had miscalculated the situation is well known. He was soon claiming that his letter to Thieriot had been printed 'toutte défigurée et toute tronquée'.[40] The challenge thrown down to Geneva's pastors was taken up in an anonymous letter normally attributed to Vernet,[41] but which the influential theologian denied having written. It asserted that, although people would agree that Servetus's execution had been unfortunate, they would not accept Voltaire's violent expressions. At the time of the trial tolerance was unknown, and heretics were punished by the civil authorities. Moreover, the purified Christianity of Geneva had actually helped the rise of tolerance, a fact Voltaire ought to have realised. The anonymous letter further asserted that Calvin was a great man despite his defects. He was a lawyer, imbued with the legal prejudices of his time, and should not be so harshly condemned for what was, after all, 'l'erreur commune du siècle'.[42]

[40] Best.D7261, to Jacob Vernes, *c.* 15 May 1757.

[41] cf. Chaponnière's comment: 'Hé oui, le style est l'homme même' (*Voltaire chez les calvinistes*, p.82). Florida (p.181, n.19) does not find this argument conclusive.

[42] Best.D7272, 30 May 1757. It may be remembered that this was the argument also used by Haller: cf. above, p.83.

129

It was hardly to be expected that Voltaire would accept these strictures good-humouredly, but an attempt was made to smooth the affair over and to restore the uneasy truce between him and the religious establishment of Geneva.[43] On 19 July Vernet told Théodore Tronchin that he had asked the *ancien syndic* Saladin whether he (Vernet) should forward to Voltaire a *projet de lettre* which the *philosophe* could then send to the Consistory (Best.D7319). It may be remembered that this was a procedure Voltaire had already adopted to the satisfaction of both sides regarding *La Pucelle*. Vernet wrote to Tronchin again on 22 July pointing out that he had attempted to stop any polemical writings: 'je souhaite cõe vous que toute cette noize soit absolum̄ᵗ étouffée' (Best.D7322). The pastor added that he could understand the angry reaction in some quarters, but concluded: 'que cela soit fini et vivons en paix'. The tone of both Vernet's letters regarding Voltaire is moderate and courteous, and his desire for peace would seem perfectly genuine.

But Voltaire was now aroused. He refused to believe that most pastors of Geneva shared the views expressed in the anonymous letter. 'Nos calvinistes ne sont point du tout attachez à Calvin, il y a ici plus de philosofes qu'ailleurs', he had insisted to Thieriot on 2 June (Best. D7275). In fact it took some time before he formed the opinion that most Genevese pastors were hypocrites who merely lacked the courage of their convictions. Voltaire's immediate reaction to the anonymous letter was to concentrate his anger and resentment on Vernet, whom he believed to be its author and whom he had obviously mistrusted ever since the pastor had warned him not to meddle in Geneva's religious affairs. He insisted that reactionaries like Vernet were in the minority (Best.D7357) and maintained a defiant attitude, encouraged by the fact that a theatre at the gates of Geneva was attracting great support from the citizens.[44] Yet Voltaire did not hit back at his anonymous critic. His correspondence for August 1757 does not even mention the *âme atroce* affair, and on 2 September he told François Tronchin: 'Je me flatte que la tracasserie de Servet est anéantie, du moins elle l'est par mon silence' (Best.D7364).

It is clear that the Tronchin family played an important part in assuring that the affair was damped down and it is also obvious that they can only have been acting with the approval of Geneva's all-important *Petit conseil*, who expressed the wish that no more should be

43 Florida, pp.184 ff., has a very full account of this.
44 Best.D7338, D7355, D7362. Cf. above, p.98, n.3.

said on the subject.[45] Indeed, perhaps the most significant fact to emerge from the affair is that the Tronchins and other members of the Council agreed, to all intents and purposes, with Voltaire, and virtually prevented Vernet from defending Calvin, even in a moderate way. Voltaire had promised Tronchin to preserve silence on the matter, and the promise was kept although he encouraged Bertrand and Polier to refute the anonymous letter on his behalf.[46] We must look in a little detail at the correspondence between Vernet and the Tronchins in order to appreciate how divided were the Council and a respected pastor on this matter. On 11 September Vernet had asked Th. Tronchin to lend him certain manuscripts relating to the Servetus case. 'He was refused,' Besterman tells us, 'and on 12th sent Tronchin a series of questions concerning Calvin and Servet which he asked to have answered from the manuscripts' (Best.D7382, commentary; see also D.app.157). Vernet had also made other advances, as Raymond Naves explains (p.42):

Désireux de prendre Voltaire en défaut sur un point d'histoire, il projette d'écrire un ouvrage sur Calvin et, comme les documents du procès Servet sont dans les archives de Conseil, il en demande communication à De Chapeaurouge, secrétaire d'Etat. Le 12 septembre, le Conseil délibère et refuse: le compte rendu dit sèchement: 'Le Conseil n'a pas trouvé convenable qu'il lui donnât ladite communication.'

Vernet had no doubt learned quickly of the Council's hostility, and this presumably explains his modified request to Tronchin of 12 September. But in Besterman's opinion, 'Tronchin presumably expressed further doubts' (Best.D7382, commentary) and in an important letter dated 13 September Vernet restated his position. He denied having been author of the anonymous letter: 'On doit y reconnaître les traits de jeunes mains, qui sont en grand nombre.' He further claimed to have tried to prevent its publication. There were many mistakes in the chapters 'Genève et Calvin' and 'Calvin et Servet' of the *Essai sur les mœurs*, Vernet asserted, adding that he was correcting

[45] on 12 September the *Petit conseil* declared that 'il désire que l'on n'écrive plus sur cette matière' (Naves, p.42).

[46] cf. Voltaire's letter of 9 September 1757 to Bertrand: 'Mon cher téologien, mon cher philosofe, mon cher ami vous avez donc voulu absolument qu'on repondît à la lettre du mercure de Neuf Chatel. Mr Polier de Bottens qui méditait de son côté une réponse, vient de m'aprendre qu'il y en a une qui paraît sous vos auspices' (Best.D7371). Voltaire is presumably referring to the 'Réponse à la Lettre insérée dans le Journal Helvétique de Juin, adressée à Mr. de Voltaire', *Journal helvétique*, Neuchâtel (August 1757), pp.156-62 (Best.D7371, commentary; Roulet, p.68).

these in the form of a moderate letter addressed to Formey.[47] Tronchin's reply must have seemed a slap in the face, and it put Geneva's
leading pastor in a well-nigh impossible position. He told Vernet that
he hated the whole affair and was determined to stop it. Vernet had
seemed to agree with him in July, but must since have changed his
mind. Calvin's cause was indefensible,[48] and provided marvellous
ammunition for someone like Voltaire. Vernet's zeal was preparing
many mortifications for the Protestants of Geneva. The Council
favoured silence, since any dispute would harm religion. Personalities
would be hurtful and Vernet must be prepared to take what was dealt
out to him. In the face of this implacable hostility on the Council's part
Vernet could only defend himself as if he had been the sole guilty party.
It was impossible, he claimed, to prevent the anti-Voltaire letter from
being printed abroad. He had thought that Voltaire would write a
letter of explanation to the Consistory, and his own letter (presumably
the one to be addressed to Formey) was moderate. Vernet and his
colleagues were planning a work to defend religion and Calvin if possible – surely this was a worthwhile enterprise? Silence would imply
acquiescence – the pastor obviously understood Voltaire's tactics
very well – and Vernet promised he would not descend to personalities
(Best.D7389, 20 September).

One might imagine that it would have been discouraging enough for
Vernet to be told that the Council of Geneva agreed with Voltaire's
opinion of Calvin. Yet more unpleasantness was in store for him. As
we shall see, it seems clear from the Besterman edition of Voltaire's
correspondence that the Tronchins were letting Voltaire read Vernet's
letters or at the very least telling him what they contained. On 21
September Jean-Robert Tronchin-Boissier added his weight to the
debate in an attempt to dissuade Vernet from taking further action.
Voltaire had not been attacked honourably, claimed Tronchin. He
would be forced to reply to any public criticism by Vernet, and he would
be able to say that Vernet had edited the *Essai sur les mœurs* (in which
the chapters unfavourable to Calvin appeared). Tronchin stated that
the author of the anonymous letter was the aggressor in this dispute.

[47] Best.D7382, 13 September. This was subsequently published in Vernet's *Lettres critiques d'un voyageur anglois.*
[48] Best.D7383, 13 September. Tronchin's exact words deserve to be quoted: 'La cause de Calvin est insoutenable, ce qui nous reste à faire c'est d'en rougir. Je vous ai déjà dit que nous devions souhaiter que Dieu lui fît miséricorde.'

Calvin's action would always be odious. What could be gained by continuing the affair? The personal attacks Vernet had been warned about had in fact begun, and there is little doubt that Voltaire himself had introduced them, for he now considered Vernet as his personal enemy. On 23 September he took up the point made by Tronchin-Boissier and in a letter to Théodore Tronchin insisted that Vernet had invited him to Geneva, had been the self-appointed editor of Voltaire's history, the *Essai sur les mœurs*, and that not only had the pastor written against a work he had edited, he had also contradicted 'ses propres sentiments universellement reconnus' (Best.D7396, 23 September). Tronchin immediately repeated these allegations to Vernet in a letter written the next day, proof positive of how closely he was supporting Voltaire and accepting his arguments. In a two-edged compliment, he agreed that Vernet could not be considered the author of the anonymous letter, '*puisque dans le fond vous pensés cõme moi* [...] *sur l'affaire de Servet*' (Best.D7398, 24 September). Voltaire's good faith had obviously disappeared now in the heat of battle, for, as Vernet pointed out tellingly in his reply to Théodore Tronchin, he had in fact corrected Voltaire's *Histoire*, but only the first two volumes concerning medieval history; they did not include 'une peinture du Calvinisme comme d'une Religion ennemie de la Monarchie, & beaucoup de sottises sur nos Réformateurs' (Best.D7404, 29 September).

The wind had obviously been taken out of Vernet's sails by the Tronchins' attitude. He could now do little other than justify his personal position and attitude, saying that he had always acted honestly with Voltaire, whose coming to Geneva he had both desired and feared. Vernet claimed that he had been forced to defend his religion, but now ill-health prevented him from undertaking the work in defence of Calvinism mentioned in an earlier letter, although he was willing to assist others (Best.D7404). It is impossible to see this as anything other than a tactical withdrawal, if not a defeat, in the face of such violent opposition by the Council. Vernet was in fact following advice given to him by the *syndic* Calendrini, whose clear directive shows conclusively that the Tronchins were not the only prominent Genevese citizens to share Voltaire's views:

La conduite de Calvin est telle que l'on veut que tout soit enseveli dans un profond oubli. Calvin n'est pas excusable [...] Servez-vous de la raison tirée de votre maladie pour nous dispenser d'un ouvrage qui ne peut être que nuisible à la religion, à la réformation et à votre patrie, ou qui serait peu conforme à la vérité.[49]

Théodore Tronchin's final letter to Vernet contrived to sound even more Voltairean than his earlier ones. He expressed his pleasure that the Consistory had taken no firm resolution and declared that it was impossible to hide the pointlessness of theological disputes; only irreligion profited from them. 'Conservons nos mœurs, Mr.,' he concluded, 'elles seront le vrai soutien de notre Religion' (Best.D7409, 4 October). Had Voltaire dictated this letter himself, it would have been difficult for him to have expressed his religious opinions in a more characteristic way.

Thus, to all intents and purposes, ended the *âme atroce* affair. Voltaire had not succeeded in his original purpose of inducing the Genevese clergy as a whole to break with Calvin, but he had scored an important victory through the anti-Calvinist stand taken by the Council. He refused in any case to believe that the protesters had been more than a small number of reactionaries led by Vernet, for he was satisfied that many ministers held the most liberal of views. Towards the end of October, after a period in which he had obviously been taking stock of the situation, Voltaire told Bertrand with quiet satisfaction: 'Les brouillons qui ont répondu avec amertume à vos sages insinuations sont désaprouvez de leurs confrères, et ont excité l'indignation des magistrats' (Best.D7428). Above all he considered the refusal of the Council to let Vernet see the records of Servetus's trial as a great triumph, and he frequently mentioned this example of the Genevese government's good sense in his subsequent correspondence and published works. The attack on Vernet had probably been basically unjustified and was unfair in the way it was carried out.[50] But whereas the pastor had been able to refute convincingly allegations that he had connived in the anti-Calvinist views of the *Essai sur les mœurs*, the letter to Bertrand

[49] Geneva, *Arch. gen.*, PH suppl.208., quoted by Naves, pp.42-43 (no date given).

[50] Voltaire also exaggerated somewhat the extent to which his opponent had been discomfited, commenting in the same letter to Bertrand: 'Il se meurt de chagrin, je le plains, et je me tais.' One may be permitted to doubt both the suggestion that Voltaire sympathised with Vernet's position and the claim (also made in Best.D7428) that Vernet was covered with confusion by the letters Voltaire had produced. No doubt the Council's hostile attitude in the affair and the personalities directed against him had dismayed Vernet, but his subsequent opposition to Voltaire and the latter's angry reaction were to prove amply that this influential pastor was still a force to be reckoned with: cf. below, pp.173-77.

contains another charge, not yet made during the *âme atroce* affair, but which Vernet would soon find it more difficult to deny: 'Ajoutons pour couronner l'œuvre que c'est un antitrinitaire qui veut aujourd'hui justifier la mort de Servet' (Best.D7428).

iv. *The 'sociniens honteux'*

D'Alembert's article 'Genève', published in November 1757 as part of the *Encyclopédie*'s seventh volume (Naves, p.34), brought to the attention of Europe the paradox that several Genevese pastors, the successors of Calvin, were more heterodox than Servetus, whom the Reformer had caused to be burned for his antitrinitarian views. Coming so soon after the *âme atroce* affair, the storm caused by these allegations finally ruined lingering attempts to maintain a *modus vivendi* between Voltaire and Geneva's clergy. For Voltaire had been d'Alembert's host at *Les Délices* in August 1756,[51] and he was accused of having inspired the encyclopedist's article.[52] Convinced as he was that most pastors were in fact Socinians, Voltaire reacted by renewing his charges of priestly hypocrisy and by abandoning all hopes of support from the religious establishment of Geneva in his attempts to encourage 'enlightened' religion. The religious establishment there was henceforth definitely identified with *l'infâme*.

D'Alembert's notorious article is so well known that it will be sufficient merely to recall the most controversial of his remarks regarding 'la religion de Genève'. Several pastors not only reject the divinity of Christ and deplore Calvin's treatment of Servetus, the encyclopedist stated, they have also abandoned any belief in Hell:

Pour tout dire en un mot, plusieurs pasteurs de Genève n'ont d'autre religion qu'un socianisme parfait, rejetant tout ce qu'on appelle mystères et s'imaginant que le premier principe d'une religion véritable, est de ne rien proposer à croire qui heurte la raison [. . .][53]. La religion y est presque réduite à l'adoration d'un seul Dieu, du moins chez tout ce qui n'est pas peuple; le respect pour Jésus-Christ et pour les Ecritures sont peut-être la seule chose qui distingue d'un pur déisme le christianisme de Genève.

---

51 according to Chaponnière (*Voltaire chez les calvinistes*, p.62) he arrived on 10 August, and Naves (p.20, n.71) thinks he left 'au début de septembre'.

52 Best.D7512, Voltaire to d'Alembert, 12 December 1757.

53 René Pomeau (*La Religion de Voltaire*, p.304) points out that 'Jacob Vernes dans la *Préface* de son *Catéchisme Universel* ne dit rien d'autre'.

How much truth was there in the accusation that 'une confédération impie' had been formed between Voltaire and d'Alembert?[54] As Ronald Grimsley points out:

There has been considerable discussion about the relative responsibility of d'Alembert and Voltaire in the composition of this article, some critics insisting that d'Alembert was little more than Voltaire's scribe, others seeking to leave the ultimate responsibility with him.[55]

Of all the accounts describing this incident that of Raymond Naves (pp.18-21, 34-50) remains the most scholarly and authoritative,[56] and on many points it will be sufficient to summarise and briefly discuss his conclusions. On this particular question Naves (p.48) sees Voltaire as having inspired the article, 'qui devait être pour lui un moyen indirect de sonder définitivement les esprits genevois, et aussi de les diriger, peut-être malgré eux, dans le sens de la tolérance et du déisme'.[57] He also considers that Voltaire inspired certain secondary details. In other words, during the discussions Voltaire had with d'Alembert at a time when he was still highly enthusiastic about Geneva's clergy (an enthusiasm marred only by the ban on his theatricals), the idea was already forming in his mind to test out the reality of the pastors' liberalism. This, as we have just seen, was the tactic employed in the *âme atroce* affair, although by then Voltaire's determination to force the issue into the open had been strengthened by developments in Lausanne during the winter of 1756.

[54] *The Encyclopédie of Diderot and d'Alembert*, ed. John Lough (Cambridge 1954), pp.95-96.

[55] *Jean d'Alembert (1717-83)* (Oxford 1963), p.53.

[56] Florida, pp.192-208, also has a clear and well-balanced appreciation.

[57] the passage on Geneva's lack of a theatre is an obvious example, but Naves also mentions the defence of inoculation, a comment on burial hygiene ('On enterre dans un vaste cimetière assez éloigné de la ville, usage qui devrait être suivi partout'), praise of the spirit of concord among Geneva's pastors, and slightly unfavourable comments on the sacred music and chants of Geneva (p.44). Grimsley considers that d'Alembert might already have been interested in inoculation before his visit to *Les Délices*. Naves's other points seem reasonable, although it is only fair to say that Voltaire was subsequently to delight in refuting these suggestions one by one, which might indicate that he personally had not been their source. At any rate he certainly rebuked d'Alembert later for the too favourable account he had given of the ministers' spirit of concord and generosity (cf. Best.D4790). Moreover, as regards Genevese worship, it is known that d'Alembert attended at least one service during his stay, and he might therefore quite easily have formed his own impressions, especially since most of Voltaire's scathing criticisms of psalm-singing were made at a later date.

The opinion formed by d'Alembert, after talking with Voltaire and meeting several ministers and prominent members of the laity,[58] thus coincided with the optimistic views of his host, and this was the basis on which d'Alembert composed the section of his article dealing with religion.[59] However, as Naves pertinently observes (p.43): 'l'article *Genève* est anachronique; par ses éloges sans réserve du clergé calviniste, il représente l'opinion de Voltaire six mois plus tôt'. For, although d'Alembert underwent Voltaire's influence in forming his opinion, 'la rédaction dans son ensemble est certainement de d'Alembert' (p.45). Naves's reasons for this conclusion are based on the style of the article and on d'Alembert's character and subsequent reactions to criticism levelled at him by the ministers.[60] It is certainly true that Voltaire himself regarded stubborness as one of the main traits of his friend's personality, as we can see from an amusing comment to Thieriot: 'C'est d'ailleurs un drôle de corps que notre ami Protagoras; *il est tètu comme une mule*, il est tout plein d'esprit, il est charmant.'[61] Perhaps the most convincing proof of d'Alembert's authorship put forward by Naves is that:

l'article n'a pas été connu de Voltaire dans sa rédaction avant qu'il fût publié, il suffit d'y lire la citation de la fameuse lettre à Thieriot: on y voit l'*âme atroce* dans sa version la plus primitive. C'est que d'Alembert ignorait la rectification de Voltaire, et il cite le texte dans son intégralité sans se douter que la reprise du mot, origine de controverses et d'injures depuis plusieurs mois, était une maladresse enorme à l'égard des pasteurs. Jamais Voltaire ne l'aurait laissé passer s'il avait eu connaissance du manuscrit.[62]

[58] 'Jacob Vernet, auquel son frère, banquier à Paris, avait recommandé cet académicien de trente-quatre ans, lui amena plusieurs pasteurs et savants' (Chaponnière, *Voltaire chez les calvinistes*, p.62). D'Alembert dined with the councillor Jean-Louis Du Pan (Naves, p.19, n.64). The pastors he met were, according to Chaponnière (p.63), Vernet, de La Rive, Lullin, Vernes and Moultou (cf. also Naves, p.19).

[59] 'La partie politique de l'article fut prise, selon Vernet, dans un mémoire que d'Alembert se fit envoyer de la ville' (J. S. Spink, *J.-J. Rousseau et Genève* (Paris 1934), p.153; cf. also Chaponnière, *Voltaire chez les calvinistes*, p.62).

[60] pp.46-47. Naves argues very convincingly here. He shows how d'Alembert refused to retract and wished to take sole responsibility for the article. He lists the times d'Alembert returned to the theme of the Genevese pastors' religious views (four separate occasions in print between 1758 and 1767), and concludes: 'D'Alembert n'a pas lâché prise. L'article *Genève* est pour lui un des actes importants de sa vie' (Naves, p.47, n.65).

[61] Best.D9132, 11 August 1760, my italics. Cf. also the letter to Vernes of 12 January 1758: 'Mr. Dalembert n'est pas homme à se laisser conduire' (Best.D7580).

[62] Naves, p.47. This interpretation would seem to be borne out by mme Denis's letter to Théodore Tronchin of 5 January 1758: 'Mon oncle après avoir lu l'article de Geneve en a été inquiet, trouvant que Dalember l'avoit sité très mal à propos' (Best.D7560). It is of

Voltaire, then, was unaware of the actual form and wording of the article, though he had a good idea of what d'Alembert intended to say in it. Recent experiences with the Genevese clergy had prepared him for the attitude the pastors were to take, though this did not prevent him from redoubling his indignation at what he saw as convincing evidence of their hypocrisy and bad faith.[63] A tone of aggression toward the ministers in general and toward Vernet in particular evident in Voltaire's correspondence from the beginning of the affair[64] demonstrates his new confidence in the government of Geneva. Nor was this optimism misplaced. Maintaining the negative attitude it had shown Vernet a few months earlier, the Council decided on 9 December not to take any firm attitude concerning the article (Naves, p.55). Moreover, the split between the political and ecclesiastical authorities of Geneva was to be further aggravated. The Council expressly ordered that it should not be mentioned in the *Déclaration de la compagnie des pasteurs* which had been drawn up by a special commission (cf. Best. D7500) with the intention of refuting d'Alembert's allegations. Small wonder then, after such a convincing demonstration of clerical isolation, that Voltaire concentrated his former enthusiasm for Geneva as a whole on its enlightened Council, whose views on Calvin and religious disputes in general were so akin to his own! As he observed to Thieriot on 7 December 1757, somewhat exaggerating the extent of the Council's feelings: 'Comptez qu'il est heureux de vivre avec des magistrats qui vous disent, nous détestons l'injustice de nos pères et nous regardons

course possible that, as often happened, the good lady's pen was being directed by Voltaire, but the content of the letter would seem to indicate the contrary. Tronchin is congratulated for the moderating influence he has acquired over Voltaire, and mme Denis sighs long-sufferingly: 'vous ne ferez jamais de cure si singulière que celle de mon Oncle sur cet article, tous ses amis jus qu'à vous y avaient échoué'. Voltaire himself also claimed that d'Alembert had committed an indiscretion by mentioning the *âme atroce* incident, but as it was in his interests not to be thought behind the article, this evidence is much less convincing than mme Denis's letter.

[63] cf. the language of Best.D7512, quoted above p.112. According to Naves (p.49): 'cette violence et cette grossièreté montrent assez l'étendue de la déception: Voltaire en veut d'autant plus aux calvinistes qu'il avait fondé plus d'espoirs sur eux'.

[64] his first uncomplimentary reference to the pastors is in Best.D7490 (2 December), and Voltaire received the article between 24 and 27 December (Best.D7490, commentary, n.1). Theodore Besterman wrongly corrects Naves for allegedly saying 'that Voltaire received vol.vii on 20 or 21 December'. What Naves actually says is that 'le fameux tome vii arrive aussitôt après son [Voltaire's] départ, le 20 ou le 21' (p.37). In note 18 of the same page he points out: 'D'autre part, il quitte Genève avant que le tome vii y soit arrivé, et il ne le recevra à Lausanne que vers le 25.'

avec exécration ceux qui veulent la justifier.'[65] Only Geneva's pastors were relegated to the outer darkness of hypocrisy and intolerance.

Voltaire's angry, indigant reaction to the ministers' denials soon gave way to a more moderate attitude. On 8 January 1758 he assured Théodore Tronchin that d'Alembert would not retract, but since the worthy doctor was 'le secrétaire d'un comité de pères de l'église', he offered him some advice to bring the affair to a peaceful conclusion. Why do the pastors themselves not compose 'un article de Lelio Socini, pour la lettre L du tome prochain?' They could 'expliquer la trinité bravement, et [...] dire qu'ils la croyent, et qu'on s'est trompé à l'article de *Genève*' (Best.D7568). It was obviously not in Voltaire's interest to adopt too intransigent a stand, for this might alienate his friends in the Council who wished the affair to be forgotten quickly. Since d'Alembert had made him 'le Plénipotentiaire de l'Encyclopédie' (Best.D7607, 28 January 1758), it was easy for him to assess the situation in Geneva and to take action accordingly. On 12 January he wrote gaily to Tronchin from Lausanne: 'Il n'y a plus guères d'autodafé, et il y a fort peu de fé. Mon cher philosophe, vous ne serez point brûlé' (Best.D7579). 'Moquez-vous de tout, et soyez gai', he urged d'Alembert on 19 January (Best.D7607). By 23 February he was telling Tronchin's brother François: 'Voylà l'affaire de votre confession de foy finie. Tout le monde doit être content' (Best.D7647). Absolutely convinced that the ministers' hypocrisy was plain for all to see, Voltaire 'se contentera de savourer leur embarras'.[66] Appearances were all-important at Geneva, he assured d'Alembert (Best.D7592, 19 January 1758). After the previous year's furore: 'Je me suis contenté de dire à mes amis que *l'âme atroce* avait été en effet dans Calvin, et n'était point dans ma lettre. Les magistrats et les prêtres sont venus dîner chez moi comme à l'ordinaire.' Voltaire and Tronchin would patch up the affair between them, providing d'Alembert would permit 'seulement les politesses avec ces sociniens honteux'. On 7 March Voltaire reiterated his opinion to d'Alembert that the Genevese pastors were obviously unorthodox, but that no one cared about this any longer: 'Berne, Zurik et la Batavie

[65] the Council was not quite so solidly in Voltaire's camp as he would have wished. Cf. mme d'Epinay's comment to Grimm: 'La grosse nièce trouve fort mauvais que tous les magistrats n'aient pas pris fait et cause pour son oncle' (Best.D7588, January 1758).

[66] Naves, p.49. Moreover, Voltaire was as usual spending the winter at Lausanne, happily engaged in his theatricals: 'Nous avons établi l'empire des plaisirs et les prêtres sont oubliez', he boasted to d'Alembert on 7 March (Best.D7666).

crient que la vénérable compagnie [. . .] est plus que socinienne, mais cela ne fait aucune sensation' (Best.D7666).

What are we to make of Voltaire's allegations? This question is perhaps the most vital of all in understanding his relationship with Switzerland's pastors. If he was correct, we must surely revise the judgement of previous critics who have usually attributed his conduct to a misunderstanding of the nature of liberal Calvinism or, more simply and conveniently, to that congenital weakness, 'la malice voltairienne' (Naves, p.40). On what, if anything, did Voltaire base his charges of hypocrisy, and were they justified?

First and foremost in shaping the *philosophe*'s opinions had naturally been his conversations and contacts with Calvinist pastors. As Voltaire insisted to Elie Bertrand on 27 December 1757, d'Alembert 'ne dit que ce qu'il leur a entendu dire vingt fois' (Best.D7536), and Voltaire himself had had much longer to familiarise himself with the clergy's views. Although it is not possible to regard such subjective judgements as convincing proof, one would be foolish to overlook the fact that during the most bitter phases of his disagreements with the pastors, Voltaire continued to have cordial relations with some of their number. Jacob Vernes's case at the time of the 'Genève' controversy is particularly significant. According to some critics[67] he was distressed by d'Alembert's article. He it was who persuaded Rousseau to compose a reply,[68] and on 12 December 1757 Vernes wrote to the encyclopedist registering his protest: 'Dire que nous n'avons pas beaucoup de foi à l'Ecriture Sainte, c'est dire que nous ne sommes que des fourbes qui annoncent au peuple une parole qu'ils ne croient pas eux-mêmes.'[69] Relations between Vernes and d'Alembert were already rather strained owing to another dispute connected with the *Encyclopédie*.[70] In any case, as

---

[67] cf. Chaponnière, *Voltaire des les calvinistes*, pp.70-71; Pomeau, *La Religion de Voltaire*, p.306, n.140; Spink, *J.-J. Rousseau et Genève*, p.153.

[68] Paul Chaponnière, 'Un pasteur genevois ami de Voltaire: Jacob Vernes', *Rhl* (1929), xxxvi.186.

[69] a copy of this letter was communicated by M. P. L. Bader to Chaponnière (*Voltaire chez les calvinistes*, p.70). Vernes also says that d'Alembert is exposing Geneva's pastors to reproaches from their colleagues abroad and sowing the seeds of division.

[70] cf. Best.D7499, commentary, n.1: 'In a letter to the *Mercure de France* (Paris décembre 1757), pp.97-98, Alembert defends himself against an accusation that he had advocated usury in his article 'Arrérages' in the *Encyclopédie*; this quite unjustified remark had been made anonymously by Vernes in a 'Lettre sur la dissertation suivante [Sur l'amour de l'estime]', *Choix littéraire* (Genève &c 1756), vi.161.

Paul Chaponnière pertinently observes (*Voltaire chez les calvinistes*, p.70):

Jacob Vernes, que sa jeunesse, ses madrigaux galants et son admiration pour Voltaire désignent singulièrement à la défiance du corps ecclésiastique, et qui de ce fait doit se disculper plus vivement, s'indigne, comme le peut faire un homme dont on interprète les idées de manière à lui nuire cruellement.

In other words, d'Alembert's comments were all too correct as far as Vernes was concerned, and the pastor's protests must be interpreted as a prudent gesture he could ill avoid making. The true state of affairs can be seen much more clearly in Vernes's continuing contacts with Voltaire.

On 29 December 1757 Voltaire wrote to him: 'Oui je vous tiens mon ami, et tout jeune que vous êtes je vous fais mon prêtre. Je signe votre profession de foy' (Best.D7540). René Pomeau thinks that Vernes had sent Voltaire his *Catéchisme* as a protest against d'Alembert's article,[71] but this is not at all certain. The *Catéchisme* was sent by 28 October 1757, well before d'Alembert's article even appeared in print (cf. Best.D7437). In any case m. Pomeau himself admits that the *Catéchisme* was a 'pièce peu justificative',[72] and the fact that Voltaire was willing to accept it 'à condition que [. . .] vous n'y changerez jamais rien' (Best.D7540) hardly says much for its orthodoxy. Vernes does seem to have made some form of protest to Voltaire, but what is certain is that his amicable relations with the *philosophe* were not interrupted (cf. below, pp.178-80), despite Chaponnière's claim that after the publication of the *Lettre à d'Alembert* Vernes realised that 'la place d'un pasteur est aux côtés de Rousseau' ('Un pasteur genevois', p.186). All the evidence we have suggests that Vernes seemed to accept without a murmur the many compromising compliments Voltaire paid

[71] 'D'après la lettre de Voltaire, Best.6841 [i.e. Best.D7540], J. Vernes fut ému de l'article *Genève*. Il envoya à Voltaire son *Catéchisme*' (*La Religion de Voltaire*, p.306, n.140).

[72] Pomeau, *La Religion de Voltaire*, p.306, n.140. Finally published in 1774, the *Catéchisme destiné particulièrement à l'usage des jeunes gens qui s'instruisent pour participer à la Ste-Cène* was indeed a 'liberal' work. Addressing himself to members of all Christian denominations, Vernes stresses the social utility of religion, which, he claims, leads us to happiness in this world. Although he accepts the miracles related in the Bible, Vernes's tone is noticeably rationalistic: Christ's nature is inferior to that of God the father, the Holy Ghost is not a person, there is no mention of the trinity, and doubt is cast on the eternity of Hell. Geneva's *Compagnie des pasteurs* caused the work to be examined by a commission, and it was duly censured (see Edouard Dufour, *Jacob Vernes 1728-1791: essai sur sa vie et sa controverse apologétique avec J.-J. Rousseau* (Geneva 1898), pp.30ff.).

him.[73] In the very same letter, for example, Voltaire continues (Best. D7540, my italics):

Or ça carissimé frater in deo *et in Servetto*, êtes vous bien fâché dans le fonds du cœur qu'on dise dans l'enciclopédie que vous pensez comme Origene, et comme deux mille prêtres qui signèrent leur protestation contre le pétulant Atanase? [. . .] Allez allez vous n'êtes pas si fâchez.

The pastor does not seem to have taken these suggestions amiss, for on 12 January 1758 Voltaire assured him: 'Ce n'est pas que je ne pense avec vous que la conduitte de Calvin envers Servet fut une atrocité abominable' (Best.D7580). If Voltaire's assessment of this pastor's views was mistaken, Jacob Vernes appears to have done very little to enlighten the great man.

Among the other Genevese ministers, David Claparède (1727-1807) had also gained the distinction of appearing unorthodox to Voltaire.[74] Likewise Antoine-Jacques Roustan (1734-1808), who had collaborated with Jacob Vernes in writing a history of Geneva highly critical of Calvin's conduct towards Servetus, a work whose publication was forbidden by the *Petit conseil* (Dufour, pp.18-19). Another unorthodox Calvinist well known to Voltaire was Firmin Abauzit (1679-1767), who though not a pastor, was director of the Bibliothèque de Genève and enjoyed considerable prestige in the city.[75] Voltaire had good reason also to doubt the orthodoxy of some Swiss pastors. Both he and d'Alembert can only have been strengthened in their views by the compliant attitude and doctrinal audacity displayed in Polier's articles for the *Encyclopédie* (cf. above, p.125). Not only Polier but also Elie Bertrand had been prepared to help Voltaire after his first attack on Calvin (cf. above, p.131). Although most commentators have argued that Voltaire exaggerated the Swiss clergy's 'liberalism', we must observe that the evidence available in his correspondence provides a not insignificant amount of justification for the views he

[73] cf. for example Best.D7437 and D7509. In the former letter Voltaire praises Vernes's *Catéchisme* for 'la modération avec la quelle elle est écritte'. One could multiply such references from subsequent letters Voltaire wrote to Vernes.
[74] cf. Best.D7509, to Vernes, *c*. 10 December 1757: 'J dubb you and friend Clappared, my bishops', and Best.D7174, quoted above, p.124.
[75] see E.-G. Léonard, *Histoire générale du protestantisme*, iii.58. Abauzit, a native of Uzès, settled in Geneva after the repeal of the Edict of Nantes. Not only Voltaire, but also Newton and Rousseau were loud in their praise of him; cf. Pierre-Maurice Masson, *La Religion de Jean-Jacques Rousseau* (Paris 1916), i.205-207. For Voltaire's contacts with Abauzit see Mina Waterman, 'Voltaire and Firmin Abauzit', *Rr* (1942), xxxiii.236-49.

formed. If anyone was to blame for the 'misunderstanding', it was certainly not Voltaire himself.

Jacob Vernet later attempted to explain d'Alembert's mistaken impression of the pastors' religious views through their reluctance to contradict a famous guest:

Souvent de jeunes Ecclesiastiques, par respect, par timidité, ne contredisent pas formellement des discours hardis & d'un certain ton, quoiqu'ils les dèsaprouvent en eux mêmes; c'est un rôle de patience auquel ils sont souvent exposés: Et alors qu'arrive-t-il? Un incrédule, qui se pique de finesse, croit aisément qu'ils en pensent plus qu'ils n'en disent: malgré l'injustice qu'il y a à prendre un tel silence ou un tel embarras pour une vraye connivence.[76]

This explanation, which might be convincing if one had no other evidence of Genevese unorthodoxy apart from the allegations made by Voltaire and d'Alembert, has been accepted by some critics. But more significant, perhaps, is a letter of 28 December 1757 to d'Alembert from the young teacher Lesage, which proves that some Genevese may have gone farther than indulging in compromising silences:

M. de Voltaire ou d'autres personnes peuvent vous avoir entretenu de ces matières, mais je ne me rappelle pas qu'il en ait été question entre nous. Si cependant votre mémoire, meilleure que la mienne, vous fournissait quelque imprudence de ma part sur cet article, je vous prie de vous ressouvenir aussi que je suis un pauvre diable de laïque qui, n'ayant pas été à portée d'étudier à fond ni les dogmes ni les opinions secrètes de ceux qui les prêchent, ne peut en avoir parlé que sur quelque ouï-dire, de sorte que mon autorité serait jugée d'un poids infiniment petit pour la justification de votre assertion, et que, cependant, la citer en premier serait causer bien des chagrins à un honnête homme auquel on a confié jusqu'à présent une partie de l'instruction de la jeunesse.[77]

Such a comment, if true, is surely at least as telling as the indignant official denials made by the *compagnie des pasteurs*.

In any case, rather than young and indiscreet pastors or laymen, it was Vernet himself who bore the brunt of Voltaire's and d'Alembert's

[76] *Lettres critiques d'un voyageur anglois*, 2nd ed. (Utrecht 1761), letter 5, p.28.
[77] Chaponnière, *Voltaire chez les calvinistes*, p.68. The letter is BPU, MSS. suppl.517, f.151. Lesage had been trying to get some of his scientific work published in the *Encyclopédie* (Florida, pp.197-98). Chaponnière (p.66) also mentions 'certain *petit prêtre* dont parle Cramer, sans le nommer, qui s'en allait lisant par la ville un recueil de facéties voltairiennes'.

joint attack. As I have already indicated (above, p.135), Voltaire considered it a little bizarre for Vernet, whom he regarded as an antitrinitarian, to defend the execution of Servetus. When attacks on the 'Genève' article began, Voltaire and d'Alembert tirelessly drew attention to this paradox. Voltaire's letter of 8 January (Best.D7564) uncompromisingly lists the charges:

Que veulent dire ceux qui vous reprochent d'avoir trahi le secret de Genève? Est ce en secret que Vernet, qui vient d'établir une commission de prêtres contre vous, a imprimé que la révélation *est utile*? est-ce en secret que le mot de *Trinité* ne se trouve pas une fois dans son catéchisme?

These allusions are to Vernet's *Traité de la vérité de la religion chrétienne, tiré du latin de mr J. Alphonse Turretin,* first published in 1730. It had not passed unnoticed by Voltaire that in the second edition, which appeared in 1748, the title of book I was changed to 'de la grande utilité d'une révélation' whereas it had originally read 'De la nécessité et des caractères de la révélation'.[78] Other significant alterations in the direction of 'liberalism' had occurred.[79] It is in fact probable that d'Alembert had been referring specifically to Vernet in one passage of his article: 'aussi quand on les presse sur la nécessité de la révélation, ce dogme si essentiel du Christianisme, plusieurs y substituent le terme d'utilité, qui leur paraît plus doux.'[80]

Jacob Vernet was not the only pastor affected by the allegations of Voltaire and d'Alembert. The *compagnie des pasteurs* had espoused his cause at its meeting of 23 December, but the *Déclaration* which the special commission produced was hailed by Voltaire as entirely justify-

---

[78] Pomeau, *La Religion de Voltaire*, pp.295, 503. Many citizens of Geneva had also noticed this. Florida (p.153) explains that Vernet 'had made the change to meet the professional criticism of several friends and theologians who had pointed out that to proclaim the necessity of revelation logically removed the entire point of the *Traité* which was to demonstrate the truth and superiority of Christianity'. For those too faint-hearted to tackle Vernet's long and rather verbose treatise, Florida (pp.147-55) gives a useful summary, showing the differences between the various editions.

[79] 'le chapitre sur le "Mystère de la Trinité" disparaît. Le Christ n'est ni consubstantiel ni coéternel au Père; le Saint-Esprit n'est pas une personne, mais la force surnaturelle de Dieu' (Pomeau, *La Religion de Voltaire*, p.295).

[80] Lough, *The Encyclopédie*, p.95. Vernet later admitted that he was the pastor concerned, but declared that the change of wording was of no importance: 'y auroit-il la moindre équité, la moindre pudeur, à prétendre qu'un Ecrivain qui établit si fortement la vérité & l'excellence du Christianisme, & le besoin que nous avions d'un tel secours bien supérieur à tous les efforts de la sagesse Payenne, soit un écrivain favorable au Déisme?' (*Lettres critiques d'un voyageur anglois*, 3rd ed. (Copenhagen [Geneva] 1766), i.221).

ing d'Alembert's remarks (Best.D7652, 25 February 1758). Moreover, the caution and evident embarrassment of the pastors, and the lack of a downright statement of orthodox Calvinist or Protestant beliefs in the document they produced, provided a fertile ground for Voltaire's witticisms. It will be sufficient to quote a small example of the *Déclaration* to understand his glee (quoted in Vernet, *Lettres critiques*, 2nd ed., between letters 3 and 4, p.43):

le terme de *respect pour* JESUS-CHRIST & *pour l'Ecriture,* nous paroissant de beaucoup trop foible, ou trop équivoque, pour exprimer la nature & l'étenduë de nos sentiments à cet égard; nous disons que c'est avec Foi, avec une vénération religieuse, avec une entiére soumission d'esprit & de cœur, qu'il faut écouter ce Divin Maître & le Saint Esprit parlant dans les Ecritures [. . .], ce qui donne à notre Religion un principe plus sûr, plus relevé, & bien plus d'étenduë, bien plus d'efficace; en un mot, un tout autre caractère que celui sous lequel on s'est plu à la dépeindre.

The pastors' *Déclaration* has often been regarded as unsatisfactory and inadequate, both at the time of its composition and by subsequent critics.[81] As d'Alembert observed before receiving the document, all the pastors of Geneva had to do to establish their good faith and prove their orthodoxy was to sign 'cette petite profession de foi de deux lignes: Je soussigné crois comme article de foi, que les peines de l'enfer sont éternelles, & que Jésus-christ est dieu, égal en tout à son père.'[82]

This evident failure to make an unequivocal statement on the question of the trinity and eternal damnation tends to suggest that Voltaire and d'Alembert had come embarrasingly close to the truth in their evaluation of the pastors' religious position. Why otherwise should the *compagnie des pasteurs* have been unable to make a statement couched in more orthodox terms, one which would have both silenced their enemies and satisfied their co-religionists abroad? It is difficult to avoid the conclusion that Voltaire and d'Alembert could not have made such

[81] cf. the anonymous 'Lettre à monsieur*** au sujet de l'Extrait des registres de la vénérable compagnie des pasteurs et professeurs de l'Eglise et de l'Académie de Genève, inséré dans le Journal des Sçavans, édition de Hollande, p.400 et 521', *Bibliothèque impartiale* (1758), part three (May-June), xvii.366-82. Vuilleumier (iv.240) states quite clearly that 'cette déclaration fut jugée assez généralement faible et peu concluante à cause de ses ambiguïtés et de ses réticences'. Spink's position is more complex: he says (p.155) that the pastors were right to protest against being called Sociniens, but also comments (p.158): 'Il faut avouer que les pasteurs donnaient toute prise à l'accusation [of deism].'

[82] Best.D7607, d'Alembert to Voltaire, 28 January 1758. He made a similar proposal on 8 February (Best.D7624).

wounding allegations had the ground not been very well prepared. One must of course tread carefully in attempting to assess the religious beliefs of any individual or group, and theological developments in the twentieth century have made it even more difficult for us to say with any certainty that a refusal to accept one or other of the tenets of traditional orthodoxy prevents a man from legitimately calling himself a Christian. For the purposes of this study some standard, however arbitrary, would serve as a useful guideline in these delicate matters. The Vincentian canon[83] might seem a reasonable choice, but even here it could prove impossible to achieve agreement about what has always been believed by the Church. In the last analysis all one can do is to survey briefly the facts relating to the Genevese Church in the eighteenth century, indicate how far, if at all, its practices and beliefs differed from those of orthodox Calvinism, and finally attempt to say whether in view of this evidence, Voltaire and d'Alembert were justified according to their own lights in making the accusations they did.

From the evidence which is available we can say with a great deal of certainty that the laity's conduct, even at the beginning of the eighteenth century, would have appeared scandalous not merely to Calvin but to most normal churchgoers of our own times. Although services were still well attended, they began later than in earlier years and many people arrived only for the sermon, neglecting the reading of the scriptures which preceded it. Pierre-Maurice Masson explains:

> on fume durant le chant des psaumes; au fond du temple, c'est un va-et-vient perpétuel de gamins, qui entrent un instant pour échapper à la ronde de police et qui retournent bientôt continuer leur tapage sur la place[84]

None of this may seem very terrible, but a significant change in the rôle and beliefs of the clergy was also taking place: in 1725 the Venerable Company asked that contentious matters of dogma should not be treated 'dans les chaires' (Masson, i.198), again, on the face of it, rather a surprising development in the city which had for so long symbolised Protestant opposition to Rome and whose doctrinal edifice had been almost as impressive as that of the Catholic Church. Why were Calvinist ministers apparently losing interest in dogma?

---

[83] '*quod ubique, quod semper, quod ab omnibus creditum est* [. . .] By this triple test of œcumenicity, antiquity, and consent, the Church is able to differentiate between true and false traditions' (*Oxford dictionary of the Christian Church* (1958), *s.v.* 'Vincentian Canon').

[84] *La Religion de Jean-Jacques Rousseau*, i.10.

Calvinism in the seventeenth century had been plagued with theological disputes and had suffered generally from a growing intellectualism.[85] Toward the end of the century a reaction 'against this situation took place in Switzerland. Prominent in the movement was Turretini, whom I have had occasion to mention earlier (above, p.117) in connection with Delattre's article 'Voltaire and the ministers of Geneva'. Turretini wished essentially to simplify Christianity and to make it more accessible to the ordinary believer. Under his guidance the *Formula consensus* (cf. above, p.128) was abandoned in 1706, other Protestant denominations were allowed to hold services in Geneva, and ecumenism was encouraged.[86] Nor was Turretini alone in his experiments. Samuel Werenfels (1657-1740), who became professor of theology at Bâle, also preached the uselessness of dogmatic disputes, favoured toleration and ecumenism, even having a good word for Catholics. At Neuchâtel Osterwald (1663-1747) advocated similar measures, exerting great influence since he held the position of 'pasteur en tête' from 1696 onwards. Henri Vuilleumier coined the term 'liberal orthodoxy' to describe the teaching of these Calvinist theologians already so far from the position held by their great predecessor, yet still recognisably belonging to the mainstream traditions of Christianity.[87]

On the one hand it is obvious that the *triumvirat helvétique* had travelled some considerable way on the road leading to natural religion and *philosophie*: according to Vuilleumier (iii.568), in Turretini's publications

> se révèle la tendance à émousser les angles du dogme calviniste, à rationaliser et à moraliser la religion chrétienne, en faisant appel en première ligne au *lumen naturale*, à la raison, ou plutôt au sens commun, comme il préférait dire 'de peur d'effaroucher les gens', et à laisser un peu dans l'ombre ce qu'on

---

[85] cf. E.-G. Léonard, *Histoire du protestantisme* (Paris 1960), pp.79, 82; *Histoire générale du protestantisme*, ii.317 ff, 336 ff.

[86] see Vuilleumier, *Histoire de l'église réformée*, iii.566-67. Ironically enough, Turretini's father had been one of the promoters of the *Formula consensus*.

[87] p.552. Vuilleumier's definition of liberal orthodoxy is worth quoting: according to him 'elle [...] était libérale et pouvait passer pour progressive, non seulement en ce qu'elle revendiquait la liberté de conscience et tendait au rapprochement entre les diverses confessions protestantes, mais par le fait qu'elle mettait au premier plan de la religion du Christ les vérités rationnelles et morales, qu'elle insistait sur la parenté de l'Evangile avec la religion dite naturelle et avec la morale philosophique, tandis qu'elle reléguait au second plan les éléments surnaturels du dogme, et enfin qu'elle adoptait les résultats avérés de l'exégèse et de la critique biblique du temps'.

était convenu d'appeler, les mystères de l'Evangile, c'est-à-dire les vérités révelées.

Turretini goes even further in his *Pensées sur la religion*: 'La religion bien entendue se confond avec la loi de la nature; la religion est une philosophie, la meilleure des philosophies, qui seule nous conduit à la vraie félicité' (Masson, i.199). Osterwald's *Traité des sources de la corruption qui règne aujourd'huy parmi les Chrestiens* (1700) should also have pleased Voltaire, for in it the theologian expressed a belief that the Reformation had been a beneficial event but was incomplete, and also made clear that he liked Calvin least of all the Reformers (Vuilleumier, iii.561).[88]

Yet despite these apparent concessions to the *esprit du siècle*, Protestant historians seem in no doubt that Turretini, Werenfels and Osterwald were genuine Christians.[89] Their tactics may be criticised, but their good faith is not put in question. If one accepts Delattre's theory of cycles (cf. above, p.117), these theologians belonged to a non-dogmatic phase of Protestantism. It would seem that Jean Barbeyrac (1674-1744), though neither a pastor nor a theologian, was in a similar position. This friend of Turretini attracted Voltaire's attention to the extent that one of the *Lettres à s. a. mgr le prince de***** was devoted to him. What appealed particularly to Voltaire was Barbeyrac's defence of natural morality, toleration and the virtue of pagans, as well as his criticism of the fathers of the Church (cf. *Mélanges*, pp.1200-201). He defended himself against accusations that he wished to destroy Christianity, explains Voltaire: 'mais [...] on voit bien que Barbeyrac est plutôt le zélé partisan de la justice éternelle et de la loi naturelle donnée de Dieu aux hommes que l'adorateur des saints mystères du christianisme' (p.1201). Nonetheless, there appears to be evidence that Barbeyrac did not reject the Christian revelation but that he sought to find a happy medium between believing everything and believing nothing.[90] In short he was a 'liberal' Protestant similar to the

[88] cf. also Léonard, *Histoire générale*, iii.53.

[89] cf. Masson, i.199: 'Ce serait un lourd contresens de prendre pour un rationaliste, ou un déiste déguisé, Jean-Alphonse Turretin: il est chrétien, chrétien huguenot.' Cf. also Vuilleumier's comment on Osterwald: 'Il n'y a pas de doute; sa piété et sa foi personnelles valaient mieux que sa théologie' (iii.561).

[90] for information on Barbeyrac's life and beliefs see Philippe Meylan, *Jean Barbeyrac et les débuts de l'enseignement du droit dans l'ancienne Académie de Lausanne* (Lausanne 1938).

English latitudinarians and in fact translated Tillotson's *Sermons*.[91] Voltaire would seem nearer the truth in his assessment of Marie Huber (*Mélanges*, p.1199): 'la religion essentielle à l'homme', according to her book of the same title,

doit être de tous les temps, de tous les lieux et de tous les esprits. Tout ce qui est mystère est au-dessus de l'homme, et n'est pas fait pour lui; la pratique des vertus ne peut avoir aucun rapport avec le dogme. La religion essentielle à l'homme est dans ce qu'on doit faire, et non dans ce qu'on ne peut comprendre.

Marie Huber's religious beliefs were clearly deistic rather than Christian, and the pastors of Switzerland reacted against her teaching.[92] Yet many of them were in an ambiguous position, for if they rejected some of her ideas they shared many others. Belief in predestination had been openly abandoned – shortly after the publication of *Emile*, Vernes preached three sermons at Geneva on 'la droiture originelle de l'homme', speaking of the innate goodness of man in a way sometimes reminiscent of Rousseau (Masson, i.275). Speculative questions about the deity were avoided as much as possible, and belief in the trinity appears to have waned generally among theologians. At any rate, it is quite clear from the works of both Vernet and Vernes that neither regarded Jesus Christ as the equal of God the father, and that the Holy Spirit was no longer considered as a different 'person' or 'hypostasis' of the divine being, merely as a metaphorical way of referring to his wisdom or his action on men.[93] Justification was sought in the scriptures, where there is no mention of the term 'trinity', and where certain passages, while implying that Christ was indeed a divine being, would seem to make his status inferior to that of God the father.[94] Although claimed by Genevese

[91] it is interesting to note that Voltaire mentioned Tillotson with approval on several occasions: cf. *Dieu et les honmes*, M.xxviii.243; also *Mélanges*, pp.779, 845, 1046, 1266.

[92] Masson, i.207, n.4; 209. See A. Ruchat, *Examen de l'origénisme, ou réponse à un livre intitulé 'Sentimens . . . sur l'état des âmes séparées des corps'* (Lausanne 1733); Fr. de Roches, *Défense du christianisme contre un ouvrage intitulé 'Lettres sur la religion essentielle à l'homme'* (Geneva 1740); D. R. Boullier, *Lettres sur les vrais principes de la religion, où l'on examine un livre intitulé: 'La Religion essentielle à l'homme'* (Amsterdam 1741).

[93] cf. above, p.141, n.72 and p.144, n.79; Vernes, *Catéchisme*, 1806 edition, p.71: 'Que faut-il entendre par le Saint-Esprit, dont il est parlé dans le Symbole? – Dieu lui-même, modèle et source de toute sainteté, favorisant d'une lumière surnaturelle les hommes privilégiés qu'il avoit choisis, en divers temps, pour organes de sa sapience éternelle, et nous aidant aussi efficacement à travailler à l'œuvre de notre salut.'

[94] cf. 1 Corinthians xv.24-29, Philippians ii.5-11. The term 'trinity' was first used by Tertullian (*Encyclopaedia of religion and ethics*, ed. Hastings, *s.v.* 'Trinity'). I wish to thank mr J. Gillespie and the rev. A. W. Brown for their helpful comments in this connection.

theologians to be unassailably biblical, this position was essentially ambiguous. Indeed, had not the early Church itself found this, as it struggled to define the relationship between the persons of the godhead in that long discussion of texts and traditions which led finally to the doctrine of the trinity being elaborated?[95] Be that as it may, we can now surely appreciate the terms used in the *Déclaration* of the *compagnie des pasteurs*, at the same time expressing the deepest respect and religious veneration for Jesus, yet satisfying neither those Protestants still attached to orthodox teaching on the trinity, nor Voltaire and d'Alembert, who clearly sensed that an important step on the road away from a fundamental Christian and Protestant tradition had been taken.

Despite these developments, we must not make the mistake of classifying all the members of the clergy as 'liberal' or dechristianised: there were always at least some evangelically-minded men who protested sincerely against the deist position.[96] One of the most influential figures in the orthodox camp was in fact a layman, the celebrated naturalist Charles Bonnet.[97] But it is not unfair to say that, by the second half of the eighteenth century, Swiss Protestantism had reached a parting of the ways. With hindsight, we can perceive the beginnings of a split which has become more or less permanent in the ranks of Protestant Christians. On the one hand were the traditionalists, those orthodox believers who intended to maintain the creed of their denomination more or less intact against the attacks of 'liberal' or 'modern' elements: revitalised and brought into a position of prominence by the evangelical revival of the 1820s and 1830s, this element was to exercise great influence throughout the nineteenth century, and historical studies by its members necessarily took a dim view of eighteenth-century rationalist theologians, considered by the evangelicals to be traitors against Christianity.[98] But these 'traitors', the so-called

---

[95] cf. Henry Chadwick, *The Early Church* (London 1967), pp.77, 85-90, 114, 130, 141, 192-212, 235-36.

[96] Léon Maury (*Le Réveil religieux dans l'église réformée à Genève et en France*, p.17) mentions the following men: Bénédict Pictet (1655-1724), Antoine Maurice (1716-1795), Francillon (1731-1796), and belonging to a slightly later generation: Demellayer, Dejoux, Dutoit, Cellérier, Moulinié, and Peschier.

[97] cf. Léonard, *Histoire générale du protestantisme*, iii.58-59. Voltaire's opinion of Bonnet was far from enthusiastic: cf. Best.D16039.

[98] cf. above, p.115; Vallette, *L'Eglise de Genève à la fin du XVIIIe siècle* (Geneva 1892), p.5.

'liberals', men like Vernet and Vernes, have not always been judged so harshly.[99] From their ranks sprang those theologians who were later to adopt the findings of the German school of biblical scholarship, and who tried to adapt the Christian faith to the times in which it found itself, not turning their backs on the modern world, but trying to use its discoveries for the benefit of the Christian faith, which was itself necessarily transformed to a certain extent by this process.

Yet their very willingness to accept certain assumptions of eighteenth-century philosophy created difficulties for the Genevese pastors themselves, and even more for those who would seek to state with any certainty what exactly was their relationship to the historical tradition of Christianity. Their connections with deism on many points are unquestionable. How indeed could one draw a distinguishing line between the two? Was respect for Jesus Christ and the scriptures enough to entitle one to the name 'Christian'? The pastors of Geneva obviously thought not, or considered it prudent to reject the possibility. But how many orthodox or traditional beliefs could be jettisoned or 'interpreted' rationally before the borderline between liberal Christianity and deism was crossed? In the last analysis, it would seem that very little divided the two in many cases,[100] and that the real difference was in the opinion held about the Christian religion itself, some, like Voltaire, seeing in it the source of countless miseries for the human race,[101] others, like the Genevese pastors, who appreciated the tradition in which they had been brought up, regarding it as the basis or framework for an enlightened, socially beneficial religion which would still use recognisably Christian imagery and terminology (cf. below, pp.193 ff.).

It would then in any case have been difficult for men like Vernet and Vernes to make their exact position clear. They wished to abandon many fundamental beliefs of Calvinist orthodoxy, to make the Christian religion both more reasonable and more biblical (indeed they claimed that the two aims were synonymous)[102] yet without at the same

[99] cf. Cellérier, *L'Académie de Genève*, p.51; Dufour, p.18.

[100] one is tempted, for example, to compare the philosophical clergyman Dr Freind of *Histoire de Jenni* (see Brumfitt and Davis edition, pp.65-71) with pastors like Vernes and Allamand: for a closer study of these men and their relations with Voltaire, see below, pp.177-83, 189-98.

[101] cf., for example, his comments in the *Examen important de milord Bolingbroke* and *Dieu et les hommes*.

[102] cf. Vernet, *Lettres critiques*, 3rd ed., i.249-50.

time adopting all the philosophical assumptions of a Voltaire, above all
without appearing to share his withering scorn for nearly all forms of
organised Christianity. Yet difficult though this task was, it was surely
not impossible. The pastors could at least have attempted it. What
they actually did was quite different. In their fear of appearing to leave
the mainstream of Christian tradition, they concentrated on denying
those theological developments which in some cases they had undeniably
accepted. And the crux of the problem would thus seem to be why the
Genevese pastors clung, officially at least, to their outdated traditions
and functions, for despite their changing beliefs, Calvin's successors
attempted to maintain the spirit of his strict morality:

Comme jadis, et comme si le siècle n'avait pas marché, il [the clergy] réprime
impitoyablement les indisciplines de l'esprit et les défaillances de la chair,
proscrit, sans se lasser, cartes, danses, romans, spectacles, tous les plaisirs de
l'oisiveté, toutes les vanités du luxe; et, à force d'admonestations, de censures
grièves, de suspensions de la Sainte-Cène, souvent même de carcan ou de
prison, il sauvegarde pour quelque temps encore, sinon la stricte discipline
calviniste, du moins les principes de cette discipline.[103]

It is only too obvious how hypocritical such a conduct must have
seemed to Voltaire or indeed to any deist well informed about the
Genevese pastors' doctrinal views; indeed their position seems difficult
to defend whatever one's own religious beliefs may be. Turretini and
his colleagues clearly admitted the changes they were introducing
into traditional Calvinism. Part of Jean Barbeyrac's thought might be
used as propaganda by Voltaire, but Barbeyrac did not seek to deny
these elements, rather he frankly acknowledged what aspects of orthodoxy he found unacceptable, while claiming nonetheless that other
features of Christianity were worth preserving. Marie Huber was
plainly no longer inside the Christian fold. But the real views held by
many Genevese pastors of the 1750s and 1760s are much more difficult
to fathom.[104] Admittedly, their position under attack by a famous

[103] Masson, i.15. Masson's reaction to this priestly interference is one of approval:
'Conscience souveraine de la nation, le Vénérable Consistoire s'obstine dans son idéal
avec une ténacité qui l'honore.'

[104] 'ils ne savent plus très exactement, ou, du moins, ne disent plus très précisément, ce
qu'ils croient et ce qu'ils ne croient pas. Peut-être, au dedans d'eux-mêmes, se font-ils des
aveux qu'ils n'osent formuler, et que le sentiment de leur responsabilité, la crainte de
troubler "les bonnes âmes", arrêteront toujours sur leurs lèvres' (Masson, *La Religion de
J. J. Rousseau*, i.203-204).

deist was unpleasant and awkward to defend, but would it not have been strengthened by clearly indicating how their beliefs had evolved? In the long run, would they not have benefited from confessing frankly that they no longer approved of Calvin's actions, that they no longer believed Jesus Christ to be equal to God the father, and that eternal damnation no longer appeared to them worthy of the divinity?

But no Genevese pastor, however unorthodox his views actually were, made such a statement. There were no dissenting voices when the *Déclaration* refuting d'Alembert's article was drawn up. On the contrary, all allegations of heterodoxy were rejected, although as things turned out, the pastors' denials sounded hollow, not only to their enemies but to other Protestants as well, and it is difficult to avoid believing that some of them at least clung to their conservative image and practices out of a mixture of traditionalism and self-interest. René Pomeau (p.298) charitably describes their obstinacy as an 'attachement sentimental à la foi chrétienne qui les empêche d'aller jusqu'au bout de leur pensée'. 'Attachement sentimental' there no doubt was, though, as we have seen, this did not necessarily prevent the development of new doctrinal positions, nor can it be assumed that the internal logic of their opinions would necessarily have led the 'liberal' Genevese pastors to a complete identity of views with deists like Voltaire. In the case of some pastors, it is also difficult to avoid the conclusion that the claims of sentiment were reinforced by an attachment to the position of prestige and material well-being enjoyed by the pastoral *corps*, advantages which any fundamental change of the status quo and re-laxation of Calvinist restrictions might threaten. But that allegations concerning the unorthodoxy of many pastors were not unfounded is clear from their *Déclaration*, from their theological and other works, and from the terms employed in Voltaire's correspondence with pastors such as Vernes and Moultou.[105] Indeed, some pastors seem to have practiced a Voltairean distinction between the religion they taught and what they actually believed themselves. These lessons were not wasted on the *philosophe*. In later works propounding an Erastian doctrine for the clergy he was careful to stress that the Protestant clergy had

---

[105] cf. below, pp.178 ff. Naves (pp.146-48) is convinced of the accuracy of allegations that many Genevese pastors were unorthodox, especially as regards Vernet. He quotes the following extract from Du Pan's letter of 7 January 1758 to Freudenreich: 'Nos ministres n'ont encore rien fait pour justifier leur créance. Ils feraient peut-être prudemment de ne rien dire' (p.147, n.157).

least to lose in any further reform of religion and that its material interests would be safeguarded.[106] But the Calvinist pastors of Geneva as a body were now thoroughly discredited in his eyes, and any thought of an alliance with them was abandoned, at least for the time being.

Nonetheless, despite the obvious justification of at least some of Voltaire's allegations, many literary critics, in describing the situation, seem to have imitated the hair-splitting skill of the pastors' *Déclaration*. While most have agreed that Geneva's clergy were not completely orthodox, few have admitted unequivocally that Voltaire was correct in his opinion or have found it necessary to criticise the pastors' hypocrisy, although similar faults in Voltaire himself are ruthlessly exposed. Grimsley, for example (p.55), states quite categorically that Voltaire had 'profoundly miscalculated the real nature of the Genevan position'. On the other hand Raymond Naves clearly smells a rat: 'le Conseil n'est pas très dévoué pour défendre l'Eglise de Genève; ne se sent-il pas qualifié? Ou connaît-il trop bien les *variations* de sa doctrine?' (p.35). But instead of drawing the inevitable conclusion, he quotes with approval Chaponnière's explanation of the situation: 'Voltaire se fait des illusions sur les pasteurs; il semble avoir vu en eux des alliés dans l'œuvre à laquelle il se sentait pressé de mettre la main' (p.59). Not a word as to why, if they were indeed unorthodox, the pastors were unwilling to be allies of Voltaire. René Pomeau, on the contrary, claims (p.293) that 'A Genève et à Lausanne, on crut d'abord que Voltaire arrivait en allié.' He admits that 'la ligne de démarcation entre le déisme philosophique et la religion rationaliste n'est pas facile à tracer', yet he seems to conclude that Voltaire was nonetheless given 'une idée fausse du calvinisme genevois' (by Vernet), and, although he underlines the Socinian ideas of those pastors who had close contacts with Voltaire, Pomeau never states categorically that Voltaire was correct or justified in his allegations.[107] The reason for these hesitations is not difficult to find. Naves, Pomeau and Delattre appear to have based their accounts largely on critics like Gaberel and Chaponnière, who either refused to admit the presence of unorthodoxy among the Genevese pastors or implied that Voltaire had misunderstood the real impact of recent theological developments in the city. Had they relied more on other

---

[106] cf. esp. *Dieu et les hommes*, M.xxviii.243.

[107] the nearest he comes to it is in the following passages: 'se trompait-il tellement?' (*La Religion de Voltaire*, p.293); 'Vernet se rendait-il compte qu'il recommandait à son correspondant une double doctrine non dénuée d'hypocrisie' (p.296).

Protestant historians like Benoît and Léonard, their judgement of the 'sociniens honteux' might have been somewhat harsher and a great deal more favourable to Voltaire.

The publication of d'Alembert's article was a watershed in Voltaire's relations with the pastors of Geneva. He was now convinced that they were unorthodox – denials only served to demonstrate their hypocrisy. Moreover, although heretics themselves, they were intolerant and would persecute their opponents given half the chance. But times had changed for the better in Geneva, and the Council's enlightened attitude meant that religious persecution on the grand scale could no longer occur there. This was indeed fortunate, for the city's pastors were just the same as priests the world over, and a truthful *philosophe* was always fair game for their hypocrisy (M.i.54):

Il y avait là [in the doctrinal evolution of Calvinist theology at Geneva] de quoi se couper la gorge, allumer les bûchers, faire des Saint-Barthélemy; cependant on ne s'est pas même dit d'injures, tant les mœurs sont changées. Il n'y a que moi à qui un de ces prédicants en ait dit, parce que j'avais osé avancer que le Picard Calvin était un esprit dur qui avait fait brûler Servet fort mal à propos. Admirez, je vous prie, les contradictions de ce monde: voilà des gens qui sont presque ouvertement sectateurs de ce Servet, et qui m'injurient pour avoir trouvé mauvais que Calvin l'ait fait brûler à petit feu avec des fagots verts.

Nor was Voltaire to change his mind about the pastors of Geneva. As late as 1776 he still implied that they had been hypocritical, as we see from the *Commentaire historique sur les œuvres de l'auteur de la Henriade*, when he mentions the notorious letter to Thieriot (M.i.98):

Une de ses lettres, dans laquelle il disait que le Picard Jean Chauvin, dit Calvin, assassin véritable de Servet, *avait une âme atroce*, ayant été rendue publique par une indiscrétion trop ordinaire, quelques cafards s'irritèrent ou feignirent de s'irriter de ces paroles.

In the short term, Voltaire's reaction to the events which had taken place was to snap his fingers at the pastors now that he was sure of the government's benevolent neutrality. On about 25 March 1758 he told d'Alembert: 'Au reste on peut fort bien n'être pas l'intime ami de ces messieurs et vivre tout doucement' (Best.D7695). As yet this complete break with the clergy was confined to Geneva, but Voltaire was soon to find that it would be necessary to forgo the friendship of the pastors of Lausanne also.

Chapter 5

v. *Voltaire and The Saurin affair*[108]

In January or February 1757 Voltaire wrote to Bernard-Joseph Saurin that he understood how important it was to clear the name of the latter's father: 'Il y a encore, à la vérité, quelques vieillards [...] qui sont bien rétifs; mais j'espère les faire taire' (Best.D7137). Saurin was secretary to the prince de Conti and numbered among the *philosophes* (Naves, p.30). His father, the Protestant pastor Joseph Saurin,[109] had fled from France to Switzerland just before the repeal of the Edict of Nantes. Despite the fact that he was well received and appointed minister of Bercher, Saurin returned to France in 1681 and abjured his Protestant faith. This ex-pastor subsequently became a mathematician of some note and a member of the Royal Academy of Sciences. But he also made enemies, notably the poet Jean-Baptiste Rousseau, for Saurin had become involved in the notorious *affaire des couplets*. Saurin's enemies made enquiries about the circumstances of his departure from Switzerland, and in April 1736 (the year before Saurin's death), the *Journal helvétique* (often known as the *Mercure suisse*) printed a letter, allegedly written by Saurin to his friend Gonon, pastor at Morges. This was a letter of confession which, if genuine, proved that Saurin had been guilty of a series of petty thefts and had left Switzerland under a cloud. The letter was later reprinted several times, achieving considerable currency among the educated public in France and elsewhere. Moreover, although Voltaire appears to have had great admiration for Saurin, the article on La Motte which he wrote for the *Catalogue des écrivains* of the *Siècle de Louis XIV* tended to renew suspicions about Saurin's part in the *affaire des couplets* (Naves, p.30). Voltaire attempted to correct this impression in an article published in the *Bibliothèque impartiale* (Leyden, January-February 1753),[110] but Saurin's son asked Voltaire to re-habilitate his father in a more positive way. It was the manner in which Voltaire set about this task which ruined the good relations he had succeeded in cultivating and maintaining with the pastors of Lausanne.

[108] cf. also my article 'Voltaire et l'affaire Saurin', *Dix-huitième siècle* (1978), x.417-33.

[109] my information on Saurin's life is taken mainly from the relevant articles in the *Supplément au dictionnaire historique, géographique, généalogique, etc., des éditions de Basle de 1732 et 1733* of Moréri's *Grand dictionnaire historique* (Basle 1737-1745), and in Jacques-Georges Chauffepié, *Nouveau dictionnaire historique et critique, pour servir de supplément ou de continuation au Dictionnaire historique et critique de Pierre Bayle* (Amsterdam, The Hague 1750-1756), 4 vols.

[110] this was a reply to Haller, who had renewed allegations about Saurin's guilt (Roulet, p.105).

First of all Voltaire obtained from Polier de Bottens and from two other Lausanne pastors, Abraham de Crousaz and Daniel Pavillard, a signed certificate to the effect that 'ils n'ont jamais vu l'original de cette prétendue lettre de Saurin, ni connu personne qui l'eût vue, ni ouï dire qu'elle eût été adressée à aucun pasteur du pays de Vaud, et qu'ils ne peuvent qu'improuver l'usage qu'on a fait de cette pièce' (*Oh*, p.1207). This he inserted at the end of an article on Joseph Saurin in the *Catalogue des écrivains* of the 1757 revised Cramer edition of the *Siècle de Louis XIV*.[111] But Voltaire could not resist the chance to make 'philosophic' propaganda. Not only did he make light of the accusations levelled against the former pastor, implying that they were due to ill-feeling on the part of the Protestants and to Rousseau's attempts to blacken his enemy's character,[112] he also contrived to make Saurin appear in the guise of a *philosophe*, indifferent to the follies of Protestants and Catholics alike. Saurin died

en philosophe intrépide qui connaissait le néant de toutes les choses de ce monde, et plein d'un profond mépris pour tous ces vains préjugés, pour toutes ces disputes, pour ces opinions erronées, qui surchargent d'un nouveau poids les malheurs innombrables de la vie humaine.

These claims were not allowed to pass without protest. In October 1758 the *Mercure suisse* published an anonymous letter written at Vevey on 23 September 1758.[113] The letter contained a fierce attack on Voltaire's article and on the character he had attributed to Saurin, asserting that the declaration signed by three Lausanne pastors was either false or had been obtained under false pretences. In any case, there were still eye-witnesses that a letter from Saurin admitting his guilt had existed. If the pastors in question did sign the declaration, they cannot have realised Voltaire's intentions. Indeed, the writer showed his scorn for the *philosophe* and what he represented in no uncertain terms. It also put the three pastors in a very unenviable position. Voltaire himself replied to the anonymous letter in his *Réfutation d'un*

---

[111] cf. *Oh*, pp.1732-33. The original article on Saurin, written in 1756, contained only six lines.

[112] here Voltaire was following the example set by Fontenelle and by Saurin himself (Chauffepié, p.187, n.E).

[113] 'A mrs les éditeurs, à l'occasion d'un article concernant Saurin, inséré dans les œuvres de mr D. V.', *Journal helvétique* (Neuchâtel, October 1758), pp.361-82; Best. D7873.

écrit anonyme, dated 15 November 1758, which appeared in the December number of the *Journal helvétique*.[114] Significantly enough, Voltaire somewhat changed his position, not so much defending the character of Saurin as attempting to show that the accusations against him should not be repeated in view of the harm this might cause his family (cf. below, p.164, n.129).

It is at this point that the facts become somewhat hazy. A tradition has grown up among critics that Voltaire prevented the truth being known through a personal intervention of a particularly unphilosophical nature. Roulet's version of the incident, one of the most recent, follows the received account faithfully (p.109):

Emue de la tournure que prenait toute l'affaire, la compagnie des pasteurs de Lausanne avait exigé qu'on lui remît le registre de la classe des pasteurs d'Yverdon, afin de prendre connaissance de la copie du procès-verbal de l'instruction commencée contre l'ex-ministre. C'était peine perdue. On eut beau chercher. La pièce compromettante avait disparu. Comme le registre était confié au même Polier qui n'avait pas craint de se prêter aux manigances du philosophe, de graves soupçons pèsent sur Voltaire qui, dit-on, aurait secrètement arraché le feuillet compromettant.

Perey and Maugras,[115] Chaponnière (p.88), Heinrich Dübi[116] and Gaberel (p.12) also make these accusations, clearly implying that Voltaire was guilty, though without producing the slightest real evidence to prove their case. Desnoiresterres too (v.309) recounts the same allegations, but is very doubtful as to their veracity, as is also Naves (p.31, n.43): 'tout cela a bien l'air d'un roman', he remarks judiciously, and we shall see that his scepticism is justified. On investigation, one finds that the source of these accounts alleging Voltaire's misconduct is a book by Juste Olivier, *Voltaire à Lausanne* (Lausanne 1842). Olivier introduces his account of the incident[117] with the following comment: 'Voici encore, sur le séjour de Voltaire à Lausanne, ce que M. le doyen Bridel m'a conté comme un fait connu et encore public de son temps.'

---

[114] 1758, part 3, pp.617-25. At the end of Voltaire's *Réfutation*, the editors of the *Mercure* declared 'ne vouloir rien insérer dans la suite sur cette matière' (p.625).

[115] *La Vie intime de Voltaire aux Délices et à Ferney (1754-1778), d'après des lettres et des documents inédits* (Paris 1885), pp.235-36.

[116] 'Der Briefwechsel zwischen Voltaire und Haller im Jahre 1759', *Archiv für Studium der neureren Sprachen und Literaturen* (1910), cxxiii.361.

[117] this occurs at the end of the book in three unnumbered pages entitled: 'Note sur le théâtre et la société de Lausanne'.

This admission in itself surely devalues, to a great extent, the subsequent revelation, for Olivier published his study in 1842. The incident described allegedly occurred in 1758. Even allowing that 'M. le doyen Bridel' was quite an old gentleman when Olivier interviewed him, it is difficult to attach much importance to a rather suspect oral account made some fifty or sixty years after the event.

In any case, what exactly was the register which was supposed to be in Polier's keeping? Roulet speaks of the 'registre de la classe des pasteurs d'Yverdon', and there is indeed a gap covering 1689-1690 (the time when Saurin's letter was allegedly written). But the records for many other years are also missing, an omission explained on page nine of the register: 'Icy sont obmis les fait [sic] Classiques dês plusieurs annêes, qui ont etê êgarês pour avoir été annottês sur des papiers volants.'[118] It is also difficult to see why the records of the town of Yverdon should have been entrusted to Polier, who was *premier pasteur* of Lausanne. In point of fact, the *Archives des classes de l'Eglise vaudoise* were not brought to Lausanne until 1863. They were then kept by the *Commission synodale*, which in 1960 transferred them to their present home, the *Archives cantonales* at Lausanne.[119]

An inspection of these unpublished documents throws much new light on the Saurin affair and on Voltaire's part in it.[119a] First of all, the notion that the pastors of Lausanne felt impelled to meet and discuss matters because of the stir caused by the anonymous letter and Voltaire's reply, is shown to be quite false. The Colloque de Lausanne in fact met on 21 September 1758, two days *before* the anonymous letter was written. In this stormy meeting, attended by three laymen and fifteen pastors, not only was Voltaire's article on Saurin roundly condemned, the three pastors who had helped him were also censured and directed to publish a retraction which would have to be approved by the *colloque*. Polier de Bottens reacted violently, refusing to withdraw to allow the other pastors to consider the matter further, and protesting that the meeting had been chaired improperly. But although Polier was overruled unanimously, no firm action was taken. The affair was referred

---

[118] *Archives cantonales*, Bd.121 at Lausanne. The records of the other *classes* of the pays de Vaud are included under the same classification, and this will not be repeated each time a reference is made to them.

[119] this information was kindly provided by m. Olivier Dessemontet, *directeur* of the *Archives cantonales*.

[119a] the relevant sections are reproduced below in appendix 3.

'a l'examen des 2 autres V. Colloques pour en decider, ou qu'elle sera portée devant la V. Classe pour en juger plus outre'.

To understand what this decision meant, we shall have to say a word about the way in which the pays de Vaud's pastors were organised, for it is quite wrong to speak of the *compagnie des pasteurs*, as various critics have in fact done (cf. Perey and Maugras, p.285). There were five major groupings of pastors, called *classes*: Yverdon, Morges, Payerne, Orbe and Lausanne. Each of these assembled once or twice a year, but was further divided into two or three *colloques* which covered a smaller area and met more regularly. The meeting of pastors I have just described had thus referred the matter of Voltaire and the three pastors to its two sister *colloques*, those of Aigle and Vevey, or to the next meeting of the entire Classe de Lausanne, which would include representatives of all the three *colloques*: Aigle, Vevey and Lausanne.

At this point, things once more become obscure. The two *colloques* of Vevey and Aigle did indeed consider the Saurin affair, but their reactions were quite different. The pastors of Vevey, predictably enough, took the same point of view as their colleagues at Lausanne. Meeting on 4 October 1758, they censured Polier, de Crousaz and Pavillard, albeit in carefully worded terms, a retraction was again demanded, and the three pastors were warned severely about 'leur trop grande liaison avec un persoñage aussi dangereux que Voltaire; et dont les Discours et les Ecrits sur la Rèligion sont si peu ménagès'. Exactly one week later, on 11 October, the Colloque d'Aigle also discussed this highly controversial matter. Yet the register is strangely uninformative when compared with the lengthy and detailed comments recorded by the pastors of Vevey. The Saurin affair is relegated to the sixth item of business, and the brief minute devoted to it reveals merely that 'on a jugé à propos de suspendre toute déliberation à ce sujet jusqu'au colloque prochain du printems'.

Fortunately we do not have to rely entirely on the official registers to know what occurred at the Colloque d'Aigle's meeting, for Voltaire's correspondent, François-Louis Allamand, was a member of the *colloque* in his capacity as pastor of Bex. On 26 November he wrote to Voltaire about the Saurin affair, commenting significantly: 'Notre colloque d'octobre dernier en a très gravement délibéré' (Best.D7957). So the register's account is cryptic not because little was said but because the pastors did not wish their discussions to be recorded permanently. But why should reactions have changed so much in the short time since the meeting of the Colloque de Vevey? Had the Bernese authorities intervened to please their illustrious guest, as they were later to do in the squabbles provoked at the beginning of 1759 by Grasset's publication of his pamphlet *La Guerre littéraire de mr de Voltaire*? Voltaire was certainly on good terms with them at this time.[120] Yet the anonymous letter was not printed until the October edition of the *Mercure suisse*, and Voltaire did not comment on it until 2 November, when he told de Brenles: 'On est très irrité à Berne contre le ministre de Vévai ou de Lausane, auteur du punissable libelle inséré dans le Mercure suisse, et s'il est découvert, il portera la peine de son insolence' (Best.D7929). Some sort of action would seem to have been taken in the week between 4 and 11 October, or at the very least one supposes that a rumour of official displeasure reached the pastors of Lausanne. A more likely hypothesis than an intervention by Voltaire is that his friends in Berne anticipated him in taking action. This would explain his comments to de Brenles on 2 November and the frequency of his correspondence with Bertrand in November 1758.[121] Polier and Bertrand had both been willing to take up the cudgels on Voltaire's behalf over the *âme atroce* affair, and even if Polier resented the use to which Voltaire had put the notorious *déclaration*, he was also affronted by the *colloque*'s censure, and he could easily have let Bertrand know what had happened. If this was not the case, no doubt there were other informants who might have performed the same function. Bertrand is quite capable of having taken some action himself and then having given Voltaire an outline of what had happened, though the *philosophe* never seems to have found out the whole story. Rumours of official displeasure in Berne would easily have had time to percolate back to Lausanne by 11 October, and this would explain the attitude adopted by the Colloque d'Aigle, anxious to see which way the wind was blowing before committing itself in a way which might turn out to be compromising later.

Voltaire's letter of 27 December 1758 would seem to support this interpretation; he duly informed Saurin *fils* that the measures taken to rehabilitate his father's memory had been a complete success (Best. D8006):

[120] Voltaire had visited Berne in May 1756 (Desnoiresterres, p.145). Moreover, he had met the *avoyer* Steiger at Plombières (Roulet, p.60) and entertained the *banneret* Abraham de Freudenreich at *Les Délices* (Roulet, p.69). In December 1758 Voltaire lent the sum of 1,200 *livres* to Elie Bertrand (cf. Best.D7969).

[121] cf. Best.D7937 (11 November); Best.D7948 (20 November); Best.D7953 (27 November).

Non seulement l'article en question est imprimé dans la seconde édition des Crammer, mais il a excité la bile des vieux pasteurs de Lausane. Un prêtre, plus prêtre que ceux de Memphis a écrit un libelle à cette occasion, les ministres se sont assemblez, ils ont censuré les trois bons et honnêtes pasteurs que j'avais fait signer en votre faveur. Je les ai tous fait taire. Les avoiers de Berne ont fait sentir leur indignation à l'auteur du libelle contre la mémoire de votre illustre père, et nous sommes demeurez, votre honneur et moy, maîtres du champ de bataille.

This account of the affair is very interesting. It shows that Voltaire knew about the Colloque de Lausanne's meeting, and about the censure it had pronounced on Polier and his colleagues. But Voltaire's information had been far from complete. He thought the anonymous letter had been written *before* the *colloque*'s assembly, a fact which may account for subsequent critical confusion. Moreover, Voltaire claims to have had the Lausanne clergy silenced, but for the reasons outlined this would seem unlikely. It is clear, in any case, that he is exaggerating somewhat in this letter, as for example when he says 'Les avoiers de Berne ont fait sentir leur indignation à l'auteur de libelle', for even as Voltaire wrote these words, he was still frantically trying to discover just who the anonymous author was.

It was indeed some time before Voltaire decided firmly upon the man whom literary critics and historians have usually agreed was responsible for the anonymous letter. At first he suspected Chavannes,[122] brother-in-law of his correspondent, de Brenles, then, even more surprisingly, François-Louis Allamand, who, as we have seen, had sent Voltaire valuable information about the Colloque d'Aigle's meeting of 11 November 1758.[123] But by 7 February 1759 Voltaire had made up

---

[122] cf. Best.D8002. The reason is perhaps that Chavannes had been mentioned, in the Colloque de Lausanne's meeting of 21 September, as a man who might have seen the original of Saurin's letter to Gonon. Voltaire may have received a garbled account of the meeting and mistakenly taken Chavannes to be the author of the anonymous letter published in the *Mercure suisse*.

[123] for Voltaire's temporary hostility to Allamand, see Best.D8068 and D8084. Allamand had already told Voltaire, on 27 November 1758, that 'pour bonnes raisons' he had agreed to write a letter on behalf of his colleagues refuting an article published in the *Bibliothèque impartiale*, which had accused the pastors of 'la Suisse Françoise Réformée' of Socinian leanings (Best.D7957). It is not inconceivable that some of Allamand's colleagues, resenting his contacts with the impious Voltaire, may have circulated the rumour that he had collaborated in the anonymous letter, hoping that Voltaire would confuse this and the letter Allamand had been commissioned to write for the Colloque d'Aigle. Whether this explanation is true or not, Voltaire did apparently confuse the two

his mind where the principal responsibility lay, as he explained to de Brenles (Best.D8084):

C'est un nommé Lervêche, ci-devant précepteur de mr Constant, qui écrivit le libelle; il l'envoya à Alaman pour le corriger, il l'envoya aussi à mr. de Chavannes, à Vevey, et mr. de Chavannes méprisa cette ordure.

The 'ci-devant précepteur de mr Constant' was in fact an important member of Lausanne's clerical establishment: not only was Jean-Pierre Leresche (to give him his correct name) *doyen* of the Classe de Lausanne, he also held the same position in one of the *classe*'s three *colloques*, the Colloque de Vevey.

But why, in view of Leresche's repeated denials,[124] should one refuse to believe him innocent of the anonymous letter, particularly since Voltaire had already twice been mistaken in his attribution of its authorship? The evidence is admittedly circumstantial, but it is nonetheless significant. In the first place, we know that, although Leresche did not attend the meeting of the Colloque de Lausanne which censured Voltaire and the three pastors, he was responsible for bringing the matter to its attention.[125] Secondly, he presided over the meeting of the Colloque de Vevey which, on 4 October 1758, echoed the Colloque de Lausanne's condemnation in no uncertain manner.[126] Thirdly, Leresche attended the Colloque d'Aigle's meeting of 11 October, despite the fact that he was not a member of this body. When one adds to all this that Leresche detested Voltaire and hoped to have him expelled from Lausanne (cf. Best.D7880), that he is known to have been of an impetuous disposition,[127] that he no doubt felt a personal involvement as *doyen* of the Classe de Lausanne and responsible for the

letters, despite the full and clear information Allamand had given him on 27 November. Nonetheless, the two men were soon back on good terms: on 21 March 1759 Voltaire wrote to Allamand: 'je vous embrasse philosophiquement' (Best.D8201).

[124] cf. Best.D8160, D8197, D8208, D8211, D8222, D8223. Some of these letters became rather pathetic, as Leresche evidently feared that action might be taken against him by the Bernese authorities (cf. Best.D8211).

[125] cf. Best.D7880, Leresche to Daniel Pavillard (one of the three censured pastors), 27 September 1758.

[126] there is even a resemblance between one phrase of the *colloque*'s minutes, which speak of 'un persoñage aussi dangereux que Voltaire', and Leresche's advice to Pavillard 'sur la manière de vous diriger avec un hoñe aussi dangereux'.

[127] for an incident clearly illustrating this, see Pierre Morren, *La Vie lausannoise au XVIIIe siècle, d'après Jean Henri Polier de Vernand, lieutenant Baillival* (Geneva 1970), p.127.

clergy's honour,[128] presumptions that he was the anonymous letter's author seem, if not conclusive, then at least very reasonable. It is not difficult to imagine Leresche, dissatisfied with the outcome of the 23 September meeting, dashing off the anonymous letter to complete the work which he considered to have been left undone. The subsequent notoriety of this letter, and the relative obscurity of the *colloque*'s proceedings encouraged the formation of a garbled account of the affair, making it appear that the anonymous letter had caused the pastors of Lausanne to take action rather than vice-versa.

The unpublished evidence I have been able to present should finally give the lie to stories accusing Voltaire of petty theft or the suppression of evidence. Had Saurin's letter been in the keeping of Polier or anyone else, the assembled pastors would certainly have demanded to see it on 23 September 1758. Moreover, had there been the slightest suspicion that Voltaire had tampered with a vital piece of information, it is not hard to imagine the rumpus which would have ensued. In any case, the anonymous letter itself had implied that Saurin's alleged missive to Gonon was not kept in any public archives. Nonetheless, some critics have seemed determined to believe in Voltaire's guilt, even putting forward the argument that because the *philosophe* frankly admitted that Saurin had not been as innocent as originally claimed in the *Siècle de Louis XIV*,[129] this admission necessarily shows that Voltaire had suppressed the evidence (cf. Roulet, p.109, n.1). The logic here is difficult to follow, for if Voltaire had destroyed the proof of Saurin's guilt, why should he then choose to admit it, rendering his alleged theft completely pointless? Voltaire may indeed be criticised for trying to make philosophical propaganda out of the Saurin affair, but to portray him as an amateur thief is clearly quite absurd.

Whatever the authorship of the anonymous letter, Voltaire had learned, thanks to the series of events sparked off by his attempts of rehabilitate Joseph Saurin, that opinion in Calvinist Lausanne was much less 'liberal' than he originally thought. Although the clergy's orthodoxy was suspect in some quarters, reaction clearly won the day on this occasion. Even Polier de Bottens, despite his angry resistance at the Colloque de Lausanne's meeting of 23 September 1758, chose the path of conformity and ceased his contacts with Voltaire. The latter

128 cf. Best.D7880.
129 cf. Best.D7953, D8130. Voltaire now argued that resurrecting Saurin's guilt served only to penalise his innocent relatives: cf. Best.D.app.171.

did not hide his disappointment,[130] but in self-justification Polier could very well have echoed the words of Allamand, who, though maintaining his contacts with Voltaire, was well aware of the risks he ran and acted as prudently as possible (Best.D7957):

Ce n'est pas que j'aye honte d'un christianisme moins suisse que celui de Théodore de Beze, mais je sens aussi mon petit fagot, & j'en suis ennuyé; pour vieillir en paix, il faut tâcher de vieillir en odeur d'orthodoxie.

The end of the Saurin affair is well documented and has been fully recounted by several critics.[131] Grasset's publication of *La Guerre littéraire de mr de Voltaire* seems to have driven Voltaire into a new frenzy. Hysterically multiplying his appeals for help even after it had become clear that the Bernese government intended to intervene, he contrived to lose much sympathy, even among his friends. The far from amicable exchange of letters with Haller served further to polarise opinion in Lausanne. Voltaire had prudently abstained from staying there in the winter of 1758-1759, and the events I have been recounting can only have strengthened feelings of distaste which recent disagreements with the pastors of Geneva had already developed in him. Indeed, on 4 May 1759, Voltaire told d'Alembert, who had reprinted his article 'Genève' (Best.D8286):

Vous avez très bien fait. Mais vous faites trop d'honneur aux prédicans sociniens. Vous ne les connaissez pas vous dis-je. Ils sont aussi malins que les autres. Et les sociniens de Geneve et les calvinistes de Lausanne, et les faquirs et les bonzes sont tous de la même espèce. Je laisse faire ceux de Paris, mais pour mes suisses et mes allobroges, je les range.

Coming immediately after the controversies Voltaire had been involved in with the Genevese clergy, the Saurin affair was probably decisive in encouraging him to break his ties with Switzerland. Ferney and Tournay had already been purchased and occupied. Henceforth Voltaire would be able to indulge in baiting the Swiss pastors as much as he wished without real fear of reprisals.

vi. *Ferney – splendid isolation*

Relations between Voltaire and the clergy of Geneva as a whole deteriorated steadily between 1759 and 1761, when they reached their

---

[130] cf. Best.D7953, D8059, D8084, D8215.
[131] the fullest account is probably Roulet, pp.112 ff.

nadir. Voltaire himself was in no small measure responsible for this because of his continuing attempts to provoke and irritate the pastors. He informed the *Journal encyclopédique* that *Candide* had been written to convert the Socinians, a transparent reference not only to Leibniz and his disciples but also to the unorthodox ministers of Geneva.[132] *Candide* also contained another jibe at the Calvinist clergy: the unpleasant picture of an intolerant Dutch minister who spurns the hero appeal for charity (ed. Pomeau, p.93). The publication of Frederick II's *Œuvres du philosophe de Sans-Souci* gave Voltaire an opportunity to taunt his enemies once more:

Je ne sçais pas comment les ministres de la confession d'Augsbourg et ceux de Genève prendront une certaine épître au maréchal Keit, dans laquelle le Roy philosophe assure que L'âme est très mortelle, et ces petits vers
  Allez lâches crétiens.... etc.[133]

Later in the same year appeared the *Dialogues chrétiens*, in the second of which, he told Gabriel Cramer on 3 September, 'Vôtre professeur Vernet, Docteur en Théologie, est cruellement déchiré [...] c: à d: qu'il est peint trait pour trait' (Best.D9187). Although Voltaire strenuously denied authorship of this pamphlet,[134] and even threatened to have legal action taken at Lyon against its publisher, François Rigollet (cf. Best.D9209, D9213), there seems little doubt that he was in fact responsible for it.[135]

Nor were Voltaire's attacks confined to literature. One of the reasons he bought Ferney really seems to have been that he thought the hated

---

[132] Best.D8239, 1 April 1759: 'mon frère le Capitaine qui est le *Loustik* du Régiment est un très bon chrétien, qui en s'amusant à composer le Roman de *Candide* dans son quartier d'hiver, a eu principalement en vüe de convertir les Sociniens. Ces hérétiques ne se contentent pas de nier hautement la Trinité et les peines éternelles, ils disent que Dieu a nécessairement fait de nôtre monde le meilleur des mondes possibles, et que tout est bien. Cette idée est manifestement contraire à la doctrine du péché originel.' Cf. also Best. D8147, to Jacob Vernes (February/March 1759), where Voltaire mentions 'un livre détestable qui semble supposer le péché original [sic] et la chutte de l'homme, que vous niez vous autres damnez de sociniens'.

[133] Best.D8753, to the duchess of Saxe-Gotha, 9 February 1760. Charles Bonnet was duly horrified by the poem: 'Quelle ridicule impiété! Quelle extravagance!' he exclaimed to Haller on 23 February 1760; 'Est il possible que Voltaire vaille plus que lui, et cependant combien vaut-il peu, si nous apprécions les hommes relativement à la moralité' (Best. D8772, commentary). For another reaction see Best.D8780.

[134] cf. Best.D9194, D9195, D9198, D9201, D9202, D9204, D9218, D9226.

[135] cf. Pierre Grosclaude, *La Vie intellectuelle à Lyon dans la deuxième moitié du XVIIIe siècle* (Paris 1933), pp.283-87; also Best.D9275.

Vernet would become his vassal. On 2 June 1759 he begged François Tronchin to tell 'mon amy Vernet le tartuffe, et mon amy Sarrazin le fanatique' that the king had accorded Voltaire and mme Denis special privileges for Ferney.[136] Voltaire even took to asking his correspondents not to address their letters as if he lived at Geneva: 'Et jamais *à Geneve* s'il vous plaît, mais *par Geneve*. Voulez vous qu'on me prenne pʳ un huguenot réfugié?'[137] To Thieriot he gave the same message (Best.D8634, 5 December 1759): 'La bonne compagnie de Genève veut bien venir chez moi, mais je ne vais jamais dans cette ville hérétique.'

There was of course a very good reason why Geneva's high society continued to visit Voltaire. This was the existence of his theatre, whose popularity Voltaire considered to be the most convincing refutation of Rousseau's arguments in the *Lettre à d'Alembert* (Best.D8563). Unfortunately, the presence of a theatre so near Geneva provided the opportunity for a rather childish type of confrontation which Voltaire did his best to encourage: 'nous aurons un petit téâtre à Tourney, et vos prêtres viendront s'ils veulent nous voir jouer la comédie que nous jouons mieux qu'eux', he told Jean-Robert Tronchin and Ami Camp on 2 August 1759 (Best.D8416). He gave his entertainments a nickname which left in no doubt their role as goad to the Genevese pastors: 'Vendredy il y a anticonsistoire au châtau de Tourney, et probablement encor samedy.'[138] Yet Voltaire did not put on plays merely to annoy his Calvinist neighbours, and as time went on he began to develop more and more the idea of the theatre's social utility, a concept which had already been suggested in d'Alembert's article (cf. below, p.210). Its absence from Geneva came to represent for him not only the repressive and meaningless severity of Calvinism, but even the difference between French and Genevese life-styles. It is worth looking at some of the points he makes in favour of his thesis in order to demonstrate that Voltaire's partisanship of the theatre had wider implications than is usually supposed.

On 27 September 1760 Voltaire described the situation to the d'Argentals with characteristic irony: 'Je corromps toute la jeunesse de la

---

136 Best.D8329. Cf. also Best.D7975, D8079, D8108, D8126, D8226, D9503, D14973, commentary.

137 Best.D8633, Voltaire to d'Argental, 5 December 1759. For a similarly indignant attitude see Best.D9682 and D9684.

138 Best.D8563, Voltaire to Horace Vasserot de Vinay, 31 October 1759. He also irreverently commented that the theatre was becoming 'le troisième sacrement de Geneve' (Best.D7842).

pédante ville de Genève. Je crée les plaisirs. Les prédicants enragent'
(Best.D9268). The lapidary nature of this utterance should not conceal
from us that it expressed both one of Voltaire's main objections to
Calvinism – his intense dislike of 'la petite Eglise de Geneve, qui fait
consister la vertu dans l'usure, et dans l'austérité des mœurs'[139] – and a
corresponding desire to prove not only the harmlessness of the amusements condemned by Calvinists but also the positive good brought
about by some of them. A month or so earlier he had pointed out to
Jacques Pernetti that Christians as a whole had not always been opposed
to the theatre: 'Autrefois les évêques allaient aux spectacles: ce sont ces
faquins de calvinistes et de jansénistes[140] qui n'étant pas faits pour des
plaisirs honnêtes, en ont privé ceux qui sont faits pour les goûter'
(Best.D9164, 22 August 1760). And in a later letter to Capacelli (Best.
D9492, 23 December 1760), Voltaire developed his argument further.
Taking care to remind his correspondent of the Catholic prelates who
had supported the theatre, and appealing to the authority of antiquity,
he restated d'Alembert's arguments in favour of the theatre but went
even further than his friend: in Voltaire's opinion it should be publicly
subsidised everywhere by the municipal authorities:

Les spectacles que nous donnons chez nous, sont une bien faible imitation de
cette magnificence [of the Athenians]; mais enfin, elles en retracent quelque
idée. C'est la plus belle éducation qu'on puisse donner à la jeunesse, le plus
noble délassement du travail, la meilleure instruction pour tous les ordres des
citoyens; c'est presque la seule manière d'assembler les hommes pour les
rendre sociables [. . .]

Aussi, je ne me lasserai point de répéter que parmi vous le pape Léon x,
l'archevêque Trissino, le cardinal Bibiena, & parmi nous les cardinaux
Richelieu & Mazarin, ressucitèrent la scène.

---

[139] Best.D9561, to the marquis d'Argence, 20 January 1761. Just as he increasingly
criticised the mercenary character of the Dutch, so Voltaire also drew attention to the
inordinate profits which Genevese financiers made at the expense of France, at first sight a
rather surprising preoccupation in one often regarded as typifying the *bourgeoisie* and its
capitalist aspirations. Cf. Best.D10670, where Voltaire mentions 'Genêve la pédante, où il
n'y a que des prédicants, des marchands et des truittes', but especially Best.D19056:
Genêve est actuellement plus riche que Hambourg, elle s'est fait six millions de rentes sur
la France' and Best.D19073. An extraordinary system of exploiting the French *rentes
viagères* and *tontines* had in fact been worked out: cf. Herbert Lüthy, *La Banque protestante
de France de la révocation de l'Edit de Nantes à la Révolution* (Geneva 1959); ii.478 ff.

[140] as we have already seen (above, p.71, n.54), this linking of Calvinists and Jansenists
is in no way accidental. Indeed, it reappears several times in the 1760s and 1770s with the
Scottish Presbyterians sometimes taking the place of French or Genevese Calvinists: cf.
Best.D12788, D15003, D20447.

Two events which occurred in 1760 allowed Voltaire to push forward his attack against the Calvinists. In the first place he was able to prove that the theatreless town of Geneva was in no way morally superior because of its austerity, and secondly recent theological developments at Neuchâtel tended to demonstrate the truth of Voltaire's assertations that some of the Swiss clergy were far from orthodox. On 13 October 1762 (Best.D9308) Charlotte de Constant Rebecque told her brother François of the

avanture terrible à Geneve qui ocupe tout le monde. Mr. Vernes frère du ministre se doutant depuis longtems que sa femme [. . .] avoit une intrigue avec le proffesseur Nekrer a supris son portefeuille qu'il a trouvé plein de lettres depuis 2 ans jusqu'à présent. . . . Neker qui ne savoit rien est venus, Vernes l'a vu arriver et lui a tiré un coup de Pistolet sur l'Escalier dont il est blessé, et est parti sur le champ pour Morge où il est après avoir publié son déshonneur à tous les voisins. Necre est au lit très mal de désespoir plus tost que de sa blessure.

It is not difficult to imagine Voltaire's gleeful reaction to this scandal,[141] especially since the Venerable Consistory had just taken further action against his theatricals. The Genevese clergy, he explained to the marquis d'Argence,

s'est imaginé qu'il n'y avait de cocus dans le monde, que parce qu'on jouait la comédie. Ces maroufles s'en sont pris aux jeunes gens de leur ville, qui avaient joué sur mon théâtre de Tournay, et ils ont eu l'insolence de leur faire promettre de ne plus jouer avec des Français qui pouraient corrompre les mœurs de Genêve.[142]

The other incident was in connection with the former pastor of La Chaux-de-Fonds in the canton of Neuchâtel, Ferdinand-Olivier Petitpierre, who had recently been dismissed for preaching unorthodox

---

[141] cf. Best.D9366, to d'Alembert, 30 October 1760: 'ne croyez vous pas malgré Jean Jaques qu'il vaut mieux aller à la comédie, que de donner cette comédie?'

[142] Best.D9561 (20 January 1761). Cf. also Best.D9498, to mme d'Epinay, 26 December 1760: 'Les mécréants se déclarent contre les spectacles. Ils trouvent bon qu'on s'enivre, qu'on se tüe, qu'un de leurs bourgeois, frère du ministre Verne, cocu de la façon d'un professeur nommé Nekre, tire un coup de pistolet au galant professeur, etc. etc. etc., mais ils croyent offenser dieu s'ils soufrent que leurs bourgeois jouent Polieucte et Athalie.' Cf. also Best.D9503, D9523. According to Herbert Lüthy, Voltaire 'se montra fort déçu quand Louis Necker, ayant trouvé refuge et leçons de morale chez son frère plus grave à Paris, fit amende honorable devant le Consistoire et obtint sa réhabilitation des mains du chapelain de l'ambassade hollandaise à Paris' (*La Banque protestante*, ii.235).

beliefs, especially in connection with Hell.[143] As Voltaire put it to the marquis d'Argence, on 20 January 1761 (Best.D9561): 'un bon prêtre vient de prouver, à Neufchâtel, que l'enfer n'est point du tout Eternel, qu'il est ridicule de penser que Dieu s'occupe pendant une infinité de siècles, à rôtir un pauvre diable.'[144] The first mention of the Petitpierre case occurs in Best.D9497 (26 December 1760), with the comment: 'Apparemment que les disciples de Jean Chauvin s'étant mis à nier la divinité de Jésus, veulent affecter du rigorisme [in connection with Voltaire's theatre] afin qu'on ne les accuse pas à la fois d'une morale et d'une doctrine relâchée.' Hypocrisy was once again the motive of the clergy's reactions, in Voltaire's opinion, and he was anxious to prove how wrong they were in their evaluation of the morality of theatre-goers. An opportunity presented itself in October 1761 when Voltaire's friends let him know how ill Du Pan was, obviously hinting that it would be unseemly to continue performing theatricals at such a time. Voltaire replied with alacrity, pointing out in no uncertain terms that Calvinists were not alone in observing the *bienséances* of civilised behaviour:

Je suis très affligé de l'état du pauvre du Pan, et j'aime baucoup son père [. . .] Mes frères ne respectez que l'amitié et non pas le pédantisme. Croyez ferme-ment que les mœurs de la nation française valent bien celles de Geneve [. . .] Je vous jure que si vous mourez vendredy je ne jouerai pas la comédie.[145]

This obstinately-waged propaganda campaign with its double object of edifying the Genevese public and irritating its ministers could not fail to call forth a response from the latter. Already in October 1759, Marie-Louise Huber had written to Grimm, sensing that attendance at Voltaire's theatricals would not be permitted much longer: 'Je crois qu'il faudra aller à la première représantation [of *Tancrède*] parce que les ministres ont déjà un peu grouillé.'[146] Nonetheless, performances in which citizens of Geneva took part continued for a time, until combined

[143] for information on Petitpierre's life and family see Charles Berthoud, *Les Quatre Petitpierre (1707-1790)* (Neuchâtel 1875).

[144] Voltaire was interested enough in Petitpierre to mention him in both the *Diction-naire philosophique* article 'Enfer' and in the *Questions sur les miracles*: cf. below p.228. The affair was also to come up again in Voltaire's correspondence: cf. Best.D9498, D9503, D12534, D14117, D17339, D17370.

[145] Best.D10068, to Gabriel and Philibert Cramer, *c.* 10 October 1761.

[146] Best.D8556, commentary, 24 October 1759. But cf. below pp.205 ff. for proof that this attitude was not motivated by religious considerations only.

action by the Venerable Company and the *Magnifique conseil* taken between October 1760 and January 1761 put a stop to this practice. Two resolutions were adopted by the pastors on 9 December 1760 (Best.D.app.199, section v):

le prémier qu'il soit intimé au Sr De Voltaire une défense expresse de faire joüer ou permettre que l'on joüe dans sa maison de St Jean [i.e. *Les Délices*] aucune pièce de Théâtre, soit par représentation publique, ou par répétition.

Le second, qu'il plaise au Mag. Conseil rendre un arrêt de défenses plus étendu que les précédens, et qui interdise expressément à toutes personnes sujettes de cèt Etat de représenter aucune Pièce de théâtre tant sur le territoire de cette Ville que sur les Terres Etrangères qui sont dans nôtre Voisinage.

These resolutions were duly laid before the council, which on 24 December (Best.D.app.199, section viii) decided to assure the consistory that their representations had been favourably received and that 'le Mag. Consl se servira de son droit et de son autorité, en prenant les mesures les plus propres et les plus efficaces pour pourvoir à ce qui en fait l'objet'.

Voltaire's bluff had been called, and his anger was predictable.[147] No longer could he maintain the convenient fiction that the council was an enlightened body which took little notice of the anathemas pronounced by its clergy. Yet even during the period we have just been considering, when his attitude to Geneva was generally far from enthusiastic, Voltaire was equitable enough to remember some of its praiseworthy features. There were no difficulties about inoculation 'dans le petit païs où j'ai choisi ma retraitte', he informed François de Chennevrières on 15 December 1759 (Best.D8653). A few months later he was still more generous in his judgement, describing the 'beau lac de Genève' to Octavie Belot as 'un pays libre et tranquille où la nature est riante et où la raison n'est point persécutée' (Best.D8913, 16 May 1760). Nor did Voltaire forget that, even if Geneva was inferior to Rome and England and was 'un couvent assez ennuïeux', it contained 'des gens de beaucoup d'esprit'.[148] Though he declared in disgust to Saverio Bettinelli: 'Pour les petits pédants de la petite ville de Genève, je vous les abandonne [...] j'ai pour eux prèsque autant de mépris que pour

---

[147] cf. Best.D9498, D9523, D9561, D9562.
[148] Best.D8858, to George Keate, 16 April 1760. Cf. Best.D9523, to d'Alembert, 6 January 1761, where Voltaire speaks of 'le couvent de Geneve appellé ville'.

les convulsionaires de st Médar' (Best.D8814), to the marquis d'Argence Voltaire nonetheless expressed his willingness to pardon these barbarians, 'parce qu'il y a chez eux dix ou douze personnes de mérite' (Best.D9561, 20 January 1761). Even more surprising, at least one of these people was a minister. At no time during this propaganda war did Voltaire break off cordial relations with Jacob Vernes. Towards the end of December 1759 he sent this pastor a letter of condolence on the death of his wife (Best.D8667), and the correspondence between them appears to have continued as normal (cf. below, pp.179-80). On 20 June of the following year, writing to Duclos, Voltaire described Vernes as 'un homme de mérite' (Best.D8996). It is time to look closer at Voltaire's contacts with certain pastors to see on what basis such apparently harmonious relationships could be maintained at a time when he was in violent conflict with the official Calvinist church and had frequently expressed his contempt for its ministers in terms of the most withering scorn.

Many critics have mentioned Voltaire's contacts with one or more pastors, and a few short articles have also been published. René Pomeau includes a useful section on six pastors in his masterly study, *La Religion de Voltaire*,[149] yet despite the interesting conclusions he reaches on several points, this eminent Voltairean scholar does no more than indicate the general outlines of the topic. The space accorded to Bertrand and Paul Moultou is extremely small. There is obviously a need for a specialised study tracing the lives and work of those pastors who came into contact with Voltaire. Such a work could evaluate the extent to which both sides were influenced by the mutual contacts. This task is unfortunately beyond the scope of the present study, but an attempt will be made to describe briefly and to sum up in a general way the importance of Voltaire's contacts with five pastors: Vernet, Vernes, Allamand, Bertrand and Moultou.[150]

[149] pp.292-300, and pp.339-40. The pastors in question are Vernet, Vernes, Polier de Bottens, Bertrand, Allamand and Moultou.

[150] I do not propose to discuss Polier de Bottens in this section, partly because his contacts with Voltaire ceased relatively early (in 1759) and have already been dealt with (above, pp.125, 156-65 ff.) and partly because the topic has been closely studied in Raymond Naves, *Voltaire et l'Encyclopédie*, pp.23-33, 141-48, 185-94, and in Ira O. Wade and Norman L. Torrey, 'Voltaire and Polier de Bottens', *Rr* (1940), xxxi.147-55. The fact that Polier was a 'philosophical' pastor would seem to be proven beyond doubt.

vii. *Jacob Vernet (1698-1789)*

We have already seen how Vernet[151] tried to enlist Voltaire's support for the religious establishment of Geneva on the *philosophe*'s arrival there (above, pp.120-22), and the subsequent controversy between them over the *âme atroce* affair has been described in some detail (above, pp.129-35). The next incident was during the Saurin affair, when Grasset reprinted the anonymous letter attributed to Vernet (Best. D7272) and Vernet's letter to Formey, in his pamphlet *La Guerre littéraire de m. de Voltaire*. Although Voltaire maintained publicly that relations between himself and the pastor were still cordial,[152] it is obvious that he suspected Vernet of collusion in the enterprise if not of active support of Grasset. He apparently tried to induce Vernet to censure the use made of his writings or to disavow them altogether. 'J'ay voulu L'induire à repentir', he told Théodore Tronchin on about 10 March 1759, 'et tirer de luy une démarche honnête une fois en sa vie. S'il ne la fait pas, je l'en feray justement porter la peine' (Best.D8175). This was no idle threat, for although Vernet wrote to Tronchin in the most conciliatory terms, merely insisting that his letter to Formey was reasonable and moderate,[153] it seems that from about this time Geneva's leading theologian became one of Voltaire's *bêtes noires*. Ridicule and mockery were heaped upon him to such an extent that he almost became a Protestant Le Franc de Pompignan.

[151] Jacob Vernet became professor of theology at the Genevese Academy in 1756. His family was of Provençal origin and had settled in Geneva in the middle of the seventeenth century. See Eugène de Budé, *Vie de Jacob Vernet, théologien genevois* (Geneva 1885); Michel-Jean-Louis Saladin, *Mémoire historique sur la vie et les ouvrages de Jacob Vernet* (Paris 1790); Jean Senebier, *Notice historique sur la vie et les écrits de Jacob Vernet, pasteur et professeur en théologie* (Geneva 1807).

[152] cf. Best.D8108, and especially the fifth point in Voltaire's *Mémoire* to the Lausanne Academy in connection with the *Guerre littéraire*: 'La prétendue dispute de Mr de Voltaire avec Mr Vernet, professeur en Théologie, n'a jamais existé. Monsr de Voltaire est seigneur de la terre où Mons le professeur Vernet a une maison de campagne, et le brouillon qui a supposé un démêlé entre deux voisins et deux amis, ne peut être qu'un perturbateur du repos public' (Best.D.app.171).

[153] Best.D8112: 'on y trouve un simple éclaircissement littéraire sur l'afaire de Castalion, dont Mr de Voltaire n'a pas été bien informé'. Vernet also commented: 'n'oubliez pas d'ajouter combien je suis sensible aux expressions obligeantes dont il se sert à mon égard. Elles répondent bien aux marques de politesse que je n'ai cessé de recevoir de luid ans les liaisons que j'ai eu l'honneur d'avoir avec lui: liaisons que je regrette, & que je n'ai interrompues que par une nécessité de bienséance, depuis qu'il a imprimé sous nos yeux des choses qui nous affligent & que nous ne pouvons nous dispenser de réfuter. Mais cela ne s'appelle point avoir un démêlé: c'est une simple dissension où il n'entre rien d'ofensant, rien de personnel.'

It is indeed difficult to avoid feeling great sympathy for Vernet, who, as René Pomeau comments, 'ne se contentait pas de prêcher [...] la tolérance; dans ses débats avec Voltaire, la modération, le respect de l'adversaire seront des qualités dont il aura quelque mérite à ne pas se départir'.[154] Vernet was certainly given many opportunities to exercise these qualities. In 1760 he was violently satirised in the second of the *Dialogues chrétiens* (cf. above, p.166), and sought leave to defend himself before both the Venerable consistory and the *Petit conseil,* so grave did he consider the charges brought against him. According to his account of the affair (Best.D.app.197, section viii):

Il étoit à sa Campagne dans Une grande sécurité, & n'auroit jamais soupçonné que les traits du personnage de Ministre qui s'y trouve dépeint [...] pussent l'avoir en Vüe, Mais quelle fut sa douleur lors qu'un de ses Parents Vint l'avertir, que l'on insinuoit sourdement dans la Ville, qu'il en étoit l'objet.

Presumably Voltaire considered that Vernet had played a provocative role in the action taken against his theatricals, although there is no evidence to support this accusation. Whatever the reason, Vernet had come to symbolise for Voltaire the twin hydra of Calvinist austerity and priestly hypocrisy. He was mocked time and again as 'col tors'[155] or 'le tartuffe',[156] his honesty was called into question (cf. below, pp.175-76), and his literary efforts belittled.[157] Writing to Vernes on 26 September 1766 (Best.D13592), Voltaire commented urbanely that if Vernet's words were ever engraved, it could only be done 'avec la matière dont Ezéchiel faisait son déjeûné' (i.e. excrement). The portrait of Vernet in *La Guerre civile de Genève* aptly sums up Voltaire's opinion of him (M.ix.518):

> Du noir sénat le grave directeur
> Est Jean Vernet, de maint volume auteur,
> Le vieux Vernet, ignoré du lecteur,
> Mais trop connu des malheureux libraires,
> Dans sa jeunesse il a lu les saints pères,

---

[154] *La Religion de Voltaire*, p.295. Cf. also Delattre, *Voltaire: correspondance avec les Tronchin*, p.247: 'Le zèle de Jacob Vernet pour les lettres françaises méritait mieux.'
[155] cf. Best.D7568, D9218, D13426.
[156] cf. Best.D7367, D7428, D7568, D8329, D9204, D9218, D16762.
[157] cf. Best.D13328, D13407, D16147.

Se croit savant, affecte un air dévot:
Broun[158] est moins fat, et Needham[159] est moins sot.

It is only fair to point out that, despite Voltaire's continuing ire, Vernet's attempts to defend his conduct and character were of an altogether more gentlemanly nature than the attacks to which he was subjected. His *Lettres critiques d'un voyageur anglois*, first published in 1761, ran to three editions, the last and most extended of which appeared in 1766.[160] The publication of each of these editions called forth attacks from both Voltaire and d'Alembert,[161] but it was in 1766 that the reaction was most violent.[162] Voltaire replied in June 1766 with his *Lettre curieuse de m. Robert Covelle* (M.xxv.491-96), repeating old accusations about Vernet's collaboration in the *Essai sur les mœurs* and renewing by implication[163] charges he had made to Théodore Tronchin in 1759: 'Nous verrons si celuy qui a supposé des lettres et un testament de Giannoné pour voler ses manuscrits chez mr Turretin [...] osera soutenir ma présence ou celle de mes valets.'[164] In the opinion of André Delattre, 'C'était pure calomnie.'[165] Nonetheless, it was a

[158] a Scots ecclesiastic who was pastor of the English Church in Utrecht. After visiting Geneva in 1760-1761 he agreed to sign the preface of Vernet's anonymously published *Lettres critiques* (cf. below, n.160) as editor. When, on 29 March 1762, Voltaire commented in a letter to d'Alembert which was subsequently published in the *Saint-James chronicle* (17 July 1762) and the *Gentleman's magazine* (July 1762): 'Mon cher et grand Philosophe, vous avez donc lu cet impertinent petit libelle d'un impertinent petit Prêtre qui était venu souvent aux Délices et à qui nous avions daigné faire trop bonne chère' (Best.D10394), Brown took this insult as referring to him, although it was almost certainly meant for Vernet. Brown defended himself in a letter to the *Bibliothèque des sciences et des beaux-arts* (Best.D11077, 8 March 1763). Voltaire returned the compliment in Best.D12811 and in the *Guerre civile*, where, perhaps prompted by Brown's over-touchy defence of himself, Voltaire actually did accuse the pastor of the conduct he had denied: 'Ce prédicant écossais venait souvent manger chez l'auteur, sans en être prié; et c'est ainsi qu'il témoigna sa reconnaissance' (M.ix.518, n.3). Cf. Eugène Ritter, 'Voltaire et le pasteur Robert Brown', *Bpf* (1904), liii.156-63.

[159] cf. below, p.228, n.281.

[160] the first edition contained only two letters; the second, six (M.xxv.492, n.2); the third edition was augmented to thirteen letters, and this was the version Voltaire owned (*Ferney catalogue*, no.2922).

[161] cf. at the time of the first edition Best.D10394 and of the second Best.D10906.

[162] cf. Best.D13320, D13328, D13345, D13352, D13407, D13424, D13426, D13698, D13702.

[163] 'Nous lui dîmes tous d'une voix que nous étions fort aises de voir enfin un manuscrit qui lui appartînt' (M.xxv.492).

[164] Best.D8079, c. 3 February 1759. Voltaire had already made these charges in a letter to d'Alembert of 29 December 1757 (Best.D7539).

[165] *Correspondance avec les Tronchin*, letter 374, n.4.

serious accusation, and once more Vernet felt it necessary to go through the ritual of justifying himself before the pastors and magistrates of Geneva, publishing a sixty-three page pamphlet entitled *Mémoire présenté à monsieur le premier syndic*,[166] to which Voltaire, in turn, replied with a *Declaration* dated 5 July 1766. But still the affair did not rest: 'Vernet ayant composé un nouveau mémoire à sa louange, Voltaire refit une autre déclaration avant même que Vernet eût imprimé sa pièce.'[167] One may legitimately wonder why Voltaire took so much time and trouble in refuting 'Socin Vernet',[168] when he had declared to Thieriot that 'Son livre [i.e. the *Lettres critiques*] est entièrement ignoré' (Best.D13328, 30 May 1766). On 13 June 1766, in a letter to d'Alembert, Voltaire answered this very question, showing by his reply that Vernet was not so insignificant as the *philosophe* would have liked to imagine: 'Je sais que vous dédaignerez à Paris les coassements des grenouilles du lac de Genève, mais elles se font entendre chez toutes les grenouilles presbytériennes de l'Europe, et il est bon de les écraser en passant' (Best.D13345).

But had Voltaire really crushed Vernet?[169] His continuing irritation at Vernet's literary output would seem to imply that even he himself was not convinced of this.[170] Despite the unpleasant personal nature

---

[166] 'On trouve à la suite du mémoire un *Extrait des registres du conseil* (du 8 juillet); un *Extrait des registres de la vénérable compagnie* (du 20 juin), et un *Extrait des registres du vénérable consistoire* (du 3 juillet)' (M.xxv.491, n.1).

[167] M.xxv.499, n.1. The new *Déclaration* was dated 23 August 1766.

[168] this was d'Alembert's nickname for him: cf. Best.D13424.

[169] this at any rate is the claim made in Best.D13698 (to d'Alembert, 29 November 1766): 'A l'égard de l'ami Vernet, il est dans la boue avec Jean Jacques, et ni l'un ni l'autre ne se relèveront.'

[170] 'Ah! le beau livre que Vernet à écrit sur le *contrains les d'entrer* et sur le contrains les d'entendre', he commented to Moultou on 1 August 1769 (Best.D15791), and the work in question, on the title page of which Voltaire wrote 'très ennuieux bavard', is identified by Theodore Besterman (Best.D15791, commentary, n.2) as *Réflexions sur les mœurs, la religion, et le culte* (Geneva 1769) (*BV* 3428). Voltaire was sufficiently angered by this work to reply to it in a leaflet entitled *Mr Jean Vernet, pasteur et professeur* (1769) (Best. D15820, commentary, n.4: this pamphlet is not recorded by Bengesco), and even as late as 1777 he was ready to make a sarcastic quip at Vernet's expense. In a letter to Meister (Best.D20824, 4 October 1777), Moultou recounted the following anecdote, occasioned no doubt by the recent appointment of Necker as 'adjoint au Controlleur général [des finances]' together with Taboureau Des Réaux (cf. Best.D20365): '*Votre république, monsieur* [Voltaire was addressing a Genevese at table], *doit être bien glorieuse* [. . .]: *elle fournit à la fois à la France un philosophe pour l'éclairer* [no doubt Rousseau], *un médecin* [Tronchin] *pour la guérir, & un ministre pour remettre ses finances, & ce n'est pas l'opération la moins difficile. Il faudrait*, a-t-il ajouté, *lorsque l'archevêque de Paris mourra, donner ce siège à votre fameux ministre Vernet, pour y rétablir la religion.*'

of the attacks which Vernet suffered, there is no evidence to suggest that he ceased to be a respected member of the Genevese republic. In emphasising supposed defects in Vernet's character, Voltaire may even have weakened his case by diverting attention from the pastor's doctrinal views to his private life. As we have seen, Vernet's theology was distinctly unorthodox; he could legitimately be accused of hypocrisy or at the very least of applying double standards in his defence of Calvin's conduct toward Servetus. He was clearly a Socinian, if by this term it be understood that he considered the status of Christ to be inferior to that of God the father. Moreover, in his enthusiasm to collaborate with a great author, Vernet had certainly encouraged Voltaire to come to Geneva, and his letters had probably contributed to forming in Voltaire's mind the impression that the pastors of Geneva were more willing to compromise with deism than they actually were.[171] Once Voltaire arrived, Vernet had second thoughts. He tried to compromise with the *philosophe* and then decided that he must defend the religious *status quo*. But owing to his advanced theological position Vernet was certainly open to attack on the grounds that he was no longer an orthodox Calvinist. Perhaps the most surprising aspect of Voltaire's relations with Vernet was that after mercilessly pointing out the inconsistency of the minister's position at the time of the 'Genève' controversy, Voltaire later almost entirely switched his attention to making scurrilous personal attacks on Vernet. These were obviously unsuccessful, and in consequence Voltaire not only made a permanent enemy of Geneva's most eminent theologian and abandoned any hope of a compromise with official Calvinism, he also forfeited the moral superiority he might so easily have retained by showing his Protestant opponent a little more of the tolerance he so passionately advocated for Vernet's Huguenot brethren in France.

viii. *Jacob Vernes (1728-1791)*

When Voltaire arrived at Geneva in 1754 Jacob Vernes had been a pastor for only three years.[172] The young man had travelled widely and was

---

[171] one wonders, for example, why, in a letter to Voltaire of 9 February 1754, Vernet signed himself as 'Professeur en Histoire & non bibliothècaire' (Best.D5663). Why had he not simply said he was a pastor? It seems unlikely that Vernet was ashamed of his ministry, but it must certainly have appeared to Voltaire that he regarded it as secondary to his literary interests.

[172] Paul Chaponnière, 'Un pasteur genevois', p.182; see also, for general information on Vernes and an appreciation of his religious position: Dufour, *Jacob Vernes (1728-1791)*.

keenly interested in literature; from 1755 to 1760 he was to edit a periodical called *Le Choix littéraire* (Chaponnière, 'Un pasteur genevois', p.182). It might therefore be expected that Vernes should have given a warm welcome to Geneva's famous guest. But this was not so: Vernes at first avoided meeting him in the mistaken belief that such conduct would please Rousseau. Soon, however, the pastor was attracted into Voltaire's orbit, and he passed from one extreme to another, now larding with flattery any articles in the *Choix littéraire* where Voltaire might be mentioned. Paul Chaponnière gives an illuminating example of this (p.184):

Ainsi Roustan, qui lui avait envoyé son 'Examen historique des IV beaux siècles de M. de Voltaire,' ayant écrit: 'M. de Voltaire ne compte que quatre âges dans le monde . . .' Vernes imprime: 'Le premier des écrivains, M. de Voltaire . . .' Roustan disait: 'M. de Voltaire écrit en homme de lettres . . .' Vernes ajoute: 'qui les aime et qui en est l'honneur.' Lorsque Roustan s'écrie: 'Je somme à présent M. de Voltaire de justifier tant de calamnités et de crimes, ou j'en tire contre lui cette conséquence accablante et inévitable . . .' Vernes édulcore cette attaque directe: 'Si comme je le pense, il est impossible de justifier tant de calamnités et de crimes, j'en tire cette conséquence inévitable.'

From the first Voltaire seemed to take to Vernes, perhaps sensing that this was not the man to be shocked by indiscretions, accidental or otherwise. In 1756 we see him praising Vernes's *discours* on the Lisbon earthquake and trying to persuade the pastor to attend Voltaire's theatricals at Lausanne.[173] It was to Vernes that one of the uncomplimentary letters regarding Calvin was addressed, and as we have seen (above, pp.140-42), far from breaking off relations with Voltaire as a result, Vernes seems to have continued his visits even after the storm of protest broke.[174] Matters became more serious during the controversy over d'Alembert's article 'Genève', and Vernes's conduct at this time indicates clearly that his relationships with both Voltaire and Rousseau were based firmly on self-interest. The pastor tried to persuade Rousseau to intervene, at first unsuccessfully, and although he received a letter from Voltaire denying that the latter had inspired d'Alembert's article (Best.D7580, 12 January 1758), Chaponnière tells us that Vernes 'affirme précisément à Rousseau la collaboration de Voltaire à l'article

[173] Best.D6709, 29 January; cf. Best.D7174 and D7209.
[174] cf. this note sent to him by Voltaire on 30 August 1757: 'Si vous voulez voir un aveugle et un manchot je vous attends mardy Messieurs les lévites' (Best.D7360).

'Genève' ('Un pasteur genevois', p.186). This action might not be so hypocritical had Vernes's views really been misrepresented by d'Alembert, but it is clear that they had not. He it was who had introduced Voltaire to the erudite and unorthodox Abauzit (Chaponnière, pp.184-85), and two undated letters by Voltaire written possibly in 1757 (Best. D7544 and D7545) show that the three men did not confine their discussions to pious commonplaces (Best.D7545):

A propos avez vous lu dans les constitutions apostoliques, cette prière: *o dieu éternel, Dieu unique, père du christ et du st esprit?*
Y a t'il rien de plus net et de plus décisif?

So, at the very time Vernes was complaining to d'Alembert that the latter had misrepresented the pastors of Geneva, he was receiving, apparently without protest, letters in which the doctrine of the trinity was clearly called into doubt.

Lest it be thought that this accusation is not established by the evidence adduced so far, it will be sufficient to consider the letters Vernes and Voltaire continued to exchange between the end of the 'Genève' controversy and the beginning of the campaign on behalf of Calas's family. The fact that Vernes was the only Genevese pastor in regular epistolary contact with Voltaire during this period anyway speaks for itself. Towards the end of 1758 the *philosophe* urged Vernes to continue his history of Geneva,[175] and an earlier reference to this projected work shows that it was not all one might expect from a Calvinist pastor: 'Vous avez raison de dire que Calvin joue le rôle de Cromwel dans l'affaire de l'assassinat de Servet.'[176] Moreover, Voltaire later asked Vernes to help him locate the letter in which Calvin expressed the hope that Servetus would be given a 'capitale judicium' (Best.D8120, February 1759). As well as these uncomplimentary references to Calvin, we find further speculation about the trinity. In October 1759 Voltaire told his correspondent: 'Il est clair comme le jour que le père est plus grand que le fils. Nous nous accorderons' (Best.D9228). The two themes were combined when on about 5

[175] cf. Best.D7925, a letter which Theodore Besterman considers to have been written in October or November 1758.
[176] Best.D7437, 28 October 1757. Cf. Chaponnière, *Voltaire chez les calvinistes*, p.80: 'Vernes, dans une *Histoire de Genève* non imprimée et rédigée avec le pasteur Roustan, écrit à propos de Servet, que Calvin "fit une chute affreuse", que "l'esprit du temps l'a perdu." Roustan surenchérit: "Calvin fut inexcusable de n'avoir pas secoué toutes les erreurs de sa première religion." ' Cf. above, p.142.

November 1760 Voltaire stated: 'Vous me feriez un extrême plaisir de me preter le galimatias d'Atanase. Je le soupçonne d'être aussi fou que celuy de Calvin et de Servet' (Best.D9385). In any case, the terms in which Voltaire referred to Vernes, and the fact that the latter permitted himself to be regularly addressed in such a way, leave little doubt that this Genevese pastor was at the very least a Unitarian and probably shared more of Voltaire's deistic beliefs: 'mon cher téologo-philosofe',[177] 'mon prêtre aimable',[178] 'Prêtre de Citere et non de Calvin',[179] 'tout soy disant prêtre que vous êtes',[180] 'Je vous embrasse en *Deo solo*' (Best.D9971, 25 August 1761). Perhaps most significant of all is a letter of 1 October 1761 concerning the *Ezour Vedam* which sums up in the clearest possible way Voltaire's opinion that Vernes and other pastors were Socinians, but were afraid to acknowledge this publicly: 'Vous seriez bien étonné de trouver dans ce manuscrit quelques unes de vos opinions, mais vous verriez que les anciens brachmanes qui pensaient comme vous et vos amis avaient plus de courage que vous' (Best. D10051).

Despite the complicity so obvious from these letters, Vernes also tried to remain on good terms with Rousseau, whom he invited in 1761 to stay at his new parish of Céligny.[181] But after the condemnation of *Emile*, Vernes, apparently fearing that his orthodoxy would again be called into question, attacked his former idol in two works: 'les "Lettres sur le Christianisme" de J.-J. Rousseau, puis les "Dialogues" sur le même sujet' (Chaponnière, 'Un pasteur genevois', p.186). This gesture provoked a fierce reply from Rousseau, who was convinced that Vernes was also responsible for the virulent pamphlet *Le Sentiment des citoyens* (cf. below, p.218, esp. n.266). The break between the two men was therefore final, and no further obstacle would seem to have remained to threaten the good relations between Voltaire and Vernes. Contacts were maintained after the beginning of the Calas campaign, although Vernes was not one of Voltaire's major collaborators. But between 6 August 1764 and 26 September 1766 there is a gap in their correspondence, and a letter of 16 July 1766 from Vernes to Louis Salles confirms that this is not due merely to the disappearance of some letters:

[177] Best.D7712, probably written in April 1758.
[178] Best.D8119, probably written in February 1759.
[179] Best.D8120, also probably written in February 1759.
[180] Best.D8147, probably written in February or March 1759.
[181] Chaponnière, 'Un pasteur genevois', p.186. Vernes had been elected on 30-31 January 1761 (Best.D9971, n.6).

'je n'ai plus aucune liaison avec Mr. de Voltaire, et j'ignore si j'en serois bien reçu' (Best.D13418, commentary).

It is impossible to say which of the two men was responsible for this change, although it would not have been surprising for Voltaire to have reacted indignantly when he found out about his friend's continuing contacts with Rousseau. Perhaps Vernes was embarrassed by the disclosures Rousseau had made. A third possibility is that Vernes was annoyed that the *Sentiment des citoyens* had been attributed to him when he knew it was really by Voltaire.[182] At any rate, relations between the two were soon as cordial as they had ever been. In a letter of 4 November 1766, Voltaire apparently invited the pastor to join the colony of *philosophes* he hoped to establish under Frederick II's protection at Clèves (Best.D13651). Not only was Vernes reinstated with his former honours, new and even more prestigious titles of philosophic distinction were accorded to him: 'mon cher philosophe',[183] 'Mon cher prêtre philosophe et citoyen . . . mon cher huguenot',[184] 'mon cher philosophe huguenot',[185] 'Monsieur le philosophe prêtre',[186] 'Prêtre d'un Dieu père de tous les hommes, prédicateur de la raison, prêtre tolérant',[187] 'Le brave ennemi d'Athanase et de la tirannie';[188] 'Si Athanase vous avait ressemblé nous ne serions pas où nous en sommes', Voltaire assured Vernes on 13 November 1768 (Best.D15312). It is difficult indeed to find any evidence for René Pomeau's assertion that 'Certaines audaces de Voltaire l'inquiéteront' (*La Religion de Voltaire*, p.298).

Indeed, the debates between the two men were no longer confined to dogmas like the trinity but were extended to the very basis of religion

---

[182] Charles Dardier (*Esaïe Gasc*, pp.53-55) thinks that Voltaire tried to give the impression that the *Sentiment* was by Vernes: cf. also below, p.218, n.266.

Rousseau had the *Sentiment des citoyens* reprinted with his own comments added (Jean Guéhenno, *Jean-Jacques: grandeur et misère d'un esprit*, 2nd ed. (Paris 1962), ii.137; Best.D12365). Vernes responded by printing his correspondence with Rousseau (*Lettres de monsieur le pasteur Vernes à monsieur J.J. Rousseau avec les réponses* (Geneva 1765): *Ferney catalogue*, B2919), to which Voltaire referred slightingly in a letter to Moultou of 7 April 1765: 'Vôtre ami Vernes a fait imprimer je ne sais quelles lettres de lui et de Jean Jaques, qui ne sont pas assurément des Lettres de Ciceron et de Pline' (Best.D12530).

[183] Best.D15002, c. 5 May 1768, and Best.D15946, 9 October 1769.

[184] Best.D14143, 25 April 1767.

[185] Best.D14399, 1 September 1767.

[186] Best.D15180, 1 August 1768.

[187] Best.D14797, 1 March 1768.

[188] Best.D14889, 28 March 1768. The reference to 'tyrannie' is no doubt to be explained by Vernes's attitude in connection with the *natifs*: cf. below, pp.231-32.

itself. 'Coupez si vous pouvez toutes les branches gourmandes, antées sur un arbre salutaire', Voltaire told Vernes in 1766, 'n'en laissez subsister que le tronc qui a été planté par Dieu même depuis que l'univers existe' (Best.D13651, 4 November 1766). This passage fits into the mould we might expect of Voltaire encouraging a liberal Protestant minister to further purify and simplify his version of Christianity. But the positions would seem to be reversed in Best.D15180, written on 19 August 1768, Voltaire apparently arguing that Christianity will not disappear, while Vernes seems to think it has already done so in many quarters:

Je crois avec vous que le tems des usurpations papales est passé, c'est à dire qu'on n'en fera plus de nouvelles; mais une partie des anciennes durera encor longtems. Le christianisme, dites vous, est aboli chez tous les honnêtes gens; oui, le christianisme de Constantin, le christianisme des pères; mais le christianisme de Jesu subsistera. Vous avez grande raison d'appeller Jesu le premier des Théistes, car il ne reconnaissait qu'un seul Dieu, et comme vous avez fort bien dit, si on lui impute des sottises ce n'est ni sa faute ni la vôtre.

A plausible interpretation is, however, possible. Vernes was not announcing to Voltaire with any satisfaction the fact that Christianity was 'aboli chez tous les honnêtes gens' – this was a simple observation and a state of affairs he lamented. In fact, although he was very far from the mainstream of Calvinist orthodoxy and was not afraid to indulge in antitrinitarian banter with Voltaire, Vernes shared with his illustrious correspondent a detestation of atheism and a fear of its social consequences: this much is clear from his moral novel, *Confidence philosophique*.[189] Though of a vastly inferior literary quality, this tale reminds one in some ways of the *conte*, *Histoire de Jenni*, which Voltaire was to publish in 1774. Both establish a clear and unequivocal connection between atheism and vice, the main difference being that Voltaire's

---

[189] first published in 1772, Vernes's novel was most successful, going through five French editions, and being translated into English, German and Dutch. A young innocent, Torman, is corrupted by Dorivart, who like him works as an assistant to the virtuous merchant Olban in Amsterdam. Torman turns to atheism and debauchery. Eventually he seduces the wife of an English merchant who had taken pity on him, and makes her pregnant. Mme Herbert dies in torment, overcome with remorse and bitterly regretting that she had been persuaded by Torman's atheistic arguments.

Vernes's touchiness about atheism is clear from his reaction to the publication of d'Holbach's *Système de la nature*; cf. Voltaire's remarks to him in this connection in Best.D16335 (7 May 1770).

young hero is redeemed by his enlightened father whereas Vernes's protagonist persists, unrepentant, in his wickedness.

Whatever the significance of this parallel, it is obvious that a considerable similarity existed between the two men's views on religion. Vernes, unlike Voltaire, was attached to the forms and traditions of Christianity, but even the impious *philosophe* was prepared to compromise a little ('le christianisme de Jesu subsistera'), and fundamentally both he and Vernes considered it necessary to preach to the masses a faith more elaborate than that which they believed themselves. In doing this did not Vernes fit perfectly the description he had given of 'des fourbes qui annoncent au peuple une parole qu'ils ne croient pas eux-mêmes' (cf. above, p.140)? What more Voltairean pastor could the *philosophe* have wished to meet? The irony is completed by the fact that Vernes, whom Voltaire urged in March 1768 to renounce his ministry,[190] obtained help from him later in the same year in obtaining a new parish, Sacconex (cf. Best.D15002, *c.* 5 May 1768). Who could blame Voltaire for believing in priestly hypocrisy when he had a living illustration of it in the shape of Jacob Vernes?

Several critics[191] have assumed that Voltaire was annoyed by the publication of *Confidence philosophique* and that there was a break in relations between him and Vernes, but this seems unlikely. At the most there was only a slight difference in emphasis, and as Voltaire remarked on 14 August 1773 (Best.D18516):

Heureusement les honnêtes gens ne disputent plus. La morale est la même par tout, parconséquent voilà la source des bêtises et des horreurs tarie d'un bout de L'Europe à l'autre chez tous les honnêtes gens. C'est tout ce que j'ai demandé à Dieu dans mes prières depuis environ vingt ans.

There is little indication from the tone of this letter that Voltaire and Vernes parted company because the latter felt a belated desire to repudiate the views of his impious correspondent. Now, as at most times in his life, Jacob Vernes would have fulfilled just as appropriately and perhaps more honestly the role of a Voltairean 'maître de morale' than that of a Calvinist pastor.

---

190 Best.D14889, 28 March 1768: 'Je voudrais que vous fussiez philosophe sindic, et que vous cessassiez d'être un petit Sinésius qui prêchait des bétises dont il se moquait. Croiez moi, troquez vîte vôtre maudit rabat de prêtre contre un rabat de conseiller.'

191 Pomeau, p.298; Gaberel, pp.163-64; Dufour, p.24. None of these critics gives any convincing evidence to back up the assumption.

ix. *Elie Bertrand (1713-1797)*

The contacts between Elie Bertrand, pastor of the French Church in Berne,[192] and Voltaire were more clearly based on mutual self-interest than appears to have been the case with the other pastors Voltaire knew. From the outset Bertrand rendered the *philosophe* important services: helping entertain him in Berne in 1756 (cf. Best.D6873), defending him during the *âme atroce* controversy (cf. above, p.131), using his influence to ensure that Voltaire was supported by the government at the time of the Saurin affair. Indeed, it seems as if Bertrand had originally taken the initiative in introducing himself to Voltaire (cf. above, p.122, n.28), and, as Louis Roulet (p.65) points out, the pastor was far from being a nonentity: 'Lorsqu'il présente ses hommages au philosophe français, il est membre des Académies royales de Berlin et de Goettingue, et fait aussi partie de la Société des beaux-arts de Leipzig.' For his part Voltaire wrote to the encyclopedists in May 1758 (cf. Best.D7729) recommending Bertrand as an eminently suitable collaborator, praised the Berne *Gazette* of which Bertrand was occasionally editor (Best. D12585, 6 May 1765), encouraged the pastor to contribute to the *Questions sur l'Encyclopédie* (Best.D16242, 19 March 1770), and tried to find a suitable position for Bertrand's son or nephew.[193] He also helped his correspondent to become a member of the Académie des sciences de Lyon (Roulet, p.68). Given the rather mercenary nature of this relationship and the fact that René Pomeau comments: 'Voltaire le considéra toujours comme un naturaliste, plutôt que comme un philosophe' (*La Religion*, p.300), one might perhaps he tempted to dismiss it as of minimal value for investigating Voltaire's contacts with Protestantism. To do so would, however, be a great mistake.

Despite the fact that Bertrand was willing to take advantage of Voltaire's influence to further his career, he seems not to have accepted without a qualm all the *philosophe*'s religious views. In about March 1756 he replied to a letter in which Voltaire had rejected the 'tout est

[192] for information on Bertrand see: Charles Berthoud, 'Les deux Bertrand', *Musée neuchâtelois* (Neuchâtel 1870), vii.53-64; Paul Dumont, 'Jean-Elie Bertrand 1713-1797', *Revue de théologie et de philosophie* (Lausanne 1905), xxxviii.217-69; Roger de Guimps, *Elie Bertrand d'Yverdon* (Yverdon 1855); F. J. Crowley, 'Pastor Bertrand and Voltaire's Lisbonne', *Mln* (1959), lxxiv.430-33; Roulet, pp.64-68.

[193] cf. Best.D18017 (18 November 1772), commentary, n.1: 'Voltaire perhaps meant Jean Elie, who is described by reputable authorities (including Voltaire himself; see Best.D17507) sometimes as Elie's nephew and sometimes as his son.'

bien' philosophy (Best.D6738, 18 February 1756), pointing out that natural religion was not sufficient for man as we know him: 'il est aussi indispensable qu'il y ait une déclaration céleste, accompagnée de promesses & de menaces, pour diriger les intentions secrètes, les passions cachées, et pour réprimer les mouvements intérieurs capables de porter au mal' (Best.D6789). Voltaire should attack fanaticism, he went on, but a reasonable form of Christianity was necessary for the maintenance of society. Another letter also written in about March 1756 claimed that Voltaire failed to distinguish true Christianity from its harmful accretions (Best.D6790). At first sight, Bertrand's arguments might seem to resemble the advice Vernet had given Voltaire not to undermine the liberal Calvinism of Geneva, but the *philosophe* does not appear to have resented Bertrand's views.[194] Perhaps the Bernese pastor had made a more favourable personal impression on Voltaire than had Vernet. Or perhaps Voltaire admired the fact that Bertrand sometimes admitted frankly that the clergy had been mistaken, as at the time of the *âme atroce* affair, when his correspondent declared: 'J'ai quelquefois honte de ma robe, mon cher Monsieur, quand je vois des gens qui la portent se déshonorer par des cabales, dont l'envie est la première cause et la malignité le soutien' (Best.D7365, 2 September 1757).

In fact, clear speaking on both sides characterised the correspondence between Voltaire and Bertrand. Events during the Saurin affair drove the former to such a fury that on 5 January 1759 he sent Bertrand a letter which was no less than a general attack on Protestant intolerance, expressing the pent-up anger which Voltaire had so carefully suppressed at the beginning of his stay in Geneva. He criticised the penal laws against Catholics in England, Denmark and Sweden. Admittedly the Catholics had similar anti-Protestant laws, 'mais nous n'avons fait que vous imiter' (Best.D8029). Voltaire himself as a Catholic had been unable to buy land openly in Switzerland, and a Protestant who changed religion would lose all his property. Even the most private practice of Catholicism was absolutely forbidden in Bernese territory. Moreover:

N'avez vous pas chassé des ministres qui ne croyaient pas pouvoir signer je ne sais quel formulaire de doctrine? n'avez vous pas exilé, pour un oui et un non, de pauvres memnonistes pacifiques, malgré les sages représentations

---

[194] cf. Best.D6818 (6 April 1756): 'J'y [to Berne] viendrai lire le catéchisme dont vous me parlez, car en vérité je me sens un peu de votre Relligion, je suis indulgent comme vous, j'aime Dieu et le genre humain, et je ne damne personne.'

des états généraux qui les ont accueillis? n'y a-t-il pas encore un nombre de ces exilés, tranquilles dans les montagnes de l'évêché de Basle, que vous ne rappelez point?

The dismissal of Petitpierre (cf. above, p.169-70) is also referred to, and Voltaire concludes: 'Vous n'êtes pas plus sages que nous, convenez en, mon cher philosophe.'

This onslaught against Protestantism was not merely the result of Voltaire's losing his sense of proportion over a series of annoying and localised incidents. After the execution of Calas, Bertrand and Voltaire returned to the subject of tolerance in an exchange of letters which is of the greatest importance for understanding Voltaire's attitude toward Protestantism. On about 15 December 1763 Bertrand claimed that it was Christianity itself which was responsible for the growth of tolerance, but genuine Christianity, not 'les passions qu'elle [cette religion de paix] condamne déguisées sous le masque du zèle', which Christ himself had condemned in the Pharisees. The aim should be to make all men true Christians, not to attack religion, and 'la tolérance qui ne sera établie que sur l'indifférence pour toute doctrine, laissant subsister toutes les passions, se démentira tôt ou tard' (Best.D11562). About a week later Bertrand returned to the subject, urging Voltaire to attack intolerance, persecution, fanaticism and superstition, but adding a note of caution: 'respectez la révélation, ce système moral si admirable communiqué du ciel aux mortels, afin d'assurer leur bonheur sur la terre' (Best. D11576, c. 20 December 1763).

Voltaire's reply was emphatic. Despite their preaching of fraternal love, Jews and Christians have always acted as if inspired by hatred for those who disagree with them: 'Jésus Christ me paraît, comme à vous, doux et tolérant; mais ses sectateurs ont été dans tous les temps in-humains et barbares' (Best.D11580, 26 December 1763). Moreover, in this respect Protestants are less defensible than Catholics:

Lorsque nous vous persécutons, nous papistes, nous sommes conséquents à nos principes, parce que vous devez vous soumettre aux décisions de notre mère s^te église. Hors de l'eglise point de salut. Vous êtes donc des rebelles audacieux. Lorsque vous persécutez, vous êtes inconséquents, puisque vous accordez à chaque charbonnier le droit d'examen.

These strictures prove conclusively that Voltaire's attack on Calvin in connection with the Servetus case had not merely been designed to annoy the Calvinist pastors of Geneva because of their refusal to allow a theatre in the city. They were part of a reasoned and logical critique of Protestantism which must make one view with caution the suggestion that Voltaire was prepared to look more favourably upon this form of Christianity than upon Catholicism. This may be true in general terms, when the benefits brought about by Erastianism in Protestant countries are taken into account, but, as we see clearly here, Voltaire sometimes accused the Protestants of being worse than their papist rivals (cf. above, pp.94-95).

It is also obvious from the surviving correspondence that Bertrand had not been wholly in favour of the *Traité sur la tolérance*. He had already criticised the idea of inspiring tolerance through indifference to dogma, which was in fact the very tactic Voltaire had favoured in his treatise. On 30 December 1763 Voltaire expressed his dismay to Bertrand that while the work was finding favour with Catholics it might displease those on whose behalf it had been composed (Best.D11590). A few days later he referred to another criticism made by Bertrand: 'Vous ne trouvez pas, mon cher ami, que la plaisanterie convienne dans les matières graves.' As might be expected, Voltaire was quite unrepentant, assuring his correspondent that he was perfectly capable of distinguishing between superstition and religion (Best.D11631, 8 January 1764). Betrand apparently expressed further doubts when the *Dictionnaire philosophique* was published. Once again he was firmly repudiated, Voltaire emphasising the unfortunate Polier's collaboration in a way well calculated to embarrass one of his Protestant colleagues: 'Un de ces articles est écrit de la propre main d'un des premiers pasteurs de votre religion réformée, ou prétendue réformée. Tout cela vous regarde, et non pas moi.'[195]

In view of the frequent criticisms to which Bertrand subjected Voltaire's deistic opinions and the attempts the pastor made to defend the liberal form of Protestantism he professed, one is rather surprised to read the following conclusion to the short paragraph René Pomeau devotes to him: 'Parti du catéchisme d'Ostervald, dans ses *Institutions chrétiennes* de 1753, le ministre bernois aboutit, mais en 1777

---

[195] Best.D12284, 1 January 1765. Voltaire mercilessly repeated to numerous correspondents the fact that Polier was the author of 'Messie', which appeared in the *Dictionnaire philosophique*. These allegations were made mainly at the time of the *Dictionnaire*'s appearance in 1764, but Voltaire repeated this tactic after La Barre's execution: cf. Best. D12137, D12138, D12149, D12152, D12159, D12162, D12164, D12166, D12173, D12178, D12187, D12192, D12201, D12221, D12284, D13502, D17809.

seulement, au pur eudémonisme de l'*Essai philosophique et moral sur le plaisir*. Enfin un prédicant renonçait à Jésus-Christ' (*La Religion*, p.300). Yet, assuming that Pomeau's interpretation is correct, there are indications even in Bertrand's championing of Christiantiy which show that a further evolution of his ideas was possible. The very defence he made of revelation in Best.D6789 (cf. above, p.185) justified religion more in terms of social utility than according to an independent, transcendental scale of values. Moreover, the description he gave in 1763 of Christianity could equally be applied to Voltairean deism: 'qui appelle tous ses disciples à faire usage de leur raison pour examiner & croire ce qu'ils trouvent conforme à ses lumières [...] en leur déclarant qu'ils seront jugés selon ce qu'ils auront fait soit le bien soit le mal, & non suivant ce qu'ils auront cru.'[196] It may not be irrelevant to point out that the opinion expressed here by Bertrand is also a direct negation of justification by faith, one of the basic tenets of traditional Calvinism.

Louis Roulet observes (pp.65-66) that it is no easy matter to analyse Bertrand's philosophy, despite the prolixity of his writings. Outwardly he was as respectably orthodox as one could wish, and were it not for his relations with Voltaire and the late work mentioned by Pomeau, his faith would probably never have been questioned. Quite apart from the services Voltaire rendered Bertrand, it is easy to appreciate how attractive any scholar would have found the prospect of corresponding with France's leading man of letters. The existence of such contacts can hardly be taken as evidence that Bertrand had a secret penchant towards deism which became obvious only in the late 1770s. However, we do have concrete evidence in a letter Voltaire wrote Bertrand that the pastor was not above falsifying the truth to suit his own ends. On 19 March 1770 Bertrand was thanked for an article he had contributed to the *Questions sur l'Encyclopédie*: 'Je ne sais rien de mieux pensé, de plus méthodique, de plus vrai', Voltaire exclaimed: 'Vous avez été prêtre, et vous immolez la prêtraille à la vérité, et à l'intérêt public.'[197] In his textual notes to the letter, Theodore Besterman points out that Bertrand changed the phrase 'Vous avez été prêtre' to 'Vous avez été un esprit juste et un cœur droit', and it appears that this was not an isolated forgery on the pastor's part. If Bertrand was capable of such actions

---

[196] Best.D11562. Cf. the article 'Dogmes' of the *Dictionnaire philosophique*: 'Je vis une foule prodigieuse de morts qui disaient: "J'ai cru, j'ai cru"; mais sur leur front il était écrit: "J'ai fait"; et ils étaient condamnés' (ed. Benda and Naves, p.173).

[197] Best.D16242. The article in question was on 'Droit canonique'.

there is no guarantee that he did not similarly disguise or conceal his religious beliefs. If he was already unorthodox during the period in which he corresponded with Voltaire, it is in any case unlikely that he would have compromised himself by admitting this, even by implication, when he had seen how badly things had turned out for Polier de Bottens. Thus, in his letters Bertrand confines himself to supporting Voltaire's attacks on Catholicism, and protests when these are extended to Christianity as a whole. The prospect of 'converting' Voltaire to a reasonable alliance with liberal Protestantism may not have been absent from the pastor's mind when he lectured him on the merits of the more enlightened forms of Christianity.[198] But it must be emphasised that Bertrand's real position remains doubtful. Despite Pomeau's affirmations, Bertrand seems to have defended his religion more effectively than many of his colleagues, but for exactly what motives it is difficult to say.

x. *Allamand (1709-1784)*

The real beliefs of François-Louis Allamand, a country clergyman who served several parishes in the pays de Vaud, have also presented something of a mystery.[199] René Pomeau (p.299) summarises the position as follows:

Gibbon, qui le fréquenta à Lausanne, et le tenait pour un grand esprit, le croyait secrètement sceptique: 'petit curé de campagne qui trompe ses paroissiens'. Eugène Ritter et Henri Vuilleumier sont au contraire persuadés de la sincérité de sa foi. Ni pleinement orthodoxe, ni franchement sceptique, Allamand semble avoir été l'une de ces âmes inquiètes comme il y en eut tant au dix-huitième siècle.

Doubts as to Allamand's orthodoxy have been strengthened by the fact that, when a young man, he was involved in a controversy with the

---

[198] cf. Bertrand's letter of 16 March 1759 to Haller, written at the height of the Saurin affair during the controversy between Haller and Voltaire. Although he states that one of Voltaire's letters 'est négligée au point d'être ridicule', Bertrand steers a skilful course between the two rivals, deciding in favour of neither Voltaire nor Haller (for example, he expresses polite dismay that the latter should have allowed the correspondence to become public), and he comments significantly: 'Je voudrois pouvoir corriger V., je croirois faire une bone œuvre . . .' (Best.D8193, commentary).

[199] for information on Allamand see Eugène Ritter, 'Le pasteur Allamand', *Revue historique vaudoise* (1903), xi.289-301; Paul Maillefer, 'Voltaire et Allamand', *Revue historique vaudoise* (1898) vi.300-10, 321-32, 353-65; Vuilleumier, iv.287-300. Allamand was ordained in 1732, and after spending several years abroad was successively pastor of Ormont-dessus, Bex, and Corsier. In 1773 he was appointed professor of Greek and moral philosophy at the Lausanne academy.

oppressed French Protestants whom he advised to abandon their illegal practice of assembling 'au désert'. Moreover, as we have seen (above, pp.122, 162, n.123), he expressed his sympathy for Voltaire over the condemnation of the *Délices* epistle and also gave him as much support as he dared during the Saurin affair. Does their correspondence give us any clue as to Allamand's real position?

A reading of the letters exchanged between the two men in the first four years of their acquaintance might tend, if anything, to support the view that he was insincere in his vocation. The pastor refers flippantly to his ministry several times,[200] laments the enormous amount of preaching he has to undertake, presenting many of his pastoral duties as boring,[201] and extending his apparent scepticism to priests and pastors in general: 'aprés demain, je prêcherai sur le Repos du sabbath; ce sera le violer en le recommandant, mais les Prêtres ont toujours eu ce privilège, & ils l'ont quelquefois étendu à tout le Decalogue' (Best.D6318). Indeed, at first sight, Allamand would seem to be made very much in the mould of Vernes, a career pastor who kept his real opinions to himself, caring very little what he actually preached to his flock, providing that this rather tedious exercise guaranteed him a secure existence (Best.D6169): 'Hérétique pour Hérétique, j'aime autant le pain de Calvin que celui d'un autre, & que mes Païsans ne s'embarrassent pas, si leur liberté est d'indifférence ou de spontanéïté, pourvu que je les déclare prédestinés au salut, quand ils pratiquent les dix Commandemens' (Best.D6169).

Yet on closer investigation Allamand turns out not to be as lacking in religious convictions as the last quotation might suggest. At any rate, although he tried to impress Voltaire with his broadmindedness and tolerance, Allamand was not afraid to include in his letters comments which were unlikely to receive the seal of philosophic approval. On 20 June 1755, for example, a passing reference to Tronchin allowed Allamand to express his scepticism regarding materialist explanations of the soul.[202] And when, towards the end of the Saurin affair, Voltaire asked Allamand to forget he was a pastor when writing to him (Best.

[200] cf. Best.D6208 (17 March 1775) and Best.D6318 (20 June 1755).

[201] cf. Best.D6169 (17 February 1755), where he complains of 'l'orage de fonctions Pastorales qui me fera jusqu'à Pâques une Prison de ma paroisse'. Cf. also Best.D6493 (15 September 1755).

[202] 'je voudrais qu'on me dit, pourquoi dans ce siècle où le Corps et l'âme ne sont qu'un, il est aussi rare que dans le précédent, que ce qui est remède pour l'un, le soit aussi pour l'autre?' (Best.D6318, 20 June 1755).

D8201, 21 March 1759), Allamand not only failed to do this, in his reply he defended himself and his colleagues, claiming that priests resemble kings, 'qui ne font pas le centième du Bien qu'ils peuvent, mais qui en font toujours plus que de mal' (Best.D8206, 23 March 1759). Later in the same year Allamand hopefully enquired whether it would be possible to hold Protestant services at Ferney (Best.D8421, 6 August 1759), and, undismayed by the negative answer he received,[203] the pastor even dared to extol the virtues of preaching and the Bible, though at the same time he criticised his colleagues for their narrow-mindedness (Best. D8448, 20 August 1759). Yet it would be premature to conclude from these passages that allegations regarding his unorthodoxy have been entirely unfounded. Even while defending the utility of the clergy and of preaching, Allamand does so in terms of social justification well calculated to appeal to Voltaire (Best.D8206):

témoin votre château de Fernex que vous n'auriés pas le courage de bâtir, s'il n'y avait personne pour édifier en l'air celui qui fait la sûreté de tous les châteaux de la Terre, & qui durera plus qu'eux. Nous vivons de cela: mais ne devons nous pas vivre aussi bien que vos mâçons.

Here is Voltaire's argument of a 'dieu rémunérateur et vengeur' in a nutshell, but it is cunningly used against its priest-hating advocate. Allamand is surely asking how such a socially desirable doctrine can be preached to the unsophisticated masses, untouched by the writings of a *philosophe* like Voltaire, without the aid of an institutionalised clergy. But is his argument merely the skilful attempt of a pastor, himself convinced that the priesthood was divinely ordained, to ensnare Voltaire in his own reasoning by making him recognise the utility of the Protestant clergy as it already existed? Or was this Calvinist minister prepared to envisage the establishment of a priesthood on lines likely to appeal to a deist?

This question is of the greatest interest, and one is at a loss to understand René Pomeau's assertion that

dans sa correspondance [Allamand] évita longtemps toute discussion philosophique. On se demande même la raison pour laquelle il entretint, pendant

---

[203] 'Je ne peux faire dire la messe publiquement aux Délices, ny avoir un prêche public à Tourney et à Ferney' (Best.D8442, 16 August 1759). Voltaire was here saying exactly the opposite of what he had told Jacques-Bernard Chauvelin on 3 June 1759: 'je pourrais même, si j'étais calviniste, avoir un prédicant dans mon château' (Best.D8334).

des années, un commerce épistolaire où il n'échangeait guère avec son illustre correspondant que des propos de politesse.[204]

In fact the reverse is true. It was with François-Louis Allamand more than with any other Protestant pastor that Voltaire discussed the rôle and utility of an organised priesthood. Far from having accepted, 'sans mot dire, toutes les brochures anti-chrétiennes de Voltaire' (Pomeau, p.299), Allamand subjected several of the *philosophe*'s works to an intense scrutiny, praising those features of which he approved, but also censuring other parts and adding his own suggestions. Nor does Voltaire seem to have spurned Allamand's opinions, for he replied, sometimes in detail, to his correspondent's critique. It is this debate that I must now summarise briefly.

The publication of Voltaire's *Traité sur la tolérance* was not regarded by all Protestants as an unmitigated blessing,[205] and Allamand was one of those who expressed some misgivings. There were certain 'malices' in the work, he felt. A 'gros Suisse' would have distinguished between private and public religion. No one has a right to tamper with the former, but the State has a right to take from the Gospels what it needs for a national religion (Best.D11621, 5 January 1764). Perhaps, in view of this distinction, we can appreciate a little better why Allamand wrote his *Lettres sur les assemblées des Religionnaires* – the French Huguenots ought presumably to have contented themselves with 'private' worship and not broken the laws against public assemblies (cf. above, p.190). Allamand's letter to Voltaire continued with a semi-humorous attempt not so much to convert[206] the *philosophe* as to encourage him to make a compromise with Christianity: 'Croiés moi, Monsieur, il est un Christianisme qui mérite que vous en preniés connaissance [...] Le beau coup de fillet que je ferais là si vous vouliés un peu mordre à l'hameçon, avec trois ou quatre de vos amis, & le Vicaire savoyard!' (Best.D11621). Voltaire's reply was unpromising,[207] but the tone in

---

[204] Pomeau, *La Religion*, p.299. Florida (p.168) reaches a similarly surprising, and quite mistaken conclusion: 'They sporadically wrote one another until 1772, but their letters hardly ever moved beyond matters of scenery, health, and other commonplaces.'

[205] cf. Paul Rabaut's letter of 30 December 1763 to Court de Gébelin (Best.11590, Commentary). Cf. also Best.D11571 and Charles Coquerel, *Histoire des églises du désert* (Paris 1841) ii.339.

[206] 'Ne vous fâchés pas, j'appelle, comme les autres, un bon chrétien, celui qui l'est à ma mode, & le vrai christianisme, celui que je trouve, moi, dans le N.T.'

[207] 'Vous dites qu'il y a un peu de malice dans ce livre, j'y vois aucontraire trop de respect pour la malice de ceux qui imposent un joug impertinent à l'esprit humain, et trop

which he addressed Allamand must have more than compensated the pastor for any disappointment felt by the latter: Vos Lettres me font grand plaisir; et quand il vous passera par la tête quelque idée que vous ne vouliez pas communiquer à votre consistoire, adressez la moi hardiment, je ne vous excommunierai pas' (Best.D11629, 8 January 1764).

Allamand did not hesitate to follow this advice. In July 1768 he wrote to Voltaire after reading the *Conseils raisonnables à m. Bergier*. As in the case of the *Traité sur la tolérance* there were features which had worried Allamand. He did not agree that the author's friends (i.e. the other *philosophes*) were not interested in the clergy's benefices. Things would go further than these reformers expected, he warned. Allamand then asked to be allowed to visit Voltaire, and his request demonstrates that the two men were not discussing these questions for the first time: 'Après tout, c'est une chose à voir & à entendre qu'un Ministre de village qui prêche depuis 36 ans, à qui vous demandiés, il y en a trois, s'il était Philosophe, qui n'a pas osé répondre à la Question, & qui demande présentement à capituler' (Best.D15128, 5 July 1768). In his reply Voltaire tried to reassure Allamand that the *Conseils raisonnables* had not been written with Protestants in mind, 'mais apparemment pour de jeunes garçons catholiques qu'on veut empêcher de se faire moines, et pour de jolies filles qu'on craint de voir s'enterrer toute vivantes dans un cloitre' (Best.D15131, 8 July 1768). He added that he would be delighted to see Allamand. Before this meeting took place the pastor wrote Voltaire a letter which is perhaps the most significant of their entire correspondence, containing nothing less than a proposal for co-operation in setting up a new, philosophical religion, but one which would accept the historical framework it had inherited from Christianity (Best.D15147, 19 July 1768).

Allamand had not been entirely reassured by Voltaire's explanations, for he considered that freethinkers were concerned to attack more than merely monks and convents. Indeed he expressed his own willingness to dispense with the doctrine of Hell, and agreed that many other aspects of Christianity deserved to be ridiculed. He was reassured by the fact that 'la Profession du Thëisme[208] reconnait formellement un DIEU

de complaisance pour des imbéciles qui se soumettent aux fripons' (Best.D11629, 8 January 1764).

[208] no doubt the *Profession de foi des théistes* (1768), M.xxvii.55-74.

193

REMUNERATEUR, aussi la Voilà déjà d'accord avec Hebreux xi.6'. But the pastor also sounded a note of warning: 'Je demande seulement qu'après s'être assés épanouï la rate à nos dépends, on veuille bien revenir à des principes fixes, prendre l'affaire aussi sérieusement qu'elle le mérite, & ne pas tant se presser de mettre tout à bas.' There were very few things in the *Traité sur la tolérance* or the *Conseils raisonnables* with which he could not agree. But two lines in the latter work pleased him very much, and he commented significantly: 'Mon secret est là. Il y a, sans doute, une autre manière d'établir le xsme.' Theodore Besterman identifies these two lines as the following: 'Que feriez-vous d'un homme qui aurait empoisonné dix mille moutons?'[209] The Biblical story in question is that of Christ's casting out evil spirits into a herd of swine which promptly drowned themselves (Mark v. 11-13). Such apparently senseless waste particularly irritated Voltaire, who singled out this miracle for special attention.[210] Allamand is thus by implication accepting Voltaire's criticism of New Testament miracles as a whole, despite the fact that these prodigies were still regarded, by apologists both Catholic and Protestant, as one of the major proofs of Christianity. The pastor of Corsier is also expressing the need to find a new basis for religion (presumably in place of revelation), a need of which he has been conscious for many years, 'sans avoir cessé un instant d'être chrétien à ma mode'. He goes on:

La question serait de voir si l'Auteur des Conseils & moi, nous nous sommes rencontrés sur cette autre manière de s'y prendre; ou, en deux mots, s'il n'y aurait pas moyen d'arréter & d'exécuter un Plan de Religion Universelle, capable de faire le bonheur du genre humain, & la gloire éternelle de la Philosophie, sans oublier celle de JESUS CHRIST dont nous mangeons le pain de 1700 ans, & qui avait, assurément, saisi la bonne idée; car ce n'est pas sa faute si, après lui, sa parole a été faite Chair.

One sentence in particular gives Allamand hope that Voltaire might share his views about Christ: 'Ah, si nous voulons imiter J. CH. soions martyrs & non pas bourreaux', and beneath the rapturous praise Allamand dispenses at this point one can surely detect a genuine desire to

---

[209] M.xxvii.46 (Best.D15147, commentary, n.6).

[210] cf. the *Examen important de milord Bolingbroke*: 'Le plus beau [miracle] de tous, à mon gré, est celui par lequel Jésus envoie le diable dans le corps de deux mille cochons, dans un pays où il n'y avait point de cochons' (*Mélanges*, p.1045). According to N. Torrey (*Voltaire and the English deists* (Yale 1930), p.77), Voltaire referred to the Gadarene swine on at least twenty-six different occasions.

inspire in his correspondent a more accommodating attitude toward the founder of Christianity if not toward his disciples and their subsequent excesses.

Most critics might assume that Voltaire paid scant attention to this proposal made by an obscure country pastor from the pays de Vaud. Was it not just the sort of naivety to excite his ridicule, a convenient piece of compromising evidence Voltaire could use against the Protestant clergy just as he had publicised Polier de Bottens's heretical views (cf. above, p.187, esp. n.195)? In fact, surprising as this may seem, Voltaire appears to have been impressed by Allamand's arguments. At any rate the letter in which he told Vernes that 'le christianisme de Jesu subsistera' was written just after Allamand's visit.[211] One is even tempted to suspect some connection between these discussions with Allamand and the more conciliatory attitude toward Christianity in general and the person of Jesus in particular which some critics have noted in Voltaire's works at the end of the 1760s.[212] But this is only speculation. What is clear from his correspondence is that Voltaire now had the highest regard for Allamand and wished that other Protestant pastors 'pouvaient [lui re]ssembler, et substituer comme lui la morale [aux a]bsurdités'.[213] He was obviously prepared to make some concessions, for when Allamand criticised the harsh punishment imposed by the Bernese authorities on a blasphemer (Best.D15181, 19 August 1768), Voltaire replied that this had perhaps not been a mistake: 'Il faut peut être que la canaille respecte ce qui n'est fait uniquement que pour la canaille' (Best.D15185). Moreover, Voltaire had entrusted Allamand with a very dangerous work, the *Examen important de mylord Bolingbroke*, which the pastor took back with him to Corsier. Allamand also promised to read 'de sang froid, & la plume à la main' (Best.D15181) other pamphlets Voltaire intended to send him. The debate was to continue.

A reading of the letters exchanged between Voltaire and Allamand in the late 1760s and early 1770s shows that the pastor returned several times to the theme of reorganising religion on more 'philosophic' lines

[211] Best.D15180, 19 August 1768: cf. above, p.182.

[212] cf. *L'Ingénu and Histoire de Jenni*, ed. Brumfitt and Davis, pp.xxxviii-xli; Richard Fargher, *Life and letters in France: the eighteenth century* (London 1970), p.150.

[213] Best.D15185, 24 August 1768. Cf. also Best.D15757 (18 July 1769), where Voltaire pays tribute to Allamand's wisdom and scholarship: 'Les livres ne peuvent qu'amuser Monsieur Allamand et ne peuvent rien lui apprendre.'

and of discussing the rôle the clergy might expect to play in such a development. Allamand resumed his practice of sending Voltaire comments on passages in the *philosophe*'s works which particularly interested him, and it is surely to the pastor's credit that he was not afraid to make points which might annoy Voltaire. Thus he cunningly underlined the importance of moderation after reading one of Voltaire's most virulent attacks on Christianity:

Entre nous [. . .] j'entrevois qu'il [the *Examen important*] serait plus dangereux s'il était moins passioné, & cette passion que je déteste dans les Xñs, m'étonne toujours dans les ennemis du Xsme. [. . .] à quoi sert d'être Philosophe, si on n'est pas plus maître chés soi qu'un Théologien.[214]

On 25 January 1770 Allamand defended the Jews and refuted several of Voltaire's statements in *Dieu et les hommes* (Best.D16113). Later in the same year he subjected the *philosophe*'s reasoning on free-will to a searching examination, basing his criticisms on passages from the *Questions sur l'Encyclopédie* article 'Dieu' (Best. D16725, 24 October 1770). But Allamand's letters always contrived to balance criticism with praise, or with comments likely to please Voltaire.[215] And twice more the philosophical pastor returned to the subject which fascinated him: a reasonable reform of religion which would build rather than destroy. On 25 January 1770 he made a new plea for serious consideration of his ideas. Despite the criticisms put forward by Voltaire and the deists:

reste toujours le fond des choses qui ne laisse pas d'être d'une importance infinie, & de démontrer que la Religion a grand besoin d'être rendue plus utile au monde, & plus digne du siècle que vous avés éclairé; mais, de grâce, travaillons y donc sérieusement, & de sang froid; Prennons même les *Propositions honnétes* de l'œuv. Théol. pour préliminaires, & qu'on forme un congrès qui offre enfin au genre-humain en articles clairs et précis la Religion dont il a besoin. Je me persuade que quatre Plénipotentiaires que vous nommeriés régleraient en trois jours sous votre médiation, tous les articles de la Paix universelle.

The idea of Voltaire presiding at a congress of enlightened theologians is, to say the least, picturesque. But Allamand was prepared to go even

[214] Best.D15181. Cf. Best.D16113: 'N'y aurait il donc rien à gagner [. . .] à dessaler un peu ce qui a été lâché dans ce ton d'aigreur, & à donner aux disciples de J.Ch. l'exemple de la douceur & de la débonnaireté qu'il s'attribue, & dont il s'est rarement écarté?'

[215] cf. Best.D16113: 'il est clair que la Théologie n'est autre chose que *peur de la raison*', and in the same letter he calls Voltaire 'un des plus admirables chefs d'œuvre de celui qui a fait toute L'armée des Cieux'; cf. also Best.D16725.

further. On 24 October 1770 he declared to Voltaire his willingness to abandon even the name of Christianity (Best.D16725):

Vous m'avés vraiment soulagé à bien des égards, en vous déclarant si haute-ment, & avec cet air de franchise, pour la Religion; car si vous ne la voulés que raisonnable, utile à la société, consolante pour les gens de bien, & faite à suppléer à l'impuissance de touts les autres freins de la méchanceté, je ne veux non plus que cela; & peu m'importe le nom qu'on donnera à cette Religion pourvû qu'elle soit tout cela.

Was Allamand then merely a 'petit curé de campagne qui trompe ses paroissiens',[216] a pastor who, like Vernes and perhaps Bertrand, was prepared to make his living by preaching a religion in which he did not personally believe? At first sight this would certainly appear to be the case, but one is loath to place Allamand in the same category as some of the other pastors Voltaire knew. His relationship with Voltaire was not based on self-interest and he did not alter the *philosophe*'s letters with a view to publication as did Bertrand. Nor did he tacitly accept all Voltaire's jibes against Christianity, as Vernes seems to have done. Throughout the years he consistently maintained an independent position and, as we have seen, was not afraid to disagree with Voltaire. Allamand was certainly unorthodox, but not in a negative or destructive way: enthusiasm to build something new and more worthwhile on the historical foundations of Christianity characterises his thought. It also seems fair to assume that Allamand was exaggerating when, on one occasion, he told Voltaire that it did not matter what name the new religion was given. For throughout the pastor's correspondence we see his attachment to the name and spirit of Christianity, if not always to its history and dogma.[217] His references to Christ are always respectful,

[216] Gibbon's opinion of him as reported by Pomeau; cf. above, p.189.

[217] cf. Vuilleumier, iv.292: 'Nous n'avons pas le droit de mettre en doute sa sincérité quand, peu d'années avant d'être appelé au professorat, il fait cette déclaration: "Ce que je crois en fait de Religion, je le crois très sérieusement, et depuis quarante ans; ce n'est plus, *parce que mes prêtres m'ont dit de le croire*, c'est parce que je me suis bien convaincu, à force *d'y rêver*, que la Religion de Jésus-Christ, je dis, la Religion de Jésus-Christ, est vraye et divine."' Allamand's statement is an extract from *L'Anti-Bernier* (i.121), which was published in 1770. There is an obvious similarity between these sentiments and those expressed some months earlier to Voltaire in Best.D15147 (cf. above, pp.193-94). Vuilleumier's summary of the ideas expressed in Allamand's works – a defence of redemp-tion by Christ but hostility toward the doctrines of the trinity, predestination and eternal damnation, coupled with a great amount of toleration for other denominations – also fits in with the opinions developed in letters to Voltaire, and would seem to prove fairly conclusively that Allamand was no hypocrite.

sometimes reverent.[218] In August 1759 he told Voltaire that he liked the Bible precisely because it had something different to say for each era (Best.D8448, 20 August 1759). And even at the time when he was making the most adventurous proposals to Voltaire, Allamand was still thinking of the *philosophe*'s eternal salvation: 'Il pourrait bien être damné pour les siens; mais il ne l'est pas encore [. . .] Qui sait donc si le Coche ne m'apportera point à la fin quelque Œuvre Philosophique qui sera bonne chrétienne?' (Best.D16113, 25 January 1770).

With his interesting attempts to conciliate *philosophie* and religion, to escape from the narrow unyielding dogmatism of traditional Christianity while at the same time preserving its better features, Allamand is surely a forerunner, in many ways, of some contemporary theologians. Though his letters were often verbose and stylistically inelegant, Voltaire must always have found their content stimulating and original. His affection for the pastor seems to have been genuine, and it is unlikely that he ever regretted having told Allamand, as early as 15 January 1755: 'c'est avec de tels Pasteurs qu'il me faudrait vivre et mourir' (Best. D6085).

xi. *Paul Moultou (1731-1787)*

It was the Calas case that brought about close contacts between Voltaire and Paul Moultou.[219] As an important member of the committee set up to co-ordinate action taken on the family's behalf, Moultou collaborated closely with the *philosophe*.[220] Along with Jacob Vernes he was consulted by Voltaire regarding the *Traité sur la tolérance*, and it is quite clear from the subsequent correspondence between the two men that Moultou was a major channel of information for Voltaire regarding the state of French Protestantism. Indeed, by 1769, Moultou had acquired a fair amount of influence on his own account, not only passing on useful tips to Voltaire but sometimes presenting him with an agreeable *fait accompli*. On 13 December 1769 Voltaire commented (Best.D16039):

Je vous fais mon compliment sur vos deux galériens. Si c'est par mad. la Duchesse Danville que vous êtes parvenu à cette bonne œuvre, cela prouve qu'elle a du crédit auprès de Mr de st Florentin. Si c'est par vous même vous ferez casser la révocation de l'édit de Nantes.

---

[218] Cf. Best.D15147 and Best.D16113.

[219] cf. Pomeau, *La Religion*, pp.339-40; Bernard Gagnebin, 'Voltaire et l'intolérance d'après ses lettres au pasteur Moultou', *Les Musées de Genève* (1951).

[220] Edna Nixon, *Voltaire and the Calas case* (London 1961), pp.134-36.

During the first years of Voltaire's stay in Geneva, however, Moultou appears to have steered fairly clear of him.[221] Perhaps at this stage he disapproved of the celebrated deist. At any rate on 14 March 1759 an unidentified correspondent wrote to Moultou from Turin in connection with the *Essai sur les mœurs*, informing the pastor that he had told the bishop of Pignerol (Best.D8182, commentary):

que je coñaissais quelcun qui travaillait à réfuter sa partie de l'histoire qui regarde les Juifs et je lui avouai que c'était l'Autheur [des] thèses sur les miracles,[222] il m'assura qu'il estimait cet Autheur et q[u'il] serait charmé de lire encore de ses ouvrages.

But the main reason for Moultou's lack of contact with Voltaire was no doubt that he was one of Rousseau's most enthusiastic supporters[223] and according to Theodore Besterman the pastor was partly responsible for giving Rousseau the impression 'that Voltaire had foreknowledge of his condemnation' by the Genevese authorities (Best.D10556, commentary). In a letter to Rousseau Moultou claimed to have triumphantly defended his friend's honour 'chez Madame Danville' where he had met Voltaire by chance, adding: 'V^e resta müet, il demanda qui j'étois, il y a [. . .] six ans que je ne l'avois pas rencontré.'[224] Such a position is readily understandable in a committed supporter of Rousseau who avoided seeing Voltaire, but Moultou's attitude after the beginning of the Calas affair, when, as we have seen, he came into frequent contact with Voltaire, is rather more questionable for, as Theodore Besterman tells us, 'Moultou wrote to Rousseau on 21 August 1762, attacking Voltaire in his characteristic manner, finding the *Sermon des cinquante*

---

221 indeed Moultou seems rather to have written off Voltaire during this period: in about May or June 1760 he wrote to Vernes: 'L'Acakia de Voltaire n'inspire que de l'horreur. L'Ecossaise est coñe tout ce que V. fait aujourdhuy, Le dernier souffle d'une belle vie, mais ce n'est qu'un souffle' (Best.D8951, commentary).

222 Moultou had published his *Dissertatio de epocha qua videntur miracula desiisse in ecclesia christiana* at Geneva in 1754 (Best.D8182, n.5).

223 cf. Guéhenno, ii.91-145. In 1762 Moultou informed Rousseau of the burning of *Emile* and the *Contrat social* in Geneva and assured him that his popularity with the lower classes was immense. The following year, after Rousseau's renunciation of his Genevese citizenship, Moultou wrote to him: 'J'ai pleuré sur votre patrie, mais je vous ai admiré' (Leigh 2701), and he expressed similar admiration when the *Lettres de le montagne* were published in 1764: 'J'ai lu vôtre livre; ce sont les gémissements d'un héros [. . .] Genève même qui vous rejette, Genève un jour S'honorera de vous [. . .] Cette Prophétie est aussi Sure que votre gloire' (Leigh 3770).

224 Leigh 1961, 7 July 1762.

disgusting, and implying that he was keeping Voltaire at arm's length' (Best.D10684, commentary). In fact Moultou seems to have kept his options open with the two great men: as late as 1772 he was still in regular contact with Rousseau,[225] and despite the fact that he had received personal help from Voltaire, who had conceived the highest regard for him, Moultou still felt able to refer to him in terms far from complimentary.

On about 25 December 1762 Moultou congratulated Voltaire on his work against intolerance (Best.D10859); indeed the Calas affair prompted many Protestants to revise the unfavourable impression they had formed of him (cf. Best.D10439 and D10538). Yet it is evident from other letters written at about the same time that Moultou did more in his visits to Ferney than praise Voltaire's efforts in favour of the French Huguenots. A tone of complicity similar to that found in the *philosophe*'s letters to Vernes is evident in many of those to Moulton, and the two pastors' names are in fact coupled together several times by Voltaire, as when he invited Moultou to stay with him 'auprès d'une église qui est dédiée à dieu seul en grosses lettres', adding: 'Si votre frère l'anti-atanasien Verne veut être de la partie nous ne dirons pas grand bien des évêques d'Alexandrie, et encor moins des juges de Toulouse.'[226] This passage clearly implies that, at the very least, Moultou was not offended by the expression of antitrinitarian views, and another letter in which Voltaire addresses the pastor as 'mon cher frère en un seul dieu' confirms this impression even more explicitly.[227] Moultou resembled

---

[225] *Correspondance générale de J.-J. Rousseau*, ed. Théophile Dufour (Paris 1924-1934), xx.155; cf. Leigh 2577 (Moultou to Rousseau, 30 March 1763): 'Vôtre morceau sur les Protestants de France [*Lettre à Christophe de Beaumont*] est un morceau admirable. Vôltaire vient de fére sur le même sujet un livre abominable, il devient touts les jours plus fol.' The reference is presumably to the *Traité sur la tolérance*, in whose preparation Moultou was himself involved. It is only fair to point out that Moultou had been trying to reconcile Rousseau with Voltaire in February and March 1763, but Rousseau reacted indignantly to this suggestion and Moultou did not insist (cf. Best.D11114, commentary; Leigh 2489, 2548, 2557, 2560).

[226] Best.D10942, possibly written about 23 January 1763; cf. also Best.D10988: 'J'ai envoié à votre ami L'arien un petit chapitre tout à fait édifiant'; cf. also Best.D12530 and D14797. The fact that Moultou was still on friendly terms with Vernes although, as was also true in the case of Voltaire, Vernes had already broken with Rousseau, makes it all the more clear that in matters of friendship Moultou tried to keep his options open as long as possible, whatever apparent contradictions this involved.

[227] Best.D11074, 7 March 1763. Moultou also shared with Vernes the distinction of being saluted in a way reserved for Voltaire's most philosophic correspondents. This

Vernes in yet another respect: just as Voltaire encouraged Vernes to persevere with his history of Geneva, so he urged Moultou to let the world see something from his pen: 'de tous les livres celui que j'ai le plus envie de lire, c'est un certain ouvrage sur quatre premiers siècles d'absurdités, auquel travaille un homme dont l'esprit et la raison sont soutenus par la science, et qui ne veut tromper personne.'[228]

The last phrase of Voltaire's compliment was not entirely without foundation, for in one important respect Moultou acted in a very different way from Vernes. It was obvious that Moultou's status as a pastor conflicted with the beliefs he held by the mid-1760s, and as early as 1764 Voltaire urged him to renounce the cloth, painting a glowing picture of the future Moultou could look forward to:

Je prévois qu'il est impossible qu'un homme de vôtre mérite et de vôtre probité, reste dans ce malheureux tripot, et je crois qu'il viendra un temps où vous irez vous établir dans la France, vôtre patrie. Rien ne vous sera plus aisé que d'être de l'académie des belles Lettres, vous serez aimé et considéré à Paris.[229]

---

involved a juxtaposition of fathers of the Church on the one hand and philosophers, heretics or even pagan divinities on the other, leaving no doubt where Voltaire's real sympathies lay. Best.D15769 (to Moultou, 22 July 1769): 'Je vous embrasse toujours en Zeleucus, en Confucius, en Platon, en Marc Aurele, et en Augustin, en Jerome, en Athanaze' may seem ambiguous, but when compared with other similar letters its meaning becomes transparent. Cf. Best.D14399 (to Vernes, 1 September 1767): 'Je vous embrasse en Jehova, en Knef, en Zeus, point du tout en Athanase, très peu en Jérôme et en Augustin.' Cf. also Best.D7540 (to Vernes) and Best.D8536 (to d'Alembert). Voltaire also 'embraced' Moultou in Zwingli (Best.D14878).

[228] Best.D11609, probably written at some time during 1763 or 1764; cf. Best.D10857. A subsequent letter (Best.D12530, 7 April 1765) mentions only the first three centuries of the Christian Church, but although Moultou was obviously an expert on the subject (cf. below, p.202), the work does not appear ever to have been completed, despite renewed compliments and encouragement from Voltaire: 'Quand serai-je assez heureux pour lire quelque chose de vous?' (Best.D16908, c. 1770/1771). The same is true of a work apparently connected with religious tolerance, which Moultou mentioned to Voltaire in 1776, explaining that 'Mon ouvrage n'est encore que dans ma tête & dans mes recueils,' where, Theodore Besterman comments, it remained (Best.D20195, commentary).

[229] Best.D12087, 15 September 1764. It is interesting to note that Rousseau had already made a similar suggestion about a year earlier: 'Vous songez à changer de pays, c'est fort bien fait à mon avis. Mais il eut été mieux encore de commencer par changer de robbe, parce que celle que vous portez ne peut plus que vous deshonorer' (Rousseau to Moultou, 15 October 1763, Leigh 2969, Dufour, x.168). According to Dufour (n.1), however, Rousseau's advice was not well received on this occasion: 'Le présent billet dut déplaire à Moultou, qui cessa sa correspondence avec Rousseau et ne la reprit que quatorze mois plus tard (le 23 décembre 1764), à la publication des *Lettres de la Montagne*.'

A year or so later Voltaire was even more positive, reporting to d'Argental that Moultou 'compte même, en partant de Genève, remercier les pédants ses confrères, et renoncer au plus sot de[s] ministères' (Best.D12361, 30 January 1765). It is not absolutely certain that these claims were correct – Voltaire might merely have been trying to help Moultou obtain more easily the passport he needed for a trip to Montpellier[230] – but by June 1766[231] Moultou had definitely resigned his office as a clergyman and was congratulated accordingly by the *philosophe*: 'Je bénis Dieu et vôtre raison supérieure qui vous ont tiré de la caverne infernale où vous étiez si malheureusement engagé. Il n'est plus permis à un honnête homme d'être de cette bande' (Best.D13352, 14 June 1766). Moultou later[232] even went as far as to have his name removed from the register of pastors, thus entirely severing his connection with Geneva's Venerable Company.

By the second half of the 1760s Moultou seems to have taken over from Vernes the position as Voltaire's main Protestant *confident*. Partly, no doubt, this was because of his excellent contacts with French Protestantism, but their relationship was also based on other, more scholarly, interests. Voltaire frequently plied his friend with questions about the primitive Church, for he was convinced that the early Christians 'n'étaient précisément que ce que sont aujourd'hui les Quakers' (Best.D16058, 25 December 1769), and it was to Moultou that he turned for facts to corroborate this, especially in connection with the original role of bishops. Moultou's reply in the shape of a long, detailed and extremely erudite letter[233] can leave us in no doubt that Voltaire was justified in placing so much confidence in the ex-pastor's scholarship. It also helps us to understand why Voltaire was keen that Moultou should collaborate with him, presumably in a role similar to that originally occupied by Polier de Bottens. Theodore Besterman places the following undated letter from Voltaire to Moultou in 1763 or 1764, and if he is correct, it is possible that Moultou participated in the composition

[230] cf. Best.D12343, D12355, D12360, D12361, D12378, D12386, D12393, D12406.

[231] there appears to be some doubt about the date when this actually occurred. René Pomeau says it was on 4 July 1766 (*La Religion*, p.340, n.134), but Theodore Besterman places it in 1765 (Best.D18418, commentary).

[232] on 6 August 1773 (Pomeau, p.340, n.134; cf. also Best.D18418, commentary).

[233] Best.D16066, *c*. 30 December 1769. Moultou had earlier written Voltaire another very scholarly letter on the New Testament (Best.D11728, 29 February 1764). The *philosophe* continued to discuss these matters with Moultou: cf. Best.D16069, D16452, D16460, D16461.

of the *Dictionnaire philosophique*, for he exclaims (Best.D11608): 'Vraiment, mon cher philosophe, vous rendrez un grand service à la raison. Faites ces trois articles [. . .] Jetez les fondements de la raison, soyez en l'apôtre' (Best.D11608). We are on firmer ground with Voltaire's letter of 20 December 1769 in which he offered to insert Moultou's material on the early Church 'par ordre alphabétique dans le supplément qu'on fait à l'Enciclopédie' (Best.D16050). A few days later he made an even more precise request: 'Faites l'article *Apôtre*, qui rectifiera celui qui est déjà fait, et *Tems apostoliques*, qui n'est pas fait' (Best.D16069, 1 January 1770). It was in fact in connection with *Questions sur l'Encyclopédie* that Voltaire was most anxioux to obtain Moultou's help, and a further letter gave Moultou *carte blanche* to write whatever he liked for this work (Best.D16147, 13 February 1770).

It is not clear whether Moultou, by writing some articles for the *Questions*, actually lived up to the literary expectations Voltaire had so clearly conceived for him, but he did achieve a certain amount of notoriety in the role of editor. Moultou was one of those who prepared for publication the works of Abausit, 'le socinien Abausit',[234] to whom Voltaire had referred with such affection.[235] Moreover, Ripert de Montclar, author of a *Mémoire théologique et politique au sujet des mariages clandestins des protestans de France*, was distantly related to Moultou, who was engaged in a controversy with the clergy which followed Ripert's death (cf. Gaberel, pp.96-97). A *protégé* of Moultou's also struck a blow in the cause of tolerance which delighted Voltaire. This was Jacob Heinrich Meister, of whose book *De l'origine des principes religieux* Voltaire commented: 'Un temps viendra où sa brochure sera le catéchisme des honnêtes gens.'[236]

One's final judgement of Moultou is hedged about with the same ambiguities that confront us when trying to evaluate the religious position of the Genevese pastors as a whole. We have clear evidence of his unorthodoxy, if this is assessed according to traditional standards, and his withdrawal from the ministry indicates anyway that he no longer

---

234 cf. Best.D14809: Moultou edited the *Œuvres diverses de m. Abauzit* (London 1770-1773). This project is referred to in Best.D16039 and D16050.

235 cf. Best.D7544, Voltaire to Vernes, written in 1757 or 1758; also above, p.142.

236 Best.D15769, 22 July 1769. Cf. also Best.D17998, D17999, D18004, and Yvonne de Athay de Grubenman, *Un cosmopolite suisse: Jacques-Henri Meister* (Geneva 1954), pp.37-38.

felt any vocation to preach the gospel. The ex-pastor's erudition was put at the disposal of Voltaire, thereby associating Moultou by implication with the use which was made of it, namely a systematic attack on the Christian religion. Yet there are surprises in store for anyone tempted to regard Moultou as merely a pale reflection of his collaborator. On 24 January 1772 he wrote to Voltaire in connection with the *Lettres de Memmius à Cicéron*, which mme Necker had praised in a recent letter to him. Moultou agreed with her judgement, but added the following qualification: 's'il [Memmius=Voltaire] relève nos espérances en nous prouvant invinciblement un Dieu que ce siècle affecte de méconnaître, pourquoi ne se livre-t'il pas davantage à l'espoir de l'immortalité qui doit le séduire beaucoup plus qu'un autre?' (Best. D17569). This defence of immortality seems based more on a Rousseauistic appeal to sentiment than on a Voltairean form of reasoning, for although Moultou does comment: 'Au fond toutes les conclusions de la métaphysique sont suspectes d'erreur', he goes on: 'choisissons donc l'erreur qui console', emphasising that he is not interested in this belief merely because it can be used as a check on man's criminal tendencies, but because 'l'existence n'est odieuse qu'au supersitieux & au méchant, elle est si douce à l'homme de bien'.

Thus, although Moultou's contacts with Rousseau had now ceased, his religious thought seems to have been increasingly influenced by the ideas of his former idol. On the other hand, Moultou's conduct toward Voltaire, which, as we have noted, left something to be desired in the mid 1760s, appears to have improved considerably. The glowing description Moultou gave of Ferney[237] may provide a clue as to his own religious position: what Moultou admired in Voltaire was above all his work in favour of tolerance. The *philosophe*'s rationalistic attitude toward religion may have appeared too destructive to Moulton, who preferred the new sentimental approach made popular by Rousseau, a position impervious to the traditional attacks of reason. But Moultou was certainly a deist, even if his position differed somewhat from that of Voltaire, and the latter could well be satisfied with this erudite Protestant whose beliefs had caused him to renounce his ministry. Was this not the shape of things to come?

This brief survey of Voltaire's contacts with five Protestant pastors allows us to reach certain tentative conclusions. In the first place there

---

[237] Best.D19639, Moultou to Meister, 1 September 1775.

is no common pattern in the relationships: Jacob Vernet reacted against Voltaire's ideas and became one of his most hated enemies; Jacob Vernes and Paul Moultou on the other hand played a deferential and largely passive rôle, almost as if they were disciples of the great man, although of the two Moultou was somewhat more independent. Elie Bertrand and François-Louis Allamand fell into yet another category, eager for one reason or another to be in contact with Voltaire, yet not afraid to criticise his religious ideas or to suggest improvements. But whatever the position of each individual pastor, one thing is certain. When Voltaire accused the pastors of Switzerland of unorthodoxy, he was perfectly justified in his assertions, at least as far as his personal contacts with them were concerned. All five pastors spoke in terms which a deist could understand and respond to, one justifying religion in terms of its social desirability, another apparently prepared to teach elements of dogma he did not personally accept, and a third proposing the establishment of a new philosophical religion for the benefit of mankind. It is indeed possible to argue that the pastors with whom Voltaire came in contact were not representative of the clergy as a whole, but what we cannot do is to assert that he had completely misunderstood the religious position in Protestant Switzerland, and had been 'carried away by his own brand of fanaticism'.[238]

xii. *Geneva and Voltaire: the social and political element*

Although I have been concerned to demonstrate that Voltaire's accusations against the Genevese clergy were fully justified in some cases, nothing would be more unfair than to consider the pastors and their beliefs in a vacuum. It is crucial to appreciate that, even more so than in many other societies, developments in belief and changes in conduct among the members of the Genevese pastoral corps were conditioned by the political and social movements of which they were a part. These wider conflicts will now be described briefly, and we shall also see the inconsistencies of Voltaire's attitude toward the clergy becoming apparent when he is dealing with the political situation in Geneva.

The 1760s witnessed a renewal of the political and social unrest which had dogged Geneva throughout the eighteenth century but whose roots

---

[238] Delattre, 'Voltaire and the ministers', p.244, quoted above, p.117.

went much deeper.[239] Calvin himself had played an important part in codifying or redrafting the republic's constitution in a way which favoured the aristocracy.[240] This bias was strengthened as time went on, and when Voltaire arrived in Geneva the city had to all intents and purposes become an oligarchy.[241] Four councils existed, but the *Petit conseil*, whose membership of twenty-five was restricted to a limited number of families, controlled the executive and legislative power of the republic. The *Conseil des soixante* played a minor advisory role in relation to the *Petit conseil*, and had little influence. Similarly, the *Conseil des deux-cents* (or *Conseil des CC*) was a purely consultative body, and its members were in any case nominated by the *Petit conseil*. The powers of the *Conseil général*, which met only once a year, had become largely decorative, and it could no longer provide an effective check on the *Petit conseil*'s actions. Its sole important prerogative was to elect yearly the four *syndics* who were the executive officers of the republic, although even here the choice was limited to the officially presented candidates who had to belong to certain families in order to be eligible. Repeated efforts were made to reduce the executive's power, but these attempts were always treated as seditious by the *Petit conseil* and repressed vigorously. In 1707 and 1734-1738 Geneva was close to civil war, and on both occasions the magistrates had to rely on foreign intervention to maintain the status quo (Spink, pp.13-15, 25-29; Gay, pp.194-95). After the 1738 *médiation* by France, Berne and Zurich, peace returned for a while, but the right, accorded to the Genevese *bourgeoisie*, of 'représentation',[242] inevitably brought about renewed conflict with the *Petit conseil*, which refused to take account of these manifestations of public opinion.

[239] cf. Spink, pp.9-29, 246-56; Michel Launay, 'Jean-Jacques Rousseau, écrivain politique', *Au siècle des lumières* (1970), pp.77-136, to which all references in this section will be made (this article appears also as chapter 1 of Michel Launay, *Jean-Jacques Rousseau: écrivain politique (1712-1762)*, Grenoble 1971); Peter Gay, *Voltaire's politics: the poet as realist* (Princeton 1959), pp.190 ff.

[240] Wendel, *Calvin*, pp.80-81. Cf. the praise given to Calvin by Rousseau (*Du contrat social, ou principes du droit politique*, édition Garnier Frères (Paris 1962), p.261, n.2), but, as Rousseau admits and Spink makes clear, although Calvin was a member of the commission which drew up the edicts of 1543, he was not the city's legislator. On this point d'Alembert's article 'Genève' certainly gives the wrong impression (cf. Lough, p.85).

[241] Spink (p.8) comments that the Genevese constitution 'n'était démocratique qu'en apparence, et [...] elle était vicieuse à sa naissance'.

[242] the *bourgeois* opponents of the *Petit conseil* were hence nicknamed *représentants*, and the magistrates and aristocrats hostile to their pretensions, *négatifs*.

Mention has been made of the *bourgeoisie*, and it is indispensable at this point to enumerate the five classes or orders traditionally found in Geneva.[243] At the top came the two privileged classes, the *citoyens* and the *bourgeois*, who alone were members of the *Conseil général*. The *citoyens* were those Genevese born in the city of parents who already belonged to this class. Michel Launay tells us (p.99):

Le bourgeois était celui qui, sans être Citoyen, avait obtenu des 'lettres de bourgeoisie', moyennant finance: ces lettres de bourgeoisie lui donnaient droit de vote au Conseil [i.e. the *Conseil général*], mais non pas droit d'être élu aux principales magistratures.

The *natifs* had also been born in the city, but of parents who were neither *citoyens* nor *bourgeois*. The *habitants* were foreigners who had purchased the right to live in Geneva, 'et qui payaient des impôts plus lourds que les Citoyens et Bourgeois'. Finally came the *sujets*, men who for one reason or another had drifted to Geneva and were unable to pay the necessary sum to become *habitants*. The right of 'représentation' had been given only to the *bourgeois* by the mediation of 1738, and the troubles of the 1760s were distinguished by the emergence of demands put forward by the *natifs* also, a development resisted by both the other parties, aristocrats and *bourgeois* alike, with tragic consequences for the tiny republic. It must not be imagined that the relationships between these various classes were conditioned merely by internal events. A major exacerbating factor was the close identity of interests and attitudes between the aristocracy and the French government. Indeed, in many ways Geneva came to resemble a client state rather than an independent power. For one thing, the French kings were represented not by an ambassador but by a *Résident* who exerted enormous political influence over Geneva's government: this minister was treated with the greatest deference and was accorded exceptional privileges.[244] In the financial field too, the tiny republic rendered great services to France. Genevese bankers had helped to fill Louis xiv's coffers in times of need,[245] and the

[243] Launay, p.99; Gay, p.190. D'Alembert mistakenly says: 'On distingue à Genève quatre ordres de personnes' (Lough, p.87).

[244] cf. Launay, pp.126-29: 'L'un d'eux, vers 1703, profita de son immunité diplomatique pour faire du trafic sur les métaux précieux, dont le commerce était sévèrement réglementé à Genève à cause de l'industrie horlogère et l'orfèvrerie; et M. le Résident était choqué que les Citoyens de Genève eussent le mauvais goût de protester contre ce trafic' (pp.126-27); cf. also Lüthy, *La Banque protestante en France*, i.49.

[245] cf. Lüthy, i.126-39. Genevese contributions to the French army in Italy made in 1701 and 1702 were unpopular in the city itself and caused diplomatic pressure to be exerted on

Petit conseil acted vigorously to suppress manifestations of popular opinion, which were consistently anti-French: for example, bonfires were lit to celebrate William of Orange's victory at the battle of the Boyne, since this represented a defeat for Louis XIV (cf. Launay, pp.125-26). We can now begin to understand the depths of resentment caused by attempts to introduce French culture, especially the theatre,[246] to Geneva, for more than anything else this underlined the dominance of one particular class and reminded other Genevese of disabilities to which they were subject. The sumptuary laws, for example, were not so much an illustration of the persisting influence of Calvinism on all sections of the community as a constant and deliberate reminder of the class divisions outlined earlier, for the higher reaches of Genevese society were largely unaffected by these measures. In 1711, for example, the *Petit conseil* had divided the city's population into three 'conditions', for each of which different sumptuary regulations applied, and this state of affairs lasted until 1772 when the sumptuary laws were revised. The following excerpt from the Council's *Ordonnances somptuaires* is typical, and shows how little affected were the aristocracy by Calvinist austerity: 'Permettant néanmoins aux personnes de la première condition, les cadres dorés aux miroirs, et aux portraits de leur famille, un bord de galon sur l'équipage à cheval, sur le manteau des hommes allant à la campagne, et sur l'habit de cheval des femmes.'[247]

The reaction of the aristocracy's enemies, in the face of this blatant discrimination, was to take refuge in an austere, Calvinist type of nationalism. By opposing the establishment of a theatre, they were

it by the allies. The *Petit conseil* had to forbid these transactions, but they continued to be carried out in the name of private citizens. Eventually, reprisals were taken against Genevese trade in the Holy Roman Empire.

[246] Voltaire and d'Alembert were not the only advocates of this development. In 1737 Jean Du Pan recommended its introduction to the *Conseil des deux cents*, arguing that: 'Le Théâtre, malgré le préjugé que l'on a contre, est tellement épuré, qu'il châtie et corrige en badinant les mauvaises habitudes et les ridicules, avec beaucoup plus de succès que les Prédications les plus austères' (Launay, p.117). According to Launay, the establishment of a theatre in Geneva was one of the aristocracy's 'préoccupations politiques les plus constantes' (p.116).

[247] Launay, p.111. Gaberel, however (*Voltaire et les Genevois*, pp.30-31), though giving no evidence to support his claims, maintains that conditions were the same for everyone: 'Du reste, si l'action du tribunal moral institué par Calvin, sous le nom de Consistoire, était rude à notre point de vue moderne, ce corps se montrait rigoureusement impartial, ne faisant aucune distinction entre les classes sociales, et censurant ou punissant avec une égale sévérité le premier magistrat et le plus mince bourgeois, le millionnaire et le paysan, le chef militaire et le simple soldat.'

taking their revenge on those Genevese exempt from many of the provisions laid down by the sumptuary laws, as well as defying the French *Résident* and the nation he represented. Similarly, the aristocracy sometimes concealed political motives behind a moral façade, as in the case of the bourgeois 'cercles'. These informal gatherings, praised by Rousseau in the *Lettre à d'Alembert* (*Du contrat social*, ed. Garnier, pp.202-208), were anathema to the *Petit conseil*, for not only were they unruly, it was also feared that political discussions went on there. Thus social, political and moral issues in eighteenth-century Geneva became interconnected in a way which at first sight appears rather surprising. The pastors were in a particularly ambiguous and invidious position. Socially and culturally they were usually classed with the pro-French aristocracy. In 1704 and 1705, for example, François Delachanas violently attacked the 'Ministres pleins d'orgueil', 'Messieurs les mondains Prédicateurs' and their 'pompeuse prédication'. He also railed against 'l'indécente fausse perruque frisottée et farinée de Messieurs les Pasteurs'. Popular indignation even extended to the French Protestant refugees, accused of importing 'jeux de cartes, bibliothèques, académie, cette belle science décousue, cette science sublime' (Launay, pp.115-16). And indeed, it is often to the influence of the Huguenots that the liberalisation of Genevese theology has been attributed (cf. Vuilleumier, iii.179ff), a fact which draws to our attention an important paradox: the faithful of Geneva in many cases remained more Calvinist than did their pastors. Michel Launay points out that 'les diatribes de Delachanas contre les pasteurs n'impliquent aucun attiédissement, chez lui, de la foi calviniste' (p.116). No doubt the pastors were aware of the ambiguity of their position, and their efforts not to become estranged entirely from the majority of Geneva's inhabitants were coincidentally responsible for some of their disagreements with Voltaire in the late 1750s.

Rousseau's dedication of his *Discours sur l'inégalité* to the Republic of Geneva could only revive in 1754 disagreements which had lain dormant since the mediation of 1738. Although he referred to the city's magistrates in the most respectful of terms and exhorted the republic's various classes to live together in peace and harmony, Rousseau's analysis and discussion of inequality in the body of the work doubtless caused many inhabitants of Geneva to reflect upon their own situation. The process had in fact begun whereby Rousseau was to become the darling of Geneva's *bourgeoisie*. He also exercised an attraction over some of the younger pastors,[248] a development encouraged by his defence of the ministers in the *Lettre à d'Alembert*. In my discussion of the article 'Genève' I concentrated mainly on d'Alembert's description of the pastors' religious beliefs and the ensuing controversy, but it contained another recommendation which was debated even more hotly: the establishment of a theatre. D'Alembert had claimed (Lough, p.90):

Par ce moyen *Genève* aurait des spectacles et des mœurs et jouirait de l'avantage des uns et des autres: les représentations théâtrales formeraient le goût des citoyens et leur donneraient une finesse de tact, une délicatesse de sentiment qu'il est très difficile d'acquérir sans ce secours.

In other words, the rough though honest manners of Geneva would gradually be refined until they approximated more closely to those of Parisian high society.

The quandary of the pastoral *corps* in this situation is only too obvious, for their position in Genevese society was somewhat paradoxical. Traditionally, links between Church and civil authority had been close, and it was therefore in the pastors' interests to support the *Petit conseil*. This they had normally done (cf. Launay, p.98) at the risk of incurring unpopularity among the population at large. But in the 1750s a radically new situation developed: Voltaire's presence apparently induced the government to dissociate itself from the pastors on two important occasions: over the *philosophe*'s attack on Calvin, and the profession of faith composed in connection with d'Alembert's article 'Genève'. Thus some pastors may have re-examined their commitment to a pro-French, unpopular aristocracy which was on the whole anti-Calvinist and seemed to regard religion mainly as a useful check on the actions of the populace. Moreover, despite the progressive theology of at least some pastors, a continuing sympathy with the moral aims of Calvinism and a realisation that Voltaire wished to change Geneva's religious life very radically, probably caused many of them to concur in Rousseau's condemnation of the theatre. Voltaire's policy of deliberate irritation exacerbated matters further after 1758, and encouraged the ban on his theatricals. Thus the united front between pastors and govern-

---

[248] Jacob Vernes and Paul Moultou are the most obvious examples. The *Lettre à d'Alembert* was approved by Perdriau, Roustan, Sarrasin, and even by Vernet, though the latter showed a little less enthusiasm than some (Spink, pp.167-68). Another fervent admirer of Rousseau's was Jean-Ami Martin (1736-1805) (Spink, pp.161-62).

ment was restored in 1760, but it is worth emphasising that the pastors'
position was not entirely a foregone conclusion, for although the
theatre had traditionally been forbidden in Geneva, many respectable
attempts to introduce it to the city had been made before Voltaire's
arrival, and not all pastors had looked unfavourably on these efforts.[249]

In his reply to d'Alembert's arguments, Rousseau significantly
struck an austere and patriotic note; his defence of the pastors' beliefs
was apologetic and ambiguous, but as regards the theatre issue he felt on
safe ground. That this was the preserve of the aristocracy and generally
unpopular with the rest of Geneva's population is clearly indicated in the
minutes of the meeting at which the *Petit conseil* decided to forbid
citizens of the republic to take part in Voltaire's theatricals. Since it was
the Venerable Consistory which had requested this measure, it might
appear to be a clear case of clerical influence, and this indeed was how
Voltaire interpreted the situation. As late as 19 July 1763 he complained
to the duchess of Saxe-Gotha that 'le conseil [. . .] est un peu l'esclave
des prêtres' (Best.D11313). Yet it seems certain nonetheless that political rather than religious motives prompted the council to adopt these
measures and that it acted reluctantly, for the excellent reason that those
Genevese being censured belonged to the same social class as the
magistrates and were in many cases related to them. On closer investigation we find that the Venerable Company's arguments did carry
great weight with the Council, but this was probably for the very good
reason that no one was better aware of the social and political implications of this question than Geneva's pastors, as the following extract
from the minutes of the consistory's meeting of 27 November 1760 will
make clear. It was decided (Best.D.app.199):

qu'il est contre la décence publique et bien affligeant pour tout bon Citoyen,
que des personnes destinées par leur naissance, leur éducation, et leurs talens,
au Government de l'Etat, se produisent sur un théâtre presque public[. . .]

Que si l'ordre de personnes qui ont représenté, semble rassurer sur la
plus grande partie de ces inconvéniens, leur éxemple cependant peut être
suivi par gens de tout état et sans principes, qui pourroient donner le plus

---

[249] cf. Launay, p.117; in 1737, when theatrical performances were allowed for a time out
of deference to the French mediator, 'Les pasteurs, loin de jouer leur rôle de gardiens de
l'austère tradition calviniste, doivent eux-mêmes se refréner, et éviter la tentation et le
scandale en s'interdisant par avance, ou plutôt en interdisant à leurs épouses d'assister au
spectacle: "La Vénérable Classe a fait un règlement qui interdit la comédie aux Ministres,
à leurs femmes et aux proposants"' (Launay, p.117, quoting the unpublished *Journal de
Perdriau,* Mss. de la Société d'histoire et d'archéologie de Genève, n.6).

grand scandale. Qu'ainsi la société a un intérêt pressant, que les Conducteurs de l'Etat et l'Eglise s'unissent pour s'opposer à des plaisirs aussi dangereux, qui causent depuis longtemps beaucoup de murmure [sic] parmi nous.

Nothing could evoke more explicitly than such a passage the political motives which on this occasion (as on so many in the past) caused Geneva's magistrates and pastors to adopt a common policy. Nor did Voltaire himself remain completely unaware that the motivation of the Council was at least partly political, for on 27 February 1765 he described the incident to Richelieu in specifically non-religious terms (Best.D12422):

Il est vrai que la faction ennemie du conseil de Genêve, trouva mauvais, il y a quelques années, que les enfans des magistrats de la plus illustre et de la plus puissante république du monde se déshonorassent au point de venir jouer quelquefois la comédie chez moi.

When one reflects that the party opposed to the council was composed mainly of *bourgeois représentants*, it is easy to appreciate how Voltaire became the unwitting enemy of this class over an issue whose wider implications he did not at first grasp. The hostility is all the more understandable in view of the close identification with the *bourgeoisie*'s political aspirations of Voltaire's rival, J.-J. Rousseau.

These considerations thus help us to understand why the theatre issue, at first sight a rather trivial question, divided Geneva into two factions for so long. To Voltaire the matter originally seemed straightforward: a clear case of clerical obscurantism which he attempted to discredit by demonstrating that the theatre was a positive force for moral improvement. But things were not really as simple as this. One hesitates to tax Voltaire with ignorance, but it is true nonetheless that just as both he and Montesquieu oversimplified the political situation in England, partly through insufficient experience of the institutions they were describing, so too Voltaire appears to have been at first unaware of the social and political overtones of the moral and cultural questions in which he became involved in Geneva. As the personification of French culture he was naturally identified with the aristocracy,[250] and this probably explains to some extent the indulgent attitude the *Petit conseil* showed him during the 1750s. On the other hand, to many Genevese he symbolised the hated French domination inside and outside their republic,

---

[250] Gay, *Voltaire's politics*, p.196; Chaponnière, *Voltaire chez les calvinistes*, pp.108-12.

and they consequently rallied to Rousseau when he took up the cudgels on behalf of traditional values of austerity and patriotism.

The question of the theatre marked the beginning of Voltaire's involvement in Genevese politics, an involvement which was to reach its height in the mid 1760s. But the main catalyst of political events in the city during this period was Rousseau, and many issues were often complicated or obscured because of the rivalry between him and Voltaire. In 1762 *Emile* and the *Contrat social* were banned in both France and Geneva.[251] Although the correspondence shows us Voltaire referring to this event in reasonably sympathetic terms,[252] he was immediately accused by Charles Pictet of having solicited the condemnation of Rousseau's works in Geneva, clear evidence of the influence Jean-Jacques's supporters thought Voltaire had with the *Petit conseil* and of the hostility with which they viewed him.[253] Further accusations were made when Rousseau was expelled from Bernese territory on 9 July.[254]

---

[251] *Emile* was condemned in Paris on 9 June and in Geneva on 11 June (Best.D10517, commentary). On 19 June both *Emile* and the *Contrat social* were lacerated and burned by Geneva's public executioner, and a warrant was issued for Rousseau's arrest, should he return to the city (*Œuvres complètes de Jean-Jacques Rousseau*, ed. Bernard Gagnebin and Marcel Raymond (Paris 1959-1969), iii.clxii; Guéhenno, ii.97).

[252] in 1761 Voltaire complained to d'Alembert that Rousseau had accused him of corrupting Geneva, and also claimed that Rousseau was in league with the pastors, 'pour m'empêcher d'avoir un téâtre à Tournay' (Best.D9743), but when he found out about the condemnation of Rousseau's books Voltaire commented to Gabriel Cramer: 'Puis que ce bâtard du chien de Diogene est malheureux, il faut lui pardoner' (Best.D10543, *c.* 30 June 1762). Cf. also Best.D10507.

[253] Best.D10523, 22 June 1762. Pictet also claimed that Voltaire 'a fait à Geneve plus de Déistes que Calvin n'y a fait de protestants'. Voltaire replied in moderate terms (Best. D10578). The upshot of Pictet's action was that he was deprived of membership of the *Conseil des deux-cents* and ordered to make an apology (Gay, p.200). Small wonder that Rousseau's supporters identified Voltaire with the aristocracy.

[254] cf. Best.D10565, commentary, which reproduces a letter of 7 July 1762 where Julie von Bondeli claims that Voltaire is responsible for Rousseau's misfortunes. On 15 July her correspondent, Johann Georg Zimmermann wrote in a similar vein to Haller (Best. D10588, commentary), and these rumours quickly filtered through to Geneva. D'Alembert also seems to have believed the allegation: cf. his letter of 9 September 1762 (Best. D10697) to Voltaire, the latter's reply (Best.D10705), and a much later letter of d'Alembert (Best.D12287). Theodore Besterman (Best.D10697, n.8) believes that Voltaire had no part in the persecution of Rousseau, either in 1762 or later, in 1765, as has also been claimed. In connection with the latter incident he refers to Bernard Gagnebin, 'Voltaire a-t-il provoqué l'expulsion de Rousseau de l'île Saint-Pierre?', *Annales de la Société Jean-Jacques Rousseau, 1943-1945* (Geneva 1947), xxx.111-31. One must also point out that many critics, even some fairly hostile to Voltaire, have taken the same view: cf. Chaponnière, *Voltaire chez les calvinistes*, pp.120-21; Gay, p.200, n.30; Guéhenno, ii.91; Spink, pp.216-17.

There is evidence that criticism of Voltaire in Geneva was fairly general about this time despite his action in favour of the Calas family, and a letter of 12 July 1762 from the French *Résident*, the baron de Mont-péroux, to Choiseul (Best.D10583) indicates that the *Petit conseil* was displeased by rumours that it was indebted to Voltaire in several ways. For his part, Voltaire was becoming less enthusiastic about a body which appeared willing to yield on occasions to clerical influence, and it seems clear that he did not realise immediately that measures against his theatricals might have been a necessary step taken to placate public opinion, although Jean-Robert Tronchin, apologising on about 1 January 1761 for the action which had been taken, admitted as much to him: 'tout se réduit à éprouver un des inconvéniens qui se rencontrent dans une Rép^e, où les mœurs sont différentes de celles d'une Monarchie, *et où l'opinion de la multitude est prépondérante*' (Best.D9512, my italics). Voltaire's earlier admiration for the city fathers had by now largely vanished, and scornful references to 'la petitissime, et pédantissime république de Geneve' are to be found in his correspondence at the end of 1762 and the beginning of 1763.[255]

Perhaps even more significant was Voltaire's reaction to an event of the following year, which marks the beginning of the political evolution whereby he increasingly became estranged from the *Petit conseil* and looked with more favour first on the *bourgeois* then on the *natifs*. This event again concerned Rousseau, who had been disgusted by the lack of concrete support he had received from his fellow-countrymen. On 12 May 1763 he therefore wrote to the first *syndic* of Geneva, renouncing his Genevese citizenship, an action which finally encouraged the expression of mass protests and representations to the *Petit conseil* by members of the *bourgeoisie*:[256] the first protest occurred on 18 June 1763, when about forty *citoyens* and *bourgeois* waited on the first *syndic*, but the number of Genevese involved in subsequent representations rose dramatically to reach a total of about 450 (Best.D11376, commentary). Voltaire reported these demonstrations in terms of great satisfaction – the following account to the duchess of Saxe-Gotha is typical:

Si votre altesse s^e peut se plaire aux petits objets qui marquent de l'humanité, je lui dirai que Jean Jaques Rousseau, condamné dans la ville de Calvin pour avoir fait parler un vicaire savoiard, Jean Jaques qui s'était débourgeoisé de

---

[255] Best.D10843; cf. Best.D10670, D10922.
[256] Guéhenno, ii.115-20; *Œuvres complètes*, iii.CLXIV-CLXVII; Best.D11286, D11306, D11313.

Geneve a trouvé des bourgeois qui ont pris son parti. Deux cent personnes parmi les quelles il y avait deux ou trois ministres ont présenté pour luy requête au magistrat. Nous savons bien qu'il n'est pas crétien, disent ils, mais nous voulons qu'il soit notre citoien.²⁵⁷

Yet despite a growing awareness of the political motives behind the *bourgeoisie*'s support of Rousseau, one feature which consistently characterised Voltaire's attitude was a marked tendency to exaggerate the clergy's role, or indeed sometimes to attribute the Genevese troubles of the 1760s to entirely religious causes.²⁵⁸ Thus to Damilaville on 23 August 1763 he observed (Best.D11379, my italics):

Mon cher frère, ne bénissez vous pas Dieu de voir le peuple de Calvin prendre si hautement le parti de Jean Jaques? Ne considérons point sa personne, considérons sa cause. Jamais les droits de l'humanité n'ont été plus soutenus. Il n'y a point d'éxemple de pareille avanture *dans l'histoire de l'Eglise*.

And two days later he commented to Helvétius: 'Le dogme fatal de la tolérance infecte aujourd'hui tous les esprits, les trois quarts de la France, au moins, commencement à demander la liberté de conscience, on la prêche à Genêve' (Best.D11383). Were one to judge only from these examples, it might be possible to suppose that Voltaire saw events in Geneva merely as part of the battle against *l'infâme*, with political issues playing a very minor if not insignificant role. The lengths to which this oversimplification could extend are amply demonstrated by the following statement, made to d'Argental as late as 20 January 1766: 'un peuple tout entier s'est élevé contre ses magistrats, parce qu'ils avaient condamné le vicaire savoyard' (Best.D13126).

²⁵⁷ Best.D11286, 30 June 1763. Cf. also Best.D11306 (to Damilaville), D11313 (again to the duchess), D11376 (to Damilaville), D11377 (to the duc de Praslin), and D11383 (to Helvétius).

²⁵⁸ cf. Best.D10581, to d'Alembert, 12 July 1762: 'voylà ces prédicants qui obtiennent qu'on brûle son livre [*Emile*] et qu'on décrète l'auteur '. This was perhaps unfair comment in connection with the events just described, for in condemning Rousseau's books the *Petit conseil* acted on its own without consulting the Consistory. The latter indeed made no official comment on *Emile*, a fact to which Rousseau himself drew attention in the *Lettres de la montagne* (*Œuvres complètes*, iii.689-90). In October 1763, however, the Consistory declared unanimously 'que le magn. Conseil n'avoit donné aucune atteinte aux droits du Ve Consistoire dans l'affaire de Rousseau; estimant au surplus que le silence qu'il avait gardé dans cette occasion devoit être regardé comme une preuve suffisante et non équivoque de ses sentimens à cet égard . . .' (Dardier, *Esaïe Gasc*, p.44). Almost the only other action taken by the pastoral *corps* as a whole during the early 1760s was, on 9 February 1765, to wait 'on the Council to assure it of their own confidence, respect and Christian patience in the matter of the recent outrageous publications' (Best.D12406, commentary, n.1).

Here no doubt we can find an explanation for the importance attached by Voltaire to the rather insignificant case of Covelle. The latter was a watchmaker, who, summoned before the Consistory for having fathered a child on one mlle Ferbot, a miller's daughter, refused to follow the tradition of kneeling before the assembled ministers. His appeal against this custom was upheld and Voltaire considered him a hero of the philosophic battle against *l'infâme*.[259] Covelle subsequently served as Voltaire's mouthpiece in the *Questions sur les miracles*, in which he put forward sternly Erastian views, and also became the protagonist of *La Guerre civile de Genève*, a mock epic poem which significantly reduced the whole Genevese problem to a straightforward clash between clergy and people.

Nonetheless, despite his constant suspicion of pastoral involvement, we may assume that the political motivation of the actors in Geneva's drama was becoming steadily more obvious to Voltaire. On 18 January 1763 he told d'Alembert that the condemnation of Emile 'a été une affaire de parti dans la petitissime république' (Best.D10922). And on 28 September of the same year he gave the same correspondent another entirely non-religious explanation of the situation: 'Jean Jaques il est vray a été condamné mais c'est parce que dans un petit livret intitulé contract social, il avait trop pris le parti du peuple contre le magistrat' (Best.D11433). A few days later he explained to Pierre Rousseau why the citizens had protested: 'ils disent qu'un citoien de Genève est en droit de tourner en ridicule la religion chrétienne tant qu'il veut, et qu'on ne peut le condamner qu'après avoir conféré amiablement avec lui' (Best.D11440), and although Voltaire tirelessly drew attention to the paradox that 'les ministres du st évangile sont du party de Jean Jacques après qu'il s'est bien moqué d'eux',[260] it is obvious that he is not only making a propaganda point against ministers of the Christian

---

[259] cf. Paul Chaponnière, *Voltaire chez les calvinistes*, p.145; M.xxv.406, n.4; Best. D11805, D11837, D14963; Gay, *Voltaire's politics*, pp.204-205; Jean-Pierre Ferrier, 'Covelle, Voltaire et l'affaire de la génuflexion', *Bulletin de la Société d'histoire et d'archéologie de Genève* (Geneva 1946), viii.217-25.

[260] Best.D12302, to d'Argental, 10 January 1765. In fact d'Alembert's previous assessment of the situation was probably nearer the mark: 'On prétend que Rousseau fait actuellement trois partis dans la sérénissime république: les ministres pour l'auteur & contre le livre [*Emile*]: le conseil pour le livre & contre l'auteur; et le peuple pour le livre & pour l'auteur; vous y ajouterez sans doute un 4e parti, contre le livre & contre l'auteur' (Best.D10622, 31 July 1762). What Voltaire particularly resented was the suppression of the *Vicaire savoyard*, which was the only part of *Emile* to his taste. Cf. Best.D11376: 'Je ne serais pas fâché de voir une guerre civile pour le vicaire savoiar.'

religion but also expressing his enthusiasm at this example of the defence of free speech and the right to dissent in a civilised society.[261] In fact the terms used here by Voltaire somewhat resemble the adage attributed by legend to him but never precisely located in his works: 'I disapprove of what you say, but I will defend to the death your right to say it.'[262] It is pleasing to note that the spirit if not the letter of this statement is at any rate expressed in Voltaire's correspondence, especially in connection with his arch-enemy Rousseau.

A sudden worsening of his relations with Rousseau paradoxically helped Voltaire to appreciate even better the political nature of the *bourgeoisie*'s demands, and henceforth he was no longer tempted to consider the *représentants* as merely the 'parti de Jean Jacques' (Best. D12178). Hitherto Voltaire had viewed the author of *Emile* with a mixture of incomprehension and contempt, but had not seemed completely hostile when Rousseau's misfortunes began in 1762. Relations between them deteriorated steadily, however, Rousseau convinced that Voltaire was poisoning his fellow-countrymen's minds against him[263] and Voltaire that Rousseau was mischievously trying to foment political trouble in Geneva as a form of revenge for his exile.[264] Suddenly, on 26 December 1764, we have clear evidence that Voltaire was using his remaining influence with the *Petit conseil* in an attempt to have Rousseau condemned in a new and even more damning way; the populace should be silenced, he told Gabriel Cramer, and the councillors should even encourage 'adroitement tous les ministres à faire des rep-

---

[261] cf. Best.D11383, to Helvétius: 'un citoyen de Genève peut écrire ce qu'il veut, pourvu qu'il donne de bonnes explications'. Cf. also Best.D11377.

[262] R. Fargher, *Life and letters in France* (p.151), observes that this statement appears to have been invented by Tallentyre in 1907.

[263] cf. Rousseau's letter of 27 July 1762 to the comtesse de Boufflers (Best.D10611, Leigh 2040): 'Le poète Voltaire et le jongleur Tronchin ont admirablement joué leur rôle à Genève et à Berne, et vous pouvez bien croire qu'ils ne m'oublieront pas à Berlin.' Cf. also Best.D12365.

[264] there was certainly some truth in Voltaire's belief. Rousseau's letter of 26 May 1763 to Marc Chappuis had virtually invited the *bourgeoisie* to take action on his behalf: 'Si cinq ou six bourgeois seulement eussent protesté on pourroit vous croire Sur les sentimens que vous leur prêtés [. . .] on ne juge pas les hommes sur leurs pensées, on les juge sur leurs actions' (Leigh). Moreover, Jean Guéhenno comments that when Rousseau later visited Thonon: 'l'objet principal du voyage, le seul peut-être, avait été de rencontrer à Thonon les chefs des Représentants. On régla les circonstances de la publication des *Lettres de la montagne* et de la réponse que les Représentants eux-mêmes comptaient faire aux lettres de Tronchin. On convint d'un code pour la correspondance à ce sujet. C'était une vraie conspiration' (ii.132).

résentations' (Best.D12265). What had brought about this unlikely alliance between Voltaire and the pastoral *corps* of Geneva? It seems clear that the cause had been the publication of the *Lettres écrites de la montagne*,[265] in which Rousseau fired broadsides against all sections of the Genevese community: the *Petit conseil*, the pastors and, of course, Voltaire himself. The latter told Damilaville on 31 December 1764 (Best.D12276): 'Dans ce Libelle, J: J: fâché qu'on ait brûle Emile, m'accuse d'être l'auteur du Sermon des Cinquante. Ce procédé n'est pas assurément d'un philosophe ni d'un honnête homme.' This was putting it mildly, for the *Sermon* had been condemned in both France and Geneva and its author was theoretically liable to the death penalty. Little wonder, then, that Voltaire's attacks against Rousseau became even bitterer, and it is unfortunately more than likely that the vitriolic pamphlet, *Le Sentiment des citoyens*, was composed by him.[266]

At the beginning of 1765 Voltaire left *Les Délices* permanently, a clear indication that he no longer felt at ease in Geneva. Now he had against him not only the defenders of Calvin, anti-French elements of the population, and Rousseau's supporters – some members of the *Petit conseil* were also subjecting him to violent criticism. Du Pan, for example, wrote to Freudenreich on 31 December 1764: 'Voltaire mérite bien qu'on brûle ses ouvrages. Cet homme nous a bien fait du mal. On ne va plus chez lui. Ses connoissances lui font une visite ou deux par an, afin de ne pas rompre absolument' (Best.D12276, commentary). But no

---

[265] these were a reply to the *Lettres écrites de la campagne*, published by the *procureur général* of Geneva, Jean-Robert Tronchin, a work which expounded the *négatif* point of view. According to Chaponnière, the *représentants* 's'empressèrent de répandre le bruit que ces lettres [écrites de la campagne] avaient passé "par les mains de Voltaire", sans doute pour exciter Rousseau à répondre' (*Voltaire chez les calvinistes*, pp.135-6; the phrase quoted by Chaponnière is from a letter of 30 September 1763 (Leigh 2945) sent by de Luc to Rousseau).

[266] the pamphlet caused Rousseau great distress (cf. Guéhenno, ii.135-8), since it revealed that he had abandoned his children at the *Enfants-trouvés* in Paris, and recommended that he should either be incarcerated as a madman or subjected to the death penalty. Rousseau was convinced that the *Sentiment des citoyens* was by Jacob Vernes, who had in 1762 published his *Lettres sur le christianisme de J.-J. Rousseau*, refuting the religious ideas of *Emile*, an action which Jean-Jacques regarded as treachery. Nonetheless, the *Sentiment des citoyens* has usually been attributed to Voltaire. Theodore Besterman, on the other hand (Best.D12332, n.1; D12531, n.1), thinks that Voltaire's authorship is doubtful, although even he admits that at least part of a letter to François Tronchin composed about 25 December 1764 (Best.D12262) 'was written or dictated by Voltaire'. This would seem to be conclusive, for the letter concerned, both as regards style and content, bears a close resemblance to the *Sentiment des citoyens*.

sooner had Voltaire apparently withdrawn from the Genevese scene than he began to take a keen and active interest in the fortunes of the *représentants*. No doubt this development was due partly to his disenchantment with the *Petit conseil*. As he told the d'Argentals: 'il importe fort peu pour la France que Genève soit aristocratique ou Démocratique. Je vous avoue que je penche àprésent assez pour la Démocratie, malgré mes anciens principes, parce qu'il me semble que les magnates ont eu tort dans plusieurs points' (Best.D12933, 14 October 1765). Indeed, it appeared to Voltaire that the *Petit conseil* of the tiny republic was definitely suffering from delusions of grandeur: not only had it insulted the empress Catherine II by ordering the return to Geneva of some young ladies who had been recruited to teach French in Russia,[267] it had also shown a churlish disregard for etiquette when the governor of a neighbouring French province, the duc de Randon, visited the city (Best.D12933, to the d'Argentals). Voltaire's references to the *Petit conseil* became progressively stronger. On 11 October 1765 he declared to the d'Argentals: 'Il y a dans ce conseil trois ou quatre coquins, c'est à dire trois ou quatre dévots fanatiques qui ne sont bons qu'à jetter dans le lac' (Best.D12928), and a couple of weeks later he went as far as to claim to d'Argental that he had never been on social terms with the members of the *Petit conseil*: 'Car excepté les Tronchin et deux ou trois autres, ce tripot est composé de pédants du seizième siécle. Il y a beaucoup plus d'esprit et de raison dans les autres citoyens' (Best.D12952, 26 October 1765).

Moreover, not only was Voltaire now thoroughly disenchanted with the magistrates he had formerly admired, the way was also open for him to take a greatly increased interest in the fortunes of the *bourgeoisie*, for Rousseau, suspected by Voltaire of political intervention in the affairs of Geneva, had now left Switzerland. Voltaire himself declared that his role was the opposite of Rousseau's: he wished to calm down the situation rather than stir up trouble, he told the marquis de Florian on about 16 November 1765 (Best.D12988). Such a claim would doubtless inspire scorn in many critics, and it must be admitted that Voltaire's new attitude was probably motivated, at least in part, by a desire to

---

[267] Best.D12899, to the d'Argentals, 23 September 1765. The ladies got no farther than Berne. It must be said in fairness to the Genevese authorities that, according to Gaberel (p.50), m. de Bulow, who was in charge of the operation, 'a essayé de débaucher quelques personnes', and this was apparently why the *Petit conseil* decided to oppose his mission.

annoy the *Petit conseil* and to cut an important Genevese figure. Nonetheless there is also evidence that he was now taking a genuine interest in the political struggle developing before his eyes. On 13 November 1765 Voltaire invited members of both factions to a dinner at Ferney, and there is no doubt that the various proposals he made subsequently were conciliatory rather than inflammatory, especially if one takes into account the letters he wrote to various *représentants* (cf. Best.D12995, to de Luc). The *Propositions à examiner pour apaiser les divisions de Genève* and the *Réflections sur les moyens proposés pour appaiser les troubles de la ville de Genève*, which he composed on behalf of the *représentants*,[268] show a detailed knowledge of Geneva's political history and contain sensible and practical suggestions which the *Petit conseil* might have adopted with advantage.[269] Moreover, Peter Gay argues convincingly that the *Idées républicaines* were composed at this period rather than in 1762 as has usually been assumed.[270] In point of fact the *Petit conseil* politely refused Voltaire's overtures (cf. Best. D12999), but the *bourgeoisie* changed radically in its attitude to him. Even d'Ivernois took part in negotiations with him, informing Rousseau on 23 December 1765 of Voltaire's efforts (Best.D13058), and receiving a reply not intended to discourage this new policy: 'Quel que soit l'homme qui vous [i.e. the Genevese] rendra la paix et la liberté', exclaimed Rousseau, 'il me sera toujours cher et respectable' (Best.D13073).

The period of Voltaire's maximum involvement in Geneva's politics had now arrived. On about 5 April 1766 he received a letter from Georges Auzière, one of the leaders of the *natifs*, asking for his help and advice (Best.D13240). The aristocracy had at times allied itself with this class against the *bourgeoisie* (Launay, p.80), but the promised

---

[268] Best.D12996, commentary, n.1. The former was published by Fernand Caussy in 'Voltaire pacificateur de Genève', *Revue bleue* (Paris, 4 January 1908), 5th ser., ix.9-15.

[269] Voltaire proposed that 'when 700 Citizens, supported by three lawyers of a university of their choice, demand the interpretation of an obscure law, the improvement of a neglected law, the Council of Twenty-Five shall take the representation to the Council of Two Hundred and the first syndic shall convoke the General Council for action' (Gay, p.213).

[270] cf. *Mélanges* (p.140): 'Beuchot date avec vraisemblance cet opuscule de 1762, année de la publication du *Contrat social*, dont les *Idées républicaines* sont, pour leur plus grande partie, une critique.' One of Gay's most telling points in *The Party of humanity: studies in the French Enlightenment* (London 1954), pp.55-96, is that there is a specific reference to the Covelle case which, as we have seen, occurred in 1763. Cf. also Gay's article 'Voltaire's *Idées républicaines*: a study in bibliography and interpretation', *Studies on Voltaire* (1958) vi.67-105.

rewards for its co-operation had never materialised. The *natifs* therefore hoped that they would be included in the proposals made by the new commission of mediation, again composed, as in 1738, of plenipotentiaries from France, Berne and Zurich. During the recent troubles the *natifs* had largely supported demands put forward by the *bourgeoisie*, but when the mediators arrived at the beginning of 1766, the *natifs* decided that this action had been fruitless and were at last emboldened to put forward some demands on their own behalf.[271] To all intents and purposes, the *natifs* represented a section of the Genevese working class, composed largely of watchmakers and other craftsmen, and it is surely to Voltaire's credit that he was ready to help members of the 'populace' which he had so often anathematised. Some critics have in fact doubted his good faith and regarded his intervention in favour of the *natifs* as spiteful meddling in Genevese internal affairs.[272] Yet it seems fairly clear that Voltaire made a distinction between the Genevese *natifs*, with whose standard of education he was visibly impressed, and the lower classes of other countries, whose ignorance was a breeding ground for religious fanaticism.[273]

Whatever his motives, Voltaire composed a *compliment de circonstance* to be read out to the French plenipotentiary, and advised the *natifs* on how to present their case in the most favourable light (Gay, *Voltaire's*

[271] 'les Natifs ont aidé les Bourgeois dans leur lutte politique mais n'ont rien obtenu en échange. On s'est servi d'eux, on les a dupés, ils n'ont été que les instruments des Bourgeois' (extract from a *Mémoire* concerning the *natifs* transmitted to Voltaire by Sylvestre in April 1766, quoted by Launay, p.107).

[272] cf. Launay, p.110; Lüthy, ii.107. Other critics, however, have taken a more generous view of Voltaire's conduct: cf. Caussy, 'Voltaire pacificateur de Genève', p.9; Jane Ceitac, *Voltaire et l'affaire des natifs: un aspect de la carrière humanitaire du patriarche de Ferney* (Geneva 1956), pp.61-62, cited below, p.222. Cf. also the attitude of Geneva's new French *Résident*, reporting to the duc de Praslin: 'Je prévois que ma conduitte vis-à-vis de luy [Voltaire] ne sera pas sans épines. Il veut le bien; il est abordable par plus d'un endroit, je tâcherai qu'il ne nuise à rien, en lui persuadant qu'il peut faire beaucoup (quoted by Desnoiresterres, vii.9).

[273] cf. Best.D14039, textual notes (Voltaire to Linguet, 15 March 1767): 'les parisiens seraient étonnés s'ils voyaient dans plusieurs villes de Suisse & surtout dans Genève, presque tous ceux qui sont employés aux manufactures passer à lire le temps qui ne peut être consacré au travail. *Non, monsieur, tout n'est pas perdu, quand on met le peuple en état de s'apercevoir qu'il a un esprit.* Tout est perdu au contraire quand on le traite comme une troupe de taureaux. Car tôt ou tard ils vous frappent de leurs cornes. [During the religious wars in England and France . . .] Le peuple ignorant & féroce était mené par quelques docteurs fanatiques qui criaient: tuez tout au nom de dieu.' Cf. Gay, *Voltaire's politics*, pp.220 ff. For a useful discussion of Voltaire's attitude toward the masses see Roland Mortier, 'Voltaire et le peuple', *AE*, pp.137-51.

politics, p.288). His involvement was soon discovered and he was censured both by the *Petit conseil* and by the French representative (cf. Best.D13274, n.1). Jane Ceitac, who examines Voltaire's contacts with the *bourgeois* and *natifs* in a wealth of detail which would be out of place in this study, observes that Voltaire's action could have provoked severe reprisals on the part of the French government (he was in fact warned by Choiseul on 12 May 1766 (Best.D13298) not to become involved in the affairs of Geneva). She is in no doubt that his conduct was determined by basically humanitarian motives (p.61):

Si l'incident n'eut pas de suites pour Voltaire, remarquons, malgré tout, qu'il avait exposé sa tranquillité, et que les conséquences auraient pu être graves pour lui. Le geste d'humanité qu'il avait fait en faveur d'une classe de déshérités fut taxé de malveillance. Pourtant, Voltaire aurait pu apprendre à ses dépens que l'on n'est pas 'humain' impunément.

The mediation had no more success than Voltaire's personal attempts in restoring peace to the political life of Geneva. In december 1766 the *représentants* rejected the plan of pacification, and the French government replied by blockading the city's frontiers in 1767.[274] Voltaire remained unpopular in many Genevese circles. In the late 1760s he encouraged the building of Versoix which, it was hoped, would not only be a town where religious tolerance was practised but also a dangerous commercial rival for Geneva.[275] When the fall of Choiseul caused this project to be abandoned and renewed political troubles broke out in Geneva, Voltaire induced many disgruntled *natifs* to settle at Ferney, subsequently giving his colony of watchmakers publicity on a European scale.[276] But, despite these remaining connections, by the early 1770s Voltaire had stopped trying to play any part in the city's internal affairs. Tragic miscarriages of justice in France, and in particular the La Barre case, had anyway helped him to keep a sense of proportion as regards the importance of Geneva's political strife.

[274] Gay, *Voltaire's politics*, p.230. An edict of conciliation was finally accepted on 11 March 1768, but political troubles continued to dog the tiny republic, especially during the early 1770s.

[275] cf. Ira O. Wade, 'The search for a new Voltaire: studies in Voltaire based upon material deposited at the American philosophical society', *Transactions of the American philosophical society* (Philadelphia 1958), xlviii.94-105; also Fernand Caussy, *Voltaire seigneur de village* (Paris 1912); J.-P. Ferrier, *Le Duc de Choiseul, Voltaire, et la création de Versoix-la-ville* (Geneva 1922).

[276] cf. a plethora of letters written in the early 1770s: e.g. Best.D16281, D16282, D16299, D16313, D16314.

Even before the disaster at Abbeville he told Damilaville that the troubles had been exaggerated (Best.D13059, 25 December 1765), and to the duchess of Saxe-Gotha he was even more affirmative: 'Ces troubles sont fort pacifiques, les Genevois sont malades d'une indigestion de bonheur' (Best.D13197). Moreover, the philosophic revolution was proceeding apace: 'Il y a beaucoup de tracasseries politiques à Genève, mais je ne connais pas de ville où il y ait moins de calvinistes que dans cette ville de Calvin.'[277]

Yet despite, or perhaps because of this encouraging development, Voltaire was all the more concerned to protect Geneva's citizens against clerical interference in their affairs. We have noted his tendency to exaggerate the importance of religious motives in the troubles of the 1760s.[278] Time and again he failed to appreciate that individual pastors could have political opinions just like other citizens, and that their association with a given group was not necessarily proof of a priestly conspiracy to gain effective power in the republic. Convinced as he was by events of the 1750s that the pastors were hypocrites, Voltaire lost no opportunity of vilifying Calvin in his works and of pointing out examples of intolerance in Geneva's history which could be attributed to the Reformer's unwholesome influence. The *Dictionnaire philosophique* article 'Dogmes', for example, first printed in 1765, contains a vitriolic attack on Calvin, who is judged even more harshly than the cardinal de Lorraine, one of the prime movers of the *Ligue* during the

---

[277] Best.D13374, to d'Alembert, 26 June 1766. A decade later Voltaire was able to report an even more satisfactory development to d'Alembert: 'Il n'y a pas longtemps que des polissons qu'on nomme ministres ou pasteurs ont présenté une requête aux polissons de je ne sais quel conseil de Genève pour obtenir une augmentation de leur pension, et une diminution du nombre de leurs prêches, attendu disaient ils que personne ne venait plus les entendre' (Best.D19910, 8 February 1776; cf. n.5 to the letter for corroboration of this claim. There was also a lack of candidates for the clergy).

[278] cf. above, pp.211 ff. It is significant that when troubles began again in 1770, Voltaire showed the same ambiguous attitude in his accounts of the incidents, at first regarding them as political in nature (cf. Best.D16153, D16154, D16155, D16156, D16159, D16160, D16161, D16168, D16169), then implying that the clergy were at the bottom of the affair (cf. Best.D16170: 'On s'est mis à tirer sur les passants dans la sainte cité de maître Jean Calvin [. . .] Tout celà est abominable; mais les prédicants disent que c'est pour avoir la paix.'), later stating categorically to several correspondents that 'il ne s'agissait point de religion' (Best.D16195; cf. also Best.D16214), but then once again referring to the troubles in 'L'église militante de Calvin' (Best.D16285). One is forced to conclude that, although Voltaire realised the basically political nature of these disturbances, he could not resist blackening the clergy's name on many occasions.

French religious wars.[279] Here as elsewhere, the execution of Servetus is recalled. Voltaire's message is plain: although they no longer shared Calvin's doctrinal beliefs, Geneva's pastors retained his lust for domination, a domination best achieved by tirelessly censuring the most harmless amusements and pastimes, as the Reformer himself had done, so that every aspect of national life should be open to clerical interference.

xiii. *Antoine*

The persistence of intolerance at Geneva, diagnosed by Voltaire as an inevitable consequence of Calvin's influence, was perfectly illustrated by the case of Nicolas Antoine (1602-1632), whose execution is mentioned many times in Voltaire's works[280] and is twice related at some length: in the *Commentaire sur le livre des Délits et des peines* (1766), and in the article 'Miracles' (1771) of the *Questions sur l'Encyclopédie*. Both accounts are of interest, for not only are the pastors of Geneva cast as chief villains on each occasion, we can also see how Voltaire varied his attack on *l'infâme* as the occasion demanded, sometimes giving a sober account of Christian intolerance so that the reader heartily sympathised with the victims of persecution, sometimes, in a more general condemnation of religious 'enthousiasme', widening his scope to include the fanatics who suffered as well as the fanatics who persecuted.

The earlier account begins by stressing the similarity between martyrs of differing faiths and the fact that they all believed in the same God, then Voltaire recounts briefly the story of Antoine, which he claims to have read in a 'manuscrit très curieux', part of which is related by one Jacob Spon (*Mélanges,* p.799). Antoine was originally a Catholic, converted first to Protestantism, but who later became convinced of the truth of Judaism. By this time, unfortunately, he was a pastor in Geneva. Unable to reconcile himself to 'la secte de Calvin qu'il était obligé de prêcher', Antoine was eventually tried before the 'conseil de la ville', acting on the advice of the clergy. A small number of pastors wished to have pity on him, but the majority voted that he be burned alive, and the sentence was carried out in 1632. The story is told simply, with fewer ironic comments than might be expected. Voltaire's purpose

---

[279] cf. above, p.66. A similarly violent and thoroughgoing attack on Calvin is also to be found in Voltaire's correspondence for this period, in two letters to the *président* Hénault (Best.D14779, Best.D14832).

[280] cf. M.xviii.265; Best.D7579 and D8185. For information on Antoine see Léonard, *Histoire générale du protestantisme*, ii.238.

is to illustrate the extent of Calvinist fanaticism, and the sober, almost dignified tone of his account heightens the effect. We are, however left in no doubt as to the depth of his feelings, since he sums up: 'Il faut cent ans de raison et de vertu pour expier un pareil jugement' (p.800).

The second account of the affair is quite different. By 1771 Voltaire is no longer concerned, as he had been in the *Commentaire sur le livre des Délits et des peines*, to point out a classic case of injustice, but to strike as many blows as he can for the good cause. The technique is a sort of detached attack, rather as in *Candide* and some of the other *contes*, both on *l'infâme* (here represented by the Calvinist clergy) and on its victims, who are portrayed as equally fanatical and unenlightened. Antoine, though his heroism is stressed, and the Genevese pastors, though their cruelty is emphasised even more than in the previous account, are both made to seem ridiculous to the point that we can no longer take completely seriously what Voltaire has elsewhere shown to be a tragedy. Antoine is quite simply mad, 'saintement fou' like Fox in the *Lettres philosophiques* (ed. Lanson, i.32), and Voltaire's deliberate intention is to illustrate that both the 'infortuné prêtre' and the 'conseil des prédicants' were equally blind and mistaken in their beliefs and actions. Antoine's trial allows Voltaire to make a passing attack on clerical influence in the state, and an indirect comment on the contemporary situation in Geneva, for 'le petit conseil de Genève, qui ne faisait rien *alors* sans consulter le conseil des prédicants, leur demanda leur avis' (M.xx.92, my italics). The case for tolerance and leniency was put by 'les plus sensés de ces prêtres', but the majority of the pastors were inflexible in demanding the death penalty: 'à ce mot de tolérance grinçant des dents beaucoup plus qu'Antoine au nom de Jésus-Christ, et charmés d'ailleurs de trouver une occasion de faire brûler un homme, ce qui arrivait très-rarement.'

At the end of the story Voltaire comments that Antoine's courage at his death was remarkable – 'jamais martyr ne consomma son sacrifice avec une foi plus vive' (M.xx.93) – implicitly suggesting that all other martyrs may have been equally mistaken. Moreover, 'cela prouve évidemment que sa folie n'était autre chose qu'une forte persuasion', a conclusive demonstration that Voltaire is here illustrating the folly of 'enthusiasm' just as much as he is attacking intolerance. If there were no idiots like Antoine, the priests would have no one to martyr. It is worth noting that in both accounts there is a small number of pastors

225

who put forward the reasonable and humanitarian case against executing Antoine. This is doubtless because Voltaire, as we have seen, remained on good terms with several Swiss ministers, despite his ups and downs with the pastoral *corps* as a whole, and it must have been difficult, even for him, to see these generally mild and studious men in the role of bloodthirsty, persecuting inquisitors.

xiv. *The* Questions sur les miracles

Nonetheless, despite his friendship with individual pastors, Voltaire's attitude towards Geneva's clergy and its influence in the city was hostile, as I have shown in some detail. Indeed, perhaps the best example of this tendency to exaggerate the rôle played by the pastors in Geneva's political affairs is to be found in the *Questions sur les miracles* (1765), which contains a virulent outburst of wrath against the city's Calvinist ministers. Two incidents especially had aroused Voltaire's ire: the Covelle affair (cf. above, p.216), and the treatment received by Rousseau in Switzerland, and more particularly at Môtiers-Travers near Neuchâtel. It goes without saying that Voltaire's sympathy for Rousseau was not particularly great, as is evident in the *Questions*, but what did annoy him was the clergy's high-handed and authoritarian attitude to the unfortunate author of *Emile*, and this provided him with an excellent opportunity for attacking their pretensions.

The *Questions sur les miracles* sees the two incidents mentioned above as showing up the pastors in their true colours, and seizes the opportunity of delivering what is, despite its humorous style and presentation, Voltaire's longest and most emotional attack upon them, in which his Erastian principles are given their most extreme statement. He points out how a priest or pastor should behave: his role should be primarily that of a minister of morals whose *raison d'être* is to preach virtue and avoid trouble-provoking theology (M.xxv.383-84):

N'est-il pas évident que la vertu vient de Dieu, et que les dogmes viennent des hommes qui ont voulu dominer? Vous voulez être prédicant, prêchez la justice et rien de plus. Il nous faut des gens de bien, et non des sophistes. On vous paye pour dire aux enfants: 'Respectez, aimez vos pères et mères; soyez soumis aux lois: ne faites jamais rien contre votre conscience; rendez votre femme heureuse; ne vous privez pas d'elle sur de vains caprices; élevez vos enfants dans l'amour du juste et de l'honnête; aimez votre patrie; adorez un Dieu éternel et juste; sachez que, puisqu'il est juste, il récompensera la vertu et punira le crime.'

Voilà, continua-t-il, le symbole de la raison et de la justice.

By doing this, they will not, Voltaire tells the Genevese pastors, become rich and powerful, but 'vous aurez la considération convenable à votre état, et vous serez regardés comme de bons citoyens, ce qui est le plus grand des avantages'. This is, in fact, more or less the blueprint for a Voltairean deist minister. In earlier days, he might have hoped for voluntary support from the Calvinist ministers, who did indeed when preaching concentrate on morality almost to the exclusion of theology, but now his disillusion with them leads him to think that a show of authority will be necessary to force them to be more co-operative.

Fortunately, at Geneva reason is better established than in many places, and the pastors have their hands tied. One of them remarks glumly in the ninth letter of the *Questions* (M.xxv.405-406):

Nous en ferions tout comme les autres, si nous avions à faire à des sots; mais notre peuple est instruit et malin; il laisse passer les anciens miracles qu'il a trouvés tout établis. Si nous nous mêlions d'en faire pour notre compte, si nous nous avisions, par exemple, d'exorciser des possédés, on croirait que nous le sommes; si nous chassions les diables, on nous chasserait avec eux.

Voltaire again emphasises that the clergy must be subservient to the state, and then expresses himself almost as a Quaker might. Indeed, one cannot help remembering Andrew Pitt's exposition of the universal priesthood of all believers in the first *Lettre philosophique*, for Voltaire argues that the laity has not lost its rights, and that an established priesthood is a convenience of civilised society which in no way alienates each man's competence to perform sacerdotal functions himself (cf. Lanson ed., i.24). Priests, indeed, are merely the servants of society, and if only they could give up their ideas of power and domination, they would realise that the role he is advocating for them is preferable to their past ambitions (M.xxv.409).

Speaking in the thirteenth letter as 'Covelle à ses chers concitoyens', Voltaire urges the citizens of Geneva to defend their liberty against the pretensions of their clergy: 'ce ne peut être aujourd'hui que dans un violent transport au cerveau, que des hommes vêtus de noir puissent prétendre nous rendre imbéciles pour nous gouverner' (M.xxv.418). Again using arguments which recall Quaker ideas, Voltaire claims that, in the last resort, priests can be dispensed with altogether, and he quotes the example of Pennsylvania to back up his assertion. The Calvinist ministers as a body are quite incorrigible. In Neuchâtel, as well as in Geneva, they are the source of trouble and injustice, a fact demonstrated by the case of Petitpierre, a 'pauvre pasteur de campagne', who, as we have seen, was humane enough to reject the idea of eternal damnation and to substitute for it a kind of purgatory, and was forced to exile himself in England, despite his complete orthodoxy on all other points (cf. above, p.170). The sixteenth letter of the *Questions* contains a further outburst against the ministers and against ecclesiastical power and influence in Geneva. Do the pastors think that the Reformation has made no difference to the status of priests?: 'Les meurtres, les empoisonnements, les parricides d'Alexandre vi, l'ambition guerrière et turbulente de Jules ii, les débauches et les rapines de Léon x, nous révoltèrent: nous brisâmes l'idole; mais nous n'avons pas prétendu en adorer une nouvelle' (M.xxv.429). The clergy are now only a kind of civil servant and their submission to the government should be complete in all fields, even that of dogma: 'Il y a des choses dont on ne doit que rire; il y en a contre lesquelles il faut s'élever avec force [...] riez des sottises; mais éclatez contre la persécution. L'esprit persécuteur est l'ennemi de tous les hommes: il mène droit à l'établissement de l'Inquisition' (M.xxv.430-31). This last point is illustrated in the final letter, which recounts the trial, before the Neuchâtel Consistory, of Needham, the Jesuit 'aux anguilles'.[281] Here are echoes of Calvin's persecution of Servetus, and of the condemnation of Antoine. Sentenced by the Consistory to be stoned, Needham is defended by 'M. du Peyrou, homme de bien, qui, n'étant pas prêtre, fait beaucoup de bonnes œuvres' (M.xxv.448), and finally manages to escape while the pastors are digesting the decision of the governor of Neuchâtel's lieutenant: 'Oh bien [...] lapidez-le donc; mais que ce soit le plus absurde de vous tous qui jette la première pierre.'

xv. *Conclusion*

To sum up briefly the complicated and constantly changing relationship between Voltaire and the religious establishment of Geneva is no easy matter. His original enthusiasm for Calvin's city has often been described, and we have seen how, after becoming rapidly disenchanted with 'la prètraille de Jehan Chauvin',[282] he nonetheless retained his respect and admiration for the city's magistrates. Yet even this qualified approval was to disappear as Voltaire became involved in the vortex of Genevese politics, identified first with the *bourgeois* then with the *natifs*,

---

[281] John Needham was an Irish Jesuit whose theories on spontaneous generation were anathema to Voltaire: cf. Best.D15189, D15199, D15413.
[282] Voltaire uses this expression in Best.D13158.

in both cases supporting groups opposed to the *Petit conseil* he had earlier praised so enthusiastically. But this new hostility to the latter body was not compensated by any lessening of Voltaire's scorn for Geneva's pastors. On the contrary, the *philosophe* became steadily more embittered as far as they were concerned: in the *Questions sur les miracles* he railed at every aspect of the pastors' role, determined to prove their unworthiness as spiritual guides of the population and the necessity of having them controlled in the strictest way by the civil authorities. The violence with which Voltaire advocated this reform was perhaps encouraged by the fact that he considered great things already to have been achieved in Geneva, and the possibility of finally destroying Calvinism there and replacing it with a reasonable form of deism to be within his grasp.

But there was another side to Voltaire's contacts with the Calvinist pastors of Switzerland. His cordial relationships with individual ministers, even men like Bertrand who were unwilling to accept without protest his attacks on Christianity, show that the growing hostility and bitterness I have just described cannot be regarded as an inevitable consequence of Voltaire's stay in Geneva. Indeed, such an apparently trivial factor as personality may have played an important part in triggering off Voltaire's opposition to the views of his Protestant hosts. Jacob Vernet notably failed to gain Voltaire's confidence: his moderately phrased proposal that the famous deist should support Geneva's enlightened religion (cf. above, p.120) was not unlike similar comments by Bertrand (cf. above, pp.184-85), yet the latter's remarks received quite a different reception. Once initial hostility had developed, it was all too easy for Voltaire to find in remaining manifestations of Calvinist morality confirmation of his worst fears regarding its austerity and harshness, and at the same time proof of the hypocrisy of those pastors who continued to enforce such a morality while rejecting the theological foundation on which it was based. And indeed, Voltaire was surely correct in his evaluation of this inconsistency,[283] although he

[283] Voltaire himself pointed out, in a letter to Bertrand (Best.D11580; cf. above, p.186) that Protestantism was founded on the individual's right to interpret the scriptures. Yet, as any student of the Reformation can see, new dogmatic edifices – Lutheran, Anglican, Calvinist – were quickly erected, and dissenters could be severely punished. The position of 'liberal' eighteenth-century pastors was even more equivocal, for they had apparently accepted the rights of the *esprit de libre examen* as far as theology was concerned, yet continued to impose a rigid system of petty Calvinist restrictions, even though a fundamentally new style of morality was gaining general acceptance.

does not seem to have grasped the social and political factors which caused the clergy's intransigence. Yet should a Voltaire who himself preached to the multitude beliefs which he did not necessarily share,[284] have been so shocked or surprised at the position of Geneva's 'enlightened' clergy? What, one may ask, is the basic difference between the Anglican priest Freind, who acts as Voltaire's spokesman in *Histoire de Jenni*,[285] and a liberal Genevese theologian like Vernet? The former, like the latter, emphasised the moral demands imposed by religion, prudently leaving aside awkward dogmas such as the trinity, on the grounds that they were unbiblical and irrelevant to the development of true piety.

We must conclude that in the 1750s the time was not yet ripe for an alliance between Voltaire and the pastors of Geneva. Had they, at the same time as liberalising their theology, been willing to renounce their allegiance to Calvin and revise some of their more rebarbative moral rules, especially in connection with the theatre, Voltaire's attitude to their hypocrisy might have been very different. And had Voltaire himself not been about to enter on his most violently anti-Christian phase, had he already been shocked and worried by the spread of militant atheism as he was to be after the appearance of d'Holbach's *Système de la nature*, the chances of collaboration might have been great indeed. That this is not merely idle speculation is surely demonstrated by the apparent change in Voltaire's attitude to Jesus in the late 1760s, possibly a consequence, at least in part, of his contacts with ministers like Jacob Vernes and particularly François-Louis Allamand, whose proposals concerning the establishment of a philosophical religion on the framework of Christianity appear greatly to have interested Voltaire. Indeed, in view of some of Allamand's statements, it would not be unlikely that the Freind of *Histoire de Jenni* was partly modelled on him, although Brumfitt and Davis (p.lviii) have convincingly argued that this tolerant and philosophical clergyman was 'to no small extent based on a historical personage', dr John Freind.[286] Nonetheless, even a partial identification

[284] 'The idea of a magistrate God who hands out rewards and sentences appears to Voltaire after about 1750 to be a necessity for the populace' (H. T. Mason, *Pierre Bayle and Voltaire*, p.84).

[285] thus Freind claims: 'L'Evangile n'agite pas cette question, et jamais Saint Paul n'écrivit le nom de Trinité' (*L'Ingénu and Histoire de Jenni*, ed. Brumfitt and Davis, p.68). In the second edition of his *Traité de la vérité de la religion chrétienne*, Vernet omitted the chapter on the trinity (Pomeau, *La Religion*, p.295).

[286] another probable influence was the eccentric bishop of Derry, Frederick Augustus

of Allamand and Freind would have been a fitting tribute to a man who, without being afraid to criticise Voltaire, consistently praised the constructive side of his religious thought and encouraged him to reach a fruitful compromise with a rationalised and purified form of Christianity.

But indications that Voltaire's attitude toward Christianity was softening at the end of the 1760s were confined strictly to his contacts with certain individual pastors and to a few passages in his published works. There was at no time any hint of a compromise with official Calvinism. Indeed, events of the 1760s only further soured Voltaire and strengthened his conviction that the clergy of Geneva sought to achieve political influence in the city as well as retaining and extending their moral authority. It was to the Anglican Church, in his opinion a model of Erastianism, that Voltaire turned his hopes, and even his most anticlerical works of this period give it grudging approval.[287] At first sight, Voltaire's determination to see the clergy's hand in every turn of Geneva's political life merely provides further evidence of his congenital hostility to Christian priests of almost every denomination. His consistent anticlerical propaganda may even have had the paradoxical effect of creating religious unrest in Geneva where none had previously existed. This, at any rate, was what Du Pan claimed to Freudenreich in about April 1762: 'Il a fait un mal incroyable dans notre ville en y faisant naître une faction composée de Ministres et de dévots. Si cette faction continue à s'échauffer, on pourra bien en venir à s'égorger pour la gloire de Dieu' (Best.D10429, commentary).

Yet it would be misrepresenting the truth to give the impression that Voltaire had no grounds whatsoever for suspecting that the clergy were sometimes involved in Genevese politics or that political events could have an influence on the republic's religious practices from time to time. In the first place, Jacob Vernes, one of Voltaire's few friends in the pastorate, is unlikely to have done anything but strengthen his already formidable prejudices. According to Chaponnière: 'Vernes qui, le 5 mars 1768, essaiera, sans succès, de faire soutenir par la Compagnie un projet de conciliation se dépite de voir "l'injustice des pasteurs ses

---

Hervey (1730-1803), who visited Voltaire on several occasions and who, as well as championing the rights of oppressed Irish Catholics, was noted by some of his contemporaries as a free-thinker: see below, appendix 5.

[287] cf., for example, the *Examen important de milord Bolingbroke* of 1767 (*Mélanges*, p.1022), and the *Lettre de milord Cornsbury à milord Bolingbroke* of the same year (M.xxvi. 305-306); also Best.D9006 and D13374 and below, pp.443 ff.

confrères", encourage Voltaire dans son action.'[288] Moreover, despite the fact, remarked on by Voltaire in his correspondence (cf. above, pp. 214-15), that a few pastors had defended Rousseau in 1762 and thus identified themselves with the *bourgeoisie*'s essentially political protest, Chaponnière and Dardier point out that most ministers sided with the aristocratic *négatifs* against the 'popular' party (cf. esp. *Esaïe Gasc*, pp.67-68). Such a development was not surprising in view of the clergy's traditional policy of supporting the *Petit conseil*. But the upshot of this polarisation was that 'les Représentants, par représailles, ne mettaient plus les pieds à l'église' (*Voltaire chez les calvinistes*, p.148). This action was no doubt warmly supported by Voltaire, and such incidents may have encouraged him to reach unwarranted conclusions regarding the importance of religious factors in the Genevese troubles of the 1760s.

Examples like this indicate that Voltaire's apparently rather jaundiced picture of the pastors' political rôle was due more to a mistaken perspective than to a fundamentally incorrect analysis. The pastoral body did have a recognisable political attitude, though this was by no means shared by all its members and was only a relatively minor element in the clash of interests between various Genevese social groups. Voltaire's error was, on occasions, to magnify the importance of the clergy's position out of all proportion. On the matter of the pastors' faith Voltaire was nearer the mark, despite their own denials and subsequent critical whitewashing. So close in fact were the views of Voltaire and some pastors that a compromise between *philosophie* and religion might not have been impossible. That such a development did not materialise was due as much to temperament as to any more fundamental reasons. There were of course some exceptions, but when it came to following their new theological beliefs through to a logical conclusion, many members of the Genevese clergy drew back aghast, hurriedly taking shelter behind the ramparts of Calvinist orthodoxy. And even those in favour of some type of reform may have feared suffocating in the Voltairean embrace if they showed themselves willing to accept philosophic ideas too openly and without a certain amount of qualification. In Voltaire's opinion, such a position was inadmissible. The pastors of Geneva, by condoning Calvin's conduct toward Servetus, incurred a share in responsibility for the Reformer's intolerance: by hypocritically refusing to acknowledge their unorthodox doctrinal beliefs, they identified themselves with *l'infâme* and were treated accordingly.

[288] *Voltaire chez les calvinistes*, p.160; cf. Dardier, *Esaïe Gasc*, p.64.

6

Protestantism in France: a civil disaster

As FAR as Voltaire was concerned, there had been no happy ending to the history of French Protestantism. Disaster had followed disaster. First the civil wars had made out of France two nations, which regarded each other with fear and suspicion. The treachery and bitterness of this period culminated in the massacre of St Bartholomew's Day. Then, after a period of uneasiness under Louis XIII, the unifying force of Louis XIV's reign offered the French a chance of a religious peace acceptable to both sides, only to shatter this hope with a senseless act of authority, both arbitrary and mistaken. The consequences of the repeal of the Edict of Nantes were to deprive the country of desperately needed manpower and skills, while at the same time Louis XIV's extreme measure failed anyway in its object of stamping out Protestantism. Although many Huguenots chose the path of exile,[1] still more remained in France as uneasy and unwilling converts to Catholicism, henceforth liable to severe penal laws should they indulge in overt acts of Protestantism and hampered in the exercise of many trades and professions by the necessity of obtaining credentials to prove their catholicity (cf. below, p.265). In Voltaire's opinion this was not only a crime against humanity but also extreme economic folly in a nation struggling to maintain its standards of living and to pay for a series of costly wars.[2]

i. The French Reformation and the civil wars

Four main sources are available in Voltaire's works for discovering his views about the French Reformation and subsequent events until the

[1] in Le Siècle de Louis XIV Voltaire points out that the French Huguenots established colonies as far afield as South Africa (cf. Best.D4787), concluding bitterly: 'Les Français ont été dispersés plus loin que les Juifs' (Oh, p.1056).

[2] in his correspondence Voltaire draws frequent attention to the pernicious effects the repeal of the Edict of Nantes continued to have on France. The following comment in a letter to Le Bault is typical: 'Mon terrain est excellent, et cependant j'ay trouvé cent arpents apartenants à mes habitans, qui restent sans culture [. . .] Voylà les déplorables suittes de la révocation de l'édit de Nantes' (Best.D7946, 18 November 1758). Cf. also Best.D10413, D14450, D15444, D19247, D19899.

reign of Louis XIV; the relevant chapters in the *Essai sur les mœurs* and the *Histoire du parlement de Paris* as well as the beginning of the chapter on Calvinism in *Le Siècle de Louis XIV* (chapter 36) and the early *Essay upon the civil wars of France*, written while Voltaire was in England in 1727. All the accounts are basically similar, although Voltaire's attitude to the Huguenots becomes perhaps slightly more favourable as time goes on. It will be sufficient for our purposes here to mention the main points Voltaire makes, in order to illustrate the dominant themes of the French religious wars as he saw them.

Voltaire begins in the *Essai sur les mœurs* by stressing that France might easily have adopted the Reformation had it not been for the Concordat of 1516 between François I and the pope, which meant that, for political reasons, the king did not favour a change in religion, despite the fact that the Concordat was generally unpopular: 'Dans toute cette affaire qui fit tant de peine à François 1er, il était nécessaire qu'il fût obéi s'il voulait que Léon x remplît avec lui ses engagements politiques, et l'aidât à recouvrer le duché de Milan' (*Essai*, ii.273). The *Histoire du parlement* makes the same point, adding that François's patronage of the arts had made his own religious policy more difficult to enforce: 'François 1er lui-même, en favorisant les lettres, avait fait naître le crépuscule à la lueur duquel on commençait à voir en France tous les abus de l'Eglise; mais il était toujours dans la nécessité de ménager le pape.'[3] His own sister was a supporter of the new religion, but his opposition to it was strengthened by another political reason: 'Le conseil du roi croyait [...] que toute nouveauté en religion traîne après elle des nouveautés dans l'Etat' (*Essai*, ii.273). Voltaire points out that this assumption was justified if one considered only Germany, but there were also the examples of Sweden and Denmark whose kings had established Lutheranism there with no difficulty whatsoever. Yet the cynical François, who is judged very harshly by Voltaire,[4] allowed

---

[3] M.xv.498. We see that François was thus in a similar position to Leo x: the encouragement he gave to the arts was, Voltaire suggests, incompatible with his desire to maintain traditional Catholicism. Cf. above, p.30.

[4] cf. the two letters Voltaire wrote in 1768 and 1769 to G. H. Gaillard in connection with the latter's *Histoire de François 1er* (see Best.15284, n.4). In the first (Best.D15284, 2 November 1768) Voltaire calls François 'ce brave chevalier et [...] ce pauvre roi' and compares him unfavourably to Charles v, who did not burn any Lutherans: 'il leur accordait la liberté de conscience après les avoir battus en rase campagne'. Voltaire's next letter (Best.D15614, 28 April 1769) dismisses Gaillard's attempted defence of François. Once again the superiority of Charles v is emphasised, and Voltaire describes the inhuman

persecution against the heretics to begin, apparently almost by accident: 'Les évéques, les parlements, allumèrent les bûchers: il ne les éteignit pas. Il les aurait éteints si son cœur n'avait pas été endurci sur les malheurs des autres autant qu'amolli par les plaisirs [...] la religion ne l'embarrassait guère' (*Essai*, ii.274). He hypocritically allied himself with the Protestant princes of Germany while the persecutions against the Protestants were at their height in France: 'et quand les princes luthériens d'Allemagne ses alliés lui reprochèrent d'avoir fait mourir leurs frères qui n'excitaient aucune trouble en France, il rejetait tout sur les juges ordinaires'.

Another event of François's reign was the massacre at Mérindol and Cabrières of the remaining Waldensians, though Voltaire does not blame the king for this new atrocity.[5] The greatest responsibility was to be attributed to the violent persecution carried out by the parlement de Provence, whose *premier président* d'Oppède and *avocat général* Guérin caused the deaths of thousands of innocent people, despite the fact that the king's decree had merely authorised the execution of nineteen heretics. It is interesting to note that Voltaire seems to shift some of the blame for the event onto the Protestants. Had they not been such busybodies, he implies, the Waldensians might well have been left in peace (*Essai*, ii.275):

Ces Vaudois jouissaient de ce calme, quand les réformateurs d'Allemagne et de Genève apprirent qu'ils avaient des frères (1540). Aussitôt ils leur envoyèrent des ministres [...] Alors ces Vaudois furent trop connus. Les édits nouveaux contre les hérétiques les condamnaient au feu.

But, for all its severity, the government's attempts to prevent the new religion spreading were completely unsuccessful: 'Ces exécutions n'empêchaient pas le progrès du calvinisme. On brûlait d'un côté, et on chantait de l'autre en riant les psaumes de Marot, selon le génie toujours léger et quelquefois très cruel de la nation française' (*Essai*, ii.277). Voltaire is surely also suggesting that, in some way, the Protestants wished on themselves the extent of the persecution they underwent by refusing to keep silent and conform outwardly, as one feels sure a prudent *philosophe* would have done. The Huguenots' numbers

tortures to which François subjected the unfortunate Lutherans. A 1769 addition to the *Essai sur les mœurs* includes similar details (*Essai*, ii.274).

5 several references to these massacres occur in Voltaire's correspondence: cf. Best. D5858, D11744, D12552, D13521. Louis Trenard ('Voltaire, historien de la Réforme en France', p.158) considers that Voltaire was influenced by Bayle in the importance he accords them.

were indeed increased by their heroic sacrifices, but one feels that, for Voltaire, the price paid was an unreasonable one, especially since the Protestants were recruiting converts for Calvinism, which he obviously regarded as a prejudiced, rather than an enlightened form of belief: 'Les martyrs font des prosélytes: le supplice d'un tel homme fit plus de réformés que les livres de Calvin', he states (*Essai*, ii.278) after describing the death of Dubourg, and this is a theme which recurs in his explanations of the growing number of Protestants. Undoubtedly he was right: martyrs did produce more martyrs and increase the rate of conversions. Yet Voltaire seems to have no conception of the necessity these Protestants martyrs felt to witness to their faith: to him the phenomenon was a kind of lunatic mathematical law, a symptom of the madness which had overtaken France and which religion can always produce if not held in check by the state, or, even more effectively, by reason. It was one of the irrational features about the Protestants which appealed to him least. He could certainly admire a man like Dubourg, 'juge intègre, homme d'une vie irréprochable, et citoyen zélé' (M.xv.505), whose death is often cited in his works[6] as an example of intolerance and who was made the mouthpiece of Voltaire's criticism of the Roman Church in his pamphlet *Discours du conseiller Anne Dubourg* (M.xxviii. 469-72), but at the same time he could not understand the need for Dubourg's death (cf. above, p.89) and probably put it down to the power that fanaticism could exert, even over the actions of such an outstanding man, once it had become widespread and generally accepted in society.

In fact Voltaire's sympathies are never wholly with the Huguenots. Although he has portrayed the *réformés* as harassed inhumanly by the authorities, he does not seem to consider them justified in taking up arms to defend themselves. His attitude could almost be that of a traditional Gallican: approval for the Protestants' attacks on abuses in the Church, and a desire for independence from Rome, but no sympathy with a party whose aims were to disobey the laws and to flout openly the royal authority. The government could, and should, have avoided the religious wars by treating the Protestants less severely: 'on pouvait conserver de bons sujets, en leur laissant la liberté de conscience. Il eût importé peu à l'Etat qu'ils chantassent à leur manière, pourvu qu'ils eussent été soumis aux lois de l'Etat: on les persécuta, et on en fit de

---

[6] cf. M.vii.184; xxvii.49, 65; xxx.548; Best.D7534, D12819, D13651, D14779.

rebelles' (*Essai*, ii.481-82). The emphasis here is all on the social and political disadvantages which were caused by persecution: the Huguenots themselves are dismissed as a group of bizarre eccentrics, whose moral code was austere and unpalatable.[7] Perhaps the most significant point, however, is that Voltaire does not appear to condemn intolerance in itself, on principle, but argues that in this case it was a mistaken and ineffective policy.

Admittedly, his attitude to the Protestants is more favourable in the pamphlet *Du protestantisme et de la guerre des Cévennes*. There Voltaire states categorically: 'Il est constant que ceux qui se disent réformés en France furent persécutés quarante ans avant qu'ils se révoltassent; car ce ne fut qu'après le massacre de Vassy qu'ils prirent les armes' (*Mélanges*, p.1278), but this is in a work written in 1763 at the time of Voltaire's maximum involvement with the Calas case, and it is not surprising that the Protestants are less harshly treated than elsewhere. *Le Siècle de Louis XIV*, in contrast, explains the religious wars and the progress of Protestantism as a result of political faction: if the government had remained strong, there would probably have been no serious outbreaks of violence:

On ne vit point les luthériens et les calvinistes causer de grands troubles en France sous le gouvernement ferme de François Ier et de Henri II. Mais, dès que le gouvernement fut faible et partagé, les querelles de religion furent violentes. Les Condé et les Coligny, devenus calvinistes parce que les Guise étaient catholiques, bouleversèrent l'Etat à l'envi. La légèreté et l'impétuosité de la nation, la fureur de la nouveauté, et l'enthousiasme, firent pendant quarante ans du peuple le plus poli un peuple de barbares.[8]

[7] cf. Best.D11060, Voltaire to the marquis d'Argence, 2 March 1763: 'Rien ne fut plus atrabilaire et plus féroce que les huguenots, parce qu'ils voulaient combattre la morale relâchée.'

[8] *Oh*, p.1044. Cf. the *Essay upon the civil wars of France*, where Voltaire also stresses the importance of political considerations in the conversion to Calvinism of sixteenth-century French Protestant leaders. This early work is, however, somewhat fairer to the Calvinists than is *Le Siècle de Louis XIV* in that it advances other motives of consequence apart from mere political expediency: 'The Superstition, the dull ignorant Knavery of the Monks, the overgrown Power of *Rome*, Men's passion for Novelty, the Ambition of *Luther* and *Calvin*, the Policy of many Princes; all these had given rise and countenance to this Sect, free indeed from Superstition, but running as headlong toward Anarchy, as the Church of *Rome* towards Tyranny. The Protestants had been unmercifully persecuted in *France*; but it is the ordinary effect of Persecution to make Proselytes; their Sect increased every day amidst the Scaffolds and Tortures. *Condé, Coligny*, the two Brothers of *Coligny*, all their Adherents, all who were oppressed by the *Guises*, turned Protestants at once; they united their Griefs, their Vengeance, and their Interests together, so that a Revolution both in the State and in Religion was at hand' (Studies on Voltaire (1965), xl.667).

By 1768 Voltaire was much better aware of the Huguenots's under-priveleged position in contemporary France, and he had already intervened many times on their behalf (cf. below, pp.304 ff). Yet although the *Histoire du parlement* excuses the Protestant leaders from direct responsibility in causing the religious wars, the very fact that so much importance is attached to political factors means that the attitude expressed by Voltaire in earlier accounts is but little changed (M.xv.507):

François de Guise et le cardinal de Lorraine son frère [. . .] étaient les maîtres absolus de l'Etat [. . .] Les princes du sang, écartés et humiliés, ne purent se soutenir contre eux qu'en se joignant secrètement aux protestants, qui commençaient à faire un parti considérable dans le royaume [. . .] Louis de Condé frère d'Antoine de Bourbon, roi de la Basse-Navarre, entreprit d'ôter aux Guises un pouvoir qui ne leur appartenait pas, et se rendit criminel dans une juste cause par la fameuse conspiration d'Amboise.

Although Voltaire does not deny the strength of the Huguenots' religious convictions, he makes it clear that it was the political direction given to them by powerful princes which made them a force to be reckoned with (cf. *Essai*, ii.482-83).

That Voltaire's view of the religious wars was determined by basically political motives is again illustrated when he criticises Catherine of Medici's semi-indulgent attitude towards the Huguenots (*Essai*, ii.487):

Elle commença par indiquer le colloque de Poissy entre les catholiques et les protestants: ce qui était mettre l'ancienne religion en compromis, et donner un grand crédit aux calvinistes, en les faisant disputer contre ceux qui ne se croyaient faits que pour les juger.

Not a word about the merits or otherwise of the Huguenots' religious position. The fact that the *Histoire du parlement* is slightly more favourable to Catherine is presumably because in that work Voltaire is concerned to discredit the *parlements* by showing that they opposed all the more tolerant edicts made during this troubled period of French history (cf. M.xv.510-14).

Voltaire goes on to describe the general Protestant uprising after the massacre of Vassy. Although we might expect this event to increase his sympathy for the Huguenots, the assassination of the duc de Guise, attributed by him to a type of fanaticism which, in its beginnings at least, was specifically Protestant (cf. above, pp.87-88), confirms his attitude of suspicion and dislike towards them. They were just as much to be condemned as the Catholics (cf. *Essai*, ii.490). Even the massacre of St Bartholomew's Day, which he describes as 'ce qu'il y a jamais eu de plus horrible' (M.xv.527), and for which his aversion is well-known, afflicts him more as a crime against humanity than as one against the Protestants. In their connection, he notes that the massacre was ineffective and served merely to increase their determination to resist (*Essai*, ii.497):

S'il pouvait y avoir quelque chose de plus déplorable que la Saint-Barthélemy, c'est qu'elle fit naître la guerre civile au lieu de couper la racine des troubles. Les calvinistes ne pensèrent plus, dans tout le royaume, qu'à vendre chèrement leurs vies.

A passage in chapter 173 of the *Essai sur les mœurs* ('De la France sous Henri III') shows Voltaire in perhaps his most anti-Huguenot frame of mind. Their attempts to practice an unnecessarily harsh type of morality made them into virtually a separate nation, and this harmful development was reinforced by their republican aspirations (*Essai*, ii.516):

Les protestants, au contraire, qui se piquaient de réforme, opposaient des mœurs austères à celles de la cour; ils punissaient de mort l'adultère. Les spectacles, les jeux, leur étaient autant en horreur que les cérémonies de l'Eglise romaine; ils mettaient presque au même rang la messe et les sortilèges; de sorte qu'il y avait deux nations dans la France absolument différentes l'une de l'autre, et on espérait d'autant moins la réunion que les huguenots avaient, surtout depuis la Saint Barthélemy, formé le dessein de s'ériger en république.

Voltaire is quite positive about the Huguenots' political ambitions, and emphasises that they retained these in the France of Louis XIII (*Essai*, ii.579):

L'amour de la liberté, si naturel aux hommes, flattait alors les réformés d'idées républicaines [. . .] Le commandant général qu'ils devaient choisir, en cas de guerre, devait avoir un sceau où étaient gravés ces mots: *Pour Christ et pour le roi*: c'est-à-dire, contre le roi. La Rochelle était regardée comme la capitale de cette république, qui pouvait former un Etat dans l'Etat.

This state of affairs persisted even after the conciliatory Edict of Nantes, which, generous though it was, had not succeeded in satisfying the Protestants: 'les calvinistes qu'il [Henri IV] avait quittés, se cantonnant contre les ligueurs, se ménageaient déjà des ressources pour résister un jour à l'autorité royale' (*Essai*, ii.541).

Voltaire's views in this context are a logical development of the opinions he expressed when first describing Calvin and his Reformation. Calvinism represented a complete break with the past, and the new type of morality it preached was bound to cause continued trouble in both Church and state; in fact, as we read in *Le Siècle de Louis XIV*, 'le calvinisme devait nécessairement enfanter des guerres civiles, et ébranler les fondements des Etats' (*Oh*, p.1063). Voltaire's opinion of the Huguenots during the French civil wars is, therefore, of a party which originally contained men fanatically opposed to the Roman Church, men who were justified in criticising the abuses they saw. Later, however, they became politically important and a danger to the state because of the support given them by powerful noblemen. The Huguenot party was a source of faction and national disunity. Even the abjuration of Henri IV, which Voltaire approves as the only practical course open to him, proves that statesmen like Henri were prepared to use religion as a means rather than considering it as an end in itself.[9] Despite the fact that Voltaire's cosmopolitanism has often been considered to be one of his most characteristic features, he was also a patriotic Frenchman, and there is every indication that he fully supported Richelieu's policy towards the Huguenots as it is outlined in the *Essai sur les mœurs* – the destruction of their power was necessary before the French nation could regain its full strength and successfully pursue the traditional foreign policy: 'il fallait abattre et désarmer tout le parti, avant de pouvoir déployer en sûreté ses forces contre la maison d'Autriche, en Allemagne, en Italie, en Flandre, et vers l'Espagne' (*Essai*, ii.598).

ii. *The repeal of the Edict of Nantes and the Camisard uprising*

Normally Voltaire refuses to hold Louis XIV at all responsible for the tragedy of the repeal. An early letter to Frederick of Prussia illustrates

[9] cf. Best.D7875 and D10602: in these letters Voltaire appears to think that Henri's action was not sincere, but nonetheless implies that it was justified for reasons of state. And in a marginal note on his copy of Rousseau's *Contrat social* referring to Henri's conversion, Voltaire states quite simply 'sa raison fut la couronne de france' (George R. Havens, *Voltaire's marginalia on the pages of Rousseau* (New York 1933), p.68). But this opportunism certainly did not reduce Voltaire's enthusiasm for the king: on 1 March 1751 he told Sophia Wilhelmina of Bayreuth that she was the first person who had ever valued Sully above Henri IV: 'Pour moy homme très faible', he went on, 'j'avoue que j'aime mieux les faiblesses de ce bon roy que touttes les vertus austères de son ministre' (Best. D4409). This opinion should be borne in mind in view of the over-enthusiastic picture of Calvinist leaders like Sully and Mornay which Voltaire was supposed by some to have painted in *La Henriade*.

in a characteristic way Voltaire's ambiguous reaction to the most disastrous event of Louis xiv's reign: on the one hand dismay at the loss of manpower sustained by France and the consequent enrichment of neighbouring countries, but on the other hand a shifting of the blame from Louis xiv himself onto one or another of his advisers or ministers. Louis xiv 'ne lut jamais', Voltaire tells Frederick (Best.D1255, *c.* 15 January 1737): 'et s'il avoit lu, s'il avoit sçu l'histoire, vous auriez moins de français à Berlin, votre royaume ne se seroit pas enrichi en i686 des dépouilles du sien, il auroit moins écouté le jésuite le Tellier'. Writing a few years later to baron Hervey of Ickworth, Voltaire went even further to disculpate Louis xiv, claiming that the king was a great man 'malgré un million d'hommes dont il a privé la France, & qui tous ont été intéressés à le décrier'. The mass exodus of Protestants is now made to sound beneficial to the European family of nations in general: even Louis's mistakes have been useful! (Best.D2216).

The *Anecdotes sur Louis XIV* (1748) shows Voltaire similarly determined to defend the Sun King against the reproaches of historians. All the accounts written in Holland are biased, because their authors were themselves Protestants, he claims once more. Louis xiv's action was not as serious as that of Philip iii, when the Spanish monarch had driven out the Moors, 'ce qui avait fait à la monarchie espagnole une plaie inguérissable'.[10] He wished the Huguenots to stay in France and be converted. Voltaire's personal enquiries to cardinal Fleury show that Bâville, the intendant of Languedoc, was responsible for the whole affair. The latter's exaggerated claim to have abolished the sect in his province, despite the fact that there were still 80,000 Huguenots there, easily persuaded Louis xiv that the same thing could be done in the kingdom as a whole. So, again, the king's part in the repeal is minimised, and Bâville takes over from Le Tellier the rôle of chief villain.

Such extreme indulgence as that shown in Best.D2216 and the *Anecdotes* was not always to be maintained in Voltaire's references to the repeal of the Edict of Nantes, but in *Le Siècle de Louis XIV* he is still prepared to go a long way toward condoning the king's personal position, and he shows but little sympathy for the Huguenots' plight. Louis did not realise that the political situation had evolved and the

[10] elsewhere, Voltaire's opinion is different, and he often compares the two, as in Best. D14450 (to Shuvalov, 30 September 1767), where the two events appear to have had equally disastrous consequences: 'L'Espagne s'est détruite elle même en chassant les Juifs et les Maures. La plaie de la révocation de l'édit de Nantes saigne encore en France.'

Huguenots were no longer dangerous, Voltaire explains: under Mazarin they took no part at all in the Fronde, despite the attempts of various factions to enlist their support. Moreover: 'Les fêtes magnifiques d'une cour galante jetaient même du ridicule sur le pédantisme des huguenots. A mesure que le bon goût se perfectionnait, les psaumes de Marot et de Bèze ne pouvaient plus insensiblement inspirer que du dégoût' (*Oh*, pp.1048-49). The king, however, knew little about the Huguenots and his prejudice against them was not completely unfounded: 'Louis XIV, nullement instruit d'ailleurs du fond de leur doctrine, les regardait, non sans quelque raison, comme d'anciens révoltés soumis avec peine' (*Oh*, p.1049). This explained his systematic attempts to undermine their religion. At first a 'caisse des conversions' run by Pellisson was tried, but this proved largely unsuccessful. Nonetheless, false reports persuaded the authorities to use force and the subsequent *dragonnades* caused the first migrations to begin: all this time the clergy kept up constant pressure on the government to continue its anti-Protestant measures. If only the government had turned its attention abroad, it would have realised that times had changed: 'tout prouvait qu'un roi absolu pouvait être également bien servi par des catholiques et par des protestants' (*Oh*, p.1052). After all, the king had loyal Lutheran subjects in Alsace: 'Louis XIV [. . .] pouvait tolérer dans ses Etats le calvinisme, que le temps aurait pu abolir.'

Yet this sensible policy was not followed. Persecution continued and the Huguenots began to hold open-air assemblies in some areas. The ensuing punishments did not have the desired effect: 'Tout cela inspirait la terreur, et en même temps augmentait l'opiniâtreté. On sait trop que les hommes s'attachent à leur religion à mesure qu'ils souffrent pour elle.' Voltaire no more suggests a reason for this phenomenon than he did when talking of the civil wars (cf. above, pp.235-36), but it provides a useful practical argument against persecution, since it was France's enemies who benefited from the talents and skills of the *émigrés*. Moreover, Voltaire points out that at this time Louis XIV was on the worst of terms with the pope, and keeping the Calvinists would have been a way of opposing the papacy's pretensions. But half measures were not good enough for the king: 'Louis XIV, conciliant les intérêts de sa religion et ceux de sa grandeur, voulut à la fois humilier le pape d'une main et écraser le calvinisme de l'autre' (*Oh*, p.1053). Voltaire goes on to describe the unpleasant details of the *dragonnades* and blames Louvois for these atrocities.[11] The Edict of Nantes was finally repealed, but instead of imprisoning the Protestant ministers, the government made the mistake of exiling them: 'c'était s'aveugler que de penser qu'en chassant les pasteurs, une grande partie du troupeau ne suivrait pas' (*Oh*, p.1054). And so began the massive emigration of French talents and manpower: over 50,000 families, he calculates, left France in three years. The prince of Orange and the duke of Savoy formed regiments of Protestant soldiers; altogether France lost 500,000 inhabitants. Moreover, the sacrifice of so many useful citizens achieved nothing: the 400,000 Calvinists left in the kingdom had only been converted by force. Continued persecution merely rallied them to their faith, and led to a fresh disaster, the Camisard uprising.

Voltaire's indulgent attitude to Louis XIV is maintained in *L'Ingénu* (1767); according to professor S. B. Taylor, this is because Voltaire was aware that the government of the day was considering some easing of the anti-Protestant laws, and he wanted to plead their case discreetly without at the same time compromising their chances of obtaining at least a degree of legal recognition.[12] Be this as it may, Voltaire had become acutely aware over the previous few years of the effect that imprudent statements might have on his Huguenot contemporaries, so it would be surprising, here and at other times, if Voltaire had not abstained from attaching personal blame to Louis XIV, purely for tactical considerations in his fight to achieve religious toleration. Yet the terms used in Voltaire's letter to Formey (Best.D4961, 29 July 1752) seem to indicate that his admiration for Louis's qualities was real, and that he did believe that the king had been misled. At any rate, it is the Jesuits, especially the king's confessor, the père de La Chaise, who are blamed in *L'Ingénu*, together with Louvois, who dispatches 'de tous côtés des jésuites et des dragons' (ed. Brumfitt and Davis, p.2). But a change was to occur before the end of Voltaire's life: a letter to d'Argental of 23 January 1769 (Best.D15444), while still providing an

[11] cf. Best.D4961 (to Formey, 29 July 1752): 'Il faut bien regretter qu'un roi qui avait des sentiments si grands & des principes si sages, n'ait pas consulté son propre cœur au lieu d'écouter des prêtres & Louvois, quand il s'agissait de perdre quatre ou cinq cent mille sujets utiles.'

[12] see 'Voltaire's *L'Ingénu*, the Huguenots and Choiseul', *AE*, pp.107-36, and below pp.333-52. I have also discussed this question in 'Voltaire, Gilbert de Voisins's *Mémoires* and the problem of Huguenot civil rights (1767-1768)', *Studies on Voltaire* (1978), clxxiv.7-57.

escape clause for the king, concentrates on the intolerance of Louis's action and on its disastrous consequences with a directness very different from the tone of Voltaire's earlier references to the repeal: 'Je suis tous les jours témoin du mal que l'intolérance de Louis xiv, ou plutôt de ses confesseurs a fait à la France.' And his attitude to Louis xiv hardens considerably in the *Discours de Me Belleguier* (1773). This deplores the fact that the king was not enlightened enough to realise the disaster he was bringing upon himself and his kingdom. The entire passage is worth quoting, for Voltaire cogently lists all the economic, military and social disadvantages which, in his opinion, resulted from this misguided act of authority (M.xxix.17):

Louis xiv, petit-fils de Henri iv, plût au ciel que ta belle âme eût été assez éclairée par la philosophie pour ne point détruire l'ouvrage de ton grandpère! Tu n'aurais point vu la huitième partie de ton peuple abandonner ton royaume, porter chez tes ennemis les manufactures, les arts, et l'industrie de la France; tu n'aurais point vu des Français combattre sous les étendards de Guillaume iii contre des Français, et leur disputer longtemps la victoire; tu n'aurais point vu un prince catholique armer contre toi deux régiments de Français protestants; tu aurais sagement prévenu le fanatisme barbare des Cévennes, et le châtiment, non moins barbare que le crime.

These are strong words, and Voltaire actually goes as far as to lay some of the blame for the repeal on Louis xiv himself; after all, he was obeyed by the entire nation and there were plenty of examples abroad of different sects co-existing together: 'rien n'était plus aisé que de soutenir et de contenir tous tes sujets. Jaloux du nom de Grand, tu ne connus pas ta grandeur'. But immediately, as if dismayed at his own boldness, Voltaire refers once again to the pope and to the Jesuits, implying that the king was, after all, influenced by them against his better judgement. Nonetheless, in this work Voltaire apportions responsibility for the repeal more realistically, no longer advancing the improbable thesis that the most powerful king in Europe was little more than the plaything of his advisers in religious matters. His most frank reference to Louis xiv's responsibility occurs in a letter to Condorcet of 20 December 1776 (Best.D20479), in which Voltaire seeks to defend Colbert against the latter's numerous eighteenth-century critics. Colbert's chief difficulty, explains Voltaire, was that he had to deal with 'un maître enivré de sa puissance et de sa gloire et [...] quand il s'agissait de trouver cinq cents millions sur le champ pour affermir cette gloire & cette puissance, il fallait les trouver et les fournir, sous peine d'être écrasé par l'impitoyable Louvois'.[13]

It would be unrealistic to expect such a harsh condemnation of France's most absolute king to appear in any of Voltaire's published works, even in the 1770s, and in any case his attitude seems to have wavered somewhat as to the extent of Louis XIV's involvement. Despite the critical attitude adopted in the *Discours de Me Belleguier*, the *Fragment sur l'histoire générale* written in the same year, 1773, comes to a rather different conclusion. Voltaire again says that the government's policy was mistaken, but quotes mme de Maintenon's niece, mme Caylus, to the effect that 'le roi *avait été trompé*' (M.xxix.275). He returns to the repeal for a last time in 1777: one of the articles he wrote for the *Journal de politique et de littérature* deals with the duc de Noailles's *Mémoires*, of which the first volume is relevant to the subject we are considering. The background to the repeal is again sketched in, the same causes as in Voltaire's other accounts are given for the king's policy. This time the tragedy is stated to be 'le fruit des sollicitations du jésuite La Chaise, confesseur du roi, de quelques évêques, et surtout du chancelier Le Tellier, et de Louvois son fils, ennemi de Colbert' (M.xxx.393). Colbert thought that the Huguenots' industry was necessary to the state, but Louis XIV was persuaded that 'il n'avait qu'à dire un mot, et que tous les cœurs se soumettraient. Il le crut, parce qu'il avait pendant quarante ans réussi dans tout ce qu'il avait voulu'. Mme de Maintenon joins the list of *responsables* for the first time in Voltaire's published works, thus bringing him into line with the traditional opinion of Protestant historiography that she, though originally a Huguenot, was the prime mover of the persecution.[14] Voltaire dismisses the feeble

[13] this is the nearest Voltaire comes to the conclusion of Jean Orcibal that Louis XIV's overweening personal pride must bear the lion's share of responsibility for the repeal of the Edict of Nantes (*Louis XIV et les protestants* (Paris 1951), especially pp.96-97).

[14] cf. Napoléon Peyrat, *Histoire des pasteurs du désert depuis la révocation de l'Edit de Nantes jusqu'à la Révolution Française (1685-1789)* (Paris 1842), i.63-64.

Towards the end of his stay in Berlin Voltaire had denied that mme de Maintenon had any part in causing the repeal: 'Pourquoi dites vous que madame de Maintenon eut beaucoup de part à la révocation de l'édit de Nantes?' he asked Formey. 'Elle toléra cette persécution, comme elle toléra celle du cardinal de Noailles, celle de Racine; mais certainement elle n'y eut aucune part. C'est un fait certain. Elle n'osait jamais contredire Louis XIV.' (Best.D5162, 17 January 1753). And in a further note to Formey written on the same day Voltaire was even more emphatic, referring him to mme de Maintenon's correspondence (Best.D5163). Yet by 1756 Voltaire had changed his mind: to the Duchess of Saxe-Gotha he spoke of 'cette femme singulière [. . .] qui naquit protestante et qui contribua à la révocation de L'édit de Nantes' (Best.D6978, 23 August 1756). At the beginning of the

and useless efforts of Pellisson, recalling sadly the fanaticism shown by the Languedoc peasants, who had not really changed since the time of the Albigensians. The repeal was thus a failure and the anti-Protestant measures of Louis XIV and his government only succeeded in resurrecting the spectre of civil war. To condemn the country to lose a significant proportion of its manpower and skills was a crime against reason and sound administration, but to stir up again the feuds and hatreds of the previous century was a crime against humanity. A mistaken policy made the spirit of the 'Welches' break out in France's most civilised era: 'On ne sait que trop qu'il résulta de ces fureurs de religion une guerre civile entre le roi et une partie de son peuple, et que cette guerre civile fut plus barbare que celle des sauvages' (M.xxx.394).

Professor J. H. Brumfitt considers that Voltaire's apparent lack of sympathy with the Protestants, and especially with the Camisard uprising, is the effort of 'a man constantly striving to achieve a fair balance'. In his article 'History and propaganda in Voltaire' he writes:

If the fanaticism of the *camisards* is strongly condemned, Protestantism itself is explained sympathetically in sociological terms as a natural reaction of the evangelical, egalitarian Christian spirit against the stratified hierarchy of the Roman Church (M.xv.15). If it had not been persecuted, it would in its more extreme manifestations, have died a natural death.[15]

While agreeing largely with the second part of this passage, I would venture to take issue with its initial assumption. There is a fundamental ambiguity in Voltaire's attitude which comes, with all due respect to professor Brumfitt, not in the attempt to achieve a fair balance, but because Voltaire is out of sympathy both with the Protestants and with the policy of persecuting them. In fact, he always had reservations about the Huguenots, and nowhere in his works, excepting those which are evident propaganda for religious toleration, did he portray them in a completely favourable manner. He agreed with some of their historical aims at the time of the Reformation, although, one feels, he considered that these aims could have been achieved much more effectively by a reformed, independent Gallican Church. On the other hand, the Calvinist austerity of the *réformés*, the 'fanaticism' they showed in their

Calas affair Voltaire was even more damning; discussing with Moultou how to gain mme de Pompadour's support, he observed: 'Le grand point est d'intéresser son amour propre, à faire autant de bien à l'état, que made De Maintenon a fait de mal' (Best.D10971, written in January or February 1763). The reason for this abrupt change of opinion on Voltaire's part is by no means apparent.

15 *Studies on Voltaire* (1963), xxiv.278.

beliefs, and their republican sentiments responsible in his opinion for the continuing wars, were anathema to him. Voltaire condemned the persecution of the Protestants in late seventeenth-century France through a love of humanity, not out of sympathy for Protestantism. The corresponding ambiguity – temporary compassion for the Huguenots whom he really disliked and temporary criticism of a government which normally enjoyed his respect – will become apparent from a short examination of the two main accounts which Voltaire gave of the Camisard uprising.

The first, in *Le Siècle de Louis XIV*, is clearly anti-Huguenot. Chapter 36 ('Du calvinisme au temps de Louis xiv') certainly begins by trying to find out why the 'esprit dogmatique' has caused so much trouble in the history of Christianity, and why 'le sang ait coulé pendant tant de siècles par des mains qui portaient le Dieu de la paix' (*Oh*, p.1041). But Protestantism itself is hardly explained 'sympathetically'. In fact Voltaire gives an account of the Reformation which shows that his feelings are mixed: he again stresses the republican views of most Protestant ministers, and says that the Reformation was easily accepted, for example, in Switzerland, but in Scotland: 'Le presbytérianisme établit [. . .] dans les temps malheureux, une espèce de république dont le pédantisme et la dureté étaient beaucoup plus intolérables que la rigueur du climat, et même que la tyrannie des évêques qui avait excité tant de plaintes' (*Oh*, p.1043). As we have seen, Louis xiv's policy of persecution was mistaken, but his basic assumptions regarding the Protestants were not entirely without foundation. Voltaire is clearly hostile to the revolt which followed the repeal of the Edict of Nantes. For a start, it was stirred up by prophecies, a time-honoured method of rabble-rousing: 'les prédictions ont été de tout temps un moyen dont on s'est servi pour séduire les simples, et pour enflammer les fanatiques'.[16]

---

[16] *Oh*, p.1057. It was entirely characteristic of prophecy that it should be accompanied by massacres of supposed enemies (cf. above, pp.85-86): in Voltaire's account it is a 'prophet' who prompts the first major act of the rebellion, the murder of the abbé Du Chaila, *inspecteur des missions*, who has incurred the Huguenots' special hatred. 'Un prophète lui crie: "Meurs donc; l'esprit te condamne, ton péché est contre toi." Et il est tué à coups de fusil' (*Oh*, p.1059). I have already (above, p.86) had occasion to quote Voltaire's reaction to an incident he describes in *La Bible enfin expliquée*. The same anecdote is referred to in *Le Siècle de Louis XIV*, in connection with the young Camisard leader Jean Cavalier, and the passage is worth quoting at this point not only for the information it gives us regarding Voltaire's views on prophecy but also because it shows that his researches into the rebellion had at one point taken on a personal nature: 'J'ai entendu

Moreover, the most ardent of all the prophets, under whose auspices the movement developed, was the exiled minister Jurieu,[17] persecutor of the *philosophe* Bayle, and in Voltaire's eyes, a symbol of intolerance: 'Il ne faut jamais oublier la persécution que le fanatique Jurieu suscita, dans un pays libre, à ce philosophe. Il arma contre lui le consistoire calviniste sous plusieurs prétextes, et surtout à l'occasion du fameux article David.'[18] Such an incident was hardly calculated to soften Voltaire's attitude towards the Huguenots; in fact, it was just as he expected: the Protestants showed themselves as intolerant as the Catholics when they had the whip-hand. Some of his indignation comes out in the article 'Philosophe' of the *Dictionnaire philosophique* (ed. Benda and Naves, p.346): 'Bayle fut persécuté; et par qui? par des hommes persécutés ailleurs, par des fugitifs qu'on aurait livrés aux flammes dans leur patrie'. One's mind goes back to Calvin, who would have been treated just as he treated Servetus, Voltaire frequently reminds us, had he ventured into France (cf. above, p.60). The only wise course for a *philosophe* was surely to distrust Protestants and Catholics equally.

Voltaire goes on to recount how some ministers began to return to France; one of them, Claude Brousson, 'avait formé le projet d'introduire des troupes anglaises et savoyardes dans le Languedoc' (*Oh*, p.1058). Voltaire shows little sympathy for the fate of this 'criminel d'état', who was, however, he informs us, considered a martyr by the Protestants, and in fact died like one:

L'intendant et les juges l'interrogèrent: il répondit qu'il était l'apôtre de Jésus-Christ, qu'il avait reçu le Saint-Esprit, qu'il ne devait pas trahir le dépôt de la foi, que son devoir était de distribuer le pain de la parole à ses frères. On lui demanda si les apôtres avaient écrit des projets pour faire révolter des provinces.

Voltaire recounts the atrocities committed by both sides, and also claims that economic reasons were an important factor in the success of the

souvent de la bouche du maréchal de Villars qu'il avait demandé à ce jeune homme comment il pouvait, à son âge, avoir eu tant d'autorité sur des hommes si féroces et indisciplinables. Il répondit que, quand on lui désobéissait, sa prophétesse, qu'on appelait *la grande Marie*, était sur-le-champ inspirée, et condamnait à mort les réfractaires, qu'on tuait sans raisonner. Ayant fait depuis la même question à Cavalier, j'en eus la même réponse' (*Oh*, p.1061).

[17] *Oh*, p.1057: 'Il promit la délivrance du peuple de Dieu pendant huit années. Son école de prophétie s'était établie dans les montagnes du Dauphiné, du Vivarais et des Cévennes, pays tout propre aux prédictions, peuplé d'ignorants et de cervelles chaudes, échauffées par la chaleur du climat et plus encore par leurs prédicants.'

[18] *Oh*, p.1137, part of the *Catalogue des écrivains* appended to *Le Siècle de Louis XIV*.

revolt: ' "Point d'impôts, et liberté de conscience." Ce cri séduit partout la populace' (*Oh*, p.1059). The chapter ends by bemoaning the persistence of fanaticism in France, whereas elsewhere, Voltaire claims, it was dying out as a result of a wise, and politically inspired, toleration.

By the time of the pamphlet *Du protestantisme et de la guerre des Cévennes* (1763), Voltaire's attitude has changed somewhat, both as a result of the Calas case, and probably also because of a realisation that his pronouncements might affect the lives of several hundred thousand of his contemporaries. However, he still rejects Protestant claims that he has been too harsh on the Huguenots and claims to have kept to a happy medium such as will only satisfy 'les esprits modérés' (*Mélanges*, p.1277). He tries to prove that the Protestants who died for their faith were in just the same situation as the early Christian martyrs; admittedly the former were false martyrs, but they were genuinely convinced of their beliefs, and the judges who condemned these Protestants were acting on the same principles as the judges of the Roman Empire, although, as Christians, they ought not to have treated their mistaken brethren so inhumanely. Voltaire now admits that the French Protestants were persecuted for forty years before they rebelled, and the Camisards are similarly excused (*Mélanges*, p.1278):

On doit aussi avouer que la guerre qu'une populace sauvage fit vers les Cévennes, sous Louis XIV, fut le fruit de la persécution. Les camisards agirent en bêtes féroces: mais on leur avait enlevé leurs femelles et leurs petits, ils déchirèrent les chasseurs qui couraient après eux.

He emphasises in vivid terms the terrible cruelty to which the Protestants were subjected. The six years of this war were far worse than the infamous proscriptions ordered by the Triumvirate at Rome, and only the obscurity of the participants has prevented the facts from becoming better known. Yet even in this relatively pro-Huguenot pamphlet, Voltaire does not neglect to show that both sides are equally mistaken: 'Jamais il n'y eut de plus grands crimes suivis de plus horribles supplices; et les deux partis, tantôt assassins, tantôt assassinés, invoquaient également le nom du Seigneur' (*Mélanges*, p.1280). Moreover, Voltaire does not condemn the government, but merely points out that it was mistaken, that the whole affair was caused by concentrating on dogma rather than on morality. And he concludes sadly: 'il est plus aisé de mener cent mille hommes au combat que de soumettre l'esprit d'un persuadé' (*Mélanges*, p.1280).

7

Voltaire and the *églises du désert*: contemporary French Protestantism and the struggle for toleration

THE generally anti-Huguenot attitude we have been encountering in Voltaire's works raises several important problems. Just what did the *défenseur des Calas* think of the French Protestants of his own times? What were his contacts with them? How much did he really help them, and what were the motives for his interventions? To answer these questions we shall have to try to set Voltaire's actions and campaigns against the background of the history of the French Protestant Churches in the eighteenth century. This in itself is no easy matter. By the time the history of these churches began to be written in the nineteenth century, an evangelical revival had taken place. The liberalism and unorthodoxy of many eighteenth century Protestants was played down, and the help given to their cause by the *philosophes* in general and by the infamous Voltaire in particular was either ignored or drastically reduced in importance. Charles Coquerel, author of the seminal *Histoire des églises du désert* (Paris 1841), illustrates this tendency perfectly. Though he is fairer than most of his fellow Protestant historians to Voltaire, the praise he gives him is far from unqualified, and he is completely at a loss to understand Voltaire's attitude towards Christianity.[1]

Coquerel's work illustrates another difficulty in dealing with this subject. Through a perfectly natural desire to do justice to the sufferings of his Protestant forbears, Coquerel comes dangerously near to the

---

[1] while on the one hand (ii.338) he mentions the 'services incontestables' rendered by Voltaire to the churches, and says that the Calas affair was 'un beau chapitre dans la vie morale de Voltaire', he also writes (ii.340) concerning Voltaire's *Traité sur la tolérance*: 'Voltaire accumule, sans fruit pour les persécutés, les épigrammes et les déductions philosophiques. Sa légèreté inexplicable en fait de christianisme empêchait que les églises ne fissent même une tentative pour lui faire comprendre sérieusement leurs malheurs.' As we shall see later, this statement is as inaccurate as it is unfair.

borderline between history and hagiography.[2] Other Protestant writers cross it,[3] and some of their writings are little more than pious declamations. Two studies by the abbé Joseph Dedieu: *Le rôle politique des protestants français (1689-1715)* (Paris 1920) and the *Histoire politique des protestants français (1715-1794)* (Paris 1925), were therefore a welcome addition to the literature on Protestant history and filled an important gap. The latter work investigated whether the Protestants' struggle for tolerance had a political side which had usually been neglected. Dedieu's studies, richly documented though in general hardly sympathetic to the Protestants, have been appreciated by more recent Protestant historians[4] who, fortunately, have combined a sympathy for their subject with a high standard of accuracy and impartiality.[5] Now we have a more complete picture of the French Protestants in the eighteenth century – of the feuds and the bitter rivalry which existed between their various factions as well as of the heroism and determination they showed in the face of persecution – and it is time to examine just how far Voltaire helped them in the battle for toleration.

i. *Before 1754*

The thinkers of the eighteenth century have often been criticised for being idealists unversed in practical affairs, dreamers whose systems bore no relation to the facts in the world around them. The special charge of Protestant historians has been that the *philosophes* did not turn their attention to the sufferings of the *églises du désert* and sometimes made generalisations which might even be harmful to them. Coquerel (ii.476-77) makes the point with some force:

on ne peut s'empêcher de se demander comment la philosophie du XVIIIe siècle, si renommée en son amour pour l'humanité, négligea de prendre en

---

[2] Coquerel either glosses over disagreements among the Protestants or refuses to discuss them at all. A statement like the following (ii.376, my italics) is typical: 'Nos pièces sont remplies des détails de ces débats, *peu intéressants*, et dont nous ne parlerons qu'autant qu'ils pourraient offrir quelques faits utiles à l'histoire.' Coquerel's treatment of the relations between the Protestants and the government is also rather lacking in impartiality. Nowhere does he admit that the Protestants were ever guilty of rebellious acts.

[3] cf. Frank Puaux, *Paul Rabaut, l'apôtre du désert* (Paris 1918); Charles Dardier, 'Paul Rabaut', *Bpf* (1883), xxxii.461-79.

[4] cf. E.-G. Léonard's comment: 'nous ne saurions trop recommander *l'Histoire politique des protestants français*' ('Le problème du culte public et de l'Eglise dans le protestantisme au XVIIIe siècle', *Foi et vie* (1937), pp.431-57).

[5] m. Léonard's own works are particularly noteworthy: see bibliography.

mains un aussi grand intérêt [the rights of the Protestants]. Comment s'est-il fait que les lois du désert se fussent dérobées aux recherches doctes et minutieuses de Montesquieu, comme les droits outragés des protestants furent omis par Rousseau dans son éloquence passionnée et même dans ses sophismes [. . .] et au milieu de tous, centre et moteur de l'enthousiasme, la grande puissance de Ferney se prenait à tous les faits, à toutes les maximes, à tous les dogmes de l'ancienne société et faisait pénétrer la philosophie jusque dans les palais et les parlements qu'elle devait ravager. C'est que la philosophie du xviiie siècle, soit par la nécessité de sa position, soit par la tendance de l'esprit français, n'eut point de caractère positif et pratique. Elle s'en tint à de grandes et belles généralités.

But is this cliché a sufficient reason? Why were the conditions and rights of the Protestants not investigated? 'Les églises du désert étaient très peu connues', says Coquerel (i.487-88), answering his own question: 'Elles jetaient un éclat privé, qui se perdait dans les masses populaires qui les composaient.' If this was true, there is little need to attempt to exonerate the *philosophes*, since they can scarcely be blamed for ignoring a problem of which hardly anyone was aware. But in Voltaire's case, is it correct to say that he had absolutely no contact with the problem before the Calas case, or that he had never thought about it before arriving in Protestant Geneva in 1754? This is the first question we must attempt to answer.

Voltaire's first known connection with a Protestant was his love affair with Olympe Dunoyer while he was an apprentice diplomat in Holland at the end of 1713.[6] Olympe's mother had left her husband and taken refuge in Holland with her two daughters, Voltaire tells us in the *Supplément au Siècle de Louis XIV*. He describes this as 'une faute que sa religion fit commettre' (*Oh*, p.1260), but this is probably only because he wishes to make the lady appear respectable, since he is refuting La Beaumelle's description of the incident. Perhaps it is also a recollection of a strategem Voltaire had himself suggested to mme Dunoyer's daughter, for when back in Paris the young Arouet had written to his 'Pimpette', advising her to appeal to her uncle, the bishop of Evreux in Normandy, for help to return to France. She should use religion as her main pretext: 'que la religion & que l'amitié pour votre famille soient vos deux motifs auprès de lui; insistez surtout sur l'article de la religion, dites lui que le roi souhaite la conversion des huguenots'

---

[6] see Marcel Fabre, 'Voltaire et Pimpette de Nîmes', *Mémoires de l'Académie de Nîmes* (Nîmes 1933-1935), i.XLI-LXIX.

(Best.D22, 20 January 1714). This not very laudable suggestion at least shows us that Voltaire was aware of the royal policy toward the Protestants.

Voltaire's next visit to Holland impressed him because of the large measure of religious tolerance he found there. In October 1722 he delightedly tells mme de Bernières of the various types of sects one can see at The Hague (Best.D128): 'Nous avons ici un opéra détestable mais en revanche je voi des ministres calvinistes, des arminiens, des sociniens, des rabins, des anabaptistes qui parlent tous à merveille et qui en vérité ont tous raison.' This religious freedom might have prompted Voltaire to reflect on the situation of his French Protestant contemporaries, and indeed French Calvinists play a major part in his epic poem *La Henriade*. But, as René Pomeau observes, 'l'un des manques les plus étonnants de cette épopée religieuse est que le calvinisme en est absent. Bourbon ne ressemble pas à un chef calviniste'.[7] This in itself is perhaps not very surprising. Even if Voltaire had thought about the French Calvinist problem, he was not personally acquainted with Huguenot circles and would not necessarily have been aware of their special characteristics. What is more serious, however, is the opinion which Voltaire puts into the mouth of the *vieillard* in the first canto, implying that Calvinism is destined to fade away:

> Un culte si nouveau ne peut durer toujours.
> Des caprices de l'homme il a tiré son être.
> On le verra périr ainsi qu'on l'a vu naître.[8]

Of course, this was not necessarily Voltaire's own opinion, but no one with an eye to the plight of the *églises du désert* would have used such a tactless phrase in a poem which sought to promote religious toleration. As we shall see shortly, French Protestant leaders were loud in their condemnation of statements like this which might be turned to the advantage of their oppressors. Voltaire was thinking of French Calvinism as a historical fact, not as a contemporary problem.[9]

[7] *La Religion*, p.108. Cf. also p.133: 'Il n'est que de voir comme il peint, ou plutôt ne peint pas, les calvinistes français dans la *Henriade*.'

[8] *La Henriade*, first canto, lines 244-46, ed. Taylor, p.378.

[9] it is just possible, however, that there is a different explanation. As O.R. Taylor argues in his edition of *La Henriade* (pp.25-26), the poem 'paraît avoir été conçu non seulement comme un panégyrique personnel, mais aussi comme une œuvre de propagande destinée à appuyer la politique intérieure et extérieure de Philippe d'Orléans'. R.E. Waller ('Voltaire and the regent', *Studies on Voltaire* (1974), cxxvii.33) is of the same opinion.

The apprentice *philosophe*'s exile in England brought him into contact with members of the French Refuge. One of the people Voltaire met was Jean Cavalier, former leader of the Camisard rebels, who in fact shared with Voltaire the distinction of having been a suitor of Olympe Dunoyer. La Beaumelle later claimed that the two men had been rivals, and Voltaire is at pains to set the picture to rights:

Cavalier, étant colonel au service d'Angleterre en 1708, passa dans les Pays-Bas et vit Mlle Dunoyer, encore très jeune. Il la demanda en mariage; cette négociation fut rompue et Cavalier alla se marier en Irlande. L'auteur du *Siècle* était alors au collège; il n'alla en Hollande qu'en 1714 et n'a connu Cavalier qu'en Angleterre en 1726.[10]

Voltaire also questioned a follower of Fatio Duillier, who had been one of the leaders of the Cévenol 'prophets' exiled in England, and who had offered to resurrect a dead man. Voltaire obviously had some respect for Duillier, whom he calls 'un des plus grands géomètres de l'Europe', but this only made his superstition more regrettable. 'Le fanatisme rend la science même sa complice, et étouffe la raison' is the *philosophe*'s comment (*Oh*, p.1062). These two contacts, far from increasing Voltaire's sympathy for the French Protestants, probably had a contrary effect, reminding him both of their history as rebels and of the recent outbreak of fanaticism on the part of the Cévenol prophets during the Camisard uprising. If, in some later works, Voltaire is to play down the rebellious nature of the Protestants, he is always tempted to consider the Huguenot masses of the south as a superstitious rabble prone to fanaticism, and the Camisard uprising is often mentioned in enumerations of the worst cases of religious fanaticism (cf. above, p.43, n.45).

But Voltaire did not meet only disreputable members of the Refuge. He lived for a while in Wandsworth, at a time when the company of fellow Frenchmen was probably especially comforting to him.[11] He was acquainted with the Rainbow coffee house. In fact Voltaire's main

Perhaps Voltaire's prediction that Calvinism would ultimately disappear was designed to support the government's policy, even if he thus tended to diminish somewhat the value of his plea for religious toleration in general.

[10] *Oh*, p.1260. R. Fargher is also rather wide of the mark, therefore, when he says that 'the Camisard commander, Jean Cavalier [...] succeeded Voltaire in the affections of Olympe Dunoyer' (*Life and letters in France: the eighteenth century*, p.131).

[11] Pomeau, *La Religion*, p.133; André-Michel Rousseau, *L'Angleterre et Voltaire*, Studies on Voltaire (1976), cxlv.138-39.

contacts with the English Refuge were literary rather than religious. There are many references in his works to Rapin de Thoyras, the Huguenot refugee who wrote on English history, and although Voltaire's attitude seems to have varied somewhat, he generally expressed his esteem for Thoyras's *Histoire d'Angleterre*.[12] The exiled poet also frequented Pierre Desmaizeaux, a correspondent of literary figures all over Europe. Desmaizeaux did have contacts with Samuel Clarke, a Protestant divine whom Voltaire greatly admired (see below, pp.427-34), but it seems unlikely that Voltaire saw any connection between the rationalist type of Anglicanism of which Clarke was the chief representative and the fanatical Camisards he probably imagined to be the characteristic manifestation of contemporary French Protestantism.

There is no evidence in Voltaire's works of the period to lead us to believe that he took any particular interest in French Protestantism during the 1740s. In 1741-1743, however, while staying in Brussels, he engaged in a correspondence with César de Missy, minister of the French church of St James's in London,[13] which may have made him feel more sympathetic toward members of the Refuge and perhaps encouraged him to regard liberal Protestantism as an intellectual ally in the struggle for religious toleration.

Nonetheless, this does not seem to have changed Voltaire's attitude to his Huguenot contemporaries in France for the time being. The *Siècle de Louis XIV* is on the whole anti-Protestant. The Camisard uprising and its attendant fanaticism are condemned, and Voltaire also suggests that Louis xiv was not wrong in assuming that the Protestants were republicans at heart. Voltaire's position in the *Siècle* was criticised by *philosophes* and Protestants alike. Writing in the *Correspondance littéraire*, Grimm commented:

[12] cf. Brumfitt, *Voltaire historian*, p.29; *Oh*, p.1197; M.i.391; Best.D12089.

[13] Best.D2539, n.2. This pastor wrote to Voltaire on literary and historical topics; he also defends Voltaire over *Mahomet*, saying that superstition, not religion, has inspired the poet's critics (Best.D2659), and in his letter of 18 November 1742 (Best.D2689) he attacks the various Christian sects for being divided on points of doctrine: 'car quand il leur échape d'articuler ce que réellement ils pensent, il ne s'en trouve jamais trois qui soient parfaitement d'accord sur tous les articles'. Missy is presumably trying to rally Voltaire to his own brand of liberal Protestantism (Best.D2659), and in doing so he has gone a long way to meet the Voltairean position. 'Nous voudrions que tous les gens de votre robe vous ressemblassent', writes Voltaire on behalf of himself and mme Du Châtelet (Best.D2559), but the attempt at conversion is politely avoided (Best.D2714).

For a brief biographical sketch and an investigation of the epistolary and literary contacts between Voltaire and de Missy see J. Patrick Lee, 'Voltaire and César de Missy', *Studies on Voltaire* (1976), clxiii.57-72.

Dans le chapitre du calvinisme, notre historien fait le tableau de toutes les atrocités et de toutes les persécutions exercées contre les protestants. Il observe que c'était là l'ouvrage du clergé: 'C'était après tout, ose-t-il ajouter, les enfants de la maison qui ne voulaient point de partage avec des étrangers introduits par force.' Quelle réflexion! On dirait que les calvinistes du royaume n'étaient pas Français, que leur état de citoyen était précaire, et que le droit est toujours du côté du plus fort.[14]

The pastor Paul Rabaut (1717-94)[15] wrote in a similar vein to his colleague Moultou in Geneva (letter of 24 October 1755, quoted in Coquerel, ii.197):

Vous connaissez, Monsieur, le *Siècle de Louis XIV* du fameux de Voltaire; je ne sais si cet auteur a voulu faire la cour à la France, mais j'ai vu avec chagrin que dans son ouvrage, sans égard à la sincérité qu'exige l'histoire, sans faire attention à ce qu'il avait mis à la tête de sa *Henriade,* sans craindre d'attirer de nouvelles persécutions à des gens, qui en ont tant souffert le plus injustement du monde, il a répandu sur nous le fiel de la plus maligne satire. C'est ce qu'il a fait principalement à l'article du calvinisme. Plus la réputation de l'auteur est grande, plus son ouvrage est lu, et plus il importe qu'il soit réfuté d'une manière triomphante.

Either Voltaire was indifferent to the fate of his Huguenot contemporaries, or he had still not realised that such historically orientated statements might have important consequences in the present and could provide help and comfort for the Huguenots' enemies. Fortunately, there is some evidence that in the late 1740s Voltaire was finding out a little more about the actual conditions under which Protestants were living in France.[16] And although this increasing knowledge was not yet translated into a more sympathetic attitude to Protestantism in Voltaire's works, his stay in Berlin was to provide just the catalyst necessary to stimulate a more active interest in the problem.

At first sight this may seem something of a contradiction in terms. For although Prussia was a Protestant country, its king was a deist who enjoyed snubbing and humiliating his clergy, a practice not likely to

---

[14] *Correspondance littéraire,* ed. M. Tourneux (Paris 1877-1882), iii.30.

[15] one of the most influential Protestant leaders in the eighteenth century: see below, pp.340 ff.

[16] cf., for example, the *Anecdotes sur Louis XIV* (1748), where, discussing the repeal of the Edict of Nantes, he mentions Lutheran families 'comme il y en a dans l'Alsace' (M.xxiii.244), thus showing that he is aware of the special situation of this province, where both Lutherans and Calvinists were tolerated: cf. also a similar comment in *Le Siècle de Louis XIV* itself (*Oh*, p.1052).

displease the anticlerical *philosophe*. Yet as in England Voltaire again came into contact with members of the French Refuge. And if these contacts were once more primarily literary,[17] the acquaintance he made with the works of Isaac de Beausobre, especially the latter's *Histoire critique de Manichée et du manichéisme* (Amsterdam 1734-1739),[18] which made a tremendous impression on Voltaire, strengthened his sincere admiration for Protestant scholarship and enlightenment, an admiration which had its roots in the English experience and which had probably also been encouraged by the correspondence with César de Missy.[19] Moreover, Voltaire was dismayed by the extent of Frederick's religious scepticism, which went much farther than his own, and although he was no more a Protestant than a Catholic,[20] it is not fanciful to suggest that at the end of his stay in Berlin he was more ready than at most times of his life to make common cause with liberal Protestantism, providing it would meet him half way.[21] There were many things to

[17] e.g. with Formey, whose religious views Voltaire did *not* respect. They corresponded about various literary topics including Ninon de Lenclos's *Mémoires* (Best.D4456) and mme de Maintenon's part in the repeal of the Edict of Nantes (Best.D5162, D5163, D5164; cf. above, p.245, n.14). The *Défense de milord Bolingbroke* (November 1752) is a reply to Formey's attacks on incredulity in the *Nouvelle bibliothèque germanique* (Amsterdam, July-September 1752, pp.77-96); cf. Best.D5055, commentary, n.1, and Best.D5061 (Voltaire to Formey, 4 November 1752). La Beaumelle's name appears in Voltaire's correspondence for the first time in this period (Best.D4492, 22 June 1751), and the two men were soon on bad terms (cf. Best.D5113, 18 December 1752).

[18] continued and edited by Formey, (cf. Best.D4756, n.1). Voltaire wrote to Formey on 2 January 1752: 'J'ai lu toute la nuit l'histoire du manichéisme. Voilà ce qui s'appelle un bon livre; voilà la théologie réduite à la philosophie. M. Beausobre raisonne mieux que tous les pères; il est évident qu'il est déiste, du moins évident pour moi' (Best.D4756). And if Voltaire showed less enthusiasm for Beausobre's *Remarques historiques, critiques et philosophiques sur le nouveau testament* (The Hague 1742) – 'Beausobre ne réussit pas si bien avec Jésus qu'avec Manes' (Best.D4821, Voltaire to Formey, February or March 1752) – the tone of Best.D4898 (Voltaire to the abbé d'Olivet, introducing Beausobre's son, 25 May 1752) is one of high praise. It refers to 'un homme illustre dans la littérature [. . .] Mr de Beausobre, philosophe quoyque ministre protestant, auteur de l'excellente histoire du manichéisme, et le plus tolérant de tous les crétiens'. Cf. also the article on Beausobre in the *Catalogue des écrivains* of *Le Siècle de Louis XIV* (*Oh*, p.1138).

[19] another Protestant Voltaire was ready to learn from was the pastor Antoine Achard; cf. Best.D4491 and D4495.

[20] 'Je n'ai pas l'honneur d'être de votre religion, et je ne suis plus de l'autre' (Voltaire to Formey, Best.D4456, c. 1 May 1751).

[21] Voltaire was still contemptuous of what he considered to be Protestant fanatics: cf. Best.D4994 where one of the titles in a list of books Voltaire sends to Walther is the 'Histoire du fanatisme, 3 Tomes', identified in the commentary, n.5, as [David Augustin] de Brueys, *Histoire du fanatisme de nostre temps, et le dessein que l'on avoit de soulever en France les mécontents des calvinistes* (Paris 1692). He also rejected strictly orthodox Protestant views such as those of Formey.

257

criticise in Protestantism, but it also had great advantages over Catholicism. The hopes Voltaire formed so quickly in Switzerland a short time later and his bitter disappointment when they failed can be better understood if they are seen as the culmination of a process which had been going on for some time, and which led Voltaire to take a more favourable attitude to those forms of Protestantism which were least superstitious.

Moreover, Voltaire's increasing interest in Protestantism was not confined to its literary and philosophical aspects. On 31 August 1751 Voltaire wrote to the duc de Richelieu from Berlin thanking him for two letters he had just received:

> vous avez les mêmes bontez pour mes musulmants que pour vos calvinistes des Cevennes. Dieu vous bénira d'avoir protégé la liberté de conscience. Faire jouer le profète Mahomet à Paris, et laisser prier dieu en français dans vos montagnes du Languedoc sont deux choses qui m'édifient merveilleusement.[22]

It seems as if Richelieu had made some reference to his lenient treatment of the Protestants in the province of which he was governor. Voltaire would hardly do anything other than approve of this attitude, but the reference is interesting all the same; it shows that Richelieu might have brought up the Protestant question at other times. Anyway, it seems that Voltaire did not forget Richelieu's comment, for on 25 November 1752 he commented again to his friend: 'Vos colonies languedochiennes n'ont pas prospéré dans les pays froids; aulieu d'augmenter depuis 1686 elles ont diminué de moitié.'[23] These two brief references show that Voltaire was now becoming acquainted a little better with the contemporary situation of the French Protestant churches, and that he may even have discussed it with Richelieu. His influential friend was well placed to give him some interesting first-hand information, as we

[22] Best.D4561. Paul d'Estrée (*Le Maréchal de Richelieu (1696-1788)* (Paris 1917), p.267) also quotes this passage, adding the following information: 'C'était à peu près la réponse prêtée à Richelieu, quand on s'étonnait à Montpellier qu'il n'adoptât pas les mesures mesquines et vexatoires prescrites par le ministre Saint-Florentin contre les protestants: "Je m'embarrasse fort peu que les hommes prient Dieu à leur manière, pourvu qu'ils ne troublent pas l'ordre public . . ." '

[23] Best.D5084. Voltaire had already mentioned this topic in the *Anecdotes sur Louis XIV* (1748). But there he underlines the loss to France of 'dix milles réfugiés français à Berlin, qui ont fait de cet endroit sauvage une ville opulente et superbe' (M.xxiii.246). Now he has had the opportunity to see that the repeal of the Edict of Nantes was as tragic for the refugees themselves as for the country which suffered the loss of their industry and skills.

shall see shortly. It is intriguing to speculate on what might have happened if Voltaire had accepted Richelieu's invitation to accompany him to Languedoc in 1755 where the *maréchal* was to open the *Etats* (see Best.D6002, n.1). Voltaire would then have been able to get his information for himself and one can only guess at the results such a journey might have had. But what was the state of the institution in which he had begun to take an interest? How had it fared since the repeal of the Edict of Nantes?

At the end of the reign of Louis xiv, the remnants of France's Protestant churches were indeed in a sorry plight. Although the government's attempt to stamp out the reformed faith had failed, the measures taken had been completely successful in destroying the organisation of the 'R.P.R.'[24] The Huguenots were leaderless, their ministers had fled, and isolated attempts to restore the situation, like that of Brousson (cf. above, p.248), had proved a failure. Moreover, many of the most fervent and talented Protestants had chosen exile, so that in a large number of regions the churches received a blow from which they were not to recover. Even in the south (especially in Languedoc) where the Protestant population was still numerous, there was little to look forward to apart from possible further outbreaks of violence like the Camisard uprising, when deviationist elements gained control because the traditional authority of pastors and consistories was lacking, and something had to provide a substitute for a population as yet unwilling to accept the spiritual leadership of the Catholic clergy. Such acts of rebellion would be implacably opposed by the government and would further discredit the Protestants in the eyes of the public at large. Moreover, the prophets and *inspirés* who flourished at such times were hardly likely to endear the Protestants to enlightened opinion. We have seen (above, p.43, n.45) how contemptuous is Voltaire when referring to these 'fanatics' of the Cévennes, and that this theme appears regularly in his works.

Yet religious life had not died out completely. In the south the Protestants still assembled for their worship *au désert*, in remote or concealed places where the troops were not likely to find them. And a young man from Villeneuve-de-Berg (in the Vivarais region) who

---

[24] 'la Religion prétendue réformée', the official designation of the Calvinist churches in France.

attended assemblies like these undertook the formidable task of re-organising and re-forming the French Protestant churches. Antoine Court (1696-1760) was determined to break the influence of *illuminés* and prophets on the Protestants, despite the fact that he had previously been associated with them himself.[25] On 21 August 1715 he held a synod of all the *prédicants* in the Cévennes (Coquerel, i.28-29). This synod, which took place at Monoblet,[26] was also attended by a small number of laymen, some of whom were appointed elders as a first step in restoring Calvinist discipline in the churches. Court considered this an essential measure if the French Protestants were to become res-pectable in the eyes of their coreligionaries abroad, let alone of the government. He was also determined that the churches should have proper pastors, duly ordained, rather than the untrained, unreliable *prédicants* who had flourished since the repeal of the Edict of Nantes. Court's chief helper, Corteiz, was therefore sent to Zurich to be con-secrated as a minister, and on his return Corteiz ordained Court himself. The reorganisation of church discipline and administration was con-tinued in further synods which were held in 1716 and 1717 (Coquerel, i.32-36), and the good work spread gradually from the Cévennes and Bas-Languedoc to other provinces and districts. At the first national synod of the *églises du désert* (1726) three provinces were represented, and at the eighth and last national synod in 1763 this number had risen to thirteen,[27] a notable achievement indeed for a movement with such humble beginnings and scanty resources.

In the early 1720s, however, the shortage of manpower was still severe. The few available pastors had to make huge rounds, holding assemblies as they went, as and when conditions were favourable. Efforts were soon made to render the situation more tolerable. On a visit to Geneva in 1724, Antoine Court appealed for men and money to help the struggling French churches.[28] He had already written to the

[25] for information on Court see Coquerel, *Histoire des églises*, i.21 ff. At this point I must express my indebtedness to Coquerel whose book is of basic importance for an understanding of Protestantism in eighteenth-century France.

[26] Samuel Mours, *Les Eglises réformées en France* (Paris 1958), p.135.

[27] church organisation was reintroduced in the following provinces, at the dates given: Dauphiné (1716), Haut-Languedoc (1736), Poitou (1744), Montalbanais (1745), the Comté de Foix (1745), Basse-Normandie (1745), Haute-Normandie (1750), Agenais (1754), Béarn (1757), Saintonge, Angoumois and Périgord (1759), Bordelais (1760), Aunis (1761), Thiérache, Picardie, Orléanais and Berry (1779), (Mours, pp.135-36).

[28] Hélène Kern, 'Le Séminaire de Lausanne et le comité genevois', *Bpf* (1962), cviii.198.

various countries of the Refuge to beg the former pastors to return to their homeland, but a deaf ear had been turned to this suggestion.[29] Now, however, a secret committee which had existed in Geneva since about 1685, mainly to help Protestant galley-slaves, showed itself willing to co-operate with Court. Then, on 30 April 1725, Benjamin Du Plan, a Protestant gentleman, was chosen as Deputy of the French churches, and his appointment confirmed by a national synod held on 30 April 1728 (Kern, pp.198-200). His task was to collect funds on their behalf in friendly Protestant countries. Court's idea was to form a permanent educational establishment where future ministers could be trained. Financial contributions were forthcoming from Holland, Zurich, Berne and England, to mention only the most important. Because of political pressure which the French *Résident* in Geneva could apply, it was out of the question that an academy should be set up there. The Bernese government, however, proved willing to allow such an establishment to be founded on its territory, and thus the 'Séminaire de Lausanne' admitted its first student in 1726. The main proviso was that great secrecy should be maintained, as Berne could not be seen to be openly helping 'rebels' against the French government. Alphonse Turretini of Geneva and Archbishop Wake of Canterbury were the two most distinguished collaborators in the establishment of this academy for the French Protestants (Chavannes, p.35). Despite the fact that in the early years teaching in the seminary was rather sketchy and later in the century far from orthodox, the foundation of this academy was a great step forward. Charles Coquerel (i.208, n.2) calculates that about a hundred ministers passed through the seminary between 1740 and 1809. In France itself the seminary's work was supplemented by 'écoles ambulantes' where a small number of would-be ministers followed a pastor on his rounds and were instructed by him.[30] Antoine Court left France in 1729 and apart from brief visits to his native country henceforth resided in Lausanne, where he looked after the interests of the seminary and its students. The French Protestants could now face the future with more confidence. Their churches, on the point of extinction in 1715, had staged a remarkable revival, and now

---

[29] J. Chavannes, 'Une école libre de théologie des temps passés: notes historiques sur le Séminaire protestant français à Lausanne', *Le Chrétien évangélique* (Lausanne 1872), xv.35.

[30] cf. Charles Dardier, *La Vie des étudiants au désert d'après la correspondance de l'un d'eux, Simon Lombard* (Paris 1893).

appeared to have the will and the manpower to regain some of their former prestige.

We must not imagine, however, that this revival went on unimpeded. Government policy toward the Protestants was never clearly fixed. Neither the ministers at Versailles nor their intendants in the provinces ever quite had the capacity or the will to undertake systematic persecution, yet they were operating within a framework of anti-Protestant laws which were completely unworkable provided large numbers of Protestants persisted in their faith. Repression was consequently spasmodic, though often violent, and depended on the conduct of the Huguenots, the frequency and size of their assemblies, the availability of troops (drastically reduced, of course, in time of warfare), and the current policy of the government. A brief review of events between 1715 and 1754 will show how chaotic the state of affairs was in the south of France, and how the Huguenots, though fiercely persecuted from time to time, were nonetheless able to regroup and expand their church organisation when the government was occupied elsewhere.[31]

The attitude of the regent was typical of the quandary in which successive governments found themselves in relation to Louis XIV's anti-Protestant laws. At first it seems that he actually considered relaxing measures against the Protestants and recalling the refugees to France. In his *Mémoires* Saint-Simon claims that he dissuaded the regent from this course of action in 1716 by warning him of the danger of restoring 'en un mot, un Etat dans un Etat' after all the political trouble the Protestants had caused in previous reigns.[32] A proposal put forward by the

---

[31] Burdette C. Poland emphasises the fact that the government misread the Protestant situation and that it was to this factor above all others that the *églises du désert* owed their survival: 'If, in the first half of the eighteenth century, before the *philosophes* succeeded in discrediting religious persecution the government had fully appreciated the real diminution in Protestant strength, it might have been persuaded to show more vigor than it did in trying to extirpate heresy in France' (*French Protestantism and the French Revolution* (Princeton 1957), p.9).

Shelby T. McCloy also points out the unwillingness of many Catholics to co-operate in the repressive legislation against the Protestants (*The Humanitarian movement in eighteenth-century France* (Kentucky 1957), p.17).

[32] *Mémoires*, ed. Gonzague Truc (Paris 1955), pp.307-12. The regent had complained about the contradictions in Louis XIV's edicts, the difficulties in applying them, 'la faute même de la révocation de l'édit de Nantes, au préjudice immense que l'Etat en avoit souffert et en souffroit encore dans sa dépopulation, dans son commerce, dans la haine que ce traitement avoit allumée chez tous les protestants de l'Europe' (p.308). It is noteworthy that although Saint-Simon declared himself against recalling the Protestant refugees and in agreement with the repeal of the Edict of Nantes, he agrees grudgingly that the way it

conseil de l'intérieur under the duc d'Antin to establish a colony of refugees at Douai in order to revitalise the economic life of the area also came to nothing, vetoed by the *conseil de conscience*[33] presided over by the cardinal de Noailles. At any rate, the regent's statement of policy toward the Protestants is reasonably benevolent in tone, though it makes no particular concessions: 'Je maintiendrai les édits contre les religionnaires [...] mais j'espère trouver dans leur bonne conduite l'occasion d'user de ménagements conformes à ma clémence' (quoted in Dedieu, *Histoire politique*, i.11). The desire for a peaceful settlement was never quite strong enough to induce a Bourbon ministry to repudiate the policy of the great Louis xiv. The Protestants nonetheless at first found some heart in the regent's statement.

So began the stop-go policy of alternately repressive and conciliatory measures towards the Huguenots which was to be so typical of eighteenth-century governments. Lord Stair allowed Protestants to worship in the British embassy in Paris and for a while the regent turned a blind eye. But the numbers of Huguenot worshippers and complaints at this scandal by Catholics soon forced him to ban the practice. A few people were imprisoned but soon released. This comparatively tolerant attitude in the capital was not matched in other parts of France. The pastor Etienne Arnaud was executed in Languedoc on 22 January 1718 (Dedieu, i.16). Yet persecution did not increase inordinately, as the court was worried by the intrigues of the Spanish minister Alberoni whose policy was to encourage a rebellion of all the Huguenot provinces in the south of France. It even seems as if the clergy had tired of applying the oppressive anti-Protestant laws, for they had to be reminded of their duty by a circular sent out in 1715 by the minister Phélypeaux de Pontchartrain (Coquerel, i.67-69).

This comparative lull in persecution was soon to come to an end. Court's reorganisation of the *églises du désert* put the clergy in the south into a panic. In 1723 the bishop of Alais addressed an alarming *Mémoire* to the government in which he claimed that the laws of the land seemed to be despised. The government was also worried, as the growth of assemblies was what it feared most, and this was just what had occurred as a result of Court's reform really getting under way. The

had been applied was not a success: 'le feu Roi avoit fait la faute beaucoup plus dans la manière de l'exécution que dans la chose même', thus implicitly agreeing about the disadvantages of the measures the regent wanted to remedy.

[33] one of the councils set up by the regent to help him in governing France.

Protestants who had remained in France after the repeal of the Edict of Nantes had as yet not been harassed in an organised manner. Even Protestants who had abjured and then publicly proclaimed their continuing attachment to the reformed faith were usually left unpunished: 'Que les protestants pensent ce qu'ils veulent, qu'ils professent même leur attachement à leur foi, mais qu'ils ne tentent pas de reconstituer l'Eglise par la restauration du culte public!' Such were the government's sentiments, in the opinion of the distinguished Protestant historian E.-G. Léonard.[34]

To avoid just such a renaissance of the Protestant churches, the government took an important step. The whole corpus of edicts issued against the Huguenots since 1685 was codified and restated in a new edict. This is usually considered as one of the most draconian measures ever taken against the Protestants,[35] and there may be some significance in the fact that the duc de Bourbon and not the reasonably moderate regent was now head of the government. Yet the government's aim does not really seem to have been to increase the severity of the anti-Protestant laws, but merely to rationalise them and mould them into a workable system. This at least is the opinion of Joseph Dedieu,[36] who claims that the famous magistrate Joly de Fleury, *procureur général* at the Parlement de Paris, was responsible for composing the edict.[37] Whether or not the new edict was more severe than those which preceded it, it highlighted the oppressive nature of the legislation weighing on the Protestants. Any pastors apprehended were liable to the death penalty, Protestants caught attending religious assemblies were to be given life sentences: the men on the galleys and the women in prison (usually in the infamous Tour de Constance at Aigues-Mortes). The edict further directed that Protestant children should be given a Catholic education, even if they had to be abducted from their parents and brought up in an institution like the *Nouvelles catholiques*, financed from fines and confiscations levied on the Protestants. There were even

[34] 'Le problème du culte public et de l'église dans le protestantisme au XVIIIe siècle', pp.432-33.

[35] Coquerel (i.146) speaks of its 'rigueurs extraordinaires'.

[36] it was also Malesherbes's opinion (cf. Pierre Grosclaude, *Malesherbes: témoin et interprète de son temps* (Paris 1961), pp.364-69, especially p.367, n.26).

[37] Coquerel does not agree. He attributes the measure to the 'incroyable légèreté' of the duc de Bourbon, who wanted to settle the Protestant problem at a stroke, and to the ambition of Lavergne de Tressan, bishop of Nantes. He does not mention Joly de Fleury (i.146-47).

laws against Protestant burials, and in order to practise a profession or to occupy an official post, it was necessary to have a certificate of Catholicity.[38] Little wonder the government found these laws unworkable when it tried to apply them, and that La Vrillière, the minister responsible for religious affairs, soon agreed with some intendants that only the most blatant assemblies would be suppressed (Dedieu, *Histoire politique*, i.31-32).

Voltaire specifically criticises the 1724 edict in the *Précis du siècle de Louis XV*. Pointing out the unfairness of French law as regards confiscation of a condemned person's goods, he comments (*Oh*, p.1558):

Ainsi, lorsqu'un père de famille aura été condamné aux galères perpétuelles par une sentence arbitraire, soit pour avoir donné retraite chez soi à un prédicant, soit pour avoir écouté son sermon dans quelque caverne ou dans quelque désert, la femme et les enfants sont réduits à mendier leur pain.

And he adds a note to qualify 'arbitraire' which is highly significant: 'Voyez l'édit de 1724, 14 mai, publié à la sollicitation du cardinal de Fleury, et revu par lui.' There is in fact no doubt at whose door Voltaire lays the responsibility for this anti-Protestant rigour. Earlier in the *Précis* he has already claimed that Fleury had been given a special brief for religious affairs at the time when the Edict was drawn up: 'Monsieur le Duc abandonna d'abord tout le département de l'Eglise, et le soin de poursuivre les calvinistes et les jansénistes, à l'évêque de Fréjus, se réservant l'administration de tout le reste.'[39] And in a later work, the *Sermon prêché à Bâle* (1768), Voltaire repeats the charge – he speaks of the 'funeste édit de 1724, que la haine languedocienne arracha au cardinal de Fleury contre les pasteurs évangéliques' (*Mélanges*, p.1275). Is this

[38] such certificates could sometimes be obtained by bribery, however. For information on the 1724 edict and on the way anti-Protestant legislation was treated by the Catholic population see McCloy, pp.11-17.

[39] *Oh*, p.1314. Malesherbes makes the same point in a letter to Rulhière (dated by Grosclaude as 12 December 1786): 'Le Cardinal de Fleuri étoit au conseil en 1724. M. le Duc [de Bourbon] ne travailloit avec le Roi qu'en sa présence. Nous l'avons vu dans les Mémoires de Villars [in religious matters] auxquelles il croyoit devoir être attaché en sa qualité d'évêque, on se concertoit sûrement avec lui.' But both Malesherbes and Rulhière were convinced that Fleury was opposed to persecution: 'Je suis parfaitement de votre avis, Monsieur, sur ce que la persécution proprement dite, c'est-à-dire les procédures criminelles, n'étoient pas du goût du Cardinal de Fleuri', wrote Malesherbes in the letter already quoted above, and Rulhière's opinion (in the *Eclaircissements historiques*) was similar: 'La sanglante persécution qu'elle [la loi de 1724] devait susciter ne s'éleva pas encore pendant la douce et tranquille administration du Cardinal de Fleury' (Grosclaude, *Malesherbes*, p.367, especially n.28; cf. also Michel Richard, *La Vie quotidienne des protestants sous l'ancien régime* (Paris 1966), p.236; Coquerel, i.403 ff.

just another example of Voltaire's prejudice against the clergy, or did he have a valid reason for attributing the anti-Protestant measures of the government to Fleury? I can unfortunately give no firm answer to this question, but there are indications that Voltaire was not guided merely by blind prejudice. Speaking about the repeal of the Edict of Nantes in the *Anecdotes sur Louis XIV*, Voltaire tells us that he had made some enquiries in high places (M.xxiii.245):

J'ai demandé à M. le cardinal de Fleury ce qui avait principalement engagé le roi à ce coup d'autorité. Il me répondit que tout venait de M. de Baville, in-tendant du Languedoc, qui s'était flatté d'avoir aboli le calvinisme dans cette province, où cependant il restait plus de quatre-vingt mille huguenots.

This story rings true, as it is not the usual reason given by Voltaire for the tragedy (cf. above, pp.240-46, and he is not therefore using Fleury's name merely to give his own ideas added prestige. Is it fanciful to sup-pose that the cardinal may have given Voltaire some information on his own policy toward the Protestants, or, if this was not the case, that Voltaire had made enquiries on the subject with other ministers during his term as historiographer of France? Whatever the real truth of the matter, we have genuine evidence here that before 1750 Voltaire had begun to take an interest in the lot of his Protestant contemporaries in France, and we can demonstrate the absolute falsity of a statement like the following: 'Nulle part nous ne voyons que les événements qui désolaient alors les Eglises du Désert aient obtenu un mot de sym-pathie à cette époque de Voltaire.'[40]

The 1724 edict dismayed the Protestants at first. Appeals for Dutch and British intervention were vain, but it was soon found that the laws were unenforceable, and the steady rebuilding of the Protestant churches continued. The number of ministers in Languedoc rose sharply and in the 1730s organised Protestant worship spread to many new areas.[41] Predictably enough, the government's reply was spasmodic repression, directed mainly against assemblies and ministers. The pastor Alexandre

[40] Champendal, *Voltaire et les protestants de France*, p.42. Champendal is referring to the period before Voltaire took up residence in Geneva. He also mistakenly claims that the Protestants are not mentioned at all in the *Précis du Siècle de Louis XV*: as we have just seen, this is quite untrue. There is also a reference to them in the *Histoire de la guerre de 1741*: cf. below p.269.

[41] Despite Voltaire's assertions to the contrary, Fleury's period as chief minister is regarded by most commentators as one in which the Protestants were subjected to a minimum of persecution: cf. Coquerel, i.212-13.

Roussel was executed in Montpellier on 30 November 1728 and his colleague Pierre Durand (only a *prédicant*) suffered a similar fate in 1732. The expansion of the *églises du désert* did not please the clergy any more than the government. In 1737 a letter was sent from the *curés* of the Cévennes to cardinal Fleury, complaining that they were being threatened and intimidated by the Protestants, who despised the law (Dedieu, i.62-63). Yet in a typical change of policy (or perhaps merely through indifference), Fleury and his government did nothing (Coquerel, i.264). The Protestants moreover were encouraged by a rumour that a secret article in the last peace treaty had granted them liberty of conscience and that they would be allowed to rebuild their *temples* in 1738 at the latest.

The beginning of 1741 put the Court into a panic; it was thought that ministers were arriving from Geneva and that enemy agents were stirring up the southern provinces to revolt. Rigorous measures were applied for a short time, but the government soon saw that the Huguenots were unrebellious, and harshness gave way to leniency. The bishop of Uzès complained that the Protestants were assembling so near his palace that he could hear them singing their psalms, but no action was taken against the miscreants (Dedieu, i.68). It even seems as if the government was trying to do something about the vexed question of Protestant marriages. Joseph Dedieu tells us that:

Depuis 1738 le maréchal de Richelieu, encouragé par le roi, cherchait à élaborer un projet acceptable pour l'Eglise et les réformés. Au mois de juillet 1738, une conférence solennelle s'était ouverte en son palais, où assistaient M. de Bernage et les évêques de Lavaur, de Mende, Alais, Uzès, Viviers, Montpellier, Castres et Nîmes. Les prélats, ayant rédigé un copieux mémoire, attendaient une suite à ce projet. Pour une cause inconnue, la conférence n'en eut aucune.

Another meeting was held on 6 April 1741, but by this time the government was too worried about the War of the Austrian Succession to have time for other matters.[42]

The new intendant of Languedoc, Lenain, was a humane man who was inclined to moderation in his conduct towards the Huguenots. Unfortunately, the outbreak of the War of the Austrian Succession encouraged some of the Protestants, especially the pastor Viala and

[42] Dedieu, i.69; cf. Paul d'Estrée, *Le Maréchal de Richelieu*, p.125: 'Richelieu, pour ses débuts, avait voulu renoncer à la manière forte; et sa tolérance avait été fort appréciée des huguenots.'

his colleagues in Haut-Languedoc, to abandon the precepts of non-resistance which Antoine Court had always recommended. The bishops of Castres, Lavaur, Montauban and Toulouse all complained to the government of a sharp change in the behaviour of Protestants after the entry of England into the war on 29 March 1744. Protestant assemblies, larger than ever, were now armed, and Catholics took up arms to defend themselves. According to Dedieu (i.80 ff), the revolt had become general and civil war seemed near. Prayers were said to have been held openly for the success of the armies of Maria Theresa. The king was worried because there were not enough troops available to put down the Protestants. When Lenain did go onto the offensive at the beginning of September, he found it relatively easy to stop the assemblies and by the end of the year his new policy had been an un-expected triumph. Lenain's military governor, Richelieu, distinguished himself by the severity of the fines he imposed on the unfortunate Huguenots. It was nevertheless to the same Richelieu (among others) that the Protestants of Languedoc wrote, at the end of 1745, denying that a *cantique* praying for the success of British arms was the work of the Protestants, and asking him to intervene in their favour.[43]

Other areas also had their share of trouble. In Dauphiné a Protestant minister was supposed to have read out, on 7 June 1744, an edict of tolerance signed by the king. When informed of this, Louis xv was furious, and the *parlement* of Grenoble was instructed to show the Protestants by its actions that the rumour was untrue (Dedieu, i.113). The prisons of Grenoble were filled and two pastors executed: Louis Ranc on 5 March 1745 and Jacques Roger, one of the original restorers of the *églises du désert*, on 22 May;[44] Roger was supposed to have been the prevaricating minister in question. This was not the last execution of a Protestant pastor in those troubled times, but Dedieu (i.140-41) points out that there are two sides to the question:

La psychologie protestante nous montre des fidèles accablés de douleur, mais ardents de foi religieuse, et dont l'ardeur s'exalte avec le redoublement des souffrances. La psychologie des gens du roi, attachés à la poursuite des huguenots, ne se comprend que si l'on voit en eux des juristes, étroits si

---

[43] Coquerel, i.358-59. They wrote also to the prince de Dombes, to Saint-Florentin (the minister responsible for Protestant affairs), to m. de Manibam (*premier président* of the Toulouse *parlement*), and to Lenain.

[44] Coquerel, i.346. Roger had started preaching even before Antoine Court, in 1708 (Coquerel, i.347).

l'on veut, mais scrupuleux, et des justiciers. Le juriste veille au salut des lois, au maintien des textes incorporés à la constitution du pays. Le justicier s'étonne de trouver devant lui des rebelles, qui, sous le manteau de la religion, agitent bien d'autres idées.

The Protestants were indeed still considered as potential rebels, and not only by the government. In October 1746 the Court was convinced that a general rebellion was about to break out in the southern provinces, encouraged by France's enemies. Voltaire himself briefly mentioned the same strategy in the *Histoire de la guerre de 1741* (1745), though he was later (cf. below, p.329) to berate La Beaumelle soundly for suggesting that such a rebellion on the part of the Protestants was possible (*Oh*, p.1648):

Le projet des ennemis et surtout de l'Angleterre, était d'envahir la Provence, de ruiner le port de Lorient et avec lui la compagnie des Indes, de se saisir de Port-Louis qui aurait tombé après Lorient, de mettre la Bretagne à contri-bution, de faire soulever les calvinistes vers la Rochelle comme vers le Lan-guedoc et le Dauphiné.

In point of fact the Protestants made no attempt to rise against the government even after Provence had been invaded, but despite this proof of loyalty, the government could do no better after the war than to return to its usual vacillating policy. Lenain was instructed that 'il fallait se fixer à "une conduite mêlée de fermeté et de douceur"' (Dedieu, i.189).

There were at last some signs, however, that attempts were being made to find a more permanent settlement of the Protestant question, especially with regard to the problem of Protestant marriages, and Voltaire's friend Richelieu was intimately involved in these moves. In July 1749 he, the chancellor, Saint-Florentin (who was *ministre de la maison du roi* and therefore in charge of Protestant affairs) and Lenain met to discuss the question, a *mémoire* on Protestant marriages having been prepared by the archbishop of Narbonne. Unfortunately, the *ordonnance* of 17 January 1750, which was a direct result of the meeting, promised little hope to the Protestants: it merely attempted to suppress public assemblies and relegated civil rights to the background. Lenain had apparently spoken in favour of the Huguenots, but his hand was weakened by the fact that large assemblies continued to be held in Languedoc, and anyway he died shortly afterwards, on 28 December 1750 (Dedieu, i.207).

A more violent attitude towards the *réformés* in Languedoc was adopted in the interim before the arrival of Lenain's successor Saint-Priest. In 1751, for example, a new order was made that all children of *nouveaux convertis* should be baptised by a priest within fifteen days (Coquerel, ii.37-39). It is possible that this renewal of coercion angered the Huguenots, who were by now becoming accustomed to a measure of semi-toleration, and that the ensuing reaction on their part was responsible for the serious repression of 1752. At any rate, an assembly of about four hundred Protestants presided over by the pastor Lafon was broken up by a detachment of soldiers on 28 March 1751. The Protestants seem to have fought back, some were killed, and the new intendant was incensed (Dedieu, i.226-29). Claude Chaumont, whose case had been pending since 20 December 1750 and for whom Voltaire was later to intercede (cf. below, pp.302-304), was sentenced to life on the galleys as a reprisal. The 'massacre de Lézan', as the incident just described was called, had also put the Protestants into an ugly mood, and new reprisals were taken against Catholics, especially priests. Things were going from bad to worse. The *proposant* Bénézet was captured, and hanged at Montpellier on 27 March 1752 at the age of twenty-six (Coquerel, ii.50-51). Some pastors now went around accompanied by bands of armed men. Many *curés* fled from the country-side and sought refuge in the towns of Languedoc.

Yet the repression and increased violence on both sides were ultimately to have a good effect. The government now became convinced that the trouble was largely due to the rigid attitude of the clergy in their administration of the sacraments to the Protestants (Dedieu, i.254). Moreover, the southern bishops, under pressure from the Court, accepted a compromise on the question of baptisms and marriages (Coquerel, ii.72-73). Richelieu was again the government's 'strong man' in this difficult situation in Languedoc. On 18 October 1752 Saint-Florentin advised the intendant that Richelieu would soon be arriving, and that he was well informed of the king's intentions. Richelieu's first task was to re-establish public order and to force the Languedoc episcopate to accept a political solution. The working out of a *modus vivendi* with the bishops was in fact no easy matter; both Richelieu and Saint-Priest were irritated by the prelates' intransigence,[45] but a movement of exile had now started, and it was essential

---

[45] cf. Grosclaude, *Malesherbes*, pp.358 ff, especially p.359; also below, n.46.

to halt this. At a conference in Languedoc Richelieu declared that 'l'ordre public, le bien public et les liens les plus sacrés de la société exigent nécessairement une loi commune, invariable et uniforme, pour assurer l'état [des protestants]'.[46] This was encouragement indeed for the Protestants, and we now see why Voltaire had, in 1751, referred to the maréchal's 'bontez' for his Calvinists.

As I have already pointed out, Richelieu has not left a reputation for his tolerant behaviour toward the Huguenots – quite the opposite.[47] Yet this is due at least in part to his unenviable position as executor of government policy. A compromise had been achieved with the bishops, but it was not one which would be to the Protestants' liking: the strict requirements for baptism and marriage were to be relaxed but only in return for energetic measures against pastors and a complete ban on all religious assemblies. It was Richelieu who had to apply this ban when he arrived in Languedoc in February 1754 to open the *Etats provinciaux*, and he was necessarily unpopular among the Protestants because of this, even though he also showed fairness in trying to keep the bishops

[46] cf. Armand Lods, 'Le maréchal de Richelieu persécuteur des protestants de la Guyenne (1758)', *Bpf* (1899), lxviii.33-42. Bachaumont reports in the *Mémoires secrets* (xxxiv.226) that in 1752 Richelieu had written a letter which sought to persuade the government to guarantee civil rights to the French Protestants. In a letter of 5 December 1752 to m. Royer of the *comité wallon*, Antoine Court described the initiative as follows: 'M. de Richelieu allant aux Etats et passant à Nimes, dit à un Gentilhomme Catholique de cette ville là, que la Cour avoit de bonnes intentions à l'égard des Protestans, mais qu'elle étoit embarrassé sur les moyens qu'il y avoit à prendre pour les tranquiliser; il ajouta que *les Evêques sont des diables*, et en même tems il chargea ce Gentilhomme de réfléchir là dessus et d'en conférer avec quelques Protestants.' The gentleman in question contacted Paul Rabaut through a member of the Nîmes Consistory and asked him to prepare a *mémoire* on Protestant civil rights which the gentleman himself would give to Richelieu (Bib pf, 392, letter 83: quoted, with modernised spelling, by Lods, p.41, n.2).

[47] despite the evidence to the contrary just quoted, n.46, Lods's thesis in the article in question is that Richelieu, 'qui ne songeait qu'à ses plaisirs et à ses maîtresses' (p.41), persecuted the Huguenots in Guyenne merely because 'il a cru se rendre agréable à l'Eglise romaine, gagner son salut' (p.42). It does not seem to have occurred to Lods that, although Richelieu was a notorious lecher, he might sometimes in fact have turned his attention to other things, and that the persecution of the Protestants might have had a political motive with which Richelieu was in agreement. The *maréchal* seems always to have considered the Protestants' assemblies as dangerous manifestations which should be prevented if possible, but he saw that this was impracticable as long as the Protestants were denied basic civil rights. Paul d'Estrée, who quotes the same extract from the *Archives wallonnes* as Armand Lods, is somewhat fairer in his assessment of the situation, commenting that 'la politique d'apaisement, préconisée par le gouverneur Richelieu, n'avait pas trouvé d'écho, sinon à la Cour, du moins dans l'épiscopat' (*Le Maréchal de Richelieu*, p.284).

to their part of the bargain. Opposition persisted and it was decided that it would not be possible to force all the *nouveaux convertis* to regularise their *état-civil* in the present circumstances.

Meanwhile the debate concerning the Protestants, hitherto mainly restricted to those intimately concerned with applying the appropriate legislation, was gaining more public attention. In May 1751 the bishop of Agen had addressed a letter to the *Contrôleur général* Machault in which he protested because a passport had been given to a Huguenot merchant allowing him to return to France. The bishop also denounced the Calvinists as basically hostile to the monarchy. Antoine Court replied to these accusations in *Le Patriote françois et impartial, ou réponse à lettre de mr le contrôleur général contre la tolérance des huguenots, en date du 1er mai 1751* (2 vols, Villefranche 1753), and again in the *Lettre d'un patriote sur la tolérance civile des protestants de France et sur les avantages qui en résulteroient pour le royaume* (n.p. 1755). Voltaire himself was indirectly drawn into the debate, as Court also rejected assertions similar to those of the bishop of Agen as to the republican nature of Calvinism which Voltaire had made in the *Siècle de Louis XIV*.[48] An eloquent plea for tolerance was also made by Turgot in *Le Conciliateur* (1754). This enlightened young magistrate went farther than Voltaire, since he completely rejected the idea that it was dangerous to allow the Huguenots to hold religious assemblies.[49] Thus opened, the debate about the position of the Huguenots went on for several years and was to culminate in the *Traité sur la tolérance* (1762) and in the other works Voltaire wrote on behalf of the Protestants after the Calas case. The government was also reconsidering its position. Saint-Florentin had realised in 1752 that he was in an *impasse* and had asked Joly de Fleury to write him a *mémoire* on the situation. This was to herald a series of dissertations which distinguished magistrates and administrators prepared for the government in the long years before the Edict of Toleration was promulgated in 1787. Voltaire was to combine and popularise both types of writing, giving the somewhat dry legal arguments an appealingly journalistic flavour, and thus completely dominating pro-Huguenot writing from 1762 until the rehabilitation of Sirven in 1771.

[48] cf. above, p.256, for a similar comment by Rabaut.
[49] cf. below, pp.318-19. It must be pointed out that although this work was attributed to Turgot by Dupont de Nemours, Morellet considered it to have been composed by Loménie de Brienne, who in 1754 was *grand-vicaire* at Rouen.

But all this was in the future. On 12 December 1754 Voltaire was on his way to Geneva from Lyon, hoping to find a peaceful and secure place of exile in Switzerland. Writing to Antoine Court, the Genevese pastor Etienne Chiron describes an interesting incident which happened on the great man's journey:

Je [ne] vous écris ces deux lignes que p̄ vous dire que Mr De Voltaire a raconté ici à un de mes amis que passant à Nantua il vit arrêter et lier un homme assés bien mis parce qu'il n'avoit point de passeport, et ql avoit été trouvé avec une Carte de Géographique où étoit écrit *évités le Fort de la Cluse*. Que Mr De Voltaire et Madame sa Nièce avoit sollicités inutilement son élargissement; qu'on leur avoit répondu que ce pouvoit étre un Ministre, qu'alors ils avoient dit que l'intention du Roi étoit qu'ils sortissent du Roy^me et qu'ils répondroient aux vüës du Roi en favorisant leur évasion. Mais que le Commandant n'avoit point voulu entendre raison.[50]

This account of Voltaire's efforts to help a suspected Protestant refugee, written to the restorer of the French Protestant Churches, is symbolic of the close relations the *philosophe* was soon to have with his Huguenot contemporaries. His clever argument shows a knowledge of the government's usual policy: determination to rid the country of Protestant pastors, but at the same time reluctance to enforce the full rigour of the anti-Protestant laws, unless it was considered that an example was absolutely necessary. Voltaire was obviously unaware of a recent change in tactics, determined by the government's fears of a new exodus of refugees,[51] but his interest in the plight of the Huguenots is clearly attested by his conduct on this occasion.

An initial period of indifference or mild hostility to the Huguenots which persisted in the *Siècle de Louis XIV* and which was largely due to Voltaire's suspicion of the Protestants as potential rebels and fanatics, had now largely given way to a more sympathetic attitude. Respect for

[50] Best.D6037, *c.*19 December 1754. The man appears not to have been a pastor: cf. Best.D6037, commentary.

[51] 'En mars [1752], vingt fugitifs passent en Angleterre, en juin, le pasteur François, du Vivarais, conduit à Genève un groupe de cent quatorze réformés, ce qui frappe si douloureusement la Cour qu'on envoie à M. de Tavannes, commandant en Bourgogne, l'ordre de vérifier avec scrupule les passeports' (Dedieu, i.253). It appears that security had also been strengthened for non-religious reasons: 'On ne peut entrer dans aucune ville de la Bresse et même dans la Bourgogne qu'après un long examen. La terreur des Mandrins [a type of bandit] cause toutes ces perquisitions. Il seroit convenable que nos pauvres frères qui voudroient fuir la persécution évitassent cette route' (letter from Chiron to Antoine Court, 27 December 1754, quoted by Charles Dardier in 'Voltaire agissant en faveur des protestants en 1754', *Bpf* (1883), xxxii.605).

273

certain literary figures of the Refuge, admiration for Protestant learning, and contacts with pastors like César de Missy and Antoine Achard had all contributed to this change and had probably convinced Voltaire that the French Protestants were, by and large, respectable men worthy of sympathy, although he still distrusted and feared a certain type of popular Huguenot fanaticism. Voltaire may also have made some enquiries, during his term as historiographer of France, into the motivation of government policy toward the *nouveaux convertis*: at any rate he questioned cardinal Fleury about the reasons for the repeal of the Edict of Nantes, and other information may also have been forthcoming. By the late 1740s there are indications, few but conclusive, that Voltaire was now better informed on the Protestant question. Finally a letter written while Voltaire was in Berlin shows us that some discussion of the Huguenot problem had taken place between him and Richelieu, who was one of the chief agents of government policy in the Protestant south. Voltaire no longer regarded the problem merely in historical terms. He still had a lot to learn about the conditions the Huguenots lived under and Geneva would provide him with a wealth of new information, but the ground was now prepared and the important change in attitude had already been made.

Coquerel's criticism of the *philosophes* is therefore inaccurate, at least as far as Voltaire is concerned, although it is true that at the beginning of his life Voltaire did share Parisian society's ignorance of the persecution suffered by the *églises du désert*. Discussing the execution of eight Protestant ministers between 1745 and 1762 – 'de pauvres gens du Poitou, du Vivarais, de Valence, de Montauban' – Voltaire adds bitterly: 'On ne sait rien de cela dans Paris, où le plaisir est la seule chose importante, où l'on ignore tout ce qui se passe en province et chez les étrangers' (*Mélanges*, p.599 – this is an extract from the *Traité sur la tolérance*). This passage may very possibly contain a note of self-reproach. Yet it would be as superficial and misleading to maintain that Voltaire had no experience of the Huguenot problem before arriving in Geneva, and that he formed all his attitudes to it there, as it would be to say that he arrived in England a poet and returned to France a sage.[52]

ii. *1754-1762*

Voltaire's initial enthusiasm for the 'philosophical' atmosphere of both Geneva and Lausanne is well known and it is undeniable that contacts

[52] John Morley, *Voltaire* (London 1891), p.58.

with the Swiss clergy and laity in both towns increased his awareness of the situation of the French Protestants. Diplomatic pressure from the French government had in fact attempted to discourage the Genevese clergy from maintaining close contacts with the *églises du désert*,[53] but it is unlikely that this policy had succeeded. Genevese opinion closely followed the fortunes of the French Protestants throughout the eighteenth century, and Huguenot refugees still looked to Calvin's city as their natural place of sanctuary. Voltaire is bound at least to have heard frequent rumours of what was going on in the Protestant south, and the change in perspective caused by living in Geneva probably showed him that the Huguenot problem was more important than he had previously realised. Disagreements with the Genevese pastors might soon have distracted his attention from the problem, but in Lausanne his honeymoon period with the clergy lasted longer. His friend, the *premier pasteur* Polier de Bottens, was director of the Lausanne seminary from 1754 to 1783 (*Histoire des protestants en France*, p.234). Though great secrecy was maintained and Polier may never have spoken to Voltaire about the seminary itself,[54] it is more than probable that he discussed the fortunes of the *églises du désert* on more than one occasion. Moreover, Antoine Court himself was still living in Lausanne, and although there is no evidence that he ever met Voltaire, this is not completely out of the question. At any rate Voltaire was later of some use to Court's son, whom he called 'un bon parpaillot' (Best.D11134, to Damilaville, 28 March 1763; cf. below, p.351).

[53] 'Lorsque, après la paix de 1738 (traité de Vienne), le ministre du roi déclara que Louis xv était offensé de la correspondance qui se poursuivait entre Genève et ses sujets rebelles, le Conseil de Genève donna ordre à la Compagnie des pasteurs de cesser toute correspondance avec les ministres et synodes français' (Kern, p.198).

[54] it is impossible to say whether or not Voltaire was aware of the existence of this institution. There are no direct references to it in his works or correspondence, but Voltaire would anyway have tried to be discreet about such a matter. In the *Mémoire présenté au ministère de France* (1767), La Beaumelle is criticised for saying that 'il s'est formé un séminaire de prédicants, sous le nom de ministres du désert' (M.xxvi.364), but this evidence is inconclusive. Firstly, Voltaire is refuting La Beaumelle's assertions about the French Protestants (most of which are correct) presumably because he thinks it politically dangerous for the Huguenots that these facts be widely known (cf. below, pp.329-30). Secondly, there is no evidence that by 'Séminaire' La Beaumelle is designating the institution at Lausanne. He too may have been unaware of its existence, for secrecy was preserved to a remarkable extent. Although spies' reports filtered through to the French government in the course of the century, the bishop of Lausanne (residing at Fribourg) was still unaware of the Seminary's existence in 1787 (Chavannes, p.86).

Voltaire's correspondence gives us indications from time to time that his attention was being turned to the religious problems of France: on 24 September 1756 Voltaire wrote to Rouvière thanking him for his book on the possible reunion of the Protestants with the Catholic church.[55] The correspondence for the next two years is full of Voltaire's disputes with the clergy in Geneva and Lausanne, but contains nothing of specific interest as regards the French Protestants. Voltaire had not lost interest in the problem, however. Towards the end of 1758 he wrote to Thieriot (Best.D7995, 24 December) asking him to send Caveirac's 'justification de la st. Bartelemy'.[56] This work was an extremist contribution to the debate on the Protestant question which had begun earlier in the 1750s (cf. above, p.272). It was a reply both to Antoine Court's *Lettre d'un patriote* and to the *Mémoire théologique et politique au sujet des mariages des protestants de France* (1755). Court's *Lettre d'un patriote* was favourably reviewed in the *Correspondance littéraire* in March 1756, and in his article Grimm takes up his cudgel on behalf of the Protestants in no uncertain manner.[57] Enlightened opinion in the capital could no longer be said to be unaware of the problem and would henceforth be a force to be reckoned with. The *Mémoire théologique et politique* is also praised by Grimm, who shows himself in a very anticlerical vein.[58] Composed mainly by Ripert de Montclar, *procureur général* of the Toulouse *parlement* (the theological part was by the abbé Quesnel), the *Mémoire* proposes that the policy of toleration should be applied to the Protestants. Their marriage banns should be published before a *tribunal de justice* and the marriages celebrated in the presence of a magistrate. In the author's opinion, the clergy themselves should ask the king to adopt this policy because they profane the sacraments when they administer them to Protestants, whose only motivation is fear of the anti-Huguenot laws (cf. below, pp.334ff). Caveirac replied

[55] Best.D7006, 24 September 1756. The book was M.P.D.R. [P.D. Rouvière], *Essai de réunion des protestants aux catholiques-romains* (Paris 1756).

[56] Jean Novi de Caveirac, *Apologie de Louis XIV et de son conseil, sur la révocation de l'édit de Nantes ... avec une dissertation sur la journée de la s. Barthélemi* (n.p. 1758).

[57] 'Si, grâce à la philosophie, nous frémissons sur les maux infinis que la révocation de l'édit de Nantes a causés au royaume, qu'avons-nous fait pour les réparer et pour en prévenir les suites? Rien. [...] malgré nos beaux discours [...] les ministres des protestants sont encore conduits aux supplices [...] Trois millions de citoyens ne peuvent jouir de la protection que le gouvernement leur doit qu'en se couvrant de l'odieux masque de l'hypocrisie' (*Correspondance littéraire*, iii.193).

[58] 'On dit que le gouvernement aurait adopté ses idées, sans l'opposition de plusieurs évêques; comme s'il appartenait aux prêtres de décider du bien de l'Etat' (iii.192).

violently, praising the repeal of the Edict of Nantes, playing down the number of refugees, repeating accusations that the Protestants were rebels and traitors who helped France's enemies in time of war, and claiming that the St Bartholomew's Day massacre had been a political rather than a religious measure and that the number of victims had been greatly exaggerated.

All this was grist for Voltaire's mill. The campaign against *l'infâme* was brewing, and Caveirac was just the sort of enemy Voltaire loved to pit himself against. The work was sent by Thieriot on 25 January 1759 (Best.D8065), and in February we see Voltaire questioning the Genevese pastor Jacob Vernes as to the truth of Caveirac's assertions. Are there not at least five hundred French families established in Geneva, he wants to know (Best.D8119), and not merely fifty, as Caveirac claims? Further letters in the same month show us Voltaire asking d'Alembert for information about Caveirac, and it was not slow to come (Best.D8129, D8139).This intolerant Catholic pamphleteer may even have rendered the Huguenots a service, for Voltaire was now on the worst of terms with the clergy of both Geneva and Lausanne, and Caveirac's *libelle* drew his attention to the fact that the Protestants were not all grim ministers who condemned the theatre and defended Calvin's fanaticism. At a critical stage of Voltaire's anticlerical development, he was reminded that his Huguenot fellow-countrymen, far from being synonymous with *l'infâme*, were in fact its unfortunate victims.

In the southern provinces of France, the firm line which the Court had decided to take at the time of Richelieu's intervention had soon been compromised. The maréchal de Mirepoix, Richelieu's replacement as governor of Languedoc, intended to stop all the Protestant assemblies by means of a system of hostages. He also wanted to get rid of the pastors, and when Paul Rabaut refused, in 1756, to go into voluntary exile, Mirepoix condemned Fabre and Turge to the galleys for life, as a reprisal.[59] The *maréchal's* policies soon changed radically, however, when he saw that these harsh measures were achieving nothing, and until his death in 1757 Mirepoix provided the spectacle of a provincial

[59] Jean Fabre, born in Nîmes in 1717, became famous because he offered to suffer punishment in place of his father, who was almost eighty and who had been arrested at a service held *au désert* on 1 January 1756. The offer was accepted, and Fabre served six years on the galleys, finally securing his release on 21 May 1762 at the instigation of Choiseul. A play entitled *L'Honnête criminel* based on Fabre's story was subsequently composed in 1767 by Fenouillet de Falbaire (see Eugène and Emile Haag, *La France protestante*, 2nd ed. (1877), vi.206-207; cf. below, pp.352-53).

governor applying a policy of indulgence which was not really approved of either by the government or by his own subordinates. The situation was further complicated by the outbreak of the Seven Years' War in 1756, which meant that it would be impossible for the government to apply repressive measures as no troops were available to enforce them.

The war also prompted a curious initiative.[60] Negotiations with a view to improving the Huguenots' position had been carried on in 1755 between Protestant leaders and the prince de Conti, a member of the royal family, but these contacts had been broken off by the Protestants, who feared that they might become involved in rebellious activities (Coquerel, ii.201ff.). A prime mover of the initiative had been Le Cointe de Marcillac, an officer in Conti's service, who for many years acted as a Protestant 'agent' in Paris (Coquerel, ii.201; cf. below, pp.346-47). One of his friends, 'un nommé Herrenschwand, grand juge des gardes suisses, protestant de naissance', was told about the affair, and repaid this confidence by promptly informing the government of the situation (Hugues, p.299). Herrenschwand then became a sort of 'double agent', and undertook a trip around France at the end of 1757 to gain the Protestants' confidence and at the same time collect information for the government regarding their activities (Hugues, pp.300ff).

On his return, Herrenschwand, realising that the Conti affair was now dead, attempted to prolong his usefulness by promoting a new project, of interest both to the government and to the Protestants:

Le Sr Herrenschwand [. . .] a cru devoir, dans les circonstances présentes [i.e. an acute financial shortage caused by the war], leur [to the Protestants] insinuer le projet d'un don gratuit à Sa Majesté d'environ vingt-cinq millions; il a eu le bonheur de voir ses vues approuvées généralement, et il ne doute pas un moment qu'à l'aide des soins qu'il se donnera ultérieurement à ce sujet, et moyennant les ménagements convenables dont il serait nécessaire d'user dans l'exécution, la chose ne réussisse de la manière qu'on pourra le désirer.[61]

Herrenschwand himself would acquaint influential Protestants with the plan and instruct them to set about collecting the *don gratuit*, once the

---

[60] see Edmond Hugues, 'Un épisode de l'histoire du protestantisme au XVIIIe siècle', *Bpf* (1877), xxvi.289-303, 337-50, on which my account is largely based; cf. also E.-G. Léonard, *Histoire ecclésiastique des réformés français au XVIIIe siècle* (Paris 1940), pp.64-67; *Histoire générale*, iii.26; Coquerel, ii.344-51.

[61] letter of 19 September 1757 from Herrenschwand to mme de Pompadour, quoted by Hugues, p.341.

indispensable royal permission had been accorded. Mme de Pompadour placed Berryer in charge of the affair and apparently lost interest in it, but Herrenschwand contrived to revive this by April 1758 and also succeeded in attracting the attention of the war minister, the duc de Belle-Isle. In the next few months, however, the idea of a *don gratuit* gave way to a more daring notion: the establishment of a Protestant bank which would lend money to the government on fixed interest rates. Herrenschwand

avait gagné à ses idées deux protestants, les nommés Rey et Boudon, ce dernier, originaire de Clairac, et il avait arrêté le plan suivant. Sous la raison sociale, Rey, Boudon et Cie, ils constitueraient à Paris une maison de commerce, ils émettraient des actions, feraient appel aux religionnaires et aux réfugiés de tous les pays, et avec l'argent protestant ils prêteraient au roi.[62]

Despite this major change, the project was accepted by the government, and on 11 March 1759 Belle-Isle wrote to Boudon, one of Herrenschwand's associates, advising him not to attempt too much at the outset:

Je conçois que votre établissement ne peut être précipité; aussi je n'ai compté que sur les ecours que vous m'avez rendus possibles. Je désire même *que vous vous conduisiez dans les provinces avec la plus grande circonspection.* En conséquence, je serais fort satisfait si votre premier établissement est de trois à quatre millions, pourvu que vous y apportiez toute la diligence que les circonstances rendront nécessaire.[63]

Rumours were apparently widespread in Paris, both in Protestant circles and beyond, and in April 1759 Rey and Boudon left the capital in order to collect subscriptions in the provinces. They had already sent out copies of a letter to them from Belle-Isle dated 4 February 1759, and they took with them subscription forms for interested parties (Hugues, pp.345-48). A first setback occurred at Nîmes, however,[64] and neither Boudon nor Rey was able to inspire enough confidence among provincial Protestants to make a success of the projected bank (Hugues, p.349). Similar ideas, with the object of securing at least a tacit admission that the Protestants were useful citizens and had a right to exist, continued to be mooted for several years, but on each

---

[62] Hugues, p.344. The proposed interest was 6% per annum.

[63] Hugues, p.345; quoted also by Coquerel, ii.345, who gives the letter's date as 1 March 1759.

[64] Rey was refused permission to hold a Protestant assembly *au désert* in order to explain to local Protestants the plans for establishing a bank (Hugues, p.348).

occasion these come to nothing, partly because of inability of the various Protestant groups to agree with one another, and partly because of changes in government policy (see below, pp.349-52, 380-81).

This affair is particularly interesting as it demonstrates conclusively that Voltaire was by this time well informed about the affairs of the French Protestants. No doubt rumours were circulating in Geneva as well as in Paris, and Voltaire must have been keeping his ear fairly close to the ground, for his first reference to the affair is on 10 April 1759, only six weeks after the duc de Belle-Isle had written to Boudon giving his approval for the project. But not only did Voltaire get wind of events very quickly, his information had also been accurate, although he could not bring himself to believe it all. He wrote to Elie Bertrand:

Je serais très surpris qu'il y eût un Boudon député des protestants auprès du roy. Il n'y a point de protestans en France aux yeux de la cour, il n'y a que des nouvaux convertis. On ne connaît pas plus de corps de protestants que de corps de Turcs. Si par hazard il y en a dans les provinces on veut n'en rien savoir. Ny le clergé ny la noblesse ny le tiers état, ny les parlements n'ont le droit d'avoir un député résident à la cour.[65]

This was an accurate description of the government's usual attitude toward the Protestant question, but Voltaire was wrong in this instance, as we have seen. He re-expressed his incredulity at the reports in letters to Jean-Robert Tronchin (Best.D8260, 13 April 1759) and to mme de Fontaine. When he wrote to his niece on 15 April (Best.D8261), Voltaire seems to have had more information, for he is slightly less sceptical about the whole affair, and it is only rumours of the actual amount of money to be lent that he rejects out of hand:

Il y a des gens qui prétendent à Genève que les huguenots de France prêtent cinquante millions au roi, et qu'ils obtiennent quelques priviléges pour l'intérêt de leur argent. Mais je doute que les bons huguenots aient cinquante millions; et je souhaite que mr de Silhouette les trouve, fût ce chez les Turcs.

Voltaire may have been right when he refused to believe this report, since there seems to be some doubt as to the figure actually agreed on.[66] In any case he obviously followed the outcome of these negotiations with interest, and soon reported to Bertrand (Best.D8295) and to Jean-

[65] Best D8255. These very cogent reasons are strikingly similar to those given by the Protestants of Bordeaux for failing to support the venture (Hugues, p.348-49).

[66] we have seen (above, p.278) that Herrenschwand (quoted by Hugues) had referred to twenty-five million *livres*, but Léonard, who also mentions the Protestant bank, speaks of fifty millions, and slightly changes the name of the proposed company to 'Boudon, Rey & Co., avec siège à Nîmes' (*Histoire générale*, iii.26).

Robert Tronchin (Best.D8296, 12 May) that 'on dit que la grande affaire du petit Boudon ne va pas trop bien'. No further references to the affair appear in Voltaire's correspondence, but the accuracy of his information and the speed with which he alluded to these events is at least indicative of an intelligent interest in the fortunes of the French Protestants.

The year 1760 saw a more concrete instance of Voltaire's concern for his Huguenot contemporaries. On 23 June he complained, in a letter to d'Argental, that he had received no reply from Richelieu, to whom he had applied for a passport on behalf of a 'huguenot de Guienne'.[67] The Protestant in question was very probably a businessman, for on 6 July Voltaire lamented to the same correspondent that Richelieu had left for Bordeaux without replying or sending the passport 'que je lui ai demandé pour un pauvre Diable de Gascon hérétique, et voilà mon hérétique sur le point d'être ruiné' (Best.D9043). Turgot's visit to *Les Délices* later in the year[68] no doubt gave Voltaire an opportunity to discuss the Huguenot problem with someone who combined his own humanitarian concern for the persecuted with practical experience of the problem and a depth of knowledge which Voltaire himself was as yet unable to rival.

There are, unfortunately, indications that Voltaire still did not see the religious position in the south of France in its true light, or that he underestimated the severity with which the anti-Protestant laws might still be applied, for on 4 January 1761, in a letter to Cideville, he recounted his campaign against the curé Moëns, and commented: 'Je suis occupé àprésent à procurer à un prêtre un employ dans les galères. Si je peux faire pendre un prédicant huguenot, *sublimi feriam sidera vertice*' (Best.D9520). This quip was unfortunate, to say the least, coming only a few months before the execution of Rochette, and it lays Voltaire open to the charge not merely of flippancy, but of a callous unconcern as regards the treatment meted out to the Huguenot pastors who were caught by the authorities. There were, however, extenuating circumstances. In the first place, we know from Voltaire's whole career that his humanitarianism was genuine and that however tenacious and unreasonable his literary feuds and vendettas might be, real cases of

[67] Best.D9007. Voltaire brought up the matter again in Best.D9010 (27 June) and was reassured by d'Argental (Best.D9018) on 30 June.

[68] Voltaire wrote inviting Turgot on 26 October (Best.D9351) and informed the d'Argentals in November (Best.D9390) that his guest had arrived. Earlier in the year Voltaire had also had as his guest the vicomte de Saint-Priest, who was *intendant* of Languedoc: cf. Best.D9293.

injustice always prompted him to take an active and sympathetic concern. In making such a comment, therefore, it is unlikely that he expected a Huguenot minister ever to be executed again in France. He knew, of course, that this law was still in force, but the government's vacillating policy toward the Protestants and the general growth of philosophical enlightenment had probably convinced him that such barbaric legislation would no longer be applied. Recent contact with someone like Turgot had no doubt strengthened Voltaire's optimism as regards the Huguenots' future to the point where he thought it would be quite in order to indulge in a piece of harmless banter at their expense.[69]

The other explanatory factor is that at the time he wrote this letter to Cideville, Voltaire was more annoyed than ever with the Genevese clergy for their opposition to his theatricals. In fact, it is quite clear to anyone reading his correspondence that Voltaire was thinking of these gentlemen rather than the pastors of the *désert* when he spoke of hanging 'un prédicant huguenot'. The situation was not helped by the fact that Haller had mentioned the precarious situation of French Protestant ministers during his exchange of letters with Voltaire in 1759, in a way particularly designed to arouse the latter's ire. The debate had turned to yet another discussion of Calvin's responsibility in the Servetus affair. Arguing that Calvin was merely following the laws of his time, Haller compares him with 'Un Magistrat qui fait pendre en 1759 un Ministre sous la Croix'. The law he executes is just as cruel, but there is 'rien de plus commun en France, et rien de moins remarqué' (Best. D8282, written in April or May 1759). Though Haller's argument on the point in question is singularly unconvincing – it could in fact have been used by a Catholic like Caveirac to justify the repressive anti-Protestant laws – it ought at least to have drawn Voltaire's attention to the very real dangers which still threatened French pastors. Unfortunately he does not seem to have taken it seriously, and Haller's attempted justification of Calvin no doubt merely served to increase Voltaire's feeling of irritation against the Protestant world in general. The Rochette case was therefore a salutary shock in that it showed Voltaire that the severest anti-Protestant laws might still be applied, and it is to his credit that, despite the pique he felt against the Swiss clergy, he revised his judgement so quickly and intervened in such skilful and determined way. Voltaire's behaviour in this instance and

[69] Fargher, p.130, points out that Voltaire was in a similar 'gay, sprightly, lighthearted, ironic mood', in *Pot-pourri*, after the reversal of the judgement against Calas.

in the Calas and subsequent cases where he interceded in favour of Protestants was to atone amply for any flippant remarks which had escaped him.

iii. *The Rochette case*

François Rochette was a young Protestant minister aged twenty-six.[70] Arrested at Caussade on 14 September 1761, he was transferred first to Cahors and then Toulouse, the local Protestant population having unwittingly made the case much more serious through trying to release him by force: indeed, three Protestant gentlemen were also arrested and tried with him. Despite this unwelcome development, it seemed unlikely that he would be executed as the letter of the law required, since the spread of enlightened ideas was tending to moderate punishments inflicted on the Huguenots. Every attempt, moreover, was made to intervene in his favour, appeals being sent in particular to both Rousseau and Voltaire, asking them to use their influence on his behalf.

Voltaire has often been criticised for his attitude in this affair, but, as I have tried to show in more detail elsewhere,[71] I think such attacks are quite unjustified, for he was far from idle. In particular, he wrote three times to Richelieu (the first letter has been lost, the second, Best. D10095, is dated 25 October, and the third, Best.D10178, 27 November), showing considerable skill in the arguments he used to enlist the duke's support. The 'désinvolture choquante' with which he has been charged (Pomeau, *La religion de Voltaire*, p.325) can be explained by the fact that Richelieu had complained about Voltaire's previous letter – 'Vous dites Monseigneur que mes lettres ne sont point gaies' – and Voltaire therefore adopts a tone which, at first sight, may not appear in keeping with the subject he is raising. Yet a study of his letters to Richelieu shows clearly that, faced with his noble friend's arrogance and extraordinary sense of self-importance, Voltaire was often reduced to presenting serious requests so larded with flattery or disguised with amusing comments that it is easy for a twentieth-century reader to lose sight

[70] for information on the Rochette affair see O. de Grenier-Fajal, *Rochette et les trois frères Grenier* (Montauban 1886); Daniel Ligou, 'Essai d'interprétation psychologique des événements de septembre 1761 à Caussade', *Congrès régional des Fédérations historiques du Languedoc* (Carcassonne 1952), pp.169-75; *Documents sur le protestantisme montalbanais* (Toulouse 1955); Coquerel, ii.267-97.

[71] in my 'Voltaire, Richelieu and the problem of Huguenot emancipation in the reign of Louis xv', *Studies on Voltaire* (1979), clxxvi.97-132.

of Voltaire's original intention. It is surprising that Rousseau, rather than Voltaire, has not come in for more disapproval, since *his* attitude was quite clear. Though himself at least nominally a Protestant, he refused to intervene, explaining in two letters to Jean Ribotte (Leigh 1521 and 1615) that, although he sympathised with Rochette, the latter had been at fault in attending illegal assemblies and that a Christian should know how to suffer and accept the consequences of his actions.

Voltaire's main tactic to persuade Richelieu to intervene was a political rather than a humanitarian one. We have seen that the *maréchal* had already gained a considerable knowledge of the situation in Guyenne and Languedoc, and Voltaire plays on the political capital to be gained if Richelieu could obtain Rochette's pardon. The king's standing with the Protestants would rise: 'Et si c'est vous monseigneur qui obtenez cette grâce du roy, vous serez l'idole de ces faquins de huguenots. Il est toujours bon d'avoir pour soy tout un party' (Best.D10178, 27 November 1761). That Richelieu was not deaf to such suggestions can be seen from the fact that he did try to intervene, and its even seems that he may have sent a message to the Protestants through Voltaire, for the latter wrote to Ribotte on 27 November in terms which sound very much like an official declaration of policy (Best.D10177):

Vous ne devez pas douter, Monsieur, qu'on ne soit très indigné à la cour contre les assemblées publiques. On vous permet de faire dans vos maisons tout ce qui vous plaît, celà est bien honnête. Jesus christ a dit qu'il se trouverait toujours entre deux ou trois personnes assemblées en son nom, mais quand on est trois ou quatre mille, c'est le diable qui s'y trouve. J'ai tout lieu d'espérer que les personnes qui approchent sa Majesté, fortifieront dans son cœur les sentiments d'humanité et de bonté qui lui sont si naturels.

Despite the attempts of Richelieu and others, Rochette and the three Protestant gentlemen were executed at Toulouse on 19 February 1762, the last occasion a Protestant pastor was condemned to death in France during the *ancien régime*. But the atmosphere this case had created in Toulouse and the surrounding area was soon to culminate in another execution, that of the Protestant merchant Jean Calas. And it was surely Voltaire's attempts to help Rochette, combined with his disgust at the latter's death (cf. Best.D10353), that made him ready to espouse the case of Jean Calas so enthusiastically, turning it into one of France's *causes célèbres*, and definitively emerging as a champion of Huguenot toleration.

iv. *The Calas case: Voltaire's attitude crystallises*

On 9 March 1762 Jean Calas was broken on the wheel for the alleged murder of his son, Marc-Antoine, and opinions have differed ever since as to whether he was guilty or innocent of this crime.[72] The trial and execution have usually been regarded as a miscarriage of justice, resulting from the bigoted attitude of the parlement de Toulouse, a zealously Catholic body determined to bring about the death of the Protestant suspects in its power. This textbook opinion is due, in no small part, to Voltaire's own subsequent propaganda in connection with the case. Calas's fate in fact marks a watershed in Voltaire's relationship with the Protestants. Henceforth he would no longer be merely a sympathetic, but mainly uninvolved and distant spectator of the Huguenots' misfortunes; he would become the determined and tireless champion of their civil liberties. It is therefore crucial to appreciate the way in which Voltaire formed his opinion of the Calas case, since the views he held were to be important not only in shaping his own future strategy but also in discrediting religious intolerance throughout Europe. The facts of the Calas case are well known to students of the eighteenth century and I do not propose to discuss them further here, except insofar as the case itself and the three year campaign to clear Calas's name help us to understand Voltaire's new relationship with the Protestants and the constantly changing tactics he adopted in the struggle to help them.

The first point to note is that Voltaire was not immediately convinced of Calas's innocence. In fact his original reaction was quite the opposite. Despite his attempts to help Rochette, Voltaire had not forgotten the prophets and *illuminés* who flourished during the Camisard uprising. Even in 1762 his mistrust of the Huguenot rabble has not completely disappeared and he seems perfectly ready to accept the Calas affair as just one more example of Protestant fanaticism. Voltaire first mentions the affair in a letter to Antoine Le Bault, dated 22 March (Best.D10382). Once again he establishes a direct connection between Protestant fanaticism and the pernicious influence of the Old Testament, a part of the Bible in which the *réformés* were so well versed (cf. above, pp.85-88). Moreover a laconic reference to the Protestants' austere morality of

---

[72] I do not propose to list here the numerous books and articles which have been devoted to the Calas case. For a bibliographical comment see above, p.13, n.1.

the type Voltaire frequently makes in connection with Calvin or the pedantic ministers of Geneva (cf. above, pp.67ff), underlines his hostility:

Vous avez entendu parler peut être d'un bon huguenot que le parlement de Toulouse a fait rouer pour avoir étranglé son fils. Cependant ce saint réformé croiait avoir fait une bonne action, attendu que son fils voulait se faire catholique, et que c'était prévenir une apostasie. Il avait immolé son fils à dieu, et pensait être fort supérieur à Abraham, car Abraham n'avait fait qu'obéir, mais notre calviniste avait pendu son fils de son propre mouvement, et pour l'acquit de sa conscience. Nous ne valons pas grand chose, mais les huguenots sont pires que nous, et deplus ils déclament contre la comédie.

A few days later, when Voltaire had heard different accounts of the story, he was less categorical, but he still showed no inclination to accept the innocence of Calas precipitately, without first making well sure of the facts. He asks cardinal de Bernis's opinion and says that whoever is reponsible, 'Il faut regarder [. . .] avec des yeux d'horreur' (Best.D10386). On the same day, 25 March 1762, he wrote to Fyot de La Marche in Paris (Best.D10387), asking him to ascertain the truth of the affair from the *intendant* of Languedoc, Saint-Priest. A similar request for information is contained in a letter of 27 March to the d'Argentals (Best.D10389): 'Ne pouriez vous pas engager M. le comte de Choiseuil à s'informer de cette horrible avanture qui déshonore la nature humaine, soit que Calas soit coupable soit qu'il soit innocent?' The letter to d'Alembert of 29 March shows us Voltaire at his most scathing as regards both Catholics and Protestants, but by 4 April he had made up his mind. On that day he wrote to Damilaville, and the belligerent tone of the letter heralds the beginning of Voltaire's campaign against the Toulouse judgement and the fanaticism which inspired it (Best. D10406):

Mes chers frères, il est avéré que les juges toulousains ont roué le plus innocent des hommes. Presque tout le Languedoc en gémit avec horreur. Les nations étrangères qui nous haïssent et qui nous battent, sont saisies d'indignation. Jamais depuis le jour de la st Barthélemi rien n'a tant déshonoré la nature humaine. Criez, et qu'on crie.

Once again the Protestants were on the right side in the battle against *l'infâme*. What had caused this change of heart?

Voltaire's initial hesitation in making up his mind is a convincing refutation of those who have accused him of taking up the affair from cheap journalistic motives. He is supposed by some to have seen that it was readily exploitable in the philosophic battle for tolerance, and to have found out from his friends in high places that there would be no danger involved in pressing for a retrial. His main motive would therefore have been the prestige he knew he would gain from defending the unfortunate victim of a judicial blunder. If one accepts the view of Voltaire's detractors, he can take little credit for his campaign in favour of Calas. He can at best be praised for an adroit exercise in enlightened self-interest.

These strictures do not square with the facts, though each of them contains its share of half truth. Voltaire did use his immense journalistic skill in the ensuing campaign, which explains why it was such a success. The cause of toleration in general, and of the Protestants in particular, was helped enormously by the public interest Voltaire's propaganda generated in the case. And Voltaire's own popularity did, of course, receive a spectacular boost from his role as defender of the innocent oppressed. Already, on 7 May 1762, before the campaign had really begun, Julie von Bondeli wrote from Berne to Johann Georg Zimmermann: 'Voltaire s'est si bien conduit dans toute cette affaire, que depuis lors il est réconcilié avec tout Genéve.'[73] Moreover, as I have already pointed out (above, p.14), Voltaire's subsequent popularity with the masses was closely associated with his action on behalf of unfortunates like Calas. Voltaire's campaign to rehabilitate the memory of Calas is, in fact, one of the most praiseworthy episodes in his life, and he must be given due credit for his attitude and behaviour in the affair. His involvement was not the result of a cynically calculating decision, the attempt to enhance his reputation by associating himself with a cause he knew to be espoused already by influential members of French society. Voltaire's efforts were the result of a personal conviction, and, as his correspondence shows us clearly, he might have run a considerable risk in taking the stand he did.

Indeed, the letters sent to Voltaire by his influential friends and some of the other reports he received, far from immediately reassuring him about the case, either left him no wiser than he already was or actively discouraged him from taking any further part in the affair. The very day that Voltaire opened the campaign in favour of Calas with his

[73] Best.D10439, commentary, cf. also Théodore Tronchin's approving remarks to Jacob Vernes in his letter of 29 June 1762 (Best.D10537, commentary).

letter to Damilaville, he reported to Constant d'Hermenches that 'un homme de poids' to whom he had written about the case, had replied: 'que nous importe qu'on ait roué un homme, quand nous perdons la Martinique' (Best.D10405). Richelieu wrote Voltaire a long letter on the subject, but, comments the *philosophe* to the d'Argentals, 'il n'est pas plus au fait que moi' (Best.D10445, 15 May 1762). Chazel had told Voltaire on 12 May that 'il n'est pas une seule personne sensée dans cette province qui ose porter un jugement assuré'.[74] Similarly, cardinal de Bernis did not think 'un protestant plus capable d'un crime atroce qu'un catholique', but he added that his brother in Toulouse had been unable to find out any more information about the affair and Bernis said he would not believe 'que des magistrats s'entendent pour faire une horrible injustice' (Best.D10455, 18 May 1762). The duc de Villars was even more positive. He wrote to Voltaire from Aix on 26 May 1762 to the effect that he knew Calas was guilty and had already ill-treated one of his sons – even the Protestants had to admit this. The judges had in fact been very indulgent, which explained the ambiguity in the judgement. The duke's logic might have persuaded Voltaire a few weeks earlier, and he might also have agreed with cardinal de Bernis's comment about the judges. Now, however, Voltaire was convinced of the innocence of Calas; he told the d'Argentals that uncertainty remained only because the Toulouse *parlement* was covering up its mistake (Best.D10445), and he endorsed the duke's letter 'étrange lettre du duc de Villars qui croit les Calas coupables' (Best.D10472, textual notes).

Voltaire's decision had therefore been made despite indications that his championing of Calas might be a dangerous and unpopular course of action in the opinion of many influential people.[75] On 5 June 1762 he

[74] Best.D10443. Cf. Best.D10446, to cardinal de Bernis: 'Toutes les Lettres que j'ai du Languedoc sur cette affaire se contredisent.'

[75] on the other hand it is true that mme de Pompadour wrote to the duc de Fitzjames on 27 August 1762 expressing her distress at the way in which Calas had been treated: 'Vous avez raison, Monsieur le Duc, l'affaire de ce malheureux Calas fait frémir. Il falloit le plaindre d'être né huguenot, mais il ne falloit le traiter pour cela comme un voleur de grand chemin '(Best.D10677; cf. also Edna Nixon, *Voltaire and the Calas case* (London 1961), pp.139-40). Nonetheless, this letter was written long after Voltaire had taken his decision about the Calas affair. Moreover, it is unlikely that he knew of such attitudes in the early stages of the campaign. On 5 June 1762 he wrote to d'Argental asking his friend to find out through Choiseul the attitude of Saint-Florentin (Best.D10489). And on 7 June he repeated his request: 'M. le comte de Choiseuil ne sera t'il point curieux de savoir de mr de Saint Florentin la vérité touchant l'horrible avanture des Calas, supposé que M. de St

told Ribotte that for two months he had made 'les plus grands éfforts auprès des premières personnes du Royaume, en faveur de cette malheureuse famille qu'il a cru innocente. Mais on les croit tous très coupables. On tient que le parlement a fait justice et miséricorde' (Best. D10490). What clearer proof of Voltaire's good faith could one ask for? The risks were real and Voltaire was prepared to face them. But if his change of heart had not been a cold, calculating decision, dictated by reasons of philosophical and personal expediency, what was the explanation? Reports from the Protestant side had also come flooding in to Voltaire. He was therefore much better informed than when he first received news of the affair, but if he had definitely decided that Calas was a Huguenot fanatic, no amount of potentially biased evidence from Protestant sources would have been sufficient to change his mind. It seems that it was Voltaire's interview with Donat Calas that left him without a doubt as to the innocence of the *roué de Toulouse*. 'Je suis peu édifié de votre indiférence sur l'horrible avanture de Calas', he chided the Protestant banker Ami Camp on 14 April (Best.D10412), 'J'ay parlé à son fils une heure entière. Il me paraît impossible que son fils soit coupable.' As in other cases of judicial injustice, Voltaire identified himself with the sufferings of the victims, and this explains, at least in part, the extraordinary tenacity with which he carried out the campaign to clear Calas's name. As René Pomeau puts it, 'Voltaire a cru, parce que Donat Calas a pleuré.'[76]

It is worth pausing for a moment to reflect on the enormous amount of time and effort Voltaire spent on the Calas case. To say that his activity was prodigious is a commonplace, but the facts oblige us to respect this description. In 1762, well over a quarter of the letters printed in the definitive Besterman edition of Voltaire's correspondence (186 out of 628) mention Calas in one way or another. This number includes references made by Voltaire's correspondents also, but the overwhelming majority are by the *philosophe* himself. In 1763 the number of letters connected directly with the campaign or mentioning Calas in some way was about 131 out of 730; in 1764, 39 out of 680, and in 1765, 115 out of 804: in all, from 1762 to 1765, approximately 473 letters out of a total of 2,845 printed in the definitive Besterman edition. The effort deployed

Florentin en soit instruit' (Best.D10493). This is not the tone of a man who knows that he has the government's support.

[76] *La Religion*, p.328. The emotional nature of Voltaire's involvement in the Calas affair is stressed in Pomeau's account of the episode (pp.326-32).

on behalf of the Sirven family is also impressive. Though slightly fewer, the letters span a longer period: from 1763 to the end of 1770, some 334 letters mention Sirven and his case. These statistics are in themselves an eloquent tribute to Voltaire's energy and attest the determination with which he pursued his humanitarian goal.[77]

v. *The consequences of the Calas affair: initial optimism*

The essentially emotional basis of Voltaire's involvement in the Calas affair had an important consequence. He began to see the Protestants as people actually suffering from persecution rather than merely as an abstract religious and political problem. This is not to argue that he had been unaffected by earlier cases of repression, but Rochette, for example, was a pastor carrying out an illegal occupation. He had been trained abroad and could be regarded as a potential rebel. Jean Calas, the *bon père de famille*[78] and paragon of bourgeois virtue and normality, was a different matter. The cruelty of the laws was there for all to see. In the last analysis, the Toulouse merchant had suffered his horrible death merely for what he was and what he believed. The *philosophes* were in a similar position. Their existence was not proscribed, but they were liable to the same threat of arbitrary violence on the part of the establishment. They, like the Protestants, were a challenge to the status quo of the *ancien régime,* though, as we now see clearly, the Protestants were a legacy of its troubled past whereas the ideas represented by the *philosophes* were a far more dangerous threat to its future. At the time, however, this difference was less apparent, and both Protestants and *philosophes* were aware that all forms of dissidence might be persecuted with equal, though spasmodic, ferocity.[79] It is clear that even in the comparative safety of Ferney Voltaire at times still felt very insecure, as when he precipitately crossed the Swiss border after La Barre's execution, ostensibly to take the waters at Rolle (cf. Best.D13409). Less obviously than in the La Barre case, but just as surely, Voltaire felt himself threatened by the treatment meted out to Jean Calas.

But it was not only Voltaire and the *philosophes* who could identify with the *roué de Toulouse.* Every middle-class Frenchman, every respectable merchant and *père de famille* could consider the case and shake his head in dismay at the brutal judicial murder of one of his fellows.

[77] see appendix 2 for a list of these letters.
[78] Voltaire uses this expression in Best.D10394.
[79] cf. Elie Galland, *L'Affaire Sirven*, p.245.

This was why the case was so perfect to exploit in favour of Protestant civil rights. Jean Calas was not politically dangerous. He had attended no rebellious assemblies. His religion was a private matter in the four walls of his home. If most people could be brought round to thinking that *bourgeois* respectability was more important than harmless sectarian beliefs, then the day of – at least limited – toleration was at hand for the Protestants. The prosecution had, of course, made great play out of the religious element. Indeed, as things turned out, it became the basis of the whole case. But the accusation of fanaticism was successfully turned back against the authorities themselves. In Voltaire's propaganda the fuse was taken out of what had always been an explosive mixture, for particularly Protestant elements of Calas's religion were played down or disappeared altogether (cf. below, pp.292-93). So long as *bourgeois* opinion imagined the Protestants to be fanatical rebels fighting against the king and the possible cause of a civil war, this class could be relied on to support the attitude of the authorities. But the spectacle of an ageing family man broken on the wheel for a well-nigh inconceivable crime, was an altogether more disturbing image. And when his wife, *éplorée* and virtuous, came to the capital and could be seen in the salons of Paris, the *dénouement* of this *larmoyant drame bourgeois* could not seriously be in doubt.

I have pointed out, however, that Voltaire's intervention was not merely an attempt to capitalise on a situation ripe for exploitation. He had already experienced the emotions he tried to provoke in others and was totally committed in the action he took. In the past, Voltaire had probably felt a rather vague sympathy for his French Protestant contemporaries, while at the same time deploring their fanaticism. Henceforward he would still be rather suspicious of some of their religious manifestations, but the Calas case had promoted them to the forefront of his attention, both as victims of *l'infâme* and of arbitrary power. They were a sizeable minority of respectable people against whom the laws discriminated unfairly. They must be helped, and this Voltaire now set out to do.

Describing Voltaire's conduct at the time of the Roux-Roubel case (cf. below, pp.368-71), Charles Dardier comments: 'le vieux patriarche ne fit rien. La gloire qu'il avait recueillie de l'affaire Calas lui suffisait; il n'en chercha point d'autre.'[80] This sort of charge has often been

---

[80] *Un procès scandaleux à propos d'un mariage béni au désert* (offprint from *Etrennes chrétiennes*) (Geneva 1881), pp.39-40.

levelled against Voltaire by Protestant historians and commentators. Even in Dardier's time and earlier, some evidence was available to discredit this view conclusively (cf. below, p.371, n.202), and we now have a mine of new information in the definitive Besterman edition of Voltaire's correspondence. Anyone reading through the letters written after 1762 must be struck by the great number and diversity of the references to Protestantism in France, betokening an interest which remained firm throughout the rest of Voltaire's life. A brief review of these themes will demonstrate once and for all the absurdity of such criticisms as Dardier's.

The Calas case was followed by an initial optimism on Voltaire's part as regards the future of the French Protestants. In a letter written in August or September 1762 he told Philippe Debrus that he was by then sure the Calas family would obtain justice.[81] As regards the Protestant galley-slaves (on whose behalf Debrus had obviously asked him to intercede), 'il faudra un peu plus de temps et d'adresse'. But Voltaire's letter ends on a very encouraging note: 'pour faire cesser la persécution, il faudra la protection la plus secrète et la plus puissante; j'ose l'espérer pour l'honneur de la France.' Voltaire was now basing his optimism to a large extent on the good will of enlightened members of the ruling classes.

I have tried to show that Voltaire was at first unsure about the attitude of his influential friends, and that some of them actually tried to discourage him from taking a hand in the Calas case. Voltaire was already hard at work in an attempt to change this opposition. Choiseul had probably been favourable from the first, and mme de Pompadour also ranged herself in the philosophic camp (cf. above, p.288, n.75). Richelieu paid a visit to Ferney in October 1762 and Voltaire was able to convince the *maréchal* of Calas's innocence (Nixon, pp.162-63). But personal contacts were not enough: Voltaire was busy with a work he hoped would prove acceptable to a sufficient number of *hommes en place* to effect a real change in the Protestants' fortunes. This work was the *Traité sur la tolérance*.

Already, on about 28 July 1762, in connection with Donat Calas's *Mémoire*, Voltaire had written to Théodore Tronchin that it was necessary for a Protestant to speak with moderation and to try to disarm the prejudices against Calvinism in France: 'il m'a paru qu'un protestant

---

[81] Best.D10683. The editor is unable to date this letter more precisely.

ne devait pas désavouer sa religion, mais qu'il devait en parler avec modestie' (Best.D10613). Voltaire was obviously trying to gain as many allies as he could for the Protestant cause, and he hoped he could count the pro-Jansenist *parlements* among these. On the very next day he wrote again to Tronchin (Best.D10616):

entre nous, je sçais s'il est mal d'exposer en une seule page tout ce qui peut rendre la religion des Calas excusable aux yeux des Jansénistes, qui dans le fond pensent assez comme Claude, Evêque de Turin.[82] Il me paraît que tous les parlements de France, excepté celui de Toulouse, marchent à grands pas vers un protestantisme mitigé.

These then were Voltaire's main tactics in the *Traité*: to make Protestantism seem as socially innocuous as possible and to stress the advantages which a policy of toleration would bring to the nation.

The first argument is presented with some force. The Protestants are no longer made of the same stuff as their rebellious ancestors; they are peaceable, law-abiding citizens (*Mélanges*, p.575):

Les huguenots, sans doute, ont été enivrés de fanatisme et souillés de sang comme nous; mais la génération présente est-elle aussi barbare que leurs pères? Le temps, la raison qui fait tant de progrès, les bons livres, la douceur de la société, n'ont-ils point pénétré chez ceux qui conduisent l'esprit de ces peuples?

It would be difficult to ask a more rhetorical question. The Huguenots' assemblies, feared by the government as potentially rebellious, are not mentioned.[83] Voltaire admits that there are still some fanatics 'dans la populace calviniste', but says that there are many more among the Jansenist convulsionaries (p.581). He points out the cruel treatment suffered by Protestant pastors in France, emphasising the harmless religious function they carry out,[84] and he further claims that in no Protestant country are Catholic priests treated anything like as badly. Europe has changed entirely in the last fifty years, and in many countries formerly ravaged by religious wars, different sects now coexist in

---

[82] cf. above, p.24, especially n.12.

[83] the nearest Voltaire comes to this is when he says that Lutherans and Calvinists must cause no disorders (*Mélanges*, p.627).

[84] 'Nous envoyons encore quelquefois à la potence de pauvres gens du Poitou, du Vivarais, de Valence, de Montauban. Nous avons pendu, depuis 1745, huit personnages de ceux qu'on appelle *prédicants* ou *ministres de l'Evangile*, qui n'avaient d'autre crime que d'avoir prié Dieu pour le roi en patois, et d'avoir donné une goutte de vin et un morceau de pain levé à quelques paysans imbéciles' (*Mélanges*, p.599).

harmony: 'le juif, le catholique, le grec, le luthérien, le calviniste, l'anabaptiste, le socinien, le mennonite, le morave, et tant d'autres, vivent en frères dans ces contrées, et contribuent également au bien de la société' (p.576). There are points of real disagreement between Catholics and Protestants, but 'la fureur de la dispute est tellement amortie que les protestants eux-mêmes ne prêchent aujourd'hui la controverse en aucune de leurs églises' (p.583). The progress of reason has in fact at last enabled Christians of different sects to live together peaceably, and there is an example in their own kingdom which should convince the French: Alsace has a majority of Lutherans, but this leads to no civil strife (p.577). Why then should a limited toleration not be extended to Huguenots throughout France?

Having presented the Protestants and their religion in the most favourable light possible, Voltaire backs up his case with arguments likely to convince the hard-headed politicians at whom the *Traité* was largely aimed, the first being designed to appeal to those of pro-Gallican sentiments. Voltaire emphasises the good effects of the Reformation in an unequivocal manner which is distinctly different from that found in his other accounts of it (cf. above, pp.28-35, 44-48). He claims that the Protestants had been better educated than the Catholics, and for once goes on to praise the Reformers as he had never done, stressing their contribution to the progress of reason rather than to the growth of fanaticism and bloodshed in the sixteenth century: 'Ne dissimulons point que, malgré leurs erreurs, nous leur devons le développement de l'esprit humain, longtemps enseveli dans la plus épaisse barbarie' (pp.573-74). In recalling the abuses which the Protestants had justly attacked, Voltaire points a lesson for his own day and age: 'On peut [...] convenir sans blasphème que les hérétiques, en proposant l'abolition de ces impôts singuliers dont la postérité s'étonnera, ne faisaient pas en cela un grand mal au royaume, et qu'ils étaient plutôt bons calculateurs que mauvais sujets' (p.573). Gallicanism is here synonymous with practical economics.

Voltaire emphasises the expense of the 'annates, les procès en cour de Rome, et les dispenses qui subsistent encore aujourd'hui'. This was the sort of language to which one might expect the eternally bankrupt Court to pay attention. Voltaire had always emphasised the tragic economic effects of the repeal of the Edict of Nantes, and the same attitude is evident in most of his polemical works to obtain social recognition for the oppressed Huguenot minority. In the *Traité sur la tolérance* Voltaire does not push this argument into too great a prominence – it would, after all, seem a little out of place in what purports to be almost a semi-theological work – but he outlines the economic advantages clearly enough. The state's interest is to have a high population. What would one lose 'à voir la terre cultivée et ornée par plus de mains laborieuses, les tributs augmentés, l'Etat plus florissant?' (p.580). Germany would be a desert 'si la paix de Westphalie n'avait pas procuré enfin la liberté de conscience'. Finally Voltaire puts forward the most tempting prospect of all. In return for a basic minimum of civil rights, 'nous savons que plusieurs chefs de famille, qui ont élevé de grandes fortunes dans les pays étrangers, sont prêts à retourner dans leur patrie' (p.581). This inflow of capital would be a great advantage to the nation. On the question of toleration, politics and humanitarianism are for once in accord: 'l'humanité le demande, la raison le conseille, et la politique ne peut s'en effrayer' (p.583).

The *Traité*, however, is not merely a pamphlet arguing in favour of Huguenot toleration written from a moderate Protestant standpoint. Although Voltaire does claim (Best.D11632) that the work is by 'un protestant assez instruit, qui demande que ses frères puissent cultiver la terre en France, au lieu d'enrichir les pays étrangers', it is obvious enough that its author is a *philosophe*. This is plain from the characteristic attacks on some of the basic tenets of Christianity, attacks which were unacceptable to both Catholics and Protestants alike. For although Voltaire had submitted his work to the scrutiny of some Protestant ministers,[85] it was soon found to be very far from pleasing the majority of their colleagues. Paul Rabaut[86] was to write rather suspiciously to Court de Gébelin on 30 December 1763: 'On m'écrit de geneve que mr. de Voltaire a mis, aujour un ouvrage en faveur de la tolerance; je serois bien curieux de le lire. il y avance, dit on, un singulier paradoxe, c'est que les premiers chretiens ne furent point persecutés.'[87] The

---

[85] on 4 January 1763 Voltaire wrote to Gabriel Cramer: 'On lui renverra incessamment le traitté sur la tolérance, sur lequel on a consulté des ministres du St Evangile, et qui par conséquent sera approuvé de Dieu et des hommes' (Best.D10882).

[86] successor of Antoine Court and leader of the French Protestants during the second part of the eighteenth century. Born at Bédarieux near Montpellier, Rabaut studied at Lausanne in 1741, became acquainted with Court who was in exile there, and on his return to France rapidly assumed a position of importance.

[87] Bib pf, Collection Coquerel, Papiers Rabaut, 318, f.6; photocopy Theodore Besterman (Best.D11590, commentary). See appendix 3 for another example of hostile Protestant reaction to the *Traité* and the identity of the pastors consulted by Voltaire.

references to the Roman Catholic church are certainly more moderate than Voltaire's usual utterances,[88] but the effect of these passages on most practising Catholics would be more than cancelled out by the attacks on martyrs and false legends (chapters 9 and 10). In fact, as might be expected, the improvement in conditions which Voltaire claims has taken place in the previous fifty years[89] is attributed neither to Protestants nor to Catholics: 'La philosophie, la seule philosophie, cette sœur de la religion, a désarmé des mains que la superstition avait longtemps ensanglantées, et l'esprit humain, au réveil de son ivresse, s'est étonné des excès ou l'avait emporté le fanatisme' (p.577). Not a very surprising statement on Voltaire's part, perhaps, but why does he jeopardise the success of his campaign by taking the risk of alienating both Protestants and Catholics? Is this a result of blind philosophic prejudice, or is there another reason?

Two important letters to the pastor Paul Moultou written in January 1763 not only answer our question but also admirably sum up Voltaire's attitude to this type of polemical writing. Voltaire was still doing his homework for parts of the *Traité*. On 2 January he asked Moultou what the latter knew about the *Accord parfait* mentioned by 'ce fripon d'abbé de Caveirac' (Best.D10877). The book was obviously lent to Voltaire, as he wrote again to Moultou on 5 January (Best.D10885) with some interesting reflections on the work, of which he had read a large part 'avec attention'. He admits that there are some good things on the subject of toleration, but thinks the book has one great defect: 'c'est qu'il dit continuellement que les catholiques ont toujours eu tort, et les protestans toujours raison; que tous les Chefs des catholiques étaient des monstres, et les chefs des protestants des saints'. This is a pitfall Voltaire himself obviously did not intend to fall into in the *Traité*, a fact which, to a large extent, explains his moderate language and demands: 'quand on attaque violemment une secte en demandant grâce', he observes, 'on

[88] e.g. he praises the *corps des évêques* in France, which, he says, 'est composé de gens de qualité qui pensent et qui agissent avec une noblesse digne de leur naissance: ils sont charitables et généreux, c'est une justice qu'on [doit] leur rendre' (*Mélanges*, p.577), but it is rather too obvious from the context that this compliment is made for propaganda reasons.

[89] 'On ne craint plus en Hollande que les disputes d'un Gomar sur la prédestination fassent trancher la tête au grand pensionnaire. On ne craint plus à Londres que les querelles des presbytériens et des épiscopaux, pour une liturgie et pour un surplis, répandent le sang d'un roi sur un échafaud. L'Irlande, peuplée et enrichie, ne verra plus ses citoyens sacrifier à Dieu pendant deux mois ses citoyens protestants' (*Mélanges*, pp.576-77).

obtient la haine, et point de grâce'. Voltaire urges Moultou to write on
tolerance: the *Accord parfait* will never be read at Court as it is too long
and declamatory: 'il faut être très court, et un peu salé, sans quoi les
ministres et mad^e de Pompadour, les Commis et les femmes de Chambre,
font des papillotes du livre' (Best.D10885). This is a maxim which
Voltaire plainly took to heart in the *Traité*, as he explains to Moultou
in Best.D10897 (9 January 1763):

J'ai beaucoup retravaillé l'ouvrage en question; je me dis toujours, il faut
tâcher qu'on te lise sans dégoût; c'est par le plaisir qu'on vient à bout des
hommes; répands quelques poignées de sel et d'épices dans le ragoût que
tu leur présentes, mêle le ridicule aux raisons, tâche de faire naître l'indifférence, alors tu obtiendras sûrement la tolérance.

The tactic had been explained even more clearly in Best.D10885 (5
January 1763):

Sous un autre gouvernement, je n'aurais pas osé hazarder quelques petites
notes, dont il est très aisé de tirer d'étranges Conséquences; mais je connais
assez ceux qui gouvernent, pour être sûr que ces conséquences ne leur dé-
plairont pas. Je pense même qu'il n'y a d'autre moien d'obtenir la tolérance,
que d'inspirer beaucoup d'indifférence pour les préjugés, en montrant
pourtant pour ces préjugés mêmes, un respect qu'ils ne méritent pas.

Here then is the reason for the moderate tone Voltaire employs when
speaking of the Catholic Church in the *Traité*, and at the same time for
the attacks there on its historical foundations. Voltaire felt sure enough
of the government's attitude, and he wished to inspire tolerance through
indifference among the people who counted. He probably saw himself
in a rôle like that of Michel de L'Hospital, the French chancellor he had
portrayed as a voice of reason in the religious wars of the sixteenth
century. L'Hospital had tried to influence the *politiques*, men who despised the extremism of both Catholics and Protestants (cf. *Essai*,
ii.484).

Voltaire's initial optimism over the prospects of improving the
Huguenots' position was therefore grounded in the support he thought
the government was willing to give to this policy. On 25 February 1763
he wrote again to Moultou: 'Je suis sûr que mr le controlleur général,
mr le Duc de Praslin, mr le Duc de Choiseuil, mad^e de Pompadour ont
de très bonnes intentions; il faut assurément en profiter' (Best.D11043).
On 3 April, in another letter to Moultou, he discussed how he would
send out copies of the *Traité* to people in high places (Best.D11148).

Panic had been caused for a time by the *Toulousaines*,[90] a virulent work in favour of the Calas family written by Antoine Court's son, Court de Gébelin. None of the rules of prudence Voltaire had so carefully followed himself was respected, and he was afraid that the *Toulousaines* would ruin everything, for on 7 March the first real progress in the Calas campaign had been achieved,[91] and if the *Toulousaines* were published Saint-Florentin, 'qui n'est déjà que trop prévenu contre les Calas', would be able to tell the king that the Protestants were seditious and attacked the *parlements* indiscriminately. Moreover, Gébelin had linked the Sirven affair with that of the Calas family, and this could be fatal.[92] Voltaire explained his policy to Vernes: 'Les ouvrages qu'on peut écrire sur cette matière délicate, ne peuvent être confiés qu'à des personnes sûres, et qui sont en état de servir' (Best.D11097). Fortunately, Gébelin was prevailed upon to withdraw his work, at least for, the time being, and on 4 April Voltaire again expresses his optimism, this time to Végobre. Discretion is necessary among the Protestants in the *midi* because there is real hope for the future. The ministers are in favour of tolerance; only one is against it, 'et on le fléchira'. Voltaire was further encouraged by the appointment of Maupeou, who he thought would be favourable to the Protestant cause, as vice-chancellor and *garde des sceaux* (cf. Best.D11470, n.1). A letter from the duc de Choiseul, written on 27 November 1763, shows that Voltaire's statements were not just wishful thinking but that he had good reason for his confidence in at least some members of the government. The minister informed him of the success of the *Traité* (Best.D11518):

Madame de Pompadour, madame de Gramont, tous ceux qui ont lu, ou liront le livre de votre prêtre, en ont été enchantés; chacun se dit après l'avoir lu: il faut convenir qu'il a raison, et j'ai toujours pensé de même; je me garde bien de vous dire mon avis sur le fond de la matière (car le livre m'a fait un plaisir infini à lire).

[90] *Les Toulousaines ou lettres historiques et apologétiques en faveur de la religion réformée, et de divers Protestants condamnés dans ces derniers tems par le Parlement de Toulouse, ou dans le Haut Languedoc* (Edimbourg [Lausanne] 1763).

[91] 'un conseil extraordinaire [. . .] composé de tous les ministres d'Etat, de tous les conseillers d'Etat, et de tous les maîtres des requêtes [. . .] admettant la requête en cassation a ordonné d'une voix unanime, que le parlement de Toulouse enverrait incessamment les procédures, et les motifs de son arrêt' (Best.D11097, Voltaire to Vernes, 14 March 1763).

[92] many Protestants were in agreement with Voltaire: on 31 June 1763 one of the elders of the Montauban church wrote to Rabaut asking that the *Toulousaines* should be suppressed (Coquerel, ii.494), and the work was in fact banned in Geneva.

This was heady praise indeed, coming from someone of Choiseul's importance, and on 4 December Voltaire delightedly informed his *anges* of the good news: 'Monsieur le Duc De Choiseuil me mande qu'il en est *enchanté*, ainsi que mad^e De Grammont, et Mad^e De Pompadour. Peut être qu'un jour ce livre produira le bien, dont il n'aura d'abord fait voir que le germe' (Best.D11528).

Voltaire's efforts in the Protestant cause during 1763 had not been entirely restricted to writing and distributing the *Traité sur la tolérance*. He made enquiries about the marquis de Gouvernet, Charles-Frédéric de La Tour Du Pan de Bourbon, who in 1727 had married mlle de Livry, one of Voltaire's former mistresses.[93] The couple lived in Paris, in the rue Condé, and mlle Livry was still known under her maiden name, 'attendu que nous ne marions point les maudits huguenots en face de l'Eglise, avec les bénis catholiques'.[94] Voltaire was also keeping his attention on the Protestant south. In a letter to Ribotte, he makes a passing reference to the holding of a synod, which may very possibly have been the last national synod to take place under the *ancien régime*.[95] On 12 September he told Végobre that he had written to Richelieu 'le plus fortement que j'ai pu, en faveur de Mr Carbon', and he assured him of the *maréchal*'s protection (Best.D11412). About six weeks later, Voltaire asked Végobre to pass on his compliments to 'Mr de Carbon. Mr le M^al de Richelieu qui est malade aux eaux, ne m'a point encor répondu sur ce qui regarde ce gentilhomme. J'aurai l'honneur de lui écrire dès qu'il sera de retour à Bordeaux' (Best.D11470). Dedieu provides us with some interesting information about the gentleman in question (*Histoire politique*, i.381):

[93] 'Vous sçavez peut être qu'il a le malheur d'être huguenot, mais il pourait nous être fort utile' (Best.D11046, Voltaire to Philippe Debrus, *c.* 25 February 1763). For information on the marquis, see Best.D11098, n.1.

[94] Best.D11098, Voltaire to Debrus, 14 or 15 March 1763. It is not clear from these references exactly why he wished to contact the *marquis*, but the matter is elucidated by a comment made many years later in a letter Voltaire wrote to Bernard-Joseph Saurin. Perhaps m. de Gouvernet had still been jealous of him – at any rate he had refused to help the Protestant cause which his former rival was supporting: 'J'ai toujours oublié de vous demander, si Mlle de Livry nôtre ancienne amie vit encor. Je me souviens que du tems de l'avanture horrible des Calas j'écrivis à Mr de Gouvernet pour le prier de s'intéresser à cette famille infortunée. Il ne me fit point de réponse, et ne voulut point voir Mad^e Calas; il ne mérite pas de vieillir, cependant je ne souhaitte pas qu'il soit mort' (Best.D17585, 2 February 1772; cf. also Best.D11186).

[95] 'Il est fort aise que vos protestants assemblent des synodes et serait encore plus aise que les philosophes en assemblassent' (Best.D11436, 28 September; cf. below, p.381).

Le duc de Fitzjames, successeur du maréchal de Thomond en Languedoc, s'était chargé de plaider, devant le Secrétaire d'Etat, la cause du réfugié Carbon, dont un frère était conseiller au parlement de Toulouse. Malgré le vif désir de complaire au nouveau gouverneur, Saint-Florentin s'opposa nettement au retour du réfugié: 'On ne pourrait, disait-il, refuser la même permission à un nombre infini de personnes qui viendraient moins pour augmenter le commerce et la population, que pour semer l'erreur sur la religion et l'esprit républicain sur le gouvernement, qu'elles auraient gagné pendant leur séjour en pays étranger.'

Saint-Florentin had written this letter on 15 August, and it seems likely that an appeal was then made to Voltaire on Carbon's behalf, after the failure of the duc de Fitzjames's efforts. Voltaire's intervention was more successful, for on 9 December he was able to report to Végobre: 'Mr Le Maréchal de Richelieu me mande qu'il accorde toute sa protection à mr de Carbon, et que si on voulait lui faire la moindre peine, il l'en ferait avertir' (Best.D11546). Richelieu does in fact seem to have taken Carbon under his wing, for just over a year later, Voltaire was to write to his friend Moultou, who was also hoping to stay for a time in the south of France (Best.D12308, 11 or 12 January 1765):

pour vous rassurer je vous dirai que lorsque mr Carbon s'en retourna avec sa famille, je demandai un passeport à mr le mᵃˡ de Richelieu, qui m'envoia faire faire avec mon passeport, et qui me dit que pourvu que ce mr Carbon n'ameuta point le peuple et ne priât point Dieu la bayonnette au bout du fusil, il serait le très bien venu. Il est aujourd'hui très tranquile et très heureux dans sa patrie; et cependant il était violemment soupçone d'être apôtre.

The eighteen months or so after the Calas affair were by and large, therefore, a time of optimism. After a short period of doubt, Voltaire became convinced of the good intentions of the government. The position of the Protestants seemed likely to improve quickly. On 5 January 1763 he told Moultou he thought that 'l'avanture des Calas peut servir à relâcher beaucoup les chaines de vos frères qui prient Dieu en fort mauvais vers' (Best.D10885). A similar opinion was expressed to Debrus on 14 March: 'On songe à eux plus qu'ils ne pensent, *et je vous répète ce que je vous ai dit depuis six mois, qu'il poura naître un grand bien de l'horrible mal qui s'est commis.*'[96] Towards the end of the year, however, a change occurs. On 9 December Voltaire confides in Végobre that Court de Gébelin is in Paris under an assumed name. Voltaire has

---

[96] Best.D11093; cf. also the letter of 15 February to cardinal de Bernis (Best.D11009).

given him introductions to several influential people, and he assures Végobre that 'il y a des hommes en place qui sont tout aussi zélés que moi'. But Voltaire's former optimism seems to have waned a little. He fears that Gébelin will try to rush things too much: 'plus cette affaire est importante, plus elle demande des ménagements extrêmes.' And on 30 December the tone is definitely one of a certain discouragement: 'La Tolérance me tient aussi un peu en échec. Il y a un homme qui travaille à la cour en faveur des huguenots, et qui probablement ne réussira guère. On me fait craindre que la race des dévots ne se déchaîne contre ma tolérance. Heureusement mon nom n'y est pas' (Best.D11593, Voltaire to the d'Argentals). The popular outcry which followed the Calas case and the campaign led by Voltaire had no doubt somewhat discomfited the forces of reaction. Now, however, they were re-forming and making themselves felt. They had in Saint-Florentin a reliable foothold in the government. The letter from Choiseul congratulating Voltaire on the *Traité* should indeed have given him an indication that it would not be quite so easy to win tolerance as he had supposed. Choiseul recounts how he has tried to give temporary employment in France to Germans who were to be colonists in French Guyana: 'j'ai essuyé un refus presque total et me suis attiré une tracasserie énorme, parce que, après avoir pensé à tout, j'ai oublié qu'il y avait quelque Allemand dans le nombre qui avait le malheur d'être luthérien' (Best. D11518). If even the plans of such a powerful minister could be thwarted by the clergy, it was plain that Voltaire would have to revise his opinion: a radical change in the situation of the Protestants would not be achieved in the immediate future.

vi. *Fluctuating hopes and fortunes: 1764-1766*

The beginning of 1764 saw Voltaire in a more realistic mood concerning the prospects of the *Traité sur la tolérance*. On 8 January he wrote to the Swiss pastor Allamand, giving a full account of the situation. There is perhaps a slight note of disappointment in Voltaire's tone, but it is accompanied by a more qualified and sensible optimism than he had been displaying in the previous year (Best.D11629):

On m'a dit que les premières personnes de France, c'est à dire, celles qui ont le plus de crédit, approuvaient cet ouvrage, et que cependant il n'aura pas tout l'effet qu'on s'en était promis. Il poura servir à relâcher un peu, et à rendre plus légers, les fers dont [on] accable cinq ou six cent mille malheureux, qui n'ont d'autre crime que d'être un peu opiniâtres.

A letter to Végobre written on about 10 January expresses similar sentiments. Voltaire says he is sorry not to be able to do more for the Protestants. He does not despair of opening the eyes of the Court, but at the
moment 'les finances pressent plus que la religion' (Best.D11635).
However, this fact may help the situation of Protestant refugees when
the government realises that Huguenot money is just as good as Catholic
money. The *Traité* then was having a less immediate effect than Voltaire
had hoped,[97] but he did not relapse into an unproductive pessimism.

On 27 January, an interesting request for information was made to
Jean Ribotte in Montauban: 'S'il y a quelque sotise nouvelle, monsieur
Ribote est prié d'en faire part à celui qui rit de toutes les sotises qui sont
frivoles, et qui tâche de réparer celles qui sont barbares' (Best.D11666).
Voltaire the pragmatist did not intend to forget about the Huguenots,
and his interest in Protestant affairs in the years succeeding the Calas
case was very wide-ranging, to say the least: interventions with the
authorities, references in the *Dictionnaire philosophique* and other
important works, nothing was neglected in his efforts to make the plight
of the Protestants better known and to improve their conditions.

Already, in January 1764, Voltaire was turning his attention to the
case of the Sirven family.[98] He informed Végobre that he had seen
Sirven and suggested that a safe-conduct to the court might be a good
idea, so that Sirven could go and plead his case in person. On 4 March
Voltaire expressed his surprise to Damilaville at a report that the Protestants of Alsace were being troubled by the authorities – this was
not Choiseul's intention, he claimed (Best.D11747). The *philosophe* was
also keeping up with the theoretical debate about the rights of Protestants. He asked Moultou about Turmeau de La Morandière's *Principes
sur le rappel des Protestants en France*. Voltaire criticised this work for not
being liberal enough, although he admitted that he had not yet read it,
and that he might be mistaken. But perhaps the most significant development of 1764 in the Protestant cause was Voltaire's success in achieving
the liberation of the galley slave Claude Chaumont.

According to the letter of the law (the 1724 edict–cf. above, pp.264-65),
any adult male Protestant caught attending an illegal assembly was
liable to be sentenced to the galleys for life. In practice, however,
severity was the exception rather than the rule, and the rigour of the
edicts was applied only when it was felt that an example should be made.

---

[97] cf. also Best.D11663 and D11664 where Voltaire expresses comparable ideas.
[98] the most comprehensive study on this topic is Elie Galland, *L'Affaire Sirven*.

Moreover, not all those condemned to the galleys were actually sent there. According to Coquerel 'il paraît [...] qu'on exécutait au plus un tiers des condamnations' (i.432). Unfortunately for Claude Chaumont, however, he was one of those upon whom sentence was put into effect, and his ordeal began in 1751 (cf. above, p.270). Conditions on the galleys at the turn of the eighteenth century had been terrible, and many Protestants died at their task.[99] As the *siècle des lumieres* progressed, however, the lot of the Protestant galley slaves improved a little, though it was still hardly a life to be envied. Money was sent to them from Protestants all over Europe and from their French brethren also. By the 1760s some more favoured prisoners did not have to work on the galleys at all, but were allowed to run small businesses in Toulon. Moreover, the number of slaves had fallen dramatically as the century wore on. Small groups were released periodically as a result of interventions from Protestant powers or personalities. A case in point occurred in 1755 during the visit to the south of France of the margrave and margravine of Bayreuth. A *placet* by Paul Rabaut appealed to them to intercede with the government on behalf of the Protestant slaves, and as a result of their efforts several *galériens* were freed (Coquerel, ii.412-14). It also appears that the duc de Richelieu forestalled his friend Voltaire in this charitable activity, for a letter dated 28 September 1755 written by the galley-slave Bonnafous to his son claimed that Richelieu ' "solicitait fort et ferme à la cour", en faveur des protestants des galères' (Coquerel, ii.410). According to Coquerel's figures there were forty-eight Protestant slaves at Toulon in 1753; by 1759 this had fallen to forty-one, and by 1764 to a mere twenty, although, as we shall see shortly, the number referred to by Voltaire himself was somewhat larger. Despite these advances there was still opposition in the government to a policy of liberalism. Prompted by Paul Rabaut, the duke of Bedford, English plenipotentiary in the 1762 peace negotiations, canvassed for the release of the Protestant galley-slaves and the women who were still imprisoned in the tour de Constance. Choiseul apparently agreed to this request: thirty-seven men and twenty women were to be released, but this was counting without Saint-Florentin, who turned down the idea out of hand (Dedieu, *Histoire politique*, ii.11-15). An

[99] for the most comprehensive study on Protestant galley-slaves see Gaston Tournier, *Les Galères de France et les galériens protestants des XVIIe et XVIIIe siècles* (Musée du désert 1945-1949); also S. Mours, 'Note sur les galériens protestants (1683-1775)', *Bpf* (1970), cxvi.178-231.

intervention on the same lines by the duc de Praslin was also turned down. Much obviously depended, therefore, on the tug of war for power among various members of the government and on their standing when any particular request for clemency was made. Sometimes Saint-Florentin was able to stand firm, sometimes he was overruled by the other ministers.

Voltaire's intervention on behalf of Chaumont in 1764 seems to have been made at a particularly favourable moment. The rapid success of his request must have surprised even the *philosophe* himself. It was from Louis Necker that the appeal to help Chaumont had come, and Voltaire replied on 11 January in a typically bantering, irreverent way. He says he is writing to Choiseul on behalf of 'vôtre martyr le cordonnier', but he is not sure whether this matter is in Choiseul's department (Best. D11637). On 15 February Voltaire is boasting to Damilaville that the *Traité sur la tolérance* has already delivered a few *galériens*, 'condamnés pour avoir entendu en plein champ de mauvais sermons de sots prêtres calvinistes' (Best.D11699). These rather exaggerated claims probably refer only to Chaumont, as on the same day Voltaire announced to Necker that he would be very pleased for Chaumont to come and make him a pair of shoes (Best.D11700). No wonder Voltaire felt proud of having obtained the release of a galley-slave in under a month.

This success made Voltaire feel that it would be comparatively easy to obtain freedom for the rest of the Protestant slaves. He therefore asked Necker to supply him with a list of the *galériens*, and the phrasing of this request demonstrates that Voltaire did not only intend to be well informed – his campaign would not be lacking in characteristic irony either (Best.D11700, 15 February 1764):

Ayez la bonté, Monsieur, de m'envoier les noms, surnoms, mêtiers, galêres, numéros, de vos martirs de la sottise, condamnés à ramer par le fanatisme; il ne serait pas mal de spécifier en marge, les mérites de chaque particulier. Par éxemple, Isaac, pour être allé armé, entendre la parole de Dieu. Jacob, pour avoir donné un souflet à un prêtre. Daniel, pour avoir parlé irrévérentieusement de la présence réelle, etc.

Voltaire promises that he will send the list to the government, and do his very best to prevent any more Protestants being dispatched to the galleys. Probably on the same day he wrote to Necker, Voltaire observed to Moultou that it was a pity only one galley-slave had been released whereas there were still twenty-three in irons 'pour avoir prié dieu mal à propos' (Best.D11702). The next day he informed Végobre of Choiseul's intervention in favour of Chaumont, and added: 'Il a quelques compagnons, dont je ne désepère pas de briser les fers et les rames. L'esprit de Tolérance commence à s'introduire sur les ruines du fanatisme. Bénissons en Dieu' (Best.D11706). On 1 March Voltaire asked Végobre for information about another galley-slave 'Paul Achard, natif de Chatillon au département de Grenoble, lequel (par parenthèse) est aux galères depuis l'année 1745.' Was he any relation to 'Mr. Achard, citoien de Genêve'?[100] It seems that the *philosophe* was already planning a second intervention on the heels of the first, but, as had already happened in connection with the *Traité*, Voltaire's hopes, at first very high, were soon to be somewhat disappointed.

The bad news was obviously received by Voltaire just after 1 March, perhaps in a letter from Choiseul himself, for on 4 March he told Végobre sadly: 'Vous savez qu'en France les circonstances des affaires changent prèsque tous les jours; et ce qu'on pouvait hier on ne le peut demain' (Best.D11748). And writing to Necker the next day, he commented: 'Je crains bien, Monsieur, de ne pas m'élever plus haut que la cheville du pied, et d'être obligé de m'en tenir à la délivrance du pauvre cordonnier' (Best.D11750). On 6 March Voltaire received a visit from the *pauvre cordonnier* in person, and the scene, described to Paul Rabaut by Etienne Chiron, who presented Chaumont to the *philosophe,* not only provides a delightfully amusing glimpse of Voltaire *chez lui,* it also confirms that Chaumont's case was exceptional: 'Une seule lettre que j'ai écrite à m. de Choiseul a opéré cet élargissement; mais aussi c'est le seul galérien pour lequel j'ai écrit et pour lequel j'oserai écrire.'[101] The balance of power and circumstances had obviously changed subtly in the government. Saint-Florentin had no doubt resented Choiseul's intervention and had taken steps to prevent its repetition. Perhaps this is why Chiron adds towards the end of his letter: 'Il faut prendre garde

[100] Best.D11740. Paul Achard, born at Chatillon in Dauphiné in 1710 and condemned by the Toulouse *parlement* on 9 February 1746 'pour avoir sauvé un prédicant', was in fact one of the last Protestant galley-slaves to be released, in 1775 (*La France protestante,* i.30; vi.213).

[101] Best.D11751. Coquerel (ii.426-27) accepts Voltaire's statement at face value and comments: 'On voit [. . .] que Voltaire lui-même avait pris ses précautions [. . .] pour bien faire comprendre qu'il n'entendait pas se mêler davantage du sort des galériens du désert [. . .] Aussi, même après cette haute intervention, qui aurait pu être suivie d'une amnistie bien plus générale, les compagnons d'infortunes du galérien délivré restèrent dans le bagne de Toulon.' Fortunately, we shall soon see how mistaken Coquerel's opinion is regarding Voltaire's conduct and intentions.

305

de ne pas trop publier certains détails, qui pourraient peut-être choquer une personne qu'il faut extrêmement ménager.'

Despite this setback Voltaire had taken the plight of the galley-slaves to heart, and he conceived an ingenious solution to the problem.[102] In a long and detailed letter to Louis Necker, Voltaire outlines his proposals. He emphasises again the exceptional nature of Choiseul's intervention on behalf of Chaumont: 'le ministre à qui je m'adressai [. . .] a eu besoin de beaucoup d'adresse pour réussir aussi vite qu'il a fait dans une chose qui n'est pas de son ministère' (Best.D11785, 19 March 1764). It will be impossible to do likewise for the other twenty-four Protestant slaves, the majority of whom had been condemned by *parlements*. However, Voltaire has put forward his own propositions in view of Choiseul's 'prédilection pour la nouvelle Colonie de la Guiane'.[103] The proposal is basically that the *galériens* should agree to go to Guyana as colonists, taking with them members of their families and friends, if possible. The 20,000 *livres* which Necker has mentioned as available to help obtain liberty for the slaves could be used to buy provisions, tools and other necessaries, though the ministry would probably help. In Voltaire's opinion the Protestants ought not to ask permission to build a *temple* or to take pastors with them. This they should do secretly: 'il faut qu'ils se présentent comme cultivateur soit d'indigo, ou de cochenille, ou de cotton, ou de soye, ou de Tabac, ou de sucre, et non comme le peuple de Dieu passant les mers pour aller chanter les pseaumes de Marot' (Best.D11785). The governor in Guyana will be a tolerant man. In fact it was to be Turgot's brother, Etienne François.[104] Voltaire urges Necker to find out the galley-slaves' attitude as soon as possible, since there is no time to lose. One can never be sure about anything, but he thinks the minister will be able to make this plan succeed. Vol-

---

[102] news of his initial success had got through to the *galériens*, as he tells Turgot: 'Les 24 martirs s'imaginèrent que j'avais tout pouvoir sur la Meditérranée; ils me firent écrire qu'ils pouraient donner quinze ou vingt mille francs pour obtenir leur délivrance' (Best. D11786, 19 March 1764).

[103] the interest shown by Choiseul and his cousin, the duc de Praslin, was not without justification: 'Le premier soin du Gouvernement, lors des études préparatoires et bien avant aucun commencement d'exécution, avait été la concession aux ducs de Choiseul et de Praslin de toutes les terres comprises entre la rive gauche du Kourou et la rive droite du Maroni. C'étaient environ cent soixante kilomètres qui leur étaient livrés en toute propriété, pour eux et leurs successeurs, avec droit de pêche et de chasse et tous les privilèges accordés aux vice-royautés' (Pierre Calmettes, *Choiseul et Voltaire* (Paris 1902), p.175).

[104] Best.D11785, n.1. Choiseul later described this man as 'un fol et fripon en même temps' (Calmettes, p.197).

taire's opinion is perhaps best summed up in the comment: 'Il me parait qu'il vaut mieux s'enrichir à la Cayenne, que d'être enchainé à Marseilles' (Best.D11785).

That this enterprising plan came to nothing was certainly a blessing in disguise for the men he was trying to help, although Voltaire could not possibly know this at the time. He wrote to Turgot on 19 March (Best.D11786) explaining the proposals he was making on behalf of the Protestants and asking for the support of Turgot and his brother. By 6 April he still had not heard from Necker. Voltaire therefore wrote again emphasising that he must know about the *galériens'* intentions as soon as possible. Guyana is a marvellous country, he claims: the Protestants would have freedom of conscience there – and could make a lot of money! 'Ce qui après la liberté et les pseaumes de Marot est une fort bonne chose' (Best.D11813). As it turned out, Choiseul's colony was a terrible failure and ended in total disaster. Within two years practically all the colonists had perished.[105] The Protestant galley-slaves would appear to have retained the prophetical insight of the Camisard *illuminés*, for they apparently turned down Voltaire's offer – 'Mes gens ont préféré les galères à la Guiane', he informed the d'Argentals in disgust. The account he gives of the incident is worth quoting: 'Ils avaient promis de s'embarquer avec chacun mille écus. Croiriez vous que ces drôles là quand il a fallu tenir leur parole ont fait comme les compagnons d'Ulisse qui aimèrent mieux rester cochons que de redevenir hommes?' (Best.D11930, 17 June 1764). Are we to believe that Necker had written again in the intervening weeks to accept the offer on behalf of the slaves, who subsequently had changed their minds again? Or was this wishful thinking on Voltaire's part? Necker's original slowness in replying does not seem to imply that the galley-slaves had been particularly attracted to the idea of becoming colonists. As far as one can tell, therefore, Voltaire's story to the d'Argentals seems a pure fabrication. He was no doubt piqued by what he saw as the unreasonable refusal of a generously conceived plan, and he did not

[105] cf. Best.D11518 and Calmettes, pp.188-90. On 14 July 1763 three ships and 127 colonists had arrived at Cayenne. Unfortunately, organisation was chaotic and nothing had been achieved by the time eleven more ships arrived under the command of m. de Chauvalon, on 22 December 1763, bringing another 429 emigrants. In all 9,000 colonists arrived, virtually without food or other resources. The chevalier de Turgot did not even visit the colony until December 1764, and he left again the following April with the 900 surviving emigrants.

scruple to make the Huguenots' part in this affair seem more damning than it really was.

On another front, however, things were going well: 'Cette horrible avanture des Calas a fait ouvrir les yeux à beaucoup de monde. Les exemplaires de la tolérance se sont répandues dans les provinces, où l'on était bien sot. Les écailles tombent des yeux, le règne de la vérité est proche' (Best.D11930). Propaganda in favour of toleration had originally been addressed mainly to the influential few in control of France's destinies. But Voltaire was now beginning to realise the powerful effect of the Calas campaign on public opinion, and as the 1760s went on he periodically expressed his conviction that the growing enlightenment would help the cause of toleration. He was not therefore disposed to sulk because one of his plans in favour of the Huguenots had not had the success he had hoped for. Encouraging news came that the famous advocate Elie de Beaumont had undertaken the defence of one Potin, a Protestant who had married abroad and the validity of whose union was now being questioned. 'J'ai reçu le factum pour Potin et pour l'humanité', Voltaire told Damilaville on 28 May (Best.D11896), and he sent it off to Végobre on the same day (Best.D11897). Further details were forthcoming on 9 June, when Voltaire informed Végobre, a little over optimistically: 'Mr. Beaumont l'avocat, qui plaide actuellement la légitimité du mariage du sr Potin compte gagner sa cause au Parlement de Paris, et l'arrêt obtenu mettre en sûreté les mariages des protestans, sans autre formalité.'[106] Voltaire also wrote to Beaumont himself, commenting on the stupidity of the legislation in this matter, and expressing a wish that 'Il viendra peut être un temps où il y aura des loix. Nous n'avons guères jusqu'icy, que des recueils d'arrêts qui se contredisent' (Best.D12015, 26 July 1764).

Moultou's name has often been mentioned in the preceding pages as one of Voltaire's main correspondents on the Protestant question. In 1765 he comes into prominence in his own right, for on 11 January Voltaire wrote to the duc de Praslin asking for a passport for Moultou so that he could go to Montpellier for reasons of health.[107] This 'philo-

---

[106] Best.D11917; cf. also Best.D11956, D12008, D12587 for other brief references to Potin and his case.

[107] Best.D12306. Cf. also Leigh 3951 (Moultou to Rousseau, 30 January 1765): 'La santé de mon pére qui va de mal en pis, le determine a faire un voyage a Montpellier, il espère d'y trouver des Secours plus efficaces que ceux qu'il avoit icy [. . .] Come nôtre voiage sera de Six mois au moins, je prends avec moi ma feme et deux de mes enfants.'

sophe des plus décidés et des plus aimables' (Best.D12309) was obviously rather worried about the risk he would be taking. On 11 or 12 January (Best.D12308) Voltaire reassured him by pointing out that Carbon had experienced no difficulties at all on his return to France (cf. above, pp.299-300), and on 23 January he added that 'La petite avanture de mr Jalabert arriva dans un temps suspect, et il y eut des circonstances particulières qui n'ont rien de commun avec la situation présente'.[108] Moultou was obviously concerned to make clear to the authorities that he was a pastor, and this had been causing Voltaire some difficulties (Best.D12343, 23 January 1765):

Vous savez bien, mon cher philosophe, que j'écrivis le vendredi, et qu'en conséquence de la rage que vous aviez d'être intitulé ministre du St Evangile, j'écrivis encor le samedi. On me mande en réponse de la Lettre du vendredy que vous aurez vôtre passeport. Mais je tremble, je vous l'avoue, que la Lettre du samedi n'ait tout gâté. Il est très certain qu'avec un passeport du ministre vous auriez été dans la plus grande sécurité.

The passport did in fact take more time to come, and Moultou did not set off on his journey until the middle of March. Voltaire's efforts on behalf of his friend are attested by frequent references to Moultou's passport in the letters of this period (cf. Best.D12345, D12355, D12360, D12361, D12378, D12386, D12393, D12406).

A rather more significant event than Moultou's visit to Montpellier also took place in March 1765. This was the reversal, on 9 March 1765, of the Toulouse *parlement*'s judgement against Jean Calas. Voltaire's campaign had been crowned with success, and it was probably this heartening news which caused him to write in great spirits to Elie Bertrand: 'Il se fera sans doute un jour une grande révolution dans les esprits. Un homme de mon âge ne la verra pas, mais il mourra dans l'espérance que les hommes seront plus éclairés et plus doux' (Best.D12503, 26 March 1765). On 16 April Voltaire reported to Damilaville that the king had given mme Calas a pension and that the Protestants were at his feet (Best.D12552). He espressed his confidence about the future once more in a letter to the marquis d'Argence, written towards the end of the year. But what seemed to be a reasonably based optimism was to be shattered again, this time at the beginning of 1766, by the profound shock Voltaire experienced as a result of the La Barre case.

---

[108] 'this is no doubt a reference to Jallabert's journey to Montpellier for his health in 1743' (Best.D12343, n.3).

Nonetheless, despite a nervous period in the first months of the year, Voltaire continued his efforts to help the Protestants. Most of his energies in 1766 were directed to obtaining relief for the family of Jean-Pierre Espinas, a Protestant who had been condemned to the galleys in 1740 and released in 1764 (*La France protestante*, vi.265). Voltaire described the family's plight to mme de Saint-Julien on 14 September (Best.D13555):

Le père a été vingt trois ans aux galères pour avoir donné à souper et à coucher à un prédicant; la mère a été enfermée, les enfans réduits à mandier leur pain. On leur avait laissé le tiers du bien pour les nourir; ce tiers a été usurpé par le receveur des domaines.

This particular campaign shows that Voltaire did not always have an easy time when he tried to intervene with the authorities, and also that he was not quickly discouraged from attempting to right an injustice. At first he wrote to Richelieu, sending him a *mémoire* about the Espinas family and asking him to give it to Saint-Florentin (Best.D13502, 19 August 1766). Voltaire wrote again to his *héros* on 15 September to remind him about the Espinas (Best.D13560), and a further letter, dated 8 October, attempts to forestall the criticism that he was taking too much interest in the Huguenots by stressing the human misery caused by persecution and its effect on an *homme de bien*:

Vous me demanderez de quoy je me mêle de solliciter toujours pour des huguenots. C'est que je vois tous les jours ces infortunez, c'est que je vois des familles dispersées et sans pain, c'est que cent personnes viennent crier et pleurer chez moy et qu'il est impossible de n'en être pas ému.[109]

An unfavourable reply was received from Richelieu, but this did not prevent Voltaire from despatching yet another appeal to the worthy duke at the risk of incurring his even greater displeasure (Best.D13632, 28 October 1766).

Voltaire had also written to mme de Saint-Julien on 14 September (Best.D13555), and the lady was tactfully asked on 28 October whether she had received a letter sent to her about a month earlier: 'Je crois que je vous parlais encore d'un galérien' (Best.D13631). Meanwhile, Voltaire had told Moultou on about 14 September that he thought mme d'Enville was the only person who could achieve anything in this

[109] Best.D13602. This could throw a new light on Richelieu's character. Did Voltaire seriously think he was likely to be moved by such considerations? Perhaps the *maréchal* was not quite so cynical as is usually affirmed.

matter. An extremely courtly exchange had also taken place between Voltaire and the duc de Nivernois, who had been responsible for releasing Espinas from the galleys.[110] The duke implied that his influence over Saint-Florentin was not very strong, but assured Voltaire that he would inform him immediately of the outcome of his efforts. Finally, on 15 December, Voltaire was able to congratulate mme de Saint-Julien: 'cette famille obtient par vos bontés une pension sur son propre bien dont on lui arrache le fond pour avoir donné il y a vingt six ans à souper à un sot prêtre hérétique' (Best.D13737).

This affair gives us a fascinating insight into the devious ways Voltaire now had to venture into to obtain any concession from the government in favour of the Protestants. The significant thing about the Espinas affair is that all the people Voltaire canvassed had, or could be expected to exercise, some influence over Saint-Florentin. The *ministre de la maison du roi* was now in a minority among his colleagues in favouring a fairly strict application of the edicts and opposing the granting of any major concessions to the Protestants, though even he was prepared to accept some rationalisation of the situation regarding civil rights, as we shall see when we come to consider Gilbert de Voisins's *Mémoires* (cf. below, pp.335 ff.). His position was becoming more and more difficult, as Joseph Dedieu explains (*Histoire politique,* ii.16): 'Saint-Florentin faisait ainsi front de tous côtés à de puissants adversaires. Il se défendait, mais comme une bête traquée.' Yet although force of events sometimes compelled him to be lenient, especially as regards illegal assemblies, his department gave him overall control of policy in Protestant affairs and it was a very difficult matter to persuade him to part with any of his prisoners. We have already seen (above, p.303) that it was he who had opposed Choiseul when it was proposed to release the remaining *galériens* in 1762. The very fact that he was in such a minority no doubt made him harden his attitude in certain cases, and the support of Choiseul was therefore not necessarily a help when one was interceding on behalf of Huguenot prisoners or clients. Indeed it might prove to be quite the opposite as Voltaire, was apparently finding out.

Voltaire had learned that Saint-Florentin was not any easy man to deal with at the beginning of the Calas campaign. Time had caused his attitude to harden, and by 1765 he had begun to refer to Saint-Florentin in terms of bitter hatred and contempt. 'J'ai bien peur qu'il

[110]Voltaire wrote to the duke on 29 September (Best.D13594) and the duke replied on 3 October (Best.D13598).

[the duc de Praslin] ne se croie obligé de conférer avec mr le Cte de st Florentin, c'est se noier dans son crachat', he observed urbanely to Moultou in connection with his friend's passport (Best.D12386, 7 February 1765). And writing to Végobre on 10 February 1766 Voltaire remarked dejectedly: 'je ne puis rien auprès de mr le cte de st Florentin' (Best.D13164). Voltaire's conduct during the Espinas affair leaves not the shadow of a doubt that he knew he was as inimical to Saint-Florentin as the minister was to him. 'J'ose encore vous conjurer de dire un mot à m. de St Florentin', he wrote to Richelieu on 28 October 1766; 'Vous ne lui direz pas sans doute que c'est moi qui vous en ai supplié' (Best. D13632). Voltaire had already expressed his scepticism as to whether mme de Saint-Julien would be able to persuade Saint-Florentin by herself: 'Si vous n'êtes pas assez forte (ce que je ne crois pas) pour toucher la pitié de mr De St Florentin, j'ose vous demander en grâce dejoindre Mr Le Maréchal de Richelieu à vous. Mr De St Florentin est difficile à émouvoir sur les huguenots' (Best.D13555, 14 September 1766). Voltaire's estimate of Saint-Florentin's attitude toward the Protestants was not changed by the reply he received from the duc de Nivernois, who, as we have already seen, implied that his influence over the minister was not very strong. The power struggle in the government was obviously going on continually, for on 12 January 1767 Voltaire wrote to d'Argental in triumph: 'Mr le Duc De Choiseuil a tiré deux hommes des galères à ma seule prière, et a forcé mr le comte de st Florentin à faire cette grâce' (Best.D13833). Voltaire's hatred now knew no bounds for the man he had castigated as 'un athée qui cherche à plaire à des fanatiques'.[111] The *ministre de la maison du roi* thus in many ways resembled a latter-day Borgia, for Voltaire explained the licence of Renaissance Italy by the argument that the leaders of Church and State were atheists who believed neither in the religion they preached and upheld nor in any morality.[112] Such a man also was Saint-

[111] Best.D13557, Voltaire to Moultou, *c.* 14 September 1766. There seems little doubt from the context that Saint-Florentin is the object of this attack. Moreover, as we shall see later (below, p.338), it appears very likely that Voltaire had Saint-Florentin in mind when he created Saint-Pouange, the powerful and unscrupulous minister who causes the tragic *dénouement* of *L'Ingénu*. Nor did Saint-Florentin's opposition to Voltaire's interventions diminish as time went on; cf. Best.D14701 (Voltaire to Végobre, 27 January 1768): 'Mr Le Duc De Choiseul parait très las de ne pouvoir rien obtenir de Mr De st Florentin.'

[112] cf. Best.D15189 (Voltaire to Villevielle, 26 August 1768): 'L'athéisme était très commun en Italie au 15e et 16e siècles. Aussi que d'horribles crimes à la cour des Alexandre VI, des Jules II, des Léon X! Le trône pontifical et l'église n'étaient remplis que de rapines, d'assassinats, et d'empoisonnemens. Il n'y a que le fanatisme qui ait produit plus de crimes.'

Florentin, who cynically maintained his position of power and influence by pandering to the superstitious Louis xv and the *dévot* faction at Court.

At the end of 1766 we see Voltaire taking stock of the Protestant question. Almost four years have elapsed since the execution of Jean Calas, and he is plainly dissatisfied with the progress achieved. In a letter to Moultou written in October or November he comments: 'prèsque tout le monde ignore que les galères sont pleines de malheureux condamnés pour avoir chanté de mauvais pseaumes' (Best.D13641). Quite apart from the Calas campaign, its accompanying pamphlets, and the *Traité sur la tolérance*, which had been directly inspired by the case, Voltaire had brought the Protestant question before the public's attention in several articles of the *Dictionnaire philosophique*, e.g. 'Catéchisme du Japonais' (1764), 'Christianisme' (1764), in the *conte Pot-Pourri* (1765), the *Commentaire sur le livre des Délits et des peines* (1766), the *Avis au public sur les parricides* (1766), and the other propaganda on behalf of Sirven. It is a truism to say that Voltaire was attempting to secure a measure of toleration for the Huguenots. But what was the nature of the tolerance he campaigned for, and just how far did it go?

vii. *Voltaire and Protestant assemblies*

A recent article by Geoffrey Adams[113] has again highlighted what would seem to be a major paradox, first raised a few years ago by mme Elisabeth Labrousse.[114] This eminent Bayle scholar tried to demonstrate that the toleration sought by the major *philosophes* of the Enlightenment was much more limited in scope and much less genuine in nature than that for which Pierre Bayle had pleaded in his works some fifty to sixty years earlier. Her reasoning was forceful: Bayle's toleration sprang from an intimate and unshakeable conviction as to the inviolable sanctity of an individual's conscience, whereas the *philosophes* usually campaigned for toleration on the grounds that it would benefit society as a whole rather than the individual. Moreover, she might have added that the *philosophes'* good faith cannot be taken completely for granted, since in some cases they were hypocritically prepared to preach to the masses a

[113] 'Myths and misconceptions: the philosophe view of the Huguenots in the age of Louis xv', *Historical reflections* (1974), i.59-79.

[114] see her 'Note à propos de la conception de la tolérance au xviiie siècle', *Studies on Voltaire* (1967), lvi.799-811.

religion, designed to cement the social order, in which they did not themselves believe.[115] Mr Adams has turned his attention to *philosophes* and Huguenots in the age of Louis xv, and has found disturbing evidence that the former regarded their Calvinist contemporaries as 'republican, fanatical and bigoted'. In other words, despite their theoretical attachment to toleration, Montesquieu and Voltaire in particular tended to perpetuate attitudes held, during the reign of Louis xiv, by men like Bossuet. He claims, moreover (p.59), that:

The persistence of a simplistic and prejudiced view of the Calvinist world in the minds of France's leading philosophes, peculiar in itself, was seriously to impede the efforts of the Huguenots to interest the most influential thinkers of their time in their struggle for toleration, at least until Voltaire's intervention in the Calas affair during the 1760s.

Mr Adams's contentions provide a useful starting point for my own consideration of Voltaire's attitude to Huguenot public worship. There is certainly an apparent paradox, for Voltaire's dislike and suspicion of Protestant assemblies continued well after the Calas case. Let us sum up the position briefly. It should by now be patently obvious that he wished for full recognition of the right of Protestants to exist in France. Their legal status should be regularised, and their civil rights guaranteed. Voltaire asked that the Huguenots be allowed to carry out their trades without hindrance, emphasising the economic benefits which this would bring the state, and he further pleaded that they should no longer be persecuted for refusing to worship as Catholics or be penalised legally for not solemnising their marriages according to the Catholic rite. But despite all his interventions on behalf of Protestant victims of intolerance, Voltaire did not put forward the claim that public celebration of their religion should be permitted. 'Espérons pour nos frères désunis une tolérance politique que nos maîtres sauront accorder avec la religion dont ils sont les protecteurs', he was to write in 1772 in the *Réflexions philosophiques* (M.xxviii.555), where he enthusiastically took up the cause of the Huguenots' civil rights as far as marriage was concerned. Clearly, the limited nature of these demands is to be explained partly by considerations of prudence. As Voltaire recognised in the *Réflexions philosophiques*, the government could not openly reverse the religious

---

[115] see especially Ronald Boss's important article, 'Rousseau's civil religion and the meaning of belief: an answer to Bayle's paradox', *Studies on Voltaire* (1971), lxxxiv.123-93, which is discussed below, p.475, n.47).

policy of the great Louis XIV, and was anyway pledged to support Catholicism. To secure first of all a civil settlement for the Huguenots was obviously the most sensible approach, and any intelligent person would have followed it: the Protestants themselves were quick to emphasise the economic advantages of toleration. But was this the whole story? Voltaire could surely have followed this policy perfectly well without losing sight of the second objective: complete religious liberty for the Huguenots.

The answer is that this was just what he did not want. This is implicit in the following passage from the *Dictionnaire philosophique* article 'Christianisme', which appeared in 1764 when Voltaire was still actively engaged in the struggle to have the Calas judgement reversed: 'On voit [. . .] qu'il y avait des temps où les assemblées étaient prohibées. C'est ainsi que parmi nous il est défendu aux calvinistes de s'assembler dans le Languedoc; nous avons même quelquefois fait pendre et rouer des ministres, ou prédicants, qui tenaient des assemblées malgré les lois' (ed. Benda and Naves, p.127). There is no indignation or protest here – Voltaire is clearly quoting a piece of legislation which is far from incurring his censure, though this statement must be qualified by the fact that the passage in question seeks to discredit the early Christians, and this explains to a certain extent why French and English laws against illegal assemblies are invoked with approval. Be this as it may, Voltaire does not like the idea of large, outdoor religious assemblies such as those the Huguenots persisted in holding. If the Protestants are to be tolerated, they must behave like law-abiding citizens, not potential rebels. This is made clear in *Pot-Pourri* (1764): 'je doute fort qu'on rétablisse vos temples', the Huguenot m. de Boucacous is told, 'malgré toute la politesse dont nous nous piquons: la raison en est que vous êtes un peu nos ennemis' (*Mélanges*, pp.723-24). The Camisard uprising is recalled, but it is also pointed out that the Huguenots are now generally left in peace and have the liberty to carry on their trades (p.724):

Voilà une plaisante liberté! dit M. de Boucacous; nous ne pouvons nous assembler en pleine campagne quatre ou cinq mille seulement, avec des psaumes à quatre parties, que sur-le-champ il ne vienne un régiment de dragons qui nous fait rentrer chacun chez nous. Est-ce là vivre? Est-ce là être libre?

In actual fact, the *dragons* often did more to the Protestants found attending assemblies than merely send them home; those apprehended were liable to be sentenced to the galleys for life. Voltaire here chooses to ignore this, though he cannot have been unaware of the situation since he had already intervened with the authorities on behalf of Chaumont and other galley-slaves before this passage was written. His spokesman in *Pot-Pourri* continues: 'Il n'y a aucun pays dans le monde où l'on puisse s'attrouper sans l'ordre du souverain, tout attroupement est contre les lois. Servez Dieu à votre mode dans vos maisons; n'étourdissez personne par des hurlements que vous appelez musique.' Why should the Huguenots expect to be allowed to hold outdoor assemblies, when even in Protestant England they would not have this prerogative?[116]

Voltaire was not alone in holding these opinions. A letter written to Choiseul in 1763 has many points of similarity with his views: l'état, dont les loix defendent et punissent indistinctement toutes assemblées illicites sera sans cesse exposé aux périls que ces loix ont voulu prévenir. Des assemblées formées par un faux zele et sous pretexte de religion sont plus dangereuses que toutes autres.' What are the English doing for their Catholic subjects, Choiseul's correspondent asks: 'ils ne souffriroient certainement pas chez eux des assemblées de Catholiques au nombre de 2 et 3.000 hommes, comme nous en avons ici un grand nombre de protestantes' (AN, O'459, ff.9-11; Dedieu, *Histoire politique*, ii.12-14). It may seem rather startling, to say the least, that the author of this letter was none other than Saint-Florentin, Voltaire's archenemy in the battle for Protestant toleration and civil rights. What can possibly explain the similarity of their opinions on this topic? An obvious answer is that Voltaire was aware that these views were held by certain members of the government, and that although people like Saint-Florentin were extremely hostile to Protestantism as such, they were nonetheless able to perceive the practical anomalies of the situation, and may therefore have been prepared to make some compromises as regards Protestant civil rights. Voltaire therefore thought it was advisable not to make his demands too unreasonable at the outset and decided not to press for legalisation of Protestant assemblies.

There may indeed be some truth in this interpretation. Voltaire

[116] Voltaire was evidently unaware of the size and frequency of Methodist assemblies in England at this period; cf. W. H. Fitchett, *Wesley and his century* (London 1925), p.162: 'The open air services begun by Whitefield were attended, almost instantly, with startling results. His first audience numbered 200, the second rose to 3,000, the third to 5,000 and the crowds swiftly extended to vast gatherings of 20,000 people.'

was very much aware of the government's thinking on the Protestant question, among other things because of his contacts with Richelieu. When, in 1761, Voltaire scolded Ribotte over Huguenot assemblies – 'Vous ne devez pas douter, Monsieur, qu'on ne soit très indigné à la cour contre les assemblées publiques' (Best.D10177) – he was very possibly passing on an admonition from Richelieu,[117] though the tone of the letter suggests that Voltaire himself was in agreement with the advice. Several years later Voltaire adopted a similar tone when writing to Richelieu himself about the Espinas family. On 8 October 1766 (Best.D13602) he had anticipated criticism from the *maréchal* for taking too much interest in the affairs of Huguenots. The criticism was made nonetheless, and Voltaire replied: 'Je conviens de tout ce que vous me dites sur ces plats huguenots et sur leurs impertinentes assemblées. Savez vous bien qu'ils m'aiment à la folie et que si j'étais parmi eux j'en ferais ce que je voudrais? Cela paraît ridicule, mais je ne désespérerais pas de les empêcher d'aller au désert' (Best.D13632, 28 October 1766). Discouraging Protestant assemblies was obviously an aim dear to the *maréchal*'s heart. We have already seen (above, pp.269-72) that it was he who attempted to put into practice the new government hard line of banning all illegal gatherings in 1754, and that he had been concerned to find an answer to the Huguenot problem since 1738. In 1766 he was involved in another interesting incident; as Joseph Dedieu tells us (*Histoire politique*, ii.107):

Vers ce même temps, le duc de Richelieu, qui n'apportait cependant aucune acrimonie dans son attitude à l'égard des réformés, se déclara hostile à toutes les demandes tendant à ramener la liberté du culte public, sous le prétexte que les protestants reconnaissaient qu'il n'était pas essentiel à leur culte. Les affirmations du maréchal avaient ébranlé déjà les bonnes dispositions du prince de Beauvau et de Boutin, intendant de Bordeaux. La question soulevée était d'importance. Les réformés de Sedan, ralliés à la thèse du maréchal compliquaient une situation difficile. Gébelin, sollicité de donner un avis, en référa aux autorités de Genève qui éludèrent la question. Les directeurs de Neuchâtel déclarèrent au contraire le culte public d'une nécessité indispensable. Gébelin put alors agir auprès des protecteurs du protestantisme, qui avaient été sur le point de se fourvoyer.

117 Voltaire goes on to say: 'On vous permet de faire dans vos maisons tout ce qui vous plaît, celà est bien honnête.' In Best.D10055 (to Ribotte, 5 October 1761) Voltaire had said: 'Il [Richelieu] laisse la plus honnête Liberté, mais il ne veut pas qu'on en abuse.' The repetition of the word 'honnête' suggests that Richelieu might have used it in an earlier letter to Voltaire in which he explained his attitude toward the Huguenots.

In this connection it is significant that in 1761 Voltaire had also tried to tempt Richelieu to intervene in favour of Rochette by arguing that he would become 'l'idole de ces faquins de huguenots' (Best.D10178, 27 November; cf. above, p.284). Moreover, Voltaire was later to submit to the duke proposals concerning the regularisation of Protestant marriages. On 16 September 1772 he wrote to Richelieu emphasising with characteristic flattery his friend's unique qualifications in the matter. As former *commandant* of Languedoc and as present governor of Guienne, he has had ample evidence of the unsatisfactory nature of current legislation, 'et Monsieur le Maréchal de Richelieu qui a rendu de si grands services à l'état, est peut être aujourd'hui le seul homme capable de fermer les plaies de la révocation de l'édit de Nantes'. At the end of the letter Voltaire insists again on the prestige to be gained from settling so ticklish a question: 'J'ose vous assurer que vous seriez l'un et l'autre [Richelieu and the chancellor] bénis de la nation' (Best. D17915; cf. below, pp.361-62).

Political considerations therefore explain to some extent the terms Voltaire uses regarding Huguenot assemblies when he is writing to Richelieu. But this is not the whole story. It is very probable that Voltaire in his turn was influenced to some extent by Richelieu's views. After all it was probably the latter who first drew his attention to the Huguenot problem in the south of France, and Voltaire cannot have dismissed his friend's experience altogether, especially since Richelieu's apparent anticlericalism (cf. above, p.271, n.46) must have helped to make his views more acceptable. Such an influence would partly explain Voltaire's conservatism on this topic, and it is an attitude which may seem to need some clarification, for as early as 1754 Turgot had championed the rights of the Huguenots to public worship, and dismissed objections that their assemblies were, or would become, seditious:

Mais les assemblées qui sont nécessaires pour chaque Religion, ne pourront-elles pas devenir dangereuses? Oui sans doute, si vous les proscrivez; on n'y sera occupé alors que des moyens de se soutenir et de venger sa foi opprimée. Mais laissez aux hommes la liberté de se trouver dans les mêmes lieux pour offrir à Dieu le culte qu'ils jugent lui être agréable; & leurs assemblées, quel que soit ce culte, ne seront pas plus dangereuses que celles des Catholiques. Toutes peuvent servir de prétexte à des esprits séditieux, aucune n'en servira lorsqu'elles seront libres; et si quelqu'un mal intentionné venoit à en abuser, il seroit facile d'arrêter les progrès du mal. Les assemblées des Protestans sont

secrettes, parce qu'elles sont défendues; autorisées, elles seraient aussi publiques que les nôtres; pourquoi veut-on que l'assemblée d'une secte soit
plus nuisible à l'Etat que l'assemblée d'une autre? qu'en Angleterre ce soit
celle des Catholiques, en France celle des Protestans, par-tout celle qui ne
pense pas comme le Prince. Toute assemblée civile qui est séditieuse doit
être interdite; toute assemblée religieuse doit être permise.[118]

These generous liberal views certainly make the opinions of Voltaire
and Richelieu seem reactionary.

Of course it is in a way unfair to compare their positions. Though the
two have much common ground, Richelieu's attitude was prompted by
military and political motives and he had none of Voltaire's passionate
concern for the victims of intolerance. Yet even he had been prepared
to allow the Huguenots 'la plus honnête liberté', that is to practice a
culte privé inside their houses. Voltaire develops this point in *Pot-
pourri*. He emphasises that the Protestants must be content with private
worship, but symphathises once more with the disabilities to which
they are subject (*Mélanges*, p.725):

Faites ce qu'il vous plaira dans vos maisons et j'ai parole de M. le gouverneur
et de M. l'intendant qu'en étant sages vous serez tranquilles[...] Je trouve
très mauvais que vos mariages, l'état de vos enfants, le droit d'héritage, souffrent la moindre difficulté. Il n'est pas juste de vous saigner et de vous purger
parce que vos pères ont été malades.

This again seems almost a passing on of the government's views to the
Protestant public, and the sort of governor or intendant mentioned was
not just a figment of Voltaire's imagination – many officials interpreted
the edicts and *ordonnances* with an engaging benevolence, as the following example will show. In 1763 a Protestant school was set up at Mazères
in the comté de Foix. Local Catholics complained about this to the
marquis de Gudannes, *commandant* of the province, who summoned
two of the teachers to appear before him. He ordered them to close the
school, and also complained because it was situated opposite a Catholic
school run by the *ignorantins*. He told them:

Personne ne vous empêche de servir Dieu dans vos maisons à votre manière;
élevez vos enfants chez vous; enseignez-leur à craindre Dieu, à honorer
le roi, à aimer leur patrie, à vous respecter. Vous êtes attachés à votre religion;
vous voulez la transmettre à vos enfants; cela est bien raisonnable; mais
instruisez-les dans vos maisons et non dans une école publique. Lorsque vous

[118] *Le Conciliateur, ou lettres d'un ecclésiastique à un magistrat* (Rome 1754), pp.36-37.

voudrez faire quelque enterprise, prenez mon conseil. Regardez-moi tous comme votre père, comme votre meilleur ami.[119]

Interpreted by officials like this, the anti-Protestant legislation was not always as draconian as has sometimes been supposed. Unfortunately, Voltaire's seemingly illiberal attitude may have gone even farther than dislike of assemblies. In the *Dictionnaire philosophique* article 'Caté-chisme du Japonais' (1764), he specifically approves the policy of ex-cluding dissident minorities from responsible positions in the state. Everyone may have religious liberty providing they obey the laws and do not assemble 'quatre ou cinq mille' strong, but 'Il n'y a que ceux qui mangent à la royale qui soient susceptibles des dignités de l'Etat: tous les autres peuvent dîner à leur fantaisie, mais ils sont exclus des charges' (ed. Benda and Naves, pp.93-94).

The toleration Voltaire was fighting for seems to have been distinctly limited, therefore. In part, as I have observed, this was probably in order to make his proposals more acceptable in government circles. But there was more to it than this. Voltaire was definitely opposed to the Huguenots' assemblies. A *bourgeois* at heart, he was shocked by such rebellious disobedience to the laws of the land. As a historian, he could not but remember with distaste the religious wars of the sixteenth century; as a supporter of the *thèse royale* in France, he classed the Huguenots of the past among the chaotic forces which had weakened the monarchy and France itself; and finally as a privileged member of the social order, he regarded with suspicion the peasants who were the backbone of the *églises du désert*. The fanaticism of the Camisard rebels never completely left his mind, and Voltaire, like government officials, feared that the Huguenots' assemblies would encourage and fortify the superstitious and rebellious opinions of the rabble. The *procureur général*'s objections to points made by Paul Rabaut in *La Calomnie confondue* (written in connection with the Calas case), might almost be regarded as a paraphrase of the views expressed by Voltaire in the *Dictionnaire philosophique*, were it not for the fact that they were made two years before the *portatif* appeared: 'Où sont donc [. . .] ces *augustes lois* qui obligent les sujets à faire des *assemblées* proscrites dans tout Etat policé, assemblées illicites par la forme de leur convocation, par le nombre de ceux qui les composent, par le lieu où elles se tiennent, et par tout ce qui se pratique contre les ordres du souverain?' (quoted by

[119] letter to a Protestant gentlewoman, mme Nicol, quoted by Coquerel, ii.366.

Coquerel, ii.323). It is not only Voltaire's published works which show a distrust of Protestant political motives. 'Je n'ai jamais dit, révérence parler, *que les huguenots étaient par principe ennemis des rois*', he commented to Moultou on 9 January 1763. 'Je crois cependant, entre nous, qu'il en est quelque chose' (Best.D10897; cf. above, p.64, n.33). This admission at a time when Voltaire was writing the largely pro-Protestant *Traité sur la tolérance* explains only too well his reticence on the matter of Huguenot public worship.

Moreover, it must not be thought that Voltaire and the French government were alone in attacking open-air assemblies. Many Protestants had themselves severely criticised this practice. Some, like Bayle, considered such assemblies to be rebellious acts contrary to the obedience a loyal subject owed to his sovereign. The philosopher of Rotterdam's dispute on this subject with Pierre Jurieu, who held violently opposed views, is well known, but Bayle was not a voice crying the wilderness. During the reign of Louis XIV and for many years before, the French Calvinist church had preached passive obedience, and even after the repeal of the Edict of Nantes many Protestants continued to believe this teaching, a convincing demonstration that their reasoning was not merely based on considerations of political expediency. Many of the pastors who had emigrated refused to recognise the legitimacy of the revival instituted by Antoine Court in 1715, and condemned its attendant assemblies. In 1719, m. de Claris Florian, a minister of the Huguenot Church in London, wrote to Court complaining of

l'entreprise de certains protestants qui, sans vocation, sans science, sans une piété bien connue, ont osé prendre l'encensoir, porter la main sur l'arche, s'ériger en ministres et en pasteurs, prêcher dans les bois et les maisons, administrer le baptême et la Sainte-Cène et abuser de la simplicité d'un peuple plus lâche que religieux, plus impétueux que fidèle et moins partisan de la discipline que du désordre.[120]

There were harsh words from a man who was writing from the safety of a country of refuge to one who risked his life daily, but many exiled pastors like him shared similar views. The 'cowardice' of the Protestants still in France, according to such people, consisted in their staying in a

---

[120] 'Lettre de Pierre de Claris à Antoine Court,' *Bpf* (1885), xxxiv.76. Claris had been an abbé who abjured his Catholic faith and became a minister of the Refuge. After explanations from Court, Claris subsequently changed his attitude (Mours and Robert, *Le Protestantisme en France*, p.114).

321

country where it was illegal to profess their religion publicly, and the remedy was to go into exile; 'Sortez de Babylone' was the Biblical precept which was invoked.[121] E.-G. Léonard explains:

Pour ceux qui ne se décideraient pas à partir, il fallait leur interdire les assemblées. Ils devaient vivre enfermés dans leur maison, gémissant de leur lâcheté, implorant la force du Dieu de force, ne laissant ignorer à pas un de ceux parmi lesquels ils vivent qu'ils sont protestants, eux et leurs enfants, et souffrant avec joie toutes leurs épreuves. Suivis, ces conseils eussent, de toute manière, définitivement tué l'Eglise réformée de France: or, ils étaient approuvés, à en croire la lettre, par Abbadie et par Saurin, c'est-à-dire, par deux des pasteurs le plus savants de l'ancienne Eglise.[122]

The situation was indeed difficult for the Protestants remaining in France who believed in the necessity of public worship, when they were not only persecuted by the government, but also criticised and attacked by their brethren of the Refuge.

The split in the ranks of the Protestants was exploited only too eagerly by the government, as might be expected. On 20 April 1719 Jacques Basnage published his *Instruction pastorale aux Réformés de France sur la persévérance dans la foi et la fidélité pour le souverain*. This followed the line taken by Bayle on the necessity of obedience to the sovereign on the part of those Protestants still in France, and the work had been composed at the instigation of the French ambassador to the Netherlands (where Basnage was in exile), because the authorities at Versailles were worried by the rapid increase in the number of Huguenot assemblies. The *Instruction* was immediately reprinted by cardinal Dubois and distributed among the Protestants by the French government.[123] Unlike Claris and Saurin, Basnage did not advise the Protestants to leave France – a course of action which would hardly have gained government support – but he recommended that they abstain from their assemblies and content themselves with private and family worship in their own homes. The religious foundation of political

---

[121] 'La plume nous tombait des mains, toutes les fois que nous la prenions pour leur [to the French Churches] déclarer, que nous n'avions d'autre direction à leur donner, que celle que le Saint-Esprit donne lui-même à tous ceux qui sont dans leur cas: "*Sortez de Babylone, mon peuple, de peur qu'en participant à ses péchés, vous ne participiez à ses plaies,*" (*Apoc.*, *18.4*).' This comment made by the famous pastor Jacques Saurin is quoted by Coquerel, i.250.

[122] 'Le problème du culte public et de l'église dans le protestantisme au xviiie siècle', *Foi et vie* (1937), p.439.

[123] Léonard, p.439. Cf. also Dedieu, *Histoire politique*, i.19-21.

obedience was stressed in forceful terms: 'Souvenez-vous qu'il faut obéir au souverain, non seulement par la crainte, mais par la conscience, car c'est la grande maxime de l'Evangile.'[124] The abbé Joseph Dedieu (*Histoire politique*, i.20) claims that 'pour complaire au Régent, Basnage alla jusqu'à mettre un voile sur les doctrines réputées essentielles à la vie protestante'. Be that as it may, Basnage was at pains to justify his view with frequent reference to holy writ, and it would have been difficult for the government to find more forceful support for its repressive policy. He declared:

Les apôtres s'enfermèrent dans une chambre haute, afin d'y pratiquer les devoirs d'une religion persécutée dès sa naissance, au lieu d'assembler cette foule de nouveaux convertis que la résurrection ou l'ascension de Jésus-Christ avait faits ou raffermis. Ils choisirent un petit nombre pour louer dieu [. . .] et lorsque, par un effet d'un don merveilleux, ils eurent converti dans un seul jour trois mille hommes, ils ne les attroupèrent point en sortant du temple de Jérusalem pour s'assembler dans un lieu public à la vue des Juifs qui n'auraient pas manqué de leur en faire un crime [. . .] Imitez l'exemple des saints apôtres [. . .] on pèche en suivant les mouvements trop précipités d'un zèle téméraire. Animez-vous avec vos enfants au service de Dieu, mais souvenez-vous que la multitude peut causer plus de désordres que d'édification.[125]

Allowing for the obvious difference in language and the lack of irony in Basnage's message, this is remarkably similar to the advice Voltaire was to give the Protestants, in a letter to Ribotte, at the time of the Rochette case (Best.D10177, 27 Novembre 1761):

Vous ne devez pas douter, Monsieur, qu'on ne soit très indigné à la cour contre les assemblées publiques. On vous permet de faire dans vos maisons tout ce qui vous plaît, cela est bien honnête. Jesus christ a dit qu'il se trouverait toujours entre deux ou trois personnes assemblées en son nom, mais quand on est trois ou quatre mille, c'est le diable qui s'y trouve.

The similarity is perhaps not so surprising when one reflects that both men were temporarily acting as spokesmen of the French government or its representatives.

Antoine Court and his followers were not dismayed by the preaching of the ministers of the Refuge. They pressed on with their work of

[124] Léonard, 'Le problème', p.439; 'on croirait vraiment que c'est la seule', comments Léonard.
[125] quoted by Léonard, pp.439-40. Basnage subsequently changed his mind about Protestant assemblies in France (cf. Mours and Robert, *Le Protestantisme*, p.114).

reforming the Protestant churches, and it might be thought that the obvious success of their venture would have been proof enough to other Protestants that their enterprise was pleasing to God and respectable in the eyes of their coreligionaries. But this was not so. In 1745 appeared the anonymous *Lettre sur les assemblées de religionnaires en Languedoc*, the publication of which coincided with a renewed campaign on the part of the authorities against Protestant assemblies. The letter caused a great stir among the Huguenots, and replies were forthcoming from Antoine Court, from the Swiss professor Polier and from the chaplain of the Dutch embassy, Armand de La Chapelle. Frank Puaux summarises the aims of the author as follows:

Par une comparaison audacieuse entre les Réformés qui s'assemblaient et les sept mille qui, n'ayant pas fléchi le genou devant Baal, cependant n'avaient point de culte public, il tentait de prouver que les religionnaires allaient contre les prescriptions de la loi divine. N'allait-il pas jusqu'à dire que Jésus-Christ n'avait point eu d'autre culte public que celui des Juifs et que, du reste, ses propres maximes en diminuaient beaucoup la nécessité, que les apôtres allaient de maison en maison, etc.?[126]

Who was responsible for this pamphlet? None other than François-Louis Allamand, later a correspondent of Voltaire's, who, as we have seen (above, pp.161-63, 189 ff.), supported him during the Saurin affair and in the 1760s discussed with him possible ways of bringing about a 'philosophic' reform of Christianity. If the two men ever discussed the plight of the French Protestants, as seems probable, Allamand is unlikely to have done anything but strengthen Voltaire's prejudice against Huguenot assemblies.[127]

---

[126] 'Une lettre du refuge', *Bpf* (1878), xxvii.224.

[127] when the *Lettres* were published Allamand was preceptor of the comte de Wied, and he later served as minister of three different parishes in the *pays de Vaud* (cf. above, p.189, n.199). In view of the apparent discrepancy between his attack on the Huguenots' public worship and his own later career, one might be tempted to regard him as something of a hypocrite. Yet while admitting that Allamand's intervention in the debate was unfortunate, one must point out that his own views had a certain logical consistency (cf. above, p.192) and that he was not alone in them: as we have seen, hostility to Huguenot assemblies in France was a persistent attitude among many Protestants of the Refuge. As far as Allamand was concerned, since Protestantism was the official religion of the pays de Vaud, the position there was completely different from in France. He would no doubt have also condemned illegal Catholic assemblies in Switzerland, though at the same time probably defending the right of individual Catholics to their own form of private worship. The government of Berne had in fact allowed Catholic workers to reside in its territory since the early 1750s, so the position I have just outlined was not at all untenable.

As the century advanced, divisions between the French Protestants themselves became more obvious, and it was no longer only the government and Protestant critics abroad who condemned their assemblies. We must soon look more closely at these divisions, as it is crucial to have some conception of them in order to understand the wide range of often conflicting opinions which existed among the Huguenots of the eighteenth century. At the moment it is sufficient to say that class was responsible for the worse disagreements among the Protestants. Antoine Court's work of renewal had been carried out in the south, the traditional stronghold of the French Huguenots. The Protestants of the *midi* consisted mainly of large rural groups with a preponderance of lower-class elements, and they were determined to maintain the traditional discipline and worship of the Church. They far outnumbered the Protestants of the north, but the latter, mainly urban groups, were important socially and economically; usually members of the *bourgeoisie*, they resented the control of the Church by what they considered as peasant elements in the south. From about 1740 the influence of these northern *notables* began to grow. They had been deprived of public worship for longer than the Protestants of the south, and assemblies had been few and far between in areas like Normandy. In fact, when Préneuf tried to reorganise the Church in Normandy, he met with stiff resistance from the *bourgeoisie* of the towns. His successor Gautier sent Court an account of the difficulties he had encountered when talking to Levillain, an important Rouen merchant, and his son: 'M. son fils, qui est de mon âge, d'ailleurs joli garçon et qui ne manque pas d'esprit, a été deux fois en Hollande. Il y a séjourné et malheureusement il a vu des ministres qui blâment nos assemblées et surtout nos baptêmes et mariages, en sorte que difficilement on pourra le faire revenir' (quoted by Léonard, 'Le problème', p.446). There follows a list of no fewer than six reasons why Levillain *fils* was reluctant to entrust his spiritual welfare to a representative of the *églises du désert*. The propaganda of the Protestant opponents of Court and his reform had obviously not been without effect.[128]

An influential section of French Protestantism was therefore opposed to open-air assemblies. Even in the south, 'il fallait compter sur la

---

[128] it is interesting to remember that Rousseau also condemned religious assemblies and claimed that they were not an essential part of Christianity. At the time of the Rochette affair, he observed: 'cette même parole de Dieu est formelle sur le devoir d'obéir aux loix des Princes' (Leigh 1521).

"trop grande délicatesse" de gens "qui ne sauraient courir la nuit dans les déserts" en compagnie de coreligionnaires étrangers à leurs relations' (Léonard, *Histoire ecclésiastique*, p.24). Many northern Protestants attached a minimal importance to public worship and were very critical of the activities of their lower-class southern brethren, especially of the large and unruly assemblies held *au désert*.[129]

In any case an alternative course of action was available in the north to Huguenots with means: a visit to Paris and attendance at a service in one of the Protestant embassies would satisfy those whose consciences were perhaps a little troubled by their religious isolation. Otherwise there was the *culte privé*, which was considered to be adequate.[130] Small groups were formed which were socially exclusive, but the important point to note here is that they were not necessarily restricted to members of a single family.[131] We can thus see that Voltaire's advice to Ribotte in 1761 (cf. above, p.284) was not unrepresentative, and that the government was indeed prepared to allow the Protestants a certain amount of latitude, provided they would cease their 'rebellious' acts.

Further evidence of indulgence on the part of the government is provided by a movement begun by the pastor Louis Gibert. The Protestants in the *midi* were less timid than their brethren in the north, but they too had realised that it was their open-air assemblies which the government distrusted and feared most. Gibert's reaction was that, if this were the case, the Protestants should meet in houses or other buildings. These indoor assemblies would be obviously religious and non-seditious in character. Gibert's reasoning led him to campaign for a general policy of rebuilding the Protestants' *temples*, and in support of his thesis he pointed to the favourable attitude of certain high officials. A letter he wrote to the archbishop of Canterbury in 1761 mentions

[129] 'Ils assiègent particulièrement Mme de Pompadour et Machault d'Arnouville et essaient de gagner leurs faveurs en désavouant et même dénonçant leurs indociles coreligionnaires du Midi' (Léonard, 'Economie et religion: les protestants français au xviiie siècle', *Annales d'histoire sociale* (1940), p.12).

[130] 'En matière d'organisation ecclésiastique, refusant de reconnaître l'œuvre de Court et du Désert, ils opposent aux 'assemblées' illégales et trop mêlées, dont ils font nier jusqu'à la légitimité religieuse, de petites réunions de 'sociétés', cultes demi-privés groupant dans une clandestinité complète des parents, des amis, des voisins, en un mot des gens de même classe.'

[131] 'une tradition caennaise veut que les propriétaires protestants de la rue Neuve Saint-Jean, où ils étaient nombreux, aient percé leurs murs mitoyens pour pouvoir se réunir en secret' (Léonard, 'Le problème', p.448).

des avis que feu M. le Maréchal de Mirepoix donna secrètement aux pasteurs du Bas-Languedoc, leur donnant sa parole d'honneur que, s'ils faisaient leurs exercices dans les maisons, il ne leur arrivait [*sic*] rien de fâcheux, assurances que M. le Maréchal de Richelieu donna aux protestants de son gouvernment de Guienne.[132]

Gibert's plan was adopted by the synod of Hautes-Cévennes in 1758, but the national synod of the same year rejected it, presumably for fear of alienating the government through such a bold decision, for although Gibert had been undoubtedly right in his view on assemblies, the building of Protestant *temples* would have been seen by the government as an equally provocative step. Paul Rabaut therefore suggested as a compromise that the Protestants should meet in existing buildings rather than attempt to construct new *temples*. Even this moderate suggestion was turned down by a *conférence pastorale* in 1759, but a few years later, in 1765, the local synod changed its mind (Léonard, *Histoire ecclésiastique*, p.82). The range of opinion among the French Protestants on this difficult subject is only too obvious.

Voltaire's own position on the question can now be seen as less repressive than originally appeared. Open-air assemblies were considered dangerous not only by the Catholic government of France, but also by a considerable and influential minority among the Protestants themselves. The *culte privé* which Voltaire recommended could be interpreted in many ways. Even in the prudent north, groups consisting of several families met together, and in the *midi* a very considerable number of people could be gathered under one roof. Some Protestant historians have claimed that public worship was essential, and that Protestantism in France would have died a slow death if only the *culte privé* had been available to the Huguenots.[133] Be this as it may, it is undeniable that the government's attitude in most areas allowed the Protestants a fair degree of latitude in the private practice of their devotions. The possibility of some sort of corporate religious life was not altogether precluded.

A letter written to Moultou on 11 March 1764 shows conclusively that Voltaire did not display an uncharacteristic illiberality on this matter. Speaking about the Protestant question, he comments (Best. D11764):

---

[132] Daniel Benoît, *Les frères Gibert, deux pasteurs du Désert et du Refuge* (Toulouse 1889), p.162.
[133] cf. Coquerel, *passim*; Léonard, 'Le problème', p.436.

Ce qu'on devrait proposer, ce me semble, ce serait des conditions raisonnables, moiennant lesquelles ils [the Protestants] ne seraient plus tentés
d'abandonner leur patrie. Mais on m'assure que dans le livre de Mr de la
Morandiere,[134] on avance qu'il ne doit pas être permis à deux familles de
s'assembler pour prier Dieu. C'est conseiller la persécution sous le nom de
Tolérance, mais il se peut qu'on m'ait trompé, je n'ai point vu le livre.

Voltaire's meaning is obvious. While illegal assemblies should be
banned, the Protestants must nonetheless be allowed to assemble in
their houses to worship together peacefully. And the flippant tone
of Voltaire's questions to Louis Necker about the crimes individual
galériens had committed seems to indicate that, in private, he did not
always take as serious a view of attending assemblies as he affected in
his public utterances, especially in view of the other 'crimes' Voltaire
suggests might have been perpetrated: 'il ne serait pas mal de spécifier
[...] les mérites de chaque particulier. Par éxemple, Isaac, pour être
allé armé, entendre la parole de Dieu. Jacob, pour avoir donné un
souflet à un prêtre. Daniel, pour avoir parlé irrévérentieusement de la
présence réelle, etca' (Best.D11700, 15 February 1764). Voltaire himself might quite easily have committed the last two 'crimes' and in this
letter to Necker he does not seem to be too appalled at Isaac's conduct.
The key to his attitude is surely to be found here. He condemned
the Huguenots' large public assemblies because he thought that the
religious enthusiasm generated by them might have politically dangerous consequences. But as regards the unfortunate individuals condemned for attending these assemblies, Voltaire sometimes shows a
large measure of sympathy. In his opinion they were misguided rather
than wicked, and their religious 'crimes' were laughable.[135]

---

[134] cf. above, p.302.

[135] it is surely impossible to accept the picture painted by R. Fargher (*Life and
letters in France: the eighteenth century*, p.129): 'Voltaire, the apostle of deism and tolerance, the enemy of Christian dogma, the would-be destroyer of the Church of Rome, was
born and educated a Catholic. It was as an outraged Catholic that he quarrelled with the
English Quaker Edward Higginson for rejecting the sacrament of baptism. He built a
Catholic church for his tenants at Ferney. He was loud in his praises of good parish priests.
And his last battle, fought on his death-bed, was to try and secure for himself burial in
consecrated Catholic ground [...] Englishmen old enough to remember the distrust that
Church felt for chapels in the days before paganism and ecumenical enlightenment
descended on the land may, possibly, have some inkling of what French Catholics, and
Voltaire, felt about those of their countrymen who worshipped outside the national
religion, whose seminaries and headquarters were in foreign countries, and who had borne
arms against the King.' Each of the assertions regarding Voltaire's religious beliefs is true
up to a point, but their significance has been altered by skilful editing. The pious Voltaire

Voltaire's views on the incompatibility of being a Huguenot and holding public office are more difficult to defend, but one may again suggest that Voltaire wished to be very prudent in works which he thought might have a chance of influencing official policy, especially in the years immediately following the Calas case when he considered that the government might be favourable toward some of his proposals. It was obviously out of the question to expect great advances immediately, and moderation was the only sensible course. Lest this be thought an exaggeration, it is easy to see how far Voltaire's prudence went on the Protestant question, and how well he understood the government's attitude. Such things as church organisation were not only distasteful but dangerous, and were better left unmentioned. Voltaire's literary enemy, La Beaumelle, himself a Protestant, was castigated in the *Mémoire présenté au ministère de France* (1767) for giving a remarkably accurate account of the activities and organisation of the *églises du désert*:

Il pousse la démence jusqu'à représenter par bravade ses confrères les protestants de France (qui le désavouent) comme une multitude redoubtable au trône. Il s'est formé, dit-il, un séminaire de prédicants, sous le nom de ministres du désert, qui ont leurs consistoires, leurs synodes, leur juridiction ecclésiastique. Il y a cinquante mille baptêmes et autant de mariages bénis illicitement en Guienne, des assemblées de vingt mille âmes en Poitou, autant en Dauphiné, en Vivarais, en Béarn, soixante temples en Saintonge, un synode national tenu à Nîmes, composé de députés de toutes les provinces.

Ainsi, par ces exagérations extravagantes, il se rend le délateur de ses anciens confrères, et en écrivant contre le trône, il les exposerait à passer pour les ennemis du trône; il ferait regarder la France, parmi les étrangers, comme nourrissant dans son sein les semences d'une guerre civile prochaine, si on ne savait que toutes ces accusations contre les protestants sont d'un fou également en horreur aux protestants et aux catholiques.[136]

---

described by Fargher was not particularly reverent about the sacrament of baptism in the *Lettres philosophiques*. Voltaire rebuilt the existing church at Ferney, but he added an inscription ('Deo erexit Voltaire') which was, at the very least, open to a deistic interpretation. The praise given to good parish priests is more for the social function they carry out than for any religious reasons (cf. below, p.450). Finally, Voltaire's battle to be buried in consecrated ground probably had more to do with his wish to safeguard the inheritance rights of his heirs than with any deathbed conversion or reappearance of suppressed Catholic sentiments.

[136] M.xxvi.363-64. It was just such an uprising engineered by the enemy that the government feared most, and Voltaire had himself mentioned the strategy in his *Histoire de la guerre de 1741*: cf. above, p.269.

Voltaire's tone of calculated horror at the description of things which
were widely known (but which must at all costs not be mentioned) is
perfectly matched in an official document. In 1778 the *procureur du roi* at
Caen condemned a *Lettre pastorale des Déserts de Basse-Normandie*
in the following terms:

Tout dans cet imprimé annonce une correspondance religieuse parmi les
protestants de la province que le malheur de leur naissance et les préjugés de
l'éducation retiennent dans les erreurs. S'il faut en croire le rédacteur, ils ont
des pasteurs pour les enseigner et les conduire, des assemblées secrètes où
ils se réunissent pour les devoirs de leur religion, des règlements pour les
jours de jeûne et de prières et autres œuvres de piété. Ce sont là sans doute
des exagérations de l'auteur, fruit d'une imagination échaufée. Dans le délire
qui l'agite, il ose prophétiser le rétablissement prochain du culte public de
la R.P.R.[137]

The similarity in tone between the two passages is surely significant:
even when outlining reforms which were considered by many (cf.
below, p.333ff.) to be both reasonable and necessary, it was advisable,
at the risk of incurring severe official displeasure, to conceal the extent
to which Protestantism had re-established itself in the kingdom.

Voltaire had therefore to walk a tightrope between on the one
hand the government's neurotic fear of any public manifestation of
Protestantism, and on the other the determination of Protestant
activists in the south to continue holding large, unruly assemblies
which, in Voltaire's view, were dangerous and might be potentially
rebellious. Between these two extremes there was a whole range of
more moderate opinion, in both official and Protestant circles. Voltaire's
attitude on Huguenot assemblies in fact closely resembled that of
moderate *bourgeois* Protestants. Many northern Huguenots were even
probably ready to compromise further than he, providing some arrangement on their civil rights was forthcoming.[138] Were the Protestants of
the south irreconcilable to Voltaire's viewpoint? Although their most
respected pastor, Paul Rabaut, wrote to him persuasively in 1768 to

---

[137] C. Lesage, *A travers le passé du Calvados* (Caen 1927), i.184.

[138] as we have already seen (above, p.317), the Calvinists at Sedan were prepared to
declare that public worship was unnecessary even before any concessions had been made
to them by the government regarding Protestant civil rights. E.-G. Léonard describes the
attitude of the Protestant *bourgeoisie* as follows: 'Sa grande affaire était d'arriver à quelque
arrangement qui accordât aux protestants un état-civil régulier sans leur demander
d'acte de catholicité' ('Le problème', p.448).

plead the case for allowing Protestant assemblies,[139] he too conceded (like Voltaire) that the Protestants must not ask for too much, and that there were necessary limits which they must impose on themselves. His son, the famous Rabaut Saint-Etienne, later to become president of the National Assembly, shared his father's realistic opinions, and asked for 'un culte libre, mais, "non public", dans des "maisons de prière sans décoration extérieure". Il voulait aussi que les pasteurs fussent reconnus "non comme ministres, mais comme simples citoyens" ' (Léonard, *Histoire ecclésiastique*, p.183). There was obviously a good possibility of negotiating with the government on this sort of basis, for one of the proposals in the report presented by Gilbert de Voisins in 1767 was that certain pastors be given safe-conducts, not as ministers of the Reformed Church but as private individuals (cf. below, p.336).

Saint-Etienne's moderation is not really surprising when one considers that pastors of the *églises du désert* were themselves, from the late 1750s onwards (and in many areas earlier), respectable *bourgeois* who had acquired a position of considerable prestige in some parts of the *midi*. Men like this had a lot to lose, and while they stubbornly defended what they understood to be the interests of the Huguenots, their ideas were very often substantially different from those held by the rural population they were supposed to represent. A brief extract from a letter written in May 1773 by Jean Gal-Pomaret to Olivier-Desmont, a Reformed minister at Bordeaux, criticising some of his more activist colleagues, will show how greatly the character and attitudes of many Protestant pastors had changed throughout the century: 'Nous avons quelques pasteurs qui se croiroient en droit d'aller paître les protestants transplantés à Cadix; cependant, s'ils y alloient y former des assemblées, ils auroient tort.'[140] Yet if Antoine Court and his colleagues had abstained from holding illegal assemblies in France during the years following Louis XIV's death, it is fair to say that Gal-Pomaret would never have had the chance to become a pastor.

Growing conservatism and prudence had therefore combined to make the leaders of even the *églises du désert* more willing to compromise in their demands for religious freedom. Voltaire's opinions on Protestant

---

[139] Best.D14784, 29 February 1768. The letter was addressed to Moultou, but was intended to be passed on to Voltaire and was in fact endorsed by him (see this letter, commentary, n.1).

[140] Charles Dardier, 'Lettres écrites par divers pasteurs au sujet des églises réformées de France', *Bpf* (1869), xviii.340.

assemblies must be placed in their historical context. As the 1760s progressed, many ministers and government servants became increasingly tolerant, and with men like Choiseul in power there were some hopes of improving the Huguenots' lot. Yet conservatives persisted in their views and sometimes found unexpected allies. I shall shortly be considering in some detail the circumstances surrounding the preparation of Gilbert de Voisins's *Mémoires sur les moyens de donner aux protestans un état civil en France*[141] and Voltaire's possible knowledge of the existence of this secret report. Despite the fact that it has been hailed as a great step forward in the Huguenot cause, de Voisins was very stern in his attitude toward illegal assemblies, including the following article (XII) in the *Projet de déclaration* at the end of his *Mémoires*: 'Défendons très-expressément à nosdits sujets Religionnaires toutes assemblées & attroupements entr'eux, sous prétexte d'exercice & actes de leur Religion & de prieres en commun, soit de jour ou de nuits, & en pleine campagne ou dans les maisons & habitations, & en quelque lieux que ce puisse être' (pp.140-41; cf. pp.51, 124, 131). Nonetheless, in the body of his report (p.51), de Voisins admitted just as explicitly that conditions should not be made unbearable for the Protestants and that they should be permitted religious freedom in their own houses: 'Ils peuvent prier en commun, mais entre parens, domestiques, amis, ou voisins seulement: en petit nombre, sans bruit & sans éclat audehors.' The same point is made in the second *Mémoire*:

Cette liberté domestique & privée demeurera renfermée dans l'intérieur de leurs familles & de leurs maisons. On ne s'informera point de ce qui pourra s'y passer entre'eux par rapport aux actes de religion. Chaque famille, enfans & descendans, domestiques, quelques parens, quelques amis mêmes, selon l'occasion, sans qu'on y regarde de trop près, mais toujours en petit nombre, qu'il sera peut-être à propos de borner; & sur-tout sans forme ni apparence de culte exterieur, & encore moins d'assemblées.[142]

Despite Gilbert's strong language regarding assemblies, the line of distinction between meetings in a private house and similar gatherings in

---

[141] n.p. 1787; for full title see bibliography. There are two *Mémoires* followed by a *Projet de déclaration*.

[142] pp.97-98; cf. also article II of the *Projet de déclaration*: 'notre intention est qu'ils puissent, chacun dans l'intérieur de sa maison, vivre tranquillement, sans autre gêne sur sa Religion que de s'abstenir de toute apparence de publicité, & de se renfermer, pour satisfaire à ce qui peut regarder la conscience, dans l'intérieur domestique le plus mesuré, famille, serviteurs, amis; le tout en petit nombre, tel seulement que comporte la vie privée' (*Mémoires*, pp.135-36).

a *maison de prière* does not seem very clear; perhaps the number of people attending the service was crucial, but nowhere does de Voisins give any precise indication as to exactly how many people might meet together before constituting an unlawful assembly. Given the indulgence which might reasonably be expected from government servants in the interpretation of this rule, a firm position for negotiation with the Protestants was made possible. A solution which allowed a fair degree of latitude would be acceptable to both the *bourgeois* Protestants of the north and the more conservative leaders of the south. Unfortunately, as we shall see later, de Voisins's proposals were not put into effect. The Edict of Toleration, finally granted by Louis XVI in 1787, made relatively few concessions, if considered in the context of complete religious freedom, but even then many Protestants were not disappointed, as E.-G. Léonard ('Economie et religion,' p.14) explains: 'L'Edit de tolérance de 1787, dont on s'est plu à dénoncer les insuffisances, répondait entièrement aux vœux de nos bourgeois, et Rabaut Saint-Etienne lui-même n'avait pas demandé bien davantage.'

Voltaire's attitude on Protestant assemblies demonstrates therefore how well he was in touch with the contemporary situation. His emphasis on the *culte privé* would both allay the fears of the government and at the same time satisfy a substantial element of Protestant opinion. Increasing epistolary contact with pastors like Pomaret and Rabaut from 1767 onwards may even have caused his position to become more liberal, as he came to realise that the Protestant leaders in the south were not merely ignorant hotheads,[143] but even if this was not so, Voltaire must be given credit for having shown the way to a solution which avoided the extremist views of both sides. In the 1760s and 1770s when the government was still unwilling to consider complete toleration of the type canvassed by Turgot, only a compromise like that envisaged by Voltaire had any chance of success.

viii. *Voltaire, Gilbert de Voisins's* Mémoires *and* L'Ingénu

Throughout the eighteenth century, as I have tried to show, it was primarily Protestant assemblies which worried the government, since

[143] this seems to have been his attitude at the time of the Calas case: cf. Best.D11128, Voltaire to Jean Ribotte, *c.* 25 March 1763: 'Si vous pouvez faire dire de ma part au ministre Rabot qu'il est un fou et qu'il faut qu'il se taise jusqu'à ce que le procès des Calas soit entièrement gagné, vous rendrés un très grand service et de dire aussi à vos Ministres qu'ils fassent le plus d'enfants qu'ils pourront aux servantes, mais que d'ailleurs ils soyent infiniment circonspects. Il est question de leur faire du bien pourvu qu'ils ne l'empêchent pas.'

these meetings could not fail to appear rebellious in the eyes of the Catholic majority. But the problem had other aspects which gained increasing significance as the century wore on. The 1724 edict had restated the anti-Huguenot legislation, and at every point of his life the Protestant was surrounded and harassed by a corpus of repressive measures: Protestant baptism was proscribed, children might be abducted from their parents, and most important of all, Protestant marriages, when carried out *au désert* by a Protestant minister, were illegal, any children of such a union being bastards, and theoretically unable to inherit their parents' property.

Yet paradoxically enough, it was the sheer quantity and comprehensiveness of this repressive legislation that eventually helped the Protestants to regain their civil rights. For the edict appeared quite unworkable. The government's attempts at enforcing the legislation, though sometimes violent, were spasmodic and largely unsuccessful. Not only was there opposition from the Protestants themselves, who on this issue were for once united since it threatened all classes and shades of opinion, many of the administrators and magistrates responsible for applying the law also wished to see it substantially altered. These men frequently pointed to the paradoxical situation of the clergy, required to administer the sacraments to the *nouveaux convertis*, men whom they regarded as relapsed heretics.[144] Bishops and priests indeed often refused to do this, since in their opinion it was tantamount to committing sacrilege.

It seemed therefore imperative to find a solution that would not only safeguard France's status as a Catholic country and avoid shocking the scruples of the clergy, but which would also diminish the number of invalid Protestant marriages whose numbers, by the late 1750s and early 1760s, had reached alarming proportions. As early as 1726 a proposal had been made (Dedieu, i.401-402) that Protestants should have a civil marriage celebrated before a magistrate, and similar ideas continued to be canvassed periodically in the following years. 1749 saw an effort by Machault d'Arnouville to involve the chaplain of the Swedish embassy in moves to introduce legislation in favour of the Protestants.[145] In 1752 Joly de Fleury, son of the magistrate who had probably been largely responsible for drafting the 1724 edict,

[144] cf. Lüthy, *La Banque protestante*, ii.22.

[145] see A. Salomon, 'Le pasteur alsacien C.-F. Baer, chapelain de l'ambassade de Suède à Paris (1719-1797)', *Bpf* (1925), lxxiv.423-49.

addressed a *mémoire* to the *conseil du roi,* a *mémoire* which had been requested by Saint-Florentin himself. His suggestion was that the clergy should forget their scruples and marry any *nouveaux convertis* prepared to accept the Catholic rite: this concession on the clergy's part was to be rewarded by a strict repression of Protestant marriages and baptisms. The policy of repression was attempted and failed (Dedieu, i.226-29). Ripert de Montclar's *Mémoire théologique et politique au sujet des mariages des protestans de France* (1755) marks a clear step forward in proposing that Protestant marriages should be celebrated before a civil magistrate. Though this concession might have been expected to incur ecclesiastical opposition, Montclar's assertion that priests were profaning the sacraments by administering them to non-Catholics was probably supported by a sizeable proportion of the clergy. The same year, moreover, saw two meetings between the pastor Paul Rabaut and the prince de Conti, meetings regarded with suspicion by some but significant nonetheless because they heralded a period when Protestant leaders were to gain a semi-official status. As we can see, there had been no lack of informed discussion about the problem of Huguenot marriages. How would the government go about finding a solution?

An example in fact already existed in the kingdom of France which showed that toleration was possible. This was the province of Alsace, annexed in 1648, and still enjoying the religious provisions of the Treaty of Westphalia: not only Lutherans but even Calvinists were allowed to practice their religion there (Richard, pp.284-86), and the validity of Protestant marriages, never disputed, was confirmed once more by Louis xv in 1763. Why should this limited toleration not be extended to the rest of the kingdom? Even Saint-Florentin, the Huguenots' arch-enemy, realised that something must be done (Dedieu, ii.61), and on receiving a pressing letter from Choiseul dated 1 June 1766, he asked the distinguished magistrate Gilbert de Voisins to draft a report on the question.[146] The resulting two *Mémoires* remained highly secret and were not finally published until 1787, but their preparation provoked great activity in certain government and church circles at the time. And although Gilbert de Voisins was known to have

[146] cf. Michel Antoine, *Le Conseil du roi sous le règne de Louis XV* (Geneva 1970), pp. 448-49. I have investigated Voltaire's possible knowledge of Gilbert's *Mémoires* and the other questions dealt with in the present section of this book in my 'Voltaire, Gilbert de Voisins's *Mémoires* and the problem of Huguenot civil rights (1767-1768)', *Studies on Voltaire* (1978), clxxiv.7-57, where a more detailed discussion of these problems will be found.

Jansenist sympathies and was not therefore very favourable to the political aspirations of the French episcopate, it seems as if the government wanted his proposals to have the widest possible support. The archbishop of Narbonne was summoned to Paris in October 1766 and spent three weeks working on the Protestant question with de Voisins, who was able to submit his first *Mémoire* for discussion. Saint-Florentin himself collaborated by forwarding to Gilbert anything which seemed relevant to the dossier. The duc de Choiseul and the prince de Beauvau were also party to the elaboration of the *Mémoires* and to the discussions surrounding them (Dedieu, ii.65). Gilbert would have liked the archbishop to approve his ideas, but the latter said that, as a priest, he was unable to do this. He did admit, however, that he saw the necessity for the government to do something for the Protestants regarding their civil rights on a non-religious basis. Let us look in a little more detail at the conclusions and proposals of these important *Mémoires*.

The first point to note is Gilbert's refreshing frankness, for he makes no attempt to conceal the extent of the problem. Quoting from a letter written in 1765 by the *intendant* of Languedoc Saint-Priest, he shows that both marriages and baptisms are carried out almost publicly within sight of many towns and that even rich Protestants are not afraid to attend them. To change this situation, the government would need large numbers of troops, and even if these were available, it would be an extremely difficult enterprise. Yet despite his pragmatism, Gilbert still retains something of the ambivalent attitude characteristic of Louis xv's reign, for he considers that the conversion of the Protestants to Catholicism remains 'un objet définitif' (*Memoires*, p.79). The dual and perhaps contradictory aims proposed by Gilbert are clearly stated in his first *Mémoire* (pp.49-50):

Il semble donc que le parti qu'on pourroit prendre entre les deux extrémités, seroit de maintenir l'interdiction publique & solemnelle de la Religion prétendue réformée portée par nos dernières loix; de ne point perdre de vue l'objet permanent toujours desirable, de ramener ceux qui y sont encore attachés; mais en même-temps de leur laisser comme provisoirement dans cet état où ils se trouvent une sorte de liberté domestique & privée de Religion, & sans forcer leur conscience, & sans leur ôter toute voie de satisfaire à ce qu'elle peut exiger.

Conditions might be made more bearable for the Huguenots if certain pastors were given safe-conducts 'révocables en tout temps', and which would not amount to giving them official recognition. As regards civil rights, Gilbert would like curés to baptise Protestant children without creating too many difficulties (pp.56-59). Marriages, he recommends, should be celebrated before a secular magistrate. Even religious freedom should be permitted, 'mais entre parens, domestiques, amis, ou voisins seulement' (p.51). Yet it is clear that these concessions are not brought about by any purely humanitarian spirit: they merely accept what the government could not avoid recognising in the 1760s, that chaos was being caused in several parts of France because of the legal fiction that there were no longer any Protestants in the kingdom, and that some solution had to be found for the problem. The long-term aim is still an entirely Catholic kingdom, which is clear from Gilbert's explicit re-commendation that the exclusion of non-Catholics from a variety of pro-fessions ('Médecin, Chirurgien, Apothicaire & Sage-femme, Libraire & Imprimeur') should be maintained: this discrimination 'n'est pas d'une médiocre importance pour acheminer leur retour, par la gêne où elle les met tant qu'ils perseverent dans leur erreur' (*Mémoires*, pp.121-122).

Despite the limited nature of Gilbert's proposals, they would have represented a considerable step forward had they been adopted in the mid 1760s. Yet there is something of a mystery over their fate. Almost certainly composed in 1767 (Coquerel, ii.458), the *Mémoires* had apparently commissioned by Louis xv himself, and a comment at the beginning of the second *Mémoire* claims that about this time (July or August 1767) the first *Mémoire* 'a été lu dans un Comité du Conseil [du roi], où il n'a pas été désapprouvé' (*Mémoires*, p.84). Discussions continued to be held between the prince de Beauvau and the archbishop of Narbonne, the latter eventually expressing his virtual approval of the report on a practical level, though, as a priest, he still had strong reservations. Contacts also took place between de Voisins and Lecointe, one of the Protestant agents in Paris, and we know that Choiseul was pressing for both parts of the report to be submitted. It is even possible that Lecointe met Saint-Florentin himself (cf. Dedieu, ii.73). And yet the plan to grant the Protestants a limited number of civil rights fell through. Was this due to the death of Gilbert de Voisins in 1769? Was it merely consigned to an obscure bureau at Versailles, or can we arrive at a more plausible explanation as to why the expected legislation did not materialise?

Professor S. S. B. Taylor has discussed this problem in an important article,[147] and his conclusions will provide an admirable starting point

[147] 'Voltaire's *L'Ingénu*, the Huguenots and Choiseul', *AE*, pp.107-36.

for our own investigation. For the sake of clarity, I shall summarise professor Taylor's views under four headings. Firstly he claims that important measures in favour of the Huguenots were being mooted in 1767 and were in fact partly adopted by the government. These were a direct result of Gilbert de Voisins's *Mémoires*, in fact an application of them insofar as they were accepted. The proposals on marriage were not approved because the government did not wish to alienate the clergy. Secondly, professor Taylor thinks that Voltaire was aware of all this, and that he was probably used by Choiseul and the government to control the unruly Protestants and by the Protestants to inform the Court of their views. Thirdly, professor Taylor suggests that the most sensible Protestants accepted that they could not achieve all their aims at once. They had to be content for the time being with a first step on the road to complete civil rights. His final point is that *L'Ingénu* (and other works) were remodelled as a form of discreet propaganda. Voltaire could not be too open in what he said for fear of prejudicing the Protestants' hopes of favourable legislation.

It is certainly beyond reasonable doubt that the Huguenot theme running through *L'Ingénu* is an important one. As professor Taylor observes, the action of the *conte* takes place in 1689, four years after the repeal of the Edict of Nantes, and one of the chapters is set in Saumur, a Protestant town gravely affected by the government's policies. He also draws attention to the fact that a Huguenot had taught the Ingénu French, that a Jesuit asks him whether he is a Huguenot, that he is later arrested as a Huguenot sympathiser, and wishes to go to Versailles to make the king aware of the situation. There is also a significant tribute to Choiseul. One might add that the tyrannical minister St Pouange may well be a portrait of Saint-Florentin, the minister on whom the Huguenots' destinies chiefly depended.[148] Nonetheless, the Protestant theme, as professor Taylor himself observes (p.135), is only one of a number which appear to have inspired *L'Ingénu*. Sources in Voltaire's correspondence can be found as early as 1762,[149] and there seem no conclusive

---

[148] cf. Voltaire, *Romans et contes*, ed. H. Bénac (Paris 1960), p.641, n.347.

[149] see Voltaire's comment in a letter of *c.* 29 July 1762 (Best.D10616) to Théodore Tronchin: 'je ne sçais s'il est mal d'exposer en une seule page tout ce qui peut rendre la religion des Calas excusable aux yeux des Jansénistes, qui dans le fond pensent assez comme Claude, Evêque de Turin. Il me paraît que tous les parlements de France, excepté celui de Toulouse, marchent à grands pas vers un protestantisme mitigé.' Professor H.T. Mason, 'The unity of Voltaire's *L'Ingénu*', *AE*, p.101, n.15, has already pointed out that some of the material of *L'Ingénu* might belong to an earlier date.

indications in the *conte* that Voltaire was aware of possible government moves in favour of the Huguenots in 1767. Similarly, another work which might have been expected to give some inkling of this, the *Siècle de Louis XIV* (a revised edition appeared in 1768), shows, if anything, a slightly less sympathetic attitude to the Protestants.[150]

One may certainly say with some measure of confidence that the Protestant situation in France was one of the fields which, since the early 1760s, had preoccupied Voltaire and in which he had gained a creditable amount of knowledge and experience. But is there any real evidence that he was aware of special measures being contemplated in 1767? Professor Taylor instances a letter from Voltaire to Moultou written on 24 April 1767 (Best.D14140), in which the *philosophe* rejoices at 'deux grandes nouvelles'. The first concerns the expulsion of the Jesuits from Spain, and the second obviously refers to the Protestants,

une espèce de persécutés qui peut enfin espérer de jouir des droits du genre humain, que le révérend père La Chaise et Michel Le Tellier leur a ravis.

Il faudrait piquer d'honneur Mr De Maupeou. Je réponds bien de Mr Le Duc De Choiseul et de mr Le Duc De Praslin, mais dans une affaire de législation le chancelier a toujours la voix prepondérante.

So, on 24 April Voltaire knew, or thought he knew, that the government intended to take some action on Protestant marriages. But does this prove that he had any special information about the government's intentions? Did he possess knowledge which was unknown to other interested parties? An indication that Voltaire was in no special class is given by a letter of 16 May 1767 from Paul Rabaut to Jean Pradel:

Les nouvelles qu'on débite sont fort hasardées. On ne peut y faire aucun fonds. Mes correspondances de Paris m'en auraient appris quelque chose, s'il était vrai qu'on voulût, comme en [*sic*] le débite, rétablir l'édit de Nantes. Il paraît que ces nouvelles ont pour but de faire peur au pape [. . .] Je ne doute pourtant pas que le gouvernement n'ait de bonnes intentions à notre égard, mais nous ignorons jusqu'où elles vont et quand il les manifestera.[151]

Rumours among the Protestants were obviously widespread, and the fact that Voltaire wrote to Moultou in high spirits on the topic is by

---

[150] see appendix 3 for a more detailed discussion of this question.
[151] *Paul Rabaut: ses lettres à divers (1744-1794)*, ed. Picheral and Dardier (Paris 1891-1892), ii.69-70.

itself no adequate reason for supposing that he had any special information. Moreover, he had also written to Paul Rabaut on the same day
(16 May). If, as professor Taylor suggests, Choiseul was using Voltaire
as a private channel of communication with the Huguenots, one would
surely expect to find some indication of the government's intentions in
this letter to the most respected and influential *pasteur du désert*.

In fact, it seems as if this is the first letter Voltaire had ever written to
Rabaut. His comments are optimistic, but expressed in general terms
(except to agree that the prince de Beauvau is very well disposed towards the Protestants), and although he tells Rabaut that 'une grande
révolution commence dans les esprits', this can hardly be taken as a
reference to current government action, since he adds immediately:
'Vivez assez longtemps, Monsieur, pour en voir l'accomplissement;
celà sera long' (Best.D14185, my italics). So, in a long letter of 16 May
1767 to the *de facto* head of the French Huguenot Churches, Voltaire
gives no indication that special moves were being made in government
circles to improve the Protestants' lot. Are we to assume that by 23
May he had been enlightened by Choiseul or some other correspondent
or – as seems infinitely more probable – are we to conclude that he was
no better informed than were the Protestant leaders, and that he had
merely heard rumours which were fairly widespread? In fact, what
evidence is available seems to show that, far from being at the centre of
supposed negotiations between the government and the Protestants,
Voltaire was completely uninformed about what was going on. In
letters to Chardon (14 November, Best.D14530), Damilaville (18
November, D14536 and 27 November, D14553) and Marin (27 November, D14554), Voltaire repeatedly asked his Parisian correspondents
for detailed information about the rumours he had heard. A letter of 2
December to Marmontel seems to indicate that he had at last obtained
some more precise information, but it is not until 16 December that we
can be sure. On that day Voltaire wrote to Christin in quite a different
vein, giving details of the government's measures (Best.D14591):

Deux déclarations du conseil, sans nommer les protestants, leur accordent le
droit d'éxercer toutes les professions et de négocier dans le roiaume. On a
minuté un édit pour légitimer leurs mariages; il a été quatre fois sur le tapis
mais enfin il n'a point passé à cause des conséquences.

Surely this evidence from his correspondence shows clearly enough
that, for the major part of 1767, Voltaire had no special information

about Gilbert's report or other government measures in favour of the Huguenots?

But professor Taylor has other evidence to support his thesis that Voltaire was used by Choiseul as a channel of communication with the Huguenots. This is in the form of a letter written by Seigneux de Correvon to Voltaire on 22 October 1767 'to complain of provocative actions by the authorities in terms that leave no real doubt about Voltaire's role in the matter' (Taylor, p.127):

Où est donc Mon cher Monsieur la sage et humaine tolérance dont il semblait que le Ministère eût adopté le systhème? ne voulait on que leurer les Peuples d'une vaine lueur d'espérance? et se flatoit on d'arrêter par là les émigrations? En vérité, l'on n'y conçoit rien; tandis qu'on parle de paix d'un Côté, on ne cesse d'affliger de l'autre. La conduite de mr le Prince de Beauvau et celle de Mr le Duc de Richelieu ne sont pas aisées à concilier.

Ne pouriés vous point Monsieur faire connaître à Mr le Duc de Choiseuil les inconvéniens de ces nouvelles allarmes pour *le sage but qu'il se propose?* Se pourait-il qu'on suivît en cela ses intentions et la volonte du Roy?[152]

On the face of it, this letter does appear to show that Voltaire had told Seigneux about the government's intention of relaxing the anti-Protestant legislation, and had possibly 'leaked' information about the preparation of Gilbert de Voisins's *Mémoires*. But the real explanation is quite different, for the letter is not merely a general complaint about the repressive attitude of the authorities, it is a detailed account of one incident, an incident which had been preoccupying Voltaire for several months, and which we may conveniently call the Sainte-Foix affair.

On 26 June 1767 Voltaire had written to Damilaville (Best.D14246):

On[153] me mande, mon cher ami, que les huguenots d'un petit canton en Guienne ont assassiné un curé, et en ont poursuivi deux autres. Si la chose est vrai ces messieurs n'ont pas la tolérance en grande recommandation, et on n'en aura pas beaucoup pour eux. Je ne veux pas croire cette horrible nouvelle.

The next paragraph expresses Voltaire's great fear – that this event might have an adverse effect on the chances of rehabilitating Sirven: 'Pour peu qu'ils eussent donné lieu à une émeute, ils ne feraient pas de bien à la cause des Sirven. Je pense qu'alors il faudrait tout abandonner. Mais je me flatte encor que ce n'est qu'un faux bruit.' Throughout the

---

[152] Best.D14497 (professor Taylor's italics). Gabriel de Seigneux, seigneur de Correvon, was one of the *bannerets* (or magistrates) of Lausanne.

[153] his informant seems to have been the marquis d'Argence: cf. Best.D14265.

summer and autumn of 1767 Voltaire was preoccupied with the affair. Again and again, in letters to correspondents, he expressed his fears that this unfortunate incident would wreck Sirven's chances of vindication and harm the status of the Protestants in general. As time went on he was able to piece together what had really happened: two hundred Protestants were in prison at Bordeaux, the bishop of Agen had issued a *monitoire* (the same proceeding as had been used in the Calas case), even Richelieu (who once again was an invaluable source of information for Voltaire) considered that the affair was very serious (cf. Best.D14360). Voltaire naturally wrote to his Swiss correspondents to try to obtain further details (cf. his letter of 14 August to Jean Ribotte, Best.D14367), and we may surmise that it was a similar request to Seigneux de Correvon which prompted the detailed account and accompanying reflections contained in the letter from which professor Taylor quotes in support of his thesis.

According to Seigneux, two distinct incidents had occurred in the Sainte-Foix affair. A Protestant assembly about two leagues from Bordeaux had been discovered by soldiers. As the minister had not yet arrived, an elder was reading from the New Testament, and this 'pauvre Lecteur sans caractère est condanné à la Corde, Le Maitre de la Maison aux galères, et tous les auditeurs à un banissement de cinq ans, et à la confiscation de la moitié de leurs biens' (Best.D14497). Quite independent of this, apparently, was the affair of the 'masqués de Sainte-Foy' who were suspected of being Protestants 'puisqu'ils en vouloient à un curé'. Seigneux goes on to bewail the apparent change in the government's attitude, warns of the dangers of mass emigration, and asks Voltaire to intervene in the affair with Choiseul. By remarking that 'la conduite de mr le Prince de Beauvau et celle de Mr le Duc de Richelieu ne sont pas aisées à concilier' he highlights the apparent inconsistency of government policy, for Richelieu was regarded as a 'hard-liner'[154] whereas the prince de Beauvau had gained a wide reputation for his clemency and moderation. The demand for an 'Edit fixe et irrévocable' at the end of the letter is a natural corollary of the unjust procedures Seigneux has been describing. There seems absolutely no need to connect it with the circumstances surrounding the composition of Gilbert

---

[154] Richelieu's reputation for severity was maintained after his move from Languedoc to Guyenne: cf. Paul d'Estrée, *La Vieillesse de Richelieu (1758-1788)* (Paris 1918), pp. 5-8; A. de Boilisle, *Mémoires authentiques du maréchal de Richelieu (1725-1757)* (Paris 1918), pp.237-47.

de Voisins's *Mémoires*, and it can hardly be taken as conclusive proof that Voltaire had passed on secret information to the Protestants in order to restrain them from imprudent acts at this crucial time.

Even the fact that Seigneux specifically asks Voltaire to intervene with Choiseul does not necessarily prove that he was acting as a special intermediary between the minister and Protestant leaders, for the two men were widely known to have close and cordial relations. For several years now, Choiseul had obtained special favours and privileges for the *philosophe*: what more natural than for Seigneux to suggest that Voltaire should ask his powerful friend to intervene? This conjecture appears all the more likely when one considers the extent to which Swiss Protestants thought Voltaire was capable of influencing Choiseul. When a growing diplomatic rift between France and Geneva determined Choiseul to construct a port on Lake Geneva at Versoix, in French territory, a town in which he hoped to guarantee freedom of religion, Voltaire supported the project enthusiastically (cf. Best. D15432). Not only did the Genevese find out about the plan very quickly, they almost immediately connected Voltaire with it and assumed that he had been largely instrumental in persuading the minister to adopt the project (Best.D14162, commentary). In Paris reactions were quite different. The news does not seem to have been known, or at any rate believed, for several months. Mme Du Deffand dismissed the possibility of any connection as late as 9 December. She told Walpole she had heard about the Versoix project, but added: 'je n'ai point ouï dire que Voltaire y entrât pour rien, et c'est un conte qu'on vous a fait' (Best.D14580, commentary). Seigneux de Correvon cannot have been unaware in Lausanne of the gossip buzzing through neighbouring Geneva, and this topical reminder of Voltaire's influence with the minister is surely a sufficient explanation of Seigneux's having mentioned Choiseul in the letter I have quoted.

The Sainte-Foix affair and its consequences continued to occupy Voltaire in the last months of 1767. His letter of 25 December to Olivier Desmont is highly intriguing and leads one to speculate as to whether Desmont might not have been the man arrested at Sainte-Foix and, according to Seigneux, condemned to death.[155] Voltaire is at pains to

---

[155] according to Emile Du Cailar and Daniel Benoît (*Gal-Pomaret, pasteur de Ganges* pp.160-61), Desmonts came originally from Durfort, and 'après un court ministère dans les églises de Valleraugue et d'Anduze, venait [in 1771] d'être appelé au poste important de Bordeaux'. Voltaire's letter was 'apparently addressed to Anduse' (Best.D14620, textual notes).

reassure his correspondent: 'La personne à qui vous avez bien voulu écrire, monsieur, le 17 xbr, peut d'abord vous assurer que vous ne serez point pendu [...] Nous sortons de la barbarie' (Best.D14620). How could he be so sure? Had he perhaps tried to intervene at government level? This is, of course, pure speculation, but he does at least mention Choiseul in this letter. Voltaire assures Desmonts that if the latter or his friends can perform the service of finding a brochure needed in connection with the Sirven case, he is sure that 'm. le duc de Choiseul lui-même protégera ceux qu'on exclut des offices municipaux' (Best. D14620). This will be a delicate matter, for the Huguenots do not have the same rights as the Lutherans of Alsace, and Choiseul is not in charge of Languedoc, but it will be possible to attack the *parlement* for having gone beyond its powers. What had presumably happened was that, as a reprisal for the Sainte-Foix affair, the Protestants had seen their civil rights even more strictly curtailed and had been excluded from a number of positions where they had begun to be tolerated. This interpretation does present a slight difficulty, however, for although it is corroborated in a letter from Gal-Pomaret to Voltaire (Best.D14692, 18 January 1768), it would seem that the repressive measures were taken, not by the parlement of Bordeaux as one might have expected, but by the parlement of Toulouse.

I have examined the Sainte-Foix affair at some length in order to show how much it claimed Voltaire's attention during the summer and autumn of 1767. Between 26 June and 30 October a total of seventeen letters included in the definitive edition of Voltaire's correspondence mention the incident in some form or another. Another letter, written at some time in February 1768, reminds us how seriously Voltaire had been preoccupied with the affair, both because of its possible implications for future relations between the Protestants and officialdom, and because of the immediate effects it might have on the Sirven case. The *philosophe*'s pessimism had apparently been confirmed: 'La malheureuse aventure de ste Foi aiant été depuis longtemps représentée au conseil du roi sous les plus noires couleurs, a nui beaucoup à l'affaire des Sirven comme je l'avais prévu' (Best.D14756). But Voltaire here goes further, and claims that 'Ces mêmes considérations ont empêché de signer

It is interesting to note that the Protestant community at Sainte-Foix was one of the four which later continued to hold religious services under the Terror: see Rabaut le Jeune, *Annuaire, ou répertoire ecclésiastique à l'usage des églises réformées et protestantes de l'Empire français* (Paris 1807), p.113.

l'édit qui était tout prêt, pour légitimer les mariages des réformés'. At first sight this might be taken to support professor Taylor's thesis that Voltaire had been aware all along of the government's intentions. Such a view would account for his having been so worried about the Sainte-Foix affair, because he knew it might be used as a pretext by the Protestants' enemies in the government to prevent the adoption of more liberal legislation. But if this was so, why did Voltaire give a different reason when writing to Gal-Pomaret?[156] Surely this would have been an ideal opportunity to drive home the message that the Protestants must abandon their assemblies if they were to have any hope of improving their situation?

Voltaire did, in fact, advise prudence in the holding of assemblies. In the letter already quoted, he observes: 'Il n'y a d'autre parti à prendre que celui d'attendre tout du temps. Il faudrait n'avoir que de loin à loin des assemblées publiques' (Best.D14756). This is the sole specific reference one is able to find in the correspondence for 1767-1768 which might be taken to imply that Voltaire played an active rôle in restraining the Huguenots. The comment was made, however, not to an over-zealous pastor but to Joseph Audra, the philosophic abbé who was to rejoice Voltaire's heart with his account of the advent of tolerance in reactionary Toulouse (cf. Best.D15287). What one must surely conclude is that Voltaire had been speculating as to the various possible reasons which had prevented the marriage edict from becoming law. At first the responsibility had seemed to be that of the clergy; perhaps such a report had come from one of his correspondents in Paris. But later, disappointed at the slow progress of Sirven's rehabilitation, Voltaire appears to have revived his gloomy view of the harmful effects of the Sainte-Foix incident and to have connected it with the failure of liberal elements in the government to have new legislation on Protestant marriages adopted. This speculation on Voltaire's part is far from proving that he had any inkling about the government's moves before the end of 1767.

Two final indications that Voltaire was not a priveleged channel of information between Choiseul and the Huguenots in 1767 can still be given. In the first place, the two men's relations seem to have been somewhat cool at this period: so much is clear from a letter to Damilaville

[156] 'L'édit pour légitimer leurs mariages a été quatre fois sur le tapis au conseil privé du roi. A la fin il n'a point passé *pour ne pas choquer le clergé trop ouvertement*' (Best.D14598, 18 December 1767, my italics).

dated 14 December (Best.D14587): 'Je n'aurai probablement aucune réponse de longtemps de m. le duc de Choiseul. On m'a même fait des tracasseries auprès de lui pour les sottes affaires de Geneve; mais c'est ce qui m'inquiète fort peu.' On 19 December, he made a similar comment – 'm. le duc de Choiseul me néglige beaucoup' – in another letter (Best.D14603) to the same correspondent. Choiseul had apparently taken umbrage at Voltaire's involvement in internal Genevese politics, or at least this was what Voltaire thought. It was only after encouragement from Marmontel (letter of 29 December, Best.D14628) and a letter received from Choiseul himself in January 1768 (see Best.D14664) that Voltaire regained confidence in his relations with the minister. The second, and even more conclusive, indication is a letter written by Paul Rabaut, ostensibly to Paul Moultou, but really intended for Voltaire and in fact endorsed by him (Best.D14784, 29 February 1768). Rabaut says he is aware that the government plans to improve the Protestants' conditions, 'mais je sais aussi qu'on travaille à lui faire adopter un arrangement dont les protestants ne sauraient se contenter', namely the complete banning of public worship and a reduction in the number of ministers. The pastor then puts forward four sets of reasons why this would be an unwise and retrograde step. He is fulsome in his praise of Voltaire, and goes as far as to state: 'Si la main qui nous accablait s'est relâchée, si nous jouissons de quelque tranquillité dans notre patrie, c'est à ce grand homme que nous en sommes redevables.' Yet, although he also comments on the *philosophe*'s relations with influential members of the government and observes that 'ces sages politiques écoutent monsieur de Voltaire et profitent de ses leçons', Rabaut also makes clear that no previous contacts have been made through Voltaire when he adds: 's'il voulait se donner la peine de leur inculquer quelques faits indubitables que j'exposerai ci-après', surely implying that up till now Voltaire has presented no coherent *politique d'ensemble* to the government.

Rabaut's letter is interesting for another reason also, since it reveals that he had not been consulted by the government and appeared rather to resent this. In fact, as we have seen, another Protestant, Lecointe, had been party to the negotiations, and this may explain Rabaut's hostility, for rivalry between the different Protestant representatives was often bitter. Lecointe's own position was threatened after the arrival in Paris of Antoine Court's son, Court de Gébelin, in 1763, but as 'gentilhomme de la chambre du prince de Conti' he retained a certain influence and convassed several projects, including that of a Protestant bank (Schmidt, p.44).[157] He, or other Huguenot sources, had obviously leaked accounts of the proposals to reduce and strictly control the number of ministers and ban public worship in exchange for the right to hold extended private worship in the Protestants' houses, and Rabaut, getting wind of the plan, at that stage made an approach to Voltaire. But why was he so opposed to these proposals? In his 1755 negotiations with the prince de Conti he had not been completely intransigent on the question of Protestant assemblies: he had asked that his coreligionists should be allowed, if not to rebuild their temples, at least to meet in houses or outside towns (Coquerel, ii.215). And in 1762 he appeared similarly prepared to reach agreement with the duc de Fitzjames. On the face of it, Gilbert de Voisins's proposals went some way to granting one of these conditions, and one has the distinct impression that Rabaut's objections are motivated by personal animosity rather than by a reasoned appraisal of the Huguenots' real interests. After all, if Lecointe had been consulted, this represented a loss of face for Gébelin, a close contact if not a *protégé* of Rabaut: the mere fact that Lecointe had been invited to join in negotiations from which Gébelin had been excluded was probably enough to pique Rabaut and to provoke in him a hostile reaction to reports he heard.[158]

There remains an important and at first sight perhaps a rather paradoxical question. Can we be absolutely sure that the legislation adopted by the government in 1767 resulted directly from the preparation of Gilbert de Voisins's *Mémoires*? For there seems to be a certain amount of doubt as to what the 'nouveaux édits en faveur des négociants et des artisans' mentioned by Voltaire on 27 November (Best.D14553, to Damilaville) really were. Theodore Besterman says that what this refers to is 'probably the *Edit...concernant les arts et métiers* (Paris 1767), which was registered 19 June' and which was in Voltaire's library (*Ferney catalogue*, B1153; BV2192).[159] In a note to a similar

---

[157] Paul Rabaut had strenuously opposed Lecointe's proposals on the grounds that they were 'ruineux' (Bib pf, Collection Coquerel, Papiers Rabaut, 318, ff.5-6, Rabaut to Gébelin, 30 December 1763).

[158] several years later, when Malesherbes was *ministre de la maison du roi*, Lecointe corresponded with him and proposed that he (Lecointe) should be chosen as *député* of all the Protestants. Pierre Grosclaude says that Lecointe wished to supplant Court de Gébelin and that he was supported in this by the church at Bordeaux and a few others, but that he was opposed by the churches of Bas-Languedoc. Paul Rabaut explained that it would be very imprudent to back this initiative (*Malesherbes*, p.378, especially n.12).

[159] Best.D14553, n.1.

passage in Best.D14530 (to Chardon) he comments, though without giving any reason for his opinion: 'this may well refer to certain relaxations in favour of Jews as well as Protestants'. And quite inexplicably, confronted by Voltaire's letter to Christin of 16 December 1767 in which the *philosophe* gives his correspondent details[160] of the legislation already adopted by the government, dr Besterman declares that 'the wish was again the father of the thought' (Best.D14591, n.1). Professor Taylor, however, as we have seen, rather more plausibly connects Voltaire's comments with a measure approved on 30 October 1767. Yet, after reproducing Voltaire's report to Gal-Pomaret of the various measures taken in favour of the Protestants (Best.D14598, 18 December 1767), professor Taylor (p.122) comments: 'There had been a number of *Arrêtés* or *Lettres patentes* on the subject of the regulations concerning entry to the trades and professions (23 June, 12 August, 23 August 1767).'

There is, therefore, no agreement between distinguished commentators as to which piece or pieces of legislation Voltaire was actually discussing. This must inevitably make one view with certain amount of suspicion any suggestion that the pro-Protestant measures were taken by the government on a certain date after the due presentation and discussion of Gilbert de Voisins's *Mémoires*, and one's scepticism is increased by the following consideration. As we have seen, Gilbert is very strict as regards assemblies and recommends that the sanctions against Protestants in various trades and professions should be maintained, yet he insists on the importance of recognising Protestant marriages. On 30 October and at several dates during the summer of 1767 participation in trades and professions was made easier for Protestants, but no legislation regarding their marriages was adopted. In other words, Gilbert's proposals for granting limited civil rights to the Protestants were not adopted, and his recommendations in connection with trades and professions were ignored. If the government had been guided by the *Mémoires* in 1767, it is fair to say they had signally misunderstood or distorted Gilbert's conclusions.

One is tempted to guess that disagreements and tensions inside the government, rather than opposition on the part of the clergy (no doubt expected anyway by most ministers), may explain the failure to regularise the Protestants' *état-civil* in 1767 or 1768. As early as 1764

[160] 'Deux déclarations du conseil, sans nommer les protestants, leur accordent le droit d'exercer toutes les professions et de négocier dans le roiaume' (Best.D14591).

Choiseul had been putting pressure on Saint-Florentin to review the situation. On 24 July he wrote to de Voisins that the time to act had come (AN. TT463, f.52). Is it inconceivable that Choiseul, wearied by the slow progress of the de Voisins report, tried to have some pro-Huguenot measures implemented either before it was presented to the Council or just after it was read there at the end of October 1767? Such a sudden initiative would probably have incurred the resentment and opposition of Saint-Florentin, who, now that he had acknowledged the necessity of reforming Protestant legislation, was determined that he would have a dominant rôle in framing the new laws, and wished to await the final completion of the *Mémoires* before allowing reforms to be introduced. It may, therefore, have been Saint-Florentin who discouraged the council from making any radical change on Protestant marriages in 1767, and by the time Gilbert's *Mémoires* were completed about a year later Choiseul may have lost interest, or in his turn may have been piqued by Saint-Florentin's earlier opposition.

The fact that Protestant pastors like Rabaut and Gal-Pomaret began corresponding with Voltaire about this time may have been largely coincidental. At first, during his campaign to rehabilitate Calas, they had been suspicious of the *philosophe* and his motives, and in his turn Voltaire appears to have viewed many Protestant pastors as ignorant fanatics (cf. above, p.333, n.143). But as his interventions in favour of Huguenot galley-slaves and other unfortunates multiplied, the pastors' opinion changed and they expressed their appreciation of his actions to friends in Geneva. Finally they became confident enough to address themselves directly to Voltaire, the more so perhaps since after his attempt to influence public opinion in a general way with the *Traité sur la tolérance*, he appears to have concentrated his activity on helping individual victims of the anti-Protestant laws, Sirven, Chaumont, Espinas, to mention only the most obvious.

A fundamental question must still be answered. Were disagreements among members of the government the only reason for shelving pro-Protestant legislation, or was failure partly due to the unbending attitude of Huguenot extremists? The latter would seem to be professor Taylor's view, for he declares (p.128) that:

Their public declarations of their grievances and intransigence over the matter of full freedom of worship had been a contributory factor in the failure of the 1763 *initiatives* in their favour. Voltaire and Choiseul faced bigotry on either side, in attempting to set matters right.

If these statements mean that the Huguenots, through their own division and failure to arrive at a common policy, were themselves responsible to some extent for retarding the advent of toleration, then one must agree with professor Taylor. But if, on the other hand, he is implying that Huguenot leaders were *dogmatically* inflexible or intransigent in their contacts with the authorities, one must not hesitate to take issue with him. On the first point, both Paul Rabaut and Gal-Pomaret seem to have cared very little about maintaining Calvinist orthodoxy.[161] And on the second, Rabaut in particular showed himself eager to establish a *modus vivendi* with the authorities on every possible occasion. Fierce opposition to any concessions over public worship there sometimes was, but this came not so much from the leaders of the *églises du désert* as from the Protestant masses of the south themselves. Rivalry between the various Huguenot representatives was also an important factor (cf. above, pp.346-47). We have already seen evidence of the bitter divisions between the various Huguenot representatives, and it should also be remembered that the Protestants were not a homogeneous group. In the south, the Protestant peasants, still in considerable number, demanded a maintenance of traditional worship and were in many cases more stubborn than their pastors, men like Rabaut who were conscious of their social superiority over their flock and desired a more authoritarian position (see below, p.380). In the north, as we have seen, the Protestants were numerically weak but often socially influential. They were obsessed above all by the desire to obtain a regular *état-civil*, detesting their southern brethren for the latter's intransigence, and often causing difficulties for those who tried to represent them in Paris. Class divisions became so important that in many areas Protestants of different backgrounds no longer met together for worship, but assembled in separate groups or *sociétés*.[162] The struggle between the various Protestant factions went on all through the 1760s, and it was these dissensions, largely based on class differences, which more than anything prevented the Protestants from pressing on for full legal recognition in a united front.

We have already seen that Court de Gébelin arrived in Paris in

---

[161] see E.-G. Léonard, *Histoire générale*, iii.56, *Histoire ecclésiastique*, p.105, n.3; Daniel Robert, 'Le rôle historique de Paul Rabaut', *Foi et vie* (1952), p.30; Du Cailar and Benoît, *Gal-Pomaret*, p.116; below, pp.375 ff.

[162] see Léonard, *Histoire ecclésiastique*, pp.72 ff.; Pierre Dez, *Histoire des protestants de l'église réformée de l'Ile de Ré* (La Rochelle 1926), pp.115-19.

November 1763 and that Voltaire had prevailed upon him in the previous year to withdraw the *Toulousaines,* a provocative work attacking the authorities over the Calas case (cf. above, p.298). In return for this compliant attitude Voltaire tried to smooth his path in the capital, as he reported to Végobre on 9 December 1763 (Best.D11546): 'Il m'a prié de lui faire avoir des audiances de quelques personnes qui peuvent beaucoup; je l'ai fait.' But Voltaire considered that Gébelin's task would be lengthy, and he was right. Despite meeting Saint-Florentin, possibly also Maurepas, and establishing contacts with the vice-chancellor in 1765 (Dedieu, *Histoire politique,* ii.100-106), Antoine Court's son experienced many difficulties, a considerable number coming from members of his own community. He was unable to gain official recognition from the *églises du désert* as their representative, having to content himself with the title 'correspondant des églises'.[163] The most likely explanation of this hostility is that Gébelin was seen by many to be Paul Rabaut's man, and hindering his efforts was a convenient way of combatting the latter's considerable influence and prestige, especially in the south. But even in the town of which he was pastor Rabaut had enemies, who at one point considered revenging themselves on the unfortunate Gébelin. Incredible though it may seem, the Protestant *notables* of Nîmes actually threatened to denounce him to Saint-Florentin: 'Si M. de Gébelin continue, il ne sera pas en sûreté à Paris; on sera obligé de prendre des mesures contre lui' (reported in Rabaut's letter to Gébelin of 8 October 1764, quoted by Schmidt, p.59).

With such bitter divisions between them it is a wonder that the French Huguenots ever managed to regain their civil rights before the Revolution. The failure of attempts in 1767 to better their conditions may be partly attributable to this factor, for Paul Rabaut and his *protégé* Court de Gébelin were obviously not consulted in the discussions over Gilbert de Voisins's *Mémoires,* the Protestant viewpoint being put by one of their rivals. Nonetheless, despite these internecine struggles between influential Huguenots which may have contributed to delaying their complete emancipation for twenty years, 1767 did see the first statutory improvement of the Protestants' position since the repeal of the Edict of Nantes. Voltaire's part in this change must not be underestimated, though I have tried to show that he had no special

---

[163] cf. Paul Schmidt, *Court de Gébelin à Paris (1763-1784)* (Sainte-Blaise, Roubaix 1908), pp.22-25.

knowledge of the government's intentions during the years 1767-1768. Firstly, through his propaganda in favour of the Calas family and his more general *plaidoyer* for the Protestants in the *Traité sur la tolérance*, Voltaire had drawn public attention to a class of Frenchmen who were systematically discriminated against for reasons which no longer appeared valid to many of their fellow countrymen. References or allusions to the Huguenots' plight continued to occur in his works, the most notable example being *L'Ingénu*, but he also began to concentrate on helping individual victims of the anti-Protestant laws. As he grew older, Voltaire became progressively more unlike the stereotyped image of a *philosophe* – a thinker besotted with generalisations who confined himself to a 'sentiment de philantropie universelle' (Coquerel, ii.427). Individuals increasingly claimed his attention. This is especially true in the case of French Protestantism, as we shall now see in considering Voltaire's activities during the last years of his life.

ix. *The last years*

'Plus je deviens vieux et malade moins j'ai de crédit', lamented Voltaire to Rabaut Saint-Etienne, Paul Rabaut's son, on 29 August 1768 (Best. D15194). There is probably a certain amount of truth in his comment, for no doubt a saturation point existed beyond which appeals to government officials did more harm than good. Yet the last years of Voltaire's life saw little diminution in his efforts on behalf of the French Protestants. 'Jamais je n'ai tant abhorré l'intolérance et la persécution', he told Végobre on 25 February 1768 (Best.D14777), and a brief review of his interests in the last few years of his life will show us that this was no idle boast. As usual Voltaire's thoughts and feelings found an outlet in positive, constructive action.

Towards the end of 1767, the leading dramatist of his day passed judgement on a play sent to him by a young admirer: Fenouillet de Falbaire's *L'Honnête criminel*. This incident of literary history is interesting in that it shows us Voltaire's views on the theatrical possibilities of the anti-Protestant laws and also demonstrates that, despite his many contacts, he did not always grasp immediately the full significance of contemporary allusions. For Voltaire was at first unaware that the plot was based on an actual event, the courageous action of Jean Fabre who had taken the place of his aged father when the latter had been condemned to the galleys (see above, p.277, n.59). 'Avez vous lu *l'honnête Criminel?*' he asked Damilaville on 1 December 1767: 'Il y a de très beaux vers. L'auteur aurait pu faire de cette pièce un ouvrage excellent; il aurait fait une très grande sensation et aurait servi votre cause' (Best.D14562). And writing to the author a few days later (11 December) he commented: 'Je suis fâché que votre prédicant Lisimond ait eu la lâcheté de laisser traîner son fils aux galères' (Best.D14583). A similar opinion was expressed to Chabanon on 25 December (Best.D14617). But by 16 January 1768 Voltaire had found out the actual facts of the case and he was highly indignant.[164] If the events portrayed in the play were accurate, Fabre's father was 'un grand misérable'. The revelation seems to have rather disgusted Voltaire with a play he had originally praised, even though his approval had been qualified. On 10 April 1768 (Best.D14933) mme Du Deffand informed him that she was one of the few people who disliked *L'Honnête criminel*, and Voltaire replied assuring her that he shared her opinion: 'Je n'ai pas plus pleuré que vous à la lecture de la pièce dont vous me parlez' (Best.D14964, 18 April).

The Sirven affair and the Versoix project continued to occupy Voltaire's attention in 1768. The outcome of both was still in doubt, but towards the end of the year he received a letter which encouraged him greatly regarding the progress of toleration and the possibility of ameliorating the Protestants' lot. On 2 November the abbé Joseph Audra wrote to him describing the near revolution brought about in what had been one of the most bigoted towns of the kingdom (Best. D15287):

Je connais actuellement assez Toulouse pour vous assurer qu'il n'est peutêtre aucune ville du royaume où il y ait autant de gens éclairés [...] Vous ne sauriez croire combien tout à changé depuis la malheureuse avanture de Calas. On va jusqu'à se reprocher le jugement rendu contre Mr Rochette et les trois gentilshommes.

This was heartening news indeed, and Voltaire soon passed on the information to several of his correspondents.[165] He was also concerned in the case of two students, the brothers Métayer, who were arrested near the Swiss border on their way to the seminary at Lausanne. Seigneux de Correvon, at the instigation of the pastors of Poitou, asked Voltaire to intervene: 'Gébelin, de Paris, et Chiron, de Genève,

[164] 'Je ne savais pas que l'honnête criminel éxistât en éffet, et qu'il s'appelât Favre' (Best.D14680, to Elie de Beaumont).

[165] to Lavaysse on 5 January 1769 (Best.D15414); to d'Argental on 23 January (Best. D15444) and 27 February (Best.D15490); to the Beaumonts on 14 January (D15430); and to Jean Ribotte on 26 January (D15448).

353

entreprirent de leur côté des démarches et tous ces efforts eurent pour effet de libérer les deux jeunes huguenots' (Champendal, *Voltaire et les protestants de France*, p.63). All in all, Voltaire ended 1768 in a highly optimistic mood. On 20 December he wrote to the seigneur de Villevielle attributing the revolution which was taking place to the beneficial effects of *philosophie*, for this was now reaching even the people (Best.D15377).

Voltaire was more than ever determined to play his part in the spread of enlightenment, and the enthusiasm of 1768 bore fruit in his new drama *Les Guèbres*. It is surprising that in his excellent study on Voltairean tragedy Ronald Ridgway does not underline the relevance of this 'tragédie-pamphlet' to the status of Voltaire's Protestant contemporaries. He concludes that it was

contre l'*infâme* que Voltaire a déclenché son offensive, et l'*infâme* comprend tous les ennemis de la tolérance, qu'ils soient jésuites ou jansénistes, espagnols ou français, catholiques ou calvinistes, prêtres ou laïques. Mais il est clair que le 'prétoire' dans *Les Guèbres* symbolise avant tout les juges de La Barre et le clergé qui les appuyait.[166]

Ridgway's remark is, of course, perfectly valid. As in the case of *L'Ingénu* Voltaire's attack is aimed primarily at intolerance and injustice wherever they are to be found, and the work contains many contemporary allusions. Yet in this instance we have proof that he was thinking especially about the Protestants. On 24 July 1769 he scolded mme Du Deffand for her lack of interest in toleration and explained to her quite explicitly the purpose of *Les Guèbres* (Best.D15773):

Vous n'êtes informée que des plaisirs de Paris, et je le suis des malheurs de trois ou quatre cent mille âmes qui souffrent dans les provinces. On ne veut pas les reconnaître pour citoiens, leurs mariages sont nuls, on déclare leurs enfans bâtards. Un jeune homme de la plus grande espérance, plein de candeur et de génie, m'apporta il y a près de six mois cet ouvrage que je vous ai envoié.

And Voltaire was no less definite when he wrote to mme Choiseul two days later (Best.D15776). The reply he received from mme Du Deffand contains what turned out to be a very accurate prophecy: 'jamais on ne permettra la représentation de cette pièce, avant que les changement qu'elle a pour bût ne soyent arrivés; ils arriveront un jour; mais vous

---

[166] *La Propagande philosophique dans les tragédies de Voltaire*, Studies on Voltaire (1961), xv.220.

êtes comme Moÿse, vous voyez la terre promise et vous n'y entrerés pas' (Best.D15782, 29 July 1769). Nonetheless Voltaire returned to the attack. On 16 August he asked the comte de Schomberg to persuade the duc d'Orléans to protect *Les Guèbres*: 'Henri quatre dont il a tant de choses les protégea; et la dernière scène des Guebres est précisément l'édit de Nantes.'[167] On 11 September Voltaire told mme Denis that *Les Guèbres* would not be performed at Lyons because of the large number of Protestants there and for fear of displeasing the archbishop (Best.D15885). On 13 September he scolded the marquis de Ximenès for not having prevailed upon Richelieu to have *Les Guèbres* acted at Fontainebleau (Best.D15890). To the duke himself he expressed very different views (Best.D15922), but this was obviously for reasons of prudence, and Voltaire was disappointed that his play would not have the chance to affect opinion which a public performance would have gained for it (cf. Best.D15890).

The projected development of Versoix continued to preoccupy Voltaire in 1769. He agreed with the duchesse de Choiseul that it would not be called 'la ville de tolérance', but he was nonetheless adamant as to the necessity of making it this, in fact if not in name: 'si la chose n'y est pas j'assure le maître de votre pied qu'elle ne sera jamais peuplée' (Best.D15822, 14 August 1769). On 13 December Voltaire congratulated Moultou on obtaining the release of two galley-slaves, and he asked his friend to enlighten him on a topic which was puzzling him: 'Je voudrais bien savoir comment le parlement de Toulouse a validé un mariage fait contre les loix du roiaume. Celà n'est pas dans l'ordre des possibles. Il faut qu'il y ait dans cette avanture des circonstances qui en changent totalement le fond' (Best.D16039). Voltaire was right to be puzzled, for the judgement made on 24 September 1769 in favour of the widow Marie Roubel marked an important step forward in the campaign to gain legal recognition for Protestant marriages. This lady had been married *au désert* and, on the death of her husband, some of his relations contested her right to inherit, for legally the marriage was completely invalid, a fact Voltaire obviously appreciated. Yet public opinion at Toulouse was so strong that the *parlement* finally accepted a certificate signed by Paul Rabaut as establishing the validity of the marriage (Dedieu, ii.149-51). Such a decision obviously conferred semi-official status on Protestant pastors and justifies the optimistic report of conditions in Toulouse which the abbé Audra had sent to Voltaire.

[167] Best.D15830. A similar request was made on 22 September (D15912).

Among other things 1770 saw Voltaire assuring Gal-Pomaret that, contrary to what he seemed to think, the Versoix project was advancing well, but that the Protestants must keep very quiet about it (Best.D16124, 31 January). He also wrote to Sénac de Meilhan on 1 May requesting a passport for one of the Genevese pastors, Jean Perdriau (Best.D16327). But perhaps the most important feature of Voltaire's correspondence as regards the Protestant question in 1770 is the appearance of a theme which would reappear regularly in the next few years. In April or May he informed the marquis de Jaucourt of a consoling fact (Best.D16325):

Les âmes tolérantes et sensibles seront encor fort aises d'apprendre que soixante huguenots vivent avec mes paroissiens de façon qu'il ne serait pas possible de deviner qu'il y a deux relligions chez moy. Voilà qui est consolant pour la philosophie et qui démontre combien l'intolérance est absurde et abominable.

Accounts of this edifying spectacle were sent not only to Protestant correspondents and friends, they were also addressed to influential members of the Court and government, even the redoubtable Saint-Florentin (who in 1770 had been created duc de la Vrillière).[168] After the final abandoning of the Versoix project, the existence on his doorstep of this harmonious and emancipated community consoled Voltaire, as he told Allamand on 17 June 1771: 'du moins il y a un Village de libre en France, et c'est le mien' (Best.D17249). He returned to the same theme in his *Commentaire historique sur les œuvres de l'auteur de la Henriade* (1776), where he paints a glowing picture of Ferney's religious idyll (M.i.106):

J'ai vu les femmes des colons genevois et suisses préparer de leurs mains trois reposoirs pour la procession de la fête du Saint-Sacrement. Elles assistèrent à cette procession avec un profond respect; et M. Hugonet, nouveau curé de Ferney, homme aussi tolérant que généreux, les en remercia publiquement dans son prône. Quand une catholique était malade, les protestantes allaient la garder, et en recevaient à leur tour la même assistance.

The fruits of tolerance were to be found at Ferney, even if the rest of France was still too 'welche' to cultivate them.

[168] the following is a representative, if not quite exhaustive selection of the correspondents Voltaire told about his happy colony: the comte de Schomberg (Best.D16366, 28 May 1770, and D16612, 25 August 1770); Du Pont de Nemours (Best.D16525, 16 July 1770); the Choiseuls (Best.D16615, 27 August 1770); Ribotte (Best.D16806, 5 December 1770 and D17420, 25 October 1771); Formey (Best.D17342, 26 August 1771); La Vrillière (Best.D17692, 13 April 1772); prince Golitsuin (Best.D18431, 19 June 1773).

Yet Voltaire did not succumb to the temptation of withdrawing into his private world at Ferney, thereby forgetting the plight of Protestants in France as a whole, although some commentators seem to have assumed that he did this.[169] The patriarch was convinced that what he had achieved in his domain pointed a lesson for the rest of the kingdom, and he did not relax his efforts to win toleration for the Huguenots. He continued to play his now familiar rôle as mentor to certain Protestants, passing on the information and rumours he had heard as to the government's intentions. Sometimes he had no news and frankly admitted this: 'je n'ai rien su de l'affaire de Brie'[170], he told Gal-Pomaret on 22 May 1771 (Best.D17201). But a few months later he informed his correspondent that the Protestants would be left in peace, as the government was too occupied with the *parlements* to think of persecuting the Huguenots. In any case, 'On s'appesantit plus sur les philosophes que sur les réformés', he commented: 'Mais si les uns et les autres ne parlent pas trop haut, on les laissera respirer en paix. C'est tout ce que l'on peut espérer dans la situation présente' (Best.D17401, 14 October 1771). Pomaret replied on 2 February 1772 that the Protestants in his area were 'fort tranquiles', thanks to the comte de Périgord, for whose wisdom and humanity they were full of praise (Best.D17586).

It is in itself noteworthy that Voltaire sustained an active interest in the Protestant question at the end of his life, a considerable time after the successful conclusion of the Calas case, but we should be wrong in thinking that he acted merely as the distinguished correspondent of certain fortunate Protestants. His activity was of a much more positive kind, and the concluding years of Louis xv's reign saw him make his last important and sustained attempt to better the Huguenots' position in France. In this instance he concentrated his efforts on the question of Protestant marriages, perhaps the most burning issue in the eyes of all Huguenots, whatever their social class or religious opinions. We have seen (above, pp.313-33) that civil rights had always appeared more important to him than public worship, and a series of contemporary cases focused Voltaire's attention on the ridiculous abuse that 'les Welches ne permettent pas à d'autres Welches de se marier!' (Best. D14140).

[169] cf. comments by Coquerel and Dardier, quoted above, p.305, n.101, and below, p.371, n.202.

[170] 'Après les emprisonnements de 1766, malgré la modération du pasteur François Charmusy, dont nous possédons plusieurs lettres originales, ce ministre fut arrêté en 1770, et il paraît qu'il mourut après neuf jours de captivité' (Coquerel, ii.531).

In 1765 there had been the Potin case and Elie de Beaumont's *mémoire* (cf. above, p.308). Two years later the *Avocat-général* of the Grenoble *parlement*, Servan, was successful in obtaining damages[171] on behalf of Marie Robequin, deserted by her husband Jacques Roux on the pretext that they had been married *au désert* (Coquerel, ii.455). The marriage was not declared valid, but the *parlement* requested that the king should declare it so (Puaux, p.333), and many people thought that a great step forward had been taken. Servan published two pamphlets on the topic[172] and sent them to Voltaire[173] who was moved to tears by the *avocat*'s eloquence, genuine tears it would appear, for nearly two years later Voltaire reminded Servan of the circumstances (Best.D16026, 6 December 1769):

Vous ai-je jamais dit combien de larmes interrompirent la lecture que je fesais à douze ou quinze personnes, de ce discours dans lequel vous vengiez les droits de l'humanité contre un lâche qui s'était fait catholique apostolique romain, pour trahir sa femme et la réduire à l'aumône? On m'a dit que tout l'auditoire avait éclaté en sanglots comme nous.

Moreover, as we have seen, a letter written earlier in the same year had shown Voltaire surprised when the Toulouse *parlement* had allowed Marie Roubel, widow of a Protestant and married *au désert*, to inherit, for this was tantamount to admitting the validity of her marriage (Best.D16039; cf. above, p.355).

So far Voltaire had been an interested bystander, but he was soon impelled to intervene personally. On 19 November 1771 Marthe Camp wrote appealing for his help (Best.D17460). She had married, according to the Protestant rite, Jean-Louis-Frédéric-Charles, vicomte de Bombelles, on 21 March 1766. But in 1771 her husband decided that he was free to contract a Catholic marriage with mlle de Carvoisin, 'd'une figure désagréable, âgée de quarante ans, avec mille écus de rente viagère'.[174] In her letter to Voltaire mlle Camp painted her situation and that of her four-year-old daughter in moving terms, informing him that she had gone to Paris intent on preserving her good name and

---

[171] the sum was 1,200 livres (Coquerel, ii.457; N.A.F. Puaux, *Histoire populaire du protestantisme français* (Paris 1894), p.333).

[172] the *Discours sur l'administration de la justice criminelle* (Geneva 1766) (*Ferney catalogue*, B2692), and the *Discours ... dans la cause d'une femme protestante* (Geneva 1767).

[173] he was thanked in glowing terms on 13 January 1768 (Best.D14668). Voltaire continued to correspond with Servan; cf. Best.D16026 and D17035.

[174] this is mlle Camp's own description of her rival, in Best.D17460.

defending her child's interests. Voltaire was clearly moved by the plight of 'une Dame aussi interressante et aussi vertueuse que Madame De Bombelles' as he told mme Anne Duvoisin[175] on 25 November (Best. D17470), and his keenly-developed journalistic sense told him how important public opinion would be in this case. By 25 December Marin was already informing him that he had written 'pour avoir la réponse de m. de Bombelles à la lettre de l'Ecole Royale militaire, et dès qu'on me l'aura envoyée Je vous la ferai parvenir' (Best.D17527). For when the authorities at the Ecole militaire, where Bombelles had been brought up, heard of his conduct, they asked him not to pay any further visits there (M.xxviii.553, n.1.). By 1771 actions theoretically sanctioned by the French anti-Protestant laws were not necessarily considered worthy of a gentleman.

The judgement given on 7 August 1772 highlighted this discrepancy between what the law permitted and what good conduct demanded. Although the vicomte's second marriage was declared the only legal one, mlle Camp was awarded damages of 12,000 francs and her daughter was directed to be brought up at the vicomte's expense as a Catholic. Letters written to various correspondents[176] demonstrate Voltaire's continuing interest in the case, and the outcome prompted him to compose his *Réflexions philosophiques sur le procès de mademoiselle Camp* (August 1772), in which he enthusiastically took up the cause of the Huguenots' civil rights especially as regards marriage (M.xxviii.553-58). The opening sentence of the pamphlet succinctly draws the moral of the case and its judgement: laws which are eschewed by public opinion can never really be acceptable or practicable: 'La loi commande, le magistrat prononce: le public dont l'arrêt est inutile pour l'exécution des lois, mais irrévocable au tribunal de l'équité naturelle, décide en dernier ressort. Sa voix se fait entendre à la dernière postérité' (M.xxviii. 553). In this instance the public have agreed with the ruling, which took into account the good faith of the wife; now it only remains for the nation to will an end to the separation of the Protestants from their fellow countrymen, a lamentable state of affairs which 'désole sourdement la France depuis près de cent années'. Louis XIV's measures

---

[175] née Calas. She had written to Voltaire on mlle Camp's behalf; cf. Best.D17460.

[176] to Marin on 27 April 1772 (Best.D17715); to Gabriel Cramer in July or August (Best.D17842); to mme Du Deffand on 15 August (Best.D17865); another letter, probably to Christin, on the same day (Best.D17864); to Moultou on about 24 August (Best. D17881); to Octavie de Meynières on 9 September (Best.D17905); and to Suzanne Necker on 27 September (Best.D17932).

against the Protestants have failed: 'ils ont persisté dans leur culte' (p.554). Why, anyway, should contemporary Huguenots, who are excellent citizens, be punished for the sins of their forefathers? The example of Alsace, where Lutherans and even Calvinists are tolerated, proves that there is no reason why Protestant marriages should not be allowed, and Voltaire even defends marriage between Catholics and Protestants, quoting st Paul as his authority! The second part of the pamphlet, a diatribe against the abbé de Caveirac (see above, pp.276-77), perhaps detracts a little from its overall effect, but the first section is a clear and dignified plea to end the nonsensical situation caused, in the second half of the eighteenth century, by anachronistic anti-Protestant legislation. The moderate nature of his demands is exemplified by the final sentence: 'Espérons pour nos frères désunis une tolérance politique que nos maîtres sauront accorder avec la religion dont ils sont les protecteurs' (p.555).

An event in Voltaire's own family circle brought home to him with even more force the desirability of legal reforms in connection with Protestant marriages. M. de Florian, the widower of Voltaire's niece, wished to remarry, but as his intended was a divorced Protestant whose husband was still alive, difficulties were raised by Catholic and Protestant clergy alike. Voltaire appealed to the French government through Saint-Florentin,[177] and to the pope through cardinal de Bernis (Best.D17571, 28 January 1772), asking, as mme Gallatin told Frederick II of Hesse-Cassel, for a dispensation: 'parce qu'il faut qu'il garde à vüe deux jeunes gens dont l'un à 57 ans et L'autre 37 [...] Nos ministres ne sont point satisfait de se mariage, cependant Le uns l'aprouvent et non les autres' (Best.D17591, 7 February 1772). To the indignation Voltaire felt at mlle Camp's plight was now added his natural anticlericalism, for he blamed first and foremost the bishop of Annecy who had refused to sanction the marriage (Best.D17612, to d'Hornoy, 21 February 1772). A solution was found when the two would-be partners were married by a Lutheran pastor 'vers le lac de Constance' (Best. D17669), and Voltaire did not seem to be taking the matter too seriously.

---

[177] he wrote to the minister on 12 February 1772 (Best.D17598a), informing him that Florian was thinking of marrying mlle de Normandy, who had been born in Holland of Protestant refugee parents. Voltaire said that mlle de Normandy intended to become a Catholic and asked permission for her to return to France, but Saint-Florentin refused, insisting that she should abjure the Protestant faith before her return and that her marriage should be performed in the normal way.

On 2 May he told Bernis that Florian was already married: 'On prétend que son mariage est nul; mais les conjoints l'ont rendu très réel' (Best. D17722). Yet on 16 September Voltaire made the case of Florian his chief example when he put forward to Richelieu the case for reforming the law on Protestant marriages.

It is difficult to overestimate the significance of this letter (Best. D17915), for here rather than in 1767 is Voltaire's most open attempt to influence the government directly on the Protestant question since the *Traité sur la tolérance*. The terms in which it is written make it clear that Richelieu had asked for Voltaire's advice[178] and the 'more significant passages were underlined by Richelieu or a secretary' (Best.D17915, commentary). No flattery is spared in the endeavour to convince Richelieu of the truth of Voltaire's arguments and to secure his active support for the measures suggested. Voltaire clearly hoped that his proposals, moderate as they were, would be transmitted to the chancellor, if not to the king. He says he is sure that Richelieu, because of his experience as *commandant* of Languedoc and governor of Guyenne, is in a better position than anyone to appreciate the disadvantages of the present laws, and he briefly outlines Florian's predicament. It is worth quoting the remedy Voltaire suggests in full. Would it not be possible, he asks,

de remettre en vigueur, et même d'étendre l'arrêt du conseil signé par Louis 14 lui même le 15e 7bre 1685 par lequel les protestants pouvaient se marier devant un officier de justice. Leurs mariages n'avaient pas la dignité d'un sacrement comme les nôtres; mais ils étaient valides. Les enfans étaient légitimes, les familles n'étaient point troublées. On crut en révoquant cet arrêt forcer les huguenots à rentrer dans le sein de la religion dominante. On se trompa. Pourquoi ne pas revenir sur ses pas lorsqu'on s'est trompé? pourquoi ne pas rétablir l'ordre lorsque le désordre est si pernicieux, et lorsqu'il est si aisé de donner un état à cent mille familles sans le moindre risque, sans le moindre embarras, sans exciter le plus léger murmure?

In taking as a basis for settlement an arrangement originally adopted, however briefly, in 1685, Voltaire shows himself very subtle, almost prophetic, in his argument. No French government of the *ancien régime* dared to go openly against the religious policy of the great king, and

[178] 'Mon héros est très bienfaisant, quoi qu'il se moque de la bienfaisance. Ce qu'il daigne me dire sur les mariages des protestants me touche [. . .] Puisque vous poussez la bonté et la condescendance jusqu'à vouloir qu'un homme aussi obscur que moi vous dise ce qu'il pense sur un objet si important et si délicat [. . .]'

Louis XVI was able to grant the Edict of Toleration in 1787 only by adopting the fiction that he was, as Voltaire almost implies here, returning to the original intentions of his great-grandfather.[179]

Though Voltaire explicitly denied any connection between the cases of mlle Camp and Florian (cf. Best.D17715), it is obvious that, coming so close together, they had been jointly responsible for encouraging Voltaire to put forward a new initiative regarding Protestant marriages. Florian might be mentioned in confidence to Richelieu, but Voltaire did not wish to jeopardise his career by naming him in public or semi-public utterances on the question.[180] Mlle Camp was ideal for this purpose, since in her position as a wronged woman she would only gain from publicity and she had anyway won the support of public opinion already. But lest there be any remaining doubt that the two cases were intimately connected in Voltaire's mind, it is sufficient to compare the wording of Best.D17915 (in which mlle Camp is not mentioned) with that of Voltaire's letter of 27 September 1772 to Suzanne Necker (where Voltaire puts forward the same proposals as in the letter to Richelieu). He claims that it might be possible to put the 'attendrissement universel' occasioned by the Camp affair to good use: 'peutêtre des hommes principaux ne s'éloigneraient ils pas de proposer le renouvellement de l'arrest du conseil du 15 septembre 1685 qui permit de se marier légalement devant le juge du lieu' (Best.D17932). Voltaire then adds significantly: 'Des personnes de la plus grande considération ont approuvé cette idée.' (Does he mean only Richelieu?) He tries to persuade mme Necker to canvass the proposal: 'Peutêtre enfin seriez vous plus capable que personne de la faire réussir.' But he ends on a note of prudence, realising how far Ferney is from the centre of the French administrative machine; 'Je ne vois les choses qu'à travers des lunettes de cent lieues.'

Thus we see that in the concluding years of the reign of Louis XV, despite feelings that he was somewhat isolated and perhaps not as well informed as some of his correspondents in Paris, Voltaire not only

---

[179] this was the tactic adopted later by Malesherbes. Cf. his *Mémoire sur le mariage des protestants*, 1785, p.22: 'La loi qui est à faire se trouve tout entière dans plusieurs arrêts du Conseil rendus dans le temps de la Révocation de l'Edit de Nantes [. . .] On verra que c'est alors que Louis XIV fixa la forme dans laquelle ceux de ses sujets à qui il permettait de rester protestants pourraient se marier sans donner aux ministres de leur religion le caractère d'officiers publics qu'ils avaient eu par l'Edit de Nantes et qu'on voulait abolir' (quoted in Grosclaude, *Malesherbes*, p.365, n.23).

[180] 'mon neveu étant officier, chevalier de st Louis et pensioné par le Roy, est astreint à des devoirs dont la transgression pourrait avoir des suittes fâcheuses' (Best.D17715).

maintained a strong interest in Huguenot affairs, he also put forward a plan for legalisation of their marriages very similar to the measures finally adopted in 1787. Since Best.D17915 was first printed in the Kehl edition of Voltaire's works (lxii.104-106), one is at a loss to understand comments made by some critics to the effect that, after the Calas case, Voltaire took little further interest in the plight of his Protestant contemporaries.[181] At the beginning of 1773 occurred the death of Ripert de Montclar, to whom had been attributed the *Mémoire théologique et politique au sujet des protestans de France* (1755).[182] The bishop of Apt censured the curé who had administered the sacrament to Montlcar and forced the unfortunate priest to sign a declaration that he had been wrong to do this, and that Montclar had declared submission to the bull *Unigenitus*, a retraction which the priest subsequently regretted and withdrew. Voltaire was kept informed of developments through his Genevese friend Moultou, who was, according to Gaberel, 'proche parent des Montclar'.[183] There may even be a connection between these events and the proposals Voltaire had been putting forward to Richelieu and others, for the *Mémoire théologique* too recommended a civil marriage for Protestants,

ce qui ne serait, en somme, affirmait l'auteur, qu'un retour à l'arrêt du Conseil du 15 septembre 1685, aux termes duquel les protestants pourraient se marier devant le principal officier de justice de la résidence de leurs ministres, arrêt dont l'Edit de Révocation, survenu un mois après, avait empêché l'application.[184]

Of course Voltaire's suggestions to Richelieu and other correspondents had been made several months before Montclar's death, but it is possible that Moultou had mentioned his illness to Voltaire and that the two men had discussed him, thereby prompting Voltaire to reread the *Mémoire théologique*. We do know, at any rate, that he had this and several other works by Montclar in his library at Ferney.[185] Be this as it may, Voltaire continued his propaganda on behalf of the Huguenots in 1773. Like the *Réflexions philosophiques* and Voltaire's letter to Richelieu, the chapter dealing with the repeal of the Edict of Nantes in the *Fragment sur l'histoire générale* again stresses the economic losses sustained by France as a result of the Huguenot emigrations. But nowa-

[181] cf. above, p.305, n.101; 371, n.202.   [182] cf. above, pp.276, 335.
[183] Gaberel, *Voltaire et les Genevois*, p.96.
[184] Grosclaude, *Malesherbes*, p.361.
[185] Ripert de Montclar's *Mémoire* is *Ferney catalogue* 2535.

days, says Voltaire, owing to the influence of the 'divin esprit de tolér-ance', no one is surprised to see Protestants occupying important economic positions in the state, for example as *fermiers généraux*.[186] The implication is that it is clearly ludicrous for such useful citizens to be without an *état-civil*.

Mme Necker, whose husband would soon be one of the Protestants in high places, replied to Voltaire in November 1773. Whether she in-tended this as a polite refusal of Voltaire's invitation to canvass his plans for Protestant marriage reform, or whether she merely wished to flatter him, her letter expresses in fulsome terms the belief that no one was better qualified than Voltaire himself to improve the Huguenots' lot. According to her, the Protestants were 'bien loin de la liberté de con-science qui règne à Ferney; l'on nous bénit quelquefois à Paris, mais l'on nous y damne encore' (Best.D18626). Despite mme Necker's lack of enthusiasm, it was undeniable that the situation of Protestants, in Paris and in the rest of France, was appreciably more secure and tolerable than it had been even a decade earlier. Rumours about an impending settlement continued to be spread, and Voltaire was not always *au courant*: 'Il n'a pas entendu dire un seul mot des sacrements de baptême et de mariage dont vous lui parlez', he told Ribotte on 4 February 1772 (Best.D18794). It is in fact impossible to trace clearly the sources of these reports. Sometimes Voltaire was completely uninformed, sometimes he seems to have been the source of rumours and to have known more than his Protestant correspondents.

This then was the situation in 1774 at the accession of Louis XVI: although spasmodic persecution continued in some areas, there was a general mood of optimism among the Protestants and their sup-porters.[187] Initially, it is true, uncertainty had been felt as to the young king's intentions and the policy his government would adopt. But encouraging reports about the new monarch were soon circulating, and one of these was spread by Voltaire, if not originated by him. On about 26 June he told Gabriel Cramer (Best.D19000):

il est bon de savoir que les protestants de la Gascogne aiant fait une assemblée extraordinaire dans laquelle ils ont prié dieu pour la guérison de Louis 15, et pour la prospérité de Louis 16, Montillet, archevêque d'Auch, a écrit au

[186] M.xix.276. This is an obvious reference to François Tronchin, who had become a *fermier général* at the beginning of 1762 (cf. Best.D10261, commentary).

[187] Pierre Grosclaude, 'Une négociation prématurée: Louis Dutens et les protestants français', *Bpf* (1958) civ.73-74; *Malesherbes*, pp.373-74.

roi une grande Lettre dans laquelle il lui a remontré que ces prières étaient contre les loix du roiaume, et qu'on ne pouvait punir trop sévèrement une telle prévarication. Le Roi a demandé quelles étaient ces loix, on lui a répondu que c'étaient d'anciens édits donnés dans des temps difficiles, qu'ils n'étaient plus d'usage et qu'ils dormaient. Le roi a répondu qu'ils ne fallait pas les éveiller, et s'est fait inoculer le moment d'après.

This anecdote does sound a little too good to be true – the king's conduct would almost be worthy of the hero of a Voltairean *conte* – and unfortunately Joseph Dedieu (*Histoire politique*, ii.163) has shown that the story was the result either of false information or of pure invention. Nonetheless it was repeated to two of Voltaire's main Protestant correspondents[188] and it no doubt exercised a certain amount of influence. Voltaire was on safer ground when, later in 1774 (18 September), he informed Gal-Pomaret that persecuting prelates would not be heeded: there were again hopes for a speedy settlement of the Protestant marriage question (Best.D19120). He was in a good position to be optimistic, having recently been of some practical assistance to the Huguenots. Earlier in the year, it is true, he had received an impassioned appeal from Pierre Lombard on behalf of the galley-slave Paul Achard,[189] and we have no evidence that Voltaire was able to achieve anything. But when some Protestants from Mauzevin were exiled or imprisoned at Auch for having held a prayer-meeting in a private house, an appeal was sent on 6 August to Ferney by one of them with Moultou's help, and Voltaire intervened successfully on their behalf (Champendal, p.63).

There is also firm evidence that information given by Voltaire was disseminated among the Huguenots at this time. Pierre Grosclaude ('Une négociation', pp.74-75) has established that a letter of 13 May 1775 from the pastor Chalon to Chiron *fils* at Annonay echoes in several important passages the following letter written on 11 April 1775 by Voltaire to Etienne Chiron at Geneva:[190]

---

188 to Ribotte (Best.D19001, 26 June 1774) and, in a slightly different form, to Gal-Pomaret (Best.D19048, 26 July 1774).

189 Best.D18801, 7 February 1774. This is presumably the unfortunate man whom Voltaire had already tried to help in 1764 (see above, p.305, especially n.100), and who had been on the galleys since 1745.

190 Best.D19414. Theodore Besterman gives the addressee as Etienne Chiron. In his 1958 article Grosclaude says the letter was 'sans nom de destinataire' (p.75) and makes no attempt to identify Voltaire's correspondent. In chapter xv, section 2, of his book on Malesherbes, where some of the material printed in the article reappears, Grosclaude

On a reçu la Lettre et le mémoire. On peut assurer que des ministres sages pensent sérieusement à établir la légitimité des mariages des protestants avec la seule formalité de les faire inscrire sur les régistres de la jurisdiction dans laquelle ces mariages auront été contractés. Plusieurs Evêques, non moins sages que ces ministres d'Etat, ont déjà déclaré qu'ils aprouvaient ce projet qui eut lieu pendant deux ans sous Louis 14 même.

Ce point principal étant une fois accordé, les autres ne feront pas une grande difficulté, et il faut espérer qu'à la fin on admettra une tolérance que la raison ordonne, et que la religion ne peut réprouver.[191]

La personne à qui on a écrit n'a aucun crédit, elle n'a qu'un désir extrême de voir établir cette tolérance qui est le premier lien des hommes.

Chalon invoked these reports as one reason why the Protestants should not hold a national synod and thus risk alienating the government. In this instance therefore Voltaire did act (although perhaps unwittingly) as what might be called a moderating influence on the Huguenots; yet it is possible to argue that by 1775 the Protestants' interests would have been served better if they had not allowed their completely harmless national synods to lapse, thereby further impairing the already tenuous unity between them.[192]

But what had caused Voltaire's optimism? As early as 10 January 1775 (Best.D19283) he had written encouragingly to Ribotte: 'On espère même qu'il y aura un règlement pour légitimer tous les mariages.' And when one compares the proposals outlined in the letter to Chiron with those Voltaire had already made himself, privately to Richelieu and publicly in the *Réflexions philosophiques*, we see that the similarity between them is manifest. It is difficult to avoid the conclusion that the arrival of Turgot in the ministry had given Voltaire hope that his proposals or ones very similar to them would soon be adopted. Already, during the *guerre des farines*, Turgot had sent a circular to Protestant ministers as well as Catholic priests, urging them to explain the measures

suggests that the letter was 'peut-être adressée au pasteur Chalon' (p.373, n.1). If Theodore Besterman's identification is correct, it would appear that Chiron had sent on the information to a series of correspondents, one of whom had told Chalon. This would explain why he then passed on the same information to Chiron's son who had presumably known about it before Chalon himself.

[191] this phrase is so similar to one in the *Traité sur la tolérance*: 'l'humanité le demande, la raison le conseille, et la politique ne peut s'en effrayer' (*Mélanges*, p.583; cf. above, p.295), that one wonders if Voltaire's growing optimism had encouraged him to reread this work with a view to making some further use of the arguments it puts forward in favour of the Protestants.

[192] the last national synod was held in 1763; cf. above, p.299; below, p.381.

to their flocks and to prevent violence.[193] This tacit recognition of the role played by the Huguenots' pastors was no doubt seen by many as a foretaste of more substantial things to come. The appointment on 20 July 1775 of Malesherbes to replace Saint-Florentin as *ministre de la maison du roi* (and thus in charge of Protestant affairs) made reform even more likely.

The fascinating article by Pierre Grosclaude which I have already quoted shows that the hopes shared by Voltaire and the Protestants were not merely wishful thinking. Malesherbes was contacted by Lecointe de Marcillac in August 1775, and they continued to correspond until Malesherbes's fall from the ministry (*Malesherbes*, p.383; cf. above, p.347, n.158). But more significant in Grosclaude's opinion were important negotiations carried out during the winter of 1775-1776, conducted on the Protestant side by one Louis Dutens. Born in Tours in 1730 of Protestant parents, Dutens decided to leave France after seeing his sister abducted by order of the bishop to be brought up in a convent. He went to London and subsequently exercised diplomatic functions on behalf of the British government. He was a man of letters, publishing in 1767 an edition of Leibniz.[194] In 1774 he visited France and met Malesherbes. On the latter's assuming office, Dutens was persuaded by the Protestants of La Rochelle (where his sister lived) to negotiate on their behalf. Dutens wished authority to speak on behalf of all French Protestants, and a circular letter was accordingly dispatched to other churches.[195] However, strong opposition was expressed by the Protestants of Bordeaux and Nîmes. Firstly, they observed, Dutens was or had been in the service of a foreign power, which would naturally render him suspicious to the French government. Secondly, he and the Protestants of La Rochelle wanted to make limited demands, while their brethren of the south refused to countenance any agreement which did not include freedom of worship. Furthermore they preferred to retain Court de Gébelin as their representative. Dutens's ill-starred mission finally ended with the fall of Malesherbes in May 1776. Grosclaude ('Une négociation', p.93) considers it unfortunate that 'les

---

[193] cf. Coquerel, ii.530: 'Le synode du Languedoc répondit que leurs [the Protestants'] églises étaient munies d'avance contre les menées ayant pour but de les attirer dans le parti des incendiaires qui avaient troublé la capitale et les contrées voisines.'

[194] Dutens sent this and another work to Voltaire on 20 May 1768 (cf. Best.D15028) and was thanked by him on 29 June (Best.D15105).

[195] Grosclaude reproduces *in extenso* the letter sent from La Rochelle to the Protestants of Vivarais ('Une négociation', pp.82-85).

églises aient, dans leur ensemble, accueilli avec tant de défiance la tentative désintéressée d'un homme qui savait ce qu'on pouvait obtenir dans l'immédiat et qui, bien que passé au service du roi d'Angleterre ne songeait qu'à mettre son crédit et son zèle à celui de ses anciens compatriotes opprimés'. Though Voltaire would no doubt have sympathised with Dutens's aims had he known who was carrying on the negotiations, he held a very unsympathetic opinion of the man. For this 'demi savant très méchant homme, nommé Du Temps, réfugié à présent en Angleterre', had damned himself irremediably in Voltaire's eyes and identified himself with the forces of reaction when he had published, in 1769, 'un sot Libelle atroce contre tous les philosophes intitulé *Le Tocsin*'.[196]

By the middle of 1776 the reign of Louis XVI was not living up to the hopes Voltaire and others had conceived for it. Voltaire's disappointment is evident in a letter to Gal-Pomaret, written on 8 April of that year at a time when Malesherbes was still in office (Best.D20053):

on nous avait assuré que de très sages ministres d'état s'occupaient de rétablir une ancienne loi de la nature qui veut qu'un enfant appartienne légitimement à son père et à sa mère, soit que le mariage soit une chose incompréhensible nommée sacrement, soit qu'on ne le regarde que comme une affaire humaine. Mais tout cela est renvoyé bien loin, et il faut attendre.

And in reply to a letter from Gal (Best.D20191, 25 June 1776), who assured Voltaire that he was still hopeful despite the disgrace of Malesherbes and Turgot, the patriarch revealed the hopes he had had in these 'deux vrais philosophes' when they were in the ministry: 'La tolérance était le premier de leurs principes; tous deux se sont retirés le même jour, après avoir fait tout le bien qui avait dépendu d'eux en si peu de temps' (Best.D20201, 4 July 1776).

But if the government of Louis XVI was not long under the control of *philosophes* favourable to the Huguenots, yet another Protestant marriage case, which began at the very end of Louis XV's reign and continued after Louis XVI's accession, brought comfort to the Protestants by showing them just how far the representatives of justice backed up by indignant public opinion were prepared to flout France's

---

[196] Best.D18067, Voltaire to the chevalier de Chastellux, 7 December 1772. Dutens had nonetheless visited the *philosophe* at Ferney in about April 1770 in the company of lord Algernon Percy, whose governor he was (see 'Voltaire's British visitors', ed. sir Gavin de Beer and André-Michel Rousseau, Studies on Voltaire (1967), xlix, section 101).

anachronistic laws. Henri Roux and Jeanne Roubel had been married *au désert* on 25 February 1765.[197] In 1773 Roux became dangerously ill and his wife, after a quarrel, ran off with another man. Four days later she informed her husband that she had entered the convent of the Dames des Ecoles chrétiennes and demanded that their marriage be celebrated before a priest. On 17 January 1774, Roux was summoned to appear before the Senechal, and he was ordered, if he should persist in refusing to marry 'la demoiselle Roubel', to pay interest on her dowry and 25,000 *livres* in damages (Dardier, *Un procès scandaleux*, p.9). His wife had by now abjured publicly. Perhaps the most significant fact of the ensuing case was that when mlle Roubel's advocate pleaded against the validity of Protestant marriages in general, Roux's advocate Troussel was led onto the same ground. He tried to prove that, since there were now no *nouveaux convertis*, only Protestants, the laws applying to the former could no longer be invoked against the Huguenots.[198] Most surprising of all, 'L'avocat du Roi, M. Mazer, se montra, dans son réquisitoire large et tolérant, soutenant la thèse de la validité des mariages protestants' (Schmidt, p.134). This was, of course, a major breakthrough for the Protestant cause and a development which displeased the king and his *garde des sceaux* immensely. Mazer and Troussel were summoned to Paris and threatened with dismissal. Fortunately Court de Gébelin was able to use his influence in their favour and no disciplinary action was taken (Dardier, *Un procès scandaleux*, p.33). The atmosphere of the case was heightened by the fact that it took place in strongly-Protestant Nîmes. At one point mlle Roubel had to don the habit of a nun to ensure that she was not identified by hostile crowds. Judgement was finally pronounced on 25 June 1774. Roux was ordered to pay his wife an alimony as long as she stayed in the convent. This was hardly what she had expected. Her appeal against the court's decision was rejected and she was transferred to another convent by *lettre de cachet*. Unfortunately the *garde des sceaux*'s anger at the conduct of the trial was turned against Roux and his children. A *lettre de cachet* confined his two eldest daughters to a Celestine convent in Dauphiné.

[197] for this case see especially Charles Dardier: *Un procès scandaleux à propos d'un mariage béni au désert: affaire Roux-Roubel 1774*, (offprint from *Etrennes chrétiennes*, Geneva 1886); and Paul Schmidt, *Court de Gébelin à Paris*, pp.132-39.

[198] this was an ironical twist of Louis XIV's assertion in 1685 that there were no longer any Protestants in France, only *nouveaux convertis*.

369

Voltaire had been well informed about the progress of the case. On 22 April 1774 Troussel sent him the *plaidoyers* he had composed on behalf of Roux: 'l'honnête citoyen dont on m'a confié la défense' (Best.D18904). A few days later (*c*. 30 April) the patriarch thanked him warmly, congratulating him on his eloquence in a good cause. Writing to Moultou on 6 August Voltaire expressed some surprise and doubt that the *avocat du roi* should have sided so strongly with the Protestants: 'J'ai lu sur le champ, Monsieur, le discours attribué à l'avocat du Roi de Nimes. Je souhaitte qu'en effet il l'ait prononcé et que ce ne soit une pièce suposée. Mais il ne me parait pas respirer l'impartialité nécessaire à un avocat général.'[199] Voltaire's own help was soon sought. One of Roux's imprisoned daughters was ill, and although her father was allowed to visit her, she was not permitted to leave the convent: in fact, the unfortunate Roux was not able to secure the release of his children until 1788, after the promulgation of the Edict of Toleration. A *mémoire* composed by Rabaut Saint-Etienne was to be forwarded to Voltaire through Chiron.[200] In the event mme Cramer presented it to him. The patriarch wrote an encouraging letter to Chiron, but made it clear that he was in no position to help Roux: 'La personne à qui on a écrit n'a aucun crédit, elle n'a qu'un désir extrême de voir établir cette tolérance qui est le premier lien des hommes.'[201] To mme Cramer Voltaire expressed his sympathy, at the

[199] Best.D19064. Here we glimpse another reason why Voltaire disapproved so strongly of anti-Protestant laws which were unenforceable and rejected by public opinion. Any attempt to help the Huguenots within the present system, however beneficial to individuals, could only be unfortunate in a wider context if it involved tinkering with the law and bringing it into disrepute. Voltaire obviously believed very strongly that laws should be based on consensus and should be revised if found unpopular or impracticable, but he also considered that while they were in force it ought not to be possible to evade them or to tamper with them. Cf. his doubts in 1769 over the Roubel affair (above, p.355): 'Je voudrais bien savoir comment le parlement de Toulouse a validé un mariage contre les loix du roiaume. Celà n'est pas dans l'ordre des possibles. Il faut qu'il y ait dans cette avanture des circonstances qui en changent totalement le fond' (Best.D16039).

[200] 'Chiron avait été prié de le [the *mémoire*] faire parvenir à Voltaire, et quelques semaines plus tard Paul Rabaut, impatient, lui écrivait: "Nous voudrions bien savoir ce qu'il dit et ce qu'il fait"' (Dardier, *Un procès scandaleux*, pp.36-37; Rabaut's letter was dated 5 April 1775).

[201] Best.D19414, 11 April 1775. This does not seem to have been merely a polite way of declining to help. Earlier in the year Voltaire had told Ribotte: 'il est survenu à celui qui vous répond, une affaire particulière si importante et si intéressante sur des objets de cette nature, qu'il ne peut de longtems écrire à personne, ni se mêler d'aucun autre objet. Il vous prie d'en avertir Mr de Pomaret et Mr de Pradel' (Best.D19283, 10 January 1775). As to what this 'affaire particulière' was, one can only speculate. Perhaps Voltaire was referring to his own colony of Huguenot watchmakers at Ferney.

same time explaining that he was unable to intervene for a very good reason (Best.D19423, probably written in April 1775):

Je voudrais sans doute, madame, servir ces deux demoiselles et leur digne père. Mais malheureusement je ne pourrais que leur nuire. Elles sont entre les mains d'un Pompignan, archevêque de Vienne, frère d'un Pompignan, dont les odes sacrées sont si sacrées que personne n'y touche.

In effect, it was hardly likely that Voltaire would be helped by any member of the Pompignan family after the ridicule he had heaped on them in 1761.[202]

Yet when he knew he could be of practical help to the Huguenots Voltaire was not slow to grasp the opportunity. On 3 May 1775 the pastor Daniel Armand was arrested near Château-Queyras in Dauphiné. Various attempts were made to help him: 'M. de Végobre écrivit à une dame noble, Paul Rabaut à Court de Gébelin,'[203] and Gal-Pomaret asked Voltaire to intervene. Some two months later (5 July) the latter explained to Moultou what his part in the affair had been (Best.D19547):

Il y a longtems que je sçus l'emprisonnement du pasteur Dauphinois. Mr. Pomaret m'en écrivit, et sur le champ je supliai Made la marquise de Clermont Tonnerre, gouvernante du Dauphiné, de vouloir bien interposer ses bontés et son autorité. J'ai envoié la réponse de Made De Tonnerre à Mr Pomaret.

No further action was taken against Armand, and a few months later he was allowed to escape. Voltaire could claim yet another success in the Protestant cause.

It should by now be obvious how important the question of Protestant marriages was for Voltaire in the 1770s, and he was concerned with yet two more before his death. If the difficulties surrounding Florian's nuptials had strengthened Voltaire's Erastian views, the case of Hennin, French *résident* at Geneva, drew from him some perfectly vitriolic statements against the clergy. Hennin, who wished to marry

---

202 Dardier however seems completely unable to understand this, despite the fact that he quotes Voltaire's letter to mme Cramer, and he comments as follows on Voltaire's conduct in the affair: 'Il n'aurait eu qu'un mot à dire peut-être; mais ce mot, il ne le dit pas' (*Un procès scandaleux*, p.36). 'Bien qu'il l'eût [Saint-Etienne's *mémoire*] reçu d'une main qui lui était chère, le vieux patriarche ne fit rien. La gloire qu'il avait recueillie de l'affaire Calas lui suffisait; il n'en chercha point d'autre' (pp.39-40).

203 G. Bonet-Maury, 'Le rétablissement du culte protestant dans le Queyras', *Bpf* (1907), lvi.379.

Camille Elisabeth Mallet, a Protestant, asked Voltaire[204] to find out from the baron d'Espagnac if it was true that the latter's son had been able to marry mlle His, daughter of the Hamburg banker Peter His, 'avec une simple permission du Roi, sans être obligé de faire ouvrir une si jolie porte par les clefs de St Pierre?' (Best.D19858, 11 January 1776). Hennin had received permission from the government, but, as he informed Voltaire on 27 January (Best.D19885), the comte de Vergennes had told him that 'les bruits qui ont couru et qui courent encore au sujet des mariages des Protestans rendent la Cour de Rome plus difficile que jamais'. This was too much for Voltaire, who fulminated against clerical interference in French internal affairs: 'Les gens sensés comme vous m. sauront bien se mettre audessus de toutes ces impertinences. Je vous exhorte fort à suivre votre idée très raisonable de profiter de la permission du Roi sans demander celle des singes d'Italie' (Best.D19887, 28 January 1776). There was some delay (see Best.D19902) before a reply was received from m. d'Espagnac, and when one did come it was far from reassuring.[205] But finally the difficulties were overcome; the mariage took place at Delemont on 29 April (see Best.D19885, n.2) and Voltaire sent Hennin his congratulations (Best.D20087, 26 April 1776). Earlier in the month Moultou had received a letter from Toulouse praising Voltaire to the skies 'after a judgement tending to legalise the marriage of Protestants':[206] 'Votre sublime voisin doit avoir reçu le mémoire. Rien n'est plus capable de consoler sa vieillesse et celui de Sirven. Il lui était réservé de voir luire sur la frontière qu'il habite l'aurore de la révolution que nous prépare un ministère tel qu'il n'en fut jamais dans le monde.'[207] The most surprising thing about this letter was that it was written by none other than the vicar-general of Toulouse, Jean-Marie de Grumet, who had apparently been received

[204] Hennin's original letter is lost, but he repeated his request on 27 January 1776 (Best.D19885).
[205] Best.D19915, Voltaire to Hennin, 9 February 1776: 'Mr D'Espagnac me fait dire qu'il ne peut à présent, m'aprendre les raisons pour lesquelles il n'a pas répondu à l'article que vous savez.' For the official permission given see Bibliothèque nationale, Fonds Joly de Fleury 476, pièce 5871.
[206] Best.D20044, commentary. Grosclaude mentions this incident briefly: 'l'arrêt du Parlement de Toulouse qui, le 2 avril 1776, donnait les effets civils au mariage d'un protestant fait au désert, arrêt qui fut cassé le 25 octobre, quelques mois après la retraite de Malesherbes, par le Conseil d'Etat du Roi, avec des attendus qui témoignaient de l'intolérance la plus bornée' (*Malesherbes*, p.376; the relevant records of the Conseil d'Etat are Bibliothèque nationale, Fonds Joly de Fleury 476, pièce 5870).
[207] Jean-Marie de Grumet to Moultou, 4 April 1776 (quoted in Edouard Chapuisat, *Figures et choses d'autrefois* (Paris 1920), p.176).

at Ferney, for this tolerant ecclesiastic also asked Moultou to assure Voltaire that he had not forgotten the 'accueil flatteur que j'ai reçu de lui sous vos auspices', despite the patriarch's hostility to Christianity.[208] On 15 May, after reading the *mémoire*, Voltaire wrote a letter to Delacroix, who was advocate at the Toulouse *parlement*, calling him 'l'apôtre de la justice et de l'humanité qui sont la vraie religion', and telling him gleefully: 'Voilà de ma connaissance quatre mariages de Catholiques avec des protestantes en deux mois de tems.'[209]

In the last two years of his life, Voltaire did somewhat lose touch with the evolution of the Protestant situation. This was hardly surprising for a man of his age. Yet he continued his correspondence with Gal-Pomaret, and he knew that, although the Protestants had not yet actually won legal toleration, their position was now so improved that it was only a matter of time before an Edict of Toleration was granted. Voltaire's letter to Gal of 7 February 1777 reaffirms his cautious optimism, and it is perhaps significant in view of the doubts which have been cast on the sincerity of Voltaire's religious beliefs that the letter ends gratefully attributing the progress of reason to God himself (Best.D20556):

Mon état ne m'ayant pas permis depuis quelque temps de cultiver le peu d'amis qui me restaient à Paris, je ne sais rien de ce qui s'y passe. Je vois seulement que le nombre des hommes d'état éclairés et tolérants augmente tous les jours, qu'on adoucit partout dans le commerce de la vie des lois trop sévères, qu'on souffre ou qu'on autorise les mariages entre les personnes de l'ancienne secte et de la nouvelle. Je me réjouis avec vous de ce progrès de la raison, et j'en remercie le dieu de toutes les sectes et de tous les êtres.

Appropriately enough, one of the last acts of Voltaire's public life was performed with the aid of two distinguished Protestants: Court de Gébelin and Benjamin Franklin. Court was secretary of the Masonic Loge des neuf sœurs, of which Voltaire became a member when he went to Paris in 1778. Voltaire had of course furnished Court with letters of introduction when he first visited the capital in 1763 (see above,

---

[208] 'Virgile n'était pas chrétien, j'aime et j'admire Virgile. Lucien nous persifla jusqu'à notre berceau, et je le relis avec plaisir. Enfin, Racine m'enchante, quoique janséniste: pourquoi m'interdirais-je l'hommage dû à notre Nestor littéraire?' On 12 May Voltaire graciously told Moultou: 'Je ne suis point du tout de l'avis de votre vicaire général quelque respect que j'aie pour son esprit et pour sa science' (Best.D20114).

[209] Best.D20118. It has not been possible to identify three of these marriages: one of them was obviously Hennin's.

pp.300-301). He had then called his *protégé* 'un bon parpaillot', and although subsequent contacts between them do not seem to have been very close, Voltaire retained an excellent impression of Court, whom he described to Végobre in 1772 as 'un très bon citoien qui aime la tolérance, et qui déteste la persécution' (Best.D18024). On his arrival at the lodge Voltaire asked specially to see Gébelin and in the ensuing conversation 'se glorifia de tout ce qu'il [Voltaire] avait fait en faveur des Protestants'. When the ceremony began, Voltaire was introduced 'appuyé sur Franklin et Court de Gébelin', a fitting tribute to the part he had played in advancing the cause of his Huguenot contemporaries (Schmidt, p.153).

It is pleasant to be able to record that the vicar-general of Toulouse was not the only tolerant Catholic in France. Coquerel quotes a glowing account of the good relations established between Catholics and Protestants in Mas-d'Azil as early as 1763.[210] He also mentions (ii.518): 'une lettre touchante et naïve du pasteur Durand, de Saint-Jean, où il raconte que, s'étant logé imprudemment tout près du curé et ayant pris la résolution de déménager, "le curé dit qu'il exigeait à titre de grâce que je ne sortisse point de cette maison et il m'offrit une déclaration par écrit pour me mettre à l'abri de tout événement"' (the letter was dated 25 December 1771). Everywhere the Protestants were establishing *maisons de prière*, in houses, barns or other disused buildings. The government at first made ineffective attempts to halt this, but then contented itself with spasmodic harassment. In 1768 Saint-Florentin protested when benches were taken to Protestant assemblies; the Protestants abandoned this practice but took large stones instead. Inquisitive Catholics began to attend the assemblies, which were held nearer and nearer towns, sometimes under their very walls. Indeed the period from 1760 till the promulgation of the Edict of Toleration (1787) is often called the *second désert* to distinguish it from the times of fierce persecution. It is impossible to assess how far Voltaire or the other *philosophes* contributed to this improvement.[211] As Haydn Mason re-

---

[210] 'Nous voyons tous les jours notre pasteur se familiariser avec de curés, des religieux et des gentilhommes catholiques romains, apporter les enfants, en plein midi, avec tout ordre, à notre maison d'oraison pour les baptiser; notre église est au milieu de la ville [. . .] vis-à-vis la cathédrale, où il n'y a que la halle entre; on entend d'un côté chanter les psaumes en français et de l'autre en latin, et pour dire en un mot, comme si nous avions liberté entière' (from a letter of 10 November 1763 written by the elders of the Consistory: Laborde, Boubilla, Fargues, Barbe, quoted by Coquerel, ii.372).

[211] one Protestant pastor at least was of the opinion that they should be given full credit. Gal-Pomaret wrote on 28 November 1761: 'Le commissaire qui avait été nommé

marks in his study on *Pierre Bayle and Voltaire* ('Introduction', p.xiii): 'How can one isolate beyond any doubt the part played by one author in influencing, for example, the movement towards religious toleration in the eighteenth century? Where does the genuinely characteristic contribution become merged with the body of the time?' One can say that Voltaire's works certainly affected the general climate of opinion, causing intolerance to become increasingly unfashionable. The furore caused by the Calas case and its sequel focused public attention on the Protestant problem, and this factor may have been decisive in determining the subsequent attitude of certain members of the government. Yet this is merely dealing in probabilities. One question which this book can attempt to answer with a little more confidence is the following: how far did Voltaire influence the Protestants he set out to help?

x. *Voltaire's influence on the Protestant clergy*

Once again one cannot be categorical, but it will be sufficient to consider the statements of some prominent Protestant pastors to see how Voltairean many of their doctrinal opinions actually were. Let us take as our first example Paul Rabaut, perhaps the most influential *pasteur du désert* in the second half of the eighteenth century. The classical view of nineteenth-century Protestant historians, well represented by Coquerel (ii.494), was that the *pasteurs du désert* were fervent Calvinists who fought hard against the influence of the irreligious *philosophes*: 'On trouve peu de témoignages certains sur la théologie du désert', he claims, 'sinon leur conformité générale avec les anciennes doctrines calvinistes reçues dans l'église de France.' Concerning Rabaut he is even more positive: 'On peut reconnaître, même dans ses relations de correspondance philologique avec son ami le pasteur du bas Languedoc, la couleur religieuse et comme cette ferveur du désert, qui signalait ces hommes d'une foi si vraie' (ii.499). It is true that Rabaut criticised Voltaire's *Dictionnaire philosophique* (Coquerel, ii.339), expressed reservations about the *Traité sur la tolérance*,[212] and in *La Calomnie*

par le parlement pour connaître des assemblées, qui se tiennent en Béarn, s'est comporté en homme pacifique et tolérant. Le papisme ne l'a pas fait; mais la nature, ou plutôt les Montesquieu et les Voltaire' (mss Paul Rabaut, quoted by Coquerel, ii.301).

212 'On m'écrit de geneve que M. de Voltaire a mis, aujour un ouvrage en faveur de la tolerance; je serois bien curieux de le lire. il y avance, dit on, un singulier paradoxe, c'est que les premiers chretiens ne furent point persecutés' (letter of 30 September 1763 to Court de Gébelin, Bib pf, Collection Coquerel, Papiers Rabaut, 318, f.6).

confondue (1762) refuted, with an impressive dignity and simplicity,[213] accusations that the Huguenots encouraged the murder of children who wished to abjure their faith in favour of Catholicism. Rabaut also told Jacob Vernes on 5 August 1774 that he could not accept the latter's *Catéchisme* – 'Je ne rejetterai point un mystère par la seule raison qu'il est incompréhensible' (Léonard, *Histoire générale*, iii.56). Nonetheless, the twentieth-century Protestant E.-G. Léonard passes a harsh judgement on him.[214] His sermons were dry, clothed in the language of eighteenth-century rationalism, neglecting traditional Calvinist doctrines and avoiding meditation on the Trinity (p.67). According to Léonard (*Histoire ecclésiastique*, p.105, n.3), Rabaut despised theology. Invited to sign La Beaumelle's *Préservatif contre le déisme* (which was a reply to Rousseau's *Emile*) he refused, replying 'par un trait absolument voltairien: "Je craindrais donc, Monsieur, d'être aujourd'hui la victime du zèle théologique et peut-être aussi de l'intolérance civile." '

While we may consider that Léonard's opinion of Rabaut is a little extreme, it is undeniable that he sometimes wrote and thought in a way which appears characteristic of Voltaire himself. A good example occurs in a letter to Moultou intended to be shown to the *philosophe*. On 29 February 1768, arguing that the Protestants should be allowed to continue their assemblies, Rabaut commented (Best.D14784, my italics):

Quand on pourrait sevrer les protestants de leur culte, la saine politique ne voudrait pas qu'on le fît. On l'a dit souvent *et on a eu raison de le dire :* il faut une religion au peuple; sa misère, ses occupations, son incapacité ne lui laissent guère d'autres moyens d'instruction que les exercices religieux. Privez le de ce secours, il tombera dans l'ignorance la plus grossière, dans la plus dangereuse dépravation de mœurs, et enfin dans un fanatisme qui produira les plus affreux désordres.

This may well have been merely a very skilful appeal to Voltaire couched in the terms most likely to move him, playing on his hatred of

---

[213] 'L'accusation intentée contre Calvin est une impudence qui ne mérite point de réponse. Les écrits de ce docteur ont fait l'admiration d'une partie du monde et le désespoir de l'autre. Qu'on les lise, et l'on verra que sa morale n'est autre que celle de l'évangile'. The force of this quotation is, however, modified by the fact that *La Calomnie confondue* may have been by La Beaumelle, Rabaut merely putting his name to it (Léonard, *Histoire ecclésiastique*, p.104).

[214] he speaks of Rabaut's 'orthodoxie pourtant douteuse' (*Histoire générale*, iii.56). Cf. Daniel Robert, 'Le rôle historique de Paul Rabaut', p.30: 'du point de vue du théologien, il me semble [. . .] que l'on ne peut guère défendre les "habiletés" un peu trop habiles de Rabaut à la fin de sa vie'.

fanaticism and on his fears of a second Camisard uprising. Yet there is no firm indication that Rabaut had such an intention, especially since Voltaire was not the only correspondent to whom he expressed himself in this way.[215] It is hard to avoid the conclusion that, although Rabaut was a sincere Christian according to his own lights, the *ferveur du désert* which Coquerel found in him is usually conspicuous by its absence. Rabaut was probably more affected by philosophic rationalism than he realised,[216] and judging from specific expressions and turns of phrase which he used, it is likely that Voltaire, through his writings and actions, was responsible in some measure for this influence.

Other Protestants were similarly affected. The following extract from an article written in 1766 by Court de Gébelin for the projected newspaper *L'Observateur protestant* is particularly significant. He expressed his astonishment that some citizens (Catholics) could accuse others (Protestants) 'd'être mauvais sujets, infidèles patriotes parce qu'ils ne pensent pas de même qu'eux sur des dogmes, intéressants sans doute, mais qui ne touchent point aux mœurs, aux vertus, aux devoirs' (Schmidt, p.77). That Court de Gébelin could relegate dogma to such an insignificant level, that of being merely 'interesting', makes one wonder seriously in what respects his version of Protestantism really differed from Voltairean deism,[217] especially when the latter was presented by such an accommodating spokesman as the Anglican Freind. As the end

---

[215] cf. Charles Dardier, *Paul Rabaut: ses lettres à divers*, ii.85.

[216] cf. his comment in a letter of 8 July 1768 to Court de Gébelin in connection with the possibility of establishing closer links with moderate Catholics: 'Dans ce siècle, plus que dans aucun autre, il est nécessaire de simplifier la religion, d'en écarter tout l'accessoire; alors elle sera goûtée des philosophes et à la portée du peuple' (p.89). This simplification would probably have been more pleasing to *philosophes* than to Catholics, and Daniel Robert comments: 'Tout rapprochement avec l'"œcumenisme" actuel serait profondément érroné: il ne s'agit point de théologiens qui, après avoir approfondi le point de vue de leur confession, s'efforcent de le dépasser; mais au contraire d'un point de vue confessionnel médiocrement creusé" ('Le rôle historique de Paul Rabaut', p.24; cf. below, p.382, especially n.227).

[217] whatever the truth of this assertion, Court de Gébelin's beliefs have certainly been considered inadequate by some Protestant historians; cf. N.A.F. Puaux's comment: 'Nous aimerions à trouver chez Gébelin la foi solide de son père; quoique croyant, l'atmosphère malsaine de Paris avait cependant affaibli chez lui cette sève de vie chrétienne qui nous aide à supporter nos maux et nous fait trouver le calme dans la tempête' (*Histoire populaire du protestantisme français*, p.340). According to Daniel Robert, 'Court de Gébelin poussait le syncrétisme jusqu'à croire que toutes les religions (et non pas seulement toutes les formes du christianisme) étaient fondamentalement la même religion' ('Le rôle historique de Paul Rabaut', p.24, n.8). Ideas like this must surely remind one of Voltaire's theory that behind all the major religions of the world was a basic theism.

of the *ancien régime* approached, the differences between the two became even more difficult to distinguish. Paul Rabaut's son, Rabaut Saint-Etienne, reduced the specifically Christian or Protestant element of his religion still farther than the pastors already mentioned. According to one of his Christmas sermons: 'La religion révelée n'est que la religion naturelle dévoilée aux mortels et confirmée par J.-C.'. The conscience 'n'est ni une voix secrète de Dieu qui se fait entendre à nos âmes, ni un juge placé en nous à qui notre être soit soumis. Elle n'est autre chose que le jugement que notre raison porte sur nos actions' (Léonard, *Histoire générale*, iii.69). Saint-Etienne's views on the soul are similarly Voltairean: 'Toutes les idées nous viennent des sens, c'est-à-dire que notre âme n'a aucune pensée, aucune réflection, aucun sentiment qui ne lui soient donnés par les sens' (p.70). Small wonder that, when asked his opinion on Vernet's *Thèses* in which, according to Saint-Etienne himself, 'la divinité de J-C. est formellement niée', he replied: 'Il n'y a pas là de quoi faire tant de bruit.'[218]

What had caused this astonishing dechristianisation of French Protestantism, all the more paradoxical when one considers how successfully the Huguenots had stood up to years of persecution and that they were finally to achieve legal recognition in 1787?[219] To a certain extent, admittedly, the lack of emphasis of certain doctrines is symptomatic of a genuine development in Protestant thought during the late seventeenth and early eighteenth centuries. Theologians like Turretini and Osterwald were no less genuinely Christian for wishing to change the emphasis given to certain dogmas, and for attempting to reconcile faith and reason. Yet it is difficult to view as genuinely 'Chris-

---

[218] Léonard, *Problèmes et expériences du protestantisme français* (Paris 1940), p.77; Dardier, *Paul Rabaut: ses lettres à divers*, ii.89, n.6. It is only fair to add that Saint-Etienne went on to say: 'Ce serait à présent le temps d'engager les théologiens de toutes les sectes à simplifier leur symbole, et à nous ramener au Christianisme de Jésus-Christ' (letter to Etienne Chiron of 28 October 1778, quoted in Dardier, *Paul Rabaut: ses lettres à divers*, ii.89, n.6). This might be seen as a laudable attempt to take Christianity back to its evangelical roots, but one should not forget that Voltaire was also an advocate of 'le christianisme de Jésus' (cf. above, p.182), which he interpreted in quite a different way; cf. the 1771 article Voltaire wrote for the *Questions sur l'Encyclopédie*: 'je [Jesus is speaking] leur disais simplement: "Aimez Dieu de tout votre cœur, et votre prochain comme vous-même, car c'est là tout l'homme." Jugez si ce précepte n'est pas aussi ancien que l'univers; jugez si je leur apportais un culte nouveau' (*Dictionnaire philosophique*, ed. Benda and Naves, p.612).

[219] for a penetrating and illuminating study of French Protestants and their religious and political beliefs during this period see Burdette C. Poland, *French Protestantism and the French Revolution* (Princeton 1957).

tian' or 'Protestant' a church whose leading pastors could preach such heterodox opinions as those held by Rabaut Saint-Etienne while at the same time proscribing the expression of genuinely Calvinist doctrines. This is, however, exactly what happened at Bordeaux in 1770. Although Etienne Gibert did not believe in predestination, he did insist on preaching 'la corruption irrémédiable de l'homme, la repentance et le salut par la grâce et par la mort expiatoire et le sang du Christ'.[220] He was forced to leave his church. These developments are to be explained partly by the influence which, for historical and practical reasons, the Swiss churches exercised over their French counterparts. Geneva was still considered by many to be the world capital of Protestantism, and this prestige coupled with its position as a natural centre of refuge for French Huguenots, ensured that theological liberalism there would not fail to find its echo in France.[221] It would obviously be foolish to attribute the doctrinal 'liberalism' of the *pasteurs du désert* exclusively to philosophical influence. The new attitudes in theology prepared the ground for them, so that many ideas put forward by Voltaire and other theists in the 1750s and 1760s were no longer very terrible to Protestants of Rabaut's generation. And, as we have seen in an earlier chapter (above, pp.135 ff.), some pastors became very 'liberal': in 1816 Empaytaz, a *réveilleur* (that is, an evangelical Protestant eager to re-establish Calvinist orthodoxy) wrote that no pastor he had read had mentioned the divinity of Christ since the middle of the eighteenth century (Léonard, *Histoire générale*, iii.56)! Lausanne, where the Protestant 'Seminary' was situated, was in a similar position. Indeed, some opposition to sending candidates to Switzerland was expressed by Huguenots who disliked the fashionable unorthodoxy prevalent there: these critics preferred the *écoles ambulantes* which existed in France, but their resistance proved ineffectual. Had they succeeded there is little doubt that many heterodox opinions which developed among French

---

[220] Léonard, *Histoire ecclésiastique*, p.157; cf. also Daniel Benoît, *Du caractère huguenot et des transformations de la piété protestante* (Paris 1892), p.49.

[221] this influence can already be discerned in the 'restorer' of the *églises du désert*, Antoine Court: Daniel Benoît (*Du caractère huguenot*, pp.42-43) calls him a second Calvin, but expresses reservations about his doctrine which is 'raisonneuse et didactique plutôt que communicative et vivante [. . .] Il ne paraît pas saintement préoccupé de la conversion des pécheurs [. . .] On y surprend avec regret la préoccupation de soi, et le désir de la domination. On n'y entend que rarement la note de l'humilité [. . .] Dans ses lettres ou ses Mémoires, il est plus souvent question de l'attachement à la religion que de l'amour pour Jésus-Christ.'

pastors might otherwise have been much slower in making their appearance.

But general trends in Protestant thought and the influence exercised by the Swiss churches are only part of the story. For if the French Huguenots had preserved a united front to the outside world they might have been able to withstand the attacks of the *philosophes* on their Protestant faith just as they had survived the persecution directed at them by the government for so many years. But this they were unable to do, and French Protestantism was weakened first and foremost by its internal divisions. Far from disappearing after 1760 when persecution on a large scale ceased, these disagreements were, if anything, exacerbated.[222] The oppression had generated a semblance of unity because the struggle had been restricted largely to the Huguenot masses of the south, but in the 1760s and 1770s the Protestant *bourgeoisie* felt secure enough to assert itself. Unable to agree on either aims or methods of achieving them, the Protestants saw tolerance elude them again and again. There were disagreements regarding the organisation of the churches. Traditional Calvinist discipline made of each church an independent entity whose laity had great power over their minister, and who could censure him if necessary. The *églises du désert* continued this practice, but more and more pastors resented the power of the elders, whom they regarded as peasants (Léonard, *Histoire ecclésiastique*, p.166). Both Paul Rabaut and Pomaret were in favour of an episcopal form of church government.[223] Provincial synods like that of Bas-Languedoc reacted by asserting their independence, making life difficult for distinguished pastors such as Rabaut (Léonard, *Histoire ecclésiastique*, p.101), and by opposing projects they suspected of having been made for the advantage of the more affluent northern Protestants. Often they were undoubtedly right. When Armand, the chaplain of the Dutch embassy, attempted, with French government support, to

---

[222] cf. Daniel Benoît, 'Les premiers missionaires moraves en France', *Revue chrétienne* (1891), p.827: 'La persécution avait tenu en éveil la foi des Eglises réformées du xviiie siècle. Elle avait grandi dans l'épreuve, la tolérance l'affaiblit, et les approches de la Révolution éveillèrent chez les protestants d'autres préoccupations que celles du ciel.'

[223] cf above, p.350. Pomaret observed to Dumont of Bordeaux on 17 February 1772 that the future did not look bright for 'le système de Calvin': 'Tous ceux qui pensent reconnaissent aujourd'hui qu'il faut dans l'Eglise une hiérarchie, et Calvin ne voulait qu'il y eût entre les ecclésiastiques aucune primauté' (Charles Dardier, 'Lettres écrites par divers pasteurs au sujet des églises réformées de France', *Bpf* (1869), xviii.333-34; cf. Léonard, *Histoire ecclésiastique*, pp.121-25; Daniel Robert, 'Le rôle historique de Paul Rabaut', p.26.

impose on the Huguenots an authoritarian system with himself as *de facto* bishop, disaster threatened French Protestantism[224] and Paul Rabaut joined the synods in fighting the very kind of reform he had so strongly advocated.[225] Often, however, the resistance of the synods was purely negative, and the resulting suspicion between them and some pastors can only have hindered the achievement of complete religious toleration. Another allied factor which weakened French Protestantism was, as we have seen (above, pp.229, 366) that no national synods were held after 1763 for fear of alienating the government.

The pernicious consequences which developed for French Protestantism as a result of these divisions are easy to see in retrospect. Léonard stresses that many pastors, though holding heterodox views, were devoted to pastoral care, but however laudable these activities may have been in themselves, they were of no lasting value for the life and worship of a Christian church. In any case, many pastors, though dedicated, had the barest of theological training, and were thus unable to give very satisfactory teaching to their flocks. Some of the recruits to the ministry were probably tempted by the social prestige of the position, especially in the later part of the century when very little danger threatened a pastor (Poland, p.246; Léonard, *Histoire générale*, iii.69). The results should have pleased Voltaire immensely; most pastors concentrated on the preaching[226] of virtue, neglecting theology,

[224] nearly every history of the *églises du désert* mentions the 'Armand affair'. One of the best and most thorough accounts is Léonard, *Histoire ecclésiastique*, pp.169-80; cf. also, Poland, pp.229-31, and for the part played by Gébelin, Schmidt, *Court de Gébelin à Paris*, pp.159-73.

[225] Léonard, *Histoire ecclésiastique*, p.180. The decision of the synod of Bas-Languedoc was decisive in assuring the failure of Armand's activities.

[226] some pastors even regarded preaching itself as disagreeable and time-consuming: 'Vous êtes heureux, écrivait le pasteur Barre, d'Anduze, à l'un de ses collègues, de pouvoir vous passer de faire des sermons et d'employer votre temps à des occupations plus utiles. J'en fais le moins qu'il m'est possible, mais ce moins est trop pour moi. Ce travail à la longue vous ennuie et vous empêche d'acquérir les connaissances qui sont nécessaires pour faire de bonnes compositions' (Benoît, *Du caractère huguenot*, p.49). Voltaire's correspondent Gal-Pomaret expressed a similar opinion on 23 May 1773. In fact, were this statement to come from the mouth of one of Voltaire's pseudo-Protestant religious spokesmen (perhaps the Pasteur Bourn or Jenni's father Freind) we should feel no surprise whatsoever: 'Je ne fais, Monsieur, presque plus de sermons. Eh! pourquoi tant de sermons? Saint-Jean dans ses vieux ans, n'assembloit les fidèles que pour leur dire, Mes petits enfants, n'aimés point le monde; aimés Dieu, aimés vous les uns les autres, et malgré cela il prêchoit infiniment mieux que nous ne prêchons' (Dardier, 'Lettres écrites', p.340). It is perhaps not insignificant that he goes on immediately to speak of 'le philosophe de Ferney'.

and thus at the same time coming nearer to the position of the *philosophes* and laying themselves open to influence from that quarter.

Some might argue that my analysis has been based on the beliefs and statements of a few more educated pastors, untypical of the majority of their colleagues, and that their views cannot be taken as representing those of the Protestant community as a whole. Even if this objection were true, the very fact that the pastors in question were among the most distinguished and influential of their day would in itself be somewhat disturbing. There is also some evidence, however, that a change in attitudes was taking place generally in Protestant circles. On the one hand, there was an increasing shallowness of religious belief and practices, which manifested itself in a growing desire for compromise with the Catholic church. As the pastor Olivier-Desmont put it, writing to Gal-Pomaret in 1781: 'L'indifférentisme conduit insensiblement le protestant au Catholicisme en France [...] Il faut donc prémunir les troupeaux contre un écueil si dangereux.'[227] No doubt this ecumenical tendency would have been laudable if inspired by a genuine desire for reconciliation based on a sound religious life. But one has the impression that in the weakened and divided French Protestant churches of the late eighteenth century, it was little other than a desire on the part of some to take the line of least resistance, if not a positive manifestation that many Huguenots agreed with Voltaire in finding the differences between various Christian denominations fatuous and meaningless.

These changes did not pass unnoticed. Paul Rabaut himself complained that the old Huguenot traditions were being forgotten (*Gal-Pomaret*, p.215). His friend and colleague Gal-Pomaret became very gloomy at times: 'Nous vivons dans un siècle où nous autres, ministres

---

[227] Du Cailar and Benoît, *Gal-Pomaret*, p.219. Pomaret was in agreement. 'Il est constant en effet', he told Rabaut, 'qu'un très grand nombre de jeunes ministres ne connaissent point du tout l'histoire de l'Eglise et qu'ils seraient non seulement hors d'état de défendre les intérêts de notre sainte Réformation, mais qu'ils en parlent quelquefois un peu cavalièrement. Que pensez-vous de ce couplet d'une chanson que fit un de nos jeunes pasteurs à l'occasion de la naissance du Dauphin:

> Ce ne seront point les Edits
> Qui des manteaux et des surplis
> Corrigeront la morgue austère.
> L'Episcopat, le Presbytère,
> Bientôt amis, s'embrasseront,
> Et désormais disputeront
> A qui chérira mieux ton père.'

Pomaret wishes this would come about, but considers the Catholics to be too uncompromising.

de la religion, ne sommes guère encouragés par nos troupeaux mêmes', he told Rabaut on 13 January 1784 (*Gal-Pomaret*, pp.227-28):

Les romanciers, les poètes, les prétendus beaux esprits, les écrivains qu'on dit être à la mode ont tout gâté. L'Ecriture sainte n'est plus lue; le commerce dont on parle tant attache tous les cœurs à la terre; on ne vit déjà plus que pour le corps seul; le plaisir est devenu l'idole des gens de tout état; nous donnons des sermons dont on ne profite point.

A few years earlier Court de Gébelin had consoled Pomaret over the lack of success gained by the latter's *Catéchisme*:[228]

Le petit livre que vous m'avez envoyé est un trésor précieux. J'aurais cru qu'on se serait empressé à se le procurer; mais je vois avec peine que les ouvrages de piété n'ont déjà plus de cours. Le dégoût pour les choses saintes et utiles gagne et se répand comme le goût pour le frivole et le profane. Gémir et tenter en vain d'arrêter ces progrès funestes, voilà notre ouvrage.

But not all Protestant ministers appear to have been greatly distressed by this development. More and more pastors were in fact becoming interested in politics, and Rabaut Saint-Etienne's brilliant career seems to be only the most distinguished example of a general trend. Taken in isolation, this development might seem to redound to the credit of the Protestant clergy as compared with their Catholic counterparts. But when it is considered in the context of what actually happened during the French Revolution, the real truth emerges. In the years preceding the Revolution, the French Protestant churches had been very seriously weakened. They had not proved intellectually or spiritually robust enough to remain unharmed after their flirtation with the Enlightenment.[229] Instead of absorbing new ideas and making them its own, French Protestantism itself as represented by its most distinguished pastors became virtually a travelling companion of the philosophic movement: during the most anti-Christian phase of the Revolution many Protestants showed no aversion to adopting the cult of the Supreme Being (Poland, p.205). Its distinctive Calvinist doctrines and its fundamental Protestant position were abandoned, it would appear,

---

[228] *Gal-Pomaret*, p.217; the *Catéchisme sous une forme nouvelle, ou le Catéchumène instruit et admis à la sainte communion, par M. Gal-Pomaret, pasteur de Ganges* (Neuchâtel 1779).

[229] this thesis is argued very persuasively by Poland (pp.246 ff).

without a struggle.[230] The outward shell of the Church remained, but
the fact that it no longer contained anything durable was demonstrated
when it crumbled at the first sharp blow the Revolution struck at it.[231]
Nearly all the Protestant pastors gave up their ecclesiastical functions
with little or no protest (Poland, pp.205-206). The Catholic church
had also had its 'liberals', but its resistance against the attacks made on it
was of quite a different order. The contrast was clear and decisive:
whereas substantial elements of the Catholic population kept up a
heroic struggle against secularisation, in many areas if not everywhere
the Protestants faded gracefully out of existence.

xi. *Voltaire and Gal-Pomaret*

Movements in the history of ideas often remain lifeless abstractions
unless they are placed in a living context, and it may be helpful to illustrate some of the tendencies just described as exemplified in one of
Voltaire's Protestant contemporaries, the pastor of Ganges,[232] Gal-
Pomaret. We have already met his name many times, for he corresponded regularly with the *philosophe* from the end of 1767 until just
before Voltaire's death.[233] In considering his contacts with Voltaire,

[230] during the Terror, the pastor Pierre Ribes of Aigues-Vives wrote to his wife: 'J'ai
vécu en honnête homme, en bon chrétien, j'ai fait quelque bien. J'emporte le témoignage
d'une bonne conscience.' Daniel Benoît comments: 'C'est stoïque, sans doute, c'est fier et
généreux. Mais comme on préférerait, à l'heure suprême, l'accent de la contrition et de
l'espérance chrétienne!' (*Du caractère huguenot*, p.51).

[231] cf. Poland, pp.202 ff. According to him, the laity must bear a large share of the blame
for this collapse: 'In 1793 many pastors undoubtedly abdicated their functions because
they saw the handwriting on the wall: their churches were disintegrating around them.
Under such circumstances it is easier to understand why none of them were tempted to
resist' (p.219). Poland's conclusions are largely supported by Daniel Ligou ('Sur le
protestantisme révolutionnaire à propos d'un ouvrage récent', *Bpf* (1958), civ.49): 'Les
Réformés, adeptes d'un culte purement rationaliste et moral dès le milieu de XVIIIe siècle,
n'ont guère cherché à résister à la déchristianisation et le décret du 18 floréal reconnaissant
l'existence de l'Etre Suprême et l'immortalité de l'âme a suffi à satisfaire leurs besoins
métaphysiques.' Raoul Stephan, *Histoire du protestantisme français* (Paris 1961), pp.210-
11, agrees that the Protestants did not stand up to the Terror very well, although he thinks
that there were some 'points lumineux'.

[232] a small town at the southern end of the Cévennes area.

[233] twenty-one letters appear in the definitive edition of Voltaire's correspondence.
They are (Gal to Voltaire): Best.D14577 (7 December 1767), D14692 (18 January 1768),
D16086 (11 January 1770), D16646 (14 September 1770), D17586 (2 February 1772),
D19967 (4 March 1776), D20191 (25 June 1776), D20240 (3 August 1776), D20514 (9
January 1777), D20602 (10 March 1777); (Voltaire to Gal): Best.D14598 (18 December
1767), D15432 (15 January 1769), D16124 (31 January 1770), D16723 (24 October 1770),

we shall see concentrated in one man some of the contradictions and inconsistencies which beset the eighteenth-century Protestant church in its relations with the *philosophes*.

Pomaret's real name was Jean Gal.[234] Born in 1720 in the parish of Saint-André-de-Valborgne (situated like Ganges in the Cévennes), he began to train for the ministry in 1738 and was consecrated pastor on 8 September 1748, having spent just under a year studying at Lausanne (November 1745 – September 1746). The early years of Gal's ministry were trying ones for the Protestants owing to government persecution, and Gal soon became interested in practical ways of securing toleration for his brethren. In 1751 he addressed letters to Machault d'Arnouville, Richelieu and Saint-Priest on the subject (*Gal-Pomaret*, pp.33-35). At this time he might have been considered a hard-liner, keen to keep assemblies going and eager that Protestants should persist in conducting their own marriages and baptisms. Bénézet, executed on 27 March 1752 (see above, p.270), had been one of his pupils, and Pomaret himself at one moment considered exile when the presence of troops forced him to leave Ganges. But in the ensuing years relative calm returned and Pomaret was able to cultivate his literary interests, also steadily consolidating his position within the Church until by the 1760s he had become one of the best-known and most respected pastors. In 1762 he was offered a post by the king of Denmark. But now a change was evident in Gal. He opposed the holding of the 1763 national synod because it might offend the government. 'Pourquoi s'assembler avant que de bien savoir ce que la cour veut faire de nous?' he asked Rabaut in a letter of 28 November 1762 (quoted in Coquerel, ii.338: see also Léonard, *Histoire ecclésiastique*, pp.132-33). 'Elle aime que nous marchions sans bruit, et un synode national en fait toujours beaucoup.' Both Gal and Rabaut were agreed in condemning the Calvinist organisation of the Church, and like many of his colleagues Gal wished the

D17201 (22 May 1771), D17401 (14 October 1771), D19048 (26 July 1774), D19120 (18 September 1774), D20053 (8 April 1776), D20201 (4 July 1776), D20556 (7 February 1777).

It is obvious from the extant correspondence that at least three letters from Gal are missing: between Best.D16723 and Best.D17201, between Best.D17201 and Best. D17401, and between Best.D19048 and Best.D19120.

234 Du Cailar and Benoît, *Gal-Pomaret, pasteur de Ganges*, p.7; I here acknowledge my debt to this work from which most of the ensuing information on Gal-Pomaret's life is taken. It was customary for the *pasteurs du désert* to assume a false name, originally for purposes of security, and the practice was maintained when it was no longer strictly necessary.

385

pastors to have more influence over their flocks. Building *maisons de prière* he considered to be unnecessary – Protestants should be content with assemblies as in the past.[235] By the 1760s Pomaret seems to have become more conservative and less sympathetic to the aspirations of the ordinary members of his flock. Now that the government was displaying a less intransigent attitude, pastors like Gal with much to lose if the persecution should recommence were often only too willing to compromise, sometimes becoming as timid in their demands as the *bourgeoisie* of the north.

One may sympathise with the relatively well-educated Gal[236] who felt very cut off from the rest of the intellectual world in the small isolated town of Ganges. 'Je donnerais tout au monde pour être à portée de vous voir souvent', he wrote to Rabaut, 'je ne puis ici parler avec personne: on ne s'y entend qu'à filer de la soie et à planter des vignes et des mûriers' (12 August 1768, Mss Paul Rabaut, quoted in Coquerel, ii.400). No doubt this explains his desire to correspond with famous writers, although it may also have been, as Pomaret's biographers suggest (p.97), 'pour faire diversion à sa douleur', his wife and father both having died in 1764. Rousseau exchanged several letters with him, and Gal was also on friendly terms with Voltaire's enemy La Beaumelle, but by far the most significant event of Pomaret's literary career was when he first wrote to Voltaire himself on 7 December 1767 (Best.D14577). As one might expect, the subsequent correspondence generally contains information passed on by Voltaire in response to enquiries made by Gal, although sometimes the pastor was able to bring him up to date with the situation in the provinces. The topics discussed are mostly connected with religious matters and the fortunes of Protestantism, but are nonetheless relatively wide-ranging and varied: the Sirven affair, Versoix, the Jesuits, the abbé Audra's

---

[235] 'Je n'ambitionne point de temple [. . .] et nous pouvons fort bien nous en passer', Pomaret told Rabaut in 1774 (Dardier, *Paul Rabaut: ses lettres à divers*, ii.201). In 1765 he criticised the Protestants of Durfort in Languedoc who had begun to rebuild their *temple*. 'Je pense que le gouvernement fait pour nous tout ce que les circonstances lui permettent de faire', he told Chiron, 'et si les protestants m'en croyaient, ils s'en tiendraient aux assemblées de la campagne, et ne chercheraient à se mettre à couvert que lorsque notre auguste monarque voudrait bien le leur permettre' (*Gal-Pomaret*, p.119). It is only fair to add that Pomaret later wrote in favour of these Protestants when the authorities demolished their *temple*.

[236] Coquerel (ii.400) calls him 'un esprit extrêmement cultivé'. This is perhaps a slight exaggeration.

reports on Toulouse, praise of Fitzjames, former bishop of Soissons, and of the tolerant comte de Périgord, comments on the new pope (Clement XIV), abuse of the Sorbonne, accounts of Voltaire's own colony of Protestants at Ferney, and, naturally, frequent reports on the dispositions of the government, periodic expressions of optimism regarding the Protestants' civil rights, advice from Voltaire on how they should act, and discussion of particular cases of injustice. But by far the most interesting feature of the correspondence from the point of view of this study is the frequent references made by Gal to his religious beliefs.

We must be careful to put Pomaret's statements into perspective, for he was no fool, and it was obviously in his interests to make as good an impression as possible on Voltaire in order to receive information and help for his fellow Huguenots. With this in mind we might be inclined to dismiss a statement like the following, or at any rate to attach little real significance to it: 'Vous le voïés, Monsieur, quoique nés dans des contrées pleines autrefois d'Energumènes, nous sommes raisonnables, et pourrions nous ne l'être pas dans un siècle où vous avés apris à tant de monde à raisonner' (Best.D14692, 18 January 1768). At the outset of his contacts with Voltaire, Pomaret wished to show that the Cévennes no longer harboured crypto-Camisard fanatics, an impression which was in fact slow to leave the *philosophe*. Similar considerations help us to understand the almost indecent amount of flattery heaped on Voltaire by Gal, especially in his first letter.[237] Eighteenth-century usage was more fulsome than our own[238] and expressions of respect were to be expected when one was addressing the most famous contemporary author. Rather exaggerated flattery seems anyway to have been a characteristic feature of Gal's style and did not make its appearance

[237] it will be sufficient to quote merely the beginning: 'Que j'ose, moi, ministre obscur des Cevennes, qui ne sçus jamais parler qu'un fort mauvais patois, prendre la liberté de vous écrire, à vous qui enrichissés tous les jours la langue française, & qui par la sublimité de vos pensées & la beauté de vos expressions, enchantés, pour ainsi dire le monde entier, Cela vous paraitra, sans doute, un peu trop audacieux; mais Monsieur, cette tendre humanité qui éclate dans tous vos ouvrages, m'enhardit, & me fait espérer que quelque mal conçue que puisse être ma Lettre, vous ne laisserés pas de la bien accueillir' (Best.D14577). There are many similar passages in Gal's letters to Voltaire.

[238] cf. the ending of a letter written on 21 August 1775 by Lecointe de Marcillac to Malesherbes: 'Monseigneur! ayant acquis depuis longtems l'estime de l'Europe par votre génie et par vos vertus, ayant mérité sa vénération et son attachement par votre disgrâce, fixant aujourd'huy tous les yeux, daignés être persuadé que l'affaire dont j'ay l'honneur de vous parler vous couvriroit d'une gloire immortelle' (quoted in Grosclaude, *Malesherbes*, pp.377-78).

only when he was writing to Voltaire.[239] Nor must we attach too much importance to a passage in Gal's letter to Voltaire of 11 January 1770. At first sight this would seem to be a perfect example of Voltaire's influence over the pastor; it is almost as if Pomaret were giving an account of himself and his doctrine to an ecclesiastical superior (Best. D16086):

Pasteur, comme je le suis, Monsieur, dans une ville partagée en protestans & en catholiques, je concours de tout mon pouvoir, non à les accorder sur les points de foi qui les divisent, car je ne saurois y réussir, mais à établir au-moins entr'eux un commerce réciproque de bons offices. J'ai même la satisfaction de voir que je n'i travaille pas inutilement, & c'est là pour moi le plus ravissant de tous les spectacles. Quant à ma Doctrine, j'enseigne, Monsieur, que Dieu est Esprit, & que cela étant, il ne peut se trouver chés lui que des émanations, des vertus, des opérations, des œuvres, qu'il se montre toujours à nous comme notre bien suprême, comme notre dernière fin; qu'il veut miséricorde plutôt que sacrifice; que le péché est la grande maladie de l'âme; que tant que notre âme est malade le bonheur est loin de nous; & que si nous voulons être heureux, il faut par conséquent que nous évitions le mal & que nous fassions le bien.

Yet this impression must be balanced by the fact that Gal had already given a similar account of his doctrine to La Beaumelle, though with a significant change in emphasis. [240] One trait of Gal's character was a desire to please and gain approval which, if it did not exactly turn him into a Protestant *père tout à tous*, makes it sometimes difficult to dis-

---

[239] thanking Servan for his defence of the Protestants in connection with Marie Robequin, Gal commented: 'Vous avez parlé le langage de l'humanité, le langage de la justice, le langage de la religion. Eh! qui les parla jamais plus éloquemment que vous? Qui mérita jamais mieux que vous d'être infiniment cher à tous les cœurs? Toujours vous serez dans les nôtres', etc. (*Gal-Pomaret*, p.125). And to La Beaumelle he was no less complimentary: 'Je le savais bien, Monsieur, que votre dogme favori était celui de la tolérance civile [. . .] Né, comme vous l'êtes, pour les grandes choses, daignez continuer, Monsieur, à donner des leçons au monde entier. Pour moi, je ne suis fait que pour prêcher la religion à une poignée de peuple' (p.127).

[240] 'je m'applique à la lui [religion to his flock] présenter sous les côtés qui me paraissent les plus attrayants et les plus aimables. Je lui parle de Dieu comme d'un Etre qui chérit tous les hommes et qui, dans toutes ses opérations, se propose sinon notre félicité présente au moins notre félicité future; de Jésus-Christ comme d'un Maître qui est venu nous détacher des idoles que nous nous étions faites dans notre ignorance et que nous adorions dans notre aveuglement, aussi bien que comme d'un guide qui est venu se mettre à notre tête pour nous conduire au vrai bonheur; de cette vie non comme d'un état de jouissance, mais comme d'un état de préparation à une meilleure; et de l'enfer comme d'un lieu de souffrance qui ne prendra fin que lorsque nous cesserons d'être pécheurs' (*Gal Pomaret*, pp.127-28).

tinguish his real opinions from the diplomatic utterances found in his letters.

But despite the rather contrived nature of Gal's flattery, especially in the early letters, there is little doubt that he developed a sincere affection for Voltaire, as can be seen from many of his letters. In 1770, he contributed to Voltaire's statue, and was equally anxious to express the enthusiasm of his fellow Protestants. Breaking into verse he exclaimed:

> Et les protestans de la France
> Seraient, sans doute, des ingrats,
> Si de bon cœur, ils n'aimoient pas
> L'apôtre de la tolérance
> Et le protecteur des Calas.[241]

Gal's last letter assures the patriarch that he is idolised by the Huguenots of the Cévennes (Best.D20602, 10 March 1777): 'Vous êtes plus aimé, Monsieur, dans no[s] Cevenes que vous ne sauriés croire. Tous les protestans qui s'y trouvent savent ce que vous avés fait pour eux, & tous vous ont dressé une statue dans leurs Cœurs.' Pomaret frequently sympathises with Voltaire's advanced age, wishes him a long life, and encourages him with accounts of hale and hearty old residents of Ganges aged ninety. At the beginning of 1777 (9 January) Gal laments Voltaire's silence in terms which seem to be inspired by genuine feelings rather than false politeness (Best.D20514). In one letter Gal even claimed to have followed advice given to him by Voltaire several years earlier and written a work preaching enlightened religion and virtue (Best. D17586, 2 February 1772; see below, p.390, n.244). His reward was not denied him. Voltaire congratulated him on his religious beliefs (Best. D16124), although he told Gal that he was unable to share them.[242] He assured the pastor of his esteem (Best.D20053) and on 4 July 1776 gave him the supreme accolade, calling Pomaret a 'philosophe des Cévennes' (Best.D20201).

If Pomaret was in fact a sincere Reformed Christian who, while respecting the man and his actions, disapproved of and rejected Voltaire's teachings on religion, why could he not have made this clear in

---

[241] Best.D16646, 14 September 1770. Pomaret's biographers regret these effusions: 'Ce n'est pas sans tristesse qu'on lit, sous la plume de Pomaret, ces éloges outrés à l'adresse d'un écrivain qui s'est efforcé de faire tant de mal à la religion chrétienne' (*Gal-Pomaret*, p.158).

[242] Best.D20201, 4 July 1776: 'Moi même, monsieur, qui suis si d'accord avec vous dans la morale, j'ai le malheur d'être très éloigné des sentiments que vous êtes obligé de professer.'

his letters in a dignified and tactful way?[243] Time and again, of his own accord and without any prompting from his distinguished correspondent, Gal returns to the subject of religion, but his statements seem nearly always designed to please Voltaire, as if Pomaret found it constantly necessary to justify himself. What a difference, he exclaimed on 11 January 1770, between Voltaire and so many churchmen, who preach Christianity but do not practice it: 'vous semblés le combattre, & cependant vous en faites les œuvres: aussi ne saurois-je vous dire jusqu'à quel point je vous mêts au dessus d'eux.' He then expresses the wish that men might tire of 'une dévotion qui n'a rien d'utile, pour ne se piquer que de vertus, & de vertus toujours pleines de bons fruits' (Best.D16086). The 'plan d'un ouvrage à l'usage des chefs de famille' composed by Gal in response to a suggestion by Voltaire[244] and described in Best.D17586 would not be out of place in one of the latter's own pamphlets on religion (Best.D17586, 2 February 1772):

Tout y conduit à une Religion qui présente beaucoup moins de vérités à croire, que de devoirs à pratiquer: Tout y est propre à inspirer un zèle sans fanatisme, & une bienveillance sans partialité; Tout y tend à porter les chrétiens en général à faire régner, aumoins, entr'eux une paix extérieure, s'ils ne peuvent venir à bout d'y faire régner une harmonie de sentimens.

A comment in Best.D14692 (18 January 1768) is equally Voltairean:

Par tout la tendre humanité s'empare des cœurs; par tout l'affreuse intolérance tombe; par tout l'avilissante superstition disparoit; par tout on commence à sentir que la Religion consiste moins à croire ceci ou cela, qu'à être droit dans ses sentimens, véridique dans ses paroles, fidèle dans ses promesses, juste dans ses actions, charitable dans ses œuvres.

Was then Gal, the 'philosophe des Cévennes', a hypocrite? For writing to Desmont at Bordeaux he expressed his doubts about contemporary *philosophie*[245] and encouraged the latter to refute Voltaire's ideas:

---

[243] it is significant that Gal's biographers find it necessary to ask a similar question in connection with his letters to Rousseau: 'Pourquoi notre pasteur ne se place-t-il pas au centre même de l'Evangile pour combattre celui à qui l'on ne saurait refuser, sans doute, une certaine religiosité, qui a su défendre contre des négations impies la plus noble partie de notre être et l'existence de Dieu, mais qui, d'autre part, n'a pas craint d'attaquer l'autorité même du christianisme?' (*Gal-Pomaret*, p.116).

[244] this was *Le bon père ou le Chrétien protestant* (Neuchâtel 1783), which had originally been called *Le Protestant instruit dans sa foi* (*Gal-Pomaret*, p.221).

[245] 'Nous sommes dans un siècle philosophe, mais pensés vous que la philosophie qui est tant en vogue tourne à l'avantage du christianisme? Je crois le contraire. Déjà nos troupeaux fourmillent de mécréants. Que fera-t-on, quand on aura beaucoup philosophé?

Si j'étois plus jeune et plus habile que je ne le suis, je me formerois de justes idées du système de M. de Voltaire, et je chercherois ensuite à y répandre le même ridicule qu'il a cherché à répandre sur le nôtre: ne pourriés vous pas vous charger de ce travail là? Ce grand homme traite le christianisme sans aucun ménagement dans ses nouveaux mélanges philosophiques. Je crains qu'il ne rende tout le monde déiste.[246]

Yet to other correspondents he emphasised the debt owed by Protestants to Voltaire, specifically attributing the growth of toleration to the great man's writings.[247] On 25 August 1774, for example, he wrote as follows to Soulier concerning anti-Protestant action carried out by the Bordeaux *parlement:* 'Notre même ami [Voltaire] m'écrit qu'il va se donner des mouvements pour en arrêter les effets [...] Voyez, après cela, combien sont grandes les obligations que nous lui avons' (quoted in Benoît, 'Les pasteurs et l'échafaud révolutionnaire', p.572). And when he was informed by a visitor to Ferney that Voltaire held Gal's religious views in high esteem, the pastor commented: 'Si cela est, il est donc chrétien' (letter of 2 May 1773 from Pomaret to Olivier Desmont at Bordeaux, quoted in Dardier, 'Lettres écrites', p.340).

Pomaret's dilemma in his contacts with Voltaire is understandable. A brief glance at the type of Christian he was will help us to appreciate this. It is significant that his letters to the 'philosophe de Ferney' are not the only example of Gal's expressing himself in terms which would not have displeased Voltaire. La Beaumelle found the pastor's description of his religious views insufficient (*Gal-Pomaret*, p.129). 'N'est-ce pas trop simplifier l'Evangile', he asked, 'que de représenter Jésus-Christ seulement comme un maître et un guide? Le Livre Saint ne borne pas à ce point-là nos idées et nos connaissances sur ce grand sujet.' Pomaret's biographers, Du Cailar and Benoît, comment in this connection (p.128): 'La christologie de Pomaret [...] laisse beaucoup à désirer.' To put it quite bluntly, Pomaret was a Socinian, if not *stricto sensu*, at least in the sense currently accorded to this word in the eighteenth century (see below, p.458, n.12). Though disagreeing with some

Il est fort à craindre qu'on ne retourne au fanatisme' (Dardier, 'Lettres écrites', 17 February 1772, p.336).

[246] letter of 11 January 1773, (Dardier, 'Lettres écrites', p.339).

[247] cf. Gal's comment to Pierre Soulier: 'Si M. de Voltaire n'eût donné que de gros volumes, il n'aurait pas fait le quart du bien qu'il a produit. Je dis du bien, parce que je crois que c'est principalement aux écrits de ce philosophe que nous devons la tolérance dont nous jouissons' (quoted by Daniel Benoît, 'Les pasteurs et l'échafaud révolutionnaire: Pierre Soulier de Sauve (1743-1794)', *Bpf* (1894), xliii.571).

of Voltaire's more aggressive statements on religion, Gal was in such sympathy with many of his ideas and so full of administration for his actions that he was able to write the passages mentioned above without doing violence to his own beliefs. Pomaret was not dechristianised to the extent of a Rabaut Saint-Etienne, but his doctrinal unorthodoxy is beyond question.[248]

The two main strands of Gal's Socinianism are plain. In the first place, he refused to accord to Christ equality of status with God the father. At the beginning of 1768, he explained himself as follows to La Beaumelle: 'il ne me paraît pas clair que les mots de vrai Dieu, qu'on lit dans la seconde épître de saint Jean, doivent être rapportés à Jésus-Christ proprement ainsi nommé. Il me semble qu'ils regardent plutôt le *Véritable* que nous ne connaissons pas et que Jésus est venu nous faire connaître' (*Gal-Pomaret*, pp.137-38). Secondly, Pomaret does not believe in the eternity of Hell: like the Swiss pastor Petitpierre (see above, pp.169-70) he appears to favour a notion akin to the Catholic idea of purgatory (see above, p.388, n.240). Both of these opinions are expressed to La Beaumelle, who like Gal was a Protestant and, as we have seen (above, p.391), somewhat more orthodox than the pastor himself, so there is no reason to suspect that Pomaret is watering down his beliefs as he might sometimes have been tempted to do in his correspondence with Voltaire.

On the other hand, there is no doubt that Gal was not merely a deist in Protestant clothing. His faith in Christ, whether or not the divine saviour was equal to God the father, appears warm and genuine. He told Paul Rabaut on 28 February 1774 (*Gal-Pomaret*, p.175):

sans Jésus-Christ, Monsieur, nous ne savons rien, nous ne pouvons rien; nous ne sommes qu'un bois sec, que des corps sans âme; il est notre lumière, notre force, notre pain, notre arbre de vie; son exemple vaut infiniment plus que tous les livres; il nous enseigne toutes les vertus, et ce sont des vertus qu'il nous faut pour être heureux, tant dans le temps que dans l'éternité.

As we see also from this passage, belief in an afterlife is another factor which distinguishes Pomaret's religious position from that of Voltaire and most deists. Yet despite the positive character of some of Pomaret's Christian beliefs, another confession of faith, made this time to the

---

[248] cf. *Gal-Pomaret*, pp.163-64: although the pastor Desmont's *Discours moraux* were unorthodox, they were enthusiastically praised by Gal.

Protestant pastor Olivier Desmont, illustrates how the influence of Voltairean ideas had nonetheless made an important impression on Gal. After initially expressing his veneration for Christ and the Bible, Pomaret concludes with a passage whose terms and sentiments would be just as characteristic in the mouth of Voltaire: 'on a beau faire, jamais on ne détachera les hommes de la croyance d'un Dieu, d'une Providence, d'une rétribution à venir. Mais ce qui me fait gémir, c'est le relâchement de la morale' (p.169).

This somewhat ambiguous position perhaps explains the enthusiasm expressed by Gal in connection with 'Religion', an article which appeared in the *Questions sur l'Encyclopédie* in 1771. Voltaire here presents a sympathetic view of Jesus, who is found to have disagreed on most points with later Christian teaching (ed. Benda and Naves, pp.611-13). Pomaret was obviously touched by this sign that Voltaire was not irreconcilable to some form of Christianity, and it prompted him to make an attempt to 'convert' Voltaire. Yet to use the word 'convert' is almost to overstate the case, so deferential, so apologetic is the suggestion that Voltaire adopt the teaching of the Gospel. In fact, so glowing are Gal's praises that he seems to forget his original intention and breaks out into a panegyric of the great man (Best.D19967, 4 March 1776):

Pour voir approcher la mort sans crainte & la recevoir sans émotion, il faut être, selon moi, dans la croïance des vérités Evangéliques; & je ne doute pas que vous n'y soïés. Il est vrai que vous avez formé Contr-elles plusieurs difficultés, mais on peut en faire sans être incrédule, et plus encore sans être impie.

Lorsque vous fûtes dans ces belles allées où vous trouvâtes les Numa, les Pythagore, les Zoroastre, les Socrate, & notre Rédempteur, il vous fut dit, Monsieur, par le génie qui vous conduisait, que le tems dans lequel vous deviés connaitre pleinement ce dernier n'était pas encore venu. He bien, ce tems arrivera, vous verrés Jesus-Christ dans sa gloire, & vous aurés part à son bonheur.[249] Il plaignit les pauvres pécheurs, il s'attendrit sur leurs misères, il s'empressa à les consoler. Les hypocrites sont les seuls envers lesquels il se montra dur, & vous ne fûtes assurément jamais hypocrite.

As regards good works and his teaching concerning the prime importance of morality, Voltaire was no doubt already considered by Gal

---

[249] without necessarily discounting Gal's enthusiasm here, it is not without interest to note that he was later to write to Robespierre: 'Citoyen, la nature m'a donné un petit-fils. Puisse-t-il avoir tes vertus!' (Benoît, *Du caractère huguenot*, p.50).

as one of God's chosen servants. His hostile attitude to Jesus appears to have been the only major factor which had prevented Pomaret from according to Voltaire his entire admiration, and 'Religion' seemed to indicate that even this difference between them might disappear.

By the 1770s Gal-Pomaret, like many of his fellow-pastors, was more affected by Voltairean modes of thinking than he probably realised. Even if such men believed in the preparation of the sinner through repentance and prayer for the life everlasting, this aspect of their religious life tended to be emphasised less and less: their preaching centred increasingly on the practice of virtue in this world. Dogmatic subtleties no longer interested them and in fact appeared positively harmful to many. Daniel Benoît (*Du caractère huguenot*, p.50) has aptly called their religion a 'christianisme déclamatoire'. Such men would seem to have been excellent material for the sort of clergy Voltaire had often recommended in works like the *Questions sur les miracles*. They would have been ready to accept a subservient rôle in relation to the secular authorities and to confine themselves to preaching good morality, rather than interfering in affairs of state like the Catholic clergy. Did Voltaire ever envisage the reform of Christianity in France on the lines of an expanded and purified Huguenot Church, replacing its superstitious and largely discredited Catholic counterpart? If an 'enlightened' minister had asked his advice, would he have recommended making the doctrinally co-operative Huguenot pastors the basis of the new clergy? To answer this question we must turn to a feature of Voltaire's relationship with the Protestants which we have not as yet investigated, and for which he has been criticised bitterly. Did Voltaire despise the Huguenots he helped?

xii. *The Huguenots' ridiculous characteristics*

On 15 February 1764 Voltaire wrote to Damilaville about galley-slaves who had been 'condamnés pour avoir entendu en plein champ de mauvais sermons de sots prêtres calvinistes' (Best.D11699). On 5 January 1763 he had commented to Moultou: 'Je pense enfin, que l'avanture des Calas peut servir à relâcher beaucoup les chaines de vos frères qui prient Dieu en fort mauvais vers' (Best.D10885). Such patronising and uncomplimentary references are not infrequent in Voltaire's letters or in his published works. He even went as far as to remark to d'Argence on 21 August 1762: 'Ces Calas sont, comme vous l'avez peut être déjà ouï dire, des protestants imbéciles' (Best.D10666).

The first point to make is that these references are not merely an example of the malicious m. de Voltaire's uncontrollable bent for satire and irony. It is possible to understand his motives even if one does not approve of them. Sometimes the reason for his using pejorative terms in connection with the Huguenots is obvious. When, for example, he called Rabaut a madman (Best.D11128; see above, p.333, n.143), he was angered by the possibility of his carefully planned campaign on behalf of the Calas family being ruined by the ill-considered actions of a few hasty *pasteurs du désert*. When he talked to Richelieu on 27 October 1766 of 'ces plats huguenots et [...] leurs impertinentes assemblées' (Best. D13632), he was tactfully agreeing with an opinion expressed by his correspondent in order not to alienate him further. And when he complained to Damilaville on 18 August 1766 that 'six ou sept cent mille sots huguenots ont abandonné leur patrie pour les sottises de Jehan Chauvin', his scornful terms were provoked by the fact that not twelve *philosophes* would make the same sacrifice 'à la raison universelle qu'on outrage' and set up a colony at Clèves (Best.D13500).

Voltaire's repeated mentions of the Huguenots' ridiculous charac-teristics – their obstinate singing of dreadfully translated psalms set to bad music, their insistence on assembling illegally at great personal risk to hear boring preachers – also had a definite propaganda value in the battle for toleration. Firstly, they could serve to point out the dis-parity between the ridiculous nature of the Huguenots' 'crimes' and the dreadful punishments they suffered as a result. This tactic is evident in a letter to mme Choiseul: 'Il y a dans le royaume des Francs, environ trois cent mille fous qui sont cruellement traités par d'autres fous depuis longtemps. On les met aux galères, on les pend, on les roue pour avoir prié dieu en mauvais français en plein champ.'[250] Moreover, Voltaire was probably doing the Huguenots a very good turn by making them appear figures of fun in the public mind. Their psalm-singing, perhaps the best-known Huguenot characteristic, had long held very different associations for ordinary Catholic Frenchmen. It symbolised the chaos and disorder of the civil wars, and as late as the Cévennes rebellion the Huguenots had merely to begin their psalm-singing to put their enemies to flight.[251] Voltaire was therefore

250 Best.D15776, 26 July 1769. Voltaire also made this point in connection with the Espinas family, rendered destitute 'pour avoir donné il y a vingt six ans à souper à un sot prêtre hérétique' (Best.D13737, to mme de Saint Julien, 15 December 1766).

251 'Quand ces diables-là se mettaient à chanter leur bougresse de chanson [...] nous ne pouvions plus être maîtres de nos gens; ils fuyaient comme si tous les diables avaient été à

performing a very necessary function in exorcising the fear which may have haunted many.[252] It is even possible that he had lingering doubts himself, as we can see from the description of Huguenot assemblies in *Pot-pourri* – the psalm-singing there is a very martial affair and is duly condemned by Voltaire (see above, p.315). Thus by stressing the amusing and absurd side of this characteristic feature of Huguenot worship, Voltaire was not only demonstrating to his fellow-citizens that such risible heretics were no longer a threat to the French state, he was also warning the Protestants themselves to abandon practices which could still be interpreted as subversive in some quarters. Moreover, the ridicule heaped on the Huguenots played its part in Voltaire's campaign against Christianity as a whole. The example of the Quakers had already proved that the oddities of any sect could be a useful weapon against l'*infâme*, however meritorious their other activities might be. Once again Voltaire was able to turn his irony skilfully against both the persecutors and the victims of their intolerance.

It is also possible that Voltaire had genuine aesthetic reasons for criticising Huguenot psalm-singing. Even some Protestants admitted that this could be a boisterous and rowdy practice,[253] and it was unlikely to appeal to one who had such strong views on the worship of the divinity as had Voltaire. A concern that God should be fittingly praised in words and music is manifest in *Candide*. Describing his country's religion, the *vieillard* from Eldorado explains: 'Mes amis [...] nous sommes tous prêtres; le roi et tous les chefs de famille chantent des cantiques d'actions de grâces solennellement tous les matins, et cinq ou six mille musiciens les accompagne' (Pomeau ed., p.154). Voltaire's opinions on this subject are further expressed in chapter 44 of *Dieu et les hommes*, 'Comment il faut prier dieu'. Here he insists that the theist's

leurs trousses' (E.-G. Léonard, *Histoire générale*, iii.18ff.). The 'bougresse de chanson' in question was Psalm 68, *Exsurgat Deus*: 'Que Dieu se montre seulement'.

[252] it was presumably just such a fear which produced panic among Catholics at the time of Rochette's arrest in 1761; cf. Bien, *The Calas affair*, pp.80-81; above, p.283.

[253] cf. the 'relation' of a journey through Saintonge, Poitou and Languedoc, between July and November 1768 by one Jacob Becker, a Moravian brother who lived at Bordeaux. On Whit Sunday he worshipped with the Huguenots of Saint-Savinien and wrote afterwards in his journal: 'On y chanta des psaumes qui n'avaient aucune relation avec la fête et l'on criait d'une force que j'en avais la tête toute étourdie' (quoted in Benoît, 'Les premiers missionnaires moraves en France', p.833). At a synod held on 20 September 1768, Voltaire's correspondent Gal-Pomaret 'fit remarquer que les psaumes n'étaient pas toujours chantés dans les assemblées avec toute la décence et tout le sérieux que comporte cet acte de culte' (*Gal-Pomaret*, p.142).

worship of God must be dignified: 'Loin d'abolir le culte public, nous voulons le rendre plus pur et moins indigne de l'Etre suprême [...] Louons Dieu, invoquons Dieu à la manière d'Orphée, de Pindare, d'Horace, de Dryden, de Pope, et non à la manière hébraïque' (M.xxviii. 241). Of course these remarks apply to all Christians, Catholic and Protestant alike, but it is certainly possible that Voltaire had the Huguenots particularly in mind at this point (see above, p.86, n.86). We have already seen (above, pp.85-88) that he considered the Protestants to be particularly well versed in the Old Testament, a familiarity which in his opinion encouraged both fanaticism and barbarity, and in *Dieu et les hommes* it is just this feature of Christianity's Judaic heritage, symbolised by the Psalms, that Voltaire is concerned to attack: he recalls among others the bloodcurdling verse – 'Bienheureux celui qui prendra tes petits enfants, et qui les écrasera contre la pierre' (M.xxviii.242) – the very psalm he had put into the mouth of the infamous Cromwell (see above, p.87) and had also accused the Huguenots of singing.[254] Thus Voltaire's case against Protestant psalm-singing rests mainly on two arguments: in the first place it lacks the dignity appropriate to divine worship, and secondly the texts used are barbaric and encourage cruelty and fanaticism.

These no doubt deeply-held beliefs explain the persistence of Voltaire's mockery regarding Huguenot worship. He was completely unable to understand why intelligent and cultured Protestants should cling to what he regarded as meaningless and superfluous practices: 'Celui qui a l'honneur de vous faire réponse, ne chante point de pseaume,' he told Paul Rabaut on 16 May 1767, 'mais il adore la divinité et il aime l'humanité' (Best.D14185), surely implying that the elements which distinguished the beliefs of Huguenots from those of a theist were no more than ridiculous inessentials of which a reasonable man should rid himself. When he came into contact with less educated Protestants Voltaire's patience was stretched even further: as we have already seen (above, p.304), he called the Huguenot galley-slaves 'vos martirs de la sottise, condamnés à ramer par le fanatisme' (Best.D11700). Indeed, the simple faith of unsophisticated believers was hardly likely to make a favourable impression on Voltaire, and this is probably what explains

---

[254] e.g. in *Pot-pourri* (*Mélanges*, p.724). In an extremely interesting piece of research R. Fargher has shown that Voltaire was wrong when he claimed that the Huguenots sang psalms to the air 'Réveillez-vous, belle endormie' (*Life and letters*, pp.133 ff.).

his condescending attitude to Chaumont[255] and his occasional exasperation with mme Calas.[256] Yet far from this latent hostility destroying the value of Voltaire's campaign on behalf of the Huguenots, it is surely to his eternal credit that he persevered so long and vigorously to secure toleration for men whose conduct he often regarded as excentric or downright fanatical: no more eloquent or impressive tribute to Voltaire's humanitarianism can be made than to review his efforts during the 1760s and 1770s to achieve civil rights and a measure of religious freedom for his Protestant contemporaries.

As time went on and Voltaire's contacts with pastors like Gal-Pomaret developed, his critical and mocking attitude toward the Protestants may have tended to disappear somewhat. But although he was a good friend to the persecuted Huguenots whom he helped so many times, there is little doubt that Voltaire regarded their faith, as he understood it, as abhorrent, and their church, which was in any case declining at that time, as an anachronism, of no practical use in the battle against *l'infâme*. The future lay, not with the Protestants, but with a reformed, Gallican church, freed from the control of the pope and subject to the State, shorn of the contemporary Catholic Church's unreasonable beliefs and practices. That Voltaire was willing to countenance this sort of development we shall see presently when we consider his attitude to the Anglican Church.

[255] cf. Best.D11750 (Voltaire to Louis Necker, 5 March 1764): 'J'ai vu vôtre cordonnier. Vraiment, c'est un imbécile.'

[256] cf. Best.D10810 (Voltaire to d'Alembert, 28 November 1762): 'C'est une huguenotte imbécile mais son mari a été la victime des pénitents blancs.' In mitigation, it must be said that mme Calas was capable of producing a similar effect on fellow Protestants: 'Some members of the committee (in particular m. Debrus) were apt to get impatient with Mme. Calas who, most understandably, was still suffering from shock and inclined to fall into fits of dejection and apathy' (Nixon, p.165).

Protestantism in England:
an enviable compromise

᠁᠁

i. *The development of toleration in England*

FOR many years now, critics have acknowledged and tried to assess the importance of Voltaire's stay in England as a formative influence on his thought. Such scholarship has culminated in the recent publication of m. André Rousseau's impressive study *L'Angleterre et Voltaire* (Studies on Voltaire (1976), cxlv-cxlvii): this long and stimulating work covers every aspect of the Frenchman's connection with England, both at the time of his stay there and later in his life, when frequent visits from English travellers made sure that Voltaire would be kept up to date with news, gossip and information of all kinds from his former land of exile.[1] Yet even m. Rousseau's erudition leaves some unanswered questions, particularly, it seems to me, in the field of Voltaire's relations with the Church of England and English Protestantism as a whole, and it is these I want to raise and attempt to answer – at least to some extent – in this chapter.

Most critics appear to have agreed, by and large, that Voltaire's attitude to Anglicans and the Church of England was unsympathetic. Thus, in his book on Voltaire, Theodore Besterman sums up the position as follows (pp.119-20): 'Voltaire found organised religion in England good only by contrast with that of France. As for the Church of England in itself, the author made some thoroughly Voltairean comments.' Similarly, professor Brumfitt and dr Gerard Davis state, in their introduction to two of Voltaire's *contes*, *L'Ingénu* and *Histoire de Jenni*: 'Voltaire himself, as can be seen from the *Lettres philosophiques*, was no great admirer of Anglicanism' ('Introduction', p.xl). In both these examples, the critic's opinion is quite clearly based on a reading of the *Lettres philosophiques*. And is this not what we should expect?

[1] see Sir Gavin de Beer and André-Michel Rousseau, *Voltaire's British visitors*, Studies on Voltaire (1967), xlix.

Chapter 8

Voltaire spent upwards of two years (1726-1728) in England, years which marked his attitude to that country for the rest of his life. Should we not hope to find his most characteristic views on the Anglican Church expressed in that part of the *Lettres philosophiques* which he devoted to it? If this hypothesis is correct, we shall be forced to accept the accuracy of critical views such as those I have quoted, for Voltaire's attitude in the fifth *Lettre philosophique* is patently unsympathetic. Many Anglicans, it appears, have embraced their religion merely through self-interest, to obtain a public position, which would be impossible were they members of another denomination: it is the church 'où l'on fait fortune' (Lanson ed., i.61). The Anglican clergy greedily demand their tithes, they stir up hatred against the nonconformists, and if they could, these ungrateful clerics would overthrow the Whig government which tolerates, rather than supports them. Even their good qualities are dismissed cynically. Granted, they may be more sober than their French counterparts and their conduct more decent, but this is merely because they are trained at Oxford and Cambridge, far from the temptations of London, and in any case, their age and their lack of wordly polish normally mean that they have little success with members of the opposite sex, apart from their wives. There is indeed small indication in this letter that Voltaire's views might change for the better, certainly no hint whatsoever that one of these English clerics, whom Voltaire describes as 'tous [. . .] réservés & presque tous pédants' (p.64) would one day figure prominently in his *conte Histoire de Jenni*, not in the role of an obscurantist priest, but as the triumphant defender of a reasonable form of religion. The reverend Freind is brave, tolerant, discreet: not only a match for the Inquisition and its representatives, but also for that persistent and persuasive atheist, Birton. The Church Freind represents has now become 'votre Eglise anglicane, si respectable' (ed. Brumfitt and Davis, p.65). I intend, later, to return to the importance of this *conte* and to discuss some of the possible sources for the character of Freind (see below, p.445 and appendix 5). At the moment I wish merely to emphasise the startling difference between the views expressed by Voltaire in 1734 and in 1775. And it is surely legitimate to ask why such a change had occurred. To do this, we shall have to examine Voltaire's view of the history of Protestantism in England, his reaction to the various denominations which flourished there, and his explanation, if explanation there be, of how the toleration he so admired had been achieved in England. And unless my analysis is mistaken, we shall become aware of several interesting and extremely revealing paradoxes in his attitude: as regards the Quakers, the Anglicans, and, as we shall see first, in connection with the growth of religious toleration in England.

'C'est ici le païs des Sectes. Un Anglais comme homme libre, va au Ciel par le chemin qui lui plaît.' It is still difficult to find a better illustration of Voltaire's opinion of the English religious situation than this frequently-quoted opening sentence of the fifth *Lettre philosophique* (ed. Lanson, i.61). The very existence of a large number of denominations in England, claims Voltaire, guarantees the security of religious toleration in that country. Rivalry between the differing clergies helps to keep them up to scratch. But how, one wonders, does he explain the development of this toleration? Do the circumstances in which it appeared lead Voltaire to take a more favourable view of the official Church or some of its representatives? Could this be why his attitude to them appeared to change over the years?

A systematic explanation as to why religious toleration had become established in England rather than France is never really attempted in the *Lettres philosophiques*, but one might surely expect to find some answer in the *Essai sur les mœurs*. Unfortunately, no clear picture emerges, and the resulting gap tells us as much about Voltaire's attitude to historical writing as to his opinion of the Church of England or English Protestantism in general. This is clearly a damning assertion, and I wish, therefore, to examine his attitude in some little detail before drawing any firm conclusions.

The English Reformation was certainly justified, thinks Voltaire, though he has little respect for Henry VIII and his motives, and events in England could not be compared with the dignified and reasonable way Catholicism was abolished in Geneva (see above, pp.37-38). Elizabeth I is depicted favourably, although Voltaire admits that many have found it ridiculous that a woman should have been head of the Church (*Essai*, ii.470). To counter this criticism, he emphasises her royal dignity, the competence of her administration, and points out that in Russia four women in a row have presided over the national synod. James I is praised for being tolerant and is contrasted favourably with the Presbyterians: 'Loin d'être persécuteur, il embrassait ouvertement le tolérantisme; il censura vivement les presbytériens[2] qui enseignaient

---

[2] in Best.D10897 (9 January 1763) Voltaire told Moultou that James 'regardait les presbitériens comme ennemis du thrône, et il n'avait que trop raison'.

alors que l'enfer est nécessairement le partage de tout catholique romain' (*Essai*, ii.652). Yet James was unpopular in his own time because he did not support the Protestant cause against the Catholic powers in Europe, and elsewhere Voltaire himself criticises the king for this failure.[3] Charles I's growing troubles with Church and Parliament and the Civil War itself are all explained by Voltaire in primarily, and almost exclusively, religious terms. This once again tends to make his interpretation unsatisfying for a modern reader, since, although religious affairs were very important in themselves, there was present from the outset of the Stuart dynasty an element of political ferment which finally developed into the conflict between Parliament and king. Voltaire is also unable to see that what may have sometimes appeared to him relatively small and indifferent ceremonies took their significance from the fact that they symbolised something far deeper: political aspirations which were being thwarted and traditions which were being threatened. In the case of Scotland under Charles I, for example, religious conformity was the result of the attempted subjection of a proud and stubborn people to the far-away, alien government in London. The king neither understood nor cared for the individuality of the Scottish people. What appeared to be merely a matter of a few changes in ceremony epitomised the issues at stake. G. M. Trevelyan describes the event as follows:

In large questions of national policy, the new King of Scotland never deigned to consult the nobles [. . .] The English people knew nothing of Scottish affairs, but the English Government was, after James's death, scarcely better informed. For if Charles had not been grossly ignorant, how could he have expected that, in consequence of an order from London, the whole population of Scotland would troop to the kirks on Sabbath morning, eager to take part in a service which until that moment had been regarded by them as the Mass was regarded by the English? [. . .]

Neither nobles, people nor clergy had been consulted in the destruction of their national worship. The new ritual, drawn out by the help of four Scottish Bishops, had received the finishing touches at Lambeth and had been

[3] cf. Best.D1157 (Voltaire to Frederick of Prussia, *c.* 30 September 1736): 'Dans un fatal exil Jacques laissa périr/Son gendre infortuné [the elector Palatine, cf. *Essai*, ii.653] qu'il eût pu secourir. / Ah! qu'il eût mieux valu, rassemblant ses armées, / Délivrer des Germains les villes opprimées / [. . .] Que d'aller des docteurs briguant les vains suffrages, / Au doux enfant Jesus dédier ses ouvrages.' Cf. also Best.D1999 and Best.D2125. Voltaire's opinion of James I as expressed in his correspondence (as opposed to his printed works) is invariably low: cf. Best.D10897 and the other letters already quoted.

sent down ready-made for use, like a sack of English goods. It was an order in no veiled terms that Scotland should be Scotland no more.[4]

Voltaire's account of the same episode concentrates on the senselessness of fighting for what he considers are merely trifles (*Essai*, ii.657):

La liturgie consistait dans quelques formules de prières, dans quelques cérémonies, dans un surplis que les célébrants devaient porter à l'église. A peine l'évêque d'Edimbourg eut fait lecture dans l'église des canons qui établissaient ces usages indifférents que le peuple s'éleva contre lui en fureur, et lui jeta des pierres[5] [...] Les presbytériens firent une ligue, comme s'il s'était agi du renversement de toutes les lois divines et humaines.

He does not seem to realise that, for the Scots, this is just what was at stake.

Admittedly, he does suggest one or two political motives, but these are normally portrayed as being the side-effects of a religious cause. For example, identifying the Presbyterians and Puritans as basically Calvinists, Voltaire remarks on a trait which he has consistently attributed to the followers of Calvin, from the time of the Reformer onwards (*Essai*, ii.666):

Il était visible, par ce *covenant*, que l'Ecosse et l'Angleterre puritaines voulaient s'ériger en républiques: c'était l'esprit du Calvinisme.[6] Il tenta longtemps en France cette grande entreprise; il l'exécuta en Hollande[7], mais en France et en Angleterre on ne pouvait arriver à ce but si cher aux peuples qu'à travers des flots de sang.

The Puritans, thus considered by Voltaire as synonymous with the Calvinists, are put forward as the villains of the piece: 'la fureur de la guerre civile était nourrie par cette austérité sombre et atroce que les puritains affectaient'. This pedantic austerity, a manifestation of their religious fanaticism, moved them to condemn James I's *Book of sports* 'dans lequel ce monarque savant soutenait qu'il était permis de se

---

[4] *England under the Stuarts* (first published 1904; Harmondsworth 1960), pp.175-76.

[5] the article 'Eglise' of the *Questions sur l'Encyclopédie* shows the same attitude: 'Penn voyait que les évêques anglicans et les presbytériens avaient été la cause d'une guerre affreuse pour un surplis, des manches de linon et une liturgie' (M.xviii.498-99).

[6] cf. Best.D1359 (Voltaire to Frederick of Prussia, c. 30 July 1737): 'Ne sont ce pas les presbytériens d'Ecosse qui ont commencé cette malheureuse guerre civile qui a coûté la vie à Charles I.' See also above, p.64, n.33.

[7] this oblique reference is the only time Calvinism is mentioned as having some part in the establishment of republican liberty in Holland. Cf. above, pp.100-101.

divertir après le service divin'.[8] Voltaire's attitude to those he considers
Calvinists is always the same: once again, they censure harmless diver-
sions as morally reprehensible. Sanctimonious as ever, they condemn
the marquis of Montrose, 'un des plus agréables esprits qui cultivassent
alors les lettres et l'âme la plus héroïque qui fût dans les trois royaumes'
(*Essai*, ii.677), and pronounce his damnation. The Presbyterians
indeed periodically appear in Voltaire's correspondence as a symbol
of the humourless and intransigent fanaticism which menaced France
too in the shape of the Jansenists, 'secte dure et barbare, plus ennemie
de l'autorité royale que le presbitérianisme (et ce n'est pas peu dire)'.[9]
Thus the Presbyterians are considered marginally less detestable than
the Jansenists, but the terms used by Voltaire to refer to the former are
hardly complimentary. In *Dieu et les hommes* (1769) Voltaire's dislike
of the Presbyterians reaches its peak, and he castigates them more
harshly than any other Protestant sect, even implying that they were
worse than the Catholics (M.xxviii.231):

Si les évêques ont partout usurpé les droits des princes, il ne faut pas croire
que les pasteurs de nos églises réformées aient eu moins d'ambition et de
fureur. On n'a qu'à lire dans notre historien philosophe Hume les sombres et
absurdes atrocités de nos presbytériens d'Ecosse. Le sang s'allume à une
telle lecture; on est tenté de punir, des insolences de leurs prédécesseurs, ceux
d'aujourd'hui qui étalent les mêmes principes.

To preach toleration cannot always have been easy for Voltaire.

It is against this background of inter-sectarian strife and warring
fanaticism that Voltaire describes the rise of Cromwell. The *Lettres
philosophiques*, perhaps influenced by the aura of liberty which appeared
to the exiled poet to exude from everything and everyone English, seem
to portray him as a modern reincarnation of the heady virtues of republican antiquity (ed. Lanson, ii.127-28). But Voltaire's attitude was
to evolve very considerably. A letter written by mme de Graffigny to
François Devaux on 29 December 1738 shows us Voltaire acting out the
story 'du roi d'Angleterre se sauvant des fureurs de Cromwel' (Best.

---

[8] *Essai*, ii.666. This is a markedly different judgement from the one usually made in
Voltaire's correspondence: cf. above, p.402, n.3.

[9] Best.D12788, Voltaire to the d'Argentals, 6 July 1765. Cf. Best.D14596 (Voltaire to
Chabanon, 18 December 1767): 'Si vous recevez des Jansénistes dans votre académie, tout
est perdu, ils vont inonder la face de la France. Je ne connais point de secte plus dangereuse
et plus barbare. Ils sont pires que les presbitériens d'Ecosse.' Cf. also Best.D15003 and
D20447.

D1725), which does not seem to be the action of a man who still admired the English Lord Protector. What caused Voltaire's change of attitude is a mystery, but by the time of the 1748 article, only Cromwell's vices are taken into account. For in him the full danger of religious fanaticism is illustrated, when it is affected by a man who is himself *désabusé*, having overcome his initial infatuation, and who is prepared to exploit the enthusiasm of others. Voltaire no doubt classes Cromwell along with Borgia and similar villains whom he considers as atheists, and in the *Questions sur l'Encyclopédie* (1771) he claims that these cynical rascals have been almost as dangerous as the genuine fanatics whom they have exploited: 'Borgia et ses semblables ont fait presque autant de mal que les fanatiques de Munster et des Cévennes, je dis les fanatiques des deux partis' (art. 'Dieu', *Dictionnaire philosophique*, ed. Benda and Naves, p.521). The wheel has turned full circle, and only the moderate deist can presumably be relied on to be fair and just in all his dealings. Cromwell was for Voltaire the antithesis of what a *philosophe* should be: for although more enlightened that his contemporaries, he used his *lumières* in a purely selfish and antisocial way: 'on peint Cromwell comme un homme qui a été fourbe toute sa vie', the 1748 article begins, and Voltaire goes on: 'J'ai de la peine à le croire. Je pense qu'il fut d'abord enthousiaste, et qu'ensuite il fit servir son fanatisme même à sa grandeur.'[10]

It is worth studying Voltaire's description of Cromwell in some detail, for it provides virtually the only instance where he is able to give an example of the absolute religious hypocrite.[11] Cromwell is, in fact, the complete Voltairean Tartuffe. When describing a man like Calvin the *philosophe* is not quite sure of his ground, and this hesitation translates itself as a certain ambiguity in his attitude. Sometimes the Reformer is labelled a hypocrite, as for example when he persecutes Servetus because of the latter's antitrinitarian beliefs,[12] but the hypocrisy here is,

[10] M.xviii.294. Cf. Best.D14846 (Voltaire to d'Hermenches, 17 March 1768): 'Cromwell formait des fanatiques et vous de très honnêtes gens.'

[11] an exception is a brief reference in the *Annales de l'empire* to the Anabaptist leader Muncer, who, although exploiting the credulity of his fellow men just like Cromwell, was perhaps even more cynical since, according to Voltaire, he had never been a genuine fanatic: 'Il abjura sa secte avant de mourir. Il n'avait point été enthousiaste: il avait conduit ceux qui l'étaient' (M.xiii.40). One of Voltaire's notebook fragments also links Cromwell with other religious leaders who, like him, had overcome their former fanaticism: 'Mahomet, Cromvel, Jean de Leyde *d'abord* entousiastes' (Voltaire 82, p.627, my italics).

[12] in a letter of 28 October 1757 the spirit of Cromwell is explicitly linked with this event by Voltaire, which may in fact seem a little unfair since it took place many years

as it were, localised. Calvin acted in direct contradiction to the principle of toleration he had advocated (see above, pp.60-61), but there is no suggestion that he disbelieved the faith he preached, even if driven on by the thirst for power and the desire to be a religious leader. Voltaire knew that genuine religious feeling was a part of Calvin's nature, though because this sort of conviction was lacking in his own personality he himself was totally unable to appreciate it. Yet he sensed and grudgingly acknowledged its existence, a situation which made him uneasy when attacking Calvin or other 'fanatics'. They could not all be complete hypocrites – some, like Fox the Quaker, were in fact explained away as 'saintement fou' (*Lettres philosophiques*, ed. Lanson, i.32). But Cromwell was in a different category. Voltaire had made up his mind that the Lord Protector of England had been an 'enthusiast', but had realised his error and used religion to establish his political ascendency over the madmen among whom he lived. Indeed, this was the only way to power in the times in which he found himself:

Presque tous les officiers de son armée étaient des enthousiastes qui portaient le Nouveau Testament à l'arçon de leur selle: on ne parlait, à l'armée comme dans le parlement, que de perdre Babylone, d'établir le culte dans Jérusalem, de briser le colosse. Cromwell, parmi tant de fous, cessa de l'être, et pensait qu'il valait mieux les gouverner que d'être gouverné par eux. L'habitude de prêcher en inspiré lui restait. Figurez-vous un fakir qui s'est mis aux reins une ceinture de fer par pénitence, et qui ensuite détache sa ceinture pour en donner sur les oreilles aux autres fakirs:[13] voilà Cromwell.[14]

The fact that Cromwell was originally a Puritan before becoming *désabusé* gives Voltaire the opportunity to attack not only the Protector's hypocrisy but also Calvinism itself, which is once again associated with republicanism: 'Ses principes étaient ceux des puritains; ainsi il devait haïr de tout son cœur un évêque, et ne pas aimer les rois' (M.xviii.294; cf. above, pp.64, n.33, 321, 401, n.2). Voltaire is eager to drive home the lesson of Cromwell's hypocrisy: 'Au milieu de cette guerre affreuse Cromwell faisait l'amour; il allait, la Bible sous

before Cromwell's birth in 1599: 'Vous avez raison de dire que Calvin joue le rôle de Cromwel dans l'affaire de l'assassinat de Servet' (Best.D7437, Voltaire to Vernes).

[13] cf. above, p.70, n.49.

[14] M.xviii.295-96. Cf. Best.D10413, D14039 and D11918 (Voltaire to the d'Argentals, 11 June 1764): 'Si on fait parler ce héros du fanatisme [Cromwell] comme il parlait ce serait un beau galimatias, mais c'est avec du galimatias qu'il parvint à gouverner l'Angleterre, et c'est ainsi qu'on a quelquefois subjugué le parterre.' The reference was prompted by Crébillon's play *Cromwell*.

le bras, coucher avec la femme de son major général Lambert' (M.xviii. 296). The fact that he despised the religion which had been the source of his power is illustrated by an anecdote which shows the Protector dismissing a deputation from the Presbyterian Churches; he was drinking with some notables at the time and the bottle-opener had just been lost! (M.xviii.297-98):

'Qu'on leur dise que je suis retiré, dit Cromwell, *et que je cherche le Seigneur*'. C'était l'expression dont se servaient les fanatiques quand ils faisaient leurs prières. Lorsqu'il eut ainsi congédié la bande des ministres, il dit à ses confidents ces propres paroles: 'Ces faquins-là croient que nous cherchons le Seigneur, et nous ne cherchons que le tire-bouchon.'

This anecdote had obviously made a great impression on Voltaire, as it appears twice in his notebooks, the relevant entries spanning several years.[15]

One inevitably wonders why Voltaire developed such an utter dislike for Cromwell; after all, his part in Charles 1's regicide had failed to inspire such an attitude in the *Lettres philosophiques*. Voltaire's notebooks contain at least some references to Cromwell which are not overtly hostile,[16] but in contrast he has hardly a good word to say for the Protector in his correspondence;[17] 'cet illustre fripon' (Best.D10644), 'ce héros du fanatisme' (Best.D11918), 'ce coquin de Cromvell' (Best. D11929), are only some of the damning epithets used to describe him. The *Essai sur les mœurs* gives a character sketch of him which, while largely consonant with the article we have just been studying, is rather fairer in that it makes some mention of the positive qualities, as

[15] the first occurs in the small Leningrad Notebook (Voltaire 81, p.62), most of whose entries date 'from 1726 and the next year or two' (Introduction, p.17). The second reference occurs in one of the Leningrad group of notebooks (p.371), which contain entries made between 1735 and 1750.

[16] cf. Voltaire 81, p.169: 'Le projet de faire une république de l'Angleterre et de la Holande passeroit pour bien ridicule s'il n'était pas de Cromvell.' Cf. also Voltaire 82, p.530. Other references are to Cromwell's sending queen Christina of Sweden his portrait (Voltaire 81, pp.335, 340-41), to the fact that Cromwell despised the prince de Condé (p.251), and to aspects of Cromwell's political career (cf. below, p.408, nn.19, 20). There are also two sympathetic mentions of the Protector's son Richard (Voltaire 81, p.365 and 82, p.678).

[17] the nearest he comes to it is in Best.D10644 (to Algarotti, 13 August 1762): 'Il est vrai que toutes les révolutions que j'ai vues depuis que je suis au monde, n'approchent pas de celle de Cromwell.' Although Voltaire goes on to speak of Cromwell as a fanatic, there is at least in the passage just quoted a certain grudging admiration for Cromwell's historical status, perhaps rather similar to his recognition of Luther's greatness: see above, pp.51, 54.

well as the inevitable hypocrisy, which (in Voltaire's opinion) aided Cromwell's rise to power (*Essai*, ii.682-83):

Ses mœurs furent toujours austères; il était sobre, tempérant, économe sans être avide du bien d'autrui, laborieux, et exact dans toutes les affaires. Sa dextérité ménageait toutes les sectes, ne persécutant ni les catholiques ni les anglicans, qui alors à peine osaient paraître; il avait des chapelains de tous les partis; enthousiaste avec les fanatiques, maintenant les presbytériens qu'il avait trompés et accablés, et qu'il ne craignait plus; ne donnant sa confiance qu'aux indépendants, qui ne pouvaient subsister que par lui, et se moquant d'eux quelquefois avec les théistes. Ce n'est pas qu'il vît de bon œil la religion du théisme, qui, étant sans fanatisme, ne peut servir qu'à des philosophes, et jamais à des conquérants.

The last part of this passage, from 'et se moquant' onwards, was a 1761 addition and perhaps provides the key to Voltaire's attitude to Cromwell. For Charles II, considered by the *philosophe* to have been one of these theists (although in actual fact he died a Catholic!), is described in favourable terms, and in his reign the 'sombres et sévères' sects which had triumphed under the Commonwealth were ridiculed: 'le théisme, dont le roi faisait une profession assez ouverte, fut la religion dominante au milieu de tant de religions'.[18]

Voltaire obviously considered Charles and Cromwell to be equally *désabusés*, but the difference was that the latter, instead of showing himself to be a *philosophe* of good will by embracing theism, persisted in maintaining a façade of self-interested fanaticism. Moreover, he was a violent man, who came to power and maintained himself there with the aid of the army, although one of Voltaire's notebook entries makes clear that he regarded Cromwell as a usurper, but not as a tyrant.[19] Had the Protector used his position to establish a state religion based on Erastian and reasonable principles, Voltaire's opinion of him would no doubt have been very different. His earlier enthusiasm may have stemmed from Cromwell's political achievements,[20] and as religious

[18] *Essai*, ii.687. Perhaps the king's supposed theism explains why Voltaire described him in a letter to Frederick of Prussia as 'un roi qui était honnête homme' (Best.D1359, c.30 July 1737).

[19] 'Cromwel n'abusa jamais de son pouvoir pour oprimer le peuple. Il rendit la nation florissante au dedans et respectable au dehors. Usurpateur et non tiran' (Voltaire 81, p.229).

[20] surely the following passage contains a note of admiration for Cromwell's rise from nothing rather than a snobbish criticism of his unknown origins: 'Quelle impertinence à Ramsay de dire que Cromvel révolta les anglais contre Charles premier. Cromvel n'étoit pas connu au commencement des guerres civiles' (Voltaire 81, p.250).

considerations became increasingly important for Voltaire his attitude probably changed correspondingly. In the heat of the battle against *l'infâme*, Cromwell's supposedly cynical encouragement of 'fanaticism' was complete anathema to Voltaire, and all else was obscured by this side of the Protector's character. In a letter of 13 June 1764 (Best. D11922) Voltaire asked Damilaville whether Crebillon's *Cromwell* had been a success: 'a t'il été un sublime fanatique? [. . .] un grand homme abominable?' It is hardly necessary to point out that in Voltaire's own view Cromwell was emphatically the latter.

The claim that during Charles II's reign theism became the dominant religion in the state and that, by the same token, toleration of other denominations was assured, brings us back to one of the paradoxes I have already mentioned. How, one inevitably wonders, had this surprising development occurred? Was it a reaction against the excesses of the Civil War? Had there been some other reason for such a radical change? Nowhere is this made clear. Nowhere, indeed, does Voltaire provide any concrete evidence to justify this astonishing claim. And it is surely in a situation like this that what one must, however reluctantly, call the weaknesses of Voltairean historiography become apparent. Let us make no mistake. Had he merely chronicled historical facts in a detached way, declaring himself incapable of perceiving any relationship between them, no such charge could be levelled against him. But this is the Enlightenment's most typical and most militant historian – praising, criticising, mocking, in fact taking sides in a way which would nowadays be considered unacceptable by most historians. And the corollary of this militant attitude is plain: Voltaire must surely put forward a convincing *rationale* to explain why toleration, the value with which he is perhaps above all associated, arose in such apparently unpromising circumstances. Was it as a result of growing indifference to dogma, as he later claimed in the *Traité sur la tolérance*? Voltaire would no doubt seek to imply this, and also to suggest that it was somehow the growth of reason which opened people's eyes to the frivolity of dogmatic trifles. But even if this were so (and once again Voltaire gives no indication as to why or how *philosophie* became widespread at a time he himself describes as bedevilled by theological disputes), such indifference would hardly account for the continued existence in England, some eighty years after the Civil War, of so many different denominations. Did toleration in England come about because Erastianism, the theory that the Church should be strictly subject to the

409

state, was achieved by Henry VIII and his successors? A moment's reflection will convince us once again such an explanation is scarcely feasible. After all, the spectacle of the would-be absolute Charles I, driven from power and executed by those Puritans who had risen against him and the Church which supported him, is hardly an eloquent tribute to Erastian principles. Surely it was the very fact that such all-out Erastianism did *not* succeed in England which allowed the development and continuing existence of those sects later chronicled by Voltaire in the *Lettres philosophiques*? Was it not the fact that Charles II and his successors admitted the failure of this policy and practised merely a kind of mitigated Erastianism which guaranteed the growth of toleration?

These questions are nowhere asked by Voltaire in the *Essai sur les mœurs*. Though Faguet's comment that Voltaire's philosophy contained a chaos of clear ideas has been frequently ridiculed, our present dilemma shows clearly that it contains more than a grain of truth. Certain 'idées forces' are continually put forward by Voltaire as progressive and civilising factors in the history he is chronicling. One of these is certainly Erastianism. His comments about Elisabeth I, particularly her firm treatment of the recalcitrant bishop of Ely (*Essai*, ii.470), bear this out amply. Another basic theme is the 'redeeming' rôle of theism. Voltaire has consistently suggested that: the more radical Protestants become, the more superstitions (in other words dogmas) they reject, the nearer they come to theism and the more enlightened becomes the way in which they behave. Charles II is presented as just such a theist. But once again, although Voltaire claims that 'le théisme, dont le roi faisait une profession assez ouverte, fut la religion dominante au milieu de tant de religions' (*Essai*, ii.687), he gives no evidence that this was the case, no explanation as to how such a situation arose. And most important of all, he fails completely to explain why, if this were the case, so many denominations continued to exist and flourish in England.

I do not wish to labour this point, but I think it is basic to appreciate it in order to understand the ambiguity of Voltaire's subsequent attitude to the Church of England. And there is a significant parallel. In just the same way he omits to explain how the principle of toleration became established in Holland (see above, pp.99-104). We are merely presented with a *fait accompli*.

It is possible that Voltaire himself sensed, at least to some extent, the paradox I have been trying to outline. There had surely to be some link between the follies perpetrated by the various denominations during the Civil War and the near-idealistic situation described by Voltaire at the time of his own stay in England from 1726 to 1728. And it would seem possible that, on at least some occasions, he conceived this link to be that sect which, in the *Lettres philosophiques*, he had portrayed with such a mixture of mockery and respect. The Quakers are indeed scarcely mentioned in the *Essai sur les mœurs*, but Voltaire has already made a glowing description of the Quaker settlement in Pennsylvania, which repeats and even increases the praise given to Penn's colony in the *Lettres philosophiques*. Was Voltaire implying then that the purified religious beliefs of the Quakers were almost indistinguishable from genuine theism and that they were somehow the catalyst which brought about religious toleration? I do not think this is so, although it has been argued persuasively by professor Barber (see below, pp.456-57) that Voltaire's own religious position ultimately had much in common with that of the Quakers. At any rate, the argument is never clearly presented anywhere in his works. As I hope now to show, Voltaire did idealise the Quaker contribution to civilisation as the years went by, but it was in a somewhat different domain from the one I have just been considering. The paradox deepens when we find that in later works the Anglican Church and its ministers are put forward by Voltaire as a model for other countries, when it was precisely Anglican prelates like Laud who had done their best to hinder the growth of toleration.

But I shall return to this question a little later. Let us first, having glimpsed the folly of the English religious wars through Voltaire's eyes, consider his attitude to the only Christian sect to which he was almost consistently sympathetic.

ii. *Quakers: the perfect pacifists*

Voltaire's interest in the Quakers is almost too well known to need recalling. I have already tried to show in the introductory chapter of this book that his main purpose in describing them in the *Lettres philosophiques* was to criticise the beliefs and practices of the Catholic Church, but that he was also very amused by their bizarre dress and behaviour (see above, p.18). As he grew older, this Quaker characteristic was emphasised less and less in his works, and by the end of his life it seems that he is apologising for it as a pardonable defect in otherwise wholly commendable people, rather than ridiculing the predictably ludicrous trait of a sect of enthusiasts. Voltaire has created his own legend, and more than half believes in it himself.

The various elements of Voltaire's attitude to the Quakers have been so competently analysed by professor W. H. Barber in his article 'Voltaire and Quakerism: Enlightenment and the inner light'[21] that it will scarcely be necessary to do more than comment on his conclusions. Professor Barber emphasises the importance of the two features of Quakerism which Voltaire found to be the most useful in his anti-Catholic polemic: the rejection of a priesthood and the lack of ceremonies. These criticisms gained force because Voltaire was able to show that such opinions were not incompatible with virtue; on the contrary, 'the mad, hysterical, heretical Quakers were in fact better Christians, in everyday life, than pious orthodox Catholics contrived to be' (p.87). Professor Barber suggests that the Quakers may have strengthened Voltaire's hopes that a virtuous theistic community like theirs, devoid of any remaining Christian belief, might be possible. It was certainly above all the social qualities of Quakerism which gained Voltaire's admiration. Pennsylvania was constantly portrayed as 'an enlightened Utopia of toleration, charity and equality' (p.88), whose Christianity was simple and uncomplicated and Professor Barber is of the opinion (p.89) that it was 'this Pennsylvanian Utopia which underlies Voltaire's other American paradise, the Eldorado of *Candide*'. He points out that the unacceptable side of Quakerism is still sometimes emphasised by Voltaire: the notion of direct divine inspiration, for example, is used as a weapon of ridicule against Rousseau's religious ideas, in the *Lettre au docteur Pansophe* (1766). And in the *Examen important de milord Bolingbroke* (published in 1767) 'Voltaire scornfully links the origins of Quakerism with those of Christianity itself as examples of the power of religious fanatics to win over an illiterate populace' (p.90).

Despite these lingering criticisms, professor Barber claims (p.94) that 'as always for Voltaire [...] the final, and the fundamental, emphasis is on social morality'; the similarity between Quakers and the early Christians would otherwise have been of much less interest to him, but it was also coupled with the practice of social virtue, and in Pennsylvania the Quaker policy of toleration encouraged the benefits

---

[21] *Studies on Voltaire* (1963), xxiv.81-109. For another bibliographical comment see above, p.13, n.2.

of trade. I would readily agree with the conclusion of the first part of professor Barber's article (p.97) that 'the value of the Quaker community as a living example of the actual possibility of a virtuous and theistic society is [. . .] plain'.

I must emphasise at this point that, in my opinion, Voltaire's approval for the Quakers was almost exclusively on the social, rather than the religious plane. As we have just seen, he admired their tolerance and *bienfaisance*, and the benefits which these qualities procured for the community. But despite professor Barber's attempts, in the second part of his article, to find a deeper affinity between them, it seems clear to me that Voltaire constantly rejected the Quakers' religious ideas and was fundamentally out of sympathy with them. This question is obviously basic for an understanding of Voltaire's own religious position and its relation to Protestantism, and I wish to return to it later when I shall also try to reassess other relevant elements of his religious thought (see below, pp.456-61). At the moment I wish merely to make the point that Voltaire respected the Quakers' beliefs, not for their intrinsic merits or because they were close to his own, but because the moral code inspired by these beliefs was of great benefit to society. A living proof of this was, of course, the Quaker state of Pennsylvania, to which so many laudatory references occur in Voltaire's works (see below, pp.460-61). At times Voltaire's praises of Pennsylvania are so fulsome that one wonders if a man who could be so cynical in religious matters took them completely seriously himself.[22] Pennsylvania is perhaps meant to serve the same function for the rest of the human race as the Quakers did for the French Catholic Church in the *Lettres philosophiques*: it provides an opportunity for satire and criticism. Yet Voltaire obviously believed in the basic truth of the picture he painted,[23]

[22] Edith Philips tends to think not: 'Il est vrai que Voltaire ne croyait pas aux utopies aussi facilement que certains de ses contemporains, et ce n'est pas sans ironie qu'il dit: "Guillaume Penn pouvait se vanter d'avoir apporté sur la terre l'âge d'or dont on parle tant, et qui n'a vraisemblablement existé qu'en Pennsylvanie"' ('Le Quaker vu par Voltaire', p.169).

[23] there were even rumours that Voltaire had intended to settle in Pennsylvania. In about June or July 1769 Thieriot (admittedly not the most trustworthy of sources) told Mr de Ville of Martinique: 'je vous confierai qu'en 1753 il [Voltaire] avait eu dessein d'aller fonder un établissement dans ce pays, qui, par tout ce que j'en entends dire, est digne d'être habité par des philosophes, & où l'on jouit de la plus grande & de la plus honnête liberté; mais il a préféré les environs de Genève, dont le climat ne vaut pas à beaucoup près celui de Pensilvanie' (Best.D15715, commentary).

and would have been shocked to learn the bitter truth of what life was really like in his cherished Utopia. Alfred Owen Aldridge tells us:

Shortly after the foulest and most bitterly fought election campaign in the history of the colony of Pennsylvania, during which all factions, including the Quakers, attempted to damage their opponents by misrepresentation, lies, brutal scandals and vilifications, religious and political – Franklin copied Voltaire's glowing praise of 'ces pacifiques *Primitifs* que l'on a nommés Quakers'. 'La Discorde, la Controverse, sont ignorées dans l'heureuse patrie qu'ils se sont faite et le nom seul de leur ville de *Philadelphie*, qui leur rappelle à tout moment que les hommes sont frères, est l'exemple et la honte des peuples qui ne connaissent pas encore la tolérance.' Franklin commented wryly: 'while we sit for our Picture to that able Painter, 'tis no small Advantage to us that he views us at a favourable Distance'.[24]

It does in fact seem that, as the years went by, Voltaire's critical faculties worked at something less than full capacity when he considered the Quakers of Pennsylvania. Granted that he still censured their *enthousiasme* (though he did this increasingly mildly), and that there was always the element of propaganda in his descriptions of their homeland, yet his admiration for the 'pacifiques Pensylvaniens' seems to grow more and more evident in his later works.

From the *Essai sur les mœurs* onwards indeed, Voltaire seems to be able to make a clear distinction in his mind between, on the one hand, the Quakers, who can do no wrong, and various other evangelical Protestant sects, in whom he vilifies all the manifestations of intolerance, fanaticism, and enthusiasm which he so much detested. The Puritans, for example, persecuted in England by Laud, prove themselves just as narrow-minded as the Anglican archbishop (*Essai*, ii.384):

Ces puritains, espèce de calvinistes, se réfugièrent vers l'an 1620 dans ce pays, nommé depuis la *Nouvelle-Angleterre*. Si les épiscopaux les avaient poursuivis dans leur ancienne patrie, c'étaient des tigres qui avaient fait la guerre à des ours. Ils portèrent en Amérique leur humeur sombre et féroce, et vexèrent en toute manière les pacifiques Pensylvaniens, dès que ces nouveaux venus commencèrent à s'établir.

The Puritans, however, were punished for their intolerance in a suitable manner: 'Une fille eut des convulsions en 1692 [...] la moitié des habitants crut être possédée [...] on ne vit pendant deux ans que des

24 'Benjamin Franklin and the philosophes', *Studies on Voltaire* (1963), xxiv.44.

sorciers, des possédés, et des gibets' (*Essai*, ii.385). Now the resemblance between the Independents, Cromwell's supporters, and the Quakers is almost complete as regards their articles of religious belief (*Essai*, ii.669):

La secte des *indépendants* commençait à faire quelque bruit. Les presbytériens les plus emportés s'étaient jetés dans ce parti: ils ressemblaient aux quakers, en ce qu'ils ne voulaient d'autres prêtres qu'eux-mêmes, ni d'autre explication de l'Evangile que celle de leurs propres lumières.

Why then should Voltaire wish to treat the Quakers in such a special manner, when their beliefs were shared by other Christians? The answer is that there was one fundamental difference between them, which not only explains why Voltaire was able to exclude the Quakers from the odium which he attached to other, similar sects, but which, more than anything else, explains his lasting admiration for the Quakers and his growing idealisation of them. For although the Independents were similar to the Quakers: 'ils différaient d'eux en ce qu'ils étaient aussi turbulents que les quakers étaient pacifiques. Leur projet chimérique était l'égalité entre tous les hommes; mais ils allaient à cette égalité par la violence.' The unique quality of the Quakers for Voltaire was indeed that, in his eyes, they were the perfect pacifists.

Here it may be necessary to qualify somewhat one of the conclusions reached by professor Barber in the second part of his article 'Voltaire and Quakerism'. He asserts (pp.97-98):

As a first step, two very obvious, but in fact superficial and misleading, parallels between Voltairian and Quaker attitudes may be rapidly disposed of. Both Voltaire and the Quakers are strongly opposed to war; not only from compassion for human suffering, but also because of the meaningless nature, for the individual, of the issues on which contemporary wars were fought. Voltaire's familiar ironies on this topic, indeed, are superior in literary skill but little different in tone, from those of Robert Barclay. Yet the disparity between them is in fact profound, for Voltaire is clearly not a pacifist in the Quaker sense at all; there is nothing to suggest that he would ever have disapproved of the use of violence in the genuine and necessary defence of individual life or civilised society, and his hostility to war rested primarily upon humane and rational considerations of a practical and mundane kind, not upon any spiritual view of the sacredness of the human personality and the value of self-abnegation – nor, least of all, on any desire to observe to the letter the gospel exhortation to turn the other cheek.'

Professor Barber also adds in a footnote that 'the essential difference between Voltaire's position on war and that of the Quakers is already implied in his note to *Olympie* (1763), v.vii.'[25] Plausible as this argument may sound, a reconsideration of the facts may enable us to take a rather different view. For a start, in *Olympie*, Voltaire is really, in the footnote cited by professor Barber, discussing the rights and wrongs of suicide. He claims that the taking of one's own life does less harm to society than the actions of those who serve as mercenary soldiers, and who volunteer indiscriminately for one side or another. 'Je n'entends pas, par ces homicides,' he adds hastily, 'ceux qui, s'étant voués au service de leur patrie et de leur prince, affrontent la mort dans les batailles' (M.vi.162). Presumably this is part of professor Barber's justification for claiming that 'there is nothing to suggest that he would ever have disapproved of the use of violence in the genuine and necessary defence of individual life or civilised society'. But Voltaire is merely seeking to make a distinction between two very different attitudes to fighting, that of the professional mercenary and that of the patriotic volunteer, a distinction which a Quaker would surely have been well able to appreciate, even if it only strengthened him in his fundamentally pacifist convictions, and a distinction Voltaire is virtually forced to make to avoid alienating the patriotic sentiments of the majority of his contemporaries. After all, the subject is suicide, and even a Voltaire cannot fight too many battles at once. But when he turns to the Quakers themselves, the manner in which Voltaire describes their opinion of war surely makes clear that he holds it in the greatest respect. The Quaker view is stated at some length, and in fact it closes the argument. No reply is advanced to contradict it. What clearer evidence of Voltaire's sympathy could be asked for? (M.vi.163):

Il y a un peuple sur la terre dont la maxime, non encore démentie, est de ne se jamais donner la mort, et de ne la donner à personne; ce sont les Philadelphiens, qu'on a si sottement nommés quakers. Ils ont même longtemps refusé de contribuer aux frais de la dernière guerre qu'on faisait vers le Canada pour décider à quels marchands d'Europe appartiendrait un coin de terre endurci sous la glace pendant sept mois, et stérile pendant les cinq autres. Ils disaient, pour leurs raisons, que des vases d'argile tels que les hommes ne devaient pas se briser les uns contre les autres pour de si misérables intérêts.

[25] p.97.

The question of pacifism nonetheless draws our attention to an aspect of Voltaire's thought which is plainly inconsistent. On the one hand, his historical works contain many descriptions of battles and military operations of various kinds, and despite his frequent denunciations of the evils of war, it cannot be denied that Voltaire sometimes recounts French successes with a certain amount of satisfaction.[26] No less damning for a pacifist, he followed Catherine the Great's campaign against the Turks in the early 1770s with great enthusiasm, encouraging his heroine to crush these Asiatic interlopers and deprive them of their European provinces (cf. esp. Best.D17993, D18059, D18201, D18509). He even went as far as to design a type of war chariot, apparently similar to that of Boudica, whose wheels would be equipped with swords.[27] This fiendish device would kill vast numbers of men, he assured Catherine, and he resolutely urged the empress to try out his secret weapon (cf. Best.D15487, D15664, D16290, D16348, D16490). Yet the same man apparently saw no contradiction in castigating military leaders in works like the article 'Guerre',[28] the poem *La Tactique,* and in numerous other passages of his works. The explanation of this inconsistency may be that, while greatly prizing the ideal of pacifism, Voltaire was sometimes tempted into approving a particular war for specific reasons which overrode or made him forget his scruples: in the case of the Russo-Turkish conflict he presumably thought the cause of enlightenment would be advanced by Catherine's victories. Such lapses probably made him all the more determined to take up an intransigent anti-war position in most of his published works, and in several cases, notably *La Tactique,* his poetic imagination and indignation tended to run away with him.[29] Despite his inconsistencies in this respect, the parallels between Voltaire's attitude and that of the Quakers are not necessarily 'superficial and misleading'. Nor must we assume without question that the gospel exhortation to turn the other cheek

[26] this is the case even when the outcome might unpleasantly affect Voltaire's beloved Quakers themselves! Cf. a letter to Richelieu in which Voltaire exhorted him to treat the English 'comme on vient de les traiter à Philadelfie' (Best.D6720, 7 February 1756). Voltaire also asked J.-R. Tronchin: 'La nouvelle du saccagement de Philadelfie se confirme t'elle?' (Best.D6727, c. 10 February 1756), with no apparent dismay in his tone.

[27] see Henry Meyer, *Voltaire on war and peace,* Studies on Voltaire (1975), cxliv.116-22.

[28] this appeared in the original (1764) version of the *Dictionnaire philosophique,* and additions were made to it in 1765 and 1771.

[29] Meyer (pp.51 ff.) investigates these contradictions, concluding (p.58) that for Voltaire war was a 'necessary evil'.

417

failed to inspire a sympathetic response in him.[30] What separates him from the Quakers is a difference in degree not in kind. Voltaire himself may not have managed to remain faithful to the ideal of pacifism, but for those who, like the Quakers, were content with nothing less than perfection, he had only unbounded admiration.

The pacifism of the Quakers, more than any other quality, it must be repeated, is perhaps the basic reason why they gained and retained Voltaire's whole-hearted approval. If it was purely a matter of their religious beliefs, they were liable to be dismissed like all the other Christian sects (see below, p.456). But their brethren of other denominations, from the Reformation onwards, were damned in Voltaire's eyes because of the bloodshed they had willingly caused. The article 'Guerre' of the *Dictionnaire philosophique* shows how ready most Christian clergy were to condone war (ed. Benda and Naves, p.231):

On paye partout un certain nombre de harangueurs pour célébrer ces journées meurtrières; les uns sont vêtus d'un long justaucorps noir, chargé d'un manteau écourté; les autres ont une chemise par-dessus une robe; quelques-uns portent deux pendants d'étoffe bigarrée par-dessus leur chemise. Tous parlent longtemps; ils citent ce qui s'est fait jadis en Palestine, à propos d'un combat en Vétéravie.

In contrast to this, the Quaker attitude is uncompromising – war is condemned absolutely (*Lettres philosophiques*, ed. Lanson, i.6-7):

Nous n'allons jamais à la guerre, ce n'est pas que nous craignions la mort, au contraire nous bénissons le moment qui nous unit à l'Estre des Estres; mais c'est que nous ne sommes ni loups, ni tigres, ni dogues, mais hommes, mais Chrétiens. Notre Dieu qui nous a ordonné d'aimer nos ennemis et de souffrir sans murmure, ne veut pas sans doute que nous passions la mer pour aller égorger nos frères, parce que des meurtriers vêtus de rouge avec un bonnet haut de deux pieds, enrôlent des Citoïens en faisant du bruit avec deux petits bâtons sur une peau d'âne bien tendue, & lorsqu'après des batailles gagnées tout Londres brille d'illuminations, que le Ciel est enflamé de fusées, que l'air retentit du bruit des actions de grâces, des cloches, des orgues, des canons, nous gémissons en silence sur ces meurtres qui causent la publique allégresse.

Indeed, rather than be involved in the horrors of civil war, 'les primitifs, que nous nommons quakers, ont été chercher la paix en Pennsylvanie,

---

[30] cf. a comment made to d'Argental on 4 January 1735 in connection with *Alzire*: 'S'il y a un côté respectable et frappant dans notre relligion, c'est ce pardon des injures qui d'ailleurs est toujours héroïque quand ce n'est pas l'effet de la crainte' (Best.D979).

et oublier les crimes religieux de Cromwell loin de leurs concitoyens fanatiques qui s'égorgeaient pour un surplis' (*Lettre d'un ecclésiastique* (1774), M.xxix.289). The fact that war is unknown in Pennsylvania is not the least of its attractions. In a letter to Frederick the Great (Best. D19340, 15 February 1775) Voltaire wrote: 'Quand je le loue [i.e. Frederick] d'avoir gagné des batailles en jouant de la flûte, comme Achille, ce n'est pas que je n'aie toujours la guerre en horreur; et certainement j'irais vivre chez les quakers en Pensilvanie, si la guerre était partout ailleurs.' It could be argued that this is not a serious statement and that Voltaire has his tongue in his cheek. But the fact that he naturally thinks of the Quakers and Pennsylvania in connection with pacifism is significant enough. By 1775 the two had become virtually synonymous in the ageing *philosophe*'s mind, and he thought more readily and more indulgently of this Quaker characteristic than any of the others for which he had praised them in his writings.

Pacifism is normally included in all Voltaire's references to the Quakers, except when he wished to ridicule them as *illuminés*.[31] On 4 October 1735, writing to the abbé d'Olivet, Voltaire rebuked Desfontaines for saying that Brutus (in *La Mort de César*) was a Quaker, 'ignorant que les quakers sont les plus bénins des hommes, et qu'il ne leur est pas seulement permis de porter l'épée' (Best.D923). He repeated this criticism in several other letters,[32] and returned to it as late as 1771 when he added a passage to the *Dictionnaire philosophique* article 'Critique'.[33] In the section of the *Essai sur les mœurs* praising Pennsylvania it is pointed out that the primitifs had none of the usual troubles with the Indians: 'placés entre douze petites nations que nous appelons *sauvages*, ils n'eurent de différends avec aucune; elles regardaient Penn comme leur arbitre et leur père' (*Essai*, ii.383). Starting with the article 'Méchant' of the *Dictionnaire philosophique* the Quaker characteristic of pacifism becomes even more prominent. Arguing that man's character is not as bad as is made out by orthodox theology, Voltaire comments: 'Il y a des nations entières qui ne sont point méchantes; les Philadelphiens, les Bananiens n'ont jamais tué personne' (ed. Benda and Naves, p.302). Taken as an isolated reference this would have little

[31] e.g. in the *Dictionnaire philosophique* article 'Tolérance' (ed.Benda and Naves, p.406).

[32] Best.D924, D925, D929. Desfontaines was unrepentant. He wrote to Voltaire: 'un quaker, malgré vos belles *Lettres*, est un fou' (Best.D957, c. 5 December 1735).

[33] 'Il dit à propos de la tragédie de *La Mort de César*, que Brutus *était un fanatique barbare, un quaker*. Il ignorait que les quakers sont les plus pacifiques des hommes, et ne versent jamais le sang' (ed. Benda and Naves, p.501).

significance, but the fact is that Voltaire refers increasingly to the Quakers as examples of pacifism, singling out this quality for unsparing praise, and omitting to mention their other characteristics. Often, as in the article cited, they are connected or compared with some other virtuous group, but the frequency with which Voltaire draws attention to them demonstrates conclusively his opinion that as the perfect pacifists they had no rivals. Chapter 17 of *La Philosophie de l'histoire* ('De l'Inde') emphasises that the Quakers are the only Christians who follow the unwarlike spirit of their religion.[34] The *Conseils raisonnables à m. Bergier* (1769) again asserts the unique position of Quakerism among the other varieties of Christianity (M.xxviii.38):

quelque homme puissant se met à la tête du parti; alors l'ambition crie de tous côtés: Religion! Religion! Dieu! Dieu! Alors on s'égorge au nom de Dieu. Voilà, monsieur, l'histoire de toutes les sectes, excepté celle des primitifs appelés *quakers*.

The *Sermon prêché à Bâle*, written in the same year, mentions the Quakers as one of the few tolerant peoples, and then claims that they are the only colonists never to have cheated or killed the American Indians (*Mélanges*, p.1273). A further two references to Quaker pacifism occur in 1768, the work in question being *L'A.B.C.*: 'On a vu des peuples qui n'ont jamais fait la guerre', runs the more interesting comment; 'les primitifs, que nous nommons *quakers*, commencent à composer, dans la Pensylvanie, une nation considérable, et ils ont toute guerre en horreur' (M.xxvii.331-32).

By 1773 Voltaire's preoccupation with Quaker pacifism seems to have reached a peak, for in the *Fragments historiques sur l'Inde* it is mentioned no less than four times.[35] The *Histoire de Jenni* (1775) carries the idealisation of Penn and the Quakers perhaps farther than ever before, and gives them an important place in a list seeking to demonstrate that not all men are as bloodthirsty as the majority of Christian sects: 'sans sortir du pays où nous sommes, n'avons-nous pas auprès de nous la Pensylvanie, où nos primitifs, qu'on défigure en vain par le nom de Quakers, ont toujours détesté la guerre?' (ed. Brumfitt and Davis, p.101). Though more examples exist, it is not necessary to

[34] ed. J. H. Brumfitt, Voltaire 59 (1969), p.148.
[35] e.g. M.xxix.124: 'Ces primitifs, dont la patrie est la Philadelphie dans le nouveau monde, et qui doivent faire rougir le nôtre, ont la même horreur de sang que les brames. Ils regardent la guerre comme un crime.' The other references are M.xxix.111, 207, 208.

quote them all in order to appreciate the change from Voltaire's earlier attitude, when he normally presented a broader and less idealised picture of the Quakers. What had caused this growing emphasis on one characteristic of the Quakers, to the exclusion of their more bizarre traits and even to the neglect of their other commendable, and polemically useful qualities?

There would seem to be two distinct possible answers to this question. Either Voltaire, almost unconsciously, began recalling in his later works that feature of the Quaker character which most appealed to him, so that finally he built up a kind of myth, a myth which the sceptical *philosophe* appears to have ended up believing himself. Alternatively, he may have deliberately used the Quakers' pacifism as a means to make anti-war propaganda, as an excuse to recommend to the public a humanitarian ideal of non-violence which they might otherwise consider unrealistic, without necessarily believing himself in the literal truth of the picture he was painting. This would appear to have been the opinion of one of Voltaire's correspondents, the comte de Guibert, a quick-witted and intelligent defender of the military art, which he carefully distinguished from the wars in which it was applied. His letter of 6 December 1773 in connection with *La Tactique* contains a two-edged compliment suggesting that the good count was unconvinced by the examples Voltaire had cited of peoples ignorant of war (Best.D18666):

On dit que dans vos infatigables recherches, vous venez de découvrir dans je ne sais quelle relation de voyages une nation qui vit sur le Gange et qui n'a jamais connu la guerre. J'ai besoin de lire l'histoire de cet étrange peuple pour croire qu'il puisse exister un coin de la terre où les hommes formés de bile et de sang et ayant par conséquent des sentiments et des passions, ne courent jamais aux armes. Donnez nous cette histoire. Quand même le voyageur qui vous en fournira le texte aurait pris l'état momentané de ce bon peuple pour sa situation immémoriale, vous embellirez cette fable, elle donnera des leçons aux souverains, du plaisir à vos lecteurs et un moment bien doux d'illusion à tous les honnêtes gens.

One might be tempted to share this scepticism and extend it to Voltaire's descriptions of the Quakers,[36] were it not for his reactions to the

---

[36] the comte de Guibert does not of course mention the Quakers; the people he is referring to is probably the 'anciens Gangarides', whom Voltaire mentions in the *Fragments historiques sur l'Inde et sur le général Lally* (1773) (M.xxix.208) and in *La Princesse de Babylone* (1768). Along with the 'Gentous' (M.xxix.111) and the inhabitants of Vishnapor

American War of Independence which began in 1776. For this conflict shattered the peace of Voltaire's utopia, and he was forced to come to terms with the idea that Pennsylvania was no longer exempt from the scourge afflicting the rest of mankind.[37] At first his confidence in the Quakers seems to waver: on 12 October 1775 he told Du Ponceau: 'Je suis fâché seulement que les habitants de la Pensylvanie, après avoir longtemps mérité vos éloges, démentent aujourd'hui leurs principes en levant des troupes contre leur mère partie' (Best.D19706). Moreover the *Histoire de l'établissement du christianisme,* apparently written at some time in 1776[38] contains the usual sort of comment in connection with Pennsylvania: 'Je n'ai jusqu'à présent connu de société vraiment pacifique que celle de la Caroline et de la Pensylvanie' (M.xxxi.111), but a footnote adds the cryptic comment: 'cela fut écrit avant la guerre de la métropole contre les colonies'. Has Voltaire's opinion of his perfect pacifists changed?

Voltaire's annoyance may have been intensified by the fact that Frederick had been teasing him for some time over his idealisation of the Quakers and his attacks on war.[39] In a letter of 29 September 1775 the king had specifically claimed that, although Voltaire approved of the present constitution of Pennsylvania, in a hundred years' time it would have become like that of any other country (Best.D19679). Moreover, a few months later, Frederick mercilessly put his finger on the problem which the American war was forcing Voltaire to answer: he was, he said (Best.D20007, 19 March 1776):

occupé d'aprendre si la Colonie de Penn continuera de pratiquer ses vertus pacifiques, ou si, tout Quakers qu'ils sont, ils voudront défendre leur liberté et combattre pour leurs foyers. Si cela arrive, comme il est aparent, vous serés obligé de convenir qu'il est des Cas où la guerre devient nécessaire, puisque les plus humains de tous les Peuples la font.

(M.xxix.207), the Gangarides are compared to the Quakers because of their innocence and pacifism.

[37] in the *Essai sur les mœurs* (ii.383) Voltaire had emphasised that any military activity which had taken place in Pennsylvania was in no way connected with the Quakers: 'La Pensylvanie fut longtemps sans soldats, et ce n'est que depuis peu que l'Angleterre en a envoyé pour les défendre, quand on a été en guerre avec la France.'

[38] cf. M.xxxi.43, n.1 and M.xxxi.99: 'jusqu'à cette année 1776 où nous écrivons.'

[39] his comment of 9 October 1773 is typical: 'Je ne suis qu'un demi Quaker jusqu'à-présent; quand je le serai [comme] Guillaume Pen, je déclamerai comme d'autres contre ces assassins privilégiés qui ravagent l'univers' (Best.D18581). Cf. also Best.D16731, D17370, D19679.

Voltaire's reply does not seem to be that of a man whose praise of the Quakers has been motivated purely by a desire to use them as part of his humanitarian propaganda: 'Votre Majesté a bien raison de me dire que les Anglais ne sont pas si heureux que nous. Ils se sont lassés de leur félicité. Je ne crois pas que mes chers Quakers se battent, mais ils donneront de l'argent et on se battra pour eux' (Best.D20040, 2 April 1776). Voltaire seems determined to maintain his myth, even if it is a little tarnished.[40]

Nonetheless, the *Commentaire sur l'Esprit des lois* of 1777[41] does not resolve the question, for although the blame for the conflict has been put squarely on the English government, it is still uncertain as to whether the Quakers will fall from their standards of perfection: 'Je fais des vœux ardents pour que Londres ne force point les bons Pensylvaniens à devenir aussi méchants que nous et que les anciens Lacédémoniens, qui firent le malheur de la Grèce' (M.xxx.419). But very shortly after, by the time he had written the *Dialogues d'Evhémère*, Voltaire had made his mind up that all responsibility for the war rested on the British government, and, significantly enough, he makes the dispute sound almost of a religious nature. Finally he stubbornly persists in citing the Quakers as a proof that pacifism is a practical possibility, though the terseness and latent bitterness of the final sentence of the following passage indicate the mental struggle he must have gone through before resolving the question (M.xxx.538-39):

Les primitifs, auxquels on a donné le nom ridicule de quakers, ont fui et détesté la guerre pendant plus d'un siècle, jusqu'au jour où ils ont été forcés par leurs frères les chrétiens de Londres de renoncer à cette prérogative, qui les distinguait de presque tout le reste de la terre. On peut donc à toute force se passer de tuer des hommes.

The following note added to Voltaire's description of Pennsylvania in the *Essai sur les mœurs* made its first appearance in the Kehl edition of his works and was presumably written at some time in 1777. The Quakers are once again completely exculpated: 'Cette respectable colonie a été forcée de connaître enfin la guerre, et menacée d'être détruite par les armes de l'Angleterre, la mère patrie, en 1776' (*Essai*,

---

40 Frederick could not resist making yet one more ironic comment, although he waited over a year before rubbing salt in Voltaire's wound. On 1 June 1777 he remarked: 'Nous sommes ici tranquilles et aussi pacifiques que les quakers' (Best.D20681).

41 completed by 11 June: cf. Best.D20693.

ii.384). Surely here, if ever, was a war which was justified, and yet Voltaire shows not the slightest enthusiasm in the reluctant support he finally accords to the colonists' notion of defending themselves against British troops. Thus it seems fairly clear that, although he did use Quaker pacifism as an element of his humanitarian propaganda, Voltaire was not cynically fostering public belief in a quality whose existence he rejected. The excitable, inconsistent *philosophe* genuinely prized the high ideals of his 'bons Quakers' (Best.D16069), and the part played by Pennsylvania in the American War of Independence came as a sad blow to him.

Perhaps it would be appropriate to end our discussion of the Quakers with a quotation from the *Histoire de l'établissement du christianisme*. Here Voltaire sums up his attitude to the Friends as succinctly as one could wish. Once again, their socially beneficent qualities are recalled, and, as we might expect, not least among these is their abstention from war. Yet the religious basis of their virtues is categorically rejected as 'illusions' – Voltaire makes abundantly clear that their claim to respect is not due to the fact that they resemble the early Christians, but because their behaviour gives grounds for hope of a new kind of society, if only their *mœurs* are imitated by other men (M.xxxi.105):

Ils sont jusqu'à présent sans temples, sans autels, comme furent les premiers chrétiens pendant cent cinquante ans; ils se secourent mutuellement comme eux; ils ont comme eux la guerre en horreur. Si de telles mœurs ne se corrompent pas, ils seront dignes de commander à la terre, car du sein de leurs illusions ils enseigneront la vertu qu'ils pratiquent.

In Voltaire's writings, the Quakers are a kind of goad to renewed efforts. For if an eccentric Christian sect, admittedly virtuous, but founded on irrational illusions, could give such an example to the rest of the world, what ought not theism, rooted in reason and reality, hope to achieve?

iii. *Voltaire and the English Protestant influence*

Before going on to investigate Voltaire's attitude toward England's established church, I want to look briefly at some English Protestant thinkers who are known to have influenced him, or who are at least mentioned in his works. The pertinent question in this respect is surely: was Voltaire at all impressed by the specifically Protestant characteristics of any of these writers, or was he merely interested in the non-religious areas of their thought?

1. Newton and Locke. The influence exercised on Voltaire by these two Englishmen is one of the best known and thoroughly-studied areas in the field of eighteenth-century studies. It would indeed be superfluous to describe again in detail his debt to Newton,[42] who provided Voltaire with a scientific basis for his theism, particularly in connection with the argument from design, and to Locke, who supplied a sensationalist philosophy which enabled Voltaire to reject Cartesianism and to formulate a materialist attitude toward the soul. The Frenchman's own tributes to his masters are eloquent.[43] But when one comes to consider their writings as Christians and Protestants, a very different picture emerges: Voltaire is now patronising, ironical or downright hostile. In the field of religion he feels inferior to no one, and the scientific prestige of a Newton or a Locke no longer overawes him.

Newton's religious views did have one overriding merit, in Voltaire's opinion: the great scientist was unorthodox in his beliefs regarding the trinity and could be included among the select band of distinguished Arians or Socinians so useful to quote in anti-Christian propaganda (cf. *Lettres philosophiques*, ed. Lanson, i.79, 80). But Newton had also one great defect: he had written a commentary on the *Apocalypse*. To have dealt sympathetically with any part of the Bible would, one feels, have been bad enough, but the book Newton chose symbolised for Voltaire all that was most obscure and unenlightened in the scriptures. Like the Old Testament it was full of prophecy, and such passages were always liable to be interpreted by fanatics of every time and country as referring specifically to them.[44] In editions of the *Lettres philosophiques* printed between 1739 and 1752 Voltaire added a paragraph informing

[42] for a recent study of Newton's influence see Martin S. Staum, 'Newton and Voltaire: constructive sceptics', *Studies on Voltaire* (1968), lxii.29-56.

[43] it will be sufficient to quote only two. On 18 October 1736 Voltaire told the abbé d'Olivet: 'Mon cher amy, mon cher maître Neuton est le plus grand homme qui ait jamais été, mais le plus grand, de façon que les géants de l'antiquité sont auprès de luy des enfants qui jouent à la fossette '(Best.D1174). Of Locke he said to Thieriot: 'Je trouve que ce grand homme n'a pas encor la réputation qu'il mérite, c'est le seul métaphisicien raisonable que je connaisse' (Best.D7887, 3 October 1758).

[44] cf. *Dictionnaire philosophique* article 'Apocalypse': 'les Anglais y ont trouvé les révolutions de la Grande-Bretagne; les luthériens, les troubles d'Allemagne; les réformés de France, le règne de Charles IX et la régence de Catherine de Médicis' (ed. Benda and Naves, p.33).

his readers that: 'l'Infini, l'Attraction & le Cahos de la Chronologie ne sont pas les seuls abîmes où il ait fouillé. Il s'est avisé de commenter l'Apocalypse [...] Apparemment qu'il a voulu par ce Commentaire consoler la race humaine de la supériorité qu'il avoir sur elle' (ed. Lanson, ii.61, n.222). Later editions add a longer passage in the same vein, and disparaging references to Newton's *Commentary* are not rare in other parts of Voltaire's works,[45] although he is notably less caustic about sir Isaac's views on biblical exegesis when he wishes to quote him as an imposing authority.[46] Newton's damning connection with the *Apocalypse* may even have helped to persuade Voltaire that his hero was not infallible as a scientist, for towards the end of his life we find Voltaire criticising the Englishman sharply on occasion, even in connection with physics.[47]

Voltaire's attitude to Locke's writings on religion was similarly unenthusiastic. An early reference to *The Reasonableness of Christianity* (1675) in the Small Leningrad Notebook could conceivably be regarded as neutral in tone,[48] but not so the following curt dismissal: 'Quand le célèbre Locke, voulant ménager à la fois les impostures de cette religion et les droits de l'humanité, a écrit son livre du *Christianisme raisonnable*, il n'a pas eu quatre disciples: preuve assez forte que le christianisme et la raison ne peuvent subsister ensemble' (*Le Dîner du comte de Boulainvilliers* (1767), *Mélanges*, p.1245). Nor is this the only hostile reference to Locke's book.[49] One can do little better than to echo Theodore

---

[45] cf. M.xix.2; xx.230; *Dictionnaire philosophique*, ed. Benda and Naves, pp.33, 451; Best.D4103, D15105, D18473.

[46] cf. M.xxx.159, n.1: 'On ne sait pas quel est l'auteur du livre de *Samuel*. Le grand Newton croit que c'est Samuel lui-même; qu'il écrivit tous les livres précédents, et qu'il ajouta tout ce qui regarde le grand-prêtre Héli et sa famille. Newton, qui avait étudié d'abord pour être prêtre, savait très-bien l'hébreu; il était entré dans toutes les profondeurs de l'histoire orientale.' Cf. also M.xxx.54, n.2.

[47] cf. Best.D18473: 'plus j'y pense, et plus j'ose trouver que le calcul de la densité des planètes, la comète deux mille fois plus chaude qu'un fer rouge, l'élasticité d'une matière déliée qui serait la cause de la gravitation, la création expliquée en rendant l'espace solide, et le commentaire sur l'*Apocalypse*, sont à peu pres de la même espèce.'

[48] 'Mr. Lock's reasonableness of christian relligion is really a new relligion' (Voltaire 81, p.67). In note 4 to this page, Theodore Besterman takes a different view: 'In the language of Voltaire the present comment is a severe indictment.' A remark in the *Lettres à s.a. mgr le prince de ***** is similarly ambiguous: 'C'est à tort qu'on a compté le grand philosophe Locke parmi les ennemis de la religion chrétienne. Il est vrai que son livre du *Christianisme raisonnable* s'écarte assez de la foi ordinaire' (*Mélanges*, p.1178).

[49] cf. the article 'Platon', included by Moland in the *Dictionnaire philosophique*: 'Comment Locke, après avoir si bien développé l'entendement humain, a-t-il pu dégrader son entendement dans un autre ouvrage' (M.xx.230). Cf. also M.xxxii.462.

Besterman's judicious remark: 'Voltaire admired Locke only to the extent to which the philosopher's views could be used against religion and on behalf of deism' (Voltaire 81, p.67, n.4).

2. *Samuel Clarke*. Born at Norwich on 11 October 1675, Clarke[50] was an early admirer of Newton, translating into Latin Rohault's Cartesian text-book on physics with the addition of many notes favourable to the English physicist and his theories. But Clarke's own career was in the Church: he succeeded William Whiston as chaplain to bishop Moore of Norwich in 1698 and then began a serious study of divinity in the bishop's fine library (*Dnb*, iv.443). The following year he published *Three practical essays on baptism, confirmation and repentance*, a critique of Toland's *Amyntor*, and he also made paraphrases of the gospels (published in 1701-1702).[51] It was the Boyle lectures of 1704-1705 on the being and attributes of God which brought Clarke a national reputation: in 1706 he became one of queen Anne's Chaplains in Ordinary, and in 1709 was appointed rector of St James's, Westminster. But another work was soon to spoil his chances of further promotion in the Church: the *Scripture doctrine of the trinity* (1712) aroused a storm of controversy and was censured in 1714 by the Church of England's Convocation (*Dnb*, iv.444). Clarke promised to write no more on this sensitive topic, but he also refused to accept any ecclesiastical preferment which involved subscription to the thirty-nine articles (Sykes, p.141, n.2), in other words an affirmation of orthodoxy. Nonetheless, Clarke retained friends in high places: after queen Anne's death he became a favourite of the princess of Wales, later queen Caroline, and largely at her request he defended the Newtonian theory of time and space against Leibniz in a correspondence which was published in 1717 (*Dnb*, iv.444). Despite his unorthodoxy, Clarke was

[50] for information on Clarke's life and works see J. P. Ferguson, *The Philosophy of dr Samuel Clarke and its critics* (New York 1974); *An eighteenth-century heretic: dr Samuel Clarke* (Kineton, 1976); *Dnb, s.v.* Samuel Clarke; Norman Sykes, *Church and state in England in the 18th century* (Cambridge 1934), especially pp.139-42. Professor W. H. Barber has recently published an important article on 'Voltaire and Samuel Clarke' (*Studies on Voltaire* (1979), clxxix.47-61).

[51] *Dnb*, iv.443. It is presumably *Three practical essays* to which Voltaire refers disparagingly in the article 'Platon': 'Comment un philosophe tel que Samuel Clarke, après un si admirable ouvrage sur l'existence de Dieu en a-t-il pu faire ensuite un si pitoyable sur des choses de fait?' (M.xx.230).

consulted by many younger churchmen and was generally respected. He died after a short illness on 17 May 1729.

I have given this biographical sketch of some length because for a man whose ideas were important to several figures of the French Enlightenment,[52] Clarke is little known. Even when he is mentioned, it is often merely as Newton's spokesman and the impression is given that, as an original thinker, his contribution was minimal.[53] This opinion is clearly mistaken, at any rate as regards his influence on Voltaire's religious thought. Granted that in scientific matters and even in general principles regarding the divinity Clarke is heavily dependent on ideas inferred from Newton's cosmology. Yet the religious conclusions Clarke develops from his Newtonian data are clearly his own (Staum, p.34) and his systematic investigation of the deity and its relationship with man has no parallel in Newton's works, Voltaire would appear to have been well aware of the situation. Clarke's name is often mentioned in connection with those of Newton and Locke, but Voltaire also pays tribute to Clarke's personal achievements and original contribution to the vexed subject of metaphysics, as on 8 March 1738 when he referred to 'Le docteur Clarke, qui a assez aprofondi ces matières dont Neuton n'a parlé qu'en passant.'[54]

A detailed study of Clarke and Voltaire enabling one to assess more accurately the extent to which Clarke's own speculations, as apart from the ideas he put forward on behalf of Newton, influenced the *philosophe* would obviously be desirable, but is, unfortunately, beyond the scope of this book.[55] Suffice it to say that Clarke's presence is clearly per-

[52] cf. Masson, *La Religion de J.-J. Rousseau*, i.109: 'Clarke sera le métaphysicien de Rousseau. Il lui fournira des démonstrations pour quelques thèses, d'une métaphysique élémentaire, dont Jean-Jacques fera des principes intangibles, et qu'il opposera inlassablement à la philosophie encyclopédiste.' Diderot too had read Clarke, and in the early years of his career was certainly not hostile to the English theologian – cf. Best. D3945 (Diderot to Voltaire, 11 June 1749): 'Il [Sanderson] se recommande en mourant au dieu de Clark, de Leibnitz et de Neuton.'

[53] cf. *Le Philosophe ignorant*, ed. J. L. Carr (London 1965), p.13: Clarke is here called Newton's 'mouthpiece'.

[54] Best.D1468, to prince Frederick of Prussia. Cf. also Voltaire's tribute in the article 'Platon': 'Parmi ces philosophes [in England], Clarke est peut être le plus profond ensemble et le plus clair, le plus méthodique et le plus fort, de tous ceux qui ont parlé de l'Etre suprême' (M.xx.229).

[55] professor Barber goes a long way to filling this gap. In the above-mentioned article (see p.427. n.50) he argues persuasively that Voltaire came to know Newton's specifically scientific discoveries by way of a preliminary acquaintanceship with Clarke and the latter's treatment of the more metaphysical and methodological considerations raised by Newton's discoveries.

ceptible in the *Traité de métaphysique*, the *Eléments de la philosophie de Newton*, the *Métaphysique de Newton*, several important letters to Frederick of Prussia, and, to a somewhat lesser extent, in many other parts of Voltaire's works. H. Temple Patterson's critical edition of the *Traité de métaphysique* (Manchester 1937) indicates in detail the borrowings made by Voltaire: in particular chapter two 'consists more or less of a brief summary of the first twelve Propositions of Samuel Clarke's *Demonstration of the Being and Attributes of God* [...] which Voltaire possessed in the (Amsterdam) edition of 1727' (p.18). The debt in chapter six ('Si l'homme est libre') is also great (pp.49-51), and in a series of letters to Frederick spanning the years 1737-1738 Voltaire again relied heavily on Clarke's arguments in asserting the reality of man's free will.[56] As one might expect, Clarke's influence in the *Eléments* and the *Métaphysique* is primarily as an interpreter of Newton, but Voltaire makes quite plain that this spokesman was in no way unworthy of the task entrusted to him.[57]

Voltaire later became dissatisfied with some of the metaphysical ideas put forward by Clarke and Newton,[58] and this, coupled with his rejection of free will, led to a certain amount of disillusionment with Clarke in later years. Moreover his opposition to metaphysical speculation tended to estrange him from a systematic theologian like Clarke, despite the high quality of the latter's reasoning. Voltaire's attitude on this point is bizarre: he sometimes appears to resent the fact that the excellence of Clarke's work attracts him, despite himself, to the study of a field which be believes to be beyond man's grasp and to all intents and purposes useless, yet which fascinates him nonetheless.[59] Be this as it may, critical references to Clarke occur even during the period when Voltaire's

[56] see Best.D1376, D1432, D1459, D1468, D1482, D1575. For a discussion of this correspondence see Wade, *The Search for a new Voltaire*, pp.79 ff.

[57] 'Newton, ennemi de toute dispute, et avare de son temps, laissa le docteur Clarke, son disciple en physique, et pour le moins son égal en métaphysique, entrer pour lui dans la lice' (M.xxii.408).

[58] in the article 'Platon', for example, he disagreed with the notion 'qu'il y ait un être qui pénètre intimement tout ce qui existe, et que cet être, dont on ne peut concevoir les propriétés, ait la propriété de s'étendre au-delà de toute borne imaginable' (M.xx.229), despite the fact that his own ideas as expressed in *Tout en dieu* might appear rather similar to those he rejects here (see below, p.457). Voltaire also dismissed as an unintelligible concept the theory that space is the 'sensorium' of God (article 'Espace', M.xix.2-3), and thought that Clarke was mistaken 'sur la réalité de l'infini actuel et de l'espace, etc.' (*Histoire de Jenni*, ed. Brumfitt and Davis, p.89).

[59] cf. esp. *Courte réponse aux longs discours d'un docteur allemand* (1744): 'Clarke sautait dans l'abîme, et j'osai l'y suivre' (M.xxiii.194).

enthusiasm for him was at its height. On about 15 August 1733 Voltaire told Formont that his conclusion, after rereading 'le raisonneur Clarke' is that he was 'le meilleur sophiste qui ait jamais été', a dissatisfaction apparently caused by the argument Clarke uses to prove that matter does not exist through necessity (Best.D646). In the *Métaphysique de Newton* Voltaire reproaches Clarke for playing with words when arguing about free will with Collins: his own opinion on the subject has now changed, for he claims that Clarke 'mêla tant d'aigreur à ses raisons qu'il fit croire qu'au moins il sentait toute la force de son en-nemi'[60] By the time of the *Philosophe ignorant* (1766) these criticisms have developed into a full-scale attack (M.xxvi.57):

Non, je ne puis pardonner au docteur Clarke d'avoir combattu avec mau-vaise foi ces vérités dont il sentait la force, et qui semblaient s'accommoder mal avec ses systèmes. Non, il n'est pas permis à un philosophe tel que lui d'avoir attaqué Collins en sophiste, et d'avoir détourné l'état de la question en reprochant à Collins d'appeler l'homme *un agent necéssaire*. Le prédicateur, dans Samuel Clarke, a etouffé le philosophe.

This tirade would seem to be conclusive, and after reading it one is tempted to agree with Voltaire's own claim that he had outgrown Clarke:

J'admirais, dans ma jeunesse, tous les raisonnements de Samuel Clarke [. . .] et j'aime encore sa mémoire parce qu'il était bon homme; mais le cachet de ses idées, qu'il avait mis dans ma cervelle encore molle, s'effaça quand cette cervelle se fut un peu fortifiée.[61]

Yet one would be ill advised to conclude that Voltaire's feelings about Clarke fell into any such neat pattern. Despite his annoyance at some of Clarke's beliefs and assertions, Voltaire never entirely lost the ad-miration he had conceived for the English clergyman and which had prompted so many laudatory references to Clarke during the 1730s and 1740s. In the *Homélies prononcées à Londres*. published a year after *Le Philosophe ignorant*, Clarke has again become 'le judicieux Clarke', who provides what Voltaire considers to be a valuable proof of God's existence.[62] Moreover, the *Demonstration of the being and attributes of*

---

[60] M.xxii.413: cf. a 1771 addition to the *Dictionnaire philosophique* article 'Liberté': 'Clarke ne lui [to Collins] a répondu qu'en théologien' (ed. Benda and Naves, p.564).

[61] M.xix.36, in the article 'Eternité', placed by Moland in the *Dictionnaire philosophique*.

[62] 'pourquoi [. . .] les planètes tournent-elles en un sens plutôt qu'en un autre? J'avoue que, parmi d'autres arguments plus forts, celui-ci me frappe vivement; il y a un choix: donc il y a un maître qui agit par sa volonté' (*Mélanges*, p.1122).

God was always considered highly by Voltaire (cf. M.xx.230; Best. D9754). In the anti-atheist poem *Les Cabales*, he waxed quite lyrical about Clarke's book, 'livre le plus éloigné de notre bavarderie ordinaire, livre le plus profond et le plus serré que nous ayons sur cette matière, livre auprès duquel ceux de Platon ne sont que des mots, et auquel je ne pourrais préférer que le naturel et la candeur de Locke' (M.xx.183, n.5). Here perhaps is the real key to Voltaire's attitude. Clarke's metaphysical arguments are stimulating and valuable, despite the fact that some of the Englishman's ideas tended to annoy Voltaire as he grew older. Yet compared with the certainty achieved by Locke, who had the wisdom to restrict the scope of his investigations, his compatriot appears a shade too ambitious: 'Il semble que Locke et Clarke aient eu la clef du monde intelligible. Locke a ouvert tous les appartements où l'on peut entrer; mais Clarke n'a-t-il voulu pénétrer un peu trop au delà de l'édifice?' (article 'Platon', M.xx.230).

Clarke's speculations about the nature of God thus exercised a real, though cautionary, attraction over Voltaire, but the latter was perhaps even more intrigued by an accusation he had made in the *Lettres philosophiques*, that, like Newton, Clarke was an Arian: 'Le grand Monsieur Newton faisoit à cette opinion l'honneur de la favoriser [. . .] Mais le plus ferme patron de la doctrine Arienne est l'illustre Docteur Clark' (ed. Lanson, i.79). In a 1770 addition to the *Dictionnaire philosophique* article 'Arius' Voltaire went ever further: 'Samuel Clarke, célèbre curé de Saint James, auteur d'un si bon livre sur l'existence de Dieu, se déclara hautement arien.'[63] This claim certainly represents something of an exaggeration. As we have seen (above, p.427), Clarke had difficulties with Convocation over the *Scripture doctrine of the trinity*, but unlike his friend William Whiston, 'he protested against being classed as an Arian' (Sykes, p.140). Nonetheless, Voltaire's description of Clarke was not basically inaccurate, for according to Norman Sykes, 'it is clear that he [Clarke] attributed to the Son an inferior kind of Divinity, and was therefore essentially Arian in his belief'. We must avoid the temptation of thinking that Voltaire's knowledge of Clarke's life was superficial or carelessly gleaned. He had actually met Clarke, as the *Eléments* makes clear: 'Je me souviens que dans plusieurs conférences que j'eus, en 1726, avec le docteur Clarke,

[63] ed. Benda and Naves, p.365. Cf. also *Courte réponse aux longs discours d'un docteur allemand* (M.xxiii.194).

jamais ce philosophe ne prononçait le nom de Dieu qu'avec un air de recueillement et de respect très-remarquable' (M.xxii.403). Back in France Voltaire asked Thieriot to send him 'a little pamphlet newly come out on the person and the works of Doctor Clark'.[64] This would seem to have been Whiston's *Historical memoirs of the life of dr Samuel Clarke*,[65] for in another letter to the same correspondent Voltaire adamantly maintained that Clarke had actually founded a new sect, repeating Whiston's claim that: 'Le docteur Clarke ne chantait jamais le *Credo* d'Athanase' (Best.D596, possibly written in about April 1733). Although this assertion was also denied by Clarke, it is certain at any rate that he altered the *Book of common prayer* to make certain passages more acceptable to his antitrinitarian convictions, for a copy thus amended in his own hand is still extant in the British Library (Sykes, pp.386-88).

But it is another anecdote in the *Lettres philosophiques* which has produced most critical scepticism. According to Voltaire, Clarke ruined his chances of becoming archbishop of Canterbury through the unorthodoxy of the *Scripture doctrine* (ed. Lanson, i.79-80, n.41):

Car, lorsque la reine Anne voulut lui donner ce Poste, un Docteur nommé Gibson, qui avoit sans doute ses raisons, dit à la Reine: 'Madame, M. Clarke est le plus savant & le plus honnête homme du Royaume; il ne lui manque qu'une chose. – Et quoi? dit la Reine. – C'est d'être Chrétien,' dit le Docteur Bénévole.

Lanson investigated this anecdote in his critical edition of the *Lettres*, deciding that Voltaire may have been thinking of a similar incident involving Swift, since although a Gibson did become bishop of Lincoln during queen Anne's reign, the see of Canterbury was not vacant: 'Faut-il penser', Lanson concludes, 'que l'anecdote sur Clarke est le résultat d'une série de confusions qui se firent dans la mémoire de Voltaire, ou bien qu'ici nous sommes en présence d'un arrangement artistique, dont la vérité est symbolique et non historique?'[66] Other commentators have been less charitable, but the actual truth redounds to Voltaire's credit, or at the very least proves that his artistic licence in 'arranging' the facts was not as great as Lanson supposed. The story of

---

[64] Best.D502, 9 July 1732. Thieriot was in England at the time.

[65] Lanson (*Lettres philosophiques*, i.84) is of this opinion.

[66] i.86. Lanson also comments (i.85) that: 'L'anecdote introduite en 1739 [. . .] est très suspecte', but he admits that 'Voltaire y croyait puisqu'il l'impliquait sans la conter dans sa rédaction de 1734.'

Clarke's expected preferment, of Gibson's opposition, and of the reasons for this, is substantially correct, but there are some important differences. Gibson, the 'docteur bénévole', was bishop of London and for a time held such favour with the prime minister that he was nicknamed Walpole's 'Pope' (Sykes, p.141). But this very fact is a pointer to the discrepancy between Voltaire's story and what really happened, for the queen in question was not Anne but George II's wife Caroline, the see was Bangor not Canterbury, and the year 1727, at the very time of Voltaire's own stay in England.[67] He cannot have been unaware of the queen's liking for Clarke: indeed it is even conceivable that he may have attended one or more of the weekly conferences organised by Caroline at which ecclesiastical matters were discussed.[68] Be this as it may, it seems likely that the reason Voltaire waited until after the queen's death in 1737 before including this anecdote in the *Lettres* was to avoid causing embarrassment. Even in 1739 he changed her name, but not surely because he had forgotten or wilfully invented the details of an incident which occurred *sous ses yeux*. Perhaps he was reluctant to admit that such an enlightened sovereign as Caroline had yielded to the pressure of a priest like Gibson.

In conclusion, one can safely affirm that Samuel Clarke captured the youthful Voltaire's imagination during the latter's stay in England and that he was remembered with respect throughout Voltaire's long life. Clarke's rationalistic treatment of metaphysics both impressed and irritated him, but on balance admiration seems to outweigh criticism. Moreover, the fact that Clarke was clearly unorthodox and that although this prevented his advancement to high office, he nonetheless remained a highly respected member of the Church of England, must

[67] Sykes, pp.141, 356, 384. It will be seen that Gibson's comment to queen Caroline as reported by Sykes: 'he [Clarke] is the most learned and most honest man in the Queen's dominions, but he has one defect – he is not a Christian' (p.141), is very similar to the version given by Voltaire. Unfortunately, the source of Sykes's quotation is not clear.

[68] in Best.D1320 (c. 25 April 1737) Voltaire told Frederick of Prussia: 'Je me souviens que je ne laissois pas en Angleterre d'embarasser un peu le fameux docteur Clark, quand je lui disois, on ne peut apeller démonstration un enchainement d'idées qui laisse toujours des difficultez.' Voltaire's objections were in connection with the existence of God, and it is certainly possible that the circumstances were as he describes them, since Sykes (p.142: cf. also *Dnb*, iv.445) tells us that 'there is a story that Clarke was once reduced to silence by a question put to him by a French theologian: "Could the Father annihilate the Son or the Holy Ghost." Clarke at length confessed that he could not say.' It seems very unlikely that this anecdote could refer to Voltaire's questioning of Clarke, but it does appear to suggest that the type of event described by him was liable to occur, and that Clarke was not afraid to admit his ignorance on occasion.

433

also have helped to create a more favourable image of Anglicanism in Voltaire's mind than had originally been the case when he wrote the *Lettres philosophiques*.

3. Some other English Protestants. English Protestantism, whatever its faults, doubtless appeared fortunate to Voltaire in the number of distinguished scholars and philosophers it had produced, and a brief review of some of the names which appear in Voltaire's works may not be out of place at this point. In the field of scholarship Voltaire consulted several English writers. For example, Theodore Besterman considers that he may have been influenced by Clarke's friend William Whiston in forming the opinion that the 'constitutions apostoliques' dated from the second century A.D.[69] A comment made in connection with Clarke's *Demonstration of the being and attributes of God* indicates that Voltaire was aware of Butler's correspondence with the famous theologian.[70] Voltaire was also acquainted with at least one of Derham's works,[71] and he praised Henry Dodwell, author of *Dissertationes cyprianicae* (1684), who appeared to him to have convincingly refuted Ruinart.[72] But the English cleric to whom Voltaire perhaps owed

[69] cf. Best.D7544 (to Vernes, possibly written in 1757 or 1758), commentary n.1. The work apparently referred to is Whiston's *Primitive Christianity revived* (1711). In the *Lettres philosophiques* Whiston's theories on the Flood are mocked (ed. Lanson, ii.25; cf. ii.38, n.63 and n.64), and a similar reference is made in the *Instruction à frère Pédiculoso* (*Mélanges*, p.1285). Elsewhere, however, Voltaire speaks of Whiston approvingly as being an Arian (*Examen important*, *Mélanges*, p.1020) and includes him in a list of free thinkers (*Homélies prononcées à Londres*, *Mélanges*, p.1158).

[70] M.xx.229: 'Lorsqu'il [Clarke] eut donné au public son excellent livre, il se trouva un jeune gentilhomme de la province de Gloucester qui lui fit avec candeur des objections aussi fortes que ses démonstrations.' This young objector later became a bishop and wrote *The Analogy of religion*, a famous attack on the English deists (see G. R. Gragg, *The Church and the age of reason (1648-1789)*, pp.165-67).

[71] on 26 September 1756 Voltaire wrote to Thieriot: 'Mettez moy à part je vous prie un Derhem' (Best.D7008; cf. also Best.D7049). William Derham was the author of *Physicotheology* (London 1713) and *Astro-theology* (London 1715). A comment in *Micromégas* gives the impression that Voltaire is poking gentle fun at Derham: 'je suis obligé d'avouer qu'il [Micromégas] ne vit jamais à travers les étoiles [. . .] ce beau ciel empyrée que l'illustre vicaire Derham se vante d'avoir vu au bout de sa lunette' (M.xxi.107). Several years later, however, Voltaire referred to Derham with clear approbation; in a letter to the marquis de Villevielle he mentioned a work by Bullet (Theodore Besterman identifies this as [Jean Baptiste] Bullet, *L'Existence de dieu démontrée par les merveilles de la nature* (Paris 1768)), and commented: 'Ce doyen [Bullet] est savant et marche sur les traces des Swamerdam, des Nieuventit, et des Dheram' (Best.D15189, 26 August 1768).

[72] cf. Best.D10857, Voltaire to Moultou, 25 December 1762. Similar remarks occur in the *Traité sur la tolérance* (*Mélanges*, p.592) and in the *Examen important* (*Mélanges*, p.1083).

the most in this respect was the bishop of Worcester, William Warburton. Professor Brumfitt has shown clearly how Voltaire assimilated and used to his own ends the arguments put forward by Warburton in the *Divine legation of Moses*:[73] the theory that the Jews had not believed the soul to be immortal appealed immensely to the *philosophe* and was subsequently propounded by him on many occasions.[74] But it is scarcely necessary to say that he rejected Warburton's conclusion that such ignorance proved that the Jews had been subject to a special decree of divine providence. Although Voltaire despised Warburton as a man,[75] he rifled the latter's ideas on many occasions and adapted them to his own requirements.

As regards pure philosophy, Voltaire appears to have been quite well acquainted with Berkeley's theories, although, as he told Andrew Pitt around the end of 1732, he was an admirer rather than a disciple of the bishop. Both the *Alciphron* and *The Theory of vision or visual language* (1733) are referred to in Voltaire's correspondence (Best.D558 and D1215), and the *Eléments de la philosophie de Newton* contains a 'petite ébauche' of Berkeley's ideas on how we see (Best.D1327 and D1332). Another Anglican to have gained Voltaire's esteem was Tillotson, but this was in the rather unexpected field of preaching.[76] Finally among these ranks of distinguished churchmen one must mention Swift. Admittedly Voltaire's remarks are normally concerned with Swift's literary achievements or with the anti-Christian potential of the dean's

[73] see J. H. Brumfitt, 'Voltaire and Warburton', *Studies on Voltaire* (1961), xviii.35-36; *La Philosophie de l'histoire* (Voltaire 59, *passim*).

[74] cf. especially chapters 25 and 37 of *La Philosophie de l'histoire*; articles 'Ame' and 'Enfer' of the *Dictionnaire philosophique*.

[75] on 10 August 1767 Voltaire told d'Alembert that Warburton was 'un fort insolent évêque hérétique, auquel on ne peut répondre que par des injures catholiques' (Best. D14347). This was prompted by d'Alembert's remarking (in Best.D14333, 14 August 1767) that he would have preferred Voltaire's latest attack on Warburton to be less bitter. *A Warburton* (M.xxvi.435-37) is in fact one of Voltaire's most vitriolic pamphlets; Warburton was attacked subsequently in the *Lettres à s.a. mgr le prince de ***** (M.xxvi.486-87; *Mélanges*, pp.1181-82), and in *Histoire de Jenni* he is made responsible for the atheism of Jenni and his companions (ed. Brumfitt and Davis, p.74).

[76] cf. *Dieu et les hommes*, M.xxviii.243: 'Il faut qu'ils [the clergy] lisent au peuple les beaux discours de Tillotson, de Smalridge, et de quelques autres'. In the *Relation de la mort du chevalier de La Barre* Voltaire refers to 'Le grand archevêque Tillotson, le meilleur prédicateur de l'Europe' (*Mélanges*, p.779), and similar remarks are made in the *Avis au public sur les parricides imputés aux Calas et aux Sirven* (*Mélanges*, p.845), in the *Examen important de milord Bolingbroke* (*Mélanges*, p.1046), and in the *Lettre de l'archevêque de Cantorbéry à m. l'archevêque de Paris* (*Mélanges*, p.1266).

satires,[77] but once again, as in the case of Clarke, the fact that the Church of England was tolerant enough to accommodate such men within its ranks cannot have passed unnoticed by him. Voltaire's esteem for England's national church was no doubt increased by the knowledge that so many of its clergy were literary or philosophic figures of some standing, and this may to a certain extent have tended to neutralise any hostile attitude which his enthusiasm for the English deists might have engendered.

iv. *Anglicanism: an example for the French*

For there is no doubt that Voltaire's attitude to the Church of England changed very radically from the rather disparaging one he had shown in the *Lettres philosophiques*, and many examples of this could be given. One of the most striking is to be found in the article 'Catéchisme du Japonais', which appeared in the original (1764) edition of the *Dictionnaire philosophique*. Here a surprise is once again in store for those who might see Voltaire as an all-out defender of religious toleration. For although the Quakers are accorded their customary laurels and toleration in general is praised, the principle that all religions should have equal rights is clearly sacrificed on the altar of Erastianism. In this amusing dialogue, where religious questions are transposed into culinary terms, the *Japonais* (or Englishman) refutes the *Indien* (Frenchman), arguing that toleration of non-conformist denominations is necessary. But this is a limited toleration, clearly recognising the rights and privileges of the established church (which Voltaire had tellingly ridiculed in the *Lettres philosophiques*). Moreover, there is even a measure of approval for certain penal measures against non-conformists (ed. Benda and Naves, pp.93-94):

L'INDIEN

Mais enfin il faut qu'il y ait une cuisine dominante, la cuisine du roi.

LE JAPONAIS

Je l'avoue; mais quand le roi de Japon a fait bonne chère, il doit être de bonne humeur, et il ne doit pas empêcher ses bons sujets de digérer.

---

[77] Voltaire was particularly impressed by the *Tale of a Tub* – cf. Best.D9137 (to d'Alembert, 13 August 1760): 'Le Conte du tonneau a fait plus de mal à l'église romaine que Henri VIII.' Cf. also Best.D8533 and the *Lettres à s.a. mgr le prince de* **** (*Mélanges*, pp.1185-86). For Voltaire's interest in Swift's other works see Best.D4815, D4931, D5008, D8055, D11869, D14206, D14921.

L'INDIEN

Mais si des entêtés veulent manger au nez du roi des saucisses pour lesquelles le roi aura de l'aversion, s'ils s'assemblent quatre ou cinq mille, armés de grils pour faire cuire leurs saucisses, s'ils insultent ceux qui n'en mangent point.

LE JAPONAIS

Alors il faut les punir comme des ivrognes qui troublent le repos des citoyens. Nous avons pourvu à ce danger. Il n'y a que ceux qui mangent à la royale qui soient susceptibles des dignités de l'Etat: tous les autres peuvent dîner à leur fantaisie, mais ils sont exclus des charges. Les attroupements sont souverainement défendus, et punis sur-le-champ sans rémission.

It is clear from this passage that Voltaire is condemning any sort of large, open-air gathering, such as those engaged in so dramatically by Methodists in the first flush of their movement. But what he is really referring to in this passage is his own Protestant contemporaries, and it provides yet another confirmation of the position I tried to analyse earlier: even at the height of his campaign to secure for the Huguenots a measure of civil rights which would assure the validity of their marriages and protect the status of their children, he severely condemned their illegal assemblies and seemed quite happy that they should still be subject to certain disabilities. A more detailed acquaintance with the religious problems of his own country had presumably caused Voltaire to re-examine the situation in Protestant England, where what one might call a mitigated form of Erastianism applied. The state church was dominant and its position was protected by law: yet this same law was wise enough to guarantee the existence of the many forms of Christianity. Even Catholicism was tolerated, though its legal existence was precarious. But although it allowed their existence, the state, as it were, expressed its displeasure at these denominations by rendering their adepts ineligible for many important posts. Such a situation may not appear to us very liberal or just. But it obviously appealed to Voltaire as a well-nigh ideal compromise, which at one and the same time permitted the liberty to dissent and provided a sufficient freedom of conscience, while also maintaining strict state control and ensuring that outbreaks of religious enthusiasm or violence between denominations were reduced to a minimum.

This growing approval of the institutional 'happy medium' achieved in England was obviously one of the factors which strengthened Voltaire's tendency to look with much more favour on the Anglican

Church than he had done in the *Lettres philosophiques*. But even there the tone is not completely anti-Anglican, and Voltaire's pronouncements must be viewed in the light of the polemic against Catholicism which he was conducting by implication. When the Anglicans are criticised, it is partly because of their remaining similarities with Catholicism, such as their greed and lust for domination: 'Le Clergé Anglican a retenu beaucoup des cérémonies Catholiques, & sur tout celle de recevoir les dixmes avec une attention très-scrupuleuse. Ils ont aussi la pieuse ambition d'être les Maîtres' (ed. Lanson, i.61). Their intolerance towards the various non-conformist sects also serves to remind the reader of the attitude of the French Church towards 'heretics'. Similarly, the praise Voltaire gives to the Anglican clergy is an indictment of their Gallican counterparts who lack even the respectability which characterises the ministers of the rather dull Church of England (i.64):

les Eclésiastiques sont tous ici réservés & presque tous pédans. Quand ils aprenennt qu'en France de jeunes gens connus par leurs débauches, et élevés à la Prélature par des intrigues de femmes, font publiquement l'amour, s'égaient à composer des chansons tendres, donnent tous les jours des soupers délicats & longs, & de-là vont implorer les lumieres du S. Esprit, & se nomment hardiment les successeurs des Apôtres; ils remercient Dieu d'être Protestans.

We have seen (above, especially pp.91-94) that Voltaire's attitude towards religion is consistently Erastian. He naturally seeks examples to support his point of view, and these he finds mainly in the Russian Orthodox Church and the Church of England. Perhaps the most important point about the letter 'Sur les Anglicans' is that already Voltaire is emphasising that the English Church is subject to the government, which prevents the clergy from indulging in their favourite activity, causing trouble: 'ils (se) sont réduits, dans l'obscurité de leur Paroisse au triste emploi de prier Dieu pour le Gouvernement qu'ils ne seroient pas fâchés de troubler' (ed. Lanson, i.62). The bishops still retain the right to sit in the House of Lords, 'parce que le vieil abus de les regarder comme Barons subsiste encore', but they are virtually powerless.[78] Most important of all, the government completely rejects the idea that the clergy hold office by virtue of divine right (i.63):

On [. . .] promet d'être de l'Eglise, comme elle est établie par la Loi [. . .] Ces maudits Wigs se soucient très-peu que la succession Episcopale ait

---

[78] ed. Lanson, i.62. Voltaire was mistaken on this point; cf. below, p.448, especially n.90.

été interrompue chez eux ou non [. . .] ils aiment mieux même que les Evêques tirent leur autorité du Parlement plûtôt que des Apôtres. Le Lord B. dit que cette idée de droit divin ne serviroit qu'à faire des tirans en camail & en rochet, mais que la Loi fait des Citoïens.

The *Lettres philosophiques* represent the English clergy as opposed to the civil constitution of their church (probably once again in order to criticise the pretensions of priests in general, especially the Catholic variety), but Voltaire's later works no longer stress their aspect of the English religious situation. Significantly enough, the Anglican divine Freind tells the Bachelier de Salamanque in *Histoire de Jenni* (1775): 'vous êtes esclaves d'un étranger, et nous ne sommes soumis qu'à notre raison' (ed. Brumfitt and Davis, p.65). Voltaire's historical works normally point out the beneficial effects of the Reformation in England. The religious wars were as ferocious as elsewhere, granted, but England gained enormously from the dissolution of the monasteries, the abolition of unproductive feast days, the marriage of the clergy and all the other socially-beneficent aspects of Protestantism. Moreover, the clergy in England were more fortunate than their continental brethren (*Essai*, ii.249):

La réforme en Angleterre a été plus favorable au clergé anglican qu'elle ne l'a été en Allemagne, en Suisse, et dans les Pays-Bas, aux luthériens et aux calvinistes. Tous les évêchés sont considérables dans la Grande-Bretagne; tous les bénéfices y donnent de quoi vivre honnêtement. Les curés de la campagne y sont plus à leur aise qu'en France.[79]

In Voltaire's correspondence too there are numerous references to the advantages of English life, many of which are directly or indirectly attributable to the religious settlement adopted there.[80] The implication

[79] Voltaire is clearly mistaken here as in many of the points he makes about the eighteenth-century Church of England (cf. below, pp.447-48); the income from the various bishoprics varied immensely, from princely sees like Durham (£6,000 per annum), Winchester (£5,000), and London (£4,000), to others such as Rochester (£600), Llandaff (£550), Oxford (£500), and Bristol (£450), whose incumbents found difficulty in living on the scale expected of them. Cf. Sykes, p.61.

[80] a direct connection between the Protestant religion and progress is obvious in the following lettres: Best.D8881 (to the marquis d'Argence, 28 April 1760): 'Les Anglais sont les premiers qui aient chassé les moines et les préjugez'; Best.D11418 (to Helvétius, 15 September 1763): 'Nous prenons insensiblement leur [i.e. of the English] noble liberté de penser, et leur profond mépris pour les fadaises de L'école.' Enthusiasm for England reaches a high pitch in Best.D8663, and above all in Best.D8814's rather exaggerated praise. 'Non, il n'y a point d'hypocrites en Angleterre', Voltaire told Bettinelli on 24 March 1760. 'Qui ne craint rien, ne déguise rien, qui peut penser librement ne pense point en Esclave.' But perhaps Voltaire's most eloquent tribute is the comment he made to

is clear and is backed up elsewhere: the Anglican clergy, better-off materially than other Protestant clerics, are not tempted to make sanctimonious attacks on those more fortunate than themselves and to proscribe other people's enjoyment as a sort of hypocritical compensation for their loss of power. Ministers of the Church of England escape the narrowness and extremism of the Calvinists' attitude, and their moderation is pleasing to Voltaire.

Several critics have claimed that, perhaps as a result of the growing menace of atheism, Voltaire's hostility toward the less fanatical forms of Christianity tended to soften a little from the late 1760s onwards:[81] he even seemed ready to make some concessions, especially to Protestant denominations. As early as 1752, in the *Défense de milord Bolingbroke*, Voltaire, speaking as a Protestant, assures his co-religionists that no deist wishes to make the clergy suffer materially: 'nous ne voyons pas que ni milord Bolingbroke, ni milord Shaftesbury, ni l'illustre Pope, qui a immortalisé les principes de l'un et de l'autre, aient voulu toucher à la pension d'aucun ministre du saint Evangile' (M.xxiii.554). Moreover, Protestants should be tolerant towards the deists, since they are closer to the latter than are Catholics, and thus have more chance of converting them (M.xxiii.553):

Ils [the deists] avouent tous que notre religion est plus sensée que celle des papistes. Ne les éloignons donc pas, nous qui sommes les seuls capables de les ramener; ils adorent un dieu, et nous aussi; ils enseignent la vertu, et nous aussi. Ils veulent qu'on soit soumis aux puissances, qu'on traite tous les hommes comme des frères; nous pensons de même, nous partons des mêmes principes. Agissons donc avec eux comme des parents qui ont entre les mains les titres de la famille, et qui les montrent à ceux qui, descendus de la même origine, savent seulement qu'ils ont le même père, mais qui n'ont point les papiers de la maison.

In the *Cinquième homélie* (1769), as we have already seen (above, pp.79-80), Voltaire, again apparently using a Protestant spokesman, seems to be ready to retain ceremonies like the eucharist which have clear Biblical support, provided of course that they are socially useful and are not likely to cause any sort of trouble or dispute. Written in the

Algarotti on 17 October 1763 (Best.D11465): 'J'aimerais mieux vivre dans un village d'Angleterre, que de demeurer à Rome.' The particular comparison made here surely indicates that religious considerations were often present in Voltaire's mind when he praised English liberties, even though this is not always pointed out explicitly.

[81] cf. Brumfitt and Davis, pp.xxxix-xli; Pomeau, *La Religion*, pp.438-43.

same year, *Dieu et les hommes* contains one of Voltaire's most impassioned indictments of the massacres and persecutions caused by Christianity. Despite this, he does not propose its abolition, but makes recommendations for purifying it as the basis of a universal religion (M.xxviii.238):

Nous proposons de conserver dans la morale de Jésus tout ce qui est conforme à la raison universelle, à celle de tous les grands philosophes de l'antiquité, à celle de tous les temps et de tous les lieux, à celle qui doit être l'éternel lien de toutes les sociétés.

Adorons l'Etre suprême par Jésus, puisque la chose est établie ainsi parmi nous. Les cinq lettres qui composent son nom ne sont certainement pas un crime. Qu'importe que nous rendions nos hommages à l'Etre suprême par Confucius, par Marc-Aurèle, par Jésus, ou par un autre, pourvu que nous soyons justes? La religion consiste assurément dans la vertu, et non dans le fatras impertinent de la théologie. La morale vient de Dieu, elle est uniforme partout.

Such a compromise on the part of one of Christianity's bitterest enemies may at first seem a little surprising, but it is not difficult to believe that Voltaire's amicable contacts with enlightened pastors like Allamand and his growing fear of atheism were probably sufficient to encourage this development. Voltaire attempts to calm the 'clameurs de nos ecclésiastiques', and seeks to set their minds at rest (M.xxviii.241):

Rassurez-vous, mes amis, sur la plus grande de vos craintes. Nous ne rejetons point les prêtres, quoique dans la Caroline et dans la Pensylvanie chacun de nos pères de famille puisse être ministre du Très-Haut dans sa maison. Non-seulement vous garderez vos bénéfices, mais nous prétendons augmenter le revenu de ceux qui travaillent le plus, et qui sont le moins payés.

Loin d'abolir le culte public, nous voulons le rendre plus pur et moins indigne de l'Etre suprême.

The last sentence reminds one of Eldorado, but any thought of a Quaker-type solution is obviously ruled out, as the clergy, despite their greed and self-interest, are to be retained. What seems most likely is that in *Dieu et les hommes* Voltaire was addressing himself more particularly to his Catholic fellow-countrymen and suggesting a possible future evolution for the French Church. The increase in stipend for the *curé de campagne* struggling to manage on his *portion congrue* would have been a measure welcomed by the most socially useful section of the clergy. Although, as we have already seen, Voltaire had been moved by the civil disabilities and injustices to which the Huguenots were subject, their church, not only illegal and based largely on the support of potentially fanatical, lower-class elements, but also declining spiritually and a minority organisation, can hardly have commended itself to him as a basis for future developments. It was the more representative, more powerful and socially respectable Catholic Church which must be the vehicle for any attempted purification of religion in France.

If only the policies of Gallicanism could be pushed further, the French Church freed from Rome, and the pope replaced by a French patriarch! Voltaire had always desired that this should happen, and in chapter 35 of *Le Siècle de Louis XIV* he emphasises all the economic and political advantages which would have resulted from such a policy (*Oh*, pp.1037-38):

Il y avait là [on the question of the *régale*[82]] de quoi séparer à jamais l'Eglise de France de celle de Rome. On avait parlé, sous le cardinal de Richelieu et sous Mazarin, de faire un patriarche. Le vœu de tous les magistrats était qu'on ne payât plus à Rome le tribut des annates; que Rome ne nommât plus, pendant six mois de l'année, aux bénéfices de Bretagne; que les évêques de France ne s'appellassent plus *évêques par la permission du saint-siège*. Si le roi l'avait voulu, il n'avait qu'à dire un mot: il était maître de l'assemblée du clergé, et il avait pour lui la nation.

But passions were not roused enough for a break with Rome to have been envisaged, and anyway, 'il était bien difficile de faire cette scission, tandis qu'on voulait extirper le calvinisme' (*Oh*, p.1038). Voltaire is obviously still very much in favour of this development, and it is possible to detect an echo of his own opinions in the following passage: 'L'idée de créer un patriarche se renouvela. La querelle des franchises des ambassadeurs de Rome, qui acheva d'envenimer les plaies, fit penser qu'enfin le temps était venu d'établir en France une Eglise catholique apostolique qui ne serait point *romaine*' (*Oh*, p.1039). At the end of the chapter, Voltaire points out that even the Protestants have to admit that the French Church is the least superstitious to be found in a Catholic country: 'Quelques autres superstitions, attachées à des usages respectables, ont subsisté. Les protestants en ont triomphé; mais ils sont obligés de convenir qu'il n'y a d'église catholique où ces

---

[82] 'le droit de régale [. . .] accordait au roi de France les revenus d'un évêché devenu vacant, et même la licence de nommer aux fonctions ecclésiastiques du diocèse jusqu'à l'installation du nouvel évêque' (Raoul Stéphan, *Histoire du protestantisme français*, p.159).

abus soient moins communs et plus méprisés qu'en France' (*Oh*, pp.1040-41).

The French Catholic Church was therefore ripe for just such a change, and England provided the perfect example of a state where religion was national and the pope was replaced by the head of state. What is perhaps equally significant is that Voltaire stressed that the Anglican reform had been moderate, and constituted a sort of happy medium: 'la religion anglicane conserva ce que les cérémonies romaines ont d'auguste, et ce que le luthéranisme a d'austère' (*Essai*, ii.471). Even in the 1760s, Voltaire's most militantly anti-Christian period, the Anglican Church is cited as a variety of state religion which, while far from perfect, is a notable achievement. The following passage from the *Examen important de milord Bolingbroke* (1767) provides further evidence that Voltaire did not advocate the Quaker rejection of the priesthood as a practical proposition (*Mélanges*, p.1022):

J'avertis d'abord que je ne veux pas toucher à notre église anglicane, en tant qu'elle est établie par actes de parlement. Je la regarde d'ailleurs comme la plus savante et la plus regulière de l'Europe. Je ne suis point de l'avis du *Whig indépendant*, qui semble vouloir abolir tout sacerdoce, et le remettre aux mains des pères de famille, comme du temps des patriarches. Notre société, telle qu'elle est, ne permet pas un pareil changement. Je pense qu'il est nécessaire d'entretenir des prêtres, pour être les maîtres des mœurs et pour offrir à Dieu nos prières. Nous verrons s'ils doivent être des joueurs de gobelets, des trompettes de discorde, et des persécuteurs sanguinaires.

Anglicanism, as established by law, must be retained, at least for the time being, since any change, in order to be practicable, must at the same time be gradual (p.1117):

Il y aurait du danger et peu de raison à vouloir faire tout d'un coup du christianisme ce qu'on a fait du papisme. Je tiens que, dans notre île, on doit laisser subsister la hiérarchie établie par un acte de parlement, en la soumettant toujours à la législation civile, et en l'empêchant de nuire. Il serait sans doute à désirer que l'idole fût renversée, et qu'on offrît à Dieu des hommages plus purs; mais le peuple n'en est pas encore digne. Il suffit, pour le présent, que notre Eglise soit contenue dans ses bornes. Plus les laïques seront éclairés, moins les prêtres pourront faire de mal.

Voltaire had already made more or less the same point in the *Fragment d'une lettre de lord Bolingbroke* of 1760, and had also asserted that there was a direct relationship between the material well-being of the nation

and the reasonableness of the church: 'moins notre Eglise anglicane a
été superstitieuse, plus notre Angleterre a été florissante: encore quelques pas, et nous en vaudrons mieux' (M.xxiv.155). The *Lettre de
milord Cornsbury à milord Bolingbroke* (1767) is very hard on all forms
of Christianity, but even here it is grudgingly admitted that England
is the country in which Christianity has caused the least harm, though
this is attributed to the fact that it is divided into a large number of
sects. Yet despite its defects, the Anglican Church is still preferable
to the Roman Catholic: 'Il est certain que notre Eglise anglicane est
moins superstitieuse et moins absurde que la romaine. J'entends que
nos charlatans ne nous empoisonnent qu'avec cinq ou six dogmes, au
lieu que les montebanks papistes empoisonnent avec une vingtaine'
(M.xxvi.305).

Several letters in Voltaire's correspondence show clearly that he did
regard the English religious settlement as an example for France. On
23 June 1760 he told d'Alembert: 'Je voudrais que vous écrazassiez
l'infâme, c'est là le grand point. Il faut la réduire à l'état où elle est en
Angleterre' (Best.D9006; cf. D12660). A few years later Voltaire
remarked to the same correspondent: 'On pensera un jour en France
comme en Angleterre où la religion n'est regardée par le parlement que
comme une affaire de politique' (Best.D13374, 26 June 1766). It even
seems that this Erastian ideal symbolised by the Anglican Church was
a factor in the controversial Easter Communion which Voltaire made
in 1769. At any rate it provided him with a useful argument with which
he could confront his critics after the event. On 4 April of that year he
explained to Saint-Lambert: 'J'ai déclaré expressément que je mourais
dans la religion du Roi très chrétien mon maître et de la France ma
patrie, *as it is establish'd by act of parlement.* Cela est fier et honnête'
(Best.D15570). The following day he made a similar statement to
Saurin (Best.D15572), asking the latter to reason with d'Alembert, who
had apparently been somewhat scandalised by Voltaire's confession
and the profession of faith he signed before receiving the sacraments.[83]
Although these comments may represent merely a face-saving stratagem,
they square with Voltaire's marked lack of enthusiasm regarding full
freedom of worship for the Huguenots, and it is possible that he was not
being completely insincere in his statement of loyalty to the Erastian
ideal of a French state religion similar to the Anglican Church, even

[83] cf. René Pomeau, *La Religion*, pp.443-44: 'Voltaire prétend avoir seulement affirmé
son attachement à la religion catholique en tant que religion de l'Etat.'

if this conserved some outward features of Catholicism.

I have said that even in his most anti-Christian period Voltaire was willing to tolerate Anglicanism and to acknowledge its usefulness. By the time of *Histoire de Jenni*, his attitude had become so much more favourable that he was able to put forward his arguments against atheism through the mouth of Freind, an Anglican divine. J. H. Brumfitt and M. I. Gerard Davis have shown, in their excellent critical edition of *L'Ingénu and Histoire de Jenni* (pp.lviii-lix), that the character of Freind was almost certainly taken from real life. Dr John Freind, a distinguished physician, who became a Fellow of the Royal Society (1712), and M.P. for Launceston (1722), was a close friend of Newton's and Voltaire was probably introduced to him by the earl of Peter-borough. He also had two brothers, both Anglican divines, one of whom was well known 'both as a scholar and a noble character' (p.lix). The Freind of *Histoire de Jenni* seems to partake of the qualities of both dr John Freind and his brother, and is obviously a very special person, a fact which Voltaire is careful to point out to us: 'Vous savez que M. Freind avait été député en parlement avant d'être prêtre, et qu'il est le seul à qui l'on ait permis d'exercer ces deux fonctions incompatibles' (p.72). Moreover, he is also the grandson of William Penn, 'le premier des tolérants, et le fondateur de Philadelphie' (p.72). No one, in Voltaire's eyes, could have a more respectable ancestry, and Freind obviously epitomises all the qualities which Voltaire admired: tolerance, lack of interest in useless speculation, and above all a practical concept of social virtue. Some of this credit must obviously redound to the Church of England, 'votre Eglise anglicane, si respectable', as the bachelier de Salamanque calls it (p.65). Voltaire's admiration for the wisdom and scholarship of men like Samuel Clarke (see above, pp.427-36) amply explains the sterling qualities which characterise Jenni's father.[84] We are now worlds away from the Anglican clergy as described in the *Lettres philosophiques*.

Though Freind is primarily a spokesman for Voltairian theism, the third chapter sees him giving a moderate and restrained account of an undogmatic type of Anglicanism which might have been acceptable both to the theist and to the more emancipated sort of Catholic, who, Voltaire was sure, must be numerous in France. Perhaps this explains why such a tactful account is given of the Anglican position as regards the Virgin Mary, a subject on which Catholic susceptibilities could be

[84] for another possible source see appendix 5.

most easily offended by harsh Protestant propaganda. 'Nous la révérons,' says Freind, 'nous la chérissons; mais nous croyons qu'elle se soucie peu des titres qu'on lui donne ici-bas. Elle n'est jamais nommée mère de Dieu dans l'Evangile' (ed. Brumfitt and Davis, p.67). The rest of Freind's exposition shows the same moderation. He emphasises that Protestantism is not merely a recent, temporary development of Christianity: 'C'est comme si on me disait que je ne suis pas le petit-fils de mon grand-père, parce qu'un collatéral, demeurant en Italie, s'était emparé de son testament et de mes titres. Je les ai heureusement retrouvés, et il est clair que je suis le petit-fils de mon grand-père.'[85] Anglicanism is not only as legitimate as Catholicism, it is also more reasonable and suitable for a free people: 'Nous sommes, vous et moi, de la même famille, à cela près que nous autres Anglais nous lisons le testament de notre grand-père dans notre propre langue, et qu'il vous est défendu de le lire dans la vôtre. Vous êtes esclaves d'un étranger, et nous ne sommes soumis qu'à notre raison' (p.65). Freind also emphasises one of the more obvious advantages of Protestantism, the fact that Anglican priests are permitted to marry. It is perhaps not surprising that this, more than any of the other reasons advanced, seems to convince the bachelier, who naively underlines how much more important is social utility than priestly pride and doctrinal inflexibility (p.71):

Voilà qui est fait, je suis de votre religion: je me fais anglican. Je veux me marier à une femme honnête qui fera toujours semblant de m'aimer, tant que je serai jeune, qui aura soin de moi dans ma vieillesse, et que j'enterrerai proprement si je lui survis: cela vaut mieux que de cuire des hommes et de déshonorer des filles, comme a fait mon cousin don Caracucarador, inquisiteur pour la foi.

His conversion to Anglicanism follows that of his fellow bachelors and the victims of the Inquisition saved by the English army. Later he is married to Boca Vermeja: 'le généreux Freind paya la dot des deux mariés; il plaça bien tous ses nouveaux convertis, par la protection de milord Peterborou' (p.77). Surely Voltaire here intends to point a lesson in toleration for his French readers, for *nouveaux convertis* was the official designation of the Protestants who remained in France after

[85] the argument which Voltaire adopts here was a Protestant commonplace and may indicate that he had changed his mind about statements he had made in *La Henriade* (ed. Taylor, p.378) and in *Le Siècle de Louis XIV* (*Oh*, p.1052) that Calvinism at least would die away if left to its own devices and no longer persecuted: cf. above, pp.242, 253.

the repeal of the Edict of Nantes. Freind's voluntary conversions were the opposite of those which Louis XIV's government obtained only after extreme duress, and the English divine thought of their social as well as their spiritual welfare, 'car ce n'est pas assez d'assurer le salut des gens, il faut les faire vivre'. Moreover, the superiority of Anglicanism over more extreme forms of Protestantism is symbolised by Freind's tolerant attitude towards Boca Vermeja's being the mistress of his son: 'un bon père ne doit être ni le tyran de son fils ni son mercure' (p.73). This would hardly have been the opinion of a Calvinist minister!

Anglicanism thus appears in *Histoire de Jenni* as a characteristically English solution to the problem of a state religion, a moderate institution which avoids the excesses of both Catholics and extreme Protestants. As its spokesman Freind puts it: 'Vous autres chrétiens de delà la mer britannique en tirant vers le sud, vous avez plus tôt fait cuire un de vos frères, soit le conseiller Anne Dubourg, soit Michel Servet, soit tous ceux qui furent ards sous Philippe second surnommé le discret, que nous ne faisons rôtir un rostbif à Londres' (p.63). This apparent alliance with the Church of England is interesting on several counts. In the first place, many of the factual statements Voltaire makes about it are incorrect, even in the *Lettres philosophiques*. Secondly his Erastian opinions, when considered in connection with some of his remarks about Anglicanism, are seen to be remarkably naive and uncritical. Finally, one wonders whether Voltaire was aware of the spiritual decline and pastoral inefficiency which, in the opinion of many critics, characterised the English Church in the eighteenth century.

We have already seen (above, p.439, n.79) that Voltaire was wrong in claiming that the revenues of all English bishoprics were considerable and he also rather underestimated the size of the English clergy.[86] Numbers of those taking Holy Orders were large, and since it was difficult to obtain any benefice without patronage or influence, many clerics, especially curates, were forced to eke out a precarious existence, or even to drift from town to town.[87] But perhaps the most revealing

[86] cf. Best.D18067 (Voltaire to Chastellux, 7 December 1772): 'Il n'y a que dix mille *priests* en Angleterre.' Sykes (p.187) makes clear that there was an 'admitted disproportion between the number of persons entering into Holy Orders and the benefices available'. The number of benefices in the reign of Queen Anne was in fact 'near 10,000' (Sykes, p.212).

[87] cf. Sykes, p.221: 'from Wales Dr. Wootton lamented that they were infested by "a parcel of strolling curates in south Wales, and some such there were also in north Wales, who for a crown or at most for a guinea, would marry anybody under a hedge" '.

of Voltaire's comments in this respect is when he criticises the presence in parliament of bishops, implying that the clergy as a whole are opposed to the Whig government and would like to see its overthrow.[88]

In point of fact the truth was very different. Traditionally indeed the Whigs had been the Dissenters' party, but after 1688 the situation changed and a large section of the Church supported the new religious settlement.[89] Moreover, the clergy were to a great extent in the pocket of the government, enmeshed in the same web of skilfully woven patronage as were members of Parliament and many other professional men. The parliamentary power of the bishops, far from hindering Walpole's government, in fact helped to save it in 1733 when the episcopal bench voting as a block preserved the Whig majority by a small margin.[90] Such a conduct was not only regarded as perfectly proper, it was expected of a bishop, who was required to spend the whole of the parliamentary session in London rather than remaining in his see to attend to ecclesiastical affairs (Sykes, pp.47-48). Even when he returned home he was encouraged to support the government's political interests in his diocese (pp.70-88).

The eighteenth-century Church has often been criticised for its corruption and moral decline. 'There is a worldliness', asserts J. H. Plumb, 'almost a venality, about eighteenth-century prelates which no amount of apologetics can conceal. The clerical duties of visitation ordination, and confirmation, were done only as political duties allowed. Dioceses were enormous [. . .] There were no suffragans.'[91] This picture is substantially correct, although other critics have insisted that the Hanoverian Church must be judged by the standards of its own day: some bishops had a high conception of the duties of their office, and some were on occasion bold enough to speak out against government policy, even though this was likely to ensure their staying for many

---

[88] *Lettres philosophiques*, ed. Lanson, i.62-64; cf. also the notebook fragment no.53: 'La communion anglicane est opposée au gouvernement, qui la tolère . . .' (Voltaire 82, p.699).

[89] cf. Sykes, p.34: 'The conversion of the whig party into the situation of supporters of the position of the Established Church was undoubtedly the most important factor of the ecclesiastical development of the first half of the eighteenth century.'

[90] this was in a series of votes on 17, 24 May and 2 June. On the two latter occasions, out of twenty-six bishops, twenty-four voted in favour of the government (Sykes, pp.50-51).

[91] *England in the eighteenth century*, Pelican History of England, vol.vii (Harmondsworth 1950), p.43.

years in remote or unprofitable sees.[92] As regards its spiritual life the Church was in a far from healthy state (Plumb, p.44):

the greatest danger [. . .] lay not in its refusal to reform but in its attitude to life. The way to success was in discretion and man-pleasing and the worldly virtues became heavenly ones. The most popular sermon in the eighteenth century was Tillotson's on the text: 'His commandments are not grievous,' in which he stresses that if man applies the same principles he uses in business or commerce to moral life, he will be sure – of what? A place in heaven. Evil and guilt, sin and redemption – the whole personal drama and appeal of religion – was forgotten or rationalised away and the eupeptic optimism of politicians pervaded the teaching of the Church.

The similarity between the ethic outlined here by Plumb and Voltaire's view that it was religion's prime function to encourage social virtue rather than useless theological speculation, should not pass unnoticed.[93]

The vacuum left by the established Church was quickly filled by other denominations, notably by the evangelising crusade of Methodism, which was sweeping England in the eighteenth century. There is no real hint in Voltaire's works or in his correspondence that he was aware of this situation. The name of Methodist is apparently first mentioned in *La Philosophie de l'histoire* (1765), and Voltaire seems to dismiss the sect as just one more product of the fanatical outbursts of the populace, equally ignorant and unreasonable in no matter what country (Voltaire 59, p.182):

Ne sait-on pas que dans tout pays le vulgaire est imbécile, superstitieux, insensé? N'y a-t-il pas eu des convulsionnaires dans la patrie du chancelier de L'Hôpital, de Charron, de Montaigne, de la Motte le Vayer, de Descartes, de Bayle, de Fontenelle, de Montesquieu? N'y a-t-il pas des méthodistes, des moraves, des millénaires, des fanatiques de toute espèce dans le pays qui eut le bonheur de donner naissance au chevalier Bacon, à ces génies immortels, Newton & Locke, et à une foule de grands hommes?

In the *Lettre au docteur Pansophe* of the following year Voltaire names Whitfield,[94] one of the most famous preachers associated with Methodism in its early years, though later he disagreed with Wesley over

[92] a classic case is bishop Watson, who supported both American independence and Roman Catholic emancipation, and was duly rewarded with a stay of thirty-four years (1782-1816) at Llandaff (Sykes, pp.365-78).

[93] it is also interesting to note that, among Anglican clergymen, Tillotson had been especially praised by Voltaire: cf. above, p.435, especially n.76.

[94] 'Vous deviendrez puissant en œuvres et en paroles, comme George Fox, le révérend Whitfield, etc.' (*Mélanges*, p.855).

449

predestination and broke away from the movement.[95] Later references to the Methodists in Voltaire's works merely mention them occasionally in the lists of Christian sects he frequently indulged in citing (M.xxvii.29, 111; M.xxviii.200, 240), but there is no indication that he considered them as of any more importance than 'tant d'autres *istes*' (M.xxviii.517).

Had Voltaire realised the inherent weakness of eighteenth-century Anglicanism he might indeed have rejoiced, for its decline perhaps heralded the advent of deism.[96] On the other hand, the situation could also be interpreted as a danger to over-optimistic purveyors of 'enlightened' religion. If the most purified and rational form of Christianity, far from attracting new converts, was losing vast numbers of its members to a fanatical new sect, what real hope was there that theism would ever satisfy the irrational and emotional demands of the lower classes? Moreover, despite Voltaire's hatred of the higher clergy and its pretensions, we must not forget that he regarded the village priest as fulfilling a difficult but socially useful role in many communities.[97] It seems unlikely that he would have wished French *curés* to follow the English example of laxity and indifference, had he been aware of the real situation across the Channel.

One inevitably wonders how far Voltaire had thought out the implications of the Erastianism he so strenuously advocated. In the *Lettres philosophiques*, for example, he was surely not only unfair but also somewhat inconsistent in his criticism of the Anglican Church.

[95] cf. Léonard, *Histoire générale*, iii.113: 'Un autre grand problème théologique, celui de la prédestination, opposa Wesley, arminien comme sa mère, à Whitfield, calviniste convaincu. Sans doute ce dernier, encore en 1740, lui demandait-il de s'abstenir de prêcher sur la question, comme il le faisait lui-même. Mais ses fidèles étaient moins discrets: Wesley en exclut quelques-uns et prêcha, puis publia, un grand sermon sur la *Libre grâce*, vraie déclaration de guerre.'

[96] he had indeed been correct in the *Lettres philosophiques* to emphasise the significance of Clarke's unorthodoxy. There were many other clerics in the eighteenth century who shared this divine's antitrinitarian sentiments and his wish to amend the Anglican liturgy in accordance with his beliefs. On 6 February 1772 a Unitarian petition seeking to replace the thirty-nine articles with 'a form of subscription to the Bible only' was presented to parliament, which rejected it by 217 votes to 71 (Sykes, pp.380-82). Nonetheless, 'several projects based upon his [Clarke's] original suggestions were set forth; of which that published anonymously in 1774 with the title *The Book of Common Prayer Reformed according to the Plan of the late Dr. Samuel Clarke* may be regarded as characteristic' (Sykes, p.388). For evidence that Voltaire was not unaware of these later developments see M.xxxi.93.

[97] cf. William H. Williams, 'Voltaire and the utility of the lower clergy', *Studies on Voltaire* (1967), lviii.1869-91, *passim*, especially pp.1869-72.

For England approximated closely to the model which he was later to propose for other countries, a *régime* in which the Church is completely subject to the civil authorities. Since 1689 succeeding governments had been able, with the aid of ecclesiastical patronage and preferment, to foster the growth of a generation of churchmen in the main solidly behind the existing religious settlement. Yet still the Church is judged wanting: given half a chance, implies Voltaire, the clergy would encourage revolt and sedition, for they are not content to be dependent on parliament. As we have seen, he was entirely wrong in his claims, and one must assume that while in England he had made few efforts to verify his analysis of the situation. But even if Voltaire had never visited England, if he had merely been theorising about the Anglican Church from the remoteness of Paris, would not his reasoning have been faulty? In a state where religion is subject to the government, the Church is largely what the government makes it. In the last analysis Voltaire cannot fairly praise the Whig government and the *mélange heureux* which exists between the various component parts of the English constitution (*Lettres philosophiques*, ed. Lanson, i.101) without including the Hanoverian Church, at once a product and an integral part of the system, whatever its apparent disadvantages in the eyes of the *philosophe*.

The flaw of complete Erastianism is only too obvious. Under an enlightened ruler, the clergy's power would be restrained, rationally inspired reforms introduced swiftly, and the chances of uprisings or disturbances caused by popular fanaticism would be almost entirely removed. But all princes were not made in the mould of Frederick II or Catherine the Great. What if a religious fanatic or a cynical atheist became head of state? Voltaire's reaction to Henry VIII (see above, p.37) and Cromwell (see above, pp.404-409) perhaps indicated that he was not really in favour of Erastianism in all circumstances: the proviso was that the government should itself be enlightened.[98] Unfortunately, Voltaire does not make this point explicitly – indeed it seems unlikely that he ever consciously formulated the principle. His inveterate hostility to organised priesthoods ensured that he would regard government

[98] cf. Ronald Ian Boss, 'Rousseau's civil religion', p.138: 'Voltaire's model for institutionalising [. . .] "theism" as a social religion was the Anglican church; as within the English system of government, the social religion was to be subordinated to the benevolent rule of an enlightened monarch in order to assure that the political ascendancy within the state be secular and not spiritual.'

control of almost any kind as preferable to clerical independence. Voltaire might show himself critical of Henry VIII, but it was probably inconceivable to him that the English government of his own day might have a harmful effect on the Church.

Voltaire's apprehension of the English religious situation was a fundamentally static one, although his attitude to the Anglican clergy became somewhat more favourable in later works than had been the case in the *Lettres philosophiques*. The solid virtues of state control and lack of fanaticism were what had impressed him, and the Church of England, shorn of the twin terrors of priestly domination and popular enthusiasm, was given his cachet of approval. In the largely favourable picture he painted of Christianity in England, Voltaire was presenting his suggested first step in the reform of France's religious life. This could be achieved painlessly, and would gradually prepare the nation for the more important reform to follow.

9

Conclusion

i. *Voltaire's God: a reassessment*

IN this study I have investigated Voltaire's attitude to the Reformation, the Reformers, their doctrines, and the general ethos of Protestantism, as well as his reaction to the reality of Protestantism in various countries and his efforts in favour of the French Huguenots, and I feel it is now indispensable to reconsider Voltaire's own religious views. Only by dealing with this vexed question can we hope ultimately to explain why he rejected certain aspects of Protestantism while enthusiastically accepting others, even going as far as to choose the Anglican Church as a model for religious reform in his own country. Far from being of merely marginal interest, the nature of Voltaire's religious beliefs provides a basic frame of reference for my study, without which many of the phenomena I have investigated can receive no satisfactory explanation (see above, pp.39-42, 72-73, 74-75, 89-90).

Critical debate about this subject is by no means exhausted, some scholars considering that Voltaire was really an atheist despite his protestations of theism, others not only accepting his claims but even attributing a mystical side to his idea of God. These opposing attitudes are well represented in two important articles, 'Voltaire's god', by dr Theodore Besterman (*Studies on Voltaire* (1967), lv.27-41) and professor W. H. Barber's 'Voltaire and Quakerism: Enlightenment and the inner light' (*Studies on Voltaire* (1963), xxiv.81-109). I feel that, at this point, it may be helpful to discuss briefly the conclusions of these scholars, since this may enable us to place Voltaire's religious views into some kind of perspective.

Basically, dr Besterman seeks to demonstrate that if Voltaire was a deist or theist,[1] the content and implication of his beliefs were very little

[1] dr Besterman states that, 'contrary to the generally accepted view', no distinction existed for Voltaire between the terms deist and theist ('Voltaire's god', p.30). René Pomeau, on the other hand, takes a different view: 'le théiste professe un *credo* plus étoffé que le déiste; il accepte qu'un culte soit rendu à la Divinité'(*La Religion de Voltaire*,

different from those of an atheist. A fair deal of the article is given up to a discussion of just what the term 'deist' means or has been supposed to mean. Dr Besterman (p.26) makes the point that Voltaire thought that metaphysics had a very limited value, and he also claims that Voltaire was not a man 'god obsessed. His references to the subject are relatively few, particularly in his correspondence, far fewer than to many other subjects in which he was more actively interested.' Voltaire's views evolved, dr Besterman reminds us (pp.30-33), and in such a delicate subject as this it is indispensable to evaluate the circumstances in which any particular remark may have been made, otherwise we may be misled into accepting as his true opinion what was merely a comment inspired by politeness or caution. Similarly, some of Voltaire's works may give us a more genuine and reliable insight into his personal opinions than others, and many researchers have gained a false impression because they tried to rely exclusively on the indexes of Voltaire's books 'instead of reading the great man's works' (p.33). Observing (p.38) that the *Essai sur les mœurs*, 'the work in which Voltaire concentrated the essence of his thought', almost completely neglects to mention God, dr Besterman argues strongly that Voltaire's theistic propaganda was a purely cynical exercise which he thought was beneficial to social stability: 'The fact that Voltaire insisted so often and with so much emotion on the expediency of belief, and argued so emphatically against atheism as a danger to society, clearly indicates his own disbelief' (p.40).

It is difficult to avoid the conclusion that several of the points made in dr Besterman's article appear somewhat irrelevant or pedantic. For example he criticises the 1884 *Oxford English dictionary* definition of 'deist': 'one who acknowledges the existence of a God upon the testimony of reason, but rejects revealed religion', on the grounds that 'the indefinite article is surprising, to say the least of it, for the notion that every deist could have his own god is mildly disturbing' (p.28). Despite this comment, dr Besterman expresses himself in exactly the same manner later in his article,[2] and in any case even Voltaire employs a similar turn of phrase.[3] To draw attention to his inconsistency may in

p.428). In the 'Postface' of his remarkable study (pp.476 ff.), m. Pomeau discusses dr Besterman's article and reaffirms persuasively his belief that Voltaire was a genuine theist.

[2] p.38: 'When writing against atheism in the *Dictionnaire philosophique* Voltaire argued [. . .] that it is morally much better to believe in a god than not to.'

[3] cf. Best.D13128 (Voltaire to mme Du Deffand, 20 January 1766): 'Ce n'était pas ainsi que pensaient Neuton et Platon [. . .] Ils adoraient un Dieu, et ils détestaient la superstition.'

itself appear rather petty, but it does illustrate an important fact: although he rates others for their failure satisfactorily to define deism, dr Bester-man too is guilty of many gratuitous assumptions when he is talking about God. At one point (p.29) he attacks Leslie Stephen's attempt to distinguish between constructive and critical deism on the grounds that Stephen 'was thinking solely in terms of Christian polemics, whereas for Voltaire, and indeed for all philosophers, the problem of god is nothing if not universal, existed long before Christianity, and must necessarily exist independently of this or that faith'. Nonetheless, in forming this assessment of Voltaire's religion, dr Besterman also talks as though failure to believe in a Christian-type God is clear enough evidence of virtual atheism. Toward the end of his article he quotes (in English) a remark from one of Voltaire's notebooks: 'God is the eternal geome-trician, but geometricians do not love',[4] commenting ('Voltaire's god', p.39): 'This lapidary comment pretty well sums up Voltaire's judicious agnosticism about this supposed argument for the existence of a deity.' But Voltaire's statement does nothing of the sort: all it proves is that he did not believe in a God who loved his creatures as the Christian God is claimed to do. Did dr Besterman imagine that all other religions in the world have exactly the same teaching and that a failure to believe in a God of love necessarily implied that a belief in any other kind of God is out of the question?

Several of the other conclusions dr Besterman draws from passages in Voltaire's works are equally unsatisfactory. 'Voltaire often expressed this scepticism', he remarks, having just quoted an extract from the *Dictionnaire philosophique* article 'Dieu, dieux', which includes the existence of God as one of 'a very small number of certainties' we can arrive at.[5] Admittedly, Voltaire often emphasises the fruitlessness of metaphysical speculation, but this did not prevent him from indulging

---

[4] this statement occurs in Voltaire's Leningrad group of notebooks (Voltaire 81, p.420).

[5] this is the extract given by dr Besterman (in English and without a precise reference): 'We have no adequate idea of the divinity, we merely drag ourselves from supposition to supposition, from possibilities to probabilities. We arrive at a very small number of certainties. Something exists, therefore there is something eternal, for nothing is produced from nothing. This is a sure truth on which our mind rests. Every construction which displays means and an end announces an artisan; therefore this universe, composed of mechanisms, of means, each of which has its end, reveals a very powerful, very intelligent artisan. Here we have a probability which approaches the greatest certitude; but is this supreme workman infinite? Is he everywhere? Has he a place? How can we answer this question with our limited intelligence and our feeble knowledge?' ('Voltaire's god', p.36).

in the activity himself. It is in any case noteworthy that in this quotation the attributes Voltaire mentions are of a particularly metaphysical type: he says that we cannot tell whether God is infinite or omnipresent, but he does not claim that it is impossible to know whether God is good or wise (indeed the latter would be difficult since he has just indicated that God possesses intelligence). Thus Voltaire is indeed sceptical, but this scepticism is not necessarily complete as regards God's existence, and the article 'Dieu, dieux' certainly cannot be counted as proof that Voltaire was indistinguishable from an atheist. Again, the passage cited from Best.D20158[6] is presumably supposed to indicate the lack of Voltaire's religious convictions, though it could be interpreted in quite a different manner. It begins significantly enough: 'I have long been convinced of the vast and unknown power of the author of nature.' A similar comment is also true of dr Besterman's use of a passage from Best.D16958.[7] Indeed, much of his argument seems based on quotations which, if anything, tend to prove the opposite of what he contends.[8] And certainly the assertion that Voltaire must be an atheist because he condemned atheism is well nigh inexplicable, unless firm evidence be adduced to back it up. But on one major point dr Besterman's conclusions cannot be doubted: Voltaire definitely preached a set of beliefs to which he did not subscribe himself. I shall return to this matter presently, but it may first be instructive to consider professor Barber's rather different position.

The second part of 'Voltaire and Quakerism' explores possible affinities between the Quaker belief of an Inner Light, the 'seed of Christ', which in their view was a universal human characteristic, and Voltaire's statements on the relationship between God and man, especially in the late 1760s and the 1770s. As professor Barber put it, the Inner Light was, for the Quakers, 'the opportunity of recognizing and consciously accepting a spiritual force within themselves which, if not obstructed by egotism, will transform the personality and bring it into harmony with

---

[6] Voltaire to Spallanzani, 6 June 1776. The letter refers to Spallanzani's experiments on the regenerative powers of minute aquatic animals.

[7] Voltaire to Frederick William, crown prince of Prussia, 11 January 1771. Voltaire comments: 'Le système des athées m'a toujours paru très extravagant. Spinosa lui même admettait une intelligence universelle. Il ne s'agit plus que de savoir si cette intelligence a de la justice. Or il me paraît impertinent d'admettre un dieu injuste. Tout le reste semble caché dans la nuit.'

[8] cf. also the conclusion drawn by dr Besterman from Voltaire's letter of around 10 June 1749 to Diderot (Best.D3940).

the divine purpose' ('Voltaire and Quakerism', p.102). Professor Barber also detects (p.104) in some of Voltaire's works a 'suggestion of direct inspiration' in connection with 'the teaching of an enlightened and, in a sense, inspired élite of sages throughout world history', who communicate to man God's moral law. Even more important, in *Tout en dieu* (1769), Voltaire 'presents God as not merely the creator, but as an all-pervading force in the universe, and a force which he compares, significantly, to light', and professor Barber reminds us that the parallel between Malebranche (whose influence in *Tout en dieu* is manifest) and the Quakers has not gone unnoticed. René Pomeau also considers that: 'Il y a, dans le théisme voltairien, un mysticisme des 'lumières' [...] Si l'on veut comparer la Divinité à quelque être existant, c'est la lumière qu'il faut choisir, parce que, comme Dieu, la lumière agit partout' (*La Religion de Voltaire*, p.421).[9] Is there then any connection between *Tout en dieu* and Quaker beliefs, and do Voltaire's works give us an insight into his attitude toward the doctrine of the Inner Light?

Voltaire's scepticism when confronted by the antics of *inspirés* in a Quaker assembly[10] is well known, and even in later works it seems clear that he constantly rejected any theory of direct divine inspiration, dismissing such ideas with contempt, even when they were connected with the Quakers. The *Galimatias dramatique* (M.xxxiv.75-77) for example, first published in 1765 and possibly written in 1757, ridicules the claims of all the main Christian sects to be the sole repositories of truth, and although the Quaker is perhaps treated less harshly than the others, he is included along with them nonetheless: 'tout ce qui est nécessaire', he proclaims, 'c'est d'être animé de l'Esprit' (M.xxiv.76). For a man whose brother was a convulsionary this comment was no doubt tantamount to a severe condemnation, and in any case Voltaire's constant suspicion of *illuminés*, of all those who imagined they were inspired by God, should make us very cautious before believing that the Quakers were accorded any special treatment. The several parallels drawn between the Quakers and the early Christians, and between Fox and Christ,[11] are, in a religious context, damning to both sides, merely

[9] it should be pointed out, however, that P. Henry ('A different view of Voltaire's controversial *Tout en dieu*', *Studies on Voltaire* (1975), cxxxv.143-50) considers this work to have been a sort of sympathetic investigation, by Voltaire, of the ideas of Spinoza, a philosopher he came to know well only in the late 1760s. It may not therefore entirely represent Voltaire's own ideas.

[10] *Lettres philosophiques*, ed. Lanson, i.23-25.

[11] cf. the *Dictionnaire philosophique* article 'Tolérance' (ed. Benda and Naves, p.406); *Examen important de milord Bolingbroke* (*Mélanges*, pp.1042, 1047-49).

stressing once again the imbecility of the multitude and the power of enthusiasm and fanaticism. As we have seen (above, pp.411 ff.), Voltaire's approval of the Quakers was inspired by their moral and social achievements; praise for their specifically religious ideas is normally lacking. A work written in 1772, *Il faut prendre un parti*, gives us a clue to his basic attitude. Voltaire begins by making it clear that he wishes no connection with any Christian community. A long, impressive-sounding list of them is given – despite his hostility to Christians, Voltaire always enjoyed showing off his erudition, and he never lost his curiosity for exotic sects (cf. above, p.57, n.14) – so the Quakers are included along with the rest: 'Je ne cherche point à faire un choix entre les chrétiens grecs, les arméniens, les eutychiens, les jacobites, les chrétiens appelés quakers, les anabaptistes, les jansénistes, les molinistes, les sociniens, et tant d'autres *istes*' (M.xxviii.517). But the end of the work, which gives humorous advice to the various 'istes' just mentioned, contains the following, highly significant phrase: 'nous exhortons les primitifs nommés quakers à marier leur fils aux filles des théistes nommés sociniens' (M.xxviii.551). This perhaps gives us the key to Voltaire's mature attitude towards the religious significance of Quakerism: if its *illuminisme* could be forgotten and its practical social virtues joined with the rational standpoint of the Socinians, the triumph of theism would be at hand.

Voltaire showed an interest in Socinianism and Unitarianism which, though less well known than his connection with the Quakers, was almost as long lasting.[12] That he considered these rationalist developments of Christianity to be virtually identical with theism we have

---

[12] starting with the seventh *Lettre philosophique* Voltaire often classes together Socinianism, Arianism and Unitarianism. In his writings Socinian and the other terms, although always indicating a 'liberal' and rational type of Christianity, tend to be used in two slightly different ways. On the one hand, they may have a purely militant connotation: for example the Unitarian view is used to criticise Baptism (*Dictionnaire philosophique* article 'Baptême', ed. Benda and Naves, pp.48-49), and the expression 'sociniens honteux' became a way of shaming the Genevese pastors who, in Voltaire's opinion, were afraid to admit their real beliefs. Nor was this usage limited to Voltaire's works: Zygmunt Jedryka ('Le Socinianisme et les lumières', *Studies on Voltaire* (1972), lxxxviii.823) tells us that: '*L'Encyclopédie*, plus encore que Voltaire, fait du socinianisme (article, "Unitaire") une référence et une caution rationaliste, "cartésienne" [...] et matérialiste.' On the other hand, some of Voltaire's references to Socinianism, especially those developing links between it and theism, can be regarded as constructive rather than purely critical: Socinianism appears to be a positive stage through which Christians may reach pure theism, and it is looked on with some favour for its own merits, irrespective of its convenience as a propaganda term to be used against Christianity's more traditional denominations.

already seen in connection with the Anabaptists (above, pp.39-41). The *Essai sur les mœurs* states the relationship explicitly and goes on to give a panegyric of the civilising work of theism. This passage, which dates from 1761, is worth quoting in full, as it will help to clarify Voltaire's religious position with regard to Quakerism (*Essai*, ii.687-88):

Ce théisme a fait depuis des progrès prodigieux dans le reste du monde. Le comte de Shaftesbury, le petit-fils du ministre, l'un des plus grands soutiens de cette religion, dit formellement, dans ses *Caractéristiques*, qu'on ne saurait trop respecter ce grand nom de théiste. Une foule d'illustres écrivains en ont fait profession ouverte. La plupart des sociniens se sont enfin rangés à ce parti. On reproche à cette secte si étendue de n'écouter que la raison, et d'avoir secoué le joug de la foi: il n'est pas possible à un chrétien d'excuser leur in-docilité; mais la fidélité de ce grand tableau que nous traçons de la vie humaine ne permet pas qu'en condamnant leur erreur on ne rende justice à leur con-duite. Il faut avouer que, de toutes les sectes, c'est la seule qui, en se trompant, ait toujours été sans fanatisme: il est impossible même qu'elle ne soit pas paisible. Ceux qui la professent sont unis avec tous les hommes dans le principe commun à tous les siècles et à tous les pays, dans l'adoration d'un seul Dieu; ils diffèrent des autres hommes en ce qu'ils n'ont ni dogmes ni temples, ne croyant qu'un Dieu juste, tolérant tout le reste, et découvrant rarement leur sentiment [. . .] du moins il n'y a eu jusqu'ici qu'un très petit nombre de ceux qu'on nomme *unitaires* qui se soient assemblés; mais ceux-là se disent chré-tiens primitifs plutôt que théistes.

Here then is Voltaire's ideal religion, rationalistic, universal, but unconcerned about public worship. There are resemblances with Quakerism, but also differences. The *trembleurs*, for instance, could hardly be said to have 'secoué le joug de la foi' since their religion was still firmly rooted in the Bible, though it gave great importance to the individual's interpretation of this authority. They had certainly not disturbed society, but it is doubtful whether Voltaire would have described them as completely 'sans fanatisme'. Finally, they did not hide their opinions, and like a small number of Unitarians, who are also qualified as 'chrétiens primitifs', one of Voltaire's normal appellations for the Quakers, they held assemblies.

It is not difficult to trace the progression in Voltaire's mind. The Quakers, though a Christian sect, and persisting in an 'enthusiastic' belief in direct divine inspiration, did not fall far short of his religious ideal, if judged by their good works: 'On peut, en parlant du nez et en se secouant, être doux, frugal, modeste, juste, charitable. Personne ne nie

que cette société de primitifs ne donnât l'exemple de toutes ces vertus.'[13]
The Socinians or Unitarians went one step further, and retained in their
religion only what was based on reason. To all intents and purposes, they
were virtually synonymous with pure theists, except that some Unitarians persisted in holding their assemblies. Why, then, we may ask, did
Voltaire not make use more often of the Socinian point of view in his
polemics against the established Church? The answer may be that the
Quakers provided more concrete and interesting figures in which to
embody his propaganda, and their virtue, well on the way to becoming
a legend, was generally acknowledged. Also, as we have just seen (above,
p.458, n.12), the term 'Socinian' had acquired militant connotations and
in certain works Voltaire may not have wished to use a word which
might create a purely negative impression and rule out any possibility of
rallying at least some Christians to a more rational form of theism.
Moreover, there was always the added advantage that Pennsylvania,
the Quaker utopia, could be cited in support of the argument for
tolerance. The *Profession de foi des théistes* (1768) makes quite clear,
however, that it was theism which was responsible for the happy tolerance of this American paradise. Voltaire either forgets, or intentionally
omits, the word Quaker, which does not occur in the following passage
(M.xxvii.71-72):

Puissent tous les gouvernements prendre pour modèle cette admirable loi
de la Pensylvanie, dictée par le pacifique Penn, et signée par le roi d'Angleterre Charles II,[14] le 4 mars 1681. 'La liberté de conscience étant un droit que
tous les hommes ont reçu de la nature avec l'existence, il est fermement
établi que personne ne sera jamais forcé d'assister à aucun exercice public
de religion. Au contraire, il est donné plein à chacun de faire librement exercice
public ou privé ou privé de sa religion, sans qu'on le puisse troubler en rien,
pourvu qu'il fasse profession de croire un Dieu éternel, tout-puissant,
formateur et conservateur de l'univers.

Par cette loi, le théisme a été consacré comme le centre où toutes les lignes
vont aboutir, comme le seul principe nécessaire. Aussi qu' est-il arrivé? la
colonie pour laquelle cette loi fut faite n'était alors composée que de cinq
cents têtes; elle est aujourd'hui de trois cent mille. Nos Souabes, nos Saltz-
bourgeois, nos palatins, plusieurs autres colons de notre basse Allemagne,
des Suédois, des Holstenois, ont couru en foule à Philadelphie. Elle est
devenue une des plus belles et des plus heureuses villes de la terre, et la métropole de dix villes considérables. Plus de vingt religions sont autorisées dans

[13] article 'Eglise' of the *Questions sur l'Encyclopédie* (1771) (M.xviii.498).
[14] who, we remember, Voltaire had claimed was a theist: cf. above, p.408.

cette province florissante, sous la protection du théisme leur père, qui ne détourne point les yeux de ses enfants, tout opposés qu'ils sont entre eux, pourvu qu'ils se reconnaissent pour frères.

Thus it would seem fairly clear that Voltaire was not particularly impressed by the Quaker belief in direct divine inspiration, and one must point out in fairness to professor Barber that he does not directly claim this in 'Voltaire and Quakerism'. Yet, although at one point (p.102) professor Barber states quite clearly that 'the real difference between the Quakers and Voltaire is between a spiritual or mystical and a purely intellectual conception', he nonetheless concludes (p.109) that 'the alliance derived, in spite of obvious divergences, from a deeper harmony: from a view of the world which was ultimately based on the individual's direct relationship to god, a relationship whose channels were reason and the moral sense, aspects of divinity to which man also had access'. Was there such a basic affinity between Voltaire and the Quakers, an affinity rooted in his conception of the relationship between God and man, an affinity of which Voltaire himself was not necessarily aware?

To answer this question we must review briefly the various statements Voltaire made regarding the God in which he claimed to believe. Such an exercise may enable us not only to elucidate Voltaire's affinities with the Quakers but also his relationship with other Protestant denominations and perhaps also the question of the genuineness of his belief. Spurred on by dr Besterman's warnings, I shall rely mainly on Voltaire's comments in his correspondence and on the marginalia to be found in the books he owned. The latter especially are unlikely to prove misleading as Voltaire surely had no reason to censor or hide his beliefs in such an intimate context.

First of all, one must repeat the by now banal observation that Voltaire's idea of God owed much to Newtonian science and its metaphysical framework.[15] Voltaire was convinced that the universe ran on regular, invariable, mechanistic lines, and his God provided a guarantee of the stability of the cosmos and of the validity of conclusions reached by human reason. However, the latter was strictly limited in scope, and not only a knowledge of God's attributes but also many

---

[15] in his article 'Newton and Voltaire: constructive sceptics', Martin Staum argues very convincingly the thesis that 'Newton's method and Newtonian natural theology together furnished Voltaire with evidence for the power of god and the limited, though significant capabilities of man' (p.30); cf. also Pomeau, *La Religion*, pp.190 ff.

scientific facts would always remain hidden from it.[16] Nonetheless, a certain number of truths could be discovered, even about God. The very order of the Universe proves that it was created by an intelligent being of some kind, hence the argument from design and final causes, so often invoked by Voltaire.[17] Some critics might claim that when Voltaire protested his belief in an intelligence behind nature, he was merely trying to disassociate himself from the scandal attached to d'Holbach and other atheistic *philosophes* associated with the baron. Letters to correspondents like prince Frederick William of Prussia (Best.D16958), mme Du Deffand (Best.D18511) and mme Necker (Best.D18537) would obviously fall into this category, but similar comments made to Diderot (Best.D17749), Grimm (Best.D16540) and mme d'Argental are less easy to dismiss. It appears that Voltaire's most faithful friend, d'Argental, was strongly attracted to the ideas put forward in *Le Système de la nature*,[18] and in a letter to his friend's wife Voltaire once more pointed out what he considered to be the flaws of d'Holbach's book. Why should he have taken the trouble to persuade a friend, whose loyalty was beyond question, had he not believed himself in the existence of God and the real harm done by atheism? These convictions are expressed unequivocally (Best.D17066):

il me paraît absurde de nier qu'il y ait une intelligence dans le monde. Spinosa lui même qui était bon géomètre est obligé d'en convenir. L'intelligence répandue dans la matière fait la base de son système. Cette intelligence est assurément démontrée par les faits, et l'opinion opposée de notre auteur me semble très antiphilosophique.

But of what nature was this intelligence, and could man have any contact with it? As Voltaire grew older he rejected the idea that matter had been created from nothing and came to regard the universe as an 'emanation' of God (see Pomeau, *La Religion*, p.413). The particular emphasis given by Voltaire to the relationship between God and nature distinguishes this belief from pantheism (Pomeau, p.414), but we are now a long way from the Christian teaching that God was completely separate from nature, which he created at a particular time. Another fundamental difference between Voltaire and Christians of whatever

---

[16] 'Dieu a dit à chaque homme, Tu pourras aller jusque là, et tu n'iras pas plus loin' (Best.D9484, Voltaire to Louis d'Aquin de Château-Lyon, 22 December 1760).

[17] a classic example is the article 'Fin, causes finales' of the *Dictionnaire philosophique*.

[18] 'Mr Dargental a donc toujours un grand goût pour ce système de la nature?' (Best. D17066, Voltaire to mme d'Argental, 9 March 1771).

denomination is in the importance given to man: in Voltaire's eyes the human being is a tiny, insignificant creature lost on an imperceptible speck of matter in the immensity of the universe. Yet this pygmy has imagined that everything was made for him. A comment in one of Voltaire's notebooks brings out the absurdity of man's presumption – here he reproduces the teaching of orthodox theology but transforms it into a 'Sermon prêché devant les puces': 'Mes chères puces, vous êtes l'ouvrage chéri de dieu; et tout cet univers a été fait pour vous. Dieu n'a créé l'homme que pour vous servir d'aliment, le soleil que pour vous éclairer, les étoiles que pour vous réjouir la vue, etc.' (Voltaire 81, p.349).

René Pomeau (*La Religion*, pp.213 ff., 414-16) has convincingly demonstrated Voltaire's tendency to exalt God at the expense of man. Before such immensity, all human affairs and concerns are of no account. As Voltaire told Fyot de La March on 19 May 1762:

la chaîne des évênements est immense, éternelle. Les acceptions de personnes, les faveurs et les disgrâces particulières ne sont pas faites pour une cause infinie; et dans la quantité prodigieuse de globes qui roulent les uns autour des autres par des loix générales, il serait trop ridicule que l'Eternel architecte changeât, et rechangeât continuellement les petits évênements de nôtre petit globule, il ne s'occupe ni de nos souris, ni de nos chats, ni de nos Jesuites, ni de vos flottes, ni même des tracasseries de vôtre Parlement.[19]

Prayer is not only presumptuous, but pointless: how could an infinite intelligence create laws which might subsequently be suspended, in other words will a thing and its opposite at different times?[20] Miracles are

[19] Best.D10457. Cf. *De l'âme* (M.xxix.341): if Nero murders his tutor and his mother, says Voltaire, 'cela n'est pas plus important pour l'Etre universel, âme du monde, que des moutons mangés par des loups, ou par nous, et des mouches dévorées par des araignées. Il n'y a point de mal pour le grand Etre; il n'y a pour lui que le jeu de la grande machine qui se meut sans cesse par des lois éternelles.'

[20] cf. the article 'Providence', which appeared in the *Questions sur l'Encyclopédie* in 1771: 'J'étais à la grille lorsque sœur Fessue disait à sœur Confite: "La Providence prend un soin visible de moi; vous savez comme j'aime mon moineau; il était mort si je n'avais pas dit neuf *Ave Maria* pour obtenir sa guérison. Dieu a rendu mon moineau à la vie; remercions la sainte Vierge."

'Un métaphysicien lui dit: "Ma sœur, il n'y a rien de si bon que des *Ave Maria* [...] mais je ne crois pas que Dieu s'occupe beaucoup de votre moineau [...] Si des *Ave Maria* avaient fait vivre le moineau de sœur Fessue un instant de plus qu'il ne devait vivre, ces *Ave Maria* auraient violé toutes les lois posées de toute éternité par le grand Etre; vous auriez dérangé l'univers"' (*Mélanges*, p.1307). Cf. a comment in one of Voltaire's notebooks: 'Prier dieu c'est se flatter qu'avec des paroles on changera toute la nature' (Voltaire 81, p.396).

excluded by the same argument.[21] The idea of providence too is absurd, unless we understand by this term the general arrangement of nature.[22] Anthropomorphic motives must not be attributed to God: our praise is meaningless to him.[23] By the same token, acts of martyrdom bearing witness to God are futile and unnecessary, however great the bravery of the individual concerned (cf. above, p.89). Finally, as if Voltaire is consciously turning upside down a basic idea of Christian belief, God is not love, he is incapable of love (see above, p.455).

Voltaire's scepticism over the soul is notorious, and it is quite clear from the correspondence of his last years that he disbelieved totally in the afterlife.[24] Such opinions are, of course, contrary to Christian teaching of whatever denomination, but in their absolute denial of a personal link between the individual and God, Voltaire's comments were probably even more shocking to a Protestant than to a Catholic. The Roman Church has always emphasised the necessary mediation of Church tradition, the sacraments and the priesthood, but in contrast Protestants, particularly Calvinists, have placed a direct relationship with the risen Christ at the very centre of a believer's spiritual life. The Biblical remark: 'even the hairs of your head have all been counted' (Matthew x.30) is indeed the antithesis of Voltaire's attitude. Nor must we assume that his reasoning is necessarily superior on this point to that of Protestants or Catholics. As regards prayer and miracles, divine

[21] on his copy of Houteville's *La Religion chrétienne prouvée par les faits,* beside the chapter heading 'Que les Miracles en général, & en particulier ceux de l'Evangile, sont possibles', Voltaire wrote: 'c'est a dire il est possible que dieu se contredise' (Edith Philips and Jean A. Perkins, 'Some Voltaire marginalia', *Studies on Voltaire* (1973), cxiv.39).

[22] cf. Best.D10457 (Voltaire to Fyot de La Marche, 19 May 1762): 'la providence particulière est entre nous une chimère absurde'; Best.D20588 (Voltaire to Mignot, 3 March 1777): 'Je m'abandonne à la providence universelle, n'aiant pas la hardiesse de croire à la particulière.' Cf. also Best.D16626.

[23] a passage in Pluquet's *Mémoires pour servir à l'histoire des égarements de l'esprit humain* drew forth the exclamation: 'sa gloire! comme si dieu ambitionnait d'être estimé!' ('Some Voltaire marginalia', p.70); a similar comment was made a few pages earlier. Bernard Nieuwentydt too caused Voltaire to express his ideas very clearly on this point; 'tu fais toujours dieu à ton image; tu veux que dieu soit comme un bourguemestre. Pouvons nous honorer Dieu?' (J. Vercruysse, 'La fortune de Bernard Nieuwentydt en France au xviiie siècle et les notes marginales de Voltaire', *Studies on Voltaire* (1964), xxx.223-46). Cf. also Havens, 'Voltaire's marginalia', pp.94, 109.

[24] cf. Best.D18607 (Voltaire to mme Du Deffand, 1 November 1773): 'Nôtre faculté de penser s'en ira bientôt comme notre faculté de manger et de boire. Nous rendrons aux quatre éléments ce que nous tenons d'eux, après avoir souffert quelque temps par eux, et après avoir été agités de crainte et d'espérance pendant les deux minutes de nôtre vie.' Cf. Best.D18333 (Voltaire to mme Necker, 23 April 1773).

intervention or suspension of the laws of nature at a particular moment might conceivably have been part of the divine plan from the beginning of time. Why must an infinitely intelligent being necessarily restrict itself to overseeing the physical laws of the universe? Presumably the moral laws governing its creatures are equally within its purview, and there is no contradiction involved in the belief that such an infinite being, once its existence is acknowledged, might concern itself with all its creatures, no matter how small or insignificant they may appear to us. Indeed this point brings us to what is apparently a major inconsistency in Voltaire's statements about God: how can a God who has no interest in man's affairs be regarded as the basis of human morality?

This contradiction is manifest in Voltaire's writings and cannot be discounted. On the one hand, the remoteness of God is emphasised tirelessly (Pomeau, *La Religion*, pp.213-16, 312),[25] yet equally often appears the argument that atheism is pernicious because it undermines the ethical beliefs on which human society is built,[26] thus establishing a direct link between human actions and the unapproachable deity. A belief in a God to whom human actions were no more significant than those of fleas would indeed be possible, and is in fact what many of Voltaire's statements would lead us to expect. With such a divinity, the ills of man's condition could be explained away by the immense gulf separating divine and human justice, and sometimes Voltaire appears to do this.[27] But how can such a position possibly square with his oft-repeated claims that there exists a universal moral law, common to all men and implanted in them by God?[28] If God is concerned only with the general laws of the universe and is incapable of love, why should he expend such care on an insignificant creature like man, unless the moral

[25] indeed J. L. Curtis ('La providence: vicissitudes du dieu voltairien', *Studies on Voltaire* (1974), cxviii.113) argues persuasively that Voltaire's deism passed through several stages, the influence he felt God had on human affairs becoming progressively more remote: 'la providence de 1722 garantissait un certain ordre; celle de 1772 ne garantit que celui que l'homme, en travaillant, est capable de se créer'.

[26] cf. the *Dictionnaire philosophique* article 'Athée, athéisme'; Best.D15189 (Voltaire to Villevielle, 26 August 1768): 'Mon cher Marquis, il n'y a rien de bon dans l'athéisme. Ce systême est fort mauvais dans le physique et dans le moral [. . .] Les hommes en seront-ils plus vertueux pour ne pas reconnaitre un Dieu qui ordonne la vertu? Non sans doute. Je veux que les Princes et leurs ministres en reconnaissent un, et même un Dieu qui punisse et qui pardonne. Sans ce frein je les regarderai comme des animaux féroces.'

[27] 'Quand sa Hautesse envoye un vaisseau en Egypte, s'embarrasse-t-elle si les souris qui sont dans le vaisseau sont à leur aise ou non?' (*Candide*, ed. Morize, p.222).

[28] cf. George R. Havens, 'The nature doctrine of Voltaire', *PMLA* (1925), xl.852-62.

465

law is in some way similar to the other laws governing the cosmos? Yet if this is so, surely God can no longer be said to be remote from man? And indeed, Voltaire fails to maintain the position suggested in the *conte Zadig*, that God's justice is inscrutable to human beings:[29] when he finds the argument expressed in a work uncongenial to him, his revolt is categorical. Thus, in reply to Pluquet's comment: 'Cette idée de la bonté humaine n'est pas applicable à la bonté de Dieu, qui pour être heureux n'a pas besoin, ni de l'existence ni de l'hommage de sa créature',[30] Voltaire wrote in his copy of the book: 'et comment veux-tu que nous jugions de la justice de Dieu autrement que par la notre?' ('Some Voltaire marginalia', p.70).

Another unavoidably jarring note is the presence of evil in a world supposedly created by a supreme being, and this theme is no more neglected in Voltaire's more private statements than it is in his published works. His marginalia are once again instructive in this respect, and Bernard Nieuwentydt's *L'Existence de dieu démontrée par les merveilles de la nature* inspired many interesting remarks. When the Dutch author states: 'il [God] est bon & les garantit *de tout accident facheux*', Voltaire exclaims in disgust: 'oh sot a t'il préserve d'accidents facheux douze millions d'americains egorgez le crucifix a la main, et la moitie des hommes massacres par l'autre?[31] Similarly, another remark by Nieuwentydt in connection with a 'fâcheuse maladie' calls forth the reflection: 'cela peut etre mais est ce là une preuve des bontés de Dieu!' (Vercruysse, 'La fortune de Bernard Nieuwentydt', p.239).

Critics like dr Besterman would no doubt have an answer to the apparent contradiction between Voltaire's belief in the remoteness of God and his contention that human morality is nonetheless implanted in man by this deity. Voltaire, it might be said, was insincere in the second part of this claim, merely seeking to strengthen social stability by the appeal to a 'dieu rémunérateur et vengeur'. And as regards God's function as divine organiser of the universe, this is no more than a metaphor, at best a convenient way of referring to the infinitely un-

[29] *Romans et contes*, ed. Bénac (Paris 1960), pp.55-57.

[30] Philips and Perkins, 'Some Voltaire marginalia', p.70; the work by Pluquet was the *Mémoires pour servir à l'histoire des égarements de l'esprit humain*.

[31] Vercruysse, 'La fortune de Bernard Nieuwentydt', p.238, Voltaire's underlining. Cf. also 'Some Voltaire marginalia', p.70; beside Pluquet's comment: 'L'idée de la souveraine bonté n'exige donc pas que Dieu fasse à ses créatures tout le bien possible', Voltaire wrote: 'non il ne peut pas faire des dieux tels que luy mais il pouvait faire des créatures heureuses. Tout le reste est un sophisme.'

knowable, a philosophical notion which is hardly to be confused with a belief in God as the term is normally understood. Yet it must be emphasised once more that, despite periods of profound scepticism, Voltaire's belief in a God who was at the very least an intelligence pervading and organising the universe never faltered. Thus, in his correspondence, we find him telling Frederick of Prussia (Best.D1320, *c.* 25 April 1737): 'Je ne crois pas qu'il y ait de démonstration proprement ditte, de l'existence de cet être indépendant de la matière', but a few years later, in a letter to 'S'Gravesande, he criticised Pascal for saying that he would not have had enough strength to convince atheists: 'Mais Clarke, Loke, Volf et tant d'autres ont eu cette force et assurément Pascal l'auroit eue' (Best.D2519, 1 August 1741). Similarly, on 12 October 1770, Frederick the Great was again the correspondent in whom Voltaire confided his doubts, when he confessed himself incapable of answering any of the following questions (Best.D16699): 'Y a-t-il un dieu tel qu'on le dit? une âme telle qu'on l'imagine? des relations telles qu'on les établit? Y a-t-il quelque chose à espérer après le moment de la vie?' Yet despite the doubts which could never satisfactorily be answered, Voltaire was not prepared to renounce his belief in God. Evil, pain, and misery there might be in the world, but when Nieuwentydt wrote that 'ce manque d'estime & de veneration pour le grand Créateur de toute chose, a été souvent la premiere pierre d'achoppement qui a fait broncher quelques personnes de ma connoissance, & qui a été cause ensuite de leur chute', Voltaire remarked scornfully: 'tu as donc connu de sottes gens car ils devaient conclure comme platon que Dieu est le grand et l'eternel geometre'.[32] And another passage of the same work inspired an even stronger comment: 'ce bavard donnerait envie d'etre athee, si on pouvait letre' ('La fortune de Bernard Nieuwentydt', p.238).

We must not forget, however, that Voltaire's ideas were far from static, and it is perhaps true to say that towards the end of his life the remote, architect God we have been discussing tends to be replaced by a deity corresponding more to the ideas of Malebranche and Spinoza. Might not a type of mystical contact be possible between man and a God who, like light, is present everywhere and even performs our actions for

---

[32] 'La fortune de Bernard Nieuwentydt', p.236. Beside the following passage: 'A présent, chacun étant contraint de reconnoître ici une puissance qui le préserve à tous momens d'une entière destruction, & que cette même Puissance agit selon les règles d'une sagesse merveilleuse, pouvons-nous nous dispenser d'attribuer cela à un Etre infiniment sage qui dirige tout?', Voltaire wrote quite simply: 'bon' (p.241).

us? Tempting though such an ingenious hypothesis may be, especially when argued by scholars like professor Barber and m. Pomeau, a negative answer must be given to this question. In the first place, any use of the word 'mystic' in connection with Voltaire would seem to be a profound misunderstanding. Without being unduly pedantic, one must point out that mysticism has usually been understood as a direct revelation of the godhead to an individual who has prepared himself for this experience through profound prayer and mortification and who has, in some cases, achieved the state called 'mystic marriage' with God.[33] The divine inspiration believed in by Quakers was of an essentially similar nature, in some respects sharing in the common heritage of other mystical movements.[34] But although Voltaire's effusions over the beauty of a sunrise (*La Religion de Voltaire*, pp.416-17) or his awed reverence before the star-covered night sky (pp.216-17) may indeed provide evidence that the religious dimension was not completely lacking in his character, they can hardly be considered as in any way parallel to genuine mystical experiences. Whether his belief was in a deity remote from man or in an all-present divine force, there is not the slightest real evidence to suggest that Voltaire thought any sort of direct contact with the divinity was feasible, even in the case of inspired sages like Socrates, Jesus, and Confucius. Such men, in propounding their religious teachings, merely followed the promptings of the natural law within them, interpreted by the reason which they shared, albeit to a heightened degree, with the rest of mankind. Thus, not only did Voltaire ridicule the ravings of Quakers who thought the Holy Ghost was speaking through them, he also differed significantly on an important point with the more refined ideas put forward by Robert Barclay.[35] Both Voltaire and the Quakers believed in a universal moral law implanted in man by God, they thought that human reason was in sympathy with this law and helped us to interpret it, but as regards their ideas of the nature of God, and the Quaker conviction that each man possessed Christ within him in the form of an Inner Light, a sort of appendage to reason and the conscience which enabled him to receive divine inspiration, they were surely poles apart.

It is possible to argue with Ronald Ridgway ('La propagande philosophique', pp.111-12) that the emotional side of religious experience

---

[33] *Oxford dictionary of the Christian Church*, *s.v.* 'Mysticism'.

[34] cf. Abbey and Overton, *The English Church in the eighteenth century*, i.564.

[35] for the most relevant of these ideas cf. Barber, 'Voltaire and Quakerism', pp.106-107.

normally lacking in Voltaire's writings ought perhaps to be sought in his plays and in the impassioned theatrical performances he himself delighted in giving. Another difference between his beliefs and those of the majority of Protestants and Catholics was that the notion of sin is meaningless for Voltaire,[36] although it is only fair to point out that some eighteenth-century Protestants, especially in Geneva, had already abandoned the notion of original sin (Masson, i.275). But there remains one major inconsistency in Voltaire's religious thought which in some respects he shares with traditional Calvinism and other Christian denominations: the problem of free will and determinism.

Voltaire's position on this matter is well known: in the 1730s he discussed the question in a celebrated correspondence with Frederick of Prussia, the Frenchman arguing that man did really possess free will and the prince championing determinism.[37] By the 1770s however, the rôles had been reversed,[38] and there is no question that Voltaire was totally committed to the sentiments he expressed. Once again his marginalia provide convincing proof of this. A comment made by Nieuwentydt provokes the exasperated remark: 'le hazard est un mot vide de sens',[39] and a passage from Pluquet's *Mémoires pour servir à l'histoire des égarements de l'esprit humain* calls forth the despairing inquiry: 'quest ce que liberte?' ('Some Voltaire marginalia', p.69).

I do not propose to discuss here the merits of Voltaire's deterministic beliefs, but one must observe that they cause his attitude toward Calvinism to appear unreasonable and inconsistent in at least one respect. For a man who wrote: 'comment peut-il y avoir quelque chose qui ne soit pas necessaire? dieu aurait donc fait l'inutile?' ('Some Voltaire marginalia', p.70), the actions of criminals and murderers must be conditioned absolutely by their environment, character, and the general arrangement of nature. Logically, such men can no more be criticised from a moral point of view than virtuous and self-sacrificing individuals can be praised for their noble actions. Neither group is capable of

---

[36] cf. a comment in one of Voltaire's notebooks: 'La vertu est ce qui est utile à la société. Le vice au contraire. Il y a vertu et vice, comme santé et maladie. Vertu qui ne produit rien est sottise' (Voltaire 82, p.611).

[37] cf. Ira O. Wade, *The Intellectual development of Voltaire* (Princeton 1969), pp.403-404.

[38] cf. Best.D17459 (Frederick to Voltaire, 18 November 1771): 'je me crois un être qui possède une liberté mitigée'.

[39] 'La fortune de Bernard Nieuwentydt', p.234. Cf. also p.237: apparently Voltaire underlined the word 'hasard' six times in eighteen lines.

behaving differently, and responsibility for one's conduct becomes a meaningless concept once it is conceded that no one has freedom to deviate one iota from nature's plan. The dilemmas posed by this position were not confined merely to Voltaire,[40] but what is important to note here is Voltaire's closeness to the Calvinist position. The latter thought that good works were not in themselves a proof of moral excellence and were of no avail in the individual's quest for salvation unless accompanied by faith, which was a gift of God's grace. As we have just seen, Voltaire's deterministic beliefs imply also that good deeds are no more a matter of choice than are bad deeds, and that logically, therefore, the former are no more praiseworthy than the latter are blameworthy. Certain actions may be more or less beneficial to society as a whole, but the terms 'good' and 'evil' are surely emptied of their traditional meaning once the concepts of free will and personal moral responsibility are abandoned. Thus, however much Voltaire might criticise the teaching that 'les bonnes œuvres ne valent pas un clou à souflet' and proclaim: 'Je ne suis point du tout de cet avis',[41] he was in fact deceiving himself. Indeed, in some ways his position is even more depressing than that represented by orthodox Calvinists. At least, according to the latter, apparently wicked men have just as much chance of receiving God's grace as those who seem good and virtuous, but no such escape is possible in Voltaire's scheme of things: the 'wicked' have been made thus by nature, and 'wicked' (or 'antisocial' or 'maladjusted') they may forever remain, since no direct intervention is to be expected from the remote and unapproachable author of the universe.

The implications of this belief are not only distressing on the individual level, they are also profoundly disturbing for society as a whole, and this, surely, is one of the factors which caused Voltaire to communicate to the masses very different religious concepts from those he held personally. Having attempted to uncover his private beliefs, I shall now conclude my study by trying to assess how far, in the religion he advocated publicly, he was prepared to compromise with Protestantism. A brief summary of Voltaire's opinions regarding the Protestant faith and its various denominations may be a useful preliminary.

---

[40] Diderot, for example, tried to avoid the problem by maintaining that man, although not free to act capriciously, was modifiable (cf. Arthur M. Wilson, *Diderot* (New York 1972), p.661).

[41] Best.D13932, Voltaire to Cardinal de Bernis, 9 February 1767; cf. above, p.74, n.59.

Conclusion

ii. *Voltaire and Protestantism: a temporary alliance*

There can be no serious doubt that Protestantism constitutes a major theme in Voltaire's works and correspondence, but his attitude toward it varies greatly. Sometimes it seems to be an ally in the good cause and a useful source of propaganda against *l'infâme*, for, with all its faults, Protestantism is a more rational form of Christianity than Catholicism. At other times, depressed by bigotry, intolerance, and what he sees as over-conservatism – a refusal to follow sound principles to their logical conclusions – Voltaire washes his hands of Protestantism and classes its more extreme denominations as part of *l'infâme*.[42]

This dichotomy is reflected in all his judgements. The Reformation was responsible for the advance of human reason, but this reflected no credit on the Reformers, whose overriding motive was a desire to dominate others, nor on the Protestants in general, who refused to apply reason, which they had used so commendably in attacking the abuses of the Catholic Church, to a study of the biblical basis of the Christian faith. As a historical event, the Reformation is explained mainly in non-religious terms, and no appreciation is shown of the immense spiritual need which it answered. For Voltaire, the morality of the Reformers was harsh and irrelevant to the real needs of society, and their theological speculations were as futile and meaningless as those of the Catholic doctors. Moreover, these doctrinal quibbles were the pretext for the wars and bloodshed which tormented Europe for the rest of the sixteenth century and after. Fanatical struggles over religion threatened the nascent development of learning and the arts, and put the Europeans on a lower level than savages. It would almost have been better if the Reformation had never taken place at all. Yet it had one redeeming feature which saved it in Voltaire's opinion: it had opened men's eyes to the necessity of their total independence from Rome and had thus inspired many beneficial advances in the social, political, and economic

---

[42] the nature of *l'infâme* is discussed by René Pomeau, who also reviews earlier definitions (*La Religion de Voltaire*, pp.324-25, especially p.315, n.8), and by Peter Gay (*Voltaire's politics*, pp.239 ff.). Pomeau's conclusion that 'en fin de compte, *l'infâme*, c'est le christianisme' would seem a little dogmatic, since, as we have seen, Voltaire did not completely condemn all Protestant denominations, and he was even willing to compromise with some on certain points. Surely *l'infâme* is a fluid concept, sometimes restricted merely to Catholicism or even to particular features of Catholicism, but on other occasions applied to Christianity as a whole or all organised religions, without it being possible to give any restrictive definition valid in every situation.

fields. Voltaire heatedly denied the Jesuit Nonotte's assertion that he was a Calvinist: 'il n'est pas plus pour Calvin que pour Ignace', he said of himself, but in reply he was able to state clearly and succinctly just what part of the Reformer's work he accepted:

Il ne fait pas plus de cas de Luther et de Calvin que du jésuite Le Tellier; mais il croit que Luther, Calvin, et les autres auteurs de la réforme, rendirent un grand service aux souverains en leur enseignant qu'aucun de leurs droits ne pouvait dépendre d'un évêque.[43]

Voltaire's personal experiences further coloured his attitudes to Protestantism in its various manifestations. The frustrations and disappointments of his relations with supposedly 'liberal' Swiss pastors, coupled with the resentment he felt at the Genevese government's interference with his theatrical performances, strengthened the distaste he had already conceived for Calvinism and its doctrines and set the seal on the subsequent scorn in which he held it. Sanctimonious, hypocritical and pleasure-hating, it was a form of *l'infâme* just as bad as, if not worse than papism. Geneva was saved from complete clerical domination only because its inhabitants were enlightened, would fight for their privileges, and would not allow their clergy to lead them blindfolded as priests in Catholic countries did. There was a minority of cultivated and progressive pastors in both Geneva and the pays de Vaud and with some of these men Voltaire maintained friendly contacts, but by and large he believed that, given the opportunity, Calvinist ministers would behave to their opponents just as Calvin had treated the unfortunate Servetus. Nor were the fruits of Calvinist intolerance restricted to Geneva. Holland too, the land which owed its existence to a desire for liberty, had condemned the doctrinally unorthodox Arminians, and the noble Barneveldt had been the victim of a revenge which was admittedly political, but which drew its justification from the Synod of Doordrecht and its contingent of Calvinist theologians.

The contemporary French religious situation enabled Voltaire to take a more favourable view of the Protestant Church in his own land. In the past it had been rebellious and fanatical, as one would expect of a Calvinist sect. But by the time of Louis XIV, the situation had changed and the repeal of the Edict of Nantes was a terrible blunder on the government's part. France exchanged the very real advantages of man-power and technical skill for the doubtful gain of professing only the

[43] *Eclaircissements historiques* (1763), M.xxiv.505.

king's faith, 'la religion catholique, apostolique et romaine'. Moreover, the policy was not even successful: it encouraged a disastrous outbreak of fanaticism among the Huguenots of the Cévennes, and was unable to change the religious beliefs of the majority of their brethren, whom officialdom so ironically persisted in calling *nouveaux convertis*. The situation as regards Protestant civil rights and disabilities was clearly intolerable, and Voltaire became keenly aware of the problem of the persecuted Huguenot minority, especially after the psychological and emotional shock provided by the Calas case. He intervened on behalf of many Protestants: galley-slaves, Huguenot travellers of various kinds, imprisoned pastors, and his efforts were particularly rewarded by the rehabilitations of Calas and Sirven. The question of Protestant marriages also preoccupied him, and although he appears to have been largely unaware of possible moves to effect a settlement of the problem in 1767, it is nonetheless certain that he worked out his own proposals which he forwarded to Richelieu in 1772, obviously hoping that these would influence the government and help to end a chaotic situation.

Sympathy for the social plight of the Huguenots did not imply a similar feeling toward their underground church. Large public assemblies of the sort the Protestants held *au désert* were dangerous, and the laws banning them were largely justified. Liberty to worship privately, in the home, should be enough for reasonable people – only fanatics of the populace would wish to persist in rebellious practices. Finally, the doctrinally static and spiritually declining Huguenot Church, whose numbers were in any case woefully inadequate, provided no solution for the future development of religion in France. Though many of its pastors were willing, indeed almost too willing, to listen to the philosophic message, their Church was too numerically weak and socially unrepresentative to be the vehicle for any important change. It was in the French Catholic Church that Voltaire's hopes lay. Anglicanism provided an example of what could be achieved within a national church which avoided both the superstitions of Catholicism and the excessive moral serverity of Calvinism. England also proved that an established Church, properly safeguarded by the law, was not threatened by the existence of rival, nonconformist sects, and toleration was seen to work despite the bogy of intersectarian hatred. One of the products of English toleration, the Quakers, exercised a life-long fascination over Voltaire. But while admiring the social virtues and above all the pacifism of the Friends, he rejected the irrational basis of their faith and finally preferred the more ordered structure of the Church of England, considering that it was necessary to retain a priesthood, provided it was suitably controlled. It would be a most desirable achievement if the Gallican Church could follow the course set by the Anglicans, free itself from Rome, and carry out some much-needed reforms which would benefit the whole country economically.

Yet although the Erastian Church of England could serve as a model for other enlightened countries and the credit for this necessarily reflected to some extent on Protestantism as a whole and on the legacy of the Reformation, the religious situation in many Protestant countries was by no means perfect yet: 'Le malade ne retrouve pas une santé parfaite, mais il vit dans un état tolérable à l'aide d'un régime sage' (M.xxiii.491). Indeed, the crux of Voltaire's attitude to Protestantism is that it needs a further Reformation to make it wholly reasonable, and in the *Remontrances du corps des pasteurs du Gévaudan* (1768) he represents the Protestants as desiring this themselves (M.xxvii.112):

Loin que la Suisse, Genève, la basse Allemagne, l'Angleterre, renoncent [. . .] au christianisme, tous ces pays, devenus plus éclairés, demandent un christianisme plus pur[. . .] On a fait une petite réforme au XVIe siècle; on en demande partout une nouvelle à grands cris. Le zèle est peut-être trop fort; mais on veut adorer Dieu, et non les chimères des hommes.

'Les chimères des hommes' – these are the lingering effects of clerical control, which must be stamped out. Even the Bible must now be judged by the standards of reason. After all, the *Entretiens chinois* (1768) make clear that the Protestants are superior to the Catholics mainly, if not entirely, in that they appear more reasonable. The Mandarin tells the Jesuit (M.xxvii.29):

Du moins les Européans d'Angleterre, de Hollande, de Danemark, et de Suède, ne nous disent pas que du pain n'est pas du pain, et que du vin n'est pas du vin; ne soyez pas surpris s'ils ont paru à la Chine et dans l'Inde plus raisonnables que vous.

Those features of Protestantism which are still illogical must be abolished: 'Les laïques sont instruits, et trop instruits aujourd'hui pour les prêtres [. . .] Ils croient qu'un homme ne peut pas avoir deux natures; ils croient que le péché originel fut inventé par Augustin' (M.xxvii.112). Already, in 1750, *La Voix du sage et du peuple* had gone further by suggesting that contemporary Protestantism had evolved from its origins and that the Reformers' message would no longer be of interest

474

to Voltaire's contemporaries: 'Si Luther et Calvin revenaient au monde, ils ne feraient pas plus de bruit que les scotistes et les thomistes. Pourquoi? Parce qu'ils viendraient dans un temps où les hommes commencent à être éclairés.'[44] The ninth of the *Pensées sur le gouvernement* (1756 edition) explains quite explicitly: 'La raison, en se perfectionnant, détruit le germe des guerres de religion. C'est l'esprit philosophique qui a banni cette peste du monde' (M.xxiii.525). Protestantism must show itself ready to follow reason as its only guide.

Were Protestants in fact to follow Voltaire's advice and advance even further along the path of reason, their faith would approximate more and more closely to the religion he wished to propound to the multitude and which he set forth in many of his propaganda works. It has often been demonstrated that there was a considerable difference between Voltaire's private beliefs and such utterances: his remote and largely intellectual deity was replaced by a much more positive figure, a 'dieu rémunérateur et vengeur' who would help to guarantee the moral stability of society.[45] Sometimes, as in the *Dictionnaire philosophique* article 'Athée', Voltaire quite openly states his position:

il me semble qu'il faut distinguer entre le peuple proprement dit et une société de philosophes au-dessus du peuple. Il est très-vrai que par tout pays la populace a besoin du plus grand frein, et que si Bayle avait eu seulement cinq à six cents paysans à gouverner, il n'aurait pas manqué de leur annoncer un Dieu rémunérateur et vengeur.[46]

Ronald Boss[47] has called this distinction a 'noble deceit', and has sought to show how the position of theistic *philosophes* like Voltaire and d'Alembert was inconsistent in some respects and that they themselves were not sure whether an artificial, state religion of the type they advocated could

---

[44] M.xxiii.468; cf. also the *Pensées sur le gouvernement*, M.xxiii.525.

[45] cf. Gay, *Voltaire's politics*, pp.263 ff.; Pomeau, *La Religion de Voltaire*, pp.399 ff.; Pomeau aptly calls this deity 'le Dieu gendarme des propriétaires' (p.545).

[46] *Dictionnaire philosophique*, ed. Benda and Naves, p.459; this section of the article first appeared in the *Questions sur l'Encyclopédie* in 1770.

[47] 'Rousseau's civil religion and the meaning of belief: an answer to Bayle's paradox', *Studies on Voltaire* (1971), lxxxiv.123-93. In this penetrating and illuminating article, Boss argues that such a religion, backed by the might of the state, would inevitably tend to threaten the toleration for which the *philosophes* had fought, affecting both atheists and Christians alike. This might even lead to the establishment of a civil religion akin to that described in Rousseau's *Contrat social*, where nonconformists would risk severe punishment. The position of Voltaire and d'Alembert would be doubly paradoxical were such a development ever to occur, for they did not even believe themselves in the religion whose adoption they advocated, a charge which could not be levelled at Rousseau.

really survive. Nonetheless, there is no doubt that such a reform was championed by Voltaire, and with such warmth and persistence that we must surely conclude that he was sufficiently convinced of its feasibility and necessity.[48] But my primary concern here is to establish what relation the existing Protestant religion might be expected to have with Voltaire's theism. I have already tried to show that Anglicanism provided a pattern for relations between Church and state which Voltaire thought could be adopted with profit in other countries.[49] And, as we have already seen, he appeared ready to make certain concessions to progressive Protestants. But was this a permanent development? Would the pact, if it came about, be anything more than a temporary alliance? If suitable reforms were made, was Voltaire prepared to throw in his lot with one of the more moderate forms of Protestantism and to admit that a reasonable *philosophe* could be reconciled with Christianity, if only for the practical advantages it secured? In other words, would he finally accept the plea made to him by the Genevese pastor Jacob Vernet, to respect the civic utility and social necessity of the Protestant religion? Genevese Calvinism was thoroughly and irrevocably discredited in Voltaire's eyes, but would he have been willing to respond to such an appeal if made on behalf of, say, the Anglican Church by a divine cast in the mould of the 'respectable Freind'?

Vous savez qu'il faut aux hommes une religion aussi bien qu'un gouvernement, et vous voyez que la nôtre est, par la grâce de dieu, si simple, si sage, si douce, si épurée, qu'un philosophe ne saurait en demander une plus raisonnable, ni un politique une plus convenable au bien public. Il ne faut donc pas l'ébranler, et autant il est digne d'un habile homme de couper les excrescences difformes, autant doit il prendre garde d'aller jusqu'au vif [. . .] Il serait, monsieur, bien satisfaisant pour nous de vous voir entrer dans nos vues.[50]

An answer to this question is already implied in the *Catéchisme de l'honnête homme* of 1763. Arguing, in a remarkably Protestant manner, that the reformed Churches are not a recent development[51] and are

---

[48] Voltaire's views on the reform of religion and its future are admirably expounded by René Pomeau (*La Religion de Voltaire*, pp.428 ff.).

[49] cf. the moderately favourable remarks he makes even in works like the *Examen important de milord Bolingbroke* (*Mélanges*, p.1022) and the *Lettre de milord Cornsbury à milord Bolingbroke* (M.xxvi.305).

[50] Best.D6146, 8 February 1755.

[51] 'Il me semble que la religion protestante n'est inventée ni par Luther ni par Zwingle. Il me semble qu'elle se rapproche plus de sa source que la religion romaine, qu'elle n'adopte que ce qui se trouve expressément dans *l'Evangile* des chrétiens, tandis que les Romains

nearer the spirit of the Gospel than are Roman Catholics, Voltaire once again stresses the social advantages of Protestantism: 'Les protestants réprouvent toutes ces nouveautés scandaleuses et funestes; ils sont partout soumis aux magistrats, et l'Eglise romaine lutte depuis huit cents ans contre les magistrats' (*Mélanges*, pp.667-68). He is certainly willing to make common cause with the Protestants against the Roman Church: 'Si les protestants se trompent comme les autres dans le principe, ils ont moins d'erreurs dans les conséquences, et, puisqu'il faut traiter avec les hommes, j'aime à traiter avec ceux qui trompent le moins' (p.668). This is praise, but praise which is distinctly limited. The Protestants may be better than the Catholics, but they are still deceivers. Any alliance Voltaire makes with them will be temporary and will be undertaken purely in order to make easier the eventual transition to theism. This process may not be effected rapidly, but it is nonetheless Voltaire's ultimate goal, for, despite his frequent pessimism regarding the uneducated masses, he asserts, in the second *Homélie prononcée à Londres* ('Sur la superstition'), that they are capable of being enlightened. The Reformation itself has shown this (*Mélanges*, p.1138).

On s'adresse aux peuples, et on leur parle, et, tout abrutis qu'ils sont, ils écoutent, ils ouvrent à demi les yeux; ils secouent une partie du joug le plus avilissant qu'on ait jamais porté; ils se défont de quelques erreurs, ils reprennent un peu de leur liberté, cet apanage ou plutôt cette essence de l'homme, dont on les avait dépouillés. Si on ne peut guérir les puissants de l'ambition, on peut donc guérir les peuples de la superstition.

Dieu et les hommes (1769) makes clear that the name of Christianity and its priesthood will be retained,[52] but the *Dîner du comte de Boulainvilliers* (1767) had already shown the sort of evolution Voltaire envisaged. Nothing specifically Christian, still less Protestant, would be left, except perhaps that which will linger for a while in the most superstitious part of the populace (*Mélanges*, p.1251):

Le mot de chrétien a prévalu, il restera; mais à peu près on adorera Dieu sans mélange, sans lui donner ni une mère, ni un fils; ni un père putatif, sans croire qu'on fasse des dieux avec de la farine, enfin sans cet amas de superstitions qui mettent des peuples policés si au-dessous des sauvages. L'adoration pure de l'Etre suprême commence à être aujourd'hui la religion de tous les honnêtes gens, et bientôt elle descendra dans une partie saine du peuple même.

ont chargé le culte de cérémonies et de dogmes nouveaux' (*Mélanges*, p.667).
[52] M.xxviii.238, 241.

Thus, despite a lifetime's interest in the Quakers and his qualified approval for the Anglicans, despite his friendly contacts with certain Protestant clergymen both in France and Switzerland, despite his fear of the atheistic ideas preached by d'Holbach and his followers, Voltaire's 'new sympathy with, at any rate some, aspects of Christianity',[53] does not seem to have been a stable or permanent development. For the *Histoire de l'établissement du Christianisme* (1776) is aimed at the common ground of all the Christian sects, and makes clear that what Voltaire desired most was the early introduction of a theism which, he asserted, had already been adopted by many of the crowned heads of Europe: (M.xxxi.114):

J'ose affirmer que toute la cour de l'empire russe, plus grand que la Chine, est théiste, malgré toutes les superstitions de l'Eglise grecque, qui subsistent encore.

Pour peu qu'on connaisse les autres cours du Nord, on avouera que le théisme y domine ouvertement, quoiqu'on y ait conservé de vieux usages qui sont sans conséquence.

The 'vieux usages qui sont sans conséquence' presumably refer to features of Protestantism, and the tone is very different now from the conciliatory one adopted in *Histoire de Jenni* of only the previous year. Voltaire goes on to assert that there are ten theists for every atheist 'parmi les gens qui pensent'. All representatives of the Christian faith are included in the final condemnation (M.xxxi.116):

Des fanatiques nous disent: Dieu vint en tel temps dans une petite bourgade: Dieu prêcha, et il endurcit le cœur de ses auditeurs afin qu'ils ne crussent point en lui; il leur parla, et il boucha leurs oreilles; il choisit seulement douze idiots pour l'écouter, et il n'ouvrit l'esprit à ces douze idiots que quand il fut mort. La terre entière doit rire de ces fanatiques absurdes, comme dit milord Shaftesbury; on ne doit pas leur faire l'honneur de raisonner; il faut les saigner et les purger, comme gens qui ont la fièvre chaude.

Voltaire expresses his pity for those who believe in Christianity, provided they avoid persecuting others, but it seems clear enough that he is not excepting the Protestants from those 'qui ont ainsi perverti leur raison'.

The future lay with theism, common father of all religions, and Protestantism, though useful as a temporary ally in the battle against a worse representative of superstition, was itself doomed to the same

[53] *L'Ingénu and Histoire de Jenni*, ed. Brumfitt and Davis, p.xl.

ultimate disappearance. 'J'ai fait plus en mon temps que Luther et Calvin' exclaimed Voltaire in 1768,[54] and the rivalry did not disappear. There was to be no half-hearted compromise with the enemy Voltaire had fought all his life. The Enlightenment would supersede, not complete, the Reformation.

[54] *Epître à l'auteur du livre des Trois imposteurs* (M.x.404).

Appendix 1

The Saurin affair and the Colloques of Lausanne, Vevey and Aigle

~~~~~~

i. *Extract from the minutes of the Colloque of Lausanne's meeting held on*
21 September 1758

Le V. Colloque s'est assemblè, Sous la Prèsidence de m. l'ancien Doyen DeCrousaz, Composè de mrs les Jurès Bournet, Langin & Actuaire Curtat, et de mrs les Pasteurs Vevey, Tholosan, Rivalier, Delavaux, Pavillard, Jaccaud, Secretan, Correvon, Rogguin, Curchod, Polier, Berther, Millot & Besson, en tout 18, qui ont donnè 10 [?] l'ècot du diner, exceptez mrs Delavaux, Vevey & Pavillard, ainsi reste 15£ pour la Bourse.

L'on a ouï avec édification le Sermon qu'a prononcè sur ephes.   , mr. le Pasteur DeBottens, lequel naiant traité qu'une partie de la matiére, s'est gracieusement offert à doñer la Suite au prochain ordinaire.

Rapport nous a été fait qu'on lisoit, dans la derniére Edition des œuvres de mr De Voltaire, à la Suite de l'article concernant Joseph Saurin, une dèclaration de mrs DeCrousaz, DeBottens et Pavillard, ainsi que Pasteurs de Lausanne, tendante à justifier le dᵗ Saurin des accusations quon avoit autrefois intentées contre lui. Puis les dits 3 Pasteurs Ils nous ont declarè navoir eu autre chose en vuë que de donner un tèmoignage purement nègatif, qui pût en quelque sorte servir à lever les obstacles qu'on mettoit a la fortune d'un jeune Saurin, dont on leur disoit beaucoup de bien; de n'avoir doné le dit tèmoignage qu'à la rèquisition d'un parent de ce jeune homme, & nullement sur celle de mr. De Voltaire; moins encore pour être placè en forme de preuve gènérale à larticle où il sert de conclusion. Sur quoi la plupart des membres du corps aiant dit quils avoient ouï parler de la lettre qui fut le sujet du dit témoignage: aiant même été rapporté quun ministre de la Classe avoit vü la lettre en Original: La Compagnie n'a pu, nonobstant toutes les raisons justificatives allèguèes par les dits Pasteurs de Lausanne, s'empêcher de trouver qu'il y a eu de la précipitation dans lèxpedition qu'ils ont faite de ce témoignage; ensuite de quoi elle avoit jugé, quant à eux, de leur adresser les divers avis qui pouvoient leur convenir à ce sujet; et, quant aux moyens de prevénir ou arrêter les conséquences qui pourroient rèsulter de l'abus que mr De Voltaire á fait, d'un tel acte, la d^e Compagnie avoit jugè que les d^{ts} 3 Pasteurs, 1º écriroient une lettre à mr. De Voltaire pour lui donner avis que, depuis la declaration qu'ils avoient donnée à lusage du jeune mr. Saurin, ils avoient eu occasion de voir, dans un de leurs Synodes ou Assemblées Ecclesiastiques, divers ministres qui avoient ouï parler de la lettre qui fait l'objet de d^t. déclaration (et si m. Chavanne Pasteur a montreux declare avoir vû l'original, on ajoutera) qu'il s'en trouvoit même encore un vivant de ceux qui ont vû la d^e lettre en Original, & que les droits de la verité èxigeoient d'eux qu'ils lui fissent parvenir cet avis, en le priant de le rendre public; ainsi quil l'avoit fait du premier. Qu'au surplus, ils avoient lieu de lui marquer leur juste surprise sur l'abus qu'il avoit fait de leur dit Acte; puisque, aulieu de se borner à le faire parvenir au particulier à l'usage duquel il étoit uniquement destinè, non seulement il l'avoit rendu public, mais encor & surtout il le faisoit servir de conclusion à un article qui renferme divers autres faits que la d^e lettre, & l'avançoit com̄e une preuve authentique de l'article tout entier; quainsi il semble vouloir les faire conclurre eux mêmes, par la place quil a donnée a leur d^e acte, non seulement à la non existence de la lettre, mais même à la fausseté de toutes les autres Imputations contenues en d^t article contre la personne de Joseph Saurin.

2º Que les dits Pasteurs feroient parvenir aux editeurs des divers Journaux une copie de cette lettre ou une dèclaration qui y soit rèlative, pour la rendre publique; après avoir soumis l'une et l'autre de ces pièces à lexamen du Colloque qui pourra y apporter les changemens qu'il jugera convenables; et qu'à ce dèfaut, le Corps mēme prendra le fait en main.

Sur quoi les d^{ts} 3 Pasteurs, aiant dècliné le Tribunal & mēme refusé de se retirer pour doñer lieu à nos délibèrations sur ce fait, a eté connu que toute cette affaire seroit soumise a l'examen des 2 autres V. Colloques pour en decider, ou qu'elle sera portée devant la V. Classe pour en juger plus outre. Et, sur ce que mr. De Bottens a allégué que la raison pour la quelle il ne vouloit pas se soumettre à notre jugement, étoit que mr. le Jurè Bournet avoit prèsidè en ce fait sans vocation & d'une manière irréguliére, il a ete unanimement coñu qu'àu contraire le d^t Reverend Jurè, ainsi que [?] Jurè, n'avoit rien fait qui ne fūt dans la Règle.

Notre Compagnie a encore appris avec une vive douleur que lon avoit inséré dans la Bibliothèque Impartiale, Tome XVII page 136, un article comme venant de Berne & contenant des Imputations calomnieuses à la charge des ministres du Païs de Vaud, aux quels on attribue de ne plus precher J. C, ni les articles fondamentaux de l'Evangile: Surquoi, a eté delibéré quon aviseroit aux moyens d'enlever l'Impression que de telles Imputation pourroient avoir faites & sur LL.EE. N.SS. [i.e. the Bernese authorities] & sur le Public, en faisant parvenir aux editeurs de ce Journal une déclaration pure & simple, faite au nom de tous les ministres de notre Classe, et meme des autres V. Classes lesquelles, On invitera à se joindre à nous, par laquelle on s'inscrira en faux contre de telles Imputations.

ii. *Extract from the minutes of the Colloque of Vevey's meeting held on 4 October 1758*

Quant à l'article inserè dans la Bibliothèque Impartiale Tome XVII page 136, il a etè connu qu'on ècriroit à LL EE., p^r leur tèmoigner notre surprise, et nôtre indignation sur les fausses et odieuses imputations dont il charge les ministres de la Suisse Romande.

Lecture ayant etè faite de l'article d'une nouvelle Edition des oeuvres de Voltaire (Joseph Saurin) suivi d'un Certificat souscrit de Messrs DeCrousaz, DeBottens, et Pavillard, nous avons vû avec douleur les choses scandaleuses et impies dont le dit article est rempli; Quant au Certificat qui suit, donnè par les susdits, coῆe Pasteurs de Lausanne, nous approuvons ce qui en a dèja etè deliberè par le ven: Coll: de Laus: dont ils sont membres, à cela près, qu'il nous paroît suffire que ces 3 Messrs fassent insèrer dans les Journaux un dèsaveu formel de l'usage que Mr Voltaire a fait de leur Certificat, en le mettant à la suitte d'un article, même en confirmation de tout ce qui y est contenu; Dèclarans etre dans des sentimens bien oposès; le dit article contenant entre'autres un fait qu'ils savent manifestement ètre faux, savoir que Saurin ait etè emprisôné côme Pasteur Apostat; Dèclarans en particulier qu'ils detestent les impietes contenues dans le dit article.

2° à cette ocasion, il nous a paru que les 3 susdits Pasteurs doivent ètre exhortès à etre à l'avenir plus circonspects dans l'expèdition de leurs Certificats, la facilitè qu'ils ont à cet ègard leur faisant perdre du poids qu'ils devroient avoir.

3° Il a etè rèsolu qu'on leur tèmoigneroit que l'on a vû et qu'on verroit encore plus, avec chagrin leur trop grande liaison avec un persônage aussi dangereux que Voltaire, et dont les Discours et les Ecrits sur la Rèligion sont si peu menagès.

iii. *Extract from the minutes of the Colloque of Aigle's meeting held on October 11 1758*

VI. Lecture ayant été faite d'un article que Monsr De Voltaire a ajouté dans la Nouvelle Edition de son Histoire Universelle touchant *Joseph Saurin*, Pasteur apostat de l'Eglise de Bercher, & Academicien de Paris, & de l'usage que le dit Voltaire a fait d'un témoignage de Messrs les Pasteurs de Lausanne, DeCrousaz, Polier, & Pavillard, concernant le dit Saurin, & inseré pour conclusion du dit article; on a jugé à propos de suspendre toute déliberation à ce sujet jusqu'au Colloque prochain du Printems.

VII. Quant à un article des nouvelles Litteraires du prémier bimestre [?] de la Bibliothèque Impartiale *1758* sous le titre de Berne, qui accuse le Clergé Protestant françois de la Suisse d'enseigner une morale payeñe, & de suprimer dans leurs prédications les dogmes fondamentaux du Christianisme; on a pris cette matiére importante *ad referendum*, afin d'y aviser d'autant plus meûrement.

Appendix 2

References in the definitive edition of Voltaire's correspondence to the Calas and Sirven cases

I do not claim that this is a completely exhaustive list, since not all Voltaire's references to these two affairs are clear (in most cases for reasons of prudence). Nonetheless, I think the reader of the correspondence will find it a useful guide and is unlikely to discover many supplementary references. Letters *to* Voltaire are printed in *italics*, and those letters where Calas or Sirven are mentioned in the commentary are denoted by the letter c.

a. *letters containing references to the Calas case (1762-1765)*

1762	*D10439c*	*D10537*	D10571	D10616	D10648
D10382	*D10443*	D10538	D10573	D10617	D10651
D10386	D10445	D10539	D10581	D10619	D10654
D10387	D10446	*D10540*	*D10582*	D10620	*D10655*
D10389	D10449	D10542	D10584	D10621	D10658
D10390	*D10455*	D10545	D10585	*D10622*	D10665
D10391	D10460	D10546	D10586	D10623	D10666
D10394	*D10472*	D10550	D10587	D10624	D10667
D10398	D10481	D10551	D10588	D10626	*D10669*
D10402	D10489	D10552	D10593	*D10628*	D10671
D10403	D10490	D10553	*D10595*	D10630	D10672
D10404	D10493	D10554	D10597	D10632	D10673
D10405	D10496	D10555	D10603	D10634	D10674
D10406	D10500	D10559	D10604	D10635	D10675
D10412	D10501	D10563	D10605	D10636	*D10677*
D10414	D10504	D10564	D10606	D10637	*D10679*
D10417	D10505	*D10565*	D10607	D10638	D10680
D10419	D10508	D10566	D10609	D10639	D10683
D10427	D10509	D10567	D10613	D10642	D10685
D10428	D10519	D10568	D10614	D10645	D10686
D10436	D10526	D10569	D10615	D10647	D10689

D10690	D10794	D10907	D11037	D11121	*1764*
D10691	D10795	*D10914*	D11038	*D11124*	D11633
D10692	D10797	D10920	D11040	D11128	D11648
D10697	D10802	D10922	D11042	D11134	D11650
D10698	*D10805*	D10923	*D11044*	D11135	D11666
D10702	D10810	D10924	D11046	D11140	D11668
D10703	D10822	D10925	D11052	D11141	*D11685*
D10704	D10827	D10927	D11057	D11142	D11697
D10705	*D10829*	D10929	D11060	D11143	D11700
D10707	*D10830c*	D10933	D11063	*D11145*	D11709
D10712	D10831	D10934	D11069	*D11146*	D11710
D10718	D10833	D10937	D11070	D11148	D11715
D10719	D10835	D10939	D11072	D11151	D11722
D10720	D10838	D10940	D11073	D11167	D11726
D10721	D10849	D10942	D11074	D11169	D11730
D10723	D10851	D10943	D11078	D11187	D11747
D10731	D10856	D10953	*D11080*	D11193	D11748
D10734	D10860	D10954	*D11081*	D11211	D11751
D10746	D10862	D10957	D11085	D11228	D11787
D10747	D10863	D10958	D11087	D11277	D11901
D10749	*D10864*	D10960	D11088	D11278	D11902
D10750	*D10867*	D10962	D11090	D11286	*D11907*
D10752		D10963	D11092	*D11304*	D11912
D10758		D10966	D11093	D11305	D11917
D10760	*1763*	D10971	D11094	D11307	D11918
D10762	D10874	D10980	D11096	D11328	D11919
D10763	D10875	D10982	D11097	D11342	D11923
D10764	D10876	D10989	D11098	D11347	D11927
D10768	D10877	*D10997*	D11099	D11379	*D11928*
D10769	D10878	D10999	D11100	D11432	D11930
D10771	D10879	D11001	D11102	D11436	D11947
D10772	D10885	D11004	D11103	D11468	D11950
D10775	D10890	D11005	D11107	D11470	*D11953*
D10776	D10893	D11008	D11110	D11488	D11954
D10782	D10895	D11009	D11111	D11510	D11955
D10786	D10896	D11018	D11112	D11546	D11987
D10788	D10899	D11021	D11114	D11553	D12002
D10789	D10902	D11029	D11116	D11556	D12038
D10790	D10906	D11031	D11117	D11557	

D12040	D12468	D12505	D12555	D12623	D12892
D12112	D12469	D12506	*D12556*	D12638	D12905
	D12470	D12508	D12559	D12639	*D12913*
1765	D12471	D12511	D12560	D12642	D12915
D12318	D12472	D12515	D12561	D12644	D12923
D12385	*D12475*	D12516	D12562	D12645	D12932
D12400	D12476	D12518	D12564	*D12651*	D12938
D12411	D12477	D12519	D12565	D12802	D12948
D12419	D12478	D12520	*D12566*	*D12807*	D12965
D12420	D12479	D12522	D12567	*D12822*	D12969
D12421	D12481	*D12526*	D12568	D12829	*D12970*
D12425	D12482	D12529	*D12569*	D12834	D12972
D12426	D12483	D12530	D12573	D12839	D12973
D12438	D12484	D12532	*D12575*	D12845	D13007
D12440	D12485	D12535	D12580	D12846	*D13018*
D12444	*D12486*	D12536	D12581	D12848	D13030
D12445	D12491	*D12540*	D12586	D12855	D13031
D12448	*D12496*	*D12541*	D12590	D12868	*D13032*
D12454	D12497	D12542	D12598	*D12872*	*D13049*
D12457	D12498	D12543	D12602	D12873	D13066
D12459	D12499	D12544	D12606	*D12880*	*D13072*
D12460	D12500	D12552	D12613	D12884	
D12462	D12503	D12554	D12618	D12885	

b. letters containing references to the Sirven case (1763-1770)

1763	D12421	D12498	D12559	D12602	D12813
D11096	D12425	D12500	D12560	D12606	D12825
D11097	D12426	D12501	D12563	D12618	D12873
D11098	D12438	D12503	D12564	D12623	D12902
	D12444	D12508	D12565	D12638	D12905
1764	D12445	D12511	*D12566*	D12639	D12911
D11660	D12448	D12516	D12567	D12642	*D12912*
D11697	D12459	D12532	D12568	D12644	D12916a
D11706	D12462	D12535	D12573	D12645	D12923
D11713	D12471	D12536	*D12575*	D12654	D12938
D11748	D12484	*D12541*	D12581	D12802	D12969
	D12486	D12543	D12586	D12810	D13003
1765	D12491	*D12556*	D12598	D12812	D13007
D12419					

D13014	D13342	D13468	D13594	*1767*	D14073
D13031	D13348	D13469	D13596		D14082
D13059	D13356	D13472	D13599	D13787	D14084
D13066	D13360	D13476	D13604	D13792	D14085
	D13364	D13483	D13606	D13843	D14086
1766	D13365	D13486	D13608	D13851	D14092
D13118	D13366	D13487	D13619	D13858	D14094
D13147	D13367	D13495	D13620	D13885	D14096
D13148	D13369	D13501	D13629	D13886	D14097
D13150	D13370	D13502	D13635	D13888	D14109
D13151	D13371	D13503	D13644	D13909	D14110
D13152	D13375	D13504	D13661	D13913	D14117
D13155	D13381	D13508	D13669	D13916	D14119
D13156	D13388	D13511	D13672	D13918	D14121
D13158	D13391	D13512	D13677	D13933	D14123
D13159	D13392	D13513	D13687	D13934	D14128
D13163	D13402	D13516	D13695	D13936	D14143
D13164	D13405	D13519	D13696	D13957	D14161
D13169	D13407	D13525	D13705	D13966	D14177
D13176	D13411	D13528	D13707	D13968	D14185
D13182	D13415	D13532	D13713	D13970	D14186
D13199	D13420	D13533	D13719	D13977	D14196
D13200	D13422	D13538	D13720	D13994	D14197
D13206	D13428	D13540	D13722	D13997	D14209
D13212	D13431	D13546	D13727	D13998	D14213
D13219	D13433	D13550	D13735	D14002	D14215
D13232	D13435	D13551	D13744	D14014	D14217
D13271	D13436	D13558	D13746	D14015	D14222
D13278	D13437	D13560	D13747	D14016	D14223
D13281	D13438	D13562	D13750	D14018	D14224
D13289	D13441	D13569	D13752	D14024	D14225
D13295	D13443	D13570	D13754	D14034	D14233
D13302	D13449	D13573	D13758	D14052	D14235
D13307	D13450	D13585	D13759	D14053	D14237
D13308	D13455	D13586	D13764	D14059	D14242
D13314	D13460	D13587	D13778	D14062	D14246
D13326	D13463	D13589	D13783	D14069	D14252
D13329	D13464	D13592		D14070	D14254
D13340	D13465	D13593		D14071	D14256

D14268	D14643	*1769*	D15828	D16014	D16254
D14299	D14653		D15829	D16015	D16305
D14300	D14659	D15406	D15831	D16016	D16306
D14331	D14662	D15411	D15834	D16017	D16311
D14337	D14668	D15414	D15843	D16018	D16350
D14399	D14673	D15430	D15852	D16028	D16359
D14431	D14676	D15444	D15855	D16033	D16378
D14443	D14697	D15448	D15862	D16034	D16430
D14445	D14700	D15464	D15867	D16035	D16448
D14449	D14719	D15466	D15868	D16038	D16464
D14471	D14720	D15472	D15870	D16039	D16499
D14472	D14721	D15485	D15873	D16042	D16523
D14474	D14723	D15490	D15891	D16052	D16554
D14500	D14725	D15499	D15897	D16053	D16717
D14506	D14729	D15504	D15903	D16060	D16779
D14530	D14730	D15508	D15907		D16806
D14553	D14738	D15570	D15908	*1770*	D16817
D14562	D14741	D15585	D15909	D16072	D16872
D14582	D14756	D15600	D15914	D16082	
D14587	D14762	D15607	D15915	D16086	
D14615	D14763	D15626	D15916	D16096	
D14618	D14765	D15683	D15917	D16109	
D14620	D14806	D15685	D15931	D16148	
D14623	D14842	D15688	D15948	D16152	
D14627	D14891	D15743	D15955	D16176	
	D14945	D15747	D15957	D16194	
1768	D14948	D15774	D15995	D16195	
D14635	D15008	D15812	D15999	D16196	
D14640	D15124	D15814	D16013	D16244	

Appendix 3

Protestant reaction to the *Traité sur la tolérance* and the identity of the
pastors consulted during its preparation.

We have already seen (above, p.295) that Paul Rabaut was somewhat
suspicious of Voltaire's intentions, and some other French Protestants
reacted fairly strongly against the *Traité*. On 6 February 1763 Pierre
Encontre (a *pasteur du désert*) wrote to the same Paul Rabaut:

A propos de livres, comment trouvez-vous celui que M. de Voltaire vient
de donner au public sur la tolérance? Pour moi, qui l'ai lu fort à la hâte, j'y
ai trouvé bien du bon. Mais que de poison mêlé! Et qu'il est à craindre que le
plus grand nombre, jugeant de la valeur de cet ouvrage par l'incrédulité
qu'y manifeste son auteur, ne l'improuvent entièrement, et qu'ainsi sans
produire aucun bien, il ne produise le mal d'inspirer du mépris pour nos
livres saints et pour la religion qui y est enseignée.[1]

Who, then, were the ministers who had been consulted about the
work? Coquerel (ii.338-39) again gives us the answer. 'L'influence
protestante s'enhardit un moment jusqu'au point de supposer qu'elle
pourrait peut-être guider l'esprit de Voltaire', he tells us ingenuously:
'voici ce que le pasteur Chiron, retiré à Genève, et qui avait des rapports
avec Ferney, écrivait sur le même ouvrage: "L'ouvrage de M. de Voltaire
est bien avancé et il a été communiqué à deux de mes amis particuliers,
MM. Moultou et Vernet [*sic*]. Ces messieurs y ont trouvé des traits bien
vifs et bien saillants contre la persécution, des réflexions et des raisonnements admirables, mais beaucoup aussi qui peuvent offenser et aigrir les
esprits. Ces messieurs ont fait le voyage de Ferney pour l'engager à
changer ou à retrancher ces traits piquants. Il a promis de refondre
l'ouvrage; je ne sais pas s'il tiendra parole; c'est un homme entêté,
abondant en son sens, qui ne se plie pas au conseil des autres."'
Vernet is obviously a slip for Vernes, as it is quite inconceivable that
Voltaire should ask advice on any subject from Jacob Vernet, with whom

---

[1] *Correspondance Paul Rabaut*, Bib pf, quoted by Coquerel, ii.338; cf. also Best.
D11571.

he had been at loggerheads since 1757 (see above, pp.173-77). Vernet and Jacob Vernes, his younger contemporary, have often been confused (cf. the current British Library catalogue). If Vernes and Moultou were indeed the ministers to whom Voltaire had submitted the *Traité* (and there seems little doubt that they were – Voltaire obviously discussed the work with Moultou at the beginning of 1763: cf. Best.D10877, D10885, D10897), the mystery becomes much clearer. These two gentlemen were hardly orthodox, even by eighteenth-century standards: cf. above, pp.177-83, 198-204.

Appendix 4

Le Siècle de Louis XIV: additions to and alterations of chapter 36 ('Du calvinisme au temps de Louis XIV')

∗∗∗

GUSTAVE Lanson's article 'Notes pour servir à l'étude des chapitres 35-39 du *Siècle de Louis XIV* de Voltaire'[1] and René Pomeau's edition of Voltaire's *Œuvres historiques* enable us to assess, with some degree of accuracy, whether revisions made by Voltaire for the 1768 edition of his works were affected by his supposed knowledge of the activities of Gilbert de Voisins's commission on Huguenot civil rights which was carrying on its work in 1766 and 1767 (see above, pp.333-52).

Lanson records the changes which occurred in five editions of the *Siècle*: those of 1752 (Bengesco 1185), 1757 (Bengesco 1163), 1763-1764 (Bengesco 1164), the Moland edition and Emile Bourgeois's edition (Paris 1906). His conclusions are sometimes disputed by Pomeau, and this will be indicated as appropriate. There would appear to be six passages relevant to our investigation, and I propose firstly to give the text of the Kehl edition (reproduced by both Bourgeois and Pomeau), then to indicate what additions or alterations this text shows when compared with earlier versions. In this way I hope to make clear how, if at all, Voltaire changed the emphasis in his chapter, and whether such changes as were made have any connection with the Gilbert de Voisins report.

1. Bourgeois, p.688; Pomeau, p.1043:

Le presbytérianisme établit en Ecosse, dans les temps malheureux, une espèce de république dont le pédantisme et la dureté étaient beaucoup plus intolérables que la rigueur du climat, et même que la tyrannie des évêques qui avait excité tant de plaintes. Il n'a cessé d'être dangereux en Ecosse que quand la raison, les lois et la force l'ont réprimé.

This passage does not appear in the 1752 and 1757 versions (Lanson, p.173).

[1] (Strasbourg 1924), pp.171-95.

2. Bourgeois, p.705; Pomeau, p.1054:

Paris ne fut point exposé à ces vexations; les cris se seraient fait entendre au trône de trop près. On veut bien faire des malheureux, mais on souffre d'entendre leurs clameurs.

Lanson (p.174) says that the second sentence of this paragraph did not appear in the 1752 and 1757 versions, and Pomeau states that it was added in 1761 (*Oh*, p.1724).

3. Bourgeois, p.710; Pomeau, p.1056:

On défendit aux calvinistes, en 1685, de se faire servir par des catholiques, de peur que les maîtres ne pervertissent les domestiques; et l'année d'après, un autre édit leur ordonna de se défaire des domestiques huguenots, afin de pouvoir les arrêter comme vagabonds. Il n'y avait rien de stable dans la manière de les persécuter, que le dessein de les opprimer pour les convertir.

This paragraph does not appear in the 1752 and 1757 editions (Lanson, p.174).

4. Bourgeois, p.711; Pomeau, p.1057:

dans la guerre de 1701 la rébellion et le fanatisme éclatèrent en Languedoc et dans les contrées voisines.
    Cette rébellion fut excitée par des prophéties. Les prédictions ont été de tout temps un moyen dont on s'est servi pour séduire les simples, et pour enflammer les fanatiques. De cent événements que la fourberie ose prédire, si la fortune en amène un seul, les autres sont oubliés, et celui-là reste comme un gage de la faveur de Dieu et comme la preuve d'un prodige. Si aucune pré-diction ne s'accomplit, on les explique, on leur donne un nouveau sens: les enthousiastes l'adoptent, et les imbéciles le croient.
    Le ministre Jurieu fut un des plus ardents prophètes. Il commença par se mettre au-dessus d'un Cotterus, de je ne sais quelle Christine, d'un Justus Velsius, d'un Drabitius, qu'il regarde comme gens inspirés de Dieu. Ensuite il se mit presque à côté de l'auteur de l'*Apocalypse* et de saint Paul. Ses partisans ou plutôt ses ennemis, firent frapper une médaille en Hollande, avec cet exergue: *Jurius propheta*. Il promit la délivrance du peuple de Dieu pendant huit années. Son école de prophétie s'était établie dans les montagnes du Dauphiné, du Vivarais et des Cévennes, pays tout propres aux prédictions, peuplé d'ignorants et de cervelles chaudes, échauffées par la chaleur du climat et plus encore par leurs prédicants.
    La première école de prophétie fut établie dans une verrerie, sur une montagne du Dauphiné appelée Peira. Un vieil huguenot [...]

Most of this passage was missing in the 1752 and 1757 versions, which read:

dans la guerre de 1701 la rébellion et le fanatisme éclatèrent en Languedoc et dans les contrées voisines. Il y avait déjà longtemps que dans les montagnes des Cévennes et du Vivarais, il s'élevait des inspirés et des prophètes. Un vieil huguenot [...]

Lanson (p.174) claims that the change was made in 1763, but Pomeau (*Oh*, p.1724) says that the two paragraphs 'furent ajoutés dans 61'.

5. Bourgeois, p.713; Pomeau, p.1058:

En effet, il [Claude Brousson] avait formé projet d'introduire des troupes anglaises et savoyardes dans le Languedoc. Ce projet, écrit de sa main, et adressé au duc de Schomberg, avait été intercepté depuis longtemps, et était entre les mains de l'intendant de la province. Brousson, errant de ville en ville, fut saisi à Oleron et transféré à la citadelle de Montpellier. L'intendant et ses juges l'interrogèrent: il répondit qu'il était l'apôtre de Jésus-Christ, qu'il avait reçu le Saint-Esprit, qu'il ne devait pas trahir le dépôt de la foi, que son devoir était de distribuer le pain de la parole à ses frères. On lui demanda si les apôtres avaient écrit des projets pour faire révolter des provinces; ou lui montra son fatal écrit, et les juges le condamnèrent tout d'une voix à être roué vif. (1698) Il mourut comme mouraient les premiers martyrs. Toute la secte, loin de le regarder comme un criminel d'Etat, ne vit en lui qu'un saint qui avait scellé sa foi de son sang; et on imprima le martyre de M. de Brousson.

In 1752 and 1757, according to Lanson, 'on trouve seulement, avec de fortes différences de rédaction, les trois lignes: *Il mourut ... de son sang*' (p.174).

6. Bourgeois, p.716; Pomeau, p.1060:

Le roi envoie d'abord le maréchal de Montrevel avec quelques troupes. Il fait la guerre à ces misérables avec une barbarie qui surpasse la leur.

Lanson (p.174) states that in 1752 and 1757 the phrase 'avec une barbarie qui surpasse la leur' read 'comme ils méritaient qu'on la leur fît', but Pomeau (*Oh*, p.1725) claims that all versions before the Kehl edition contained the latter phrase.

Only three of the six passages I have mentioned (nos 2, 3 and 6) appear to show some measure of sympathy for the Huguenots. No. 2 would at first sight seem to be most significant in the present context, since in its expression and content it bears some resemblance to *L'Ingénu*. None-theless, Pomeau's statement that it was added in 1761 rules out fairly conclusively any possible connection between this minor revision and the events of 1766-1767. Similarly, passage no. 3, which is in any case fairly neutral in tone, appears to have been added well before 1768, since Lanson records it as missing in only the 1752 and 1757 versions of *Le Siècle*. This comment is substantially true of passage no. 6 also, since although the change made shows more sympathy for the Huguenots, there is some disagreement about when the alteration was actually made. On the other hand, three of the passages I have quoted give clear evidence of Voltaire's continuing hostility to certain aspects of Protestantism: passage no. 1 illustrates his dislike of the moral austerity of Calvinism; passage no. 4, added in the early 1760s, emphasises his detestation of Protestant fanaticism in the Camisard uprising; and passage no. 6 deals with the Huguenots' rebellious activities.

When these two sets of passages are compared, it becomes obvious that the additions and alterations made by Voltaire to this chapter of *Le Siècle*, far from making it generally more sympathetic to the Huguenots, tend, if anything, to stress those features of Protestant history which Voltaire found distasteful or discreditable. There appears to be no evidence that Voltaire revised the work for the 1768 edition in a way designed to make public opinion more favourable to projected reforms in favour of the Protestants.

Appendix 5

A possible source for the Anglican clergyman Freind

⚜

WE have already seen (above, p.445) that Jenni's father may have been modelled partly on the historical dr John Freind and that Voltaire's admiration for Samuel Clarke may have inspired some of his qualities. But evidence also exists that his acquaintance with at least one enlightened Anglican prelate had been renewed about the time he was probably writing *Histoire de Jenni*. Frederick Hervey, fourth earl of Bristol and bishop of Derry from 1768 to 1803, visited Voltaire on several occasions (see *Voltaire's British visitors*, pp.97-98; William S. Childe-Pemberton, *The Earl bishop* (London 1924), pp.83, 104, 271), the first occasion apparently being in July 1765 (*Voltaire's British visitors*, p.97). In their critical edition of *Histoire de Jenni*, Brumfitt and Davis state that it is not certain why Voltaire chose to give the narrator the name of Sherloc: 'However, he may have been thinking of Thomas Sherlock (1678-1761) who became Bishop of London and played a prominent part in the controversy against the deists' (p.130). Yet it seems more likely that Voltaire was in fact referring to Martin Sherlock, who became bishop Hervey's chaplain and who had an interview with Voltaire in 1776. According to Sherlock's *Lettres d'un voyageur anglois* (Geneva 1779), this meeting gave evidence of the high regard in which Voltaire held Hervey, as the following comments show:

Sherlock: Vous avez connu Milord Chesterfield?
Voltaire: Oui, je l'ai connu; il avait beaucoup d'esprit.
Sherlock: Vous connaissez Milord Hervey?
Voltaire: J'ai l'honneur d'être en correspondance avec lui.
Sherlock: Il a des talens.
Voltaire: Autant de brillant que milord Chesterfield, et plus de solidité.[1]

Hervey was one of the few enlightened Church of Ireland bishops of the eighteenth century, praised by Catholics and Dissenters alike: in

---

[1] Sherlock, *Lettres*, p.140, quoted in Childe-Pemberton, *The Earl bishop*, p.271.

1774 he 'procured the introduction into the Irish Parliament of the first Catholic Relief Act, which enabled Catholics to declare their loyalty to the Crown without disavowing their spiritual allegiance to Rome' (M. A. McN. and P. J. R., *Downhill and the Mussenden Temple* (The National Trust Committee for Northern Ireland 1968), p.10). Contact with an ecclesiastic such as this can only further have strengthened Voltaire's favourable opinion of the Church of England, and it was perhaps an additional influence in the genesis of Freind's character. For further information on Hervey's activities in the field of toleration see John R. Walsh, *Frederick Augustus Hervey, 1730-1803, fourth earl of Bristol, bishop of Derry, 'Le Bienfaiteur des Catholiques'* (Maynooth 1972).

List of works cited and consulted

For list of abbreviations used see above, p.12.

i. Manuscripts

Geneva. Bibliothèque publique et universitaire. Mss. Suppl. 517. Correspondance de G.-L. Lesage.
—Mss. Suppl. 1537-1540. Lettres de Jean-Louis Du Pan à Abraham Freudenreich.
Lausanne. Archives cantonales. Bdb 53, Bdb 102, Bdb 111A (*Registres* of various *Classes* and *Colloques* of the pays de Vaud).
Paris. Archives nationales. TT.463 (Gilbert de Voisins and the preparation of his report). U.873 (documents concerning the Protestants of Alsace). O¹ 459, fs 9-11 (letter to Choiseul concerning Protestant assemblies).
—Bibliothèque de l'histoire du protestantisme français. Collection Co-querel. Papiers Rabaut. 318 (letters from Rabaut to Gébelin). 392 Correspondance d'Antoine Court, de Court de Gébelin et des professeurs du séminaire de Lausanne avec un comité de pasteurs wallons de Hollande (1734-1797), et autres pièces concernant les églises du Désert. 886 Lettres échangées entre Boudon de Clairac et le maréchal de Bellisle au sujet d'un projet de banque protestante.
—Bibliothèque nationale. Fonds Joly de Fleury 476. Pièce 5870. Pièce 5871. Lettres pattentes portant confirmation du Mariage contracté à hambourg, entre le [...] baron d'Espagnac, et la d.ᵉ Damaris his, fille d'un protestant.

ii. Printed works

'A Mrs les éditeurs, à l'occasion d'un article concernant Saurin, inséré dans les œuvres de mr. D.V.', *Journal helvétique*. Neuchâtel (October 1758), pp.361-82.

Abbey, Charles J., and Overton, John H., *The English Church in the eighteenth century*. London 1878.

Adams, Geoffrey, 'Myths and misconceptions: the philosophe view of the Huguenots in the age of Louis xv', *Historical reflections* (1974), i.69.

Aldridge, Alfred Owen, 'Benjamin Franklin and the philosophes', *Studies on Voltaire* (1963), xxiv.43-65.

Allamand, François-Louis, *L'Anti-Bernier, ou Nouveau dictionnaire de théologie*. n.p. 1770.

[Allamand, François-Louis], *Lettres sur les assemblées des Religionnaires en Languedoc*. Rotterdam 1745.

Antoine, Michel, *Le Conseil du roi sous le règne de Louis XV*. Geneva 1970.

Arnaud, Ernest, 'La jeunesse des trois fils de Paul Rabaut', *Bpf* (1879), xxviii.528-38.

'Aux éditeurs, à l'occasion d'un Article inséré dans la *Bibliothèque impartiale* sur l'état de la Religion dans la Suisse Françoise', *Journal helvétique*. Neuchâtel (November 1758), pp.501-15.

Bachaumont, Louis Petit de, *Mémoires secrets pour servir à l'histoire de la république des lettres depuis 1762 jusqu'à nos jours*. London 1777-1789.

Baldensperger, F., 'Voltaire et la diplomatie française dans les "affaires de Genève"', *Rlc* (1930), pp.581-606.

Barber, W. H., *Leibniz in France from Arnauld to Voltaire: a study in French reactions to Leibnizianism, 1670-1760.* Oxford 1955.

—'Voltaire and Quakerism: Enlightenment and the inner light', *Studies on Voltaire* (1963), xxiv.81-109.

—'Voltaire and Samuel Clarke', *Studies on Voltaire* (1979), clxxix.47-61.

Basnage, Jacques, *Instruction pastorale aux Réformés de France sur la persévérance dans la foi et la fidélité pour le souverain.* Rotterdam 1719.

Bayle, Pierre, *Dictionnaire historique et critique.* 11th ed. Paris 1820.

Beaumont, chevalier de, *L'Accord parfait de la nature et de la raison, de la révélation et de la politique, ou Traité dans lequel on établit que les voyes de rigueur, en matière de religion, blessent les droits de l'humanité et sont également contraires aux lumières de la raison, à la morale évangélique et au véritable intérêt de l'Etat, par un gentilhomme de Normandie, ancien capitaine de cavalerie au service de S.M.* Cologne 1753.

Beer, sir Gavin de, and Rousseau, André-Michel, *Voltaire's British visitors,* Studies on Voltaire (1967), lxix.

Benoît, Daniel, *Du caractère huguenot et des transformations de la piété protestante.* Paris 1892.

—*L'Etat religieux du protestantisme français dans la seconde moitié du XVIIIe siècle.* Montauban 1909.

—*Les frères Gibert, deux pasteurs du Désert et du Refuge.* Toulouse 1899.

—'Les pasteurs et l'échafaud révolutionnaire: Pierre Soulier de Sauve (1743-1794)', *Bpf* (1894), xliii.561-94.

—'Les premiers missionnaires moraves en France', *Revue chrétienne* (1901), pp.827-47.

Berthoud, Charles, 'Les deux Bertrand', *Musée neuchâtelois* (1870), vii.53-64.

—*Les quatre Petitpierre, 1707-1790.* Neuchâtel 1875.

Bertrand, Elie, 'A Mr. Luzac &c. à Leide', *Journal helvétique.* Neuchâtel (February 1759), pp.198-200.

Besnard, Philippe, *Protestantisme et capitalisme: la controverse post-Weberienne.* Paris 1970.

Besterman, Theodore, *Voltaire.* London 1970.

—'Voltaire's god', *Studies on Voltaire* (1967), lv.27-41.

Bibliothèque de Voltaire: catalogue des livres, ed. M. P. Alekseev and T. N. Kopreeva. Moscow, Leningrad 1961.

Bien, David D., *The Calas affair: persecution, toleration and heresy in eighteenth-century Toulouse.* Princeton 1960.

Boislisle, A. de, *Mémoires authentiques du maréchal de Richelieu (1725-1757).* Paris 1918.

Bonet-Maury, G., 'Le rétablissement du culte protestant dans le Queyras (1774-1810)', *Bpf* (1907), lvi.371-87.

Boss, Ronald Ian, 'Rousseau's civil religion and the meaning of belief: an answer to Bayle's paradox', *Studies on Voltaire* (1971), lxxxiv.123-93.

Boullier, D. R., *Lettres sur les vrais principes de la religion, où l'on examine le livre intitulé: 'La religion essentielle à l'homme'.* Amsterdam 1741.

Bouvier, Bernard, 'Notes inédites de Voltaire sur la *Profession de foi du vicaire savoyard*', *Annales de la Société Jean-Jacques Rousseau* (1905), i.272-84.

Bruford, W. H., *Germany in the eighteenth century: the social background to the literary revival.* Cambridge 1953.

Brumfitt, J. H., 'History and propaganda in Voltaire', *Studies on Voltaire* (1963), xxiv.271-87.

—'Voltaire and Warburton', *Studies on Voltaire* (1961), xviii.35-56.

—*Voltaire historian.* London 1958.

Budé, Eugène de, *Vie de Jacob Vernet, théologien genevois (1698-1789).* Lausanne 1893.

Calmettes, Pierre, *Choiseul et Voltaire.* Paris 1902.

Caussy, Fernand, 'Voltaire pacificateur de Genève', *Revue bleue* (1908), ix.9-15.

—*Voltaire seigneur de village.* Paris 1912.

Caveirac, Jean Novi de, *Apologie de Louis XIV et de son conseil, sur la révocation de l'édit de Nantes* [. . .] *avec une dissertation sur la journée de la s. Barthélemi.* n.p. 1758.

Ceitac, Jane, *Voltaire et l'affaire des Natifs: un aspect de la carrière humanitaire du patriarche de Ferney.* Geneva 1956.

Cellérier, J.-E., *L'Académie de Genève: esquisse d'une histoire abrégée de l'académie.* Geneva 1872.

Chadwick, Henry, *The Early Church:* vol.i of *The Pelican history of the Church.* Harmondsworth 1967.

Chadwick, Owen, *The Reformation:* vol.iii of *The Pelican history of the Church.* Harmondsworth 1964.

Champendal, Edouard, *Voltaire et les protestants de France.* Geneva 1919.

Chaponnière, Paul, 'Un pasteur genevois ami de Voltaire: Jacob Vernes', *Rhl* (1929), xxxvi.181-201.

—*Voltaire chez les calvinistes.* Geneva 1932.

Chapuisat, Edouard, *Figures et choses d'autrefois.* Paris 1920.

Chauffepié, Jacques-Georges, *Nouveau dictionnaire historique et critique, pour servir de supplément ou de continuation au Dictionnaire historique et critique de Pierre Bayle.* Amsterdam, The Hague 1750-1756.

Chavannes, J., 'Une école libre de théologie des temps passés: notes historiques sur le séminaire protestant français à Lausanne', *Le Chrétien évangélique* (1872), xv.33-45, 73-88, 119-30, 168-81.

Childe-Pemberton, William S., *The Earl Bishop.* London 1924.

Claparède, David, *Considérations sur les miracles de l'Evangile pour servir de réponse aux difficultés de mr*

J.-J. Rousseau dans sa 3e Lettre écrite de la montagne. Geneva 1765.

Clarke, Samuel, *The Works of Samuel Clarke, D. D. late rector of St James's Westminster.* London 1738.

Coquerel, Charles, *Histoire des églises du Désert.* Paris 1841.

Correspondance littéraire, ed. M. Tourneux. Paris 1877-1882.

Court, Antoine, *Histoire de la restauration du protestantisme en France au XVIIIe siècle,* ed. Edmond Hugues. Paris 1872.

—*Le Patriote françois et impartial, ou réponse à la lettre de mr l'évêque d'Agen à mr le controleur général contre la tolérance des huguenots, en date du 1er mai 1751.* Villefranche 1753.

—*Lettre d'un patriote sur la tolérance civile des protestans de France et sur les avantages qui en résulteroient pour le royaume.* n.p. 1755.

Court de Gébelin, Antoine, *Les Toulousaines ou lettres historiques et apologétiques en faveur de la religion réformée* [. . .]. Edimbourg [Lausanne] 1763.

Cragg, Gerald R., *The Church and the age of reason, 1648-1789:* vol.iv of *The Pelican history of the Church.* Harmondsworth 1960.

Cross, F. L., ed., *Oxford dictionary of the Christian Church.* London 1958.

Crowley, F. J., 'Pastor Bertrand and Voltaire's "Lisbonne"', *Mln* (1959), lxxiv.430-3.

Curtis, J. L., 'La providence: vicissitudes du dieu voltairien', *Studies on Voltaire* (1974), cxviii.9-114.

Dardier, Charles, *Esaïe Gasc, citoyen de Genève, sa politique et sa théologie.* Paris 1876.

—*La Vie des étudiants au désert d'après la correspondance de l'un d'eux, Simon Lombard.* Paris 1893.

—'Lettres écrites par divers pasteurs au sujet des églises réformées de France', *Bpf* (1869), xviii.333-44.

—'Paul Rabaut', *Bpf* (1883), xxxii.461-79.

—*Un procès scandaleux à propos d'un mariage au désert (1774)*. Geneva 1886.

—'Voltaire agissant en faveur des protestants en 1754', *Bpf* (1883), xxxii.528-9.

Dedieu, Joseph, *Histoire politique des protestants français (1715-1794)*. Paris 1925.

—*Le Rôle politique des protestants français, 1689-1715*. Paris 1920.

Delattre, André, 'Voltaire and the ministers of Geneva', *Church history* (1944), xiii.243-54.

Den Heuvel, Jacques van, 'Voltaire, Genève et l'affaire Calas', *Bpf* (1978), cxxiv.518-22.

Desnoiresterres, Gustave, *Voltaire et la société française au XVIIIe siècle*. Paris 1867-1876.

Dez, Pierre, *Histoire des protestants de l'église réformée de l'Ile de Ré*. La Rochelle 1926.

Dickens, A. G., *Reformation and society in sixteenth-century Europe*. London 1966.

Dübi, Heinrich, 'Altmann, Voltaire und Haller', *Blätter für bernische Geschichte, Kunst und Altertumskunde* (1909), v.255-64.

—'Der Briefwechsel zwischen Voltaire und Haller im Jahre 1759', *Archiv für Studium der neueren Sprachen und Literaturen* (1910), cxxiii.353-86.

Du Cailar, Emile, and Benoît, Daniel, *Gal-Pomaret, pasteur de Ganges. Son temps, son ministère, ses écrits*. Paris 1899.

Dufour, Edouard, *Jacob Vernes (1728-1791): essai sur sa vie et sa controverse apologétique avec J.-J. Rousseau*. Geneva 1898.

Dumont, Paul, 'Jean-Elie Bertrand (1713-1797)', *Revue de théologie et de philosophie* (1905), xxxviii.217-69.

Durand, Charles, *Histoire du protestantisme français pendant la Révolution et l'Empire*. Paris 1902.

Elton, G. R., *Reformation Europe 1517-1559*. London, Glasgow 1963.

Estrée, Paul d', *Le Maréchal de Richelieu (1696-1788)*. Paris 1917.

—*La Vieillesse de Richelieu*. Paris 1921.

Fabre, Marcel, 'Voltaire et Pimpette de Nîmes', *Mémoires de l'Académie de Nîmes*, 7th ser. (Nîmes 1933-1935), i.XLI-LXIX.

Falguerolles, G.-E. de, 'La Tour de Constance dans la lutte pour le rétablissement des libertés de pensée et de réunion', *Bpf* (1968), cxiv.173-291, 533-37.

—'Les prisonnières de la Tour de Constance', *Bpf* (1970), cxvi.382-420.

—'Tour de Constance et galères', *Bpf* (1970), cxvi.232-43.

Falletti, N. Charles, *Jacob Vernet, théologien genevois (1698-1789)*. Geneva 1885.

Fargher, R., *Life and letters in France: the eighteenth century*. London 1970.

Félice, G., and Bonifas, F., *Histoire des protestants de France*. Paris 1850.

Félice, Paul de, *Les Protestants d'autrefois*. Paris 1898.

Ferguson, J. P., *An eighteenth-century heretic: dr Samuel Clarke*. Kineton 1976.

—*The Philosophy of dr Samuel Clarke and its critics*. New York 1974.

Ferrier, Jean-Pierre, 'Covelle, Voltaire et l'affaire de la génuflexion', *Bulletin de la Société d'histoire et d'archéologie de Genève* (1946), viii.217-25.

—*Le Duc de Choiseul, Voltaire, et la création de Versoix-la-ville*. Geneva 1922.

Fitchett, W. H., *Wesley and his century*. London 1925.

Florida, R. E., *Voltaire and the socinians*, Studies on Voltaire (1974), cxxii.

Foulet, Lucien, 'Voltaire en Angleterre', *Rhl* (1908), xv.119-25.

—'Le voyage de Voltaire en Angleterre', *Rhl* (1906), xiii.1-25.

Frossard, Ch.-L., *L'Orthodoxie et l'Eglise réformée de France: lettres des pasteurs de Nîmes sur l'affaire Gasc en 1812*. Paris 1864.

Gaberel, Jean-Pierre, *Voltaire et les Genevois*. Paris, Geneva 1857.

Gagnebin, Bernard, 'Voltaire a-t-il provoqué l'expulsion de Rousseau de l'île Saint-Pierre?', *Annales de la Société Jean-Jacques Rousseau 1943-1945* (1947), xxx.111-31.

Gal-Pomaret, Jean, *Catéchisme sous une forme nouvelle, ou le catéchumène instruit et admis à la sainte communion, par m. Gal-Pomaret, pasteur de Ganges*. Neuchâtel 1779.

—*Le Bon père ou le Chrétien protestant*. Neuchâtel 1783.

Galland, Elie, *L'Affaire Sirven*. Mazamet 1911.

Galliani, R., ed., 'Les notes marginales de Voltaire au *Dictionnaire philosophique*', *Studies on Voltaire* (1976), clxi.7-18.

Gargett, G., 'Voltaire et l'affaire Saurin', *Dix-huitième siècle* (1978), x.417-33.

—'Voltaire, Gilbert de Voisins's *Mémoires* and the problem of Huguenot civil rights (1767-1768)', *Studies on Voltaire* (1978), clxxiv.7-57.

—'Voltaire, Richelieu and the problem of Huguenot emancipation in the reign of Louis xv', *Studies on Voltaire* (1979), clxxvi.97-132.

Gay, Peter, *The Party of humanity: studies in the French Enlightenment*. London 1954.

—'Voltaire's *Idées républicaines*: a study in bibliography and interpretation', *Studies on Voltaire* (1958), vi.67-105.

—*Voltaire's politics: the poet as realist*. Princeton 1959.

Gembicki, Dieter, 'La Réforme allemande vue par Voltaire', pp.148-155 of *Historiographie de la Réforme*. Paris, Neuchâtel, Montreal 1977.

Gilbert de Voisins, Pierre-Paul, *Mémoires sur les moyens de donner aux Protestans un état civil en France Composé de l'ordre du roi Louis XV. Par feu m. Gilbert de Voisins, Conseiller d'Etat*. n.p. 1787.

Goltz, baron Hermann von der, *Genève religieuse au XIXe siècle, ou tableau des faits qui, depuis 1815, ont accompagné dans cette ville le développement de l'individualisme ecclésiastique du réveil. ... Traduit de l'allemand ... par C. Malan-Sillen*. Geneva 1862.

Grasset, François, ed., *Guerre littéraire ou choix de quelques pièces de m. de V... avec les réponses. Pour servir de suite et d'éclaircissement à ses ouvrages*. n.p. 1759.

Grenier-Fajal, O. de, *Rochette et les trois frères Grenier*. Montauban 1886.

Grimsley, R., *Jean d'Alembert (1717-83)*. Oxford 1963.

Grosclaude, Pierre, *La Vie intellectuelle à Lyon dans la deuxième moitié du XVIIIe siècle*. Paris 1933.

—*Malesherbes: témoin et interprète de son temps, 1721-1794*. Paris 1961.

—'Une négociation prématurée: Louis Dutens et les protestants français, 1775-1776', *Bpf* (1958), civ.73-93.

Grubenman, Yvonne de Athy de, *Un cosmopolite suisse: Jacques Henri Meister*. Geneva 1954.

Guéhenno, Jean, *Jean-Jacques: grandeur et misère d'un esprit*. 2nd ed. Paris 1962.

Guimps, Roger de, *Elie Bertrand d'Yverdon*. Yverdon 1855.

Haag, E., and E., *La France protestante*. 10 vols. 1846-1858. 2nd ed. (to 'G'). 6 vols. 1877-1888.

Hastings, James, ed., *Encyclopedia of religion and ethics*. Edinburgh, Newcastle 1908-1926.

Havens, George R., 'The nature doctrine of Voltaire', *PMLA* (1925), xl.852-62.

—*Voltaire's marginalia on the pages of Rousseau*. Ohio 1933.

Havens, George R., and Torrey, Norman L., 'The private library of Voltaire at Leningrad', *PMLA* (1929), xliii.990-1009.

—'Voltaire's books: a selected list', *Mp* (1929), xxvii.i-22.

—ed., *Voltaire's catalogue of his library at Ferney*, Studies on Voltaire (1959), ix.

Henry, P., 'A different view of Voltaire's controversial *Tout en dieu*'. *Studies on Voltaire* (1975), cxxxv.143-50.

Houteville, Claude François, *La Religion chrétienne prouvée par les faits*. Paris 1722.

Huber, Marie, *Lettres sur la religion essentielle à l'homme*. n.p.1729.

Hugues, Edmond, 'Un épisode de l'histoire du protestantisme au xviiie siècle', *Bpf* (1877), xxvi.289-303, 33-7 50.

Jedryka, Zigmunt, 'Le socinianisme et les lumières', *Studies on Voltaire* (1972), lxxxviii.809-29.

Joutard, Philippe, ed., *Journaux camisards (1700-1715)*. Paris 1965.

Kamen, Henry, *The Rise of toleration*. World University Library 1967.

La Beaumelle, Laurent Angliviel de, *Préservatif contre le déisme, ou instruction pastorale de m. Dumont, ministre du Saint-Evangile, à son troupeau, sur le livre de m. J.-J. Rousseau*, intitulé Emile ou de l'éducation. Paris 1763.

Labrousse, Elisabeth, 'Note à propos de la conception de la tolérance au xviiie siècle', *Studies on Voltaire* (1967), lvi.799-811.

La Morandière, Denis-Laurian Turmeau de, *Principes politiques sur le rappel des protestans en France*. Paris 1764.

Lanson, Gustave, 'Notes pour servir à l'étude des chapitres 35-39 du *Siècle de Louis XIV* de Voltaire', *Mélanges offerts à m. Charles Andler* (Strasbourg 1924), pp.175-95.

—*Voltaire*. Paris 1910.

Launay, Michel, 'Jean-Jacques Rousseau, écrivain politique', *Au siècle des Lumières* (Ecole pratique des hautes études et Institut d'histoire universelle de l'Académie des sciences de l'U.R.S.S. 1970), pp.77-136.

—*Jean-Jacques Rousseau: écrivain politique (1712-1762)*. Grenoble 1971.

Lee, J. Patrick, 'Voltaire and César de Missy', *Studies on Voltaire* (1976), clxiii.57-72.

Léonard, Emile-G., 'Economie et religion: les protestants français au xviiie siècle', *Annales d'histoire sociale* (1940), pp.5-20.

—*Histoire du protestantisme*. Paris 1950.

—*Histoire ecclésiastique des réformés français au XVIIIe siècle*. Paris 1940.

—*Histoire générale du protestantisme*. Paris 1961-1964.

—'Le problème du culte public et de l'Eglise dans le protestantisme au xviiie siècle', *Foi et vie* (1937), pp.431-57.

—*Le Protestant français*. Paris 1953.

—*Problèmes et expériences du protestantisme français*. Paris 1940.

Lesage, G., *A travers le passé du Calvados*. Caen 1927.

'Lettre à Monsieur *** au sujet de l'Extrait des Registres de la Vénérable Compagnie des pasteurs et professeurs de l'Eglise et de l'Académie de Genève, inséré dans le Journal des Sçavans, édition de Hollande, p.400 et 521', *Bibliothèque impartiale* (1758), xvii.366-82.

'Lettre de Pierre de Claris à Antoine Court', *Bpf* (1885), xxxiv.71-82.

Ligou, Daniel, *Documents sur le protestantisme montalbanais au XVIIIe siècle*. Toulouse 1955.

—'Essai d'interprétation psychologique des événements de septembre 1761 à Caussade', *Congrès régional des Fédérations historiques du Languedoc* (Carcassonne May 1952), pp.169-75.

—'Sur le protestantisme révolutionnaire à propos d'un ouvrage recent, *Bpf* (1958), civ.23-52.

Ligou, Daniel, and Joutard, Philippe, 'Les Déserts (1685-1800)', chapter 5 (pp.189-262) of Robert Mandrou, Janine Estèbe, Daniel Ligou, and others, *Histoire des protestants en France*. Toulouse 1977.

Lods, Armand, 'Court de Gébelin et la représentation des Eglises réformées auprès du gouvernement de Louis xv (1763-1766)', *Bpf* (1899), xlviii.244-75.

—'Le maréchal de Richelieu persécuteur des protestants de la Guyenne (1758)', *Bpf* (1899), lxviii.33-42.

Lough, John, ed., *The* Encyclopédie *of Diderot and d'Alembert*. Cambridge 1954.

Lüthy, H., *La Banque protestante en France de la révocation de l'Edit de Nantes à la Révolution*. Paris 1959-1961.

Lyublinsky, Vladimir S., 'La Bibliothèque de Voltaire', *Rhl* (1958), lviii.467-88.

M.P.D.R. [P.D. Rouvière], *Essai de réunion des protestants aux catholiques-romains*. Paris 1756.

Maillefer, Paul, 'Voltaire et Allamand', *Revue historique vaudoise* (1898), vi. 300-10, 321-32, 353-65.

Mason, Haydn Trevor, *Pierre Bayle and Voltaire*. Oxford 1963.

—'The unity of Voltaire's *L'Ingénu*', *AE*, pp.93-106.

—*Voltaire*. London 1975.

Masson, Pierre-Maurice, *La Religion de Jean-Jacques Rousseau*. Paris 1916.

Maury, Léon, *Le Réveil religieux dans l'église réformée à Genève et en France (1810-1850)*. Paris 1892.

McCloy, Shelby T., *The Humanitarian movement in eighteenth-century France*. Kentucky 1957.

McN., M. A., and R., P. J., *Downhill and the Mussenden Temple*. The National Trust Committee for Northern Ireland 1968.

Meyer, Henry, *Voltaire on war and peace*, Studies on Voltaire (1975), cxliv.

Meylan, Philippe, *Jean Barbeyrac et les débuts de l'enseignement du droit dans l'ancienne Académie de Lausanne*. Lausanne 1938.

Moffat, Margaret M., *Rousseau et la querelle du théâtre au XVIIIe siècle*. Paris 1930.

Monod, Albert, *De Pascal à Chateaubriand: les défenseurs français du christianisme de 1670 à 1802*. Paris 1916.

Montclar, Jean-Pierre-François de Ripert de, *Mémoire théologique et politique au sujet des mariages clandestins des protestans de France*. n.p.1755.

Montesquieu, Charles-Louis de Secondat, baron de La Brède et de, *Œuvres complètes*, ed. Roger Caillois. Paris 1951.

Moréri, *Supplément au Dictionnaire historique, géographique, généalogique, etc., des éditions de Basle de 1732 et 1733* of the *Grand dictionnaire historique*. Basle 1737-1745.

Morley, John, *Voltaire*. London 1891.

Morren, Pierre, *La Vie lausannoise au XVIIIe siècle, d'après Jean Henri Polier de Vernand, lieutenant baillival*. Geneva 1970.

Mortier, Roland, 'Voltaire et le peuple', *AE*, pp.137-51.

Mours, Samuel, *Les Eglises réformées en France*. Paris 1958.

—'Note sur les galériens protestants (1683-1775)'. *Bpf* (1970), cxvi.178-231.

Mours, Samuel, and Robert, Daniel, *Le Protestantisme en France du XVIIIe siècle à nos jours (1685-1970)*. Paris 1972.

Mousseaux, Maurice, 'L'expédition de Villegagnon (16e siècle) et les dernières persécutions en Brie (18e siècle)', *Bpf* (1971), cxvii.414-46.

Naves, Raymond, *Voltaire et l'Encyclopédie*. Paris 1938.

Nieuwentydt, Bernard, *L'Existence de Dieu démontrée par les merveilles de la nature*. Paris 1725.

Nixon, Edna, *Voltaire and the Calas case*. London 1961.

Noyes, Alfred, *Voltaire*. London 1938.

Olivier, Juste, *Paris en 1830*, ed. André Delattre and Marc Denkinger, vol.xix of *University of California Studies in*

the romance languages and literatures (1951).
—*Voltaire à Lausanne: études d'histoire nationale*. Lausanne 1842.
Olivier-Desmont, Jacques, *Discours moraux ou sermons sur divers textes de l'Ecriture-Sainte*. The Hague 1766.
Orcibal, Jean, *Louis XIV et les protestants*. Paris 1951.

Payot, E., 'La Mission d'Albert de Haller à Lausanne en 1757', *Revue historique vaudoise* (1900), viii.65-72.
Perey, L., and Maugras, G., *La Vie intime de Voltaire aux Délices et à Ferney (1754-1778), d'après des lettres et des documents inédits*. Paris 1885.
Philips, Edith, 'Le Quaker vu par Voltaire', *Rhl* (1932), xxxix.161-77.
—*The Good Quaker in French legend*. Pennsylvania 1932.
Philips, Edith, and Perkins, Jean A., 'Some Voltaire marginalia', *Studies on Voltaire* (1973), cxiv.7-78.
Plumb, J. H., *England in the eighteenth century*: vol.iv of *The Pelican history of England*. Harmondsworth 1950.
Pluquet, François-André-Adrien, *Mémoires pour servir à l'histoire des égaremens de l'esprit humain par rapport à la religion chrétienne*. Paris 1762.
Poland, Burdette C., *French Protestantism and the French Revolution*. Princeton 1957.
Pomeau, René, *La Politique de Voltaire*. Paris 1963.
—*La Religion de Voltaire*. Paris 1956. 2nd ed. Paris 1969.
Puaux, Frank, *L'Eglise réformée de France*. Paris 1905.
—*Paul Rabaut, l'apôtre du Désert*. Paris 1918.
—'Une lettre du Refuge', *Bpf* (1878), xxvii.223-31.
Puaux, N.A.F., *Histoire de la Réformation française*. Paris 1857.
—*Histoire populaire du protestantisme français*. Paris 1894.

Quintana, Ricardo, *Swift: an introduction*. Oxford 1953.

Rabaut, Camille, *Les Assemblées du Désert sous les persécutions de Louis XIV et Louis XV. 1685-1787*. Castres 1912.
Rabaut, Paul, *Paul Rabaut: ses lettres à divers (1744-1794)*, ed. Picherdal and Dardier. Paris 1891-1892.
Rabaut, Paul, and La Beaumelle, Laurent Angliviel de, *La Calomnie confondue*. Au désert 1762.
Rabaut Le Jeune, *Annuaire, ou répertoire ecclésiastique à l'usage des églises réformées et protestantes de l'Empire français*. Paris 1807.
Read, General Meredith, *Historic studies in Vaud, Berne and Savoy*. London 1897.
Richard, Michel, *La Vie quotidienne des protestants sous l'ancien régime*. Paris 1966.
Ridgway, Ronald, *La Propagande philosophique dans les tragédies de Voltaire*, Studies on Voltaire (1961), xv.
Ritter, Eugène, 'Le pasteur Allamand', *Revue historique vaudoise* (1903), xi. 289-301.
—'Le Quaker Claude Gay', *Bpf* (1900), xlix.315-20.
—'Voltaire et le pasteur Robert Brown', *Bpf* (1904), liii.156-63.
Robert, Daniel, 'Le rôle historique de Paul Rabaut', *Foi et vie* (1952), pp.21-31.
Roches, François de, *Défense du christianisme contre un ouvrage intitulé 'Lettres sur la religion essentielle à l'homme'*. Geneva 1740.
Romane-Musculus, Paul, 'Les ancêtres réformés de Voltaire', *Bpf* (1962), cviii.28-30.
Roulet, Louis-Edouard, *Voltaire et les Bernois*. Neuchâtel 1950.
Rousseau, André-Michel, *L'Angleterre et Voltaire*, Studies on Voltaire. (1976), cxlv-cxlvii.

Rousseau, Jean-Jacques, *Correspondance complète de Jean Jacques Rousseau*, ed. R. A. Leigh. Geneva, Banbury, Oxford 1965-.

—*Correspondance générale de J.-J. Rousseau*, ed. Théophile Dufour. Paris 1924-1934.

—*Du contrat social, ou principes du droit politique*. Paris 1962.

—*Œuvres complètes*, ed. Bernard Gagnebin and Marcel Raymond. Paris 1959-1969.

—'Réponse de J.-J. Rousseau à Paul Rabaut au sujet de François Rochette et des trois gentilshommes verriers, 1761', *Bpf* (1854), ii.362-5.

Rouvière *see* M. P. D. R.

Ruchat, A., *Examen de l'origénisme, ou réponse à un livre intitulé 'Sentimens* [. . .] *sur l'état des âmes séparées des corps'*. Lausanne 1733.

Saladin, Michel-Jean-Louis, *Mémoire historique sur la vie et les ouvrages de Jacob Vernet*. Paris 1790.

Saint-Simon, duc de, *Mémoires*, ed. Gonzague Truc. Paris 1965.

Salomon, A., 'Le pasteur alsacien C.-F. Baer, chapelin de l'ambassade de Suède à Paris (1719-1797)', *Bpf* (1925), lxxiv.423-49.

Schmidt, Paul, *Court de Gébelin à Paris (1763-1784): étude sur le protestantisme français pendant la seconde moitié du XVIIIe siècle*. Sainte-Blaise and Roubaix 1908.

Spink, John Stephenson, *J.-J. Rousseau et Genève*. Paris 1934.

Staum, Martin, 'Newton and Voltaire: constructive sceptics', *Studies on Voltaire* (1968), lxii.29-56.

Stéphan, Raoul, *Histoire du protestantisme français*. Paris 1961.

Strohl, H., *Le Protestantisme en Alsace*. Strasbourg 1950.

Swift, Jonathan, *Gulliver's travels*. Harmondsworth 1967.

Sykes, Norman, *Church and state in England in the 18th century*. Cambridge 1934.

Taylor, Samuel S. B., 'Voltaire's *L'Ingénu*, the Huguenots and Choiseul', *AE*, pp.107-36.

Torrey, Norman L., *Voltaire and the English deists*. Yale 1930.

Tournier, Gaston, *Les Galères de France et les galériens protestants des XVIIe et XVIIIe siècles*. Musée du Désert 1943-1949.

Trenard, Louis, 'Voltaire, historien de la Réforme en France', pp.156-70 of *Historiographie de la Réforme*, directed by Philippe Joutard. Paris, Neuchâtel, Montreal 1977.

Trevelyan, G. M., *England under the Stuarts* (1st published 1904). Harmondsworth 1960.

Turgot, Anne-Robert-Jacques, *Le Conciliateur, ou lettres d'un ecclésiastique à un magistrat sur les affaires présentes*. Rome 1754.

Vallette, Louis, *L'Eglise de Genève à la fin du XVIIIe siècle*. Geneva 1892.

Vercruysse, J., 'La fortune de Bernard Nieuwentydt en France au XVIIIe siècle et les notes marginales de Voltaire', *Studies on Voltaire* (1964), xxx.223-46.

—*Voltaire et la Hollande*, Studies on Voltaire (1966), xlvi.

Vernes, Jacob, *Catéchisme à l'usage des j.g. de toutes les communions chrétiennes*. Paris 1774.

—*Confidance philosophique*. 2nd. ed. Geneva 1776.

—*Lettres de m. le pasteur Vernes à m. J.-J. Rousseau avec les réponses*. Geneva 1765.

—*Lettres sur le christianisme de m. J.-J. Rousseau*. Amsterdam 1764.

Vernet, Jacob, *Instruction chrétienne* [. . .] *aux dépens d'une société de gens de lettres*. Geneva 1754.

—Lettres critiques d'un voyageur anglois sur l'article Genève du Dictionnaire encyclopédique; & sur la Lettre de mr. d'Alembert à mr. Rousseau. 2nd ed. Utrecht 1761.

—*Lettres critiques d'un voyageur anglois sur l'article Genève du Dictionnaire encyclopédique et sur la Lettre de mr Rousseau touchant les spectacles.* 3rd ed. Copenhagen 1766.

—*Traité de la vérité de la religion chrétienne, tiré du latin de Mr. J.-Alphonse Turretin.* Geneva 1730-1736.

—*Traité de la vérité de la religion chrétienne, tiré en partie du latin de feu m. J.-Alphonse Turretin.* Geneva 1748-1751.

Voltaire, François-Marie Arouet de, *Candide ou l'optimisme,* édition critique avec une introduction et un commentaire par André Morize. Paris 1957.

—*Candide ou l'optimisme,* édition critique avec une introduction et un commentaire par René Pomeau. Paris 1959.

—*The Complete works of Voltaire,* ed. Theodore Besterman and others. Geneva, Banbury, Oxford 1968-.

—*Correspondence and related documents,* ed. Theodore Besterman. Geneva, Banbury, Oxford 1968-1977 (Voltaire 85-135).

—*Correspondance de Voltaire (1726-1729): la Bastille, l'Angleterre, le retour en France,* ed. Lucien Foulet. Paris 1913.

—*Dictionnaire philosophique,* ed. Julien Benda and Raymond Naves. Paris 1954.

—*Essai sur les mœurs et l'esprit des nations,* ed. René Pomeau. Paris 1963.

—*An essay upon the civil wars of France,* ed. O. R. Taylor, *Studies on Voltaire* (1965), xxxviii-xl.662-685.

—*La Henriade,* ed. O. R. Taylor. 2nd ed. 1970 (Voltaire 2).

—*L'Ingénu and Histoire de Jenni,* ed. J. H. Brumfitt and M. I. Gerard Davis. Oxford 1960.

—*Lettres philosophiques,* ed. Gustave Lanson. Paris 1909.

—*Lettres philosophiques,* ed. F. A. Taylor. Oxford 1943.

—*Mélanges,* ed. Jacques van Den Heuvel. Paris 1961.

—*Notebooks,* ed. Theodore Besterman. 2nd ed. 1968 (Voltaire 81-82).

—*Œuvres complètes.* Kehl 1784 and 1785-1789.

—*Œuvres complètes,* ed. Louis Moland. Paris 1877-1885.

—*Œuvres historiques,* ed. René Pomeau. Paris 1957.

—*Le Philosophe ignorant,* ed. J. L. Carr. London 1965.

—'Réfutation D'un Ecrit anonime, contre la mémoire de feu Monsieur Joseph SAURIN (de l'Académie des Sciences, Examinateur des Livres, & Préposé au Journal des Savans) lequel Ecrit anonime se trouve dans le Journal Helvétique du mois d'Octobre 1758', *Journal helvétique.* Neuchâtel (Décembre 1758), pp.617-26.

—*Romans et contes,* ed. Henri Bénac. Paris 1960.

—*Le Siècle de Louis XIV,* ed. Emile Bourgeois. Paris 1906.

—*Traité de métaphysique (1734),* ed. H. Temple Patterson. Manchester 1937.

—*Voltaire: correspondance avec les Tronchin,* ed. André Delattre. Paris 1950.

—*Voltaire's correspondence,* ed. Theodore Besterman. Geneva 1953-1965.

Vuilleumier, Henri, *Histoire de l'église réformée du pays de Vaud sous le régime bernois.* Lausanne 1927-1933.

Wade, Ira O., *The Search for a new Voltaire: studies in Voltaire based upon material deposited at the American philosophical society,* Transactions of the American philosophical society. Philadelphia (1958), xlviii.

Wade, Ira O., and Torrey, Norman L., 'Voltaire and Polier de Bottens', *Rr* (1940), xxi.147-55.

Waller, R. E. A., 'Voltaire and the regent', *Studies on Voltaire* (1974), cxxvii.7-39.

Walsh, John R., *Frederick Augustus Hervey, 1730-1803, fourth earl of Bristol, bishop of Derry, 'Le bienfaiteur des catholiques'.* Maynooth 1972.

List of works cited and consulted

Warburton, William, *The Divine legation of Moses*. London 1738-1741.

Waterman, Mina, 'Voltaire and Firmin Abauzit', *Rr* (1942), xxxiii.236-49.

Wendel, François, *Calvin: the origins and development of his religious thought*. Paris 1950. Tr. Philip Mairet. London 1965.

Williams, William R., 'Voltaire and the utility of the lower clergy', *Studies on Voltaire* (1967), lviii.1869-91.

Wilson, Arthur M., *Diderot*. New York 1972.

Index

(Works by Voltaire and collective works are listed without attribution; other works are followed by the name of the author in parentheses.)

Index